DUMBARTON OAKS STUDIES

XXXII

Sabas, Leader of Palestinian Monasticism

. . . ἔδει γὰρ δι᾽ αὐτοῦ ταύτην τὴν ἔρημον πολισθῆναι

. . . for through him this desert was to become a city

(*V. Sab.* 6, 90.8–10)

Sabas, Leader of Palestinian Monasticism

A Comparative Study in Eastern Monasticism, Fourth to Seventh Centuries

Joseph Patrich

DUMBARTON OAKS RESEARCH LIBRARY AND COLLECTION

Washington, D.C.

© 1995 Dumbarton Oaks
Trustees for Harvard University
Washington, D.C.

To the memory of my father, Michael

Library of Congress Cataloging-in-Publication Data

Patrich, J. (Joseph)
    Sabas, leader of Palestinian monasticism : a comparative study in
Eastern monasticism, fourth to seventh centuries / Joseph Patrich.
        p.   cm. — (Dumbarton Oaks studies ; 32)
    Includes bibliographical references and index.
    ISBN 0-88402-221-8
    1. Monasticism and religious orders—Palestine—History—Early
church, ca. 30–600.   2. Sabas, Saint, 439–532.   3. Mar Saba (Monastery)   4. Palestine—Church history.   I. Title.   II. Series.
    BR185.P38   1994
    271′.0095694′09015—dc20
                                                                93-49099
                                                                CIP

Contents

List of Illustrations

Credits. The illustrations were drawn, photographed, or granted by the following individuals and institutions:

Drawings.
        Benny Arubas, 51, 53, 54, 56, 57, 60, 61.
        Erez Cohen, 31, 33, 35, 38, 45, 47, 67.
        Tanya Gornstein, 65.
        Benny Levenstein, 30, 40, 42, 46, 50, 64.
        Raz Nicolaisku, 58, 59.
        Leen Ritmeyer, 8, 26, 37, 39, 41, 62, 66, 80.
        Anna Yamim, 1–5, 11.

Photographs.
        Radovan Zeev, 6, 7, 9, 10, 13–21, 23–25, 27–28, 48, 75, 77.
        Ilan Schtulmann, 49
        Courtesy of the Cleveland Museum of Art, 78, 79.
        Courtesy of the Israel Authority of Antiquities, 63.
        Courtesy of Princeton University Library, 70.
        Courtesy of Professor Kurt Weitzmann, 68.

All other illustrations are by the author, unless otherwise noted.

Preface

The study of desert cultures has always been of great interest to me. Within this broad research area, the flourishing of monasticism in the desert of Jerusalem is a fascinating phenomenon. The monastery of Mar Saba, suspended on cliff tops in a breathtaking location, is a mute monument attesting to this chapter of glory. The research for the present study began as an archaeological survey conducted during 1981–82 in an area surrounding this monastery. The survey was conducted on foot, and all archaeological evidence was documented and filed. As expected, it soon became evident that the most prosperous settlement occurred there during the Byzantine period, that is, from the fourth to the seventh century. Altogether, the remains of six monasteries were explored in an area of 10 × 10 km²; all of them were erected by Sabas.

At about the same time, a colleague of mine, Yizhar Hirschfeld, was surveying another area of the Judean desert and finding similar evidence of flourishing monastic settlements. The opportunity to work simultaneously in different zones of the desert, to discuss problems, raise questions, and look for answers was of great benefit to us both. Each of us decided to make the monastic chapter in his archaeological report a point of departure for a larger study of Palestinian monasticism and to write a dissertation on this vast topic, seeking for a synthesis between the archaeological finds and the literary sources. Hirschfeld's efforts were directed toward a comprehensive documentation of all the monastic remains in the Judean desert. Taking the entire Byzantine period in Palestine as a chronological unit, he aimed at studying the available sources synchronically, depicting an "average," static reconstruction of monastic life there. A comprehensive catalogue of the Judean desert monasteries and an excellent book, both based on his dissertation, appeared recently (Hirschfeld 1990, 1992).

My objective was different: to study the specific Sabaitic contribution to Palestinian monasticism. In order to define it and draw its original features, it was necessary to compare Sabas' monastic system with that of his predecessors Chariton, Euthymius, and Gerasimus. It was also necessary to trace the possible sources of influence from Egypt, Syria, and Asia Minor. All this was in an attempt to understand what was so exceptional in his system that its influence in monastic life as well as in liturgy has lasted until the present, and why his principal monastery has been inhabited almost continuously throughout history, surviving many years of Muslim rule. Such a comparative study reveals a dynamic picture of development and change throughout the Byzantine period and the existence of diverse systems rather than of "average," unitary traits.

The literary sources, mainly in Greek, are numerous, covering the entire period from the fourth to the seventh century. Many of them are also available in scholarly French or English translations. Needless to say, it was always the version of the original

PREFACE

text that counted. The most important among these sources, mainly Palestinian hagiographies that refer to the Judean desert, are also available in a Hebrew translation prepared by Dr. Leah Di Segni, a classical philologist at the Institute of Archaeology of the Hebrew University of Jerusalem. Her translations were done in conjunction with the two dissertations mentioned above, under the auspices of the Jerusalem-based Yad Yizhak Ben-Zvi Institute for the Research of Eretz Israel, Its People and Cultures. Throughout my research I benefited from her comments and critique, a result of her profound acquaintance with the literary sources as well as with the scholarly studies. All the translations of the Greek sources in this book were made by Dr. Di Segni.

My mentor, Professor Yoram Tsafrir, was encouraging and helpful throughout the work. Useful comments and proposals were put forward by Professor Lorenzo Perrone of the University of Pisa, and by Dr. Alice-Mary Talbot of Dumbarton Oaks. Both read an English translation of the entire dissertation. During my 1991–92 year as a Research Fellow at Dumbarton Oaks, I was able to transform the dissertation into a book, using the excellent resources of the Byzantine Library and gaining insights from discussions with many fellows.

In the fieldwork around Mar Saba, carried out under the auspices of the Israel Authority of Antiquities and the Hebrew University of Jerusalem, I was assisted by Erez Cohen and by Benny Levenstein, who took the measurements and drew the plans of the monastic cells. The abbot of Mar Saba, Archimandrite Seraphim, and the monks, especially Chrysostomos-Cheruvim and Chrysantos, were friendly and cooperative. Other monastic cells were discovered and explored in the framework of the Archaeological Survey of Caves, a project I have directed since 1983. Benny Arubas, who was a partner in this survey from its very beginning, took the measurements and drew the plans. Shemuel Grasiani, Eyal Naor, Hanina Kalee, and Benny Agur served successively as members of the team.

The research was supported by grants from the Hebrew University of Jerusalem, the Yad Yizhak Ben-Zvi Institute, and by the Rachel Yanait Ben-Zvi award. Research grants awarded by the Dorot Foundation and the University of Haifa helped transform the Hebrew dissertation into an English book. The dissertation was translated into English by Edward Levin, and the style of the book was greatly improved by Frances Kianka.

To all, individuals and institutions, I am deeply indebted.

The book consists of five parts. Part I contains three introductory chapters giving the historical framework and background needed for a proper understanding of the various subjects discussed in greater detail throughout the book. These will enable us to identify possible sources of influence or to define traits of uniqueness and originality in Sabas' work.

Parts II–IV constitute the main body of the book. Each part treats a different aspect of Sabas' career. Part II deals with Sabas as a founder of monasteries. The archaeological finds, the result of my survey and excavations, are described in their historical context and are accompanied by numerous illustrations. My firsthand acquaintance with the various sites where Sabas and his disciples were active enabled me to achieve a better understanding of many details of monastic life mentioned in the sources. It was also helpful in defining the traits that distinguish the Sabaite laurae from those that were modeled on the laura of Pharan.

These topics are discussed in detail in part III, which presents Sabas as an abbot and monastic legislator. As such he formulated the monks' way of life and established an administrative framework for each of his monasteries separately as well as a type of cooperative structure in which they were incorporated. Special attention is given to a study of the weekly monastic liturgy (Chap. 4), and an effort is made to reconstruct the original Rule of Sabas (Chap. 5). Information available on all the Judean desert monasteries is studied and analyzed synchronically and diachronically, on the one hand, in an attempt to trace chronological developments throughout the Byzantine period and, on the other, to point out differences or resemblances between Sabas' activities and the work of his predecessors Chariton, Euthymius, and Gerasimus. The discussion in these chapters is extended to monastic centers abroad in an effort to examine each topic in a wider scope.

Part IV examines Sabas as a religious and ecclesiastical leader: his veneration as a holy man (*hosios*) by the faithful, his status within the church establishment as the archimandrite of the monks, his struggle for Chalcedonian Orthodoxy in a tempestuous period in the history of the Church, and his activity as an emissary of the patriarchs of Jerusalem to the imperial court of Anastasius and Justinian for the welfare and strength of the Christian population of Palestine.

Part V is an epilogue containing a brief history of the Laura from Sabas' death to the end of the Byzantine period and a description of the theological struggles in which his followers had a decisive role. Affairs that took place beyond the Byzantine period in Palestine are mentioned only in order to outline the main events and point out the direction of later developments, when the region came under Muslim rule.

References are incorporated into the text and are abbreviated in the following manner:

V. Sab. 36, 123; 37, 124.5 = *Vita Sabae* (see Bibliographical Abbreviations, I), ed. Schwartz, chap. 36, p. 123 and chap. 37, p. 124, line 5.

HM VIII.V, 48 = *Historia Monachorum*, ed. Festugière, chap. VIII, para. 5, p. 48.

Perrone 1980, 141–74 = Perrone 1980 (see Bibliographical Abbreviations, II), pp. 141–74.

Part I: Introduction

1

Monasticism in Palestine before Sabas

Christian monasticism began in Palestine, the Holy Land (Fig. 1), in the early fourth century, before Christianity became the official religion of the empire.[1] The first monks known to us by name are Hilarion of Tavatha, near Gaza, who lived and was active as a monk there from 308 onward; and Chariton, a native of Iconium in Asia Minor, the founder of Judean desert monasticism. Chariton established his first monastery, Pharan, in about 330. At that time anchorites also lived among the reeds of the Jordan River. Chariton later established two other monasteries: Douka, overlooking Jericho, and Souka, not far from Thekoa. During the fourth century monasticism spread throughout Palestine, and monasteries were also established in Jerusalem, Bethlehem, and in other holy places connected with Christ's life, as well as in the lowland (Shephela) and in Sinai.

The process by which monasteries came into being, whether in the desert or in rural regions, was similar. A hermit lived in a cave or hut near a source of water; in the course of time other monks joined him and a community was formed. With donations from wealthy admirers or a legacy bequeathed to the founder (an act sometimes considered a miraculous deed of divine intervention), dwelling cells, a prayerhouse, and water reservoirs were constructed. The founder, who was the leader of the group, determined whether it would be built as a monastery of anchorites, a laura (λαύρα: literally "alley" or "lane," presumably referring to the narrow path that communicated between the monastic cells), or as a communal monastery, a coenobium (κοινόβιον, literally "common life").

During the Byzantine period, there were developments in the internal organization of these institutions. Certain variations existed even between monasteries of the same type (see below, Part III). Yet the specific features of each type are clear enough. In the laura the hermits lived during the week in cells that were remote from each other. On Saturdays and Sundays they assembled in the church, located at the laura's core, for a communal prayer and meal. In a coenobium the monks met daily in the church and in the dining room. In both types the daily schedule was divided between prayer and manual labor, which in the laura was done in the cell. Besides these two types of organized communities, there existed throughout the period under discussion, both in the desert and in the countryside, anchorites who lived without any formal connection to a monastic

---

[1] This chapter does not intend to present a detailed historical survey of the development of monasticism in Palestine, but rather to give a brief survey and define its main characteristics to the time of Sabas, with particular emphasis on the Judean desert. Thus it will be possible to evaluate correctly Sabas' contribution to this movement. For more detailed historical surveys, see the articles by Vailhé; see also Schiwietz 1913 and Chitty 1966. For the Judean desert see Perrone 1990; Di Segni 1990a, 5–46; and Hirschfeld 1992.

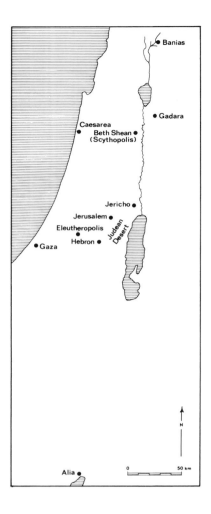

1. Provincia Palaestina. Map of main sites mentioned in the text.

community. In addition, in both monastic types—laurae and coenobia—one could find recluses who never left their cells.

In the last three decades of the fourth century, monasteries also began to be built in Jerusalem. The first monastery on the Mount of Olives was erected in ca. 370 by Innocentius, formerly a married layman of Italian origin, one of the palace dignitaries in Constantius' court. He erected a martyrion on the Mount of Olives for the bones of John the Baptist rescued from the hands of Simon Magus and his band, who had desecrated the Baptist's tomb at Sebasteia during the reign of Julian the Apostate.[2] Shortly thereafter a monk named Palladius, apparently a Cappadocian, a former disciple of Basil the Great, joined Innocentius there (Chitty 1966, 48–49). Sometime before 417, the better-known Palladius, author of the *Historia Lausiaca*, lived in the monastery for three years. In his book he relates extreme practices of mortification, similar to those of Syrian monasticism, as prevailing among some of the monks on the Mount of Olives at that time (*HL* XLIII–IV, 130–32). A more important Latin center appeared on the Mount of Olives in 375–376

---

[2] Vailhé (1899–1900a, 42–43, no. 96) also mentions the monastery of Abba Philipus in Jerusalem dating it to ca. 340. Its monks rescued the bones of John the Baptist, desecrated at Sebasteia, and sent them to Athanasius, bishop of Alexandria. This monastery is mentioned by Rufinus (*HE* II.18) and by Theodoret *HE* III.3). It seems that it was not on the Mount of Olives, and therefore is not to be identified with Innocentius' monastery mentioned above.

with the establishment of the monasteries of Melania the Elder and Rufinus. However, both Melania and Rufinus left Palestine by the end of the fourth century.

About the year 400, the monastery of Passarion was built on Mount Zion for the clergy of Holy Zion Church. Passarion also erected a large soup kitchen outside the city walls near the eastern gate. The Latin center on the Mount of Olives was given new momentum when Melania the younger erected a nunnery there (in 432) and then a monastery (in 436) with Gerontius at its head. This monastery and Passarion's were the most important ones in Jerusalem in the fifth century. Passarion's disciples established monasteries as well: Romanus near Thekoa (before 451) and near Eleutheropolis (in 457); Marcianus near Bethlehem (in 456); and Anastasius between Jerusalem and Bethlehem. Peter the Iberian established his monastery near the Tower of David (in 428); it was renowned for its welfare and charitable activities. Recluses also lived near the Tower of David, secluded in dispersed cells, along with the monks who officiated at the church of the Holy Sepulcher. These monks—the *spoudaioi* (σπουδαῖοι) of the Holy Sepulcher—were assembled in a separate coenobium only in 494 by Patriarch Elias, who established a monastery for them near the patriarchate.

Many of the Jerusalem monks, who were organized as groups (τάγμα, σπουδαῖοι) of devotees, performed rites and ceremonies in the pilgrims' and worshipers' churches in the city. They received a fixed daily allotment (διάριον) for their services and enjoyed an easy way of life (Festugière 1962b, 18 n. 6). This source of income did not exist for the monks of the desert monasteries.

Some monasteries were erected and maintained by donations from wealthy Roman matrons. Such were the Latin centers on the Mount of Olives, comprising the monasteries of Melania the Elder (375–376) and Melania the Younger (432–436), and in Bethlehem, comprising the monasteries of Paula and Jerome (386) (there was also an earlier monastery in Bethlehem, where John Cassian lived). Wealthy matrons associated with the imperial court also later took an active part in founding monasteries in Jerusalem. The most prominent among them was Eudocia, who established the church and monastery of St. Stephen north of the city walls in ca. 455. At about the same time, her colleague Bessa established a monastery and nunnery dedicated to St. Menas within the city walls. The first abbot of the monastery was Andreas, one of Euthymius' disciples; Bessa headed the nunnery. In ca. 454 a monastery was erected at Gethsemane by Flavia, who put Theognius at its head. In the same period, Hicelia, a close friend of an *hyparchos,* erected the Cathisma Church monastery next to the Jerusalem-Bethlehem road. Theodosius served as its steward at the beginning of his career.

Monastic settlements in Jerusalem and its environs prior to Sabas' activity include the monastery near the road along the Kidron ravine, where Juvenal lived prior to his nomination as patriarch in 425. This monastery was deserted by 451. Other settlements include the monastery of Eustorgius, established in Jerusalem in ca. 466 by a Cappadocian monk, where Cyriacus was first received when he arrived in Jerusalem; and a nunnery dedicated to St. George outside the city walls, with a home for the aged next to it that also served as a hostel (John the Hesychast was accommodated there in 491).[3]

---

[3] For bibliography regarding the various monasteries, see Vailhé (1899–1900a), following the reference numbers in his list: Melania the Elder and Rufinus, nos. 78, 105; Passarion, no. 90; Melania the Younger,

The monastery of Epiphanius was in the region of Eleutheropolis (Beth Govrin). Epiphanius was a native of the village of Besandûk in that region and a disciple of Hilarion. He later became the bishop of Salamis in Cyprus (367 CE). This monastery, called Old Ad (*Vetus Ad*), had been established in about 335. Like Hilarion, Epiphanius introduced into Palestine the Egyptian influence of St. Antony's disciples. Similarly, other monks, who began their monastic careers in Scetis, later settled in the region of Gaza: Porphyrius, who eventually became the bishop of Gaza (395 CE), arrived in Palestine in 377 after a five-year stay in Scetis; and Silvanus, a Palestinian, who settled with his disciples in a laura in Gerara in the northwestern Negev. Silvanus had twelve disciples in Scetis, with whom he went to Sinai (ca. 380). At Gerara he was succeeded by his disciple Zacharias (before 415). However, his most renowned disciple was Zenon, who settled in Caphar Sheartha, twenty km northeast of Gaza, after many years of leading sallies into the desert. The most famous monk who settled in the Gaza region was Abba Ishaia (see below).

We do not know which "laurae" were established by Eudocia during her second visit to Jerusalem (441/3–460) (Evagrius, *HE* I.21, 29.24). The lack of reference to them in the sources that deal with the Judean desert may indicate that they were not located in this region. They were possibly located near Eleutheropolis and Gaza, where the opponents of the Council of Chalcedon, Eudocia among them, wielded a good deal of power. In fact, Monophysite monasticism received considerable support from Eudocia. Monasteries were established on her estates in Caphar Ginatha, ca. twenty km north of Jerusalem, and in Jemania and Caphar Turban, near Eleutheropolis (Vailhé 1899–1900a, nos. 46, 59, 102). The prominent leaders of this movement in the second half of the fifth century were Peter the Iberian, who was active in the regions of Gaza and Ascalon and was nominated in 452 as the bishop of Maiumas, Romanus, and Marcianus (until his reconciliation with Patriarch Martyrius in 479). The monastery of Severus, who later became patriarch of Antioch, was also located in Maiumas.

Peter the Iberian retreated to the region of Gaza in 444 and settled in a laura not far from Caphar Tavatha, Hilarion's village of origin. Abba Ishaia had settled in the village of Beth Daltha, seven km from Tavatha, sometime between 431 and 451. Formerly a Scetiote, he introduced to this region the life-style of a recluse assisted by a disciple who attended him with food and provided news of the outside world. Abba Ishaia lived there for forty or fifty years, until his death in 489 (Chitty 1971). A coenobite community assembled around him. A nearby coenobium was that of Abba Seridos, established around the year 500. Hermits also lived in its environs. In about 514 Varsanuphius came from Upper Egypt to Tavatha, and about ten years later came John, both to live as recluses following the practice of Abba Ishaia. They maintained a correspondence with many admirers from among both monks and laity. Not far from Tavatha, the monastery of Dorotheus, a coenobium comprising a large hospital and hostel was built in the sixth century. By then all these foundations had become orthodox monasteries. But the Ju-

---

nos. 79, 80; Peter the Iberian, no. 57; St. Stephen, no. 36; Bessa, no. 11; Flavia, no. 44; the Cathisma Church, no. 20; Eustorgius, no. 41; St. George, no. 49; the *spoudaioi* of the Holy Sepulcher, no. 108; Juvenal, no. 68; Passarion's disciples: Romanus, nos. 101, 102; Marcianus, no. 71; and Anastasius, no. 5. For the monasteries of Passarion and Marcianus, see also Vailhé 1897–99, 193–98.

dean desert, not the region of Gaza, became the most important monastic center in Palestine.

Monastic life in the Judean desert was a profound spiritual experience. This was the desert of the Holy City, whose holy places were less than a day's walk distant and whose monasteries could be seen over the western horizon of the desert. Individuals of deep religious piety as well as of a high intellectual level were drawn here from all over the Christian world. In this region had walked such exemplary figures as Elijah the Prophet, John the Baptist, and Christ himself, whose teachings served as their way of life. The wild vistas of the desert were perceived as a direct contact with the Creation. It is no wonder, therefore, that their religious fervor knew no bounds. Despite the proximity to the settled land, the desert monks faithfully adhered to the way of life they had chosen. They also were deeply involved in the various theological struggles that occupied the Church of Palestine during the fifth and sixth centuries before, during, and after Sabas' time.

A lively cosmopolitan society of monks was established in the Judean desert and in the Holy City. A mixture of influences from all the monastic centers, especially from those of the East, blended to become a unique and original monastic movement of great intrinsic value. It therefore comes as no surprise that during the course of the fifth century, when Judean desert monasticism became stronger, this desert became a most important monastic center for the entire Christian world. Believers and monks flocked there from the famous older centers of Syria and Egypt.

The foundations of Euthymius, who arrived in Palestine in 406 and died there in 473, mark a new chapter in the history of Judean desert monasticism. In 411 he founded a coenobium with Theoctistus which the latter directed and for whom it was named. During his desert sallies, Euthymius founded another coenobium at Caparbaricha in the desert of Ziph, not far from Aristoboulias (ca. 422–426). He finally inaugurated his laura in 428. His disciples erected additional monasteries on the fringes of the desert and near Jericho. Some of his disciples were integrated into the ecclesiastical establishment. Two of them, Martyrius and Elias, later became patriarchs of Jerusalem.

However, the flourishing and regulation of monastic life, anchored in written rules, came into being only under Sabas' leadership. Sabas arrived in Palestine in 456 and joined Euthymius' community. In 483 he established his own laura. This new stage in the history of Judean desert monasticism will be discussed in detail later, with comparisons to the earlier stages of the movement.

The peace between the monks and the patriarch of Jerusalem, which was achieved in 479, when the "second union" within the Church of Jerusalem was agreed upon, was presumably the condition that enabled a new momentum in the building of monasteries. It was during this stage that the coenobia of Theodosius, Choziba, and Theognius and the Great Laura of Sabas were erected.

From the beginning, the laura had been the most prevalent type of monastic settlement in the Judean desert. Up to the time of Sabas, six laurae already existed there and along the Jordan River. Chariton, the first to establish monasteries in this region, had founded, as was mentioned above, three laurae in the first half of the fourth century: Pharan, Douka, and Souka. Euthymius had established his laura (428) along the lines of the one in Pharan (κατὰ τὸν τύπον Φαράν: *V. Euth.* 16, 26), a type that I shall attempt to define during the course of this work.

In the region of Jericho and the Jordan, the topographical structure is moderately hilly although cut by many rivulets, but not rocky as in the wadis of the desert. The land provides nourishment—an abundance of hearts of reed and date palms as well as water. Therefore, anchorites with no connection to any monastic community prevailed there. Such was the situation already at the time of Chariton as well as later (*V. Char.* 13, 26; *HL* XLIX–LIII, 143–45; *V. Porph.* 4, 4; *De Sync.*; *Pratum* 91, 2948). An organized community was established along the Jordan ca. 455, when Gerasimus founded a laura surrounding a coenobium. This was a monastic type different from the laura of Pharan (for a more detailed discussion of this, see below, Part III, Chaps. 3–5). At approximately the same time, anchorites also organized, along the same pattern, in the caves of the reed (τῶν καλάμων) thickets along the Jordan, thus establishing the laura of Calamon (Vailhé 1898c). The monastic center that was established in this region constituted a separate sector in the monastic movement and had its own representatives in its framework (see Part IV, Chap. 2 below).

Of a different type was the monastery of the church of St. John the Baptist near the Jordan, erected by Emperor Anastasius (491–518) on the site of Christ's baptism. Its monks received a permanent yearly allowance of six solidi from the imperial treasury (Theod., *De Situ* 20, 121). They cared for pilgrims, guided them, and served as clergy in the monastery's church. Their way of life and daily schedule differed from that of the ordinary desert monks.

The next phase of laura establishment in the Judean desert and along the Jordan River is connected with Sabas, the only one of Euthymius' disciples to establish laurae. He and his disciples founded seven, in addition to the six laurae that already existed in these areas.

Sabas and his disciples also founded six coenobia. Sabas was the first of Euthymius' disciples to establish a coenobium deep within the desert plateau. Prior to his establishment, the coenobium of Theoctistus was the only one located deep within the desert. Euthymius' second coenobium, the monastery of Caparbaricha, as well as those of his disciples Marinus and Lucas, Gabriel, and Martyrius, were established on the edge of the desert, and the double monasteries of Elias were established near Jericho. Neither Theodosius nor Theognius penetrated as far as Sabas into the desert (see Hirschfeld 1990, fig. 1, and 1992, map I). Romanus' monastery on the fringes of the desert, southwest of Thekoa, was established before the Council of Chalcedon (451); however, his monks also had cells deeper in the desert, where the New Laura would eventually be established (see Part II, Chap. 1B, below). Aposchist monks (separatists and opponents of the Council of Chalcedon) and a few Nestorians at various times occupied the Tower of Eudocia, before the establishment of the Scholarius monastery at that site (below, Part II, Chap. 2D).

Data on the size of the monastic population is very meager. According to Cyril of Scythopolis, in 516 the entire monastic population of Jerusalem and the desert totaled 10,000.[4] In large degree, however, this was after the wide expansion and settlements of

---

[4] This may be an exaggeration of Cyril or of his pro-Chalcedonian source. See also below, n. 6.

Sabas and his disciples, which greatly increased the number of monasteries in the desert and the number of monks they contained. It is clear from the brief survey above that the number of monasteries in the Judean desert (including the fringe strip) and along the Jordan was quite sparse until ca. 480: six laurae and eight coenobia.[5] A reasonable estimate of this population (including the anchorites) may be ca. 1,000–1,500 monks.[6]

There is no mention of any type of contact or relationship among the laurae of Chariton during the fourth century. The monasteries of Euthymius and his disciples, about which there is more information, were not organized in a confederate framework, as is to be found later with the monasteries of Sabas and his disciples. Euthymius also did not take pains to establish and maintain these institutions as Sabas would later do in his monasteries. Nor is there mention of any regulations that Euthymius established for them. There was, of course, an accepted pattern, an oral tradition, but there were no written, orderly rules. According to the extant sources, Gerasimus was the first abbot in the Judean desert and near the Jordan to establish regulations for his monks; Sabas would later act in a similar manner (see Part III, Chaps. 3 and 5, below).

In addition to the monks, we also hear of the "desert shepherds" and of Saracen nomads roaming the desert. Proper relations had to be maintained with each of these, lest the personal safety of the monks be jeopardized. However, this was also determined by the general state of security in the provinces of Palestine and Arabia.

The economic existence of the desert monks was based on handicrafts—the weaving of ropes and baskets from the fibers and leaves of palm trees, the traditional work of the monks (*V. Euth.* 6, 14). Most of the monks lived near inhabited regions and maintained relations with the villagers in order to market their wares, purchase food, or receive offerings from them. Even in this early phase, however, which was not sufficiently developed and organized, donations by pilgrims were a quite significant source of income. The main beneficiaries of this were the monasteries close to the main pilgrim route, which connected the holy places of Jerusalem with those along the Jordan. This was the case with the laura of Euthymius, which was once visited by a caravan of four hundred Armenian pilgrims (*V. Euth.* 17, 27; Stone 1986).

In the beginning, the monastic movement in all regions grew parallel to and was independent of the ecclesiastical establishment. In many instances tension arose between this enthusiastic and fervent society and the establishment, in whose interest it was to assimilate it into the structure of the church. Juvenal, the patriarch of Jerusalem (422–458), created a pattern for integrating the monastic movement into the ecclesiastical establishment by appointing a *chorepiskopos* as archimandrite of the monks within the

[5] The six laurae are Pharan, Douka, Souka, Euthymius, Gerasimus, and Calamon. The eight coenobia are Theoctistus, Caparbaricha, Marinus (= Photinus), Lucas, Martyrius, Elias, Gabriel, and Romanus. From the relatively few archaeological excavations conducted in desert monasteries that are historically unidentified and not included in this list, there is no monastery that can be positively dated to this period. See Hirschfeld 1990, 56–68.

[6] It may reasonably be assumed that the number of 600 monks mentioned by John Rufus as living in the monastery of Romanus (*Plerophoria* 25, 58) is an exaggeration or a distortion. In the monastery, proposed to be identified with Khirbet er-Rubei'a (Hirschfeld 1992, 43 n. 43), there is no room for such a large population of monks. Hirschfeld (1992, 78–79) estimates that there were never more than 3,000 monks in the Judean desert, including the desert of the Jordan, even at the zenith of the monastic movement. In that case, their number by the year 480 was perhaps not more than 500.

bounds of his diocese. He appointed to this position Passarion, abbot of one of the city monasteries, who was followed in this post by his successors at the head of his monastery, as well as by Gerontius, abbot of the monasteries of Melania on the Mount of Olives. These latter foundations were the most important Jerusalem monasteries at that time.

Sabas and Theodosius were the first to be chosen from, and by, the desert monks for the position of archimandrite (494). Their appointment indicates the increase in both number and power of the desert monks, as well as an increase in the importance of their representatives, the archimandrites, in the Jerusalem Church (see below, Part IV, Chap. 2). Desert monasticism began to flourish only during Sabas' time, and was in great measure a consequence of his activity in the monastic movement and in the Church of the Holy Land.

2

Eastern Monasticism: Historical Survey
and Characteristics

A brief survey of the characteristics of the eastern monastic centers outside Palestine is helpful in determining possible sources of influence and in making a comparison between them and contemporary monastic practice in Palestine as described by Cyril of Scythopolis. Acquaintance with the Justinianic monastic legislation is of particular interest in this regard. The purpose here is to point out relevant features for a comparative study rather than to depict in detail all the characteristics of each monastic center.

A. Mount Nitria, Kellia, and Scetis

These monastic settlements of Lower Egypt are the closest in structure to the laurae of Palestine, and therefore a comparative study of them is of special value. There is ample information about these centers, especially in the last quarter of the fourth century, the period of their final consolidation and flourishing.

Mount Nitria (Jebel Barnog) is located ca. 40 miles southeast of Alexandria, beyond Lake Mareotis (Evelyn-White 1932, 17–24, 43–59, 168–74). It is close to the agricultural region of the Delta, ca. 14.4 km from Hermopolis Parva (Damanhur), to the southwest (see the map, Fig. 2). Amoun, the disciple of Antony, was the first monk to settle there, ca. 315 CE (ca. 330 according to Chitty 1966, 11).

John Cassian (*Con.* III.1, 139–40; XVIII.4–6, 13–18) speaks of the existence of coenobite schools (*scholae coenobiorum*) and communities of anchorites (*congregationes anachoretarum*) as two distinct groups in the monasticism of Lower Egypt. According to him, the coenobium was a novitiate stage before a life of seclusion. Such was also the relationship between Mount Nitria and Kellia.

The monastic settlement of Kellia ("cells" in Greek) is located 10–12 miles south of Nitria. It was named after the great number of monastic cells there (Evelyn-White 1932, 24–27, 49–50, 175–78; Guillaumont 1965, 1977; Kasser 1967, 7–11; Daumas and Guillaumont 1969, 1–16). Kellia was established in 338 by Amoun of Nitria at a location chosen by Antony (*Apoph. Pat.*, Antony 34). The purpose was to find a suitable place for anchorites after the settlement in Nitria had become too large and crowded to allow true seclusion in silence. Rufinus (addition to the Latin translation of *HM* XXII) relates that the cells were quite distant from each other, thereby preventing the monk from seeing or hearing his neighbor. The cells of the settlement extended over a wide area, with some of them as much as 5–6 km from the church. The archaeological remains (see below, Part

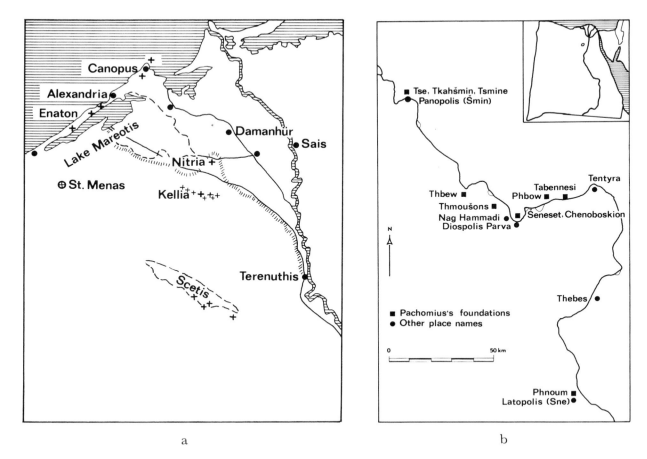

2. Egypt. Monastic centers: (a) Lower Egypt; (b) Upper Egypt.

II, Chap. 1F) indicate that the settlement later developed even further and extended over an area ca. 22 km long. Its remains include about 1,500 different complexes, including a few churches (Kasser 1967, 1972).

   The monastic center of Scetis is located deep within the western desert (Evelyn-White 1932, 27–36, 60–72, 95–124, 178–88; Guy 1964). It is ca. 40 miles south of Kellia and ca. 50 miles south of Mount Nitria, a walking distance of a day and a night (*HM* XXIII.1, 130–31). The site is on the caravan route leading from Babylon (Fustât-Cairo) to the northwest (see the map, Fig. 2a). It was established by Macarius the Great (300–390) in Wadi en-Natrun, close to the present monastery of Baramus, between 330 and 340. During the first ten years there was no priest there (Chitty 1966, 33). In 356, the year of Antony's death, it was already so densely settled that some monks left it for more se-cluded places. John Cassian lived in Scetis from ca. 385 until 399 (Chadwick 1968, 14–18). About the year 380, four distinct congregations (*congregationes/ecclesiae*) came into being around the holy men Macarius the Great, John the Little, Bishoi, and the Roman fathers Maximus and Domitius, each community with its own church and priest-leader (*Con.* X.2, 76). This basic division continued later as well.[7]

   ⁷ Evelyn-White is of the opinion that the seven priests active alongside the chief priest in Nitria reflect

In the middle of the sixth century 3,500 monks lived in the four laurae of Scetis (*Pratum* 113, 2977). *Laurae* is the usual term in this period for describing the communities of the settlement. Each had about 750–800 monks, not much more than the community of anchorites in Kellia at the end of the fourth century, which numbered 600 monks though it later expanded. These numbers are unparalleled in the Palestinian laurae, which generally numbered only several dozen monks (Hirschfeld 1992, 78–79). However, 120 monks resettled the New Laura in Palestine in 555, and in the Great Laura at the apex of its growth there were at most 250 or 300 monks. But these two Palestinian laurae are of exceptional size.

When Rufinus visited Nitria (373), about 3,000 monks lived there (*HE II*.3, 511). Some twelve years later Jerome found about 5,000 monks there (*Ep.* 22.33, 149). Palladius, who stayed in Nitria in 389–90, also mentions this number (*HL* XIII, 36–37). The author of the *Historia Monachorum* visited Nitria in 395. In Rufinus' additions to the Latin translation of this treatise (chap. XX), it is related that the monks lived in about fifty dwellings (*tabernacula*)[8] and were subordinate to one father. This indicates an average of about 100 monks in each dwelling, and a division into moderate-sized communities of monks (Evelyn-White 1932, 172). However, according to Rufinus (loc. cit.) and Palladius (*HL* VII.2, 25), some monks lived by themselves in their cells, others in pairs or small groups, while still others lived in larger groups. There is a report of a senior monk who had 210 disciples.

A dwelling in which several dozen or hundreds of monks live together is in fact a coenobium. In the extant literary sources there is no detailed information about the way of life in these coenobia or about their physical structure. It is evident, however, that they were structured quite loosely (see below), and were not well-developed and well-organized institutions such as the Pachomian coenobia, where the way of life of the monks was determined by a detailed rule that dealt with every aspect of the monk's life. In the monastic colonies of Lower Egypt there was no written, detailed set of regulations such as those of Pachomius and his successors or the Rule of Basil.[9] However, as will be explained below, these coenobia were also different from the Basilian ones that were prevalent in Palestine. The most prominent difference is that the common prayers, in which all the monks participated, were conducted in the church of the monastic colony of Mount Nitria only on Saturdays and Sundays, and not every day, as was the practice in normal coenobia.

Palladius, who arrived in Nitria at the end of 389 or the beginning of 390 and lived there for an entire year, relates (*HL* VII.2, 25) that the monks lived in different ways,

---

the actual division of the entire settlement into seven separate groups, a structure possibly expressed also in the seven bakeries that existed in Nitria according to Palladius (Evelyn-White 1932, 173 and n. 7). We do not know the reason for this division (if it indeed existed).

[8] Sozomen (*HE* VI.31.1, 286), while describing the living quarters of the monks of Nitria, uses the word Μοναστήρια, which in later periods normally denoted coenobia. During this period, however, it was also used to denote anchorite cells, and not necessarily buildings of large dimensions (Lampe 1961, 878; Evelyn-White 1932, 92 n. 13, 93 n. 4).

[9] Two sets of regulations attributed to the Monks of Nitria and Scetis dating from before the end of the 5th century apparently originated in the monasteries of Gaul in the West. They deal with regular coenobitic monasticism. See Evelyn-White 1932, 496, appendix IV.

each in accordance with his physical ability and inclination. Not everyone went to Kellia after undergoing a novitiate period. Some remained to live as anchorites at Mount Nitria (such as Nathanael or Benjamin: Palladius, *HL* XII, 35–36; XVI, 40–43). Or and Theodore are an example of two monks who lived together (*Apoph. Pat.*, Or. 1, 8).

According to the Latin addition of Rufinus to his translation of *HM* (chap. XX), the monastic colony of Nitria (which included, as was stated, several thousand monks), was subordinate to a father (*pater*). In another source (*Apoph. Pat.*, Theophilus 1), mention is also made of the abbot (ὁ ἀββᾶς) of Mount Nitria. Palladius (loc. cit.), on the other hand, speaks about a group of eight priests (πρεσβύτεροι) that administered the community, while the Eucharist was offered in the church only by the chief priest (ὁ πρῶτος πρεσβύτερος), who was also the only one among them to give sermons or rulings. He was the sole authority of judgment; the others would sit next to him in silence in the church. The chief priest was therefore the abbot of the settlement and headed the council of priests. He held this office until his death (Evelyn-White 1932, 170–71). The literary sources indicate that the chief priest regarded his position as the first among equals, and not as a leader forcefully imposing his authority on others, as a sole ruler.

A chief priest also headed each of the four congregations of Scetis; the chief among them was called in the Greek sources the "Father of Scetis" (ὁ πατὴρ τῆς Σκήτεως), a name that also appears in the Coptic sources. Later, from the fifth century, the term "*hegoumenos* of Shîhêt" appears in the Coptic sources. This title was prevalent mainly in the sixth and seventh centuries. Macarius was the first to fill this role, which was later held by his successors as head of the monastery of Macarius (see below). The "Father of Scetis" had the authority to admit or reject people who wished to join the community. The prohibition against admitting to Scetis a young monk with a face resembling a woman's is attributed to Paphnutius, Macarius' successor (*Apoph. Pat.*, Eudaemon; cf. *V. Sab.* 29, 114; *V. Euth.* 31, 50). The "Father of Scetis" also had the right to impose various punishments on monks who had sinned, such as expulsion, a temporary ban, and so on. He was the administrator of the community's life and religious ceremonies and was subordinate to the patriarch of Alexandria, whom he would visit once a year at Easter.

The monastic settlements of Mount Nitria, Kellia, and Scetis reached the peak of their growth and importance in the last quarter of the fourth century. Nitria and especially Kellia were seriously harmed during the Anthropomorphist-Origenist controversy (Evelyn-White 1932, 125–44), when Theophilus, the patriarch of Alexandria, persecuted the intellectual Origenists of these monastic settlements and brought about the expulsion of the four "Tall Brothers" and many other monks, destroying their cells (399–400). With their expulsion the settlements lost much of the reputation they had formerly enjoyed. The educated Greek element vanished with the victory of the Coptic Anthropomorphists. In the first half of the fifth century the importance of Mount Nitria began to decline, and apparently the number of monks also decreased sharply, because of the rise of other monastic centers in the area of Alexandria and Scetis. Being located in a settled region, it probably ceased already during the fifth century from being a monastic site (Evelyn-White 1932, 149, 257–63; Guillaumont 1977, 199; Kasser 1980).

After the Council of Chalcedon the community of Kellia split into supporters and opponents of the council, and a second church was erected, in order to enable each group to conduct its rites separately. John Moschus, in an anecdote from the middle of the sixth century (*Pratum* 177, 3048), speaks of Kellia as a laura headed by a priest. The excavations conducted at the site of Qusur 'Isa-South 1 on behalf of the University of Geneva (Kasser 1980) indicate that in the fifth century the settlement was interrupted. In the sixth century the site was rebuilt on a new, broader, scale, and in the seventh century, after the Muslim conquest, a period of decline began which continued until the eighth century, when the site was abandoned. But the complete history of the entire monastic settlement, taking into account the new archaeological survey and explorations, has yet to be written. Only when all this new data, accumulated since 1965, is summed up will it be possible to obtain a complete picture of its growth and decline through the different periods, using the archaeological findings to complement the literary sources. (For a general archaeological description of the entire colony and the dwelling unit of a monk, see below, Part II, Chap. 1F).

In contrast to the decline in importance of Mount Nitria and Kellia, Scetis flourished, although it suffered three attacks in the first half of the fifth century (in 407, 434, and 444) in raids by the Mazices (Μαζίκοι), barbarian tribes from the western desert. Its growth was due in great measure to the generous annual grant of wheat, oil, and other products given by Emperor Zeno to the monks of Scetis, a grant that continued until the end of the Byzantine period (Evelyn-White 1932, 224–27).

The main monastic center in Lower Egypt during the time of Euthymius and Sabas was therefore in Scetis. After the colony split into four, each congregation acted independently. The role of the head of the monastery of Macarius, the "Father of Scetis," continued, and each community continued to be headed by a priest-superior, whose authority was based in great measure on his right to remove a monk from communion. This punishment was directed mainly against those who preached erroneous religious doctrine. The duties of the head of the congregation also included providing spiritual guidance to those subordinate to him.

Here, as in Nitria and Kellia, the priest-superior of each community headed a council (συνέδριον) of elders (οἱ γέροντες), which would convene in the church of the community and deal mainly with matters of doctrine and religious discipline. This council was undoubtedly composed of clerical members—priests and deacons. It is doubtful whether it also included lay monks.

John Cassian (*Inst.* v.40, 254) mentions the *oikonomos* of Abba Paphnutius, the head of the monastery of Macarius. It may be assumed that other monasteries also had a monk who held this office. He was also responsible for the care of the sick, which was done in the church. There is no mention of a hospital in Scetis.

Unlike Nitria and Kellia, intellectual Greek-speaking monks did not constitute an important part of Scetis' population (Guy 1964, 135–37). Almost all of the monks were cell dwellers: they lived alone in their cells during weekdays and on Saturdays and Sundays met in the church. There were also recluses, however, who refrained from coming to the church. Such was the daily life in Kellia as well. The cell dwellers, or anchorites, were permitted to receive visitors in their cells from time to time. The impression gained from the *Apophthegmata Patrum* is that the monks freely associated with one another. But the semicoenobite phenomenon seen at Mount Nitria did not exist in Scetis.

The labors of the monk in his cell were the usual ones: basket weaving, fashioning mats from palm fronds, and calligraphy, the copying of books. The monks of Scetis did not weave linen fabric, as did those of Nitria, which was close to the agricultural zone in the Delta. But, as in Nitria and Kellia, the monks went into the surrounding villages to work for wages (given in kind) during the harvest season. Initially each monk marketed his products and purchased his food by himself or made use of the salt caravans as intermediaries. (Some monks in Nitria had an agent, or διακονητής, in a nearby village who took care of their needs.) Afterwards, however, this was done in a centralized manner by the *oikonomos* of each community of Scetis. There was no common garden here as there was in Nitria, but some monks had a small vegetable plot next to their cells.

According to Palladius, wine and pastry prepared by cooks were sold at Mount Nitria. The selling was probably done by peddlers who were not monks, but the monks could purchase their wares privately. Medicines and special food were distributed or sold to the sick in their cells. There were also pious people who went among the cells and supplied the sick with medicines which they purchased with their own money (*HL* XIII, 36–37). As mentioned, there was no central hospital in Scetis, and the sick were often cared for in the churches.

Festive meals connected with the weekend prayers were held in the four churches of Scetis (Evelyn-White 1932, 210–11). All members of the community would also gather there to discuss general matters when the need arose. Unlike Nitria, during the fourth and fifth centuries there was no hostelry in Scetis. Visitors stayed in the cell of their host.

As noted earlier, by the middle of the sixth century the monks of Scetis lived in four laurae (*Pratum* 113, 2977). These were formed in a process of contraction of each congregation toward its center. After the middle of the fifth century in each laura there was a fortified tower near the church, in which the monks could find refuge during the barbarian raids. In each center there was also a kitchen and storehouses for food. It is almost certain that each community had a bakery next to the church, even though they are not mentioned in the sources. (In Nitria at the end of the 4th century there were seven bakeries that supplied the needs of Kellia as well.) The monks' cells were scattered irregularly at short distances from each other. It is possible that, already among the cells, there were dwelling complexes of the *ma-nshubeh* type, which were intended for a number of disciples attached to one "father," complexes whose existence is known from later literary sources. There were also anchorites who lived in cells more distant from the laurae and maintained only loose contact with them (Cauwenbergh 1914, 122–28).

The fourth barbarian attack against Scetis, in 570, caused its complete destruction. The monks scattered to distant places and were in no hurry to return.

Anchorite life was also practiced in Upper Egypt, the stronghold of Pachomian coenobite monasticism, which will be discussed below. The anchorite settlement around the "Monastery of Epiphanius" in western Thebes (Upper Egypt), between Medinet Habu and the Valley of the Kings (see below, Part II, Chap. 1F), is an example of a colony of cell dwellers associated with a nearby coenobium. It is also contemporaneous with "The Cells" of Choziba in the Judean desert and therefore deserves our attention.

A careful analysis of the archaeological and epigraphic findings discovered in the "Monastery of Epiphanius" indicates that this was actually a hermitage of only two or perhaps three monks. Although it was the largest complex in this colony of cell dwellers, it is only in this narrow sense that the term "monastery" should be applied to it. The settlement flourished around the year 600 (Winlock and Crum 1926).

The dwelling complexes scattered over the hills, including the "Monastery of Epiphanius," were of various sizes. Such a dwelling complex was called a τόπος (place), *ma-nshubeh* (in Coptic, "dwelling place"), rarely μοναστήριον, a term more prevalent in northern Egypt, where it denotes the cell of a single monk. The shape of the dwelling complexes and epigraphic findings indicate that a few were used by individual monks, while others housed two monks or a senior monk and his disciple.[10]

In the archaeological and epigraphic findings there are no remains or mention of a church in this community. For this reason Crum assumed that for the Eucharistic ceremonies on Saturdays and Sundays the anchorites went to the church in the nearby village of Jeme (Medinat Habu) or to one of the nearby coenobia (Winlock and Crum 1926, 128–29). There is no evidence that monks celebrated liturgical rites privately in their own hermitages. In the light of this, it cannot be ruled out that the anchorites belonged in practice to a coenobite community, perhaps that of the monastery of St. Phoebammon mentioned extensively in the sources, for which a location at Deir el-Bahri has been proposed. During the weekdays they lived in their cells, outside the coenobium, but came together there for weekend prayers. Such a pattern existed in the monastery of Choziba in the Judean desert during the same period. However, regarding the "Monastery of Epiphanius" we lack explicit information on this, and it is not certain what the communal framework was.

The inscriptions indicate that a few of the monks were priests. Offices such as *oikonomos* or προεστώς, "leader," which are prevalent in the Pachomian legislation or in the deed relating to the nearby coenobium of St. Phoebammon, are not mentioned here. Epiphanius, who (in the author's opinion) headed the settlement, was given the Coptic title "great man" (Winlock and Crum 1926, 131). The impression gained from the epigraphic sources is that there was no rule obligating all the monks to follow one way of life, and apparently, as at Mount Nitria at the end of the fourth century, each monk acted in accordance with his own will and physical ability. The sources indicate that some of them were venerated monks who provided personal spiritual guidance to their disciples and admirers. Such a monk was likely to have one or more disciples (μαθητής) (ibid. 138–39).

B. The Pachomian Coenobia

Monastic communities living an organized communal life to one degree or another were in existence in Egypt even before the activity of Pachomius. Nevertheless, he is regarded as the founder of coenobite Christian monasticism because of the scope of the movement he founded and the momentum he gave to these institutions in Egypt and beyond. The rules in practice in the Pachomian monasteries were widely disseminated in their original language and in Greek and Latin translations. With appropriate modifications they shaped coenobitic life in both the East and the West (Ladeuze 1898; Bousset 1923b,

---

[10] John Climacus, who lived at approximately the same time in Sinai, recommended conducting a tranquil life alone or with one or two monks: μετὰ ἑνὸς ἢ πολὺ δύο (PG 88, 641).

236–47; Draguet 1944–45; Chitty 1966, 20–28; Ruppert 1971, 265 ff; de Vogüé 1980; Rousseau 1985).

Pachomius (290–346 CE) founded his first monastery ca. 323 in Tabennesi (see the chronological table, *Koinonia* I, 466–73), and thus at times all Pachomian monks were called Tabennesiotes. At the time of his death nine monasteries and two nunneries, scattered along the Nile in an approximately 280 km long stretch in the district of Thebais, were united in his community, the Pachomian *Koinonia* (κοινωνία).[11]

His second foundation, Phbow, established in 329, became the largest and most important monastery of the *Koinonia*. In 336/7 Pachomius moved there from Tabennesi.[12] The collection of bound books (*codices*) discovered in 1945 near Nag Hammadi belonged to the Pachomian community of the monastery of Chenoboskion (Šeneset), identified with the site of el-Qasr close to Nag Hammadi.

The population of monks was composed almost entirely of local peasants, Sahidic Coptic-speakers. Later on, however, Greek-speakers and others also joined them. As a general rule, the monasteries were established within the agricultural region of the Nile Valley and not higher, on the fringe of the desert or within it.

The available data indicate an average population of more than 300 monks in each monastery.[13] In 352, however, there were 600 monks in Phbow (Chitty 1966, 25 n. 70), and during Palladius' time the monks of this monastery numbered 1,300 (*HL* XXXII.8, 93; 1,400 in *HL* 13, 52). There were also 200–300 monks living in other monasteries during that time (*HL* XXXII.9, 94). The increased number of monks apparently led to the need to house three monks in one cell, as Palladius states (*HL* XXXII.2, 89), as opposed to the impression gained from the earlier sources that only one monk lived in each cell (*Koinonia* I, 133 n. 3 to this para. in Palladius; Chitty 1966, 22; Rousseau 1985, 79 n. 6).

The Pachomian federation, which comprised several thousand monks and about ten monasteries, was headed by its founder Pachomius and subsequently by his successors.[14]

---

[11] *Koinonia* means "community." The term also refers to the manner of life of the Jewish *Therapeutae* in Egypt, described by Philo in his *De vita contemplativa*. See S. Daniel Nataf, *The Writings of Philo of Alexandria*, I (Jerusalem 1986), 169–202, esp. p. 173 (Hebrew); E. Shürer, *The History of the Jewish People in the Age of Jesus Christ*, II, rev. and ed. G. Vermes, F. Millar, and M. Black (Edinburgh 1979), 591–93.

[12] The basilica of this monastery, located among the houses of the Egyptian village Faw Qibli, ca. 18 km northeast of Nag Hammadi, was partially excavated during 1975–80. This is a large basilica, with two rows of columns on either side of the nave. Its length is 75 m, breadth 37 m, and the thickness of its walls is ca. 1.8 m. It was established at the beginning of the 5th century and abandoned at the end of the 7th or the beginning of the 8th century. Its granite columns are scattered among the houses of the village. Its walls were made of alternating layers of limestone and fired bricks. Its dimensions are similar to those of the basilica of the "White Monastery" of Shenoute (see below). The basilica was preceded by a smaller church from the 4th century, the walls of which were made of fired bricks. This church apparently was built by Pachomius himself (Grossmann 1979; Van Elderen 1979; Lease 1980).

[13] According to Palladius (*HL* XXXII.8, 93), during his time (389–399) the Pachomian federation included many monasteries and numbered 7,000 monks; already during Pachomius' time, it had numbered 3,000 monks (*HL* VII.6, 26). Sozomen, following Palladius, also speaks of 7,000 monks (*HE* III.14.17, 120). John Cassian (*Inst.* IV.1, 122), who was in Egypt during the years 385–399, speaks of more than 5,000 Tabennesiote monks subordinate to one abbot (*abba*), while the author of *HM* (394/5) mentions only 3,000 such monks (*HM* III.1, 39). There apparently is an error in the number of 50,000 mentioned by Jerome in his introduction to the translation of Pachomius' Rule (404 CE), and it should read 5,000 (*Koinonia* II, 143, 184: *Jer. Praef.* 7).

[14] The reality reflected in the *vitae* of Pachomius, especially in the Coptic editions (in Bohairic, *Bo* and in Sahidic, *S*), but also in the main Greek translation (*Vita Prima* = *G*[1]) (Veilleux 1980 = *Koinonia* I), reveals

A similar phenomenon of thousands of monks living in many monasteries under the leadership of one person also prevailed in the monastic settlements of Nitria and Kellia. There, however, the colony was headed by a chief priest. Pachomius, on the other hand, avoided ordination, and when Athanasius visited Tabennesi and sought to ordain him, he hid among his monks (*Koinonia* I, 51: *SBo* 28; 317: *G*¹30).

The organizational and economic administration of the affairs of the entire *Koinonia* was in the hands of the *oikonomos* (οἰκονόμος) of the chief monastery, Phbow. The sense of community among the monks, the feeling that they all belonged to a single monastic society, was achieved in the assemblies held twice a year at Easter and in August, when they all gathered in Phbow. The head of each monastery delivered a report on his community, and new appointments were also made during the assemblies.

The *oikonomos* was also called "father" and, infrequently, also *hegoumenos* (ἡγούμενος); he was assisted by a deputy (*secundus*). Mention is also made of a group of monks of special status, πατέρες or *maiores*, apparently composed of the elder and more experienced monks or those who excelled in virtue. This group took an active part in the Sunday liturgy together with the house fathers (Rousseau 1985, 112–13).

The monks in each monastery were divided, according to their dwellings, into houses (οἶκοι). At times the determining factor in the division of monks among the various houses was their occupation. Jerome also speaks of an additional division, in which each three or four houses constituted a tribe (*Koinonia* II, 147: *Pr.* 15). Each house was headed by a housemaster (οἰκιακός/*praepositus*) along with a deputy. In this hierarchy we do not hear of a special status enjoyed by the priests in the monastery, as in the monastic settlements of Lower Egypt. Seemingly these northern settlements were more integrated into the ecclesiastical establishment than the southern ones. Thus, for example, the chief priest of Scetis would present himself every year at Easter to the patriarch of Alexandria, in order to report to him about the affairs of his community. Such a relationship did not exist between Pachomius and the Church establishment, although, on the other hand, there was no attempt to demolish this institutional framework, as in the ascetic movement in Asia Minor (see below).

Each week a different house provided, in rotation, the various services required by monastic life: cooking, serving food, cleaning, apportioning work, hospitality, caring for the sick, service in the church, and so on. The monks on duty each week were exempt from their regular work.

Twenty to forty monks belonged to each house; their dwellings created a barracks-like structure. The house was also supposed to include an assembly hall for lessons, discussion, and prayer. Initially one monk lived in each cell, but in a later period we hear, as was mentioned, of three monks in each cell. Such cells have been found in the excava-

---

a somewhat loose organizational framework and a high level of spirituality. In contrast, the sources from the end of the 4th century—the Pachomian Rules (which, of course, are a different type of source from the *vitae*) and the testimonies of Palladius, the anonymous author of *HM,* Jerome, John Cassian, and others—reflect a stricter and more inflexible regime and a very hierarchical, formal organization (Rousseau 1985, 77–78 and passim; Veilleux 1981 = *Koinonia* II, 11). It is specifically this later reality, however, which brings us into the 5th century, that is important here, since monasticism then began to spread more vigorously also in the Judean desert, and the comparison between these two monastic societies—that of the Judean desert and that of the Pachomian *Koinonia*—is therefore more relevant.

tions of the monastery of St. Symeon near Aswan (Monneret de Villard 1927, 14; Chitty 1966, 22 n. 28).

The monastery was surrounded by a wall, and its structure resembled that of a military camp (Chitty 1966, 22; Butler 1898, 235). In the wall there was a gatehouse, and next to it a guest room. Additional monastery buildings included: an assembly hall for prayer (generally called in the Pachomian sources σύναξις and not ἐκκλησία), a dining hall (τράπεζα) for all the monks, a kitchen, a bakery, a hospital, storehouses for food, agricultural produce, and work tools, and structures for the pigs and animals used in plowing and for transport. Camels and boats were also used for transportation.

Work played an important part in the life of the monk and in the economy of the monastery. This is a decisive difference between Pachomian and Antonian monasticism, in which the monks performed only light work in their cells (Butler 1911, 524).

There were various workshops within the monastery and agricultural labor took place outside its walls. Palladius, speaking of one of the monasteries of Panopolis (*HL* XXXII.9, 95), mentions many types of craftsmen: tailors, metalworkers, carpenters, camel drivers, swineherds, fullers, farmers, gardeners, blacksmiths, bakers, basket weavers, tanners, shoemakers, and book copyists. Each monk worked in his workshop. He also notes that from their surplus income they supplied the needs of the nunneries and prisons (*HL* XXXII.12, 96).

The apportioning of work among the monks and leading them to their place of work were the responsibilities of the housemaster. The products of their labor were collected and marketed by means of the monastery's boat, even to distant Alexandria. Marketing and purchasing goods needed by the monastery were done by monks carefully chosen for this task.

There were two mealtimes daily in the monastery's refectory: the main meal at midday, at the sixth hour, and a light meal in the evening at about the ninth hour. But according to Palladius (*HL* XXXII.11, 95), a monk could eat at any time from noon until evening. There was no obligation for all the monks to eat at the same time.

Punishments were meted out in accordance with transgressions and included a warning, a public rebuke in the dining hall, church, or house assembly hall, or confinement to the house for a period of time. Expulsion from the community was a severe punishment and was decreed for especially serious offenses such as rebellion or homosexual relations (Rousseau 1985, 95–96).

Strict attention was paid that anyone joining the community should learn to read and memorize a sizeable portion of the New Testament and the Psalter. The monks were similarly careful not to practice excessive mortifications or fasting; labor was more important. But the monk also enjoyed a degree of freedom of choice in these matters (Butler 1898, 237).

The monastery wall was intended to isolate the monks and protect them from the outside world and its temptations. In the "White Monastery" of Shenoute (see below), it was possible to leave the monastery only through a tunnel. Although it is mentioned that the monks sent their excess produce to the prison, in general we do not find in Pachomian monasticism the same degree of readiness to care for the welfare of the lay Christian society outside, by teaching, practicing medicine, providing food and lodging, etc.—activities so characteristic of Basilian coenobitic monasticism (see below).

The number of monasteries federated in the Pachomian *Koinonia* also grew after Pachomius' death, later numbering twenty-four, but the sense of unity among the monasteries weakened. Many communities in Egypt adopted his formula and regulations for coenobitic life (Winlock and Crum 1926, 127 n. 5, 137). The most important example, also for the history of the coenobitic monasticism in Egypt in later generations, is the "White Monastery" of Shenoute in Atripe. His contribution to Egyptian monasticism is regarded as second only to that of Pachomius (Leipoldt 1903; Bell 1983, 1–23).

The "White Monastery" was established about the middle of the fourth century by Pjol, Shenoute's uncle, near the ruins of ancient Atripe in the Thebais desert, not far from the present-day city of Sohag. It was so called because of the white limestone of its structure.[15] Shenoute succeeded his uncle ca. 385, and under his charismatic leadership (until ca. 466) it became a center for thousands of monks. According to the Arabic version of the *Vita Sinuthii*, written by his disciple and successor Besa, he led 2,200 monks and 1,800 nuns. Shenoute administered his monasteries with a strong hand, and his regulations, which he published in "Epistles," are more severe and all-encompassing than those of Pachomius (Leipoldt 1903, 99–106; Ladeuze 1898, 305–26; Bell 1983, 106 n. 70).[16] One of his innovations is the concept of the novitiate, establishing a preparatory period, and having new monks sign a written covenant (διαθήκη) committing themselves not to defile the body in any manner, not to steal, not to bear false witness, and not to do any act of concealed deceit. They were also asked to give up all their possessions on behalf of the community and in the service of the poor. Punishments imposed for wrongdoing included lashes on the soles of the feet. Expulsion was regarded as a very severe punishment.

Bread was baked only twice a year, on the feast of the Ascension and at Pentecost (Winlock and Crum 1926, 162). Here also labor was an important component of the daily routine of the monk and the economy of the monastery. The types of labor performed were similar to those of the Pachomian monasteries. Shenoute did not advocate great asceticism but permitted a monk to withdraw to the desert after a few years of coenobitic life, without completely cutting his ties with the community. Such was the lifestyle of the cell dwellers associated with the "Monastery of Epiphanius" near Thebes in Upper Egypt. The "White Monastery" and the monastery of St. Phoebammon near Jeme

[15] It was extensively explored by Monneret de Villard (1925–26) and others (Walters 1974, 41–42 and bibliography).

[16] Shenoute knew Greek and was even familiar with Greek culture, but he wrote in Coptic. He was the first to begin to develop original Coptic literature, and he greatly enriched the language. His literary output, which contains mainly letters and psalms (Quasten 1963, 185–87), possesses a distinctive style and rich vocabulary. Before his time this literature comprised mostly translations of the scriptures and of patristic literature, or hagiographic literature and monastic legislation. The dialect he used—the Sahidic of the Thebaid, one of the four dialects in Coptic Egypt—became the standard for Coptic literature, and only during the Middle Ages was it replaced by the Bohairic dialect as the official dialect of the Coptic Church.

Because of all this, Shenoute was regarded during the 5th century as the most important representative of Egyptian monasticism in the Thebaid district, the center of the Pachomian *Koinonia* (in 431 he accompanied Cyril of Alexandria, as his bodyguard, to the Council of Ephesus), and he had a great effect on the continued development of Egyptian monasticism, but his influence did not reach beyond Egypt. His *Vita* was never translated into Greek, and so his influence did not reach Greek- or Latin-speaking monasticism, and in the West he was not known at all.

(mentioned above) were noted for their acts of charity. As was stated, we hear less of this in the Pachomian communities (Winlock and Crum 1926, 173).

The coenobitism founded by Pachomius and modified by Shenoute was prevalent in many monasteries in Upper Egypt from his death until the Muslim conquest, although there were minor differences between one monastery and another. Work continued to be an important component in the daily routine, as did meditation. Outstanding personalities were quite rare in this period. The social reality in the monastery of Atripe, as reflected in the writings of Besa, is a sorry one: lying and stealing were common occurrences (Cauwenbergh 1914, 137–59, 171–74).

C. Syrian Monasticism

By the last quarter of the fourth century Syrian monasticism[17] demonstrated both extreme individual asceticism, on the one end, and a decisive tendency toward coenobitism on the other. Both systems prevailed in the fifth and sixth centuries as well, as is evident from Theodoret's *Historia Philotheos,* John of Ephesus' *Lives of the Eastern Saints,* and other literary sources.

While Egyptian asceticism was expressed in "natural" ways such as moderate fasting and vigils, Syrian asceticism displayed extreme forms of mortification. Besides longer periods of fasting and vigilance than those practiced in Egypt, there was a noticeable attitude of self-destruction of the body with "un-natural" mortifications: winding chains around the body; vertical binding of the body or placing it in a narrow, vertical container in order to force an erect posture, thus preventing normal sleep while lying down; exposing the body to wild beasts and snakes; choosing an extremely limited and isolated living space, at the top of a tall column or in a suspended cage; exposing the body to the ravages of weather, and so on. In the second quarter of the fourth century there was a clear tendency for every monk to adopt a certain mode of mortification, which reflects the individualistic character of this form of monasticism. Vööbus also lists the following features of this monasticism in its early stage: anchoritism—total withdrawal from settled areas and wandering in the mountains, either alone or in small groups; primitivism—a hostile attitude toward all manifestations of civilization; dwelling in the heart of nature in caves or in woods and thickets under the open sky; gathering food—fruits and wild herbs (which is the source of the Syriac term *ra'ayâ,* "shepherds," and the Greek βοσκοί, "grazers"); refraining from using fire for cooking or for light; coarse clothing made of goat hair (Vööbus 1960a, 19–35, 256–78, 292–315).

Until the middle of the fourth century we can speak of three centers of Syrian ascetics, all of them in Mesopotamia (Vööbus 1960a, 14–19).[18] Sozomen also mentions an im-

---

[17] The following survey is based mainly on the comprehensive studies by Vööbus 1960a, b, 1988; and by Canivet 1977 and to a lesser degree on Jargy 1952, 1954; Hendriks 1960; and Peña et al. 1978, 1983. For the earliest phase of Syrian asceticism see Beck 1956, 1958; Brock 1973 (repr. 1984); and Griffith 1989–90. I am indebted to Prof. S. Griffith for his comments on the present chapter.

[18] These were the Shiggar range near Nisibis (the region of Jacob of Nisibis, the first of the Syrian monks according to Theodoret [*HPh* I, 160–99], but see Bundy 1991); the Amida region; and the Harran-Edessa region, whence came the famous anchorites Abraham Qidunaia and Juliana Saba (d. 366/7), as well as Aones of Phadana, indicated by Sozomen as the first to introduce the anachorite life among the Syrians. He compares his activity in Syria to that of Antony in Egypt (*HE* VI.33–34). Regarding him see also J.-M. Fiey, "Aones, Awun et Awgin (Eugène): Aux origines du monachisme mésopotamien," *AB* 80 (1962), 53–81.

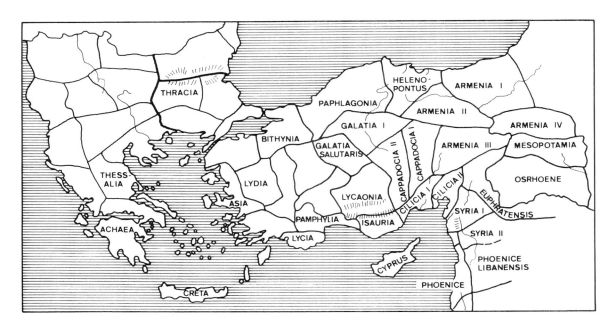

3. Asia Minor and Syria. Map of Roman provinces.

portant center named Jugaton (Ἰουγάτον) in Coele Syria. Theodoret indicates that already in the first half of the fourth century there were organized monasteries in
Osrhoene, Antiochene, and Euphratensis (see the map, Fig. 3). Additional centers developed in the second half of the century in the desert of Chalcis, in Cilicia, and in the
districts of Apamea, Zeugma, Cyrrhus, and Phoenicia (Vööbus 1960a, 224–55; Canivet
1977, 150–205).

The details of the process whereby Syrian monasticism was transformed from anchoritism to coenobitism are not known. It is clear from the *Historia Philotheos* that while
the monks of the first generation (starting with Juliana Saba, not Jacob of Nisibis; see
Bundy 1991) were anchorites, their disciples were already active in the establishment of
coenobia. Vööbus (1960a, 61–69) proposes that the process spread from Egypt via Palestine. At the same time, however, he points to an eastern—Manichaean—source of influence (ibid., 66–68). Gribomont (1965, 9–12), on the other hand, sees here the influence
of Basil the Great.

According to Vööbus' reconstruction (1960a, 61, 115–17), the transition from anchoritism to coenobitism passed through the stage of *hîrtâ*—cells arranged in irregular
fashion around the cell of the head of the community. Once the community had been
formed, it was necessary to provide it with a place of assembly for prayer and with a
storehouse for food (cf. *HPh* ii.3–5, 200–207, Juliana Saba). Physically such a settlement
of monks resembled the Palestinian laura or the semicoenobitic settlements of Mount
Nitria, Kellia, and Scetis. However, regarding the way of life of the monks, there is a
significant difference between the Syrian *hîrtâ* and the above-mentioned monastic settlements in Palestine and Egypt. The sparse information available concerning this phase of

Syrian monasticism indicates that their way of life was coenobitic, in the sense that the monks met every day for common prayers, while in the laurae in Palestine and in Egypt the community met only for the weekend prayers. During regular weekdays the monks prayed in their dwelling places.

In the monastic community of Juliana Saba, which initially numbered 10 disciples and later 100, the day began with the reciting in unison of hymns before dawn. Afterwards they all went forth to wander in pairs, spending the entire day in prayer. Toward evening they all returned to their places, and the day ended with a common evening service (*HPh* II.5, 204–7). Vööbus (1960a, 48) notes the Manichaean roots of this way of life. Work had no place in this daily routine.

A coenobium is called in Syriac *dayrâ* or *'ûmrâ*, although at times these terms are used to describe the place of seclusion of a single monk (cf. Baramki and Stephan 1935, a Syriac inscription with the word *dayrâ* denoting a hermitage, near Jericho). Close to the end of the third quarter of the fourth century there was a marked transformation in Syrian monasticism, an increasing tendency toward communal life (Vööbus 1960a, 111–23, 140–46). It is true that Egeria, who visited Edessa in April 384, does not mention large coenobitic structures in its environs. But Agapetus, the disciple of Marcianus, established two large monasteries in the Apamea district ca. 389, and his disciples established new monasteries (*HPh* III.4, 252).

With the development of coenobitism and the expansion of the communities, it became necessary to order the life of the community with rules. At first these were transmitted orally by the founder to his disciples; later the need arose to write them down and adapt them to the new developments that were taking place in the movement (Vööbus 1960a, 176–84). The individualistic nature of Syrian monasticism was also evident in this stage. It did not produce from its ranks a highly influential legislator such as Basil or Pachomius.[19] Coenobitism spread on a larger scale only later, during the fifth and sixth centuries. But there was not one, single system; differing ways of life were practiced in different monasteries. Some had a high regard for work as an essential source of the monks' livelihood, while others put their trust in heaven, depending for their existence on the generosity of the communities of the faithful, placing great emphasis on the ideal of poverty. But whatever the economic approach, both groups established their monasteries close to villages and to the agricultural region; the former in order to till the land, and the latter in order to receive contributions from the villagers. An extreme example of adherence to the ideal of poverty is Alexander Akoimetos (d. ca. 430) (Vööbus 1960a, 185–98). Rabbula (d. 435) sought to moderate and restrain, by his regulations, the rapid economic development that took place in some of the monasteries in an early stage of the expansion of coenobitism, which led to the existence of personal possessions of the monk in the monastery and various commercial transactions that he conducted privately (Vööbus 1960a, 146–58).

The coenobitic phase, with which we are more acquainted from the beginning of the fifth century on, is also characterized by the new, better planned appearance given

---

[19] On Ephraem the Syrian (d. 373), see Vööbus 1960a, 70–100; Beck 1956, 1958, 1960; Griffith 1989–90. The monastic rules attributed to him are a later work, from the 8th–9th centuries; see Vööbus 1960b, 17–23.

the new monasteries in order to adapt them to house an increasing number of monks, in place of the unorganized *hîrtâ*.

There is not much data in the *Historia Philotheos* regarding the size of the monastic population in the coenobia. Theodoret relates that in his time (about the middle of the 5th century), 400 monks lived in the two monasteries near Apamea (*HPh* III.4, 252), and in another passage he speaks of a community of 250 monks (*HPh* XXX.4, 244).

The rules of the monasteries collected by Vööbus (1960b)[20] are an important source for learning about their organization. Especially important are the rules for coenobitic monks attributed to Maruta[21] and Rabbula.[22] Their influence on the fashioning of the life of the monks went beyond the bounds of their bishoprics. At the same time, however, the increase in the number of rules testifies to the differences in the way of life between

[20] Vööbus (1960b) gathered 23 collections of monastic regulations (16 Monophysite and 7 Dyophysite-Nestorian), written in Syriac or Arabic, and published them with an English translation and a short introduction. (Several of these collections were republished by him in 1988.) Regarding the Monophysite collection I, attributed to Ephraem, see previous note. The Monophysite collections XI–XV are later than the period under discussion; collection III was for priests and collection VII was for nuns. For the other collections, which are used in this discussion, the following abbreviations have been adopted: Rabbula's Rules = collection II (ibid. 24–33), to be dated between 412 and 435; the regulations attributed to Rabbula = collection IX (ibid. 78–86); Rules for the Persians = collection X, regulations for the Monophysite monks in Persia, which originated in the Church authorities in the West, i.e., in Syria, and apparently were in force in all the Monophysite monasteries in Persia (ibid. 87–92).

The Dyophysite collections V–VII belong to the 7th and following centuries, and are not pertinent here. For the other collections used here, the following abbreviations have been adopted: Abraham's Rules = collection II, the regulations of Abraham of Kashkar (ibid. 150–62); Dadishoa's Rules = collection III (ibid. 163–75); Babai's Rules = collection IV (ibid. 176–84). The Dyophysite regulations in collection I (ibid. 115–49) were composed by Maruta, the bishop of Maipherqat (below) in 410. A corrected edition, with a more precise translation, of these regulations was published by Vööbus in 1982. This edition (abbreviated Maruta's Rules) is used herein. The numbers of the articles in Maruta's Rules are according to Vööbus 1960b, 115–49.

[21] The monastic rules attributed to Maruta are part of a larger collection of Nestorian church regulations (Vööbus 1982). Maruta, the bishop of Maipherqat on the border of Syria and Armenia, played an important role in the synod of the Church in Persia, convened in 410 in Seleucia-Ctesiphon, in the period in which friendly relations were formed between the Persian kingdom and the Byzantine Empire. In this state of affairs, the proper conditions were created for the reorganization of the persecuted Church of Persia. The Syrian Maruta aided in this, for, on the one hand, he was an expert in the affairs of the Church in Persia and was trusted by the Persian ruler, and, on the other hand, he was a man of action, involved in the Syrian Church, in the structure of which he sought to organize the Persian Church as well. And indeed, it is clear that the Nestorian canons that concern us here have their origin in the western Syrian legislation and reflect the organization proper for the Syrian monasteries in general from the point of view of a member of the ecclesiastical establishment. I.e., in these rules are formulated the proper manner, according to his opinion, for organizing life in the monastery as well as integrating the monastic movement into the Church. For this reason it is also the most detailed and methodical collection, and it presents an orderly, hierarchical monastic structure, well-integrated into the Church establishment.

[22] Rabbula was the bishop of Edessa (411–435) and one of the senior leaders of the Syrian Church during this period of struggle against Nestorius. It was said of him that he introduced monastic life into the bishop's palace. He conducted extensive correspondence with the monastic communities, even beyond the bounds of his diocese, as he sought to have coenobitic monasticism maintain the rule of poverty and tried to restrain its economic growth; this approach is also evident in his regulations. The Monophysite collection IX attributed to Rabbula (Vööbus 1960b, 78–86) includes 36 regulations. In fact, however, only the first 6 regulations are to be attributed to him. All the others belong to a period in which the coenobia were already more developed, possibly from the second half of the 5th or from the 6th century.

one monastery and another. This must be taken into consideration when one attempts to reconstruct the internal organization and the way of life of the Syrian monasteries.

The impression gained from the monastic rules is that monasteries had a very hierarchical organization. Already in the fifth century the monastic community was divided into classes, apparently four, with several ranks in each class. The passage from one rank to another within the class was a matter of seniority. Confinement to the same rank for a number of years or a demotion in rank were punitive measures (Rule attributed to Rabbula 9–10, 81). The passage from one class to another entailed ordination, appointment to a senior office in the monastery, and personal reputation. The order of seating in the church (Abraham's Rules 8, 161) also seems to be an expression of the complex hierarchy of the community.

The monastery (*dayrâ*) was headed by the *rîšdayrâ*, who was subordinate to the bishop, archdeacon, and *chorepiscopa* in whose district he lived (see Maruta's Rules XLVIII.4, 91.15–16). His appointment had to be confirmed by the bishop (ibid. XL.2–3, 85.7–11). It was his duty to care for all the needs of the monastery (Maruta's Rules XLVIII.3, 91.12–14; Rule attributed to Rabbula 34, 85) and to appoint officials for the various service tasks such as the *rabbaytâ* (see below) and the *tar'āyâ* (gatekeeper), who were subordinate to him. The allocation of service tasks and duties among the monks was done once a year, in the month of Elul (September) at the full moon, that is, in the middle of the month, in a special ceremony including a vigil and the Eucharist (Maruta's Rules XLIX, 91.20–92.6; Rule attributed to Rabbula 23, 83; Rules for the Persians 2, 89). In the Pachomian monasteries in Egypt, as noted earlier, each house fulfilled the service tasks in turn on a weekly basis. As we shall see below, the custom in Palestine was similar to that in Syria.

One rank below the *rîšdayrâ* were the three monks (*thalāthâ 'ahê dbātreh*) whose task was to care for the sustenance (*purnsa*) of everything, so that the monastery would lack nothing, and to manage the income, expenses, and affairs of the community.[23] These monks were called *mparnsānê* and were required to excel in their knowledge and fairness in managing the affairs of the community (Collection VIII.20, 75).

The *rabbaytâ* apparently was of inferior rank to them.[24] Mention is also made of a service task one rank lower than the *rabbaytâ* (Dadishoa's Rules 22, 172). The *rabbaytâ* was responsible for each monk's properly carrying out the work assigned to him (Maruta's Rules L.1–5, 92.7–16) as well as for caring for the sick (ibid. L.5, 92.16). He was also in charge of the provisions and goods in the monastery and was forbidden to waste them (ibid. L.7, 92.19–22). He was not an *oikonomos* in the regular sense of the term (see also below). The term *oikonomos* (οἰκονόμος), steward of a monastery, is not mentioned in

<hr>

[23] Rule attributed to Rabbula 7, 81; 34–35, 85. See also *HPh* III.22, 288, where "the third in the monastery" is mentioned, and also IV.10, 314, where "the second in the administration" is mentioned.

[24] In regulation 21 of collection VIII, which is from the 7th–8th century (Vööbus 1960b, 76), in addition to the *mparnsānê*, mention is made of the *rabbaytâ*. It is clear, therefore, that the *rabbaytâ* was not one of them, and was not included in the group of three in the first rank below the *rîšdayrâ*. As far as can be learned from the regulations, the *rabbaytâ* was the supervisor over the work and the cellarer, and apparently was of a lower rank than the *mparnsānê*. In regulation 16 for the Persians (ibid. 91) mention is made of the *rîšdayrâ* and the *mešablānā*, whose task was to care not only for their own reformation but also for that of the brothers. The *mešablānā* was the guide and, in this context, apparently a guide for proper monastic life.

the *Historia Philotheos,* nor is the term administrator (διοικήτης). The role of the *sā'ūrā* was to deal with the monastery's external affairs.[25]

The elders (*'ahê 'atîqê/sābê*) constituted a separate class, which was divided into several ranks (Maruta's Rules LIV.6, 97.6–7; Collection VIII.16, 74). It is quite plausible that the *mparnsānê* and possibly also the *rabbaytâ* held the senior ranks within this class (and in this case, we may speak of only three classes in the monastery). Membership in this class apparently was a consequence of prolonged excellence in the monastic life and personal reputation.

The priests (*qšīšê*) and deacons (*kōhanê/mšamšānê*) constituted a separate class, which was also divided into a few ranks (Rule attributed to Rabbula 9, 81). The remaining class was composed of the regular brothers (*'ahê*), and included no less than sixty ranks (Rule attributed to Rabbula 9–10, 81).

The routine of monastery life divided the day into three parts: services and reading, work, eating and rest (Maruta's Rules LIV.24, 99.13–15). There were only a few monasteries in which the monks did not engage in any form of work. The number of meals was determined according to the occupation of the monks. In a monastery of workers there were two meals per day, at the sixth hour and in the evening. If the monks did not work, one meal was sufficient, at the ninth hour or in the evening (Maruta's Rules LIV.18, 98.9–13; Collection XV.7, 107).

During hot summer days a detailed daily routine was prescribed: the monks would work in the early morning for as long as it was cool. When the temperature rose, they would sit for reading, until the time of the midday service. Then they would eat and rest until late afternoon when it was cooler. They would then go out to work until the time of the evening meal, which they would eat after the service (Maruta's Rules LIV.23, 99.6–12).

In the large monastery on Mount Izla near Nisibis, in Nestorian Persia, there developed a special system of cell dwellers (*'ahê dqelāytâ*: Dadishoa's Rules 15, 171) who lived outside the coenobium but belonged to its community. The founder and first abbot was Abraham of Kashkar (571–588), who was followed by Dadishoa (588–604) and Babai (604–627/8). Abraham of Kashkar (the district of his birth) is considered to be the most prominent figure in eastern Syrian monasticism.[26] There was a similar situation during this period in Choziba in the Judean desert (see below, Part III, Chaps. 3–4), a contemporary coenobium with cell dwellers living outside its walls.

---

[25] Maruta's Rules LII.1–7, 94.12–95.8; Rabbula's Rules 2–3; 27; Rule attributed to Rabbula 1–2, 80; 13, 82; Rules for the Persians 5, 89. The Rule of Maruta (XXV.6, 75.4–6) imposes upon the *chorepiscopa* the appointment of the *sā'ūrā;* thus he could ensure that the monk would be loyal to the Church establishment. It is almost certain that in practice it was the monks themselves or the *rīšdayrâ* who chose their external representatives, and only the confirmation of the *chorepiscopa* was required.

[26] In his journeys to the west he reached Scetis and Sinai. The monasticism of Scetis had a marked influence upon his community, which developed around his cave of seclusion on Mount Izla. His monastery became the most important monastery of the Nestorian Church. The reformation he introduced (which was also expressed in the garb and hairstyle of the monks) was widespread around Nisibis, where monasteries were established that followed his system. He is considered as "the head and the master of all the monks in the region of the Orient." He received the title *Rabba* (the Great) in the Nestorian Church. For historical and archaeological information about this monastic center, see J.-M. Fiey, *Nisibe: Métropole syrienne orientale et ses suffragants, des origines à nos jours,* CSCO 388, Sub. 54 (1977); S. Brock, "Notes on Some Monasteries on Mount Izla," in idem, *Syriac Perspectives on Late Antiquity* (London 1984), art. XV (= *Abr-Nahrain* XIX, Leiden 1980–81, 1–19).

The regulations of the first three monastery heads have been preserved and enable us to become acquainted with the way of life in this monastery and to follow the changes that took place there in certain areas as time passed. During weekdays the cell dwellers remained in their cells and only on Sundays and feast days met together in the church (Abraham's Rules 8, 161; Dadishoa's Rules 4, 169). A novitiate of three years in the coenobium preceded the status of cell dweller (Dadishoa's Rules 13, 170; cf. Abraham's Rules 10, 161–62; Babai's Rules 7, 179). Dadishoa explicitly ruled (regulation 7, 170) that no one who could not read books would be admitted to the monastery.

One of the responsibilities of the *rabbaytâ* was to visit the brothers in their cells once a month, and when he had the time, even more often, in order to ensure that they lacked nothing. In his absence, the monks would be visited by the brother one degree lower than him (Dadishoa's Rules 23, 173). It was forbidden to admit children to the community (ibid. 17, 171). This was an early rule of Scetis, but is also known from another Syrian set of rules (Collection VIII.5, 72).

D. Basilian Coenobitism

Acquaintance with the Basilian system is of special interest, since the leaders of Palestinian monasticism were natives of Asia Minor where Basilian monasticism prevailed. The present survey aims at pointing out their monastic inheritance, thus enabling us to see later on to what extent it was continued, modified, or abandoned.

Basil the Great (329/30–379) was one of the "Three Cappadocian Fathers" along with his friend Gregory of Nazianzus and his brother Gregory of Nyssa. They were among the senior theologians of the Church, bearing the banner of Nicaea against the Arian heresy. Born in Caesarea, the metropolis of Cappadocia (Fig. 3), to an aristocratic family, Basil received a broad secular education in Constantinople and Athens, and planned to be a rhetor like his father. But in 357, like his mother, brother, and sister, who began to lead a life of abstinence and asceticism, he also decided to withdraw from the secular world. He was baptised again and set out on a journey of learning in the famous monastic centers in Lower Egypt, Palestine, Syria, and Mesopotamia. Upon his return he distributed his possessions and began to live as a recluse on his family's estate in Annesi, on the banks of the Iris River, near Neocaesarea in the Pontus (in a landscape completely different from that of Egypt, Palestine, or Syria). His teacher in this phase of his life was Eustathius, about whose "philosophy" he had already heard quite a bit from the enthusiastic letters of his sister Macrina.

According to Sozomen (*HE* III.14.31–37, 122–23), it was Eustathius (ca. 300–377) who spread ascetic monasticism in Armenia, Paphlagonia, and Pontus. He determined for his monks what they should eat, what clothes they were to wear, what behavior to avoid and what conduct to adopt. Sozomen adds that some say he was the author of Basil's ("Small") *Ascetikon* (see below). Eustathius was born in the Roman province of Armenia. About 320 CE he stayed in Alexandria and became a disciple of Arius. There he was probably impressed by Egyptian monasticism. His own monastic teachings were directed to the lone ascetic (Gribomont 1957, 1961, 1980) and do not contain guidance for communal life. These teachings have not survived, apparently due to his semi-Arian tendencies, which were rejected by the Cappadocian Fathers and led to a breach between him and Basil in 375.

Some information about his "philosophy" and the "enthusiastic" movement (thus defined in the early sources) that it created can be gleaned from the condemnatory canons of the council of Gangra in Paphlagonia (341).[27] But the twenty canons of this council against the Eustathian ascetics are a hostile source,[28] and we cannot know to what degree they reflect his teaching or the acts of the more extreme circles in the movement, who opposed any integration of monasticism into the Church.[29]

An enthusiastic ascetic movement also existed in Constantinople. Macedonius, who later became bishop of the capital (344–359), came from these circles and maintained ties with Eustathius. Therefore, the enthusiastic movement in Asia Minor is to be viewed as a pan-Anatolian movement and not as a local phenomenon limited solely to the provinces of Armenia, Pontus, and Cappadocia (Gribomont 1980, 123–29).[30]

The spiritual profundity of this ascetic philosophy and its ties to the scriptures are reflected in great degree in the *Small Ascetikon* (see below), which, according to Basil himself, contains the teachings of Eustathius and his circle (Basil, *Ep.* 1, 2–7; 223, 295–313; Gribomont 1959).

Basil, who considered Eustathius his teacher at the beginning of his career, through reflection and study of the scriptures reached different conclusions regarding the proper system for the monastic life (Amand de Mendieta 1957; Bardy 1937). After five years in which he lived as an anchorite (357–362), when other monks began to gather around him, he saw the need for an orderly communal life. Although he was never an abbot,

[27] Eustathius and his monks were charged there with disrupting the social order by promoting celibacy, calling upon people to dissolve the marital tie and the family structure and to withdraw from the world, a doctrine that led many to abandon members of their family—spouses, parents, or children—and to leave them in distress. These ascetics also attacked the corruption they found in the ecclesiastical establishment, calling mainly for the boycott of rites conducted by married priests. Gifts were given to them by the faithful for the care of the poor and the needy, which harmed the income of the Church. Social activity was highly regarded by them (which would later be expressed also in the teachings of Basil). They preached total poverty and sought to apply this principle to the entire Christian community by encouraging slaves to flee from their masters and giving them refuge and by urging debtors not to repay their debts and to find shelter among them. These actions led, of course, to social disorder. They were also charged with violating the accepted regime of fasting: thus, e.g., they were accustomed to fast on Sunday, and the extreme among them even regarded Easter as a Jewish holiday. Their external appearance was untidy and disorderly. Men and women lived together in the same ascetic group and wore identical clothing. They also denigrated work as an essential component of the daily routine of the monk.

[28] For an English translation of these canons, see O. Larry Yarbrough, "Canons from the Council of Gangra," in V. L. Wimbush, ed., *Ascetic Behavior in Greco-Roman Antiquity: A Sourcebook* (Minneapolis 1990), 448–55.

[29] When Eustathius agreed to be ordained as bishop of Sebasteia, the metropolis of Armenia Prima (356), there were extreme monks who withdrew from his movement and went out to the snowy forests. At any rate, it is clear that the acts of the Council of Gangra, which was led by Arian bishops, did not have great influence on the common people. They did not prevent Eustathius' election as bishop of Sebasteia, and he was admired by many, including members of Basil's family and Basil himself at the beginning of his career.

[30] The Messalian movement was the continuation of Eustathian monasticism in Asia Minor in the last quarter of the 4th century and in the 5th. The Messalians (from the Syriac for "those who pray"; in Greek, εὐχῖται) originated after the middle of the 4th century in Mesopotamia, from where they spread to Syria, Asia Minor, Thrace, and afterwards to Egypt as well. According to their view, because of "original sin," there is a demon in the soul of each person, and in order to drive it away, the sacrament of baptism is not sufficient; rather, a person must pray with concentration, incessantly, until attaining the complete loss of the senses. In order to reach this, an ascetic life must be maintained as well (Vööbus 1960a, 127–39; Gribomont 1965, 18–19).

with his systematic teachings he became the founder and organizer of coenobitic monasticism in Asia Minor. He also sought to integrate the monastic movement into the bosom
of the Church (Gribomont 1965, 19–24). In 364 he was ordained a priest, and in 370 he
was elected bishop of Caesarea, the metropolis of the province of Cappadocia. In this
capacity he excelled in organizational ability and in social activities on behalf of the members of his community. He also took a forceful stand against the Arian emperor Valens
and his emissary, attempting to bring unity in the Church. His high status and reputation
greatly contributed to the growth and glorification of the monastic movement, and many
joined its ranks, adopting his monastic teaching. His system became the dominant form
of Anatolian monasticism.

Basil's monastic teaching was formulated in his ascetic writings, the Ἀσκητικά/*Ascetica* (PG 31:619–92, 869–88), his ethical ones, Τὰ ἠθικά/*Moralia* (ibid. 700–869), and in
two Rules (Quasten 1963, 211–14).[31]

Basil regarded monasticism as the only proper way of life for the Christian, and the
communal way of life, coenobitism, as the only perfect form of monastic life (*Reg. fus.* 7,
928–33). His ascetic teaching has a profound theological and philosophical foundation,
based on the scriptures (Amand 1949), and his *Regulae* were meant only to explain them.
Besides the adherence to the scriptures, at the basis of his teaching there is the love of
God and the love of one's fellow man. He therefore sought to establish his monasteries
in populated areas, among the Christian communities in the cities, towns, and villages,
rather than in distant, isolated areas.

The social framework in which the coenobium monks lived was called a brotherhood
(ἀδελφότης), a community of modest size in which ca. 30–40 monks shared a communal
life (Amand de Mendieta 1957, 39–40). Each brotherhood was autonomous; however, in
order to strengthen the ties between them, he instructed the heads of the brotherhoods
to assemble at set times and places to discuss disciplinary matters (*Reg. fus.* 54, 1044–52).
All the monasteries were subordinate to the authority of the bishop within whose see
they were located.

---

[31] The title *Ascetica* refers to a group of 13 ascetic compositions attributed to Basil, some of which are
not authentic. Gribomont (1953) studied the manuscript tradition of these compositions, including the *Moralia* and the *Rules*. The *Moralia* is a collection of 80 regulations or ethical instructions, each of which is
accompanied by a plethora of supporting texts from the New Testament. It was written when Basil lived as
an anchorite together with Gregory of Nazianzus. The two Rules took form as the outgrowth of responses
to questions directed to him by the monks he visited, which were written down on the spot by fast-writing
secretaries, and they are arranged in this manner. The earliest set of regulations, known as the *Small Ascetikon*, is dated to 358/9. The questions of the monks clearly reflect the reality of ascetic life and at times even
of Eustathian trends, which Basil sought to restrain in his responses. This early collection has not survived
in Greek, only in the Latin translation of Rufinus (PL 103, 487–554). In a later phase, when Basil had freed
himself of the influence of Eustathius and had developed the coenobite system, he expanded and adapted
this collection to his new approach (Gribomont 1953, 237–54). In this new format, the questions discussed
in the *Small Ascetikon* constitute the first 23 of the 55 paragraphs of the *Detailed Rule, Regulae fusius tractatae*
(PG 31, 889–1052), in which the principles of monastic life are discussed. The second set of regulations,
the *Short Rule, Regulae brevius tractatae* (PG 31, 1080–1305), contains 313 short paragraphs dealing with the
application of the monastic principles to everyday life in the coenobium. The two compositions together
comprise the *Large Ascetikon*. Later versions with additions also exist. The so-called *Vulgata* edition, compiled
in the 6th century, enjoyed an extremely wide circulation. Still later editions, with various additions, were
edited during the Middle Ages, and to the present day the *Regulae* of Basil remain at the foundation of
Greek monasticism (Gribomont 1953).

His system of organization was quite simple. The brotherhood is headed by the προ-εστώς (*proestos*), who must care for all the brothers as a father for his family (*Reg. fus.* 35, 1004–8). He is aided in the administration of the monastery by a deputy, who is acting head in his absence. The elder, more experienced monks, who excel in their way of life, enjoy special status in the fraternity, but it is the head of the brotherhood who decides and gives sentence, and all the monks must obey him. The principles of obedience and poverty are the two basic principles binding the monk (Amand 1949, 322–35). Other functionaries are those responsible for the workshop storehouses, for the distribution of alms to the poor, those caring for the sick, and teachers (Bardy 1937, 222–33).

Everyday life was a combination of prayer and work. Basil established a cycle of seven canonical times of prayer per day (*Reg. fus.* 37, 1009–16; see the detailed discussion below, Part III, Chap. 4A). Prayers were conducted communally in the church. In contrast to the Eustathians, he regarded work as an important component of the daily routine of the monk. The labors he recommended were: weaving, shoemaking, construction, carpentry, tinsmithing, and agriculture. He ruled that agricultural produce should serve the needs of the monastery, with the surplus being distributed to the poor (*Reg. fus.* 38, 1016–17). He did not perceive the monasteries as large production and labor centers, like the Pachomian coenobia. He permitted the educated and capable among the community to devote themselves to the study and reading of the scriptures. Permission for this had to be obtained from the head of the brotherhood (*Reg. brev.* 96, 1149; 235, 1240; 236, 1241).

Basil preached moderate modes of asceticism and moderation in fasting or vigils. The monk was not free to choose for himself his degree of asceticism or to deny himself certain foods served to all. Any deviation from the norm in the direction of excessive asceticism was perceived as false pursuit of glory (*Reg. brev.* 132, 1169–72; 137, 1173).

Basil highly regarded acts of benevolence and social welfare by the monks among the lay community: aid to the sick, the provision of lodging for travelers, care for orphans, teaching and education of children in a school near the monastery (*Reg. fus.* 15, 952–57; 38–40, 1016–21; *Reg. brev.* 155, 1184; 286, 1284; 292, 1288). In principle, a hostelry and a hospital were to be found in each Basilian fraternity (Amand de Mendieta 1957, 64).

Because of his personality and his achievements as a bishop and leader of the monastic movement, a theologian, and a religious and social reformer, as well as his extensive and profound literary activity (Quasten 1963, 204–26), he received the title "the Great." His monastic doctrine, which was translated into Latin even before the end of the fourth century, spread far and wide and was adopted by many monastic communities throughout the entire Christian world.

Basilian coenobitism differs in many respects from the Pachomian. Although Basil visited Egypt at the beginning of his monastic career, it is doubtful whether he saw any Pachomian monastery, not even the one in Canopus, close to Alexandria. Linguistically as well there is no link between the writings of Basil and the Pachomian writings that were translated into Greek. It is also doubtful whether such translations existed at such an early stage, so that they could have reached Basil. Therefore one should not overestimate the influence of Pachomius' coenobitic doctrine on Basil (Amand de Mendieta 1957, 33–34). As for Basil's teaching, it greatly influenced the monastic movement in Palestine, especially the coenobitic one, many of whose leaders were natives of Cappadocia.

E. The Organization of the Monastic Movement according to the Justinianic Legislation

The guiding principle of the Justinianic legislation on monasteries was to determine the place of the monastic movement in the structure of the Church and its subordination to it. Attempts in this direction had already been made by the Church itself. Several canons of the Council of Chalcedon, especially canons 4, 8, 16, and 24, are along these lines. This was expressed even earlier in the Pachomian Rule, in Basil's teaching, and in the Syrian regulations attributed to Maruta (410) that were enacted for the Church of Persia (Vööbus 1982).

The Justinianic legislation is different from these, since it is not ecclesiastical but civil law. It was the first comprehensive attempt at systematic state legislation focusing on the affairs of monasteries. The Justinianic legislation deals with the following matters: the mutual relationship between the monasteries and the Church, especially the subordination of the monasteries to the archbishop and bishop; the administrative organization of the monastery: the abbot, his authority and legal status, the community of monks, and various monastic functionaries; the office of *exarchos* as district supervisor of the monasteries on behalf of the bishop; the manner in which candidates are admitted to the monastery; leaving the monastery, especially due to expulsion and the conversion of belief; discipline in the monastery; and the mutual relationship, in terms of the law, between the monasteries and the state (Granič 1929–30; Frazee 1982, 271–76).

In the Justinianic legislation a comprehensive effort was also made to establish a legal system for the right of the monasteries to receive inheritances and their status in relation to the natural heirs of the monk, and to determine the legal status of the monk's property during his lifetime (Orestano 1956). There is a noticeable tendency in the legislation to bring about uniformity of structure and practice, but we cannot conclude from this that this was indeed so in every part of the empire. Many of the laws seem suitable for the situation in Constantinople and its environs but not for more remote areas. Nevertheless, the Epilogue of each law, addressed to the patriarch of the capital, states that he must circulate it among the metropolitans, bishops, and monasteries; and judicial matters also connected with the civil law, such as questions of property and inheritance, were now universally binding state laws.

For the present discussion, we are mainly concerned with those laws that bear on the organization and structure of the monasteries and their place in the Church establishment. Nearly all of these laws reflect a coenobitic reality; however, the legislation also recognizes the existence of monasteries of hermits (ἀσκητήρια) (see, e.g., *Nov.* 5.9 [535 CE]; 123.34 [546 CE]). The term *laura*, unique mainly to Palestine and to a lesser degree to Egypt, is not mentioned in the Justinianic legislation.

The basic principle establishing the subordination of the monks in each district to the bishop and that a monastery was not to be built without his prior approval (*Nov.* 5.1) was already formulated in canon 4 of the Council of Chalcedon, and Basil established it even earlier in his regulations. In Novel 5 (ibid.) it is stated that a monastery shall be established only after the bishop shall bless the site by placing a cross on it. Before giving permission the bishop must be assured that the new institution had an endowment sufficient for its maintenance. Tradition required that at least three members were necessary to constitute a monastery (*Nov.* 67; Frazee 1982, 273).

The terms most commonly used in the Justinianic legislation for denoting the abbot of a monastery are *hegoumenos* (ἡγούμενος) and, less frequently, *archimandrites* (ἀρχιμανδρίτης).[32] These terms appear frequently, with the same meaning, also in the church councils of the Justinianic period.

Each monastery had to have a *hegoumenos,* but it was forbidden that there be one *hegoumenos* for two monasteries (*Cod. Iust.* 1.3.29; *Nov.* 133.5). It was explicitly forbidden to combine a greater number of monasteries under one person's leadership. There is thus a definite trend here to prevent the formation of very large centers of power within the monastic movement.

It was the responsibility of the *hegoumenos* to supervise discipline in his monastery (*Nov.* 133.4), and all were obligated to obey him (*Nov.* 5.3). The *hegoumenos* was also responsible for the financial assets and real estate of the monastery. In the Justinianic legislation there is no *oikonomos* for monasteries, only for churches.[33] The abbot was forbidden to sell the yearly income that the monastery received as an inheritance (*Cod. Iust.* 1.3.55.2; *Nov.* 7.12 [535 CE]), and when any of the monastery's property was sold or leased, the approval of the members of the community was also required (*Cod. Iust.* 1.2.17; *Nov.* 120.6 [544 CE]; Granič 1929–30, 24).

Hagiographic literature indicates that generally a new abbot was appointed by his predecessor before his death or was chosen by the monks themselves. At times, however, this was accompanied by disagreements and quarrels, which led to the internal disintegration of the community. In order to prevent this, Justinian also gave the patriarch an active role in the process. He established that the selection of a new abbot, on the death or departure of his predecessor, would be by election (ψῆφος, ἐπιλογή) of all the monks (τὸ μοναχικὸν ἄπαν), the plenum (πλήρωμα), or by those excelling and of the highest repute among the monks, either unanimously or by majority (apparently the practice varied depending on the community). The successor would not be selected according to his seniority in the monastery, his priority in ordination, or his office or monastic rank (see below), but rather according to other criteria: personal reputation and excellence in the monastic life, true faith, chaste life, worthiness to govern, and ability to maintain discipline among the monks. He must not be a priest. It was also established that the election had to receive the approval of the bishop (*Cod. Iust.* 1.3.46.1–3; *Nov.* 5.9; 123.34). Before the Justinianic legislation we do not find that the bishop participated in the election of an abbot (Granič 1929–30, 19–22).

The community of monks was organized hierarchically. One rank below the *hegoumenos* were the first in the hierarchy (πρωτεύοντες) and the elders (γέροντες/γεγηρακότες) (*Nov.* 133.2). The abbot had a deputy (δευτεράριος), who was the second in rank (δεύτερος) or the *locum tenens* (τοποτηρητής) of the abbot during time of illness or absence (Granič 1929–30, 26; Lampe 1961–68, 1398). There is also mention of a third rank (τρί

---

[32] For additional terms, including ἡγεμών, ἀββᾶς (*Nov.* 123, chap. 34), and προεστώς (*Nov.* 133, chap. 4), see Granič 1929–30, 17–19. (The *Novellae* in the Lingenthal edition are arranged in chronological order, and their serial number is therefore different from that appearing in the edition of Scholl and Kroll. Granič refers in his edition to the *Novellae* in the Lingenthal edition.)

[33] The examples cited by Granič 1929–30, 29 n. 1, do not deal with the *oikonomoi* of the monasteries.

τον). Justinian established that the deputy does not automatically succeed the head of the monastery upon the death of his predecessor, unless he is found fit for the position and elected by the monks in the manner described above (*Cod. Iust.* I.3.46.1; *Nov.* 5.9).

It was established that each monastery would have two or three *apocrisiarii* (ἀποκρισι-άριοι), according to the size of the monastery and the scope of its affairs. These were elderly monks, subordinate to the abbot. Their task was to supervise monastic discipline (*Nov.* 133.5) and deal outside the monastery with legal matters, both of the monastery as an institution and of the monks as individuals (*Cod. Iust.* I.3.29; *Nov.* 123.42). They alone, of all the monks, were permitted to stay in the cities on behalf of the monastery. At times they were also elected to represent the monastery in church councils (Granič 1929–30, 27–29).

It was further established that in each monastery there would be at least four or five clerics, who would be chosen from among the more elderly monks who excelled in self-control. They would be ordained priests, deacons, and other ecclesiastics. Their task was to care for the church, to restrain petulant youth, and to deliver lectures upon the holy scriptures and give instruction in them (*Nov.* 133.2). For this purpose there had to be a large number of books in the monastery for the use of the monks (ibid.).

This same novel indicates that there were monasteries without churches. In such a case the monks would leave the monastery in an orderly fashion, headed by the abbot, the first in the hierarchy, and the elders, in order to participate in prayers outside its gates. They were to arrive at the church exactly at the beginning of the rite and to leave at its conclusion.

The monks were to occupy themselves not only in the study of the scriptures but also in handicrafts (*Nov.* 133.6). However, there were also monasteries of praying monks, contemplatives, whose economic existence was based on income from property and do-nations. The most famous monastery of praying monks was, of course, the monastery of the *Akoimetoi* ("sleepless ones") in the capital, where perpetual psalmody in alternating choirs day and night was maintained.

All the monks in a coenobium had to eat together and sleep together. They were to sleep in a dormitory, with each monk having a separate straw mattress. The purpose of this was to enable each monk to examine the sincerity of the intentions and acts of his fellow monks, to bear witness to their honor and modesty, and to prevent the monk from overly indulging in sleep. If there was not enough room for all the monks to sleep in one hall, they were to be divided between two or more. Separate private rooms were prohib-ited in the coenobium, except for the elderly and the weak, whose physical condition required it, or for those who had proven themselves experienced and excellent monks and who sought to maintain this type of asceticism. Permission for this, however, had to be received from the abbot. The legislation recognized the existence of anchorites and hesychasts, but recommended that all the monks, especially the young, live in a coeno-bium, where they would benefit from the example and guidance of those who were more mature (*Nov.* 5.3; 133.1; 123.36). A recluse was permitted to have one or two attendants (*Nov.* 133.1).

Each monastery was to be surrounded by strong walls, so that no one would be able to leave other than through the gates (ibid.). It was forbidden for a monastery to have more than one or two wickets (πυλίς), and a gatekeeper—who had to be a monk of advanced age, modest, and responsible—had to be stationed in each gate, to prevent the monks from leaving without the permission of the abbot and to prevent strangers from entering the monastery (ibid.). The entrance of women was forbidden, as was their burial in male monasteries (*Nov.* 133.3).[34]

[34] The prohibition of burial was not honored everywhere. In the burial cave of the monastery of Choziba inscriptions have been found testifying to the burial of women at the site; see Schneider 1931, 317–29 and the index of personal names on pp. 330–31. This monastery was also distinguished, however, from the other monasteries of the desert in that women were permitted to enter it for visits; see *Miracula* 1, 360–63.

3

Sabas' Biography

Cyril of Scythopolis completed writing his *Vita Euthymii* and *Vita Sabae* in 556 (Flusin 1983, 33).[35] At that time, the figure of Euthymius already belonged to the distant past, and therefore was vague and enveloped in an aura of idealization. Sabas, on the other hand, had died in the recent past (532), so that his personality and activity were living memories. Cyril, who as a youth had seen Sabas, learned about him from John the Hesychast as well as from some additional sources: his parents in Scythopolis; his teacher and guide George, the abbot of the monastery of Beella; Gerontius of Medaba; Paul, one of the disciples of Jeremias the Armenian; and Gregory, Sabas' nephew, who told him about his life in Cappadocia (Schwartz 1939, 374–76). All these sources are sympathetic to Sabas, as is Cyril himself. Therefore, we should read them with critical caution. At the same time, we should be aware that Cyril's compositions are not laudatory rhetorical works, with an abundance of scriptural quotations, like many other saints' lives. Cyril does not refrain from mentioning instances of revolt and opposition against Sabas' leadership, a fact that adds credibility to his narrative.

The Early Years (439–456)

Sabas was born in 439 in Cappadocia, Asia Minor, in a small village named Moutalaska (present-day Talas) (Chitty 1966, 100 n. 104), in the district of Caesarea, the capital of the province. His parents, Sophia and John, were Christians of distinguished lineage. When Sabas was about five years old, his father went to Alexandria with his military unit, the *numerus Isaurorum*,[36] and his mother accompanied him. Sabas, along with the family inheritance, was entrusted to the supervision of his maternal uncle, Hermias. However,

---

[35] The chief source for our knowledge of Sabas is this *vita*, written by Cyril of Scythopolis. Information about him is also scattered through *V. Euth.* and *V. John Hes.*, also written by Cyril. The definitive edition of these Greek texts was published by Schwartz (1939) and a French translation was published by Festugière (1962–63). I have also made use of the Hebrew and English translations by Leah Di Segni, done on behalf of the Center for the Study of the History of Eretz Israel and its Yishuv, of Yad Yizhak Ben-Zvi. My thanks to this Center and to Leah Di Segni for permission to use these translations, as yet unpublished. Price's English translation (1990) was consulted as well. The spelling of personal names is generally according to this translation, for the sake of uniformity in reference.

For comprehensive surveys on the history of Sabas, see Vailhé 1897, 1899, 1899–1900b; Phokylides 1927, 90–155; Schwartz 1939, 277–78, 374–76; Leclercq 1950, 189–96; Festugière 1962b, 145–49.

[36] The barbarian foot and cavalry units of the imperial army, which maintained their national characteristics in their equipment, arms, and methods of warfare, but were distinguished from the auxiliary by being organized in large imperial troops, were called *numeri*. See Stein-Palanque 1959, 55; Festugière 1962b, 14 n. 1. Such an army unit is also mentioned in the Nessana papyri.

the bad temper of Hermias' wife led Sabas to flee to his paternal uncle, Gregory, who lived in the village of Skandos, three miles from Moutalaska.

After three years, when the child was eight years old, a quarrel broke out between his uncles regarding Sabas and his inheritance, and the boy was transferred to the Flaviana monastery, a coenobium close to Moutalaska, in which 60 to 70 monks lived. Sabas grew up there, receiving the elementary education of a monk. Under the guidance of the abbot of the monastery, he learned the principles of monastic discipline, and within a short period of time he had learned by heart the entire Psalter, which enabled him to serve as a reader in the church (Festugière 1962b, 18 n. 6). He similarly learned the regulations of the communal life of the monks. After he had stayed for a while in the monastery, the uncles reached an agreement regarding the boy's upbringing. This apparently sprang from their fear that the inheritance would be handed over to the monastery and be lost to them. They therefore wanted to remove him from the monastery, so that he would tend the family lands and marry,[37] but they were not successful. Sabas excelled in monastic life in the Flaviana monastery, withstood various temptations, observed many fasts, and deprived himself of sleep. There is even record of a miracle that he performed there at an early age: on a winter's day, the monastery baker forgot his wet clothes in the oven, where they had been put to dry. The following day, when they began to fire the oven, the baker agitatedly remembered this. The young Sabas, however, was the only one who dared to enter the oven to remove the clothes before they were burned; he emerged unscathed (*V. Sab.* 5, 89).[38] Cyril received these details of Sabas' life in Moutalaska and in the Flaviana monastery from the priest Gregory, Sabas' nephew (ibid. 90).

After a stay of ten years in the Flaviana monastery, in his eighteenth year,[39] Sabas asked the abbot to release him so that he could go to the Holy City and live in *hesychia* (ἡσυχία)[40] in its desert. The abbot agreed to his request only after he was ordered to do so in a nocturnal vision, and Sabas set forth for Jerusalem.

---

[37] Thus Flusin (1983, 96 and n. 48) explains *V. Sab.* 2, 88.4–5. According to Festugière's translation (1962b, 15), the uncles requested only that he join his relatives.

[38] This event is reminiscent of the story of the three youths in the furnace in the Book of Daniel, chap. 3; see Flusin 1983, 193–94. Evagrius (*HE* IV.36) and Moschus (add. Mioni, no. 12), who were contemporaries, tell a similar story about a Jewish youth who was cast by his father into a furnace because he consumed the consecrated elements of the Eucharist, but who was miraculously saved. It is clear that this is a literary genre. For additional parallels, see Chadwick 1974, 48.

[39] At this stage of his life Sabas reached "the age of discretion." Although he was brought up as a youth in a monastery, only at this age did he become mature enough to decide, by his own choice, whether he wished to be a monk. Cyril as well left his house approximately at this age in order to live among the desert monks. For the canonical significance of the age in religious life, see J. Delmaille, "Age," *DDC* I (Paris 1935), 315–48; Judith Herrin and A. Kazhdan, "Age," *ODB* 36; A. Kazhdan and A. Cutler, "Childhood," *ODB* 420–21. Basil (*Ep.* 199.18, 108 in LCL ed.) states that a virgin should not be admitted to a nunnery before reaching the fullness of reason, at the age of 16 or 17. See Delmaille, "Age," 323.

[40] *Hesychia*, which means "stillness, quietness," is a technical term expressing the state of inner tranquility and quiet that results from overcoming the desires and passions. This is a necessary condition for contemplation. See *HM*, Prologue, line 20 and the interpretation of Festugière on p. 6 of his French translation, and p. 123, n. 8, in the English translation of Russell (CS 34). In *HM* the term is mentioned as characterizing the way of life of the monks of Nitria, who lived in deep silence (ἐν ἡσυχίᾳ πολλῇ). See also Flusin 1983, 118; Hausherr 1956a, 8–11; Adnes 1969, 381–99; Festugière 1962a, 55 n. 1. In the region of Gaza, the term denotes a life of seclusion; see Perrone 1988; 1990, 57–63. See also below, Part V, nn. 20–21.

First Steps in Jerusalem (Winter 456/7)

Sabas arrived in Jerusalem during the winter of 456 and was received there by an elderly monk, a fellow countryman, who brought him to the Passarion monastery, which was headed by the monks' archimandrite Elpidius. Sabas remained there through the winter months. This was one of the most important monasteries in Jerusalem at that time, and its heads also served, successively, as the archimandrites of the monks of Jerusalem (Part IV, Chap. 2, below). The monastery was located close to the Holy Zion Church, established in about the middle of the fourth century at the traditional site of the Last Supper room (Tsafrir 1975, 26; Wilkinson 1977, 171–72). Passarion established his large monastery[41] within the Wall of Zion for the staff of deacons and cantors, that is, for the devotees (σπουδαῖοι) of the Zion church (V. Petr. Ib. 35 [39 in the German trans.]; Chitty 1966, 86 n. 29). Sabas, who already knew the Psalms by heart and who was well-versed in the regulations of monastic discipline, could have joined this group as a reader, thus responding to the entreaties of the elderly Cappadocian monk who had received him in Jerusalem and had asked him to join the monastery of Passarion. Sabas refused this request, as he did to the others who brought him to their monasteries, requesting him to join the complement of monks (τάγμα) and thereby enjoy a daily living allowance (διάριον) (Festugière 1962b, 18 n. 6). This episode gives us an important piece of information about the way of life and means of support of many of the city monks. Sabas, however, did not seek financial security, nor did he desire to live as a cleric, a monk whose chief occupation was the daily liturgy, such as the deacons and cantors of the Passarion monastery, the σπουδαῖοι or the τάγμα of the Anastasis[42] or of the Cathisma,[43] and the τάγμα of the New Church of Mary[44] at a later period.

Sabas' wish was to live as an anchorite in the desert, like St. Euthymius, whom he emulated and under whose influence the "First Union" had just taken place in the Church of Jerusalem between the monks and Eudocia on one side and Patriarch Juvenal on the other, after the split between them that had occurred in the wake of the Council of Chalcedon (Chitty 1952, 22–24). The monks of the Passarion monastery took an active part in these turbulent events. Under the influence of Euthymius, the archimandrite Elpidius returned to the camp of the supporters of the council's decisions, while two other senior monks there—Marcianus and Romanus—opposed this union and detached themselves from the monastery of Passarion. Sabas was undoubtedly aware of the doctrinal issues that preoccupied the monks of Jerusalem at the time. By his decision to join Euthymius, the architect of the union, he established his place in the Orthodox camp.

[41] Vailhé 1898–99; 1899–1900a, 39–41, no. 90 (errors crept into this passage during the printing: the entry begins on p. 39 and continues on p. 41, with a passage relating to the monastery of Paula mistakenly printed in the middle). For more about this monastery see Garitte 1958, in the texts referring to May 10, June 7, and Nov. 3; Vincent and Abel 1914–26, 516–17, 905–6. According to Wilkinson 1977, 171, the Holy Zion Church was erected by John I, bishop of Jerusalem, earlier than 348.

[42] Longinus, who received Theodosius in David's Tower, belonged to the τάγμα (staff of monks) of the church of the Holy Sepulcher; these are the devotees (οἱ σπουδαῖοι) gathered later by Patriarch Elias from the cells scattered around David's Tower, for whom he established in 494 a monastery close to the patriarchate. See V. Sab. 31, 116.6; V. Theod. 236.12 and Petrides 1900–1, 1910; Vailhé 1911.

[43] Theodosius was added by the pious matron Hicelia to the staff of the Cathisma Church, which she founded; see V. Theod. 236.26–27.

[44] John Moschus (Pratum 61, 2913) tells of Leontius of Cilicia, who was one of the staff of the New Church of Mary and who did not leave the church for a period of 40 years.

After receiving permission from Elpidius, Sabas was sent, accompanied by a guide, to the laura of Euthymius (*V. Sab.* 7, 91), who was then in his eighty-second year. Sabas stayed in the laura until Saturday, when the anchorites gathered at its center. When he saw the great Euthymius coming to the church, he asked to become one of his monks. As related in *Vita Euthymii* 31, he was initially accepted, and Euthymius entrusted him to his disciple Domitian. After a short time, however, Euthymius changed his mind, explaining that, due to his youth, it was not proper for Sabas to settle in the laura and that it would be more appropriate for him to live for a few years in a coenobium. But according to *Vita Sabae* 7, Euthymius refused to accept him from the beginning, and Sabas was sent, accompanied by one of the fathers of the laura, to the coenobium of Theoctistus.

The eighteen-year-old Sabas already had ten years of experience in the monastic life and was versed in the coenobitic monastic regulations. There was then no reason to regard him as a novice monk. However, because of his youth, he was beardless, and Euthymius therefore refused to accept him, relying upon an ancient regulation of the fathers of Scetis, according to which it was not proper for a youth to be in the company of bearded anchorites (Chitty 1966, 66–67; Chadwick 1968, 11 n. 1). This precedent became a law which was also transmitted to the heads of the other laurae, and eventually, when Sabas himself headed the Great Laura, he also followed this rule (*V. Sab.* 29; see below, Part III, Chap. 5B).

In the Monastery of Theoctistus (457–473)

1. Within the Coenobium (457–469)

Upon his arrival at the monastery of Theoctistus, Sabas entrusted to him the possessions he had brought along,[45] and, according to Cyril, revealed fervent faith and great adherence to the monastic life: he was always the first to come to the church and the last to leave it. Living in a coenobium, he was given various tasks and filled a variety of positions: he assisted monks entrusted with various duties, carrying water and gathering wood, and served for some time as a mule driver (βουρδωνάριος). He faithfully fulfilled all these tasks, which entailed hard physical labor.

Despite his being cross-eyed (στραβός) (*V. Sab.* 36, 123), his appearance was impressive; he was sturdy and of great physical strength. It was the practice among the monks of the desert coenobia (*V. Euth.* 50, 72; *V. Sab.* 8, 92; *V. Geor.* 14, 110–14; 19, 118–19; 22, 121–22; *Miracula* 3, 363–64) and laurae (*V. Sab.* 40, 130) for everyone to be mobilized to reap the *mannouthion* herbs growing in the riverbeds—a plant that perhaps should be identified with the tumble thistle (Hirschfeld 1992, 89). Sabas excelled in this, and while

---

[45] Regulations have been preserved in Syria obligating the monk to give all his movable possessions and the items he brought with him to the monastery, and establishing that he has no greater right of possession than that of the other monks to these objects (Vööbus 1960b, 84.31), and that the monk is forbidden to receive from his relatives, or from strangers, any private object (ibid. 112.14). Pachomius also forbade his monks to possess any object or item of clothing besides what was used by them, and also explicitly forbade the possession of silver coins (*Koinonia* I, 338–39 and below, Part III, Chap. 3B). Regarding Dorotheus of Gaza's vacillations in ridding himself of all his property when he was in the monastery of Abba Seridos, see the introduction to the Régnault-Préville edition (SC 92, 16). For the legal situation of the right of a monk to possess private property and the developments that took place on this during the reign of Justinian, see Orestano 1956.

all the other monks reaped and carried to the monastery only one load per day, he would reap and carry three such loads.

2. The Visit to Alexandria

Once during his stay in the monastery of Theoctistus, Sabas accompanied a monk named John, a native of Alexandria, who had received permission from the abbot to visit his home in order to arrange his family affairs, since he had learned that his parents had died. These affairs obviously also included matters of the family inheritance, from which the monastery was likely to benefit. John asked Sabas to join him on his journey.

In Alexandria the tie between Sabas and his parents was renewed (*V. Sab.* 9, 92–93). His father, John, had changed his name to Conon and had become the commander of the *numerus Isaurorum.* Conon and Sabas' mother, Sophia, attempted to persuade their son to remain with them, to enlist in the regiment, and be appointed an officer with the rank of senator (or to be the priest of the regiment).[46] But Sabas would not listen. In accordance with the monastic rule of making do with little, he also rejected their offer of twenty gold coins to defray the expenses of his journey. But, in order to mollify them, he finally agreed to take three gold coins and immediately left Alexandria with his companion, the monk John. Upon his return to the monastery, he gave the coins to Theoctistus.

3. In a Cave outside the Coenobium (469–473)

After a twelve-year stay in the coenobium, when he was thirty years old (469 CE), and after the death of Theoctistus in 466 and that of his successor in 468, Sabas asked Longinus, the new abbot, to allow him to live in *hesychia* as an anchorite, in a cave outside the coenobium on the southern slope, in a cell successfully located during our survey (see below, Part II, Chap. 1F). After receiving permission for this from Euthymius, a new chapter opened in Sabas' monastic life. He would remain in his cave five days a week, depriving himself of food, engaging, in addition to prayer and contemplation, in basket weaving. On Saturday and Sunday he would join the other brothers in the coenobium, and returning to his cell on Sunday evening, he would bring with him a supply of palm shoots (βαΐων θαλλοί) sufficient for weaving fifty baskets, his weekly output. Sabas' way of life during this period, which lasted for five years, was that of a laurite monk, with the coenobium serving as a center. We have also found a similar system, of anchorites living in cells as laurites at a short distance from the coenobium, in the "cells" (τὰ κελλία) of Choziba (Patrich 1990a).

It is of interest to note that at this stage Sabas did not ask to go and live in *hesychia,* in the company of Euthymius in his laura. He rather asked to live as a cell dweller close to the Theoctistus coenobium in which he had lived until then. It is possible that he was

---

[46] *V. Sab.* 9, 92.29: στρατεύεσθαι καὶ πρεσβύτερον τοῦ νουμέρου γενέσθαι. *Presbyteros* is the Greek translation of the military rank of senator, the third in rank below the tribune among the cavalry; see Stein-Palanque 1949, 427 n. 189. In line with this, Festugière explains the text (ibid. 20 n. 8) as referring to a military rank, which is also the opinion of Flusin (1983, 96 and n. 51). Jones (1964, 632–33), on the other hand, holds that Sabas was asked to be the priest of the Isaurian battalion, an opinion shared by Chitty (1966, 94 and n. 108), since according to Sozomen (*HE* I.8.11, 19) each *numerus* had a priest and a deacon, and according to the Greek papyri of Egypt, the Latin military rank of senator was transliterated σινάτωρ and not translated into Greek (πρεσβύτερος).

enchanted by the wild landscape of Nahal Og (Wadi Mukellik) more than by the moderately hilly landscape of Euthymius' laura (Khan el-Ahmar). Indeed, Sabas would later
establish his and other laurae in an area with a similarly wild landscape. From Cyril's
description, however, it can be concluded that Sabas was not one of Euthymius' close disciples.

During this period, in which Sabas lived as a laurite outside the coenobium, he
would accompany Longinus, the abbot of his monastery, in order to take his leave of
Euthymius upon the latter's departure for the desert during Lent. At times he would
also join Euthymius on his wanderings, thereby receiving his personal instruction. Sabas,
who was not accustomed to this, once collapsed from exhaustion and thirst. Euthymius,
familiar with the desert's secrets, dug a ditch (*themileh* in Arabic), found water, and revived him (*V. Euth.* 38, 56–57; *V. Sab.* 11, 94–95).

This journey to the Rouba desert also included Domitian, Euthymius' closest disciple; Gerasimus, the head of the laura near the Jordan; and Martyrius and Elias, who
would eventually become patriarchs of Jerusalem and maintain close ties with Sabas,
aiding him in the establishment of the Great Laura and in the leadership of the monks.

A short time later Euthymius died (January 20, 473), and a new chapter unfolded
in Sabas' life: achieving spiritual independence, forging his character and spirit in wanderings in the desert, establishing his Laura, and becoming the leader of the desert
monks and all the Christians in the Holy Land.

Wanderings in the Desert and Seclusion

Domitian died one week after Euthymius. When Sabas, at age thirty-five, perceived that
the community was changing its way of life due to the death of the heads of the monastery and the lack of proper leadership, he fled to the eastern desert (*V. Sab.* 12, 95–96).
He wandered there, in the desert along the Jordan and in the deserts of Coutila and
Rouba, for four years (ibid. 15, 97; for the boundaries of these deserts, see below, beginning of Part II). During the course of his wanderings, Sabas learned to cope with the
continual difficulties of subsistence in the desert: the dangers lurking from spiders,
snakes, and beasts of prey, as well as the need to look for food and water. He maintained
the way of life of the "grass-eaters" (βοσκοί, literally "shepherds"), monks who had
adopted this type of asceticism and took their nourishment from wild plants such as
melagrion,[47] whose roots or bulbs they would uproot with a small hoe they carried, and
from hearts of reed (καρδίαι καλάμων). Sabas would keep the food he thus gathered in a
sheepskin bag (τὸ μηλωτάριον) he carried with him. In these desert regions he also became acquainted with the dwellers of the desert, the Saracens. At times he would receive
from them food richer than his usual fare: loaves of bread, cheese, and dates; on other
occasions, however, they attempted to harm him (*V. Sab.* 13–14, 96–97).

---

[47] The identity of this plant, with a root stem or a bulb, is not certain. Rubin (1982, 35 n. 49) proposed
that the allusion is to *Asphodelus microcarpus*, which is common in the Judean desert and whose roots are
edible. Sophronius identifies the *melagria* with the wild honey with which John the Baptist was nourished
(Sophronius, *Anacr.* V.24–25; PG 87.3, 3756c). In the *Suidae Lexicon* (end of the 10th century), ed. A. Adler
(Leipzig 1931), two closely related entries are cited: III, 349.16: μελαγρία; 351.15: μελεάγρια. In the first
entry it is stated that this is a plant growing in the desert, while the second entry mentions *melagria* roots
and reed cores. This information does not aid in the identification of the plant. See also Festugière 1962a,
111 n. 120; Chitty 1966, 96 and n. 125 on p. 100.

The struggle with the difficulties of existence in the desert was perceived by the monks as a battle against demons, the Devil's emissaries, who desired to create fear and arouse heresy in their hearts. The physical struggle was perceived as a spiritual struggle, which accordingly strengthened body and spirit, and overcoming these difficulties was seen as a spiritual ascent.

The life-style of monks wandering in the desert, changing their place of residence from one cave to another and subsisting on wild plants and food that came to hand, was prevalent mainly in the desert regions of Syria (Vööbus 1960a, 269–71), but it was also known in the Judean desert. Besides wandering in the desert during Lent, famous monks adopted this life-style for prolonged periods of time: Cyriacus (25 years), John the Hesychast (6 years), Abraamius and John the Scholarius (8 years), and other monks mentioned by John Moschus. These were the desert anchorites (Hirschfeld 1992, 213–22).

When Sabas was wandering in the desert of Rouba, he was joined by another monk named Anthus (*V. Sab.* 14, 97), who had previously stayed with Theodosius in the Cathisma Church. It was through him that Sabas first learned of Theodosius. After four years of wandering in the desert (at the beginning of 477), Sabas arrived at the hill of the Eudocia Tower (ibid. 15, 97–98), located on the peak of Jebel Muntar, the highest peak in the Judean desert (524 m above sea level), from which one looks out over vast expanses. It is related that in a vision an angel pointed out to him the gorge descending from the Siloam—the ravine of the Kidron—pointing to a cave on the east bank of the gorge, in which he settled. It was in this ravine that Sabas would establish the Great Laura, after five years in which he lived as an anchorite in the cave (478–483).

Abbot and Religious Leader (483–532)

The first phase in the establishment of the Laura lasted from 483 to 486 (see below, Part II, Chap. 1A). Patriarch Martyrius (478–486), who had already known Sabas during the period of the former's stay in the laura of Euthymius, aided him in this stage. During the next six years the community grew until it numbered 150 monks. Opposition to Sabas' leadership arose in the Laura during the years 486–490, and reached its peak when the rebels approached Patriarch Sallustius demanding that Sabas be deposed. But the patriarch decided in favor of Sabas (see below, Part III, Chap. 2).

In the next phase (490–501), the Laura expanded and Sabas' leadership was consolidated. The number of monks increased further (*V. Sab.* 33, 118.21–22), and additional monasteries were established for them: Kastellion (492) and the Small Coenobium (493). Hostels were established in the Laura and in Jericho (491), and afterwards a hostel was purchased in Jerusalem as well (July 494). Large water cisterns, an oven, a hospital (after 494) (*V. Sab.* 32, 117), and a large church (501) were also established in the Laura. These building projects were made possible by Sabas' family inheritance and by donations he received (*V. Sab.* 18, 103; 25, 109).

During this period a decisive change also occurred in Sabas' position in the Church of Jerusalem and among the desert monks after he was elected, together with Theodosius, to be the archimandrite of the laurites and the anchorites (before July 23, 494; see below, Part IV, Chap. 2). This was the first time that a representative of the desert monks was appointed to this position, indicating a decisive increase in their influence over the Jerusalem diocese.

Sabas was not a profound theologian, and mystical speculations did not concern him (Schwartz 1939, 374). As an abbot he was not overly strict with himself. He used to meet and dine with the heads of his monasteries in Jericho and with church officials in Jerusalem, and on those occasions appeared to be a glutton (*V. Sab.* 46, 136–37; 64, 165).

But the expansion and consolidation, on the one hand, and his appointment as archimandrite of the monks, on the other, did not appease the opposition, and in 502 he voluntarily went into a three-year exile from the Laura (503–506). At first he stayed in a cave near the River of Gadara (the Yarmuk), and afterwards in the region of Nicopolis (see below, Part III, Chap. 2). This sorry chapter in his biography came to an end only after the intervention of Patriarch Elias, who knew him from the period of his stay with Euthymius. The rebels, sixty in number, chose to leave the Laura after destroying Sabas' monastic tower in their anger, and went to live in deserted cells near Thekoa, where, after a short period of time, Sabas established a laura for them called the "New Laura." This was the first in a series of monasteries—laurae and coenobia—that Sabas founded during the years 507–511. After this date we do not hear of any further rebellion against him.

The cooperation between Sabas and Patriarch Elias increased, and the latter sent Sabas as his emissary to the court of Emperor Anastasius (winter 511–512) to intercede on behalf of the Church of Palestine in various matters and to protect Elias' standing, so that he would not be deposed under the pressure of the Monophysites. About twenty years later Sabas would be sent again, on behalf of Patriarch Peter, to the court of Emperor Justinian to deal with matters concerning the Samaritan revolt (on these journeys, see below, Part IV, Chap. 4).

Sabas died shortly after his return from his second mission in the ninety-fourth year of his life (*V. Sab.* 77, 183.17), after a short illness (Dec. 5, 532)[48] but not before he had managed to establish an additional laura, placing his disciple Jeremias at its head. When his death became known, a great crowd of monks and laymen gathered, together with Patriarch Peter and other bishops present in Jerusalem and the notables of the city (*V. Sab.* 77, 183–84). He was interred in the Laura, between the two churches, on the spot where the pillar of fire had shown him in the past the site of the Theoktistos Church.

Sabas succeeded in maintaining excellent relations with the Jerusalem patriarchs. As Euthymius before him, he led the desert monks not into confrontation with the ecclesiastical authorities but toward cooperation with them, while at the same time faithfully and forcefully defending Chalcedonian Orthodoxy. His prominent position was revealed during the great demonstration of monks at the Church of St. Stephen, in which, according to Cyril, 10,000 monks took part (end of 516). This was an act of rebellion against Emperor Anastasius and his emissaries. It was the desert monks led by Sabas and Theodosius who set the tone and dictated to Patriarch John the position to be adopted in defense of Orthodoxy.

---

[48] Cyril (*V. Sab.* 77, 184.2–183.6; *V. John Hes.* 16, 214.4–7) cites two contradictory dates for Sabas' death. One date, Dec. 5 in the 10th indiction, corresponds to the year 531, which is erroneous. The second date, in the 79th year of the life of John the Hesychast, corresponds to Dec. 5, 532, which is the correct date. See Stein 1944, 171; Festugière 1962a, 22–23 n. 1. A summary of his life is included in chap. 77: he came to Palestine at the age of 18, stayed in a coenobium for 17 years, and lived in the deserts and in the Great Laura for 59 years.

Sabas was held in great esteem by the ecclesiastical establishment and by the entire Christian population of Palestine. He was therefore chosen to disseminate throughout the country the decisions of Emperor Justinian against Monophysitism, after they had been approved by the patriarch of Jerusalem (August 6, 518), and later on Justinian's edicts of restoration in the wake of the damage caused by the Samaritan revolt (see below, Part IV, Chaps. 3–4). Cyril describes at length the warm manner in which Sabas was received on the two occasions he came to Scythopolis, the second of which he himself witnessed (*V. Sab.* 61, 162; 75, 180–81). Detailed descriptions are also extant of his ties with the people of Medaba (ibid. 46, 136–37) and with the people of Bouriron (ibid. 79, 185–86). As a holy man, he performed various miracles: causing rain to fall, healing the sick, and so on. After his death, his holy grave and his holy memory also had the power to perform such miracles (see the detailed discussion below, Part IV, Chap. 1). Cyril states, as proof of Sabas' holiness, that his body did not decompose or become corrupted; he himself saw it whole fifteen years after the time of his death, when he went down into the grave.

His followers believed that the spirit of Sabas, as is the case with saints, enjoyed great "boldness of speech" (παρρησία) before the Lord, and therefore many people came on pilgrimage to his grave to request deliverance, believing that their petitions would be granted by his intercession (ibid. 79–81, 185–87). As a token of admiration and gratitude they raised generous contributions for the Great Laura and to its subsidiary monasteries.

Sabas' Inclination toward Other Monastic Centers in the East: Asia Minor, Egypt, and Syria

In this section emphasis will be placed on the personal experience acquired by Sabas prior to his establishment of the Great Laura. An extensive examination of possible sources of influence upon the Laura itself will be postponed to the following chapters, in which various aspects of life in this laura and in the other Sabaite monasteries will be examined.

Sabas was born, as was mentioned, in Cappadocia in Asia Minor, the birthplace of Basil the Great, the founder of Greek coenobitic monasticism. From age eight to eighteen Sabas was educated in the monastery of Flaviana, close to the village of his birth. There he learned the principles of monastic discipline (ἡ τῆς μοναχικῆς πολιτείας ἀκρίβεια), and within a short time he knew by heart the fundamentals of the communal life of the monks (ἡ τοῦ κοινοβιακοῦ κατάστασις) (*V. Sab.* 2, 87–88), that is, the principles of Basilian monasticism: the place of monasticism in the bosom of the Church, and not against it; life in a community together with other monks, while being subordinate to the abbot and to the regulations; moderation in asceticism, etc. Also, in the coenobium of Theoctistus, in which he lived during his first twelve years in the Judean desert, and whose way of life had been established by Euthymius (*V. Euth.* 8–9, 16–18), it is almost certain that the Basilian system was in practice, for this was the coenobitic way of life known to Euthymius from his homeland, before his arrival in Palestine (406).

Euthymius was born two years before the death of Basil the Great (379) in Melitene, the capital of the Roman province of Armenia Secunda, bordering on Cappadocia Prima, of which Basil was the metropolitan. This was the period of activity of the "Cappadocian Fathers." Euthymius grew up in the home of the bishop of Melitene, and his teachers were Acacius and Synodius, educated church officials who would eventually become metropolitans of Melitene, and who undoubtedly were thoroughly familiar with the Basilian teaching (*V. Euth.* 4, 11; see also Flusin 1983, 111). Euthymius was an admirer of the monks (φιλομόναχος) from his childhood. When he was the priest of the church of Melitene, he was given the task of supervising the monasteries near the city (*V. Euth.* 5, 12–13: ἐπιτρέπεται φροντίζειν καὶ προΐστασθαι τῶν περὶ τὴν πόλιν μοναστηρίων). In this office he gained a good knowledge of the organization and structure of the monastic movement in the district of Melitene. Already at that time, however, he was drawn toward the life of seclusion more than to the coenobitic life (ibid. 13).[49]

Sabas, too, who grew up in a Basilian coenobium, was attracted to a more ascetic way of life. Like Euthymius before him, he also sought to live as an anchorite in the desert of the Holy City. Both of them, like Chariton (who also was of Anatolian origin, a native of Iconium [Konya] in the province of Lycaonia, bordering on the west on Cappadocia Secunda) at the beginning of the fourth century, were impelled by desire for an asceticism more extreme than that of Basil. They were perhaps inspired by the Anatolian asceticism of Eustathius or the Messalian/Euchitean movement that followed it, a movement that had members also in many of the monasteries of Melitene, the birthplace of Euthymius (Theodoret, *HE* iv.11, 229–30). In contrast, however, to these enthusiastic movements, Euthymius and Sabas always regarded the monastic movement as one integrated into the ecclesiastical establishment and not as a chiefly revolutionary social movement seeking to create a new Christian society. This approach of theirs might be attributed, in great degree, to their prior education within the framework of Basilian coenobitism.

The anchorites of the end of the fourth and the beginning of the fifth century in the provinces of Armenia and Cappadocia could also draw inspiration from Syrian anchoritism, which from the second half of the fourth century had penetrated especially into the Taron area, to the east of Melitene, and had influenced the monasticism of the Armenian kingdom (Vööbus 1960a, 353–58). But not only anchorite influences penetrated into Armenia from Syria. The Syrians also disseminated in Armenia the coenobitic way of life; the monk Maruta was especially active in this (ibid. 143). The Armenian element was the second largest ethnic component in the Great Laura (*V. Sab.* 20–21, 105–6; 32, 117–18; Stone 1986) and also in the coenobium of Theodosius, where Sophronius the Armenian served as the deputy and later the successor of Theodosius (Theodore, *V. Theod.* 18, 45). These Armenian monks also came from the kingdom of Armenia, not only from the provinces of Armenia Prima and Secunda. The Armenian monks of the Great Laura were also influenced by Syria in liturgical matters (*V. Sab.* 32, 117–18).

Ascetics of Cappadocian origin lived in Douka and its environs at the end of the fourth century (*HL* xlviii–xlix, 142–43). They were noted for their extreme modes of mortification, like the Syrian one. Syrian anchoritism was revered in the first half of the fifth century, despite its consolidation and the transition to coenobitism that took place in Syria at that time. The first three disciples of Euthymius in his laura—the Cappado-

---

[49] Seemingly because of this, Schwartz (1939, 358) was of the opinion that in his role of supervisor of country monasteries (περιοδευτής) Euthymius was in charge only of the anchorite settlements ("Anchoreten Siedlungen") close to Melitene. Cyril (ibid.), however, speaks of monasteries (μοναστήρια) in general.

cian brothers Cosmas, Chrysippus, and Gabriel—came to him in 428 after being trained for the monastic life in Syria (*V. Euth.* 16, 25–26). Domnus, the nephew of John, the patriarch of Antioch, joined the laura after them. The Syrian element in the laura of Euthymius at its start was therefore conspicuous—four of his first twelve disciples came from Syria (four others came from Euthymius' birthplace, Melitene; three came from Rhaithou in Sinai, and one was a Palestinian from Tiberias).

Euthymius' practice of going forth during Lent for sallies into the desert—a practice adopted by Sabas (see below, Part III, Chap. 5c)—originated in Syria. Similarly, there was the practice of binding the body in an erect posture in order to maintain prolonged vigilance, a practice known also in Armenia (Vööbus 1960a, 357). Among the fifth-century Syrian monks, Symeon Stylites was especially revered, even in Palestine. Eudocia turned to him initially to receive instruction regarding the correct faith and the validity of the acts of the Council of Chalcedon (*V. Euth.* 30, 47). Theodosius also made a pilgrimage to him when he was on his way to Palestine (Theodore, *V. Theod.* 3, 9–10).

Anchoritism like the Syrian type also existed in Palestine in Sabas' day. Stylite monks were rare (Festugière 1962b, 129 n. 303),[50] as were monks who adopted other extreme forms of mortification. But there were anchorites who lived in caves in the desert and near the Jordan, cut off from any community of monks. These monks would gather wild plants and roots to live on, which was the source of their name, βοσκοί (*V. Sab.* 16, 99.19). This type of monk also prevailed in Syria. Sabas himself lived in this manner from 473 to 478 and then for five more years as an anchorite, residing in a permanent cave. Later, as archimandrite, he was *ex officio* also responsible for the anchorite monks (see below, Part IV, Chap. 2). Earlier, while living in a cave outside the walls of the monastery of Theoctistus, he used to fast five days a week. However, when he became abbot he maintained, like Euthymius, that excessive asceticism was a pursuit of false glory (see below, Part III, Chap. 5c). This was in the spirit of Basil's teaching.

Euthymius had close ties with Egyptian monks, who came to visit him and related various sayings or episodes concerning the monks of Egypt. Euthymius would relate the moral of these episodes to his monks (*V. Euth.* 19, 30–31; 24, 36–37). He especially revered Arsenius, one of the senior Greek monks in Scetis (394–434), who had previously been the tutor of the princes Arcadius and Honorius in the palace of Theodosius I (*Apoph. Pat.*, Arsenius 42). Euthymius sought to copy his way of life as a monk and his personal qualities (*V. Euth.* 21, 34). Two of Euthymius' later disciples, Elias the Arab and Martyrius the Cappadocian, lived among the monks of Nitria before they joined his laura in 457 (ibid. 32, 50–51). They were preceded, as was stated, by three monks from Rhaithou in Sinai, where the influence of the Antonian monasticism of Egypt was widespread. The Antonian system continued to be vital in Palestine, as is indicated by the flourishing Palestinian laurae of the sixth century. This was primarily due to the activity of Sabas.

Sabas, like Euthymius, admired the monks of Scetis (*V. Sab.* 29, 114). He also visited Alexandria, but there is no mention that his stay there brought him into close contact with Egyptian monasticism. The schism in the Church that resulted from the Council of

---

[50] The proposal of Rosenthal to regard the thin column base located in the center of the atrium of the northern church in Shivta as a part of a Stylite column seems doubtful to me. See R. Rosenthal-Heginbottom, *Die Kirchen von Sobota und die Dreiapsidenkirchen des Nahen Ostens* (Wiesbaden 1982), 232.

Chalcedon and the clearly nationalist character that Egyptian monasticism assumed during the second half of the fifth century weakened orthodox links to Egyptian monasticism. The Egyptian monasticism of the time (Cauwenbergh 1914) was no longer a focal point and exemplar for monks and ordinary Christians, as it had been in the fourth century, when the masses flocked there from throughout the Christian world. For the same reason, Syrian monasticism also did not exert a great deal of influence on Palestine in this period. In addition, the character of Syrian monasticism changed: anchoritism increasingly gave way to coenobitism. But within the bounds of coenobitism, the Anatolian origin of the leaders of Palestinian monasticism and the Greek language, which was predominant among the monks rather than Syriac, tipped the scales in favor of Basilian, and not Syrian, coenobitism. Elements of this coenobitic system were implemented by Sabas in his laurae. This combination of the Antonian system of Egypt and the Basilian system of Asia Minor is one of the most significant features of Palestinian lauritic monasticism. Sabas was its most noteworthy architect.

Part II: The Building Projects of Sabas and His Disciples

The Geographic Background

Most of the Sabaite monasteries (Fig. 4) were located on the slopes of Jebel Muntar, the highest summit in the Judean desert, 524 m above sea level. Most of this area, especially west and south of Jebel Muntar, is drained by Nahal Kidron and its tributaries, while the area to the east is drained by Nahal Qumran (Wadi ez-Zaraniq) and its chief southern tributary, Nahal Sakekah (Wadi Abu Shu'la). Because of the central location of Nahal Kidron in this area and the location in it of the Great Laura, we have named it "the Kidron basin." The eastern section of this area (east of Mar Saba and Jebel Muntar) is, in my opinion, the desert of Rouba mentioned by Cyril of Scythopolis.[1]

Not all of Sabas' monasteries were built in the Kidron basin. The New Laura was established far from this area (see the map, Fig. 4), on the western bank of the upper Nahal Arugoth, ca. 4 km south of Thekoa. The monasteries of Sabas' disciples—Firminus, Severianus, James, and Julian "the Hunchback"—were also established beyond this area.

The Judean desert is an orographic desert, located east of the watershed line of the Judean hills, in the "Shade of the Rains" which generally progress from west to east. The multiannual average of rain decreases eastward from 400 to 50 mm. Cloud wisps over limited areas are mentioned in the writings of Cyril (*V. Sab.* 66, 167). However, it was not only the paucity of rain that prevented agricultural settlements from developing in these areas, which are not far from Jerusalem and the other settlements at the top of the Judean ridge, for water could have been brought there in aqueducts from the more rainy regions to the west. The poor quality of the soil in the desert plateau posed the major obstacle to all agricultural development.[2] The annual average temperature in Jerusalem is 17.7° C, while in Jericho it is 25.4° C.

---

[1] *V. Euth.* 38, 56; *V. Sab.* 110, 94; *V. Cyr.* 5, 225; *V. John Hes.* 11, 209; 13, 211; *V. Ab.*, ed. Peeters, 354; *Pratum* 167, 3033. The sources indicate that the desert of Rouba is south of the desert of Coutila, most of whose territory constitutes the drainage basin of Nahal Og (Wadi Mukellik), both in the eastern part of the desert plateau and in the valley of Hyrcania. Its northern boundary is to be established as the ancient Jerusalem-Jericho road, while Wadi Hashneh is the natural boundary between the desert of Coutila and the desert of Rouba in the eastern part of the desert plateau.

[2] During the archaeological survey that I conducted for the Mar Saba Map (see n. 4 below) during 1981–82, almost no traces were found of terraces or of farmstead implements so characteristic of the Negev settlements during the Byzantine period. At the same time, however, it should be noted that in rainy years the Bedouin would cultivate lands in the area of the syncline of Khan Hatrura and west of the Muntar-Mar Saba anticline, as well as small plots east of the axis of the anticline. In these areas grain was planted. From 1984 many plots, which in the past had been cultivated only in this manner, were planted with olives, irrigated by portable water tanks. This is an outstanding change in the landscape of this portion of the desert.

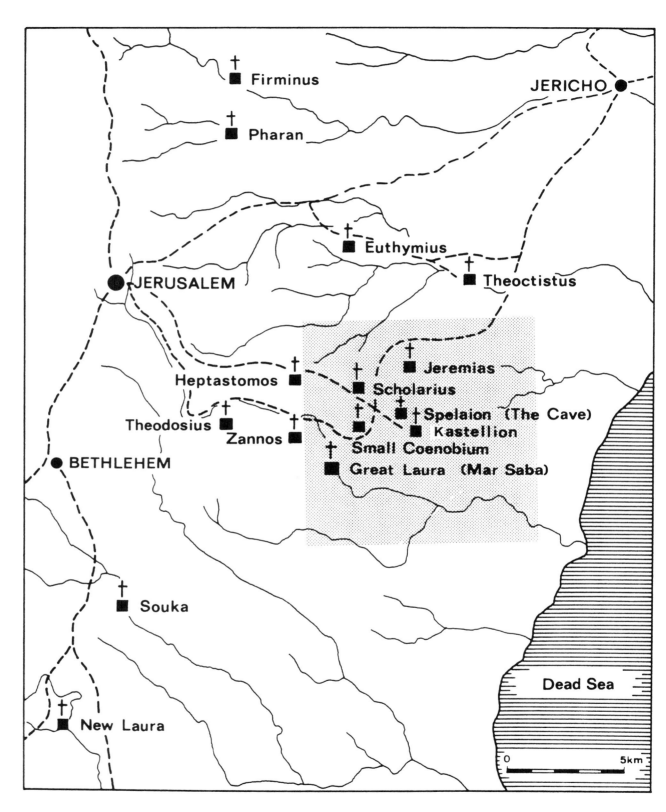

4. Sabas' monasteries in the Kidron basin and the monasteries of Chariton and Euthymius (the shaded section indicates the surveyed area).

The structural lines are: the syncline of Khan Hatrura, the anticline of Muntar-Mar Saba, and the syncline of Nebi Musa (el-Buqei'a/the valley of Hyrcania). The orientation of these lines is north-northeast, south-southwest. Therefore, parallel landscape strips were formed here, according to the main structural lines, which descend in four main levels to the Dead Sea.[3] An aerial distance of only 25 km from Jerusalem to the Dead Sea results in an altitude differential of ca. 1200 m.

In the western strip were located the settlements of the margin of the desert, Lazarion and Beth Abudisson, the monasteries to the east of Bethlehem excavated by Corbo (1955), and the monastery of Theodosius.

The desert plateau is the main area of the Kidron basin. All the Sabaitic monasteries in the basin are located in this strip. The elevation differential of the landscape has led to a deep cutting through by the wadis that drain the eastern slopes of Jebel Muntar. On the cliffs of these wadis were established the monastery of the Cave and the laura of Jeremias.

The Muntar-Mar Saba anticline created an obstacle to the course of Nahal Kidron, which was forced to break a path through the anticline. The Great Laura was established on the cliffs that were thus exposed.

The laura of Heptastomos is located close to the margin of the Khan Hatrura syncline, the monastery of the Scholarius is located on the summit of Jebel Muntar, and the Small Coenobium on the axis of the Muntar-Mar Saba anticline.

The hill of Hyrcania is part of an "island" of hard, colored metamorphic rocks that create a landscape of pointed hillocks with no stratification, parallel to the main structural lines. The ruined Hasmonean-Herodian fortress dictated the location of the monastery of Kastellion, the earliest among the monasteries in the desert of Rouba. No monasteries were established farther east.

In the Nebi Musa syncline (Hyrcania valley) which is easily crossable from north to south, remnants of large tent encampments of nomads and a large cemetery (Qubur Banat 'Utei) were traced during the archaeological survey. The relative distance of the valley from the settlements at the top of the Judean ridge or the Jericho valley and the presence of desert nomads were undoubtedly among the reasons why monasteries were not established in this strip.[4] Here, "below his monasteries" (V. Sab. 72, 175.19), Sabas intended to establish a large fortress to increase security, but he died before the plan could be accomplished. It cannot be ruled out that if the fortress had been built, monasteries would have been established also in this strip of the Kidron basin. From the raised eastern margins of the valley can be seen the Dead Sea and Transjordan. The next strip to the east is the fault scarp. No monasteries were established in this strip; however, it is possible that monks stayed there occasionally in caves during Lent.

During the course of the survey, in the entire area under discussion, including the monasteries, no remnants were found of olive presses. On the other hand, threshing floors were found at the heads of the spurs, close to the fields that had been sowed in rainy years; see Patrich 1994.

[3] For the geological structure of the Judean desert, see Rot 1969; Meshel 1973; Raz 1979. See also the geological map and the structural map of Wadi el-Qilt (Sheet 1:50,000, no. 12-1), published by the Geological Institute, Israel, 1970.

[4] See Patrich 1994.

The desert plateau, where sufficient vegetation is to be found in wintertime, also served as a grazing area for the desert shepherds, about whose existence around the monasteries Cyril speaks several times (*V. Euth.* 8, 15; *V. Sab.* 59, 160).

There are no perennial springs in the Kidron Basin, with the exception of a small flow of water at the foot of the Mar Saba monastery. According to the local tradition of the monks, this is the spring that was miraculously revealed to Sabas (*V. Sab.* 17, 101).

The Heptastomos (seven-mouthed) cistern, which is identified with Bir Sabsab (ref. pt. 1787.1258), was an important source of water before monasteries were established. Sabas drew from its waters during the first years of his seclusion in the cave in Nahal Kidron (*V. Sab.* 15, 98). Additional cisterns and reservoirs located in the Kidron basin, investigated in the framework of the survey, apparently date from the Muslim period onward (Patrich 1983, 66; 1993).

The monks could also use the water of the ravine pits, which lasts at times even throughout most of the summer, and during the winter the highground water (cf. *V. Euth.* 38, 57). Many cisterns were installed in order to supply water to the monasteries. In the laurae there were such cisterns not only in the core but also in each complex or grouping of cells. Of the two ancient aqueducts to Hyrcania/Kastellion, the longer Herodian aqueduct, which began in Nahal Kidron, has not been repaired except for a short section ca. 1.5 km from the monastery. The shorter aqueduct of Hyrcania has also been restored (Patrich 1989d).

Paths (Fig. 5)

For a solitary monk or a shepherd tending his flock, there are no especially difficult obstacles to travel in the Kidron basin except in limited sections in which the ravines are canyon-like and, of course, in the fault scarp itself. Every spur line can serve as a footpath. It is a different matter regarding routes for loaded beasts of burden—asses, mules, or she-camels. These had a defined goal: linking one monastery to another and linking all the monasteries with the centers of supply in the settlements at the top of the mountain ridge at the desert margin or in the valley of Jericho and Transjordan.

The monasteries were connected by paths that followed natural passages. Slopes difficult for passage were paved by the construction of a terrace wall that created a horizontal travel lane. The paths can be divided into longitudinal ones going from north to south, parallel to the geological structural lines of the region, and lateral paths, going from west to east.

The Muntar-Mar Saba anticline formed an obstacle for the course of Nahal Kidron eastwards and forced it to change direction to north-south. The tributaries of Nahal Kidron west of the anticline also flow in this direction. In contrast, the wadis east of Jebel Muntar flow from west to east, following the general descent of the Judean desert. Travel from north to south, west of the axis of the anticline, is therefore possible along the many spur lines. In contrast, to the east of the anticline axis, where the steep wadis form obstacles, it is possible to travel from north to south only along the foot of Jebel Muntar. This path will be called the "Road of the Monasteries." Several lateral roads lead from there to the monasteries of the desert of Rouba. Another north-south route runs along the Hyrcania valley, and a third longitudinal route, connecting the Great Laura (Mar

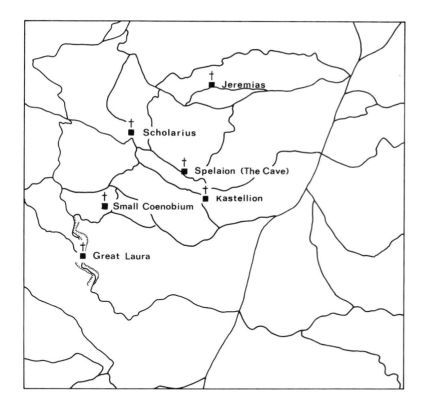

5. Paths in the Kidron basin in the Byzantine period.

Saba) with the monastery of Euthymius (Khan al-Ahmar), runs to the west of Jebel Muntar.

Three main lateral paths west of the Muntar-Mar Saba anticline connected Jerusalem and the settlements at the desert margin with the Great Laura and the other monasteries:

1. Jerusalem—Mar Saba, along Nahal Kidron. Only at the beginning of the cliff section of the Kidron, at the northern end of the Great Laura, did the route climb up to the northern bank of the Kidron.

2. Jerusalem—Abu Dis—Jebel Muntar. This is a convenient route, along the local watershed line, dividing between the tributaries draining northward into Nahal Og and those draining southward into Nahal Kidron.

3. Bethlehem—Theodosius monastery—Mar Saba. In its eastern part this road passes along the top of the southern bank of Nahal Kidron.

Four laurae and five coenobia were included in the building projects of Sabas in the Judean desert (Fig. 4). Three more laurae and an additional coenobium were constructed there by his disciples. Two other monasteries were established by Sabas outside this geographical region: one near the river of Gadara and a second near Nicopolis (Emmaus). Sabas also erected hostels for his monks in Jericho and Jerusalem, and sent funds to his village of origin in Cappadocia in order to build a church on the site of his parents' house.

1

Laurae

A. The Great Laura (483)

Previous Research

The Mar Saba monastery (Figs. 6–8), the residual core of the "Great Laura," has attracted the attention of scholars since the beginning of the geographic-historical research on the Holy Land in the second half of the nineteenth century.[5] All the studies to date make only incidental mention of the remains outside the monastery walls. Thus, for example, in the work by Phokylides (1927), which includes a detailed description of the various parts of the monastery and an account of its history from its founding to the twentieth century, about seventy pages are devoted to a description of the monastery and only three to an account of the remains located outside the monastery. Today, however, Mar Saba monastery extends over a quite limited area (ca. 60 × 100 m), while the Great Laura of Sabas' time extended over the cliffs on both banks of the Kidron, south and north of the current monastery, along a ca. 2 km section of the ravine, with dense construction.

Earlier scholars, along with later ones, for example, Meinardus (1965–66) and Compagnoni (1978, 53–63, 70–71), falsely identified the present-day monastery with the Great Laura. Thus Phokylides discusses the remains outside the walls of the monastery in a section entitled "Sites outside the Laura," Meinardus erroneously defines the monastic cell of John the Hesychast (complex 29, below) as a monastery, and Compagnoni similarly defines the "Tower of Arcadius" (complex 45, below). This basic misunderstanding also has implications for reconstructing the way of life of the monks in the Great Laura and its administration. A coenobitic way of life, and not a laurite one, is maintained in the Mar Saba monastery of today.

A detailed plan of the Mar Saba monastery has not been published until now, although already in 1897 Vailhé had published a plan of the two churches (see Fig. 12). Bagatti (1962) published a general map depicting these churches and additional chapels and their location within the area of the monastery (Fig. 22). The most detailed illustration of the monastery is presented here (see Fig. 80). Even this, however, is no substitute for a detailed plan.

---

[5] Tobler (1853–54, 837–55) gives a lengthy description of the monastery, as does Guérin (1869, 92–101). The description of Conder and Kitchener (1883, 219–20), on the other hand, is quite short. Among the historical studies, special mention should be made of those of Vailhé (1897, 1898a, 1899, and 1899–1900b). After describing the monastery, he provides a detailed historical sketch. The most comprehensive work on the monastery, however, is the monumental monograph of Phokylides (1927).

6. Mar Saba. General view from the southwest.

7. Mar Saba. Main section, view from the southwest.

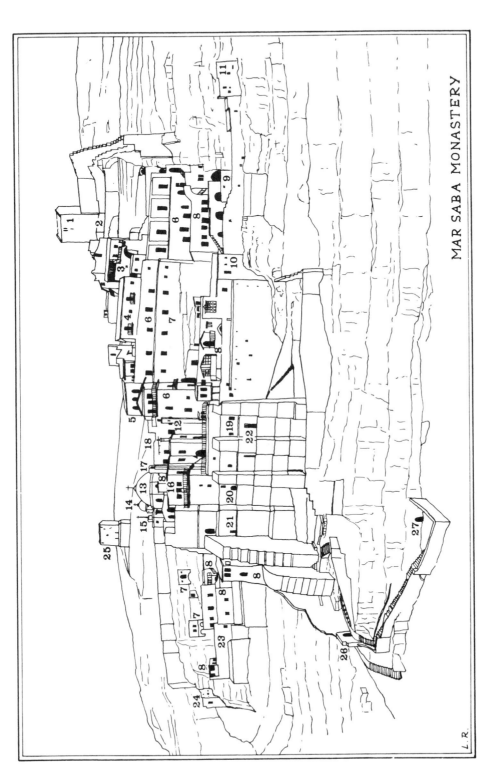

8. Mar Saba. *View from the east.*

Legend

1. "Tower of Justinian"
2. Upper water cistern
3. Deserted cells
4. Two apartments for visiting bishops
5. Guest rooms for priests
6. Hostel for visitors
7. Dwellings for monks (not occupied)
8. Dwellings for monks
9. "Palm tree of St. Sabas"
10. Lavatory
11. Chapel of St. John Chrysostom
12. Chapel of St. George
13. Dome of St. Mary Theotokos Church
14. Belfry
15. Clock room
16. Reception hall
17. Kitchen chimney
18. Bakery chimney
19. Refectory (*trapeza/aristeterion*)

20. Kitchen
21. Storeroom
22. Bakery
23. Water cistern
24. Chapel of Anna and Joachim; Sabas' *hesychasterion*
25. "Women's Tower" and Chapel of St. Symeon Stylites
26. Lower gate
27. Sacred spring

MAR SABA MONASTERY

Meinardus (1965–66) is the only scholar to provide a quite detailed description of three of the many dwelling complexes outside the walls of the monastery that belonged to the "Great Laura": the complex attributed to John the Hesychast (no. 29, below), that attributed to Arcadius the son of Xenophon (no. 45, below), and that called "Sophia's House," after Sabas' mother (no. 23, below). Compagnoni devotes less than a page to these remains, while she gives eleven pages to a description of the monastery. Important attempts to identify the remains scattered outside the monastery walls with structures of the Laura mentioned in the literary sources were made by Marcoff and Chitty (1929) and by Corbo (1958c). Ovadiah and De Silva (1981, 240–41, 253, 254) collected information and provided plans of the chapels that had already been published by Meinardus and others. Hirschfeld (1990, 31–32; 1992, 24–26) provides a short summary of the current state of the research.

The Construction of the Great Laura: A Historical Survey

In 478, at the beginning of his fortieth year (*V. Sab.* 15, 98), Sabas established his residence in a cave on the east bank of the Kidron. A tradition preserved by the monks of Mar Saba indicates its location (complex 37, below). It was difficult to climb up to the cave, and he therefore made use of a rope, which he tied to its entrance (ibid.). He lived there in seclusion for five years as an anchorite (ibid. 16, 99), bringing water from the Heptastomos cistern 15 *stadia* (2.7 km) from his cell (ibid. 15, 98). This cistern has been identified with Bir Sabsab (ref. pt. 1788.1260), located in the streambed of the Kidron next to the road leading from Jerusalem to the Laura (Corbo 1958b, 87). He successfully coexisted with the Saracens of this region, and was able to turn their curiosity and hostility into friendship, which expressed itself in their gifts of food: loaves of dry bread, cheese, and dates (*V. Sab.* 16, 99).

After five years, in the forty-fifth year of his life (ibid.), since his fame had spread, other anchorites began to gather around him, including "grass-eaters" (βοσκοί),[6] who were scattered in the area and who sustained themselves by gathering wild plants, roots, and buds. He accepted them and instructed them in the monastic life. This is the typical development pattern of a monastic community. Similar is the story of the establishment of the three laurae of Chariton, the laura of Euthymius, the coenobium of Theodosius, and others.

His first disciples included five who would later be known as founders and heads of monasteries: John, who would eventually become the head of the New Laura; James, who would later found the laura of the Towers near the Jordan River; Severianus, the future founder of the monastery near Caparbaricha; Firminus, the founder of the laura near Mikhmas; Julian the Hunchback, who would found the laura of Neelkeraba (Νεελκεραβά—the Keraba stream?) near the Jordan (see below, Chaps. 1E, 2G).

The first stage in the construction of the Laura extended over the years 483–486, during the time of Patriarch Martyrius (478–486), who knew Sabas from the period of his stay with Euthymius. Sabas gave each of those joining him a suitable place, containing a small cell and a cave. The community numbered 70 monks. Sabas served as their head, guide, and mentor (*V. Sab.* 16, 100.6: ἡγούμενος αὐτῶν καὶ ὁδηγὸς καὶ ποιμήν). On the east

---

[6] In my opinion, this is the correct meaning of the word here, rather than shepherds.

bank of the stream, not far from his cave, he established a small prayerhouse (εὐκτήριον) for its spiritual needs. A spring dug in the streambed (according to Cyril, it was revealed to Sabas by a wild ass digging with its feet) served as a source of water (*V. Sab.* 17, 101). The monks of Mar Saba have preserved as a holy site until the present day this small fountain, which is located below their monastery.

Sabas' intention from the outset was to establish a large laura on this site. Therefore, one of his first steps was to demarcate its boundaries and take possession of a long section of the riverbed and overhanging cliffs. He did this by erecting a tower "on the hill at the northern end of the ravine, after the bend" (*V. Sab.* 16, 100). The complex best fitting this description is complex no. 4 (see Fig. 26).[7]

The erection of a tower, as well as fencing off an area, in order to mark its possession by a monastery is also mentioned by Cyril in another place. Paul, the head of the Theoctistus monastery, built such a tower of demarcation in 485, twelve years after the death of Euthymius, after a rift developed between him and the monastery of Euthymius, which led to fencing off the lands of the two monasteries. Paul's tower overlooked the divided estates (*V. Cyr.* 7, 226). The boundaries of the monastery of Euthymius (τὰ μεθόρια τοῦ μοναστηρίου) are also mentioned in another passage (*V. Euth.* 59, 82.8). Cyril also tells about shepherds who grazed their flocks within the bounds of the Cave monastery; they promised to desist from grazing within the boundaries of Sabas' monasteries only after he stopped the flow of their flocks' milk (*V. Sab.* 59, 160).

I have traced boundary walls, apparently intended to demarcate lands held or claimed by the monastery, around the Cave monastery (*Spelaion*) (see Figs. 65–66) and the Scholarius monastery (see below, Chap. 2c, D, and Fig. 67). The fence surrounding the Heptastomos laura (Hirschfeld 1992, fig. 10) is unique. Boundary walls such as this have not been found around the Great Laura. Its northern limit was marked by a tower, not by a fencing wall.

In the first stage of construction, the cell of the founder, the prayerhouse, and apparently most of the cells of the other monks were located on the eastern bank of the brook. The northern tower as well was built, according to my proposal, on the eastern bank. The eastern slope of the Kidron, however, is not suitable for the erection of large monastic buildings. For logistic reasons also it was more convenient to build these structures on the west bank of the Kidron, since supplies came mainly from the west, from settlements located in the Jerusalem-Bethlehem region. For considerations of heating and lighting too, it was also preferable to erect dwellings on the west bank, which faces the rising sun, rather than on the east bank. For all these reasons, the center of the monastery was later removed to the west bank of the Kidron. It was here that the churches and other communal buildings of the core were built, and it was here that Sabas moved his dwelling, to a tower constructed for him above the *diakonikon* of the Theoktistos Church. With the further increase of the community, cells were built on both sides of the ravine; beasts of burden were also purchased to aid in the construction work and to serve the monks. In his function as *hegoumenos*, Sabas took care to supply all the needs of the monks, so that they would not be distracted by having to leave the monastery for such a purpose (*V. Sab.* 18, 102).

---

[7] Marcoff and Chitty (1929) proposed identifying the northern tower with Ras el-Baqquq, which in my opinion is the site of the Small Coenobium, while Corbo (1958c) proposed identifying complex 4 with the Small Coenobium (see Chap. 2B, below).

The small prayerhouse could no longer accommodate the growing community of monks. Accordingly, a spacious cave on the east bank was prepared, which seemed to have been built by God especially for this purpose; therefore it was called the "Theoktistos [God erected] Church." It is related (ibid. 101–2) that a pillar of fire, which appeared to Sabas in a nocturnal revelation, led him to this site. Sabas' fame spread, and many believers came to get a glimpse of him and to receive his guidance, bringing with them offerings and donations, which he used for the construction and organization of the Laura (ibid. 103). It was then necessary to build a hostel for these pilgrims near the Laura. This was done in 491 (*V. John Hes.* 5, 205).[8]

The next stage in the construction of the Laura began after two Isaurian "brothers of the flesh," the architects Gelasius and Theodulus, joined the Laura in 494.[9] They aided Sabas in constructing the large buildings in the Laura's core. These included a bakery (μαγκιπεῖον), a hospital (νοσοκομεῖον), and above them (ὑπεράνω) a large church (μεγάλη ἐκκλησία), the Theotokos Church. A courtyard (μεσίαυλον) was built between the two churches, a layout that has been preserved until the present in the Mar Saba monastery, while large water reservoirs were built in the ravine (δοχεῖα ὑδάτων μέγιστα ἐν τῷ χειμάρρῳ) (*V. Sab.* 32, 117). The large church and water reservoirs were intended to fill the needs of the growing community. The dedication of the Theotokos Church by Patriarch Elias on July 1, 501 (ibid.) marks the end of the building phase of the Laura. This was the largest and most famous of all the laurae in Palestine (*V. Sab.* 7, 91.21–22).

The construction of new cells continued in later years as well, for example, the cell that Cyril of Scythopolis built for himself (*V. Sab.* 75, 181; 82, 187). Mention is also made of the construction of a large water reservoir within a cave under the tower of Sabas in the period after his death (ibid. 82, 187). Apart from these, there is no mention of any large building project in the Laura during this period, the reign of Justinian, a period in which architectural projects flourished. Thus the physical appearance of the Laura had already been established during Sabas' lifetime.

The highest tower in the Mar Saba monastery is known as the "Tower of Justinian" (Fig. 9) on the basis of a Greek inscription engraved above the lintel of its entrance (Phokylides 1927, 70–72) (Fig. 10):

κτιτήριον
τοῦ μεγάλου Ἰουστινιανοῦ
Βασιλέως τῶν ὀρθοδόξων χριστιανῶν
ἐν ἔτε(ι) φκθ

building
of Justinian the Great
the king of the Orthodox Christians
in the year 529

[8] Its construction began, therefore, only after Sallustius had resolved the first dispute between Sabas and his monks and dedicated the Theoktistos Church (Dec. 12, 490). For further details see below, Part III, Chap. 2.

[9] On the Isaurians as skillful builders and architects, see C. Mango, "Isaurian Builders," *Polychronion: Festschrift F. Dölger* (Munich 1966), 358–65.

9. Mar Saba. Western wall and "Tower of Justinian."

ΚΤΙΤΗΡΙΟΝ ✝
ΤΟΥΜΕΤΑΛΛΟΥΙΟΥϹΤΙΝΙΑΝΟΥ
ΒΑϹΙΛΕωϹΤωΝΟΡΘΟΔΟΞωΝΧΡϹΤΙΑΝωΝ
ΕΝΕΤΕ Φ.. Κ.. ⊙ ✝

10. Mar Saba. Greek inscription on the lintel of the "Tower of Justinian."

Justinian ruled from 527 to 565 CE. The date mentioned in this inscription seemingly refers to the common Christian era (*ab incarnatione*). This era was first proposed in Rome by the Scythian monk Dionysius Exiguus ("the Short") (ca. 500–550), who established the 753rd year of the foundation of Rome (*ab urbe condita*) as the year of the Incarnation. The use of this dating system was adopted in the East by the Byzantines no earlier than the fourteenth century (Schneider 1931, 307). It is quite surprising to encounter the use of this era in an inscription in the Great Laura from such an early date. This system (*ab incarnatione*) was known to Cyril, although he did not use it as his usual dating system. Thus, for example, according to him, the date of St. Sabas' death was 524 *ab incarnatione* (*V. Sab.* 77, 183). This era of Cyril is slightly different, therefore, from the actual Christian era introduced by Dionysius Exiguus, according to which Sabas' death occurred in 532 *ab incarnatione* = CE. If the inscription refers to the conventional Christian era, then the tower was built by Justinian two years prior to Sabas' visit to his court. If, on the other hand, the reference is to the Incarnation era used by Cyril, then this corresponds to the year 537 CE. In either case, it is surprising that such a project, if it was indeed built in the Laura by Justinian, was not mentioned at all by Cyril.

From the palaeographic and epigraphic aspects, the script is not typical of the Byzantine period, and the dating system is not known in inscriptions from this period (Di Segni, personal communication). Architecturally, also, this is not a typical Justinianic fortification; the differences are noticeable in a comparison between it and the walls, for example, of St. Catherine's monastery in Sinai. The stones of the tower have a wide marginal dressing surrounding a prominent protrusion (boss), with a masons' mark on the edges (Fig. 11), a feature not characteristic of the Byzantine period.[10] The formulation of the inscription also does not suit that of the Justinianic dedicatory inscriptions (cf. Avigad 1977). In light of all these facts, there is no doubt that the inscription is not authentic and that it was engraved at a date later than that mentioned in it.

The Size and Ethnic Composition of the Population

The rate of demographic growth was rapid. The number of monks already reached 70 at the end of the first building stage (483–486). In 491, when John the Hesychast arrived in the Laura, there were already 150 monks (*V. Sab.* 19, 104; *V. John Hes.* 5, 205). More monks joined the Laura later (*V. Sab.* 33, 118.21–22). The foundation of the Kastellion monastery in 492 must be viewed as a response to the increasing population of the Laura and as an expression of care for those monks who were found to be unfit for lauritic life. The erection of the Small Coenobium in 493, on the other hand, was intended to introduce into monastic life lay people who wished to join the Laura. These building projects were solutions to real demands that arose as a result of the growth and development of the Laura; such would also be the case later on. In this manner Sabas could absorb more monks who wished to join his community but for whom there was no room in the Laura proper, or monks who were not yet fit to be accepted into the community due to their youth or lack of proper training.

[10] Masons' marks are characteristic features of Crusader architecture; see C. R. Conder, "Masons' Marks," *PEFQSt* 1883, 130–33; R. H. C. Davis, "A Catalogue of Masons' Marks as an Aid to Architectural History," *Journal of the British Archaeological Association*, 3rd ser., 17 (1954), 43–76, pls. xvii–xviii; D. Pringle, "Some Approaches to the Study of Crusader Masonry Marks in Palestine," *Levant* 13 (1981), 173–99.

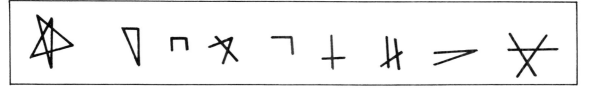

11. Mar Saba. Masons' mark on the "Tower of Justinian."

The number of the rebels against Sabas, initially 40, reached a total of 60 in 504. If it was because of them that Sabas decided to continue his exile from the Laura, going to Nicopolis, then it should be assumed that this group constituted a significant percentage of the population. If the total number of monks did not generally exceed 150, then they constituted ca. 40 percent of the community, while a figure of only 20–25 percent would result if we estimate a total population of 250–300 monks at this stage. A smaller percentage would constitute a group of rebels not significant enough to cause Sabas to leave his monastery. And indeed, on the basis of a careful study of the cell remains and of the dimensions of the Laura's churches, it is doubtful that the population ever exceeded 250–300. Moreover, it is reasonable to assume that this figure was reached only at a later date. The abandonment of the Laura by the rebels in 507 decreased the population of the Great Laura by 60 monks.

In 555, with the repopulation of the New Laura, another 60 monks were transferred for this purpose from the Great Laura. It is reasonable to assume that they constituted no more than 20–25 percent of the population of the Laura at that time. It seems, however, that the Laura returned to its earlier size within a short time by absorbing new monks. One of them was Cyril, who left the New Laura after a stay of about two years and built for himself a cell in the Great Laura (*V. Sab.* 75, 181; 82, 187). In 614, in the course of the Persian invasion, 44 of the Laura's monks were killed and others found a permanent refuge in a safer monastery near Jerusalem. Twenty monks were put to death in 797 by the Saracens. Despite these attacks, however, the population of the Laura numbered 150 monks in 808 (see below, Part v, end of Chap. 1).

The community was composed of two main ethnic or, rather, linguistic groups: Greek-speakers (most of whom came from Asia Minor) and Armenian-speakers. The latter group almost certainly included not only those from the Roman provinces of Armenia Prima and Secunda, who were undoubtedly fluent in Greek, but also those from the kingdom of Armenia, who spoke and prayed in their own tongue.

Initially, three Armenians came to the Laura (ca. 491): Jeremias and his disciples Peter and Paul. Sabas gave them the small prayerhouse on the eastern bank of the Kidron, and permitted them to pray in their own tongue on Saturdays and Sundays (*V. Sab.* 20, 105). Paul is one of the sources from whom Cyril drew his information. The first monks in Kastellion were from Melitene, the capital of Armenia Secunda (ibid. 27, 112). The number of Armenians grew, and when the large church of the Laura was dedicated in 501, they received the Theoktistos Church (*V. Sab.* 32, 117). The Armenians also included John the Hesychast and the deacon Jeremias, who accompanied Sabas to Justinian's court in the capital and who later headed the Laura named after him.

The Greek-speaking monks of the Laura and the appended monasteries came from the following provinces and cities (Schwartz 1939, 257–81, name index): Cappadocia, Isauria, Galatia, Honorias, Bithynia, Asia, Pontus, Greece, Lycia, Byzantium, and Alexandria. One monk came from the west, from Rome. A few came from Syria (Apamea), Arabia, and Phoenicia (Berythus). There were also a few from Palestine: the brothers Zannos and Benjamin came from the Hebron region; James the rebel and Stephen the anti-Origenist were Jerusalemites, Cassianus (a future *hegoumenos*) came from Scythopolis; Nonnus, the head of the Origenists, was from Palestine. The native-born monks, and certainly the villagers among them, obviously also spoke Syriac. This was not, however, one of the languages used for prayer in the Laura during the period under discussion. Regarding the appointment to key positions (priests, monastery heads, etc.), there was no noticeable preference of those from Asia Minor over native monks.

The Archaeological Remains[11]
The cells of the Great Laura were established on the cliffs of the Kidron, along a ca. 2 km section in which the ravine changed its flow from a west-east direction to a south-north direction because of its meeting with the Muntar-Mar Saba anticline, composed of hard lime geological strata. The Laura is ca. 12 km aerial distance from Jerusalem and Bethlehem, and ca. 5 km from the monastery of Theodosius. It could be reached by the three lateral paths coming from settled areas described above: (1) from Jerusalem, following the streambed of the Kidron; (2) from Jerusalem, along the Beth Abudisson-Jebel Muntar road, from which a path branches off to the south, descending along Wadi Rahwe to the Kidron; and (3) from Bethlehem, via Beth Sahur and the monastery of Theodosius.

1. *The Core of the Laura*
    The present-day Mar Saba monastery marks the core of the Laura. It is built upon high cliffs at the end of an outcrop descending steeply to the Kidron. Here the two ancient churches (Fig. 12) are located: the cave in which the Theoktistos Church was installed (at present dedicated to St. Nicholas of Myra) and the large church, the church of the Theotokos (on both churches, see below). Between them, in the courtyard separating the two churches, is located the building that houses the tomb of St. Sabas (Fig. 13). Originally Sabas was buried in the cemetery which still exists under the courtyard pavement (*V. Sab.* 78, 184). The kitchen and refectory (Fig. 14) are located at present under the level of the Great Church and to its north. This was, presumably, the site of the

[11] The Laura was surveyed by me within the framework of the Mar Saba Map survey conducted on behalf of the Association for the Archaeological Survey of Israel. The members of the team included Erez Cohen and Benny Levenstein (surveyors), Asaf Ron, Hamutal Kishon, and Efrat Schechter. During the course of our work we received the cooperation of Archimandrite Seraphim, the abbot of Mar Saba, and the monk Kerubim, along with the assistance of the Greek Orthodox patriarch, Diodorus II, and the archimandrites Timothy and Nicephorus from the Patriarchal Secretariat. In our contacts with the Patriarchal authorities, we were aided by Mr. Raphael Levi, the former Commissioner of the Jerusalem District in the Interior Ministry, and Mr. Shemuel Hamburger, Religion Staff Officer in the Civil Administration of Judea and Samaria. I am extremely grateful to all of them. For a detailed description of the findings, see Patrich 1994. The map of the Laura presents a comprehensive picture of the findings; the current chapter provides representative examples of each type of dwelling complex. See also Patrich 1988.

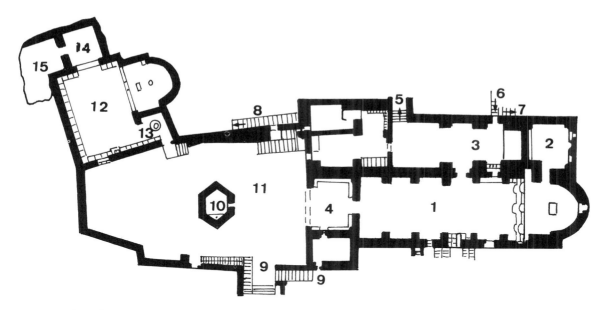

12. Mar Saba. Plan of the two main churches: the Theoktistos Church, now dedicated to St. Nicholas of Myra; the Theotokos Church, the main church.

Legend

1. Theotokos Church	9. Passage to the southern cells
2. Sacristy	10. Sabas' tomb
3. Northern narthex	11. Courtyard (cemetery underneath)
4. Narthex	12. St. Nicholas Chapel (ancient Theoktistos Church)
5. Passage to northern section	13. Baptistry
6. Staircase to refectory and kitchen	14. *Diakonikon* (display of monks' skulls)
7. Staircase to balcony	15. Repository of monks' bones
8. Open corridor to the entrance gate	

Laura's hospital during the Byzantine period. On the floor below them is the bakery (Fig. 15), apparently in the same place where it had been located in the Byzantine period, unless it was then near the hostel. The hostel was distant from the core. According to my hypothesis (see below), it is to be identified with the remains to the west of the "Women's Tower," near the road that comes from Bethlehem. The stable of the Mar Saba monastery (today in disuse) is located inside the upper gate, the one to the north of the visitor's gate. Without conducting archaeological probes, it cannot be determined when this structure was built.

The Churches

During the course of its development, the Laura had three churches: (1) a small prayer-house (εὐκτήριον) on the east bank, not far from the first cave of Sabas (its ruins or exact location are not known; possible candidates are the chapels of complexes 32 or 33 below); (2) the Theoktistos Church, in the cave; (3) the Theotokos Church, which is the Great Church. Since the Theoktistos Church was built in a natural cave, which was less exposed to the ravages of time than an aboveground structure, it may reasonably be assumed that it retained the form of the Byzantine period. According to Cyril of Scythopolis, this was

13. Mar Saba. Tomb of St. Sabas.

14. Mar Saba. The refectory (*trapeza/aristeterion*).

15. Mar Saba. The bakery.

16. Mar Saba. Church of St. Nicholas.

"a great and marvelous cave . . . on the eastern side there is an apse built by God, and on the northern side . . . a large room arranged like a *diakonikon* and an entrance from the southwest, wide and suitably open to receive the illumination of the sun's rays" (*V. Sab.* 18, 102). Cyril's description fits the present church of St. Nicholas of Myra in the Mar Saba monastery (Figs. 12, 16). Its wide opening is located today on the south side, and the rays of sunlight provide sufficient illumination indeed.

The church is almost square, ca. 11 m on each side. The apse is 2.6 m deep, and the space in front is blocked at present by an iconostasis partition, a characteristic feature of all Greek Orthodox churches. The space south of the apse serves as a baptistery, with a stone immersion basin in its center. The *diakonikon* mentioned by Cyril serves today as a display room for monks' skulls (Fig. 17), while their bones are collected in the room in the southwest corner, sealed by a metal grill. In the rock ceiling of the cave, close to the skull room, a masonry blockage is visible. Here or in the sealed charnel room was apparently the shaft that connected the *diakonikon* with the Tower of Sabas, which was constructed above this church. This shaft, by which Sabas would descend to the church, was sealed by Sabas' heirs (*Pass. XX Mart. Sab.* 47, 173). This literary source from the end of the eighth century also mentions a niche on the eastern side and a *diakonikon* on the north where holy objects were preserved—a room known as a *keimiliarcheion* or a *skeuophylakion*. This description is in accord with that of Cyril's and with the actual shape of the St. Nicholas Church.[12]

According to Cyril, the Theotokos Church (the Great Church) was built beyond the courtyard in which Sabas' tomb would eventually be erected. The relative location of the churches and the tomb at present fits this description; however, without a detailed architectural study, it is not possible to determine to what degree the Great Church of the Mar Saba monastery is founded on the original walls of the early Theotokos Church. The church (Figs. 12, 18) has a single long and high rectangular hall of the "monastic type," according to Corbo (1958a, 257) and Hirschfeld (1992, 114–17). Its length, up to the iconostasis, is 20 m, and its width is ca. 7 m. To the west there is a 6.1 × 3.65 m narthex (Fig. 19). The depth of the bema, up to the apse line, is 3.5 m. The apse protrudes slightly outward and is 3.5 m deep. Thus the total length of the church, excluding the narthex, reaches 27 m. These dimensions are larger than those of the church of the Martyrius monastery, which is 25.9 m long and 6.6 m broad.

The present roofing consists of intersecting vaults resting on piers attached to the longitudinal walls. This roofing is obviously not Early Christian but of a later period. The southern wall, which faces the wadi, is externally supported by massive pilasters, indicating that this is the weak side of the structure, whose deep foundations were undermined many times by the floods that run down in the steep tributary which empties here into

---

[12] Monastery churches built within a natural cave are also found in Khirbet ed-Deir in the upper section of Nahal Arugoth, in the monastery of Khallet ed-Denabiya in upper Wadi Makukh, and in the monasteries of Theoctistus and Sapsas (Hirschfeld 1992, 117–28). The first church of the laura of Pharan, on the other hand, was not built in a natural cave, but rather in an existing rock-cut hall that had been used by the robbers from whom the captive Chariton, the later founder of the laura, had miraculously escaped (*V. Char.* 9, 23). According to my suggestion, this hall had been excavated ca. 250 years previously, during the time of the Jewish Great Revolt against Rome, when it served as the headquarters of Symeon son of Gioras, one of the chief leaders of the revolt (Patrich 1986, 24; 1989, fig. 10).

17. Mar Saba. Church of St. Nicholas. Monks' skulls on display in the *diakonikon*.

18. Mar Saba. Theotokos Church.

19. Mar Saba. Theotokos Church, western narthex.

the Kidron. The last reinforcement of these pilasters is dated by an inscription (Fig. 20) to the year 1707.

The northern wing of the church is divided into two sections: in the east a sacristy, and in the west, a northern narthex (Fig. 21), where prayers and services that need not be conducted in the church itself are now held. It is quite possible that during the Byzantine period these two sections constituted one continuous space, which served as the *diakonikon* of the church. This is a typical arrangement for a "monastic chapel." A similar arrangement is found in the *diakonikon* of the Martyrius monastery church, which is also located as a northern wing of the church (Magen and Talgam 1990, 94, fig. 4). But because of the lack of a precise architectural study of the Great Church at Mar Saba, this proposal remains hypothetical.

At present, in addition to these two churches, the Mar Saba monastery contains five chapels (Fig. 22), all dating from a period considerably later than the Byzantine. The chapel of St. John Chrysostom (Fig. 23 and no. 11 on Fig. 8) and the chapel of Joachim and Anne (where the *hesychasterion* of St. Sabas is shown at present: no. 24 on Fig. 8 and no. 35 on Fig. 26) are located at the northernmost and southernmost points of Mar Saba. Actually, these had been dwelling complexes later transformed into chapels. This is also the case with the chapel of St. John of Damascus (Fig. 24), which was consecrated in the cell that, according to tradition, served as his dwelling and burial place. Perhaps this was

20. Mar Saba. Greek inscription on external supports of the main church.

also the case with the chapel of St. George (Fig. 8, no. 12). The chapel of the Archangels was built recently by the present abbot of the monastery, the archimandrite Seraphim. A sixth chapel, dedicated to Symeon Stylites the Elder, is located in the "Women's Tower," which was built in 1605.

The Hostel
This was built, as stated above, in 491. According to the literary sources, hostels also existed in other monasteries of the wilderness, for example, the laura of Souka (*V. Cyr.* 7, 226), the coenobium of Euthymius (*V. Euth.* 48; 59), the coenobium of Choziba (*V. Geor.* 4, 23), the coenobium of Theodosius, where there were three hostels (*V. Theod.* 13, 34–35), and others.

The hostel of the Laura was intended not only to accommodate pilgrims who came to admire the exemplary lives of Sabas and his monks, but also for the relatives, friends, and acquaintances of the monks themselves (see, e.g., *Pratum* 53).[13] The monks were also accustomed to travel at times from one monastery to another in order to become acquainted with their residents. The outstanding example of this is that of John Moschus and Sophronius.

Next to the hostel were the storerooms for the grain brought by camel caravans

---

[13] For the practice of visiting monasteries and for monastery hostels, see below, Part III, Chap. 1C.

21. Mar Saba. Theotokos Church, northern narthex.

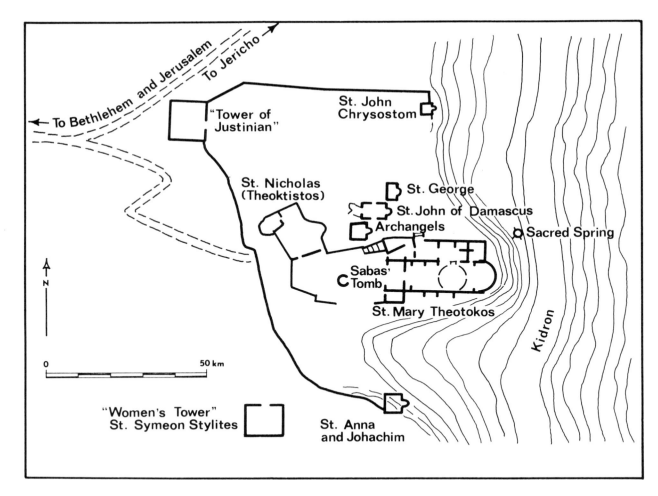

22. Mar Saba. Map of churches and chapels.

from Transjordan. The route leading there passed above the steep cliffs of the Kidron, where there was a danger of falling to the bottom (*V. Sab.* 81, 186). From the window of the hostel it was possible to throw things over the edge down to the bottom of the ravine, in a manner that was visible to Sabas from his tower (ibid. 40, 131).

In my opinion, the site of the hostel is to be identified with the ruins located ca. 100 m to the west of the Women's Tower. This site is somewhat cut off from the Laura but is located close to the road from Bethlehem and therefore conveniently accessible. It was also visible from the tower of Sabas, which was situated above the Theoktistos church.

The Water Supply

Large water cisterns were also constructed in the core during Sabas' time. The fourteen large water cisterns still in use in Mar Saba (Fig. 25) collect their water not only from the area of the monastery. Most of the water supply arrives through two aqueducts, one from the west and the other from the northwest (see the map of the Laura, Fig. 26). These are simple conduits—a dug channel and fieldstones placed on its edges—as in the Byzantine conduits in the Negev. It is quite possible that they have their beginnings in the Byzantine period. Several other large cisterns, no longer in use, are located along the streambed of the Kidron. The individual cells of the monks did not, however, receive their water

a

b

23. Mar Saba. Chapel of St. Chrysostom: (a) corridor; (b) antechamber.

a

b

24. Mar Saba. Chapel of St. John of Damascus: (a) iconostasis; (b) the saint's tomb.

25. Mar Saba. Opening of a water cistern with device for drawing water.

supply through a common aqueduct that linked the cells; rather, each dwelling complex had its own separate collecting system.

The Layout of Paths

The Laura cells were connected to the core by means of paved paths, in which rock-cut stairs were also incorporated (see the map of the Laura, Fig. 26). Two paths ran at the foot of the cliffs, on either side of the streambed. Another path ran atop the west bank of the Kidron, along the line of the present road. The three quarries located along this path are an indication of its antiquity. This path connected the roads coming from Jerusalem in the Kidron ravine with the Laura's core and hostel without passing between the monks' cells, which were located along the lower path. This path system transforms the separate structures scattered along the streambed into an integral architectonic unit—a laura. This is the architectural expression of the existence of a community of anchorites. The paths provided convenient communication between each monastic cell and the structures in the core, thereby contributing to a sense of community. It was not an encircling wall that determined the boundaries of the Laura and the monastic colony, but rather the paved paths that connected all its components.

Quarries and Lime Kiln

The mining sites, especially the quarry close to complex 25 (see Fig. 26), served in the construction of the core buildings. The dwelling complexes were built of stones collected nearby. An additional stone collecting site was possibly to the south of complex 15. The two quarries located on the east bank, in the northern part of the Laura (east of complex

9), are connected to the Herodian aqueduct leading to the fortress of Hyrcania and not to the Great Laura. Therefore these two quarries were not included in the Laura's map. A lime kiln is located below complex 43.

The Garden of the Laura

"Those who have a longtime experience of the Laura of blessed Sabas know that not even in the open air, in a garden, does a fig tree or any other tree grow, because of the hotness and dryness of the climate of the Laura. . . . And indeed, many tried to plant trees along the torrent bed, where there is a deep layer of soil, but though they water the plants during the whole winter, every year, these have hardly the strength to stay alive, owing to the excessive dryness of the climate, as I said, and the vehemence of the seasonal heat" (*V. John Hes.* 26, 221). In these words Cyril describes the harsh climatic conditions in the Laura, which prevented the growth of fruit trees. The fig tree that took root on the rock wall against which the cell of John the Hesychast was erected and even bore three figs, was regarded as a miracle, a manifestation of divine grace received by John (ibid. 25, 220).

A garden of fruit trees did exist to the north of the Laura, along the road that crosses the Kidron before the beginning of its canyon section. This garden belonged to the Small Coenobium, and its remains can be observed near Bir Ibrahim and Bir el-Baqquq, where traces of agricultural terraces, water cisterns, and structures from the Byzantine period are visible (olive trees were planted there in the late 1980s). This location fits Cyril's description (ibid. 26, 221): there is deep fertile soil there and the possibility of getting water from Wadi el-Baqquq, a small tributary of the Kidron. According to Cyril, the fathers of this monastery used to irrigate the trees with water from the wadi all winter long.

At the same time, however, it is not inconceivable that there were monks who cultivated vegetable gardens next to their cells. Although there is no explicit mention of this in the sources relating to the Great Laura, it is reasonable to suppose that efforts were made not only to plant trees but also to grow vegetables. Cyril does not mention this effort as an unsuccessful experiment. About Cyriacus we hear that he cultivated a vegetable garden next to his cell in Sousakim, a distance of 90 *stadia* (ca. 17 km) from the Old Laura, deep within the wilderness (*V. Cyr.* 15–16, 232). The vegetables in the Great Laura could have been watered during the summer months directly from the individual cisterns, as Cyriacus did (ibid.). The archaeological remains reveal the existence of small terraced plots of soil next to some of the Laura's cells, which could have served as vegetable gardens (see, e.g., the reconstruction, Fig. 41). Some of the monks follow this practice even today.

2. *The Hermitages of the Great Laura* (Patrich 1988; Meinardus 1966, 328–56)

The present-day Mar Saba monastery, with an area of 60 × 100 m², is not more than the core of the Great Laura. During the Byzantine period the Laura extended over the cliffs of the Kidron ravine, along a 2 km section south and north of Mar Saba. In the archaeological survey and excavations conducted along the ravine during 1982–83, remains of about forty dwelling complexes of monks scattered along the cliffs and about five additional buildings on the hilltops west of the Kidron were examined and docu-

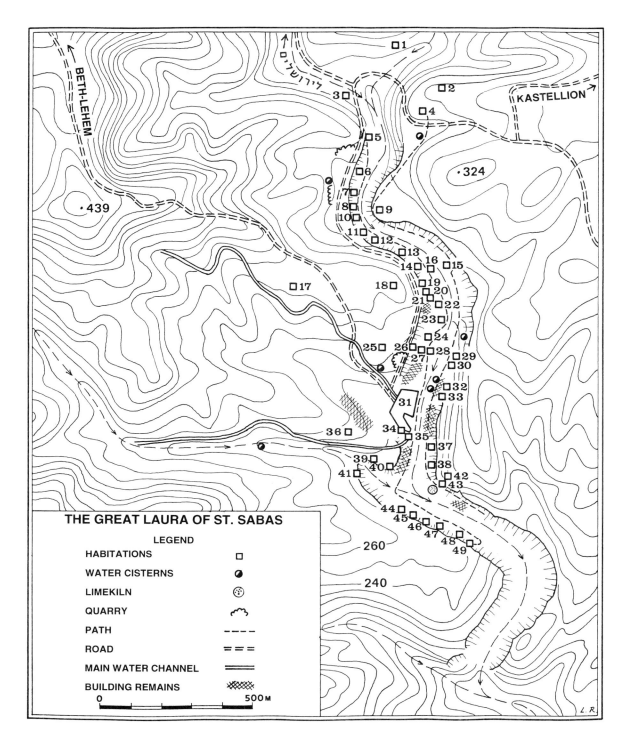

THE GREAT LAURA OF ST. SABAS

LEGEND

HABITATIONS	□
WATER CISTERNS	◐
LIMEKILN	⊚
QUARRY	⌒
PATH	- - - -
ROAD	= = =
MAIN WATER CHANNEL	═══
BUILDING REMAINS	▨▨▨

0   500 M

26. Map of the Great Laura.

mented (Fig. 26). Closer to the core of the Laura, construction was denser; today, however, it is mainly the ruins of water cisterns that are recognizable within this section. The
intensive destruction of the buildings along the first 250 m to the north and south of
Mar Saba does not permit proposing a clear plan of them without excavations. At the

same time, however, it is clear that most of the dwelling rooms were located in this section.

Further away from the center, the buildings become less dense. Yet here, despite the destruction, it is possible to isolate dwelling complexes and trace their plans. At times the preservation of the remains is remarkable and permits us to obtain a precise, detailed plan. It becomes clear that in many cases the term "monastic cell" is not suitable, since generally the hermitage is quite complex and spacious, even when it was intended for a single monk. Indeed, most of the complexes that have been examined fall into this category. A few were designed for a small group of monks, generally composed of an elderly monk and his disciple or attendant, brother monks, or monks of common ethnic origin or of similar religious inclination.

In the first phase of its history, from 478 to 483, Sabas himself and the monks who joined him lived in natural caves, which had undergone only minor construction by rock cutting and building in order to serve as dwellings (Figs. 27–29). In the second phase, when building construction began (483–486 CE), simple cells were built in overhangs against the cliff (Fig. 30) or the primitive cave hermitages were expanded and improved by additional construction on the rock ledge in front of the entrance to the cave (Figs. 31–33) (*V. Sab.* 16, 100). When a cave was located high up on the cliff, in such a manner that there was no rocky ledge in front of its opening, a tower founded on a lower level was erected, thereby creating an additional living space in front of the cave (Figs. 34–35). In some instances, the hermitage was constructed within a natural vertical cleft (Figs. 36–39).

An examination of the remains enables one to distinguish between complexes intended for a single monk and those intended for more than one. Within each of these categories, it is possible to define different types, according to the architectural nature of the complex. The classification of the cells according to the various types—ten altogether—is summarized in Table 1. These types are dispersed throughout the entire length of the Laura. There is no prevailing type of cell in any specific area.

The rock ledges upon which the complexes were located were leveled by terrace walls built at the very edge of the cliff. In this manner the monk's living space was extended. Despite the density of construction and the proximity of the complexes to each other, the trend toward seclusion is clearly visible in all the complexes: the choice of cliffs and rock ledges with difficult access, the raising of entrances, thus making the use of ladders and ropes necessary in order to climb to the complexes, and the surrounding of the complex with a boundary wall.

A few of the dwelling complexes in the Laura are more spacious and contain an elaborate chapel. However, most of the complexes that have been examined and that served as dwellings for single monks are of Type II, simple cells built on a narrow ledge parallel to the rock wall. These complexes as well are properly built, and are generally equipped with a water collecting system and an integral water cistern.

The built walls were held together with plaster and cement made of mud and lime. The main construction material was fieldstones, which were collected nearby or were brought from mining sites (see the quarries on the map of the Laura, Fig. 26). Marble was extremely rare. Roofing consisted of wood beams extended between the built walls and the rock cliff, with a plastered roof above. Roof tiles have not been found.

28. The Great Laura. Sabas' *hesychasterion*, interior.

27. The Great Laura. Sabas' *hesychasterion* (cave of seclusion), exterior.

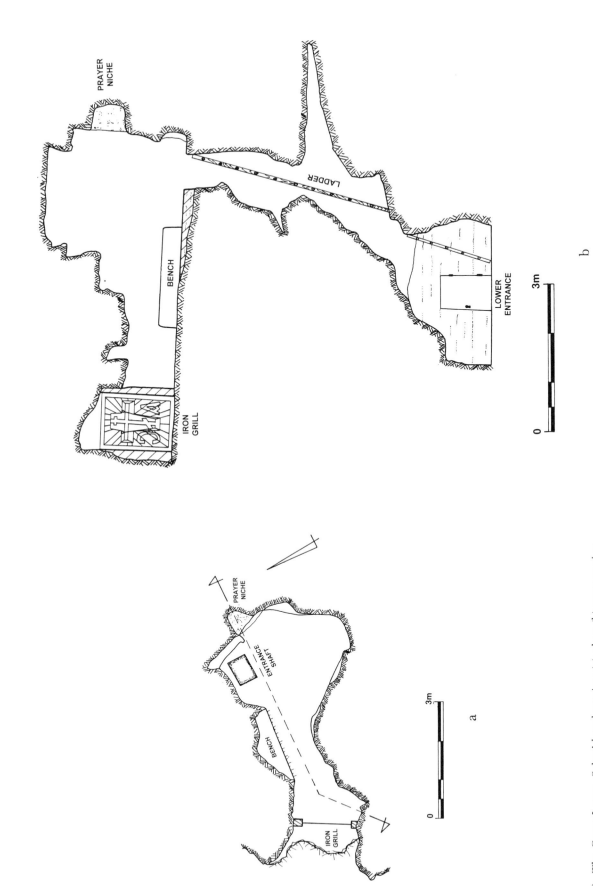

29. The Great Laura. Sabas' *hesychasterion*: (a) plan; (b) cross section.

b

PRAYER
NICHE

LADDER

BENCH

IRON
GRILL

LOWER
ENTRANCE

0   3m

a

PRAYER
NICHE

ENTRANCE
SHAFT

BENCH

IRON
GRILL

0   3m

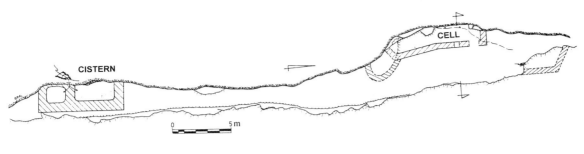

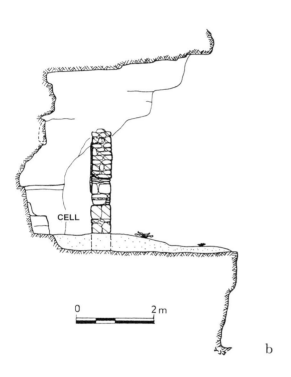

30. The Great Laura. Complex 22: (a) plan; (b) cross section.

The rock walls and masonry walls were plastered inside and out with lime plaster of good quality. A door and at times a window were inserted in the walls.[14] The floor was plastered or consisted of a mosaic. The mosaic floor, generally white in color, was made in a professional manner; underneath it was laid a bedding of lime plaster of good quality.

It is evident that these structures were planned in advance and were constructed by expert masons, not by the monks themselves. These were not destitute, miserable constructions in caves or in rock recesses. The caves were adapted for dwellings by means

[14] The hatch of the cell of John the Hesychast is mentioned a few times: *V. John Hes.* 19, 216; 21, 218; 23, 219. These sources indicate that the elderly monk guided and taught his disciples who stood beyond this opening and not within his cell; see also *Pratum* 137, 3000. In another place, mention is made of a Saracen youth who entered through the window of the cell of an elderly ascetic monk (*Pratum* 160, 3028). Mention is also made there (163, 3029) of a door of a cell of seclusion.

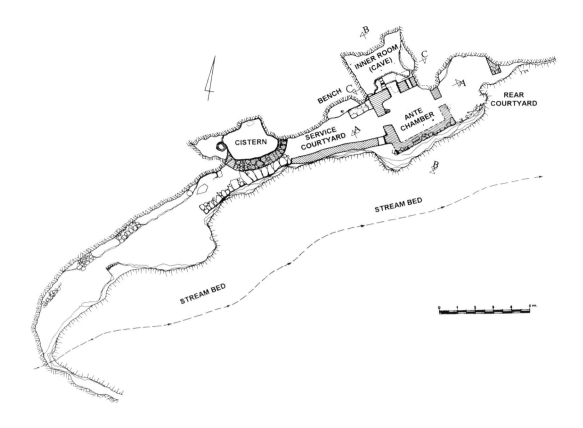

31. The Great Laura. Complex 39 ("Cave of Xenophon"), plan.

32. The Great Laura. Complex 39 ("Cave of Xenophon").

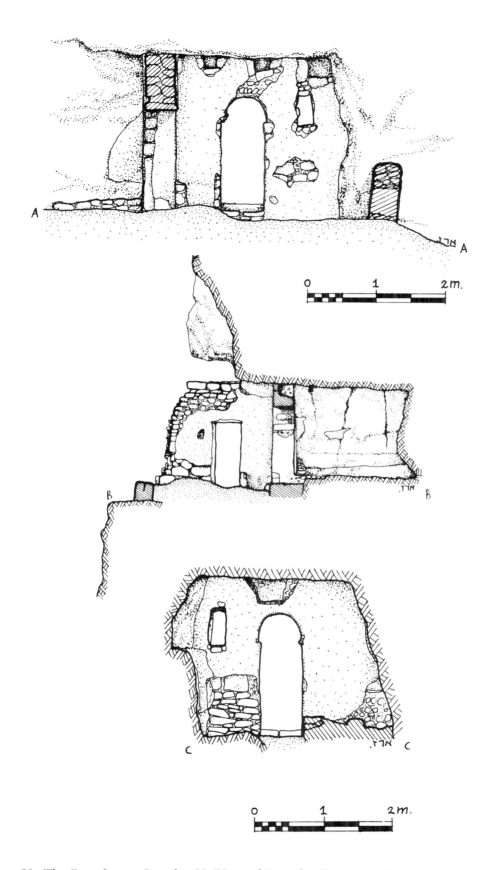

אזור

0   1   2m.

אזור

אזור

0   1   2m.

33. The Great Laura. Complex 39 ("Cave of Xenophon"), cross sections.

34. The Great Laura. Complex 45 ("Tower of Arcadius son of Xenophon"), view from the north.

of built constructions; the tendency to go outside of the cave is evident in the establishment of a forward living space, instead of excavating inward into the rock and expanding the cave. In a few instances, the dwelling and living areas are quite spacious and include a number of dwelling and service rooms and even a chapel. Generally the dwelling cell is not poor or cramped, as one might infer from a study of the literary sources alone. Various features of the hermitages are summarized in Table 2.

Prayer Chapels in the Dwelling Complexes (Patrich 1993b)
Remains of chapels or prayer niches have been found in fifteen of the complexes surveyed, both in those intended for one monk and in those intended for several. It may be assumed that each cell or complex included such a place of worship. These installations always constitute an integral part of the dwelling complex. They were intended to serve the monks during their lifetime and were not established to commemorate the monks after their death, for the monks of the Laura were not buried in the chapel within their cell, but rather in a common burial place at the center of the Laura (*V. Sab.* 43–44, 133–35; 78, 184–85).

The simplest arrangement is that of a small prayer niche rock-cut or built into the east wall of the cell. This is the case in the *hesychasterion* ("cave of Sabas"), complex 37 (Figs. 27–29).

The niches of the chapels may be entirely rock-cut (Fig. 43), partially rock-cut and partially built, or entirely built (such is the case with the cells on the western bank of the Kidron). At times a protruding rock altar (Fig. 44) takes the place of the niche. Generally the chapel comprises a separate room or space next to the dwelling room. In other in-

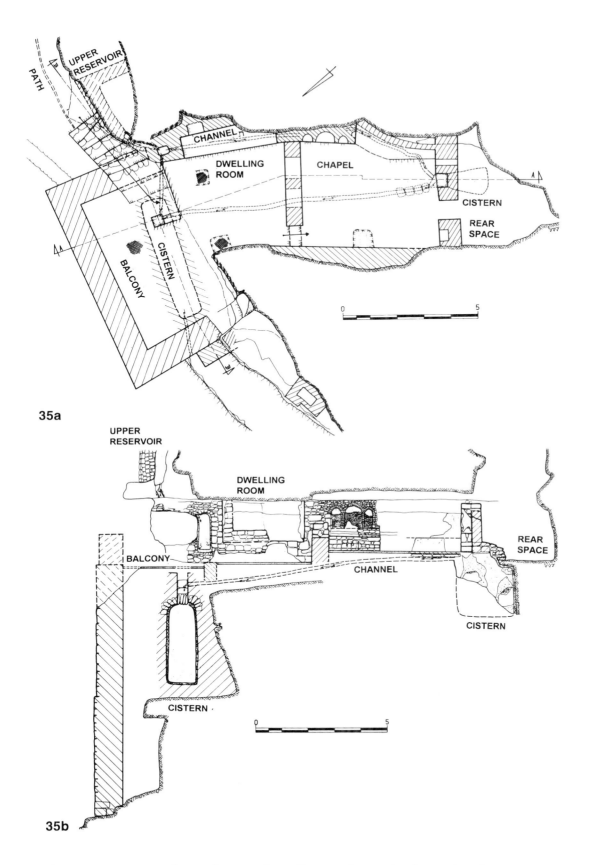

35. The Great Laura. Complex 45 ("Tower of Arcadius son of Xenophon"): (a) plan; (b) cross section.

37. The Great Laura. Complex 29 ("Tower of John the Hesychast"), reconstructed exterior.

36. The Great Laura. Complex 29 ("Tower of John the Hesychast"), general view from the west.

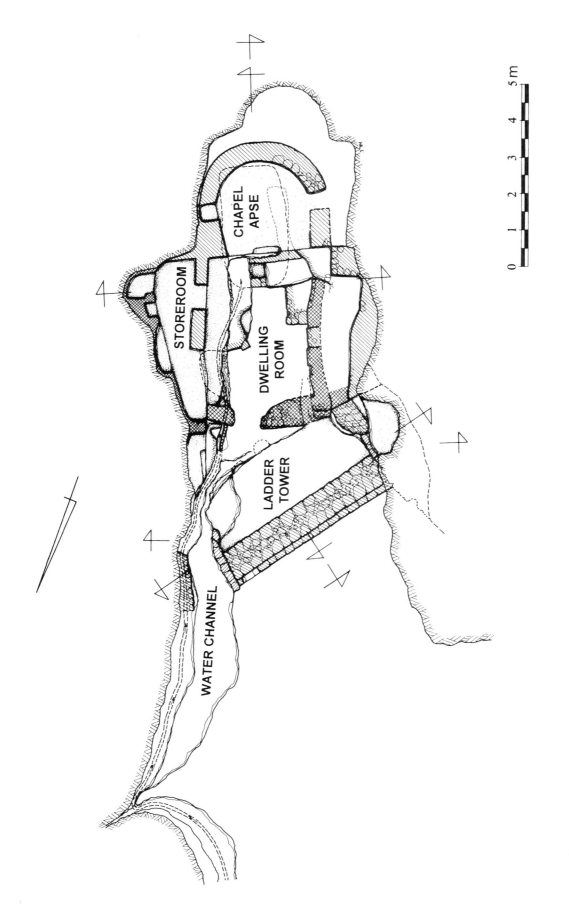

CHAPEL
APSE

STOREROOM

DWELLING
ROOM

LADDER
TOWER

WATER CHANNEL

0 1 2 3 4 5 m

38. The Great Laura. Complex 29 ("Tower of John the Hesychast"), plan.

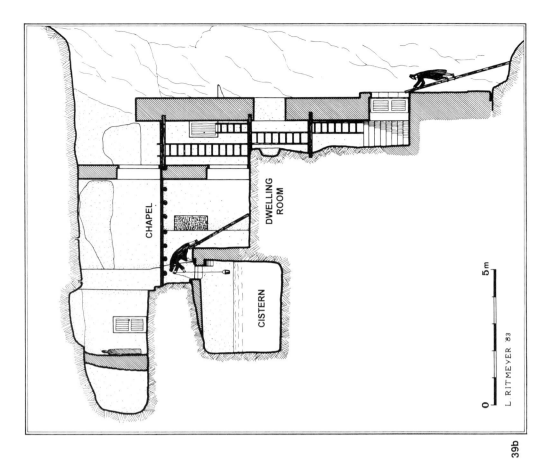

39b

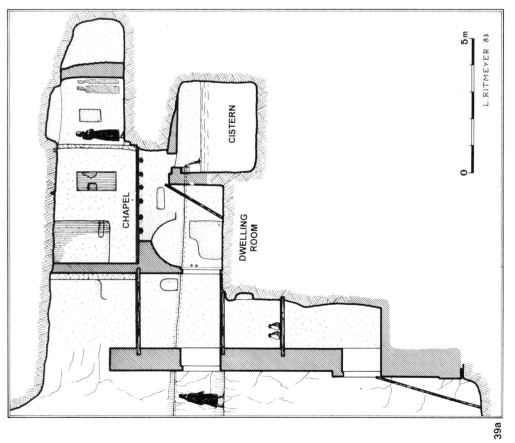

39a

39. The Great Laura. Complex 29 ("Tower of John the Hesychast"), cross sections: (a) looking south; (b) looking north.

Table 1. Typology of the Hermitages of the Great Laura*

Hermitage Type		Hermitage Number	Total
A. Hermitages intended for a single monk			34
I.	Minor modifications in a natural cave	7, 24, 37	3
II.	Construction on a narrow ledge parallel to the rock wall	6, 10, 11, 12, 13, 15, 19, 20, 21, 22, 23, 24, 44, 47	14
III.	Construction in a cave with an additional room on the rock ledge in front of it	8, 14, 35, 39, 43	5
IV.	A cave with an additional, constructed, front room on top of a tower	45, 48	2
V.	Construction within a vertical cleft	29, 30, 46	3
VI.	Construction on a moderate slope	2, 4, 5, 9, 17, 26, 38	7
B. Hermitages intended for several monks			7
I.	Construction in caves and built additions on the rock ledge in front of the caves (Fig. 40)	32, 33, 34	3
II.	Construction on a broad rock ledge (Fig. 41)	49	1
III.	Building on a moderate slope	28, 42	2
IV.	Vertical multilevel construction on the rock cliff (Fig. 42)	27	1

*There are instances in which the meager remains do not allow classification. Therefore, not all the hermitages marked on the map of the Laura appear in the present table.

stances the chapel was constructed as a second storey above the dwelling room (Fig. 39) or inside a cave. In one case there are two chapels with a similar plan in two storeys, one above the other (Fig. 45).

The chapel in complex 29, the "Tower of John the Hesychast" (Figs. 38, 39), is unique and distinguished by its plan and state of preservation. The apse was decorated with drawings of three saints. The adyton of the chapel in complex 45, the "Tower of Arcadius son of Xenophon," has an unusual shape. It is composed of three niches standing on a common base (Fig. 35).

An additional square niche is usually present alongside the prayer niche. It is generally located south or north of it and should probably be identified as a prothesis niche. This would indicate that not only the prayer of the hours but also the entire Eucharistic liturgy could have been celebrated in these complexes. In such a case the monk dwelling in the cell had to be already ordained as a priest.

The Laura's monks, who lived in their own cells during weekdays, would meet every weekend for common prayer in the churches at the center of the Laura. There were, however, monks who received special permission or an explicit order from the abbot to

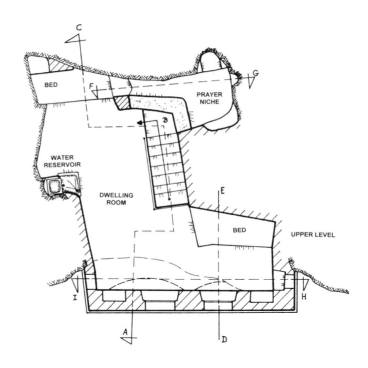

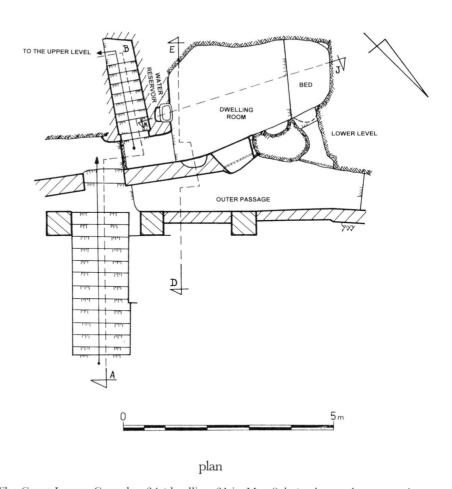

plan

40. The Great Laura. Complex 34 (dwelling 61 in Mar Saba), plan and cross sections.

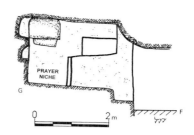

PRAYER
NICHE

G

0   2m

F

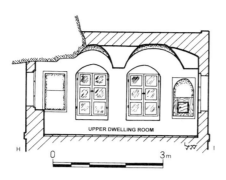

UPPER DWELLING ROOM

H   0   3m   I

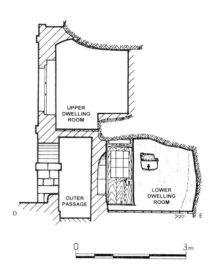

UPPER
DWELLING
ROOM

OUTER
PASSAGE

LOWER
DWELLING
ROOM

D   E

0   3m

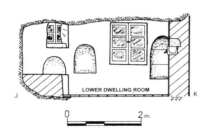

LOWER DWELLING ROOM

J   K

0   2m

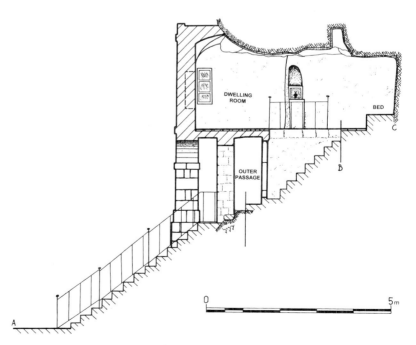

DWELLING
ROOM

BED

C

B

OUTER
PASSAGE

A

0   5m

cross sections

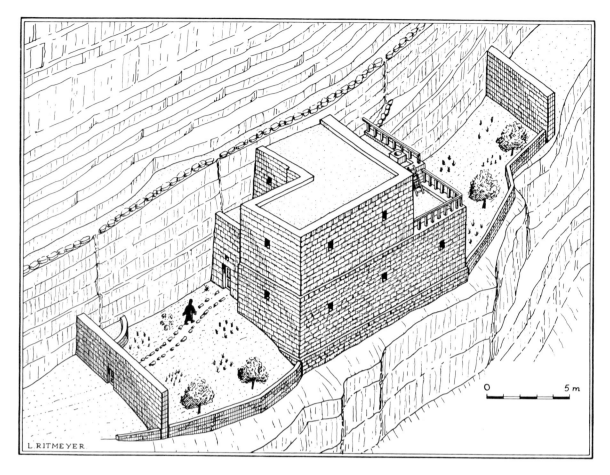

41. The Great Laura. Complex 49, reconstruction.

remain in their cells for extended periods.[15] These monks could pray and even have Communion by themselves in their cells.[16]

The artist's touch found expression in the chapels more than in the dwelling cells. The former were ornamented and beautified with colorful mosaic floors (Fig. 46), frescoes (Fig. 47), and windows with circular glass panes and stuccowork frames (Fig. 48). But in most cases the floors were plastered or of a simple white mosaic, as were the floors of the living quarters. The architectural details in the chapels were cast in cement (Fig. 49) rather than made of marble, which apparently was too expensive or luxurious.

[15] Such is the case with John the Hesychast (see below, Part V, Chap. 2A), who lived as a recluse in the Laura for 55 years. Of a different nature is the order imposed by Sabas on the monk James to seclude himself in his cell without admitting anyone except his attendant and the prohibition imposed on him not to visit the church; see *V. Sab.* 41, 132. Euthymius prohibited Gabriel, the brother of Cosmas and Chrysippus, a eunuch from birth, to leave the entrance of his cell. Only after 25 years in his cell did he leave it for the first time to go to the church of the monastery (*V. Euth.* 28, 45).

[16] Regarding a Communion held by John the Hesychast in his cell, see *V. John Hes.* 23, 219. Antony relates that George of Choziba had as an outer room a small cell, about three feet long, in which he conducted prayers and the reciting of the Psalms (*V. Geor.* 13, 109). On the conducting of common prayers in the cell, see also *Pratum* 46, 2901.

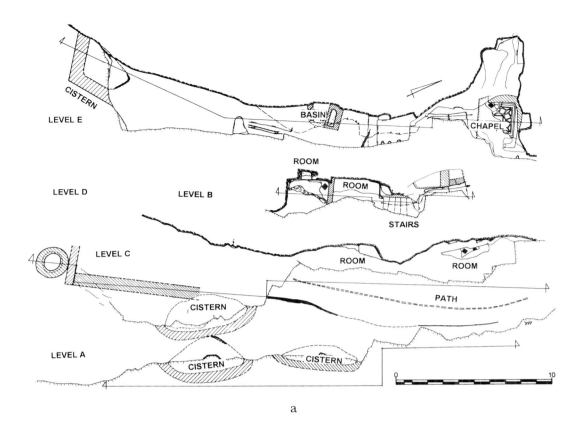

a

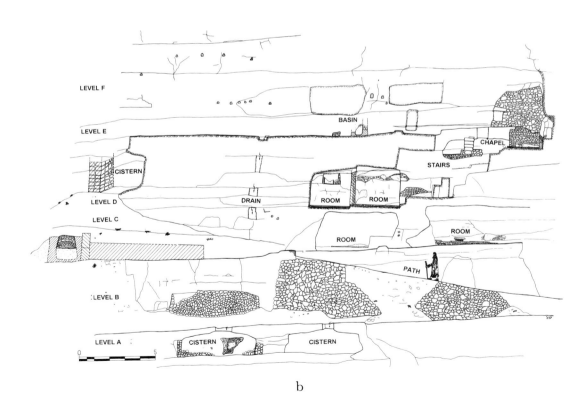

b

42. The Great Laura. Complex 27: (a) plan of the various levels; (b) elevations and cross sections.

Table 2. The Hermitages of the Great Laura—Summary

Hermitage number	Type	Living area (m²)	Chapel (pray niche)	Internal cisterns	External cisterns	Storeys (levels)	Number of monks
2	Avɪ	17.5		−		1	1
4	Avɪ	70		+	+	2(?)	1
5	Avɪ	125		+	+	n/a	n/a
6	Aɪɪ	36.5		−	+	1	1
7	Aɪ			−	−	1	1
8	Aɪɪɪ	37		−	+	(2)	1
9	Avɪ	60		?	−	(2)	1
10	Aɪɪ	30		−	+	(2)	1
11	Aɪɪ	17		−	+	1	1
12	Aɪɪ	11		+	+	1	1
13	Aɪɪ	n/a		−	+	1	1
14	Aɪɪɪ	25.5		+	+	1	1
15	Aɪɪ	22.5	(+)	−	+	1	1
17	Avɪ	210		+	−	1	1
19	Aɪɪ	?		−	+	(2)	1
20	Aɪɪ	?		−	?	1	1
21	Aɪɪ	48	+	+	+	2	1
22	Aɪɪ	16		?	+	1	1
23	Aɪɪ	98	+	−	+	1	1
24	Aɪ/ɪɪ	80	+	+	+	1	1/2
26	Avɪ	167		+	+	1(?)	1/2
27	Bɪv	20		−	+	4	3
		11		−	−		
		39	+	+	+		
28	Bɪɪɪ	n/a	+	+		2	2
29	Av	50	+	+	+	4	1
32	Bɪ	69	+	−	+	1	2
33	Bɪ	124	+	−	+	1	2/3
34	Bɪ	28	(+)	−	+	2	2
35	Aɪɪɪ	33	+	−	+	1	1
37	Aɪ	10	(+)	−	−	1	1
38	Avɪ	60		+	+	1	1
39	Aɪɪɪ	25	(+)	−	+	1	1
42	Bɪɪɪ	135		+	+	1	1/2
43	Aɪɪɪ	35	+	+	+	1	1/2
45	Aɪv	64	+	+	+	1	1
48	Aɪv	31		+(?)	−	1	1
49	Bɪɪ	168		+	+		2/3

43. The Great Laura. Complex 32, rock-cut niche
and mosaic floor of private chapel.

44. The Great Laura. Complex 33, private chapel.

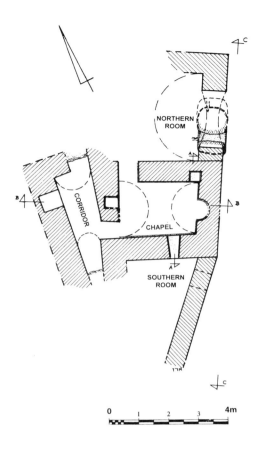

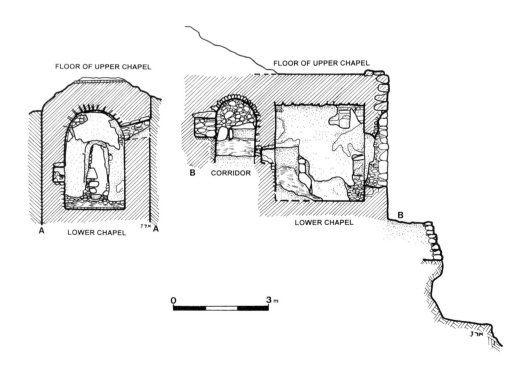

45. The Great Laura. Complex 28, the lower chapel, plan and cross sections.

46. The Great Laura. Complex 27, mosaic floor of the chapel.

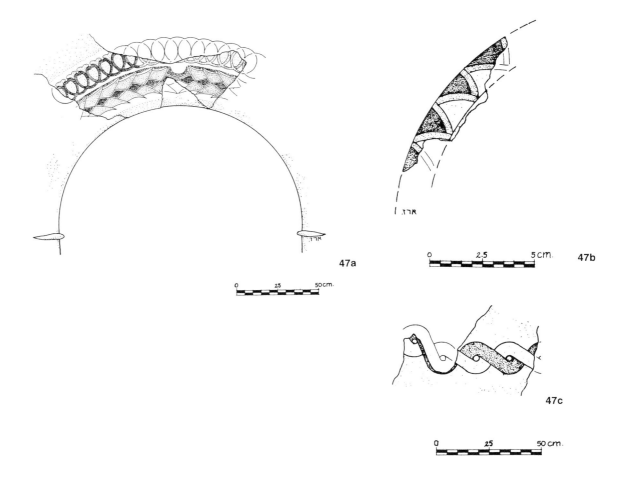

47a

47b

47c

47. The Great Laura. Complex 28, the lower chapel, painted decorations.

48. The Great Laura. Complex 28, the upper chapel, window panes and frames.

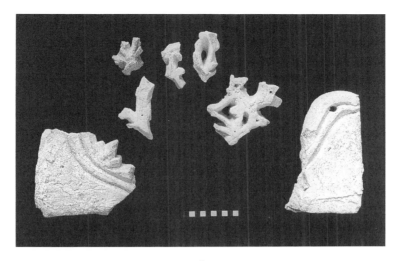

a

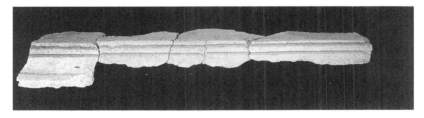

b

c

49. The Great Laura. Complex 28, the upper chapel, architectural fragments: (a) chancel screen; (b) altar plate; (c) altar legs.

The Water Supply of the Dwelling Complexes

There was no central water supply system common to all the complexes of the Laura. A separate water collecting and storage system was an integral part of each complex. This system was usually spread over three levels. In the upper level, above the dwelling complex, there were the retaining walls and ducts which collected the rainwater flowing down the slope and diverted it into the upper reservoirs. From here the water flowed down by means of built gutters to the ponds and cisterns located in the middle level, the dwelling level. Excess water was circulated from here through ducts or clay pipes to the lower reservoirs, which were located in the lower level (their inlet openings, however, were located in the middle level). In addition to the storage cisterns, sedimentation and regulation basins were also integrated into the system. The water cisterns were located close to the dwelling quarters and at times even within them, under the floor (Figs. 35, 39). It is clear from the architectural nature and quality of the dwelling complexes and water system that they were built by expert masons in accordance with a plan drawn up in advance.

The Spacious Complexes of the Laura

The dwelling complexes, as well as the other buildings of the Laura, were built on Sabas' behalf and under his supervision (*V. Sab.* 16, 100; 32, 117) or that of the *hegoumenos* who headed the Laura after his death. They were regarded as the property of the Laura. It was the *hegoumenos* who was authorized to give a cell to a newly arrived monk (*V. Sab.* 16, 100; 20, 105; 42, 132; 44, 134; *V. John Hes.* 6, 206) or to exchange the cell of an elderly monk (*V. Sab.* 43, 133). Although Sabas initiated the establishment of many monasteries, as well as hostels in Jericho and Jerusalem, the spacious complexes in the Great Laura are not consistent with the degree of restraint and moderation regarding physical needs preached by him (*V. Sab.* 28, 113; 30, 115). Although the archaeological remains are mute witnesses, they do provide more objective evidence than do the writings of Cyril on living conditions in the Great Laura.

It is possible that these complexes were built as marks of respect and honor for important monks, with funds of the Laura or from outside admirers and relatives.[17] The reference is to complexes like no. 29, in which two stages have been discerned. This complex is attributed to John the Hesychast, an Armenian monk of distinguished and wealthy origin (*V. John Hes.* 1, 201; 15, 213), who was widely admired both among the monks and among the faithful outside the monastery (see Part V, Chap. 2A, below). Another example is complex 45, erroneously attributed to Arcadius the son of Xenophon.[18] Improved chapels were also built in these elaborate complexes.

---

[17] Sabas himself viewed the building of a cell by a monk, from his private resources, as an act of religious piety equivalent to the erection of a church to God; see *V. Sab.* 28, 113. Cyril built a cell in the Great Laura with his own money; see ibid. 75, 181; 82, 187. A similar fact is related about the monk Anthimus, ibid. 43, 133.

[18] Tradition attributes hermitage 39 to a monk by the name of Xenophon; this tradition is apparently erroneous, as is that which views the hermitages of his sons, Arcadius and John, as being located close by. According to *V. Xen.* (ed. Galante), they all lived in the Old Laura, and according to the later testimony of Nicephorus Callistus (d. 1340), these monks lived in the 5th century, during the time of Euthymius, and not

The amount of comfort evident in the planning of all the cells, the superior construction, and the insistence upon equipping each cell with one or more attached water cisterns are almost certainly due to the fact that this was the Great Laura, the center of the desert monks. The funds available here for building purposes were greater than those in smaller laurae.

Whatever the explanation for this construction, the ruins of the dwelling complexes and the chapels discovered in the Great Laura cast new light on the way of life of the Laura monks. Despite the harsh conditions of the desert and the wild location on the cliffs, the monks lived under quite proper and spacious conditions, in complexes equipped with numerous water cisterns to revive the body and with magnificent chapels for the needs of the soul. The monasteries were far removed from abundance and extravagance, but living conditions were far from being poor.

Of no less interest is the existence of complexes intended for several monks, in general not more than three. In these complexes there were separate living quarters for each monk containing one or more rooms. The different cells, however, shared a chapel and water supply. The pattern of an elderly monk with a disciple or attendant living with him is known from hagiographical sources, archaeological finds, and the legislation of Justinian. But this does not seem to be the explanation for every case of this sort. Other possible explanations are that these complexes were shared by monks who were brothers, monks of common ethnic origin, similar religious tendency, or who had something else in common. Therefore, the archaeological finds indicate that not all the monks lived in cells distant from one another, but that there also were small groupings. This phenomenon is revealed in a different fashion in the laura of Jeremias in Wadi ez-Zaraniq, where the dwelling cells were clustered in three main groups. A similar phenomenon of dwelling complexes shared by a small number of monks developed in Kellia and in other monastic settlements in Egypt (see Chap. 1F, below).

B. The New Laura (507) (*V. Sab.* 36, 122–25)

Historical Sketch

The sixty monks who rebelled against Sabas and left the Great Laura settled in a ravine south of Thekoa, where they found water and remains of cells that had been built previously by the Aposchists (opponents of the Council of Chalcedon). This monastic center, whose name is not mentioned by Cyril, was undoubtedly connected with the large coenobium of Romanus, where, according to John Rufus (*Plerophoria* 25, 58), there were 600 monks. Romanus was a disciple of Passarion. His monastery near Thekoa was established prior to 451. According to this same source, following the Council of Chalcedon,

---

in the time of Sabas. The Russian abbot Daniel saw the graves of Arcadius and John in the Old Laura (the Chariton monastery), during the tour of the desert monasteries he conducted in 1106–7 under the guidance of a monk from Mar Saba (Khitrovo 1889, 48). It follows that the tradition has no historical basis.

The story of their lives has been preserved in a few manuscripts. The earliest is an Arabic manuscript preserved in the Vatican Library, written in the Mar Saba monastery in 884, which is a copy of a slightly earlier Arabic manuscript translated from the Greek original; see *V. Xen.*, ed. Graf 1910. A Greek compilation is included in the writings of the 10th-century compiler Symeon Metaphrastes (PG 114, 1014–43). An additional Greek text from the time of Metaphrastes has been discovered in Florence (ed. Galante 1903).

Romanus went into the desert three times for extended periods of prayer, until he received a revelation from heaven commanding him to anathematize the decisions of the council. As a result of his part in Theodosius' riot against Juvenal, he went into exile to Antioch, from where he was permitted to return only in 457, upon the intercession of the former empress Eudocia. He did not, however, return to his monastery near Thekoa, which was within the diocese of Jerusalem, but rather founded another large monastery near Eleutheropolis on an estate belonging to Eudocia.

Many scholars have falsely identified the remains of the cells in which the monks of the New Laura settled with the monastery of Romanus near Thekoa. Bagatti (1968, 298–99) proposed to distinguish between the two, but erred in his location of the New Laura. Hirschfeld was the first to locate the New Laura in Bir el-Wa'ar; and since the ruins in this site are not of a large coenobium, he suggested identifying the coenobium of Romanus with Khirbet er-Rubei'a (1992, 265 n. 43).

The cells of the Aposchists mentioned above were presumably abandoned and destroyed during the "Second Union" in 479, when the Aposchist leaders were deposed from heading their monasteries, and monks of their party were expelled from other monasteries as well, including from the Tower of Eudocia (*V. Euth*. 45, 67; *V. Sab*. 38, 127).[19]

The separatist monks initially rebuilt the ruins of the cells, settled them, and named the place the "New Laura." The adjacent laura of Souka from then on was called "Old Laura." Since there was no church, every Sunday they made their way to Thekoa in order to participate in the liturgy held there in the church of St. Amos. According to Cyril, they did not choose a leader for themselves, confusion and anarchy were rampant, and they quarreled among themselves. When Sabas learned where they were residing, he loaded foodstuffs on the beasts of burden of the Laura and of Kastellion, and set out toward them. He informed Patriarch Elias of their condition and requested his permission to organize them into a laura. Sabas thereby followed the terms of a decree that had already been established in the Council of Chalcedon, affirming a demand of Emperor Marcian according to which no one was allowed to found a monastery without episcopal license (Marcian's proposal: *ACO* II.1, 353; canon 4 of the council: *ACO* II.1, 355; see also Jones 1964, 933 and n. 160).

Sabas won the support of the patriarch, who gave him one *litra* of gold to finance the construction work and authority over the place and its inhabitants, since, after all, they were former members of his community. Then Sabas returned to the site with craftsmen and all the necessary materials, stayed there for five months, and built for the monks a bakery (ἀρτοκοπεῖον) and a church (ἐκκλησία), which he inaugurated in the sixty-ninth

---

[19] Cyril errs when he says that Romanus was deposed as head of his monastery as a consequence of the "Second Union." At this time (479) Romanus had not been alive for at least 15 years. This fact is learned from one of the Syriac epistles of Timothy Aelurus, which was sent from his place of exile in Gangra in Pontus (460–464) to the deacon Faustinus. The latter is defined as the successor of the blessed Romanus in the letter, which speaks of the difficult situation at the time in Palestine. It is clear, therefore, that this refers to the Romanus under discussion here. See R. Y. Ebied and L. R. Wickham, "A Collection of Unpublished Syriac Letters of Timothy Aelurus," *JTS* 21 (1970), 364–66. Cyril also erred in his dating of the establishment of the monastery of Romanus near Thekoa after the "First Union" between the monks and Eudocia, on the one hand, and Juvenal, on the other hand (*V. Euth*. 30, 49). See Chitty 1966, 89, 92, 99 n. 77; Perrone 1980, 113–14; Dan 1982, 280–82.

year of his life (507). He appointed as *hegoumenos* of the New Laura a loyal monk from the Great Laura, John the Anchorite, of Greek origin. John served in this post for seven years (507–513), and then the fathers of the New Laura, in consultation with Sabas, chose Paul, of Roman descent, as *hegoumenos*. He served in this post, unwillingly, for only six months, and then fled to Arabia, going from there to Severianus, who at that time (ca. 514) established his monastery near Caparbaricha. During his service, Origenist monks, who sowed within it the seeds of the Origenist heresy, were accepted in the monastery (see below, Part v, Chap. 2).

In 555, after the expulsion of the Origenists, the New Laura was resettled with 120 orthodox monks from the Great Laura and other monasteries. This was therefore a quite large laura. The new settlers included Cyril of Scythopolis, who was brought from the coenobium of Euthymius; Leontius, a future abbot of Theodosius' monastery (*Pratum* 4, 2856); and Abba Polychronius, from the Laura of the Towers, who became the priest of the New Laura (ibid. 5, 2856). The new settlers were assembled in Jerusalem and went forth from there, accompanied by the patriarch and the new *hegoumenos*, to Thekoa; on February 21, 555 (thus Stein 1944, 174–76; according to Schwartz 1939, 343 and Chitty 1966, 141 n. 42, the year was 554) they resettled the New Laura. John Moschus lived there during the 590s after his return from Egypt and his ten-year stay in the laura of the Ailiotes. He stayed there until leaving the Holy Land in 604 (*Prologus ad Pratum*, in Usener, *V. Tych.* 91–93; *Pratum*, add. Nissen 8, 361 n. to line 4; Chadwick 1974, 57).

Conon, the leader of the Tritheist heresy, was exiled to Palestine during the reign of Justin II, after 572. He was brought there by Photius, the stepson of Belisarius, and was imprisoned for three years in the New Laura. Photius, who was a special emissary of the emperor, was active there until his death, for a period of thirteen years, accompanied by a large entourage of monks and government and military officials whom he received from the emperor. He was known for his cruelty toward the Samaritans and the Mono-physites. According to John of Ephesus (Monophysite, died ca. 585), he was succeeded in this post by Abraham, archimandrite of the monastery called *Nea;* the reference appar-ently is to the Nea (or New) Laura, not to the Nea Church in Jerusalem (John of Ephe-sus, *HE*, iii.1.31–32, 28–30). In one of the anecdotes attributed to John Moschus (*Pratum*, add. Nissen 8, 361–65), mention is made of Abba Basil, the anchorite and priest, who was once a monk of the New Laura. Since, however, the ruler mentioned there is called "emir," it is clear that the anecdote refers to the Muslim period.

The Archaeological Remains

The New Laura was first located and identified by Hirschfeld (1985, 99–105; 1990, 36–38) in Wadi el-Jihar, which descends from the el-Kanub ridge to Nahal Arugoth. One constructed path reaches the laura from the west, through Khirbet el-Kanub, from the top of the mountain on which the villages of Se'ir and esh-Shuiukh are located. A second path arrives from the north, from ancient Thekoa, located ca. 4 km from the laura, along the streambed of Nahal Arugoth. As was stated above, before Sabas built a prayerhouse for the New Laura, the monks went there every Sunday for prayer in the church of the Prophet Amos.

This is a cliff-type laura located on a rocky slope. During the course of the survey, two complexes, comprising the core buildings of the laura, were identified in the lower portion of the wadi on its northern bank. The eastern complex (A) includes the ruins of a chapel, while the second (B), built next to a large water cistern (Bir el-Wa'ar), is an elongated courtyard complex which includes remains of various structures and installations. It has been suggested that this was the steward's building (*oikonomeion*) of the laura. The large water cistern, with a capacity of ca. 500 m³, is entirely rock-cut; it was fed by a ca. 100 m long excavated channel. It is possible that this was the water cistern found at the site by the rebel monks and that it also previously served the Aposchist monks. Besides this large cistern, an additional twelve smaller cisterns have been traced in the core of the laura. Plots of cultivated land, which constituted the garden, have been found next to each of the two complexes. One is located northeast of the chapel and the second south of the large water cistern, above the streambed, which had been dammed by a large wall.

Two dwelling cells have been located above the core; the others, more than forty in number, are scattered within a radius of not more than 400–500 m. Most of the cells, more than twenty, are scattered west of the core, ascending along the main wadi and a secondary tributary that descends from the north. These cells are between 10 and 40 m distant from each other; on the outskirts the distance is ca. 80 m. Two paths, which branch off from the main path that emerges from the core, ascend in these two wadis. About fifteen other cells are built at a lower density (ca. 30–60 m from each other), on the west bank of Nahal Arugoth, northeast and southeast of the chapel complex.

The dwellings are quite uniform (Hirschfeld 1987, 188–91, figs. 168–75). In general, they are single-room structures; at times, however, they are composed of two or three rooms. There are noticeable differences in the size of the cells. The smallest cell has an area of only 4.5 m², while the area of the largest cell is 43 m². The area of most of the cells, however, is close to the average size: ca. 21 m². One, and at times two, water cisterns have been built adjoining or under each cell. A small patch of cultivated land is also to be found next to each cell.

North of the western cells a large plot of land, surrounded by a wall in which a water cistern was constructed, has been traced. This may have served as a large orchard or garden (Hirschfeld 1992, 204). Cells 32 and 40, which are built near the two paths that descend to the laura from the west, bounded the laura in this direction. Cell 40, which is ca. 300 m west of the other cells and ca. 800 m from the center of the laura, is built on top of a peak and presumably served as an observation tower overlooking Thekoa and the desert expanses.

C. The Heptastomos Laura (510)

Historical Sketch

The Heptastomos laura had its beginnings in an incident of a breach of discipline by James, one of Sabas' monks. Cyril does not mention when this took place; it seems, however, that the establishment of the laura is to be dated prior to Sabas' first journey to Constantinople in September 511. It is difficult to imagine such a severe breach of discipline by one of his monks immediately after his return, crowned in glory, from the capital, where he presented matters concerning the Church of Palestine. In fact, the episode concerning the establishment of this laura precedes the description of Sabas' voyage to Constantinople. The misconduct of James was brought to Sabas' attention upon his return from the Lenten fast in the desert, which began on January 21 and lasted until

Easter. As a result, James was stricken by him with a fever that lasted seven months, until Sabas healed him. Consequently, this does not refer to the Lent of 511, because in October–November of that year Sabas was still in the capital. Therefore the misconduct of James should be dated to 510. Cyril relates this affair (*V. Sab.* 39, 129–30) after describing the foundation of the Scholarius monastery in 509.[20]

The story of the incident that led to the establishment of the laura is as follows. A monk named James, a native of Jerusalem, took advantage of Sabas' absence from the Laura during the Lent of 510 and, with the aid of several other monks, began to build a small prayerhouse and cells (εὐκτήριον μικρὸν καὶ κελλία) next to the Heptastomos (seven-mouth) reservoir, the cistern from which Sabas had carried water during the first years of his stay in the cave in the Kidron, situated ca. 15 *stadia* (ca. 3 km) from the Laura (*V. Sab.* 15, 98). James' intention was to establish a laura at this site. The fathers of the Great Laura, angered by this deed, were deceived by him, since he claimed that Sabas had given his consent to such an action.

The Heptastomos reservoir, located in the streambed of the Kidron, along the route leading from Jerusalem to the Laura, was regarded as a water source for it. James had thus erected his buildings within an area that Sabas regarded as belonging to the Great Laura and had done so without his permission. When Sabas returned to the Laura and learned of James' deed, he reproved him for it, but when James did not heed him, he was struck with a severe fever that lasted for seven months. It was only after he asked for forgiveness from the aged monk and expressed his repentance in the church of the Laura that Sabas revived him and in a miraculous manner put him back on his feet. James did not thereafter renew the work of construction. When Patriarch Elias learned of James' deed, an action that contradicted canon 4 of the Council of Chalcedon, which prohibited the establishment of any monastery without the permission of the district *episkopos*, he sent people to demolish the structures. Sabas, true to his policy of settling the desert with his monasteries, took some capable builder monks and constructed a prayerhouse (εὐκτήριον) with cells around it ca. 5 *stadia* (ca. 1 km) north of the demolished buildings. This was at the place indicated to him by a man called Zannagon from the village of Beth Abudisson.[21] Sabas settled there as directors two monks from the Great Laura, the Greek brothers Paul and Andreas, as well as other monks. He determined that the site would become a laura that would be called Heptastomos and continued to concern himself with the place afterward as well. Food for the fraternal meal (ἀγάπη) was brought there from the Great Laura. It may reasonably be assumed that Sabas, the archimandrite of the monks, received the patriarch's blessings for the establishment of this monastery as well as for that of his other ones. The dedication date became a feast celebrated each year on May 24 (Garitte 1958, 68, 232).

Except for this information related by Cyril, we know nothing further about the Heptastomos laura during the remainder of the sixth century. In the story of the con-

---

[20] Vailhé 1899–1900a, 539, no. 54, dates the establishment of the laura to 512.

[21] Vailhé (ibid.) is of the opinion that Sabas purchased this area from Zannagon. Regarding a possible connection between this act and the land registration conducted by the administrators of Emperor Anastasius during the same period, and the establishment of new land tax assessments in Palestine, see below, Part IV, Chap. 4.

quest of Jerusalem by the Persians (*Expug. Hier.* 6), mention is made of a monk from the Laura of Sabas, John, who lived with his disciple in a place named Heptastomos. This John saw the fall of the city in a vision, and as he was relating this to his disciple, the enemy came, seized the old man, and killed him, while his disciple fled. Later, upon his return, he found his teacher's corpse and brought it for burial in the tomb of the holy fathers (apparently in the Great Laura, the monastery of the narrator of this account, Strategius or Eustratius). Forty-four monks were killed in the Laura of Sabas during the Persian conquest (see below, Part v, Chap. 1). From this account it can be understood that during this period the Heptastomos laura was not a separate one but rather a place of seclusion for the monks of the Great Laura; apparently John and his disciple were the only monks living there at that time. The potsherds collected at the site do not date later than the Byzantine period; consequently, the laura and its structures were not reinhabited at a later period.

The Archaeological Remains
Due to its similarity with the name Zannagon, Vailhé (1899–1900a, 539, no. 54) proposed identifying the Heptastomos laura with Khirbet Zennaki or Khirbet Jinjas. The latter identification was also proposed by Delau (1899–1900, 269–70) and is accepted by modern scholars.

Corbo (1958b, 87–88) provides an extremely detailed description of the ruins in Khirbet Jinjas (ref. pt. 1798.1269) but does not include a map or plans. These were prepared by Hirschfeld (1990, 40–42; 1992, 29–30). This is a laura of the level type, located on four moderate outcrops north of the Kidron in an area surrounded by important local routes: on the north, the lateral road leading from Jerusalem to the Scholarius monastery on the peak of Jebel Muntar; on the south, the lateral road from Jerusalem to the Great Laura along the Kidron; on the east, the longitudinal road connecting the Great Laura with the Scholarius and the Euthymius monasteries along Wadi Rahwe.

This is the only laura surrounded by a 0.7–1.0 m thick boundary wall preserved to a height of one to three courses. This wall was constructed in order to define the limits of the laura and keep the desert shepherds from grazing their herds among the cells. It bounds an area of 350 dunams (1 dunam = 1,000 sq. meters), in which there are fifteen cells. This therefore was the size of the monastic population living in the laura. The cells, which are ca. 60–70 m apart, are clustered in two groups, each having a separate water reservoir. Eight cells are located north of the laura's core and seven to its south. The grouping of cells around water reservoirs is to be found in other laurae, such as the laura of Jeremias and of Firminus, both of which are cliff laurae.

The dwelling complexes generally contain two or three rooms and at times more. One hermitage, larger than the others (dimensions 10.60 × 6.70 m), is surrounded by a courtyard bounded by a low wall fence and a patch of cultivated land. It has been proposed that this may have been the cell of the director of the monastery (Corbo 1958b, 88). Several of the cells have a private water cistern in the courtyard. The average internal area of six of the cells that have been measured is 48.2 m², more than twice that of the average cell in the New Laura; however, there were also smaller cells.

In the core of the laura, we can discern the ruins of a church and appended rooms arranged around two inner courtyards, one of which served the church, while the second was possibly connected with the *oikonomeion*. The Heptastomos cistern, which has been identified with Bir Sabsab (ref. pt. 1787.1258), is located in the streambed of the Kidron, on the south bank, to which a footpath leads from the center of the laura (Corbo 1958b, 87; Hirschfeld 1987, 45, 239, and fig. 270). The water cistern was filled by long collection canals. Additional cisterns, whose mouths are sealed, have been found nearby; it is possible that this was the source of the name, the "seven-mouthed reservoir." Corbo (1958b, 85–86) proposed identifying James' buildings with the ruins of the two buildings located close to the juncture of Wadi Khariziyeh with the Kidron. The buildings stand on a hillock above the streambed. The larger of them, 11.0×14.6 m² is divided into two chambers. The second, located ca. 40 m north of the first one, is 5.30×9.60 m².

D. The Laura of Jeremias (end of 531)

Historical Sketch

Jeremias was the deacon of the Great Laura. He accompanied Sabas on his second journey to Constantinople (Apr.–Sept. 531) and was present at his interview with Emperor Justinian (*V. Sab.* 73, 178). After their return to Palestine, when Sabas distributed among his monks the gold he had brought with him from Byzantium, the deacon Jeremias left the Laura, as an expression of protest against the manner of distribution, and settled in a small dry brook ca. 5 *stadia* (1 km) north of the Cave monastery. After Sabas looked for him and found him, he saw that the site was suitable and decided to establish a laura there. With the aid of a few monks skilled in construction work, who brought with them tools, equipment, and food, a small prayerhouse (μικρὸν εὐκτήριον) and a number of cells (κελλία) were built within a few days. He appointed Jeremias to direct the place. He left with him a few brothers and entrusted them with the regulations of his own Great Laura (*V. Sab.* 74, 179.22).

The site is not mentioned in any source other than the *Vita Sabae*, written between 556 and 558. According to the archaeological remains, it seems that the site did not survive the Arab conquest, and it might have been deserted even much earlier, since it is not mentioned by John Moschus.

Previous Research

Wadi ez-Zaraniq, which begins at the northeast end of Jebel Muntar, is the chief northern tributary of Nahal Qumran. Steep cliffs have been formed in the place where the stream flows through hard lime rocks. The remains of the laura of Jeremias are scattered on both sides of the stream, along a section more than 1 km in length (Fig. 50).

The name of the wadi means rivulets or small channels of water (Palmer 1881, 357). It apparently was given this name due to the quantities of floodwater flowing during the winter in its tributaries, in several of which the rock in the streambed is completely exposed. If there had ever been a living spring here as well, its location is not known today.

The site of Khirbet ez-Zaraniq in the 1:50,000 maps refers to our cell 1. Another building is noted nearby, which refers to our cells 2 and 3 (cf. the map of the laura, Fig. 50). The members of the British survey of Palestine were of the opinion that these are recent remains (Conder and Kitchener 1883, 213). Schick was the first to report ruins of structures along the north bank of Wadi ez-Zaraniq as well. He proposed to identify them with the ruins of the Theoctistus monastery. Marti (1880, 17–19), however, indicates sev-

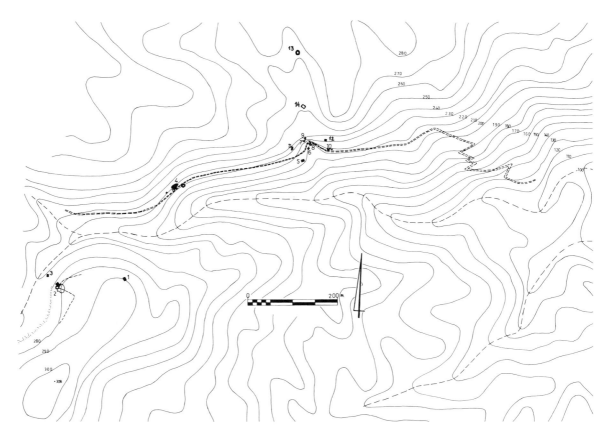

50. Map of the laura of Jeremias.

eral difficulties in this identification. Vailhé (1899–1900a, 23, no. 64) correctly identified the site with the laura of Jeremias, and this identification is accepted by all scholars (Corbo 1958d; Compagnoni 1978, 74–75). Farmer conducted a small excavation in the water cistern and the main building in the core of the laura (complex 4), but did not realize the connection between all the ruins scattered along the wadi, which together constitute the laura. His descriptions are quite accurate, but he did not include any plans or maps of the various ruins scattered along the stream. Corbo correctly defined all the components of the laura; however, his description as well is not accompanied by plans or maps.

The Archaeological Remains (Patrich 1990b)
In 1983 I conducted a rigorous survey of the site, which was followed by excavations on a limited scale[22] in the three groups of buildings that constitute the laura: in cells 2 and 3 in the western grouping; complex 4 which is the core of the laura; and cells 8 and 10 in the eastern grouping. The survey and excavations give a full and detailed picture of the layout of the laura and the structure of all its components.

[22] The excavations, held during Hanukkah (Dec.) 1984, were conducted with the participation of the scouting classes of the Nature Protection Society and the Boyer residential school in Jerusalem.

The western end of the laura is close to the "Road of the Monasteries" (see above, the geographical background). The motor vehicle road that currently circumvents Jebel Muntar from the north descends to the Hyrcania valley north of Wadi ez-Zaraniq, along the watershed line between it and Wadi Hashneh, in a relatively easy course. The ancient lateral path next to which the Muslim cemetery et-Taiyan is located passed along this same course.

The laura is composed of twelve structures arranged in three groupings, each of which has separate water cisterns (see map, Fig. 50). The western group of buildings, located on the southern side of the wadi, includes three cells (nos. 1–3). The second grouping, located on the north bank, at a distance of ca. 400 m from here, is the core of the laura (no. 4). The third grouping, also on the north bank, is ca. 300 m from the core and contains eight cells (nos. 5–12) scattered on the cliffs. The three groupings were connected by a constructed path, long sections of which have been well preserved, mainly on the north bank of the wadi. To the east, the path descends to the channel of the ravine in three switchbacks, making its way to the Hyrcania valley.

There is a line of sight between cell 1 and the core of the laura as well as with cells 5 and 10, in the eastern grouping, and with the Scholarius monastery on the peak of Jebel Muntar. It seems that its location was determined by its advantage as an observation point.

The Core of the Laura (no. 4 on the map, Fig. 50)

The archaeological finds indicate that the core of the laura had two storeys and included a church, a bakery, several dwelling cells, water cisterns, and presumably an *oikonomeion*, a kitchen, and a stable. It is built next to an upright rock cliff at the point where the rock shelf widens to a breadth of 18 m.

In the debris above the floor in one of the rooms, fragments of a mosaic floor with a geometric pattern composed of red and white squares have been found as well as a fragment of a marble colonnette, which apparently served as a leg of the altar. These fragments came from the collapse of the chapel that was on the second floor. Fragments of poorly fired bricks discovered in the excavation indicate the existence of a baking or cooking oven; however, this oven has not yet been discovered.

It is clear from Table 3 that most of the cells were quite small, with a single room and a floor area not exceeding 15 m². An exception is cell 2, which was built as a massive two-storey tower, with a large water cistern next to it. These features apparently reflect its function at the "entrance" to the laura. In a few cases there is a courtyard next to the cell, as well as a storage cave. Most of the cells did not have a cistern of their own; rather, there was a common water cistern shared by a few cells. Most of the hermitages described above were intended for only a single monk. A possible exception is complex 8, which may have served two monks. If we assume that 3 to 4 monks lived in the core of the laura, we arrive at a population of only 15 monks.

No. 13 on the map of the laura is a lime kiln located in a small tributary of Wadi ez-Zaraniq. The outer diameter of the kiln is ca. 8 m. A second lime kiln of similar dimensions (not shown in Fig. 50) was found ca. 500 m south of cell 1. Since the laura is the nearest site, it may reasonably be assumed that the kiln provided slaked lime for the construction of the laura.

Table 3. The Cells of the Laura of Jeremias

Cell number	Inner dimensions (m)	Dwelling area (m²)	Number of rooms	Water cistern	Courtyard area (m²)	Cultivated area
1	3.75 × 5	17 (34)	2	+	40	?
2	5.5 × 5.5 (2 storeys)	50	3–4	+	200	+
3	4.5 × 3.2	14.5	1	−	−	−
4	4.5 × 6	27	?	+	−	−
5	6.15 × 2.65	15	1	−	30	−
6	3.1 × 2.85	9	1	−	−	−
7	4.7 × 3.3	15	1	−	−	−
8	6.5 × 4	25	2	+	−	−
9	1.75 × 2.5	4.5	1	−	25	−
10	3.2 × 2.4	7.7	1	−	20	+(?)
11	9 × 3	25	2	−	15	−
12	3 × 3.5	10.5	1	−	30	−

Cell number	Direction of opening	Second floor	Comments
1	east	+(?)	double area, if two storeys
2	south	+	
3	east	−	
4	east (?)		on top of the large cistern
5	north	−	
6	northwest	−	
7	(?)	−	uncertainty regarding dwelling
8	north (?)		
9	north and south	−	next to a 10 m² cave
10	east	−	next to a 13 m² cave
11	north	−	
12	northwest	−	next to rock shelter used for storage

E. The Laurae of Sabas' Disciples: Firminus, the Towers, Neelkeraba

Three of Sabas' first disciples later established their own laurae: Firminus established a laura in the vicinity of Makhmas (Μαχμᾶς), James (not the one connected with the Heptastomos laura) established the laura of the Towers near the Jordan River, and Julian "the Hunchback" built for himself the laura of Neelkeraba (Νεελκεραβά) (V. Sab. 16, 99). Another disciple, Severianus, established a coenobium near Caparbaricha. The only chronological reference in Cyril's writings is to the establishment of this last coenobium, which was in the process of being built in 514/5 (*V. Sab.* 36, 124). It is possible that the other laurae of the disciples were established during this same period. This took place during the years of the difficult struggle against the Monophysite emperor Anastasius. It is not inconceivable that this spurt of monastic settlement was initiated by this combat, with the intention of driving the Monophysite or Nestorian monks out of the Judean desert, as Sabas himself had done when he established the coenobium of the Scholarius at the site of the Tower of Eudocia, where two Nestorian monks were living at that time (509) (see below, Chap. 2D). Although Cyril does not mention that such a motive was behind the establishment of the disciples' monasteries, the result, at any rate, was that additional regions of the Judean desert and the Jordan valley were settled by Orthodox monks.

Sabas himself established almost all his own monasteries within the bounds of the Kidron basin. The monasteries of his disciples were established far from the Great Laura, thus spreading Sabaitic monastic doctrine far and wide. It is clear from Cyril that these disciples venerated Sabas; these were not rebellious monks. The location of their monasteries remote from the Great Laura was not for the purpose of thus escaping Sabas' influence or intervention, as was the goal of the rebellious monks who had settled in cells near Thekoa—the site of the future New Laura—at a considerable distance from the Great Laura.

It is difficult to determine just what were the relations between the disciples' monasteries and the Great Laura or Sabas himself (cf. below, Part III, Chap. 1G). Cyril does not list them among Sabas' seven monasteries: the Great Laura, the New Laura, the Heptastomos laura, and the coenobia of Kastellion, the Cave, Scholarius, and Zannos. Sabas was personally concerned with these monasteries during all his lifetime. Cyril added to this list the monasteries of Euthymius and Theoctistus but not the disciples' monasteries (*V. Sab.* 58, 158). It is reasonable to assume that, being his disciples, they instituted Sabas' regulations in their foundations.

1. The Laura of Firminus

After Firminus, this laura was headed by Sozomen, who also was a faithful disciple of Sabas. After Sabas' death, when Sozomen as well was no longer living, this laura joined the Origenist party (*V. Sab.* 83, 188). Nestabus, a priest of the laura, participated in the synod of Constantinople in 536 (see below, Part IV, Chap. 2). Later a schism split the Origenist party, and the monks of the laura of Firminus, headed by Isidore, separated from the monks of the New Laura and joined those of the Great Laura—the anti-Origenists—headed by Conon (*V. Sab.* 89, 197; for a detailed description of these events, see below, Part V, Chap. 2A). Isidore's successor apparently was Zosimus of Cilicia, who is mentioned in one of John Moschus' anecdotes (*Pratum* 166, 3032). This source also mentions the name of an anchorite named Sabatius. In this period there were good relations between this laura and the monastery of Abba Dorotheus near Gaza and Maiumas.

In 1895 Lagrange identified Firminus' laura with the caves of el-'Aleiliyat, which were also described by Dalman in 1904–5. The core buildings, including its church and the water reservoirs, were described by Corbo (1960), and additional ruins were described by Rubin (1982). Syriac inscriptions were discovered by Marcoff and Chitty

(1929) in the el-'Aleiliyat caves, located close to the core of the laura. These caves were reexamined by a group of French scholars; a detailed description of them was provided by Patrich and Rubin (1984, with further bibliography). A Syriac inscription discovered in a Byzantine structure near 'Ein Suweinit, which probably was part of the laura, was published by Halloun and Rubin (1981). Sections of the laura further from the center were discovered by the cave survey team headed by myself, which enabled the publication, for the first time, of a map including all the components of the laura (Patrich 1989b). It appears that the monks resettled some of the caves along the wadi that originally had been prepared as hiding places at the end of the Second Temple period.

It is clear from the map (Fig. 51) that despite the fact that the water source of 'Ein Suweinit is located on the south bank, most of the cells were constructed on the north bank of the brook, which is better exposed to the sun. Here as well, as was the case regarding the laura of Jeremias, three groupings can be defined. The main grouping, the westernmost one, includes the core of the laura, the site of the church and the rest of the core structures built close to the cliff edge. On the cliff, under the western end of the core, are the caves of el-'Aleiliyat where, as was stated above, Syriac Christian inscriptions were found, along with a Greek inscription and many red-painted crosses (Patrich and Rubin 1984, 386–87).

The second grouping, considerably smaller, is located at the foot of cave 10. A rock-cut burial cave in the form of a square room, each of whose three walls contains a deep arcosolium, has been found here. Fragments of roofing tiles discovered nearby indicate the possible existence of a chapel. The third grouping is much larger. It is located close to the junction of Nahal Mikhmas (Wadi Suweinit) and Wadi al-Habibi. The remains of more than five cells and water cisterns have been discerned here. A graded rock-cut path has been discovered between caves 7 and 8, winding its way up a small, steep rivulet (Fig. 52) to a large water reservoir which supplied all the cells of the grouping. A rock-cut channel descending along the rivulet fed the lower cisterns, which were close to the hermitages. In cave 6 were found graves and a fragment of a screen plate made of reddish limestone. It served as a burial chapel. The remotest hermitage has been located on the north bank ca. 1 km southeast from here, ca. 3 km as the crow flies from the core of the laura (Patrich 1989b).

The Christian inscriptions discovered in the caves of el-'Aleiliyat and near 'Ein Suweinit indicate that at least two linguistic groups—Greek-speakers and Syriac-speakers—were living in the laura. Perhaps this is why the laura is composed of three different groupings, each including a chapel and a burial site. The different groups may have been differentiated from each other also by their religious approach to various doctrinal issues that split the Church of Palestine and desert monasticism during the sixth century.

A paved path, quite good sections of which have been preserved, connected the cells with one another and with the village of Machmas. Where necessary, stairs were also cut into the rock (Fig. 52).

2. The Laura of the Towers

The laura of the Towers near the Jordan River (ἡ ἐν τῷ Ἰορδάνῃ τῶν πυργίων λαύρα) was established by James, one of Sabas' first disciples (V. Sab. 16, 99). Apart from this, Cyril does not provide any information about this laura. At the synod of Constantinople held

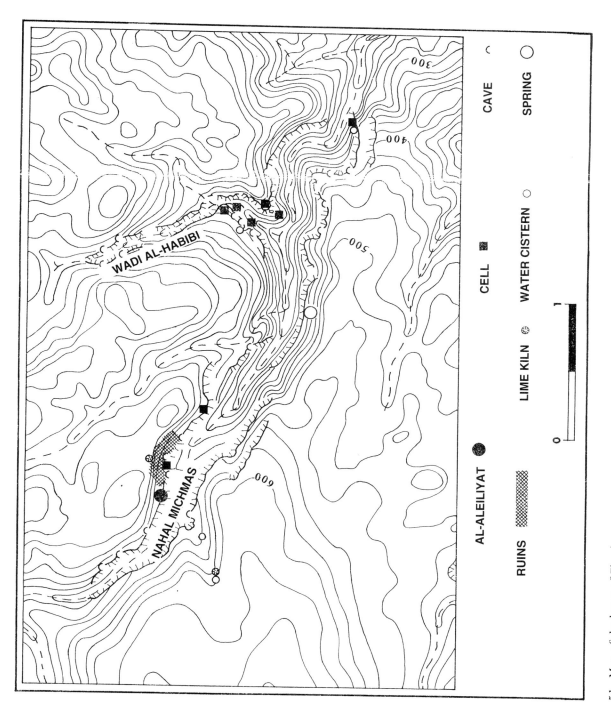

51. Map of the laura of Firminus.

52. Laura of Firminus. Rock-cut graded path.

in 536, Cyriacus, priest and *hegoumenos,* signed in the name of his monastery and in the name of all the monks along the desert of the Jordan, indicating that during this period the laura took the place of the laura of Gerasimus as the most important laura of the Jordan, second only to the Great Laura of Sabas in representing the desert monks. In addition to Cyriacus, Trajan, a priest of the same laura, also participated in this synod (*ACO* III.1; see the detailed discussion below, Part IV, Chap. 2, and Flusin 1983, 139–40 n. 259).

From the anecdotes related by John Moschus we obtain further details (*Pratum* 5–10, 2856–60; 40, 2892–93; 100, 2957). The laura was close to Calamon and Jericho. The monastic cells looked like turrets, which gave it its name. It had no hospital, and when necessary its monks were sent to the hospital in Jericho. Moschus tells the story of a pious monk who refused to be appointed abbot and mentions a steward and the *oikonomeion* of the laura. Other monks, not members of the laura community, lived in caves near the Jordan. A monk named Theodore from this laura would eventually become the bishop of Rhossus, a city in Cilicia Secunda close to Anazarbus. He also mentions a monk from the laura, Abba Theophilus, who excelled in the interpretation of the scriptures.

Federlin proposed identifying it with a large rectangular structure 52 × 37 m, which he discovered ca. 300 m southwest of 'Ein Hajla (ref. pt. 1982.1370). It contains rooms on both sides of a large courtyard, in which there is a water cistern with a barrel-shaped vault roof. He thought that the towers that gave the laura its name rose from the four corners of the structure. This structure was reexamined in the 1968 survey (site no. 74b) by Bar-Adon, who also published its plan. Hirschfeld (1990, 45–47, fig. 54) tentatively accepted this identification. It is clear, however, that the structure could have served, at most, as the core of the laura, the site of the *oikonomeion*, and the church (which was possibly the source of the colored mosaic tesserae found at the site). Rectangular structures such as this also constituted the cores of the laurae of Calamon and Gerasimus. There has not, however, been any report of remains of anchorite cells or turrets—the element defining this laura—in its vicinity. It is not inconceivable that such remains will be found in the future, since a corroborating survey of this zone has not yet been conducted. The location fits the description by John Moschus. It is not too far from Jericho and is close to Calamon ('Ein Hajla; see Hirschfeld 1990, 24–26). Therefore, only when remnants of cells are found will it be possible to confirm this proposed identification.

The laura was established in the very heart of the area of influence of the laura of Gerasimus. The later development shows that this Sabaitic institution assumed the status of priority previously held by the laura of Gerasimus among the monks of the Jordan valley. It is not inconceivable that initially this was the very reason for the establishment of the laura of the Towers in this area.

3. The Laura of Neelkeraba (Νεελκεραβά)

This laura was built by Julian "the Hunchback," near the Jordan (*V. Sab.* 16, 99), which is the only information we possess about it. On the basis of the similarity in sound, it has been proposed to identify it with the ruins of Qarawa to the north of Keren Sartaba in the Jordan valley (Vailhé 1899–1900a, 38, following the biblical atlas of Riess). The name Qarawa is the name of the Jiftlik area on the British maps, but a specific site with this name does not appear there. A thorough archaeological survey has not yet been conducted in this region. Hirschfeld (1990, 79) prefers to search for it in the area densely packed with monasteries between Jericho and the Jordan.

F. Discussion and Summary

1. Laurae and Anchorite Settlements: Parallels

In physical terms, a laura is a colony of scattered anchorite cells, which are connected by a constructed path to each other and to the core, where the church and other communal structures are built. Most of the known laurae in the Judean desert were cliff laurae, while a few, for example, the Heptastomos and Jordan laurae, were level ones (Hirschfeld 1992, 18–33).

In terms of size, the Great Laura and the laura of Jeremias represent the two extremes of the cliff laura. The laura of Jeremias, all of whose components we documented in our survey and excavations, is a small but well-organized laura: there is a well-planned core, a connecting path, and dwelling cells with water cisterns. But even the Great Laura was small in comparison with the anchorite colonies in Egypt, such as Kellia, a colony that numbered six hundred monks during the time of Palladius.

Kellia[23]

Kellia is identified with the sites of Qusur er-Roub'aiyât, Qasr Waheida, Qusur 'Isa, Qusur el-'Izeila, Qusur el-'Abid, Qusur Hegeila, and Qusur 'Ereima (Kasser 1972). The archaeological remains, explored since 1965 by expeditions from France (1965–69) and Switzerland (1965–69, 1981–83) and by the Egyptian Department of Antiquities, testify to the size and density of this colony, which extended over ca. 22 km. The collapsed cells, which were built of mud bricks, created more than fifteen hundred mounds, which are clearly visible on the ground. The mapping was done with the aid of aerial photographs, and each mound (*kom*) was given a separate number.

From the second half of the fifth century onward, instead of isolated hermitages dispersed throughout the desert, we find a process of grouping hermitages together into a compound surrounded by a wall in order to increase security. The result was a coenobium-like construction. A tower of refuge was later built. However, the monks continued to maintain the daily life of hermits, not of coenobites (Guillaumont 1977, 201). A good example of such a monastery is the final stage of *kom* 219, excavated by the French expedition (Daumas and Guillaumont 1969). Within the walls there are about ten hermitages, each comprising several rooms, grouped together and protected by a wall. The communal structures included kitchens, latrines, the courtyard, and cisterns. The earlier stage of this compound was on a more modest scale and preceded by an isolated hermitage without an encircling wall. But isolated hermitages persisted even side by side with these monasteries. However, those constructed in the late fifth to early sixth century were more spacious and elaborate than the earlier ones (see below on the Kelliot dwelling).

---

[23] For reports on the surveys and excavations at the site, see Guillaumont 1965; Daumas and Guillaumont 1969; Kasser 1967, 1972, 1980, 1982; Andreu et al. 1980; Andreu and Coquin 1981.

The main church of Kellia is apparently the one discovered at the site of Qusur 'Isa South 1, excavated by the University of Geneva (Kasser 1980). The many Greek ostraka found at the site bear the abbreviated inscription ε κ, which in one instance was written out in full: ενκλησιας κελλιων. This church already existed during the fourth century. At a later stage a second church was established close by, to the south, apparently because the community was divided into Greek and Coptic-speakers, as we learn from the inscriptions that have been discovered on the walls of the two churches. In the sixth century a large basilica was established on the site of the earlier church, while the southern church continued to function along with this. Next to these churches there were also dwelling cells and other appended buildings, including a large assembly hall. The entire complex was surrounded by a wall and had the appearance of a coenobium.

These were not, however, the only churches in Kellia. *Kom* 34 (Qasr al-Wahayda), excavated by the French expedition, was found to be a site of communal buildings. Within a wall enclosing an area of 61.4 × 44.8 m, two churches, an additional structure that possibly served as a hostelry, two massive towers (*donjons*/ğawsaq), a few dwelling cells, three wells, a garden, and cooking installations have been excavated. Many dwelling cells are scattered outside the wall.

In Egypt we also encounter anchorites living outside the walls of a coenobium while maintaining contact with it and being included in its community. Such apparently was the anchorite colony that included the "Monastery of Epiphanius" in the Thebaid, west of Luxor, as well as the cells west of Esna.

The Anchorite Colony of the "Monastery of Epiphanius" near Thebes

West of Thebes in Upper Egypt, beyond the Nile River, in the area of the famous Egyptian dynastic tombs, between Medinet Habu and the Valley of the Kings, many monastic remains from the end of the Byzantine period and the beginning of the Muslim period have been discovered. The Byzantine town of Jeme, with an area of ca. 300 × 400 m and containing a church, was located within the boundaries of the workers' camp of Medinet Habu. About 1.5 km farther to the northwest, on the hill of Sheikh 'Abd el-Kurneh, a monastic complex known as the "Monastery of Epiphanius" has been excavated (Winlock and Crum 1926, 29–39 and pls. I–III). In my opinion, this is simply a dwelling complex for a few monks (thus the quotation marks around its name). The complex has two parts, eastern and western, and was erected over six tombs from the dynastic period. The western, earlier part of the complex is surrounded by a 0.7 m thick wall which encloses a ca. 40 × 40 m area. It includes a dwelling of five rooms and a vestibule with a total area of ca. 10 × 12 m, a courtyard to its west, and two towers to its north and east. The eastern part is also surrounded by a wall, which encloses an area of similar dimensions, in which there is a residential building with an area of ca. 15 × 15 m. Additional remains, located beyond the walls, include an additional building, a few tombs, and a granary.

The epigraphic remains indicate that at the end of the sixth and the beginning of the seventh century a monk named Epiphanius, who apparently headed an anchorite settlement, lived here. About forty monastic cells have been traced on the surrounding hills. The farthest of them are 1–2 km from the "Monastery of Epiphanius." This anchorite settlement flourished during the same period in which George of Choziba and John Moschus were active in Palestine. In this region there were at least two additional monasteries of the coenobium type, one within the area of the sanctuary of Deir el-Medineh, and the other at the site of Deir el-Bakhit (Winlock and Crum 1926, pl. 1).

The monastic cells are located on high points affording a good view of the Nile valley and the valleys leading to the dynastic tombs. In many instances, the ancient tombs served as an initial core from which a complex hermitage would later develop (e.g., the dwellings in the "Monastery of Epiphanius") by additional constructions built in the entrance courtyard to the earlier tomb. Larger complexes were surrounded by a wall. They served as dwellings for several monks and were called *ma-nshubeh* (= dwelling) in Coptic. Four complexes (including the "Monastery of Epiphanius") also included towers; at times, small burial plots are found next to the dwellings, indicating that they were inhabited for an extended period (Winlock and Crum 1926, 24).

The location of the "Monastery of Epiphanius" and its ruins, which occupy a larger area than the usual dwelling complex and which include two impressive towers, and the reference to Epiphanius in the documents as a "great man" give rise to the opinion that this was actually only the center of a laura. No church has been discovered at the site, however, and scholars have proposed that on Saturdays and Sundays the monks participated in communal prayer in the nearby town of Jeme or in one of the coenobia, possibly in the monastery of St. Phoebammon (which has been proposed to be identified with the ruins in Deir el-Medineh), mentioned many times in the documents. If the anchorites did indeed go there on Saturdays and Sundays, then they can be regarded as anchorites connected to a coenobium, along the model of "The Cells" of Choziba. As was mentioned above (Part I, Chap. 2B), such a monastic practice was approved in Egypt by Shenoute, for monks who already spent several years within a coenobium.

The Anchorite Settlement West of Esna

It may be assumed that the small anchorite colony located on the mountain west of Esna (Sauneron and Jacquet 1972, fig. 1) maintained its connection to the Deir el-Shohada monastery, located on the fringes of the Nile valley, even though there was also a separate nearby church (ibid., building 11). Most of these monastic cells were located in one area, with a distance of ca. 500 m between them. A second smaller group (nos. 13–15) is located at a distance of ca. 6 km to the north. Other cells have been traced ca. 10 km to the south.

Egyptian "laurae" such as these, whose monks lived in burial caves from the Pharaonic or Roman periods, in quarries, or in built and rock-cut cells, are to be found along many stretches of the Nile valley as well as in the Delta (Martin 1966a; Walters 1974, 7–13).

Such anchorite settlements as these are distinguished from the Palestinian laurae either by the complete absence of a core (which affects the nature of communal life in the settlement) or by the coenobium serving as a substitute for the core, as was the case in Choziba in the Judean desert.

"The Cells of Choziba"

A small anchorite settlement, the size of the laura of Jeremias, sprang up outside the bounds of the Choziba coenobium: at a distance of 1 km from the coenobium, there are the remains of fifteen monastic cells scattered along the cliffs, mainly on the northern bank of the wadi (Fig. 53). The anchorites maintained in their cells a laurite way of life, while the coenobium served them as a laura core (Patrich 1990a).

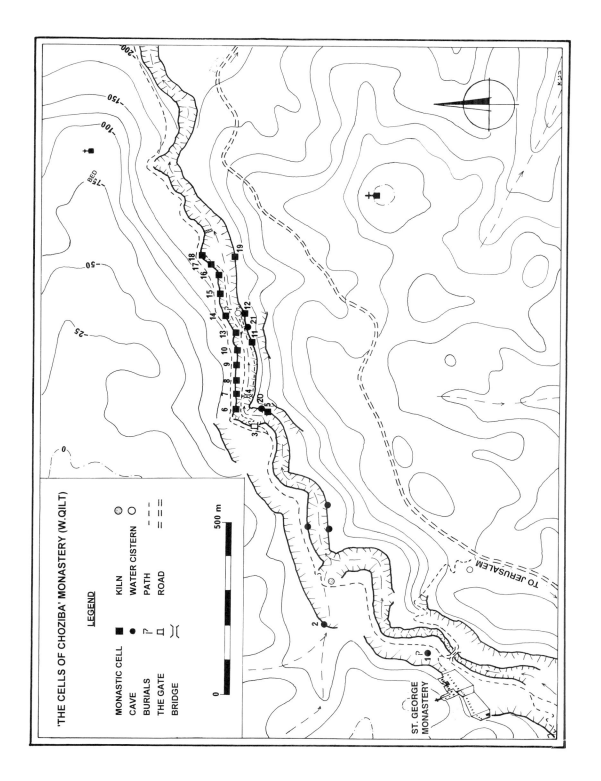

53. Map of "The Cells of Choziba."

Such a settlement did not develop outside the coenobium of Theoctistus. Cyril of Scythopolis relates, indeed, that Sabas received permission to live in a cell outside this coenobium. In the survey we conducted along Nahal Og (Wadi Mukellik), where this coenobium is located, we were able to trace outside the monastery walls just a single cell located on the southern bank of the stream. This apparently was Sabas' cell (Patrich 1988a, 68–70, fig. 24; see also below).

2. Description of Hermitages in Literary Sources Relating to the Judean Desert

Euthymius, Theoctistus, Sabas, Theodosius, Martyrius, Theognius, and other desert monks initially established themselves in caves, and only afterward did the sites develop into monasteries. The monks also lived in caves during their wanderings in the deserts of Coutila and Rouba during Lent.

A hermitage is generally called a "cell" (κελλίον) in the works of Cyril of Scythopolis, John Moschus, and other authors. In a few instances details of the limited dimensions of the cell are mentioned: Cyril relates that Martyrius and Elias left Euthymius' laura because the cells they received there were very small and uncomfortable, since Euthymius the Great had ordered that they be so made (V. Euth. 32, 51.17; 16, 26). Sabas allocated to each of his first disciples in the Great Laura a small cell and a cave (V. Sab. 16, 100); he also gave a cave and a small cell to the Armenian monks Jeremias, Peter, and Paul, who joined sometime later (V. Sab. 20, 105). More detailed is the description of Theognius' cell in his monastery, close to the Theodosius monastery, as provided by Paul of Elusa: "But very small was the cell where the beloved one used to reside when, from time to time, he came from Bitylion; and it is so low that when you come in, if you do not take care, you will knock your head against the ceiling" (V. Theog. 10, 89). The sources also mention the dwelling of a monk in a tower. Sabas built himself a tower after he left the first cave on the east bank and moved to the west bank (V. Sab. 18, 102). Theognius also built himself a small tower in his monastery and left the cave in which he had previously lived (Paul El., V. Theog. 9, 88). The regular dwelling cells in the laura of the Towers near the Jordan were of this type. Towers of seclusion were common among the Syrian recluses (see below). The towers of the Palestinian monasteries served mainly as strongholds, incorporated into the surrounding wall, overlooking the entrance gate. These were places of refuge rather than of seclusion.

3. Dwelling Complexes: Parallels from Other Sites[24]

Sabas' Cave outside the Coenobium of Theoctistus

The simplest monastic cell was a natural cave that had undergone minor construction to adapt it for use as a dwelling. Such was Sabas' first cave in the Kidron ravine (Figs. 27–29) as well as the cave in which he lived outside the coenobium of Theoctistus. This was a small natural cave with maximum dimensions of ca. 5 m (depth), 3 m (width), and 2.5 m (height). Its ground surface was leveled by a floor of wooden slats supported on three beams, which rested in depressions cut in the rock floor (Fig. 54). The cave was located in a ca. 10 m high cliff; a ladder had to be used in order to climb up to it. The

---

[24] See also Hirschfeld 1992, 176–90.

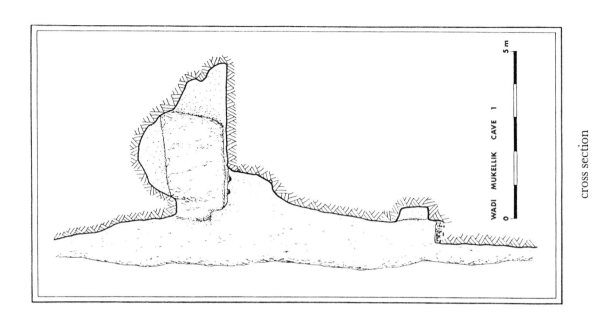

cross section

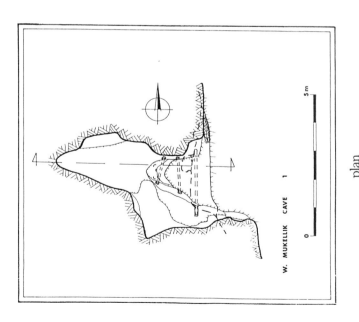

plan

54. Sabas' *hesychasterion* (cave of seclusion) outside
the monastery of Theoctistus.

fact that an anchorite settlement did not develop around the Theoctistus monastery is apparently the reason why this cell maintained its original form and was not expanded into an elaborate dwelling cell by building additions, as we have found in many of the complexes of the Great Laura. The closest water cistern is several dozen meters distant. It is located along the streambed on the north bank; above it we found Greek pilgrim inscriptions (Patrich and Di Segni 1987).

Monastic Cells in the Desert of Gerasimus (Patrich et al. 1993)

The four cells explored by us near 'Ein Abu Mahmud (ref. pt. 1957.1335), in the marl area (Fig. 55), east of Kibbutz Almog and south of the Jericho-Dead Sea road, are also monastic cells cut in the rock, without building additions.[25] They are at an aerial distance of 9 km from the Theoctistus monastery and 3.5 km from Deir Hajla (which marks the site of the monastery of Gerasimus). It is therefore reasonable that the anchorites formed a part of this community, even though the cells are at a great distance from the center of the laura. The caves were cut into the crevices and cavities in the soft marl. A characteristic feature is a long corridor that runs like a tunnel across the hillock in which the cave is cut (Fig. 56). The water supply was from the nearby tiny spring, 'Ein Abu Mahmud, whose water was collected into a constructed pool. In the east wall of the front part of cave 2 there is a rock-cut prayer niche, and around it there are engraved crosses and Greek inscriptions, in one of which the name "Ioannes" is mentioned.

Cave 3 is the most elaborate complex (Fig. 57). It was, perhaps, the residence of an admired monk who attracted others to live in his vicinity. The entire complex is rock-cut. It consists of a chapel and two living rooms located on the east side of a 15 m long corridor that interconnects them. At the other end of the corridor, two cooking stoves are cut on an elevated rock shelf (Fig. 58). A rock-cut chimney above the stove allows smoke to exit. A rock-cut bed is constructed in each room, indicating that two monks lived in this complex, presumably an elderly monk and his attendant. The entrance was blocked by a door with an elaborate locking system (Fig. 59).

Most of the dwelling cells in the various Sabaite laurae are simple structures with one or two rooms, built freely on the rock ledge on a moderately sloping area or supported on the side opposite the cliff. In the Great Laura, however, we have also found more spacious complexes. These should be compared with the dwellings of the monks in Kellia and near Esna, two sites in which the monks lived in spacious dwellings, equipped with commodities that are normally found only in houses of wealthy lay people in Egypt (Husson 1979).

The Kelliot Dwelling

The typical spacious Kelliot hermitage, which is dated to the sixth century, is composed of many rooms and a courtyard, and is surrounded by a wall (Daumas 1967, 1968,

[25] Two of these caves were brought to my attention by Asaf Gottfeld, the regional superintendent of the Nature Preservation Authority, for which I am grateful. See also P. Bar-Adon, *Excavations in the Judean Desert (Atiqot 9, Hebrew series)* (Jerusalem 1989), 87. The excavations took place in Feb.–April 1989 and Sept. 1991 with the participation of volunteers from the United States and students of the department of archaeology of the University of Haifa. The team members were Benny Arubas and Benny Agur. The expedition resided in Kibbutz Almog. Thanks are due to all.

55. 'Ein Abu Mahmud, cave 1, general view from the west.

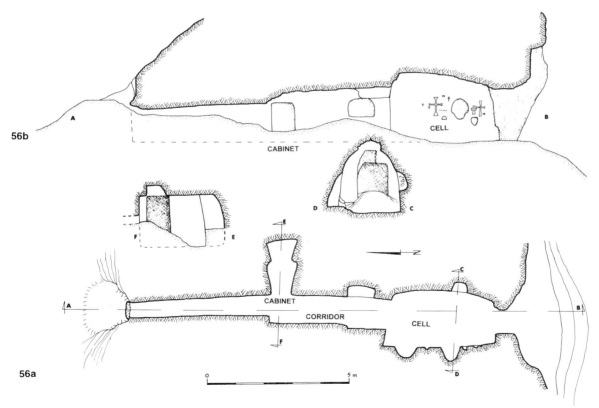

56. 'Ein Abu Mahmud, cave 2: (a) plan; (b) cross section.

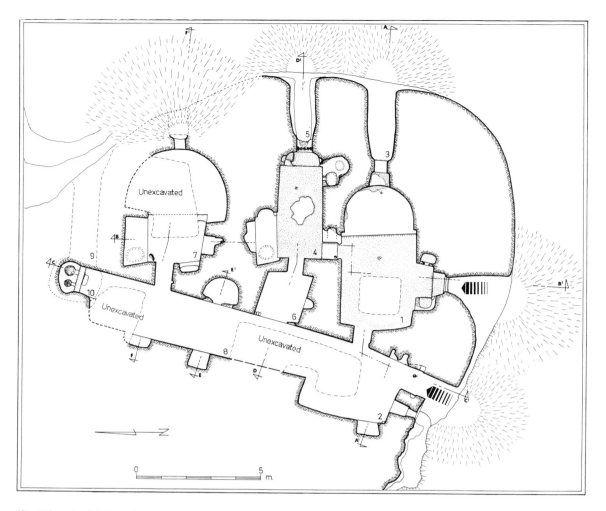

57. ʻEin Abu Mahmud, cave 3, plan.

Legend
1. Chapel
2. Entrance room
3. Window
4. Dwelling room
5. Window
6. Antechamber
7. Dwelling room of
   attendant
8. Corridor
9. Upper passage to
   chimney
10. Cooking stoves

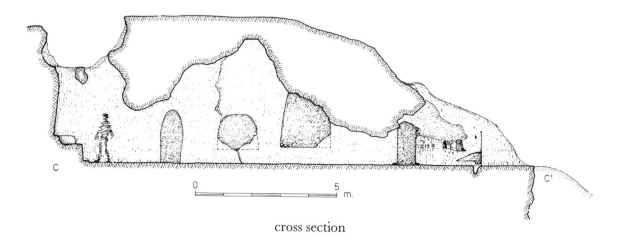

cross section

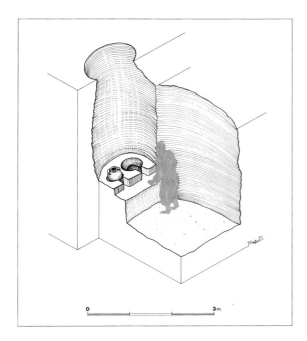

58. 'Ein Abu Mahmud, cave 3, cooking stove.

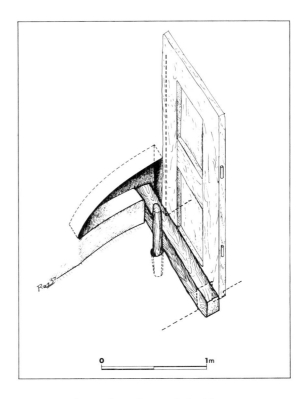

59. 'Ein Abu Mahmud, cave 3, locking system.

1969; Daumas and Guillaumont 1969; Walters 1974, 102–10; Andreu et al. 1980; Andreu and Coquin 1981; Coquin 1982). A characteristic example is the early phase of *kom* 167. A brick wall encloses a rectangular area of ca. 15 × 27.5 m. In the northwest part are the living quarters, and in the southeast corner there are water supply installations including a well, a pool, and channels. A toilet, which drains into a pit located beyond the wall, is also built there. The area between the living quarters and the well served as a garden. The spacious dwelling had two parts, each with several rooms: the larger one, which also included a kitchen and a storage area for food, was occupied by the elder or senior monk, while the smaller one, attached to it on the south side, was intended for a disciple or attendant. Each part had its own chapel (oratory). The building, with an area of 10.30 × 9.70 m, was built of bricks and plastered; the ceilings were of brick vaulting. In the walls there are many niches, which served as cupboards. The oratory is a spacious room whose walls were ornamented with frescoes. The literary sources relating to Kellia also affirm the existence of spacious dwelling complexes there (Evelyn-White 1932, 214).

The Cells West of Esna

The nine excavated cells, dated to the years 550–650 (Sauneron and Jacquet 1972), are also impressively spacious hermitages. These are subterranean complexes cut into the conglomerate stratum to a depth of ca. 3.5 m below the surface. The walls and floors are plastered and whitewashed. There are two types: the simple one, with a single prayer chapel (oratory) and courtyard, and a second type, with two chapels and two courtyards.

Hermitage no. 1 is an example of a simple complex. The staircase descending to the courtyard is always located on the south or southeast side, the direction opposite the prevailing winds. The subterranean courtyard, which was open to the sky, was the center of the complex. The oratory was always located on the north side of the courtyard, and to the west of its entrance there are two windows in the shape of an aperture which narrows toward the outside. A round pane was inserted at the narrow end. When the oratory was especially deep, a round window for light was also fixed above the entrance. In the east wall of the oratory there is a prayer niche, flanked by two additional niches. The importance of this wall is also emphasized by its drawings and inscriptions. There were additional niches in the other walls as well. At times there is a ventilation shaft in the north wall. The oratory has an attached room. On the east side of the courtyard there is a bedroom with a rock-cut and plastered bed. On the south side there is a storeroom, in which water storage jars were stored as well. The kitchen was generally equipped with elaborate cooking devices including a stove and a baking oven with an improved air circulation system.

In a double complex, such as hermitage 7, a second oratory was erected on the south side of the courtyard, parallel to the staircase, and beyond it an additional open court-yard with cooking devices and a storeroom. The double complexes apparently were in-tended for two monks, even though a second bed has not been found with certainty in such complexes.

A kitchen containing both cooking and baking devices is therefore an important and elaborate component of the highly developed monastic cells of Kellia and Esna; this obvi-ously teaches us about the way of life of the Egyptian monks who lived there. Among the secular population in Egypt, elaborate kitchens such as these were to be found only in the houses of the rich (Husson 1979). We did not find kitchens such as these even in the most developed hermitages in the Great Laura. The cells of Choziba (Figs. 60, 61), on the other hand, did have baking ovens, and cave 3 near 'Ein Abu Mahmud had cooking stoves with a rock-cut chimney.

Similarly, it is clear that a private prayer chapel (oratory) was an essential, developed component of these Egyptian hermitages. From this aspect, the private chapels we found in the hermitages of the Great Laura fit well into the general picture. Private chapels are also characteristic of the monastic cells in Bir Abu Sweira, the site of the monastic center of Rhaithou in Sinai (Tsafrir 1984; 271–73).

Monastic Cells in Sinai, Transjordan, and Syria

The cells discovered in the monastic centers of Jebel Safsafa (Finkelstein 1985) and Jebel Sirbal (Dahari 1982) in Sinai are generally small and narrow alcoves built under large boulders or in overhangs, with at least one masonry wall. Complex 250 in Jebel Safsafa is unique in that it is more spacious and is composed of a courtyard, vestibule, and a living room, while site 2 there, whose shape is that of a narrow dwelling alcove, is the prevalent type of cell (Finkelstein 1985, 55–56, figs. 13, 14, 29; plans Q, R).

The hermitage of John, abbot of Hamam Afra monastery in southern Transjordan, was in a cave containing three rooms, one of which was established as a chapel orna-mented with crosses and other ornamentations, the second served as an annex to the chapel, and the third as living quarters for the monk (Macdonald 1980). Among the

Christian monuments mentioned by Saller and Bagatti in Transjordan there are also many monastic cells.[26]

Monastic cells in Wadi el-Malih, Wadi Dfele, and el-Faranj, all in the region of Kerak, are mentioned by Canova.[27] Frank reported a hermitage with a chapel, an inscription, and a cross on the north bank of Wadi el-Hasa, not far from Ghor es-Safi (Macdonald 1980, 361–62).

Fifty towers of seclusion were explored in the limestone massif of northern Syria, between Antioch and Apamea—an agricultural region rather than a desert (Peña et al. 1980, 47–92, 165–280). The towers, of a rectangular plan, consist of two to three, and even six, storeys, each with a single room. Each tower had a door with a locking device (ibid. 64), apertures, and even wide windows. The cell in the ground floor was used by the attendant or disciples, while the cell in the upper storey served as living quarters for the recluse or as a private chapel. Only a few of the towers served more than a single monk. The storeys of each tower were separated by floors of wood or stone beams. Access from one storey to another was by means of a wooden staircase or a ladder. These towers are generally spacious hermitages, in contrast to the impression gained by reading some of the literary sources (ibid. 66). Each tower is generally surrounded by a stone fencing wall enclosing a courtyard and forming a *mandra* (μάνδρα), literally a fold. The phenomenon of tower-recluses was not familiar to Theodoret and is therefore considered to be a later development in Antiochene monasticism (ibid. 53). Some towers are dated by inscriptions to the sixth century. Some are isolated; others are appended to a monastery or church. The towers are distinguished in plan, masonry, and workmanship from simpler hermitages, and they are therefore better preserved.

A two-storey hermitage known as the "Cell of Gabriel" was explored in the abbey of Qartmin near Tur 'Abdin in the Tigris frontier. The lower storey served as a prayer chapel and the upper one as living quarters. A narrow standing niche, 88 cm deep and 22–29.5 cm wide, for perpetual standing, was constructed in the east wall of the living area. This is an architectural arrangement that reflects the extreme practice of night-long vigilance of the Syrian monks (see also below, Part III, Chap. 4A). A cavity in the wall of a charnel house served a similar purpose. This cell and another that was explored were originally inhabited by recluses who lived within the walls of the monastery. A hermit tower of three single-room storeys is located at a distance ca. 250 m to the west, outside of the monastery (Palmer 1990, 97–107, figs. 29–32, 34–36).

[26] S. Saller and B. Bagatti, *The Town of Nebo (Khirbet el-Mekhayyat) with a Brief Survey of Other Ancient Christian Monuments in Transjordan* (Jerusalem 1949), 222–33.

[27] R. Canova, *Iscrizioni e monumenti protocristiani del paese del Moab* (Rome 1954), 3–5, fig. 2; 19–22, figs. 18–20; pp. 219–22.

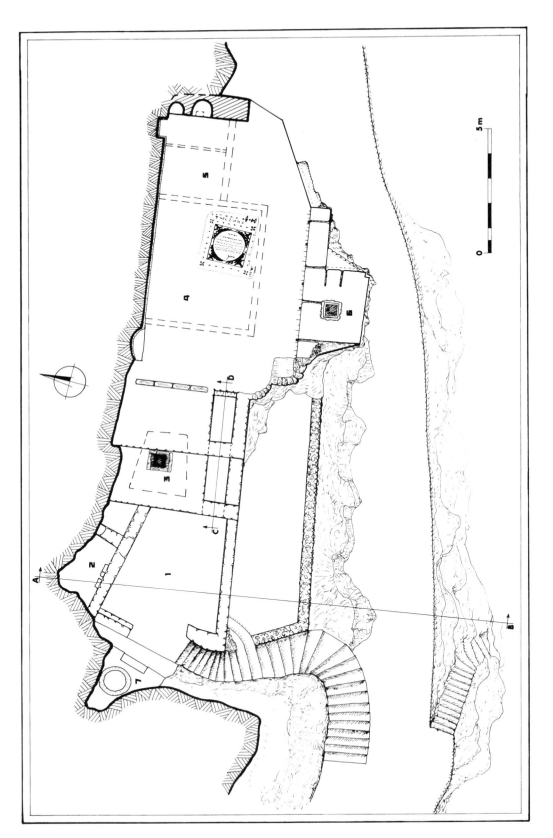

60a. "The Cells of Choziba," hermitage 13, plan.

Legend
1. Lower courtyard
2. Basin for slaked lime
3. Water cistern
4. Dwelling room

5. Private chapel
6. Water cistern under balcony
7. *Tabun* (oven)

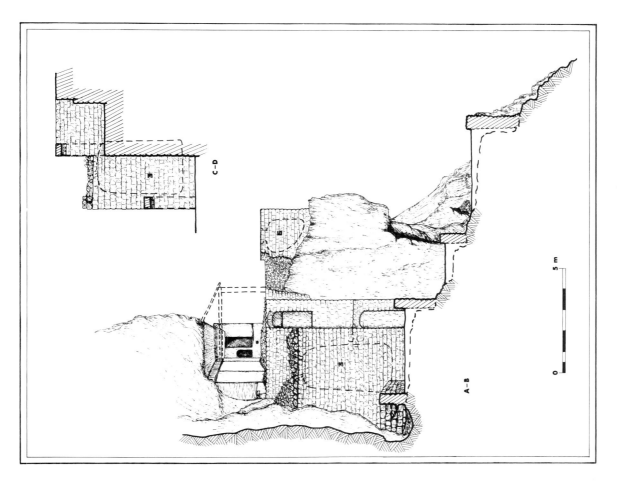

60b. "The Cells of Choziba," hermitage 13, cross section.

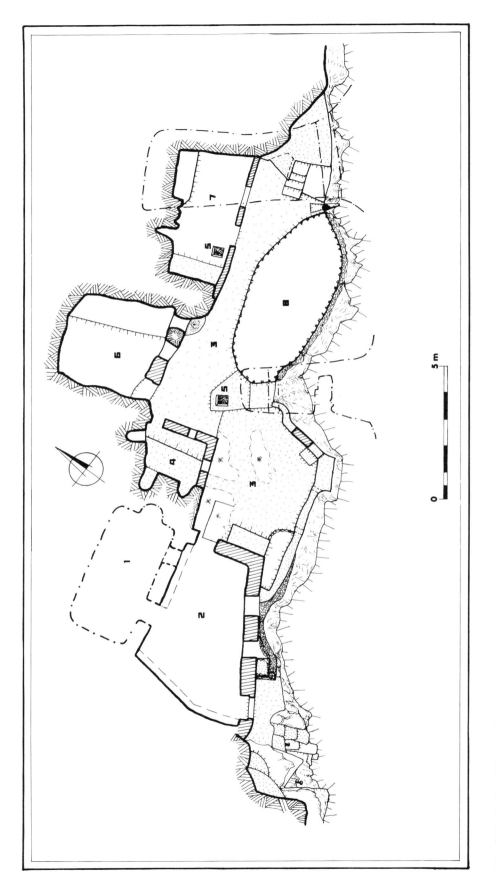

61. "The Cells of Choziba," hermitage 18, plan.

Legend

1. Private chapel
2. Dwelling room
3. Balcony
4. Bed

5. Opening of a water cistern
6. Service room
7. Working room
8. Garden

2

Coenobia

Already at an early stage of his career as an abbot, Sabas understood that coenobia should be established for those within his community who were not fit for the lauritic life. He also formulated a suitable rule for them, thus ensuring their membership in his community.

As we shall see below, in the first stage of their existence, most of the coenobia did not have more than two or three monks. In light of this, the question arises: in this early stage, is it proper to speak of a monastery, or is this simply a private hermitage in which a handful of monks lived? We also know that in the literary sources the word μοναστήριον may denote not only a coenobium but also a dwelling cell of a monk (Lampe 1961, 878; both these meanings are also valid for the Syriac terms *dayrâ* and *'ûmrâ*). What, then, is the criterion for distinguishing between these two meanings in the sources in general and in Cyril's writings in particular? When should a complex in which two or three monks lived be regarded as a monastery and not a private cell? The ultimate criterion is the existence of all the communal functions there, including weekend prayers. If the monks lived a communal life in a fixed place seven days a week and did not join the community of another monastery for weekend prayers, it is justified to view this place as a monastery, especially if the declared intent of living there was to enlarge the community and expand the buildings. It should also be noted that Cyril wrote from a retrospective view of the institutions, after the communities had grown and become full-fledged monasteries.

A. The Monastery of Kastellion (492)

The History of the Monastery

The monastery of Kastellion was founded on the ruins of the Hasmonean-Herodian fortress of Hyrcania (Patrich 1993a). The ruins of the early fortress (*castellium*/καστέλλιον), as well as the monastery established on its peak, gave the hill its name. The Arabic name Khirbet al-Mird has its source in the parallel Aramaic-Syriac name *Marda*, which also means fortress. We also know of the settlement of monks and the establishment of a monastery in an abandoned fortress in Egypt (from the history of Antony) and in Syria (Vööbus 1960a, 164–65 nn. 18, 21).

Sabas spent the Lent of 492[28] by himself at the peak of the hill of Kastellion, ca. 20 *stadia* (3.6 km) northeast of the Laura (*V. Sab.* 27, 110.5–7). In this abandoned ruin in

---

[28] *V. Sab.* 27, 110.1–3: in the 54th year of Sabas' life, two years after the dedication of the Theoktistos Church in the Laura (Dec. 12, 490; *V. Sab.* 19, 104.21 ff), in the 15th year of the indiction.

which snakes abounded and ravens (perceived as demonic creatures) nested, Sabas underwent various torments, and he sought to cleanse the site from the demons by means of the oil of the Holy Cross. It is characteristic in the writings of Cyril and in the lives of the monks that their struggle against their fears and the hallucinations they arouse is perceived as a spiritual struggle against demons and evil spirits. The Cross and the oil of the Cross are therefore efficacious in this struggle. At the conclusion of Lent he returned to the Laura. After celebrating Easter there, he took a number of fathers, went to Kastellion, and began to remove the debris and build cells from the stones there. During the course of this work a large vaulted dwelling room made of magnificent stones (οἶκον βιωτικὸν μέγαν ἀπὸ λίθων θαυμαστῶν κεκαμαρωμένον) was found under the ruins.[29] Sabas renovated it and turned it into a church. The work continued for more than seven months. In the beginning only cells and the church were reconstructed; the intent, however, was to turn the place into a coenobium. Indeed, the ruins of the buildings on the peak are arranged around a central courtyard, a structure characteristic of a level coenobium (Fig. 62).

The coenobium was dedicated on November 23, 492, the date of the death of Marcianus, abbot of the monastery near Bethlehem and archimandrite of the monks, who before his death had aided Sabas with food and manpower when the construction work at Kastellion began. The work was not completed until sometime later.

Kastellion was a coenobium for older monks who excelled in their way of life and for monks of the Laura who had misbehaved. The latter were sent there in order to mend their ways before being admitted into the Great Laura (*V. Sab.* 47, 137–38).

As the administrator (διοικητής) of the monastery, in which a considerable community lived (ibid. 27, 112), Sabas appointed a monk named Paul, a former anchorite, who was aided by his disciple Theodore. After Paul's death, Theodore assumed the administration (διοικησία) (cf. ibid. 46, 136–37), choosing as his assistant his brother Sergius and his uncle Paul, who came from Melitene in the province of Armenia. Sergius and Paul administered Kastellion one after the other and later received the bishoprics of Emmaus and of Aila, respectively. Sabas would associate with the administrators of the monasteries of Kastellion and the Cave in the hostel of the laura in Jericho (ibid.). John Moschus mentions Abba Agathonicus, an abbot of Kastellion of Galatian origin (*Pratum* 167, 3033).

During the drought of 516–521 the cisterns of the monastery—restored cisterns of the early fortress—contained sufficient water for the needs of the monks (*V. Sab.* 66, 167). The monastery had a stable and beasts of burden (ibid. 36, 123), and Sabas had purchased for it two hostelries, one in Jerusalem next to David's Citadel and the hostelry of the Great Laura, and the other in Jericho in one of the gardens that he had bought (ibid. 31, 116).

The admirers of Sabas' memory continued to contribute to Kastellion after his death (ibid. 80, 186). Some information about the monastery is also found in the *Vita Stephani*

---

[29] *V. Sab.* 27, 111.21–22. In several of the manuscripts, the phrase οἶκον βητικόν appears, instead of οἶκον βιωτικόν. Chitty (1966, 120 n. 77) prefers this formulation, interpreting it as a room in the shape of the Greek letter *beta*, i.e., a chamber with two parallel vaults. But if the church renovated by Sabas is the one which we know at present, it does not have two vaults; rather, it is a hall whose ceiling is supported by four arches extending across its width.

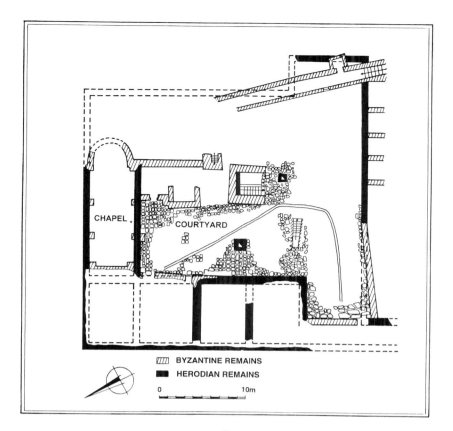

BYZANTINE REMAINS

HERODIAN REMAINS

0   10m

a

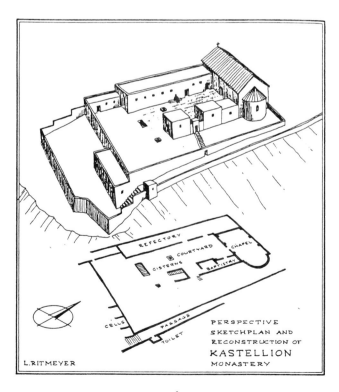

b

62. Kastellion: (a) plan; (b) reconstruction.

Sabaitae (725–794), which indicates that this was an active monastery also in the second half of the eighth century. In 749 Zacharias, the uncle of Stephen and a monk of the Great Laura, was elected *hegoumenos* of Kastellion and the Cave and died shortly afterward (ibid. IX.9, 353, ed. Garitte). Stephen had a cell there but lived there only when he left his permanent dwelling in the Great Laura and wandered in the desert accompanied by his disciples from the Laura and Souka (ibid. XVII.1–3, 365, ed. Garitte; sections 83, 131, 158, 184 in *AASS* ed.). This arrangement was possibly meant to strengthen the spirit of the community living there, since there were difficulties in obtaining a suitable abbot.

The latest testimony of a monk living there is from 1355 in a Greek inscription on the reverse of an icon from the Mar Saba monastery (see below). However, it is doubtful whether the monastery was still active at so late a period. John Phocas, who passed close to Khirbet al-Mird on his way from Jericho to the Mar Saba monastery (1185), does not mention it.

History of the Research
The identification of the monastery of Kastellion (and of the fortress of Hyrcania) with Khirbet al-Mird (ref. point 1848.1252) was proposed by Furrer (1880, 235) and Kasteren (1890, 108) and is universally accepted. Robinson and Guérin do not mention the site. The surveyors of the Palestine Exploration Fund, who visited the site in November 1873, defined it as an impressive Byzantine ruin (Conder and Kitchener 1883, 212). In 1877 Schick (in Marti 1880, pl. II) drew a quite detailed plan of the ruins on the hill and its surroundings, and proposed identifying it with the monastery of Euthymius, a suggestion which was repeated by the surveyors of the Palestine Exploration Fund (ibid. 184). Marti (1880, 19–24), aware of the difficulties raised by this identification in comparison with Cyril's description of the location of the monastery of Euthymius, proposed that Euthymius actually had two monasteries and that Cyril did not distinguish between them. Almost all other scholars have rejected this proposal, looking for the monastery of Euthymius closer to the Jerusalem-Jericho road.[30]

An orderly archaeological excavation has not yet been conducted at the site, and our knowledge of the remains is based on surveys and measurements. During the course of four visits to the site in 1912–28, Mader explored a burial cave with depictions of saints (Fig. 63), into which Kasteren had already crawled. Mader also published various finds that were discovered accidentally after several monks of the Mar Saba monastery, on the initiative of the abbot Pantalemon, renewed their residence there in 1926 and cleaned the church and the east wing of the summit. In July 1952 Bedouins discovered papyri from the monastery of Kastellion in one of the water cisterns. Following this, a Belgian expedition from the University of Louvain, headed by de Langhe, went to the site in February–April 1953 and discovered writings on papyrus and parchment in Palestinian

---

[30] Vailhé (1897–98d, 209) and Mader (1928, 45–52; 1937, 199–208) also suggested identifying Kastellion with Mount Marda, where Euthymius and his disciple Domitian established a church and altar. Chitty (in Mader 1929, 133 n. 1, and Chitty 1966, 84), Bagatti (1954b, 312–13), and Milik (1961, 23) rejected this proposal, since, according to Cyril, Sabas was the first to establish a monastery on the hill of Kastellion; they adopted the identification of Mount Marda with Masada, as had already been proposed by Delau (1899, 273–81). Pierri (1947) and Meinardus (1965–66, 340–42), on the other hand, did adopt the proposal of Vailhé and Mader.

63. Kastellion. Burial chapel.

Syriac, Greek, and Arabic.[31] In April 1960 an expedition headed by Wright (1961) stayed on the site and prepared a plan of the remains of the buildings on the summit. This plan was reexamined and corrected by me in October 1985 (Fig. 62), with the aim of distinguishing between the early remains from the Second Temple period and those from the Byzantine period. The aqueducts traced by Feldman in 1971 were reexamined by me in 1982, in order to discern the stages in their development (Patrich 1989d).

The Archaeological Remains

The hill of Kastellion/Hyrcania (248 m above sea level) rises ca. 200 m above the Hyrcania valley at the western extremity of which it is located, and is entirely isolated from its surroundings except for a ridge to its west. This ridge was narrowed by quarrying during the Herodian period. Along it ran an access path, which split off from the "Road of the Monasteries." The conduit also reached the monastery on this ridge.

Of the two conduits that fed the cisterns of the Herodian fortress, the shorter one, which comes from Wadi Abu Shu'la (Nahal Sakekah), was restored during the Byzantine period. A cross is carved in the rock near the dam in which it begins, at ca. 2 km from the monastery. Of the second, longer conduit, which comes from the Kidron, only a short

[31] See R. de Langhe, "Oude handschriften in de woestijn van Juda," in *Onze Alma Mater* 7 (1953), fasc. 4, pp. 14–19; idem, "De Leuvense expeditie naar de woestijn van Juda," ibid. 8 (1954), fasc. 1, pp. 3–5.

section, ca. 1.5 km long, might have been restored during this period. The conduit crossed the ridge at the foot of the monastery on a bridge, on the top of which can still be seen the remains of the channel, covered with reddish plaster in which potsherds are mixed. This level of the conduit could have fed only the lower cisterns, excavated in the slopes of the hill.

In the Byzantine period the monks settled in the ruined structure on the summit, which was apparently the palace of the fortress. The monastery looks like a courtyard building characteristic of a level coenobium. The north wing of the palace, with an inner width of ca. 5.5 m and a length of ca. 16 m, was transformed into a chapel. It was paved in white mosaic and roofed by four arches (Fig. 62).

Among the architectural fragments of the chapel discovered at the site are three complete marble screen posts; fragments of two screen plates, one ornamented with a cross with lilies between its branches, surrounded by an acanthus wreath, and the second ornamented with a relief of a deer (Pierri 1947, 14, fig. 2); a fragment of an altar post; a sundial, which informed the monks of the times of prayer and the daily schedule (see Fig. 76); and the cover of a *reliquiarium* (Mader 1929, 126). The room south of the chapel served as a *diakonikon* or a *baptisterium*. It had a colorful mosaic floor forming a square. The frame is of a braid between two strips of continuous wave, while the central square is divided into rhomboids by diagonal lines composed of small leaflets (Wright 1961, 10–11 and pl. v). A second, smaller panel of this mosaic floor was ornamented with birds (ibid., pl. vi).

The western wing of the structure, which had two openings to the courtyard, is now blocked by debris. Presumably this was the refectory. In the courtyard, which is paved with stone slabs, are the openings of two early water cisterns. Two staircases lead to two other cisterns. In the south side of the courtyard lies a 1 m high cylindrical immersion basin whose inner face is carved with spiral grooves. A similar immersion basin is found at present below the monastery of Qarantal, ancient Douka. A lintel ornamented with a cross and a clay oil lamp with an inscription and a cross also have been found at the site.

In the monastery of Mar Saba there is an icon depicting Jesus as Pantokrator with Mary and John the Baptist flanking him and the twelve disciples around them. On the reverse of the icon is a Greek inscription stating that it was brought to Mar Saba in 1355 (15th year of the indiction, AM 6855) from the monastery of Kastellion by a monk named Paul (Mader 1929, 128–29, pl. ii). This is the latest testimony of the dwelling in or visit of a monk to Kastellion.

In the map by Schick, who was of the opinion that this is the laura of Euthymius, nine cells appear: eight of them are west and north of the water pools to the west of the summit. It is not possible to discern anchorite cells in these places today. It cannot be ruled out that Schick interpreted shelters for shepherds and their flocks as dwelling cells of monks. This matter, however, requires further research by excavations. The monastery of Kastellion was built as a coenobium, and the dwelling cells are to be sought in the ruins on the summit. The papyri found in cistern K1 and graffiti on the walls of several cisterns indicate that the monks turned them into dwelling cells.

On the southwest side, on a level lower than that of the ruins on the summit, an oval burial cave has been found. The surveyors of the Palestine Exploration Fund had already heard of its existence, but Kasteren (1890, 108) was the first to crawl into it. Mader discovered wall paintings in the cave in 1912 and began studying them during his second visit in December 1925. Under the cave's white mosaic floor were discovered eight built burial cases arranged in two rows of four graves each (Fig. 63). The burial cases are 2 m long and 0.84 m wide. Additional graves are built into the walls of the cave. Many human bones and skulls have been found in the graves.

The walls of the cave are coated with plaster. The paintings found by Mader depict thirty-six saints, almost all of whom are desert monks of Palestine. For some of them there is virtually no other information regarding their veneration as saints; thus this series of paintings provides us with knowledge of the veneration of saints unique to Palestine. The images are identified by vertical inscriptions flanking their heads; their faces were intentionally defaced by the Bedouins. The details of the saints' bodies, clearly visible in Mader's time (1928, 1937), were later repainted by the monks of Mar Saba, so that only the general outlines are visible.

Twenty-five of the identifying inscriptions have been preserved in their entirety: on the west wall, Euthymius, Athanasius(?), Thallelaius, Martyrius, and an unidentified figure; on the south wall, Lazarus, Basil, Arsenius, Timotheus, Symeon (Stylites or Salus), an unidentified figure, Palladius, John (the Hesychast or of Choziba), Theoctistus, and George of Choziba; on the east wall, Abraamius, Marcianus, Theoctistus (II, not the companion of Euthymius), three unidentified figures, Macarius, Moses, Theodosius, Paul, Stephen, Isidore, a defaced figure, and Arcadius; on the north wall, John (the son of Xenophon[?]) and Xenophon. Sabas' name has not been preserved, but it may reasonably be assumed that he was among the images whose inscriptions were destroyed. Also found on the walls are graffiti in Greek, Arabic, and Syriac left by visitors who came to revere the saints depicted there and the monks buried in the cave. There is also a burial inscription for a monk named Andraos engraved on a tombstone (Mader 1929, 127–28).

The dating of the paintings, which were undoubtedly made during the period when the monastery was functioning, is partly dependent upon the correct identification of the saints depicted. Mader was of the opinion that the most recent saint in the series is George of Choziba, who died ca. 625. Nevertheless, he hesitated to date the paintings to the short period between this date and the conquest of Jerusalem by the Arabs in 638, since the desert monasteries had already been severely damaged after the Persian invasion in 614 (Mader 1928, 48–50; 1937, 208–11). Following Vincent, he tended to date them to the eleventh or twelfth century, while indicating the difficulty in this solution in light of the fact that there is no source from the Crusader period attesting to the continued existence or restoration of the monastery. As was stated, John Phocas, who in 1185 made his way from Jericho to the monastery of Mar Saba, passing close to Khirbet al-Mird, makes no mention of Kastellion. Mader relies upon the above-mentioned icon, brought in 1355 from Kastellion to Mar Saba, in order to prove that, despite the silence of the literary sources, it cannot be ruled out that the monastery was indeed restored during the Crusader period. Milik (1961, 26–27) is also of the opinion that the paintings are to be dated to the medieval period, noting that it cannot be ruled out that several of the saints are later than George of Choziba, such as Stephen, who was probably a Sabaitic monk in the eighth century, or Lazarus, who might have been a monk from Asia Minor who died in 1054. Mader also does not ignore these possibilities, yet they are not certain. Meinardus (1965–66, 355) accepts the opinion that the paintings are to be dated to the eleventh to twelfth century, as does Kühnel (1984, 188 n. 50), who adopts Mader's opinion in favor of this late date. Already Mader (1937, 212), and following him other scholars, noted that there is a close relationship between the paintings of the saints in the Cave of Arcadius (no. 45 on the map of the Laura) in the Great Laura and the paintings under discussion here.

However, because of the silence of the literary sources, especially that of John Phocas, it is highly doubtful whether we can speak of the restoration of the monastery during the Crusader period and attribute the paintings to it. The inscription on the icon alone does not constitute decisive evidence of the existence of a community of monks in the monastery of Kastellion; it is quite possible that the monk Paul stayed there for a short time as an anchorite or that he found the icon among the ruins while visiting the site of the abandoned monastery. One must weigh against the evidence of the icon the lack of any Crusader or Mamluk pottery at the site or any other find that could be attributed with certainty to these periods. Nor is there any architectural evidence of the later restoration of the Byzantine monastery on the summit. The monks who resettled the site in 1926 merely partially cleaned the monastery of the debris and the rubbish that had accumulated there. They reconstructed a chapel in the burial cave and built for themselves dwelling cells on the edge of the summit and in several of the cisterns.

At the same time, however, we do not necessarily have to attribute the paintings to the limited period between 625 and 638, as Mader initially proposed. The monastery of Kastellion continued to exist during the first two centuries of the Muslim conquest, as is indicated also by the Arabic papyri discovered there and by the literary sources such as the *Vita Stephani Sabaitae*. During these centuries there was significant literary activity in the monasteries of the desert, and it is not impossible that this was accompanied by artistic activity that was manifested, among other ways, in the wall paintings of the burial cave of Kastellion. In this case, the iconodule position adopted by the monks of the Laura of Sabas, with John of Damascus and in a later period Theodore Abu Qurrah, Michael the Synkellos, and the *Graptoi* brothers at their head, was also expressed in the paintings of icons on the walls of the desert monasteries. If this is so, then this constitutes an outstanding artistic find, that paintings from the iconoclastic period, or even before, did survive in a few of the monasteries of the Judean desert. Until now, only some of the earliest icons of St. Catherine's monastery in Sinai had been attributed to such an early period.[32] According to Mader (1937, 209–10), palaeographically as well the inscriptions indicate a connection to the Byzantine period.[33]

The papyri and scrolls indicate that the community of monks living in Kastellion during the seventh to ninth century was multilingual, including Greek-, Syriac-, and Arabic-speakers. This is known also from other sources. Of the papyri discovered in the

[32] K. Weitzmann, *The Monastery of Saint Catherine at Mount Sinai: The Icons, Vol. 1: From the Sixth to the Tenth Century* (Princeton 1976).

[33] Church mosaics with figurative ornamentation have recently been discovered in Jordan (Piccirillo 1988). It was suggested to date some of them to the end of the 8th century. Others are dated to the beginning of that century. These finds indicate an artistic renaissance that occurred at that period. We learn from *V. Steph. Sab.* and from *Vita Michaelis Syncelli* of close ties between the Laura of Sabas and the Christian community and monks beyond the Jordan at that period. See also Mango 1991 n. 38.

cistern K1, only those written in Arabic have been published in their entirety (Grohmann 1963; Kister 1981–82, 1982). They include a hundred mostly fragmentary texts, mainly of letters, from the first two centuries of the Hegira. They also include a section from the Koran. Most of the texts were written by Muslims, and only four were written by, or intended for, Christians. Fragments 45 and 46 are correspondence between Anba Magnille (from the Greek, Μαγνίλλιον), possibly the abbot of Kastellion, and a Muslim named Habban ibn Yusuf. These letters indicate the close relations that were formed between the monks and the Muslim population of the area.

The Syriac papyri indicate that this language served both for everyday use and as a liturgical language. They include passages from Luke 3:1, 3–4; Matthew 21:30–35; Acts 10:28–29, 32–41; Colossians 1:16–18, 20; and Joshua 22:9–11. The latter three passages were not known until then in Syriac translation. Only the passages from the Acts of the Apostles have been published (Perrot 1963). Similarly, Milik (1953, 533–36 and pl. XIX; 1961, 25 and pl. XII) published a Syriac letter from the seventh century by a monk named Gabriel (Gabril) to the head of the Laura (*lwr* in the Syriac script) of St. Sabas, asking him to pray for him, the sinner (*skl'*).

The use in Syriac of the Greek word λαύρα indicates that the Greek term was prevalent in both languages. Also of interest is the relationship of the writer to the abbot of the Laura of Sabas as his spiritual guide, and not to the head of Kastellion. It is clear that the abbot of the Laura read Syriac, but it is doubtful whether he was of Syrian origin in light of the strict care taken not to appoint a Syrian as abbot of the monastery but only as steward, as is reflected in the Sinai *Regula* (see Part III, Chap. 5D). On a plaster fragment in the burial chapel, a Syriac inscription has been identified: *Mr' ysws mšyh'*, the Lord Jesus Messiah (Milik 1961, 25).

The papyri and scrolls written in Greek include passages from the Gospels of Mark and John and from the Acts of the Apostles. The Greek language seems to have been restricted during this period, that of Muslim rule, mainly to liturgical uses.

B. The Small Coenobium (493)

The History of the Monastery and Its Research

The Small Coenobium was established for lay people who wanted to withdraw from the world and live as monks. Under the guidance of experienced monks, they were prepared for the monastic life and learned the Psalms and the order of prayer. Only after this would Sabas give them cells in the Laura. According to Cyril, the Small Coenobium was established north of the Laura (*V. Sab.* 28, 113.6: κατὰ τὸ ἀρκτῶιον μέρος τῆς λαύρας; *V. John Hes.* 6, 206.4–5: τὸ κατὰ βορρᾶν ἔξω τῆς λαύρας κοινόβιον) at a distance of 10 *stadia* (ca. 2 km) from its hostelry (*V. John Hes.* 6, 206.14: ἐπὶ δέκα σταδίοις τοῦ ξενοδοχείου).

According to Cyril (*V. John Hes.* 26, 221.4–18), the coenobium had a fruit orchard (τὰ δένδρα), alongside of which there was a path, and it was watered the entire winter with water collected and drained from the wadi near the coenobium by the monks. This data from literary sources remarkably matches the remains located at the top of a narrow, elongated, and nameless hill (ref. point 1821.1250), which extends from the northeast to the southwest, south of Wadi el-Baqquq, alongside the road connecting the Laura with

Kastellion. The area in which the site is located is designated on the maps as Ard Abu Rabbu. After the discovery of the ruins at the site, we named the hill Ras el-Baqquq.

Ruins had already been discerned at the site and described in 1928 by Marcoff. Relying on his description, Chitty proposed locating here the tower built by Sabas to mark the northern boundary of the Laura. They did not propose an identification for the Small Coenobium (Marcoff and Chitty 1929, 176–77). Corbo (1958c, 107–8) proposed identifying the Small Coenobium with the ruin denoted by the number 4 on the map of the Great Laura (Fig. 26). This, however, is the ruin of a simple hermitage, which had been severely damaged by the looting of building stones and by the construction of a road for motor vehicles, which cut off its western fringe. In my opinion, these are the ruins of the tower erected by Sabas at the northern end of the Laura to mark its boundary. Obviously, these are not the ruins of a coenobium.

Description of the Ruins
Ras el-Baqquq is a narrow, elongated hill connected to the desert plateau on its northeastern side by means of a narrow saddle. There are steep slopes on its other sides. From the hill there is a good view of the towers of the monastery of Mar Saba, the summit of Jebel Muntar, the monastery of Theodosius, and the Mount of Olives. The ruins are scattered for ca. 200 m on the summit of the hill, whose maximum width does not exceed 25 m (Fig. 64). The structures on the summit are surrounded by a wall built on the upper part of the slopes, except on the south slope, which is too steep. This is not a typical coenobium plan, since the structures are dispersed in three different locations along the summit. The eastern structure is the highest and most massive. Thick supporting walls impart to it the character of a tower with the external dimensions of 10×11 m. The middle structure is the smallest, with dimensions 5×7 m, next to which is a blocked cistern whose rolling stone has survived at the site. The westernmost structure, with dimensions 10×15 m, is divided into three chambers. To the west of it are two adjoining cisterns. It is not impossible that the building extended above these cisterns as well.

The northern slopes of the hill are partially terraced. Additional Byzantine ruins, including buildings, cisterns, and terraced plots, are located close to the mouth of Wadi el-Baqquq, where it empties into the Kidron and to its west (Fig. 64). It is clear that this was the location of the orchard of which Cyril speaks (*V. John Hes.* 26, 221.4–18). These installations could have served the fathers of the Small Coenobium to care for and water the monastery's orchard throughout the entire winter, as Cyril writes. Deep and fertile earth is still to be found here; recently (1985) olive saplings were planted in these areas. On the moderate slope descending to the Kidron to the west of Wadi el-Baqquq, remains were traced for a distance of several hundred meters of the Herodian aqueduct to Hyrcania, which also crossed Wadi el-Baqquq. It cannot be ruled out that sections of it were integrated in the Byzantine period into the irrigation system of the orchard of the Small Coenobium.

C. The Monastery of the Cave (508)
The History of the Monastery
The monastery of the Cave was established in a gorge 30 *stadia* (ca. 6 km) from the Laura,

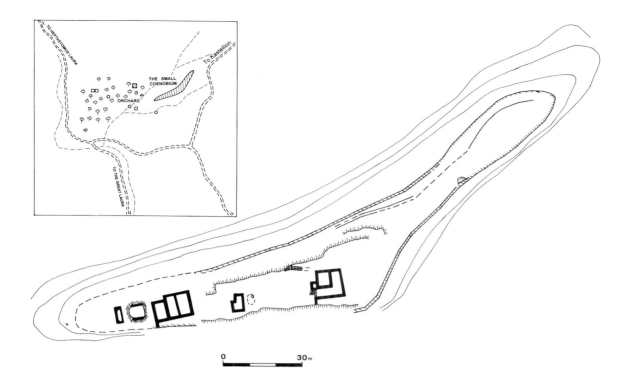

64. The Small Coenobium.

to the west of Kastellion,[34] around a cave in the north slope of the wadi, in which Sabas would seclude himself from time to time (*V. Sab.* 37, 126–27). It was here that he retired when Patriarch Elias turned down his request to ordain John the Hesychast as a priest, and it was here that the reason for the rejection was revealed to him—John was already not only a priest but also a bishop, a fact he attempted to conceal because of his humility and his desire to live as a simple monk (*V. John Hes.* 9, 208). The ordination incident took place after John had concluded a three-year term as steward of the Laura (Sept. 1, 499),[35] perhaps during a routine visit of the fathers of the monasteries to the patriarch during the annual feast of dedication of the church of the Holy Sepulcher (Sept. 13–20). The monastery of the Cave was established only nine years later.[36]

During Lent of 508, after Sabas' return from the New Laura, where he was staying for five months while occupied with its establishment, Sabas went into seclusion in this cave, accompanied by an elderly monk named Paul. Then, after returning for Easter to the Laura, he came back to the cave with Theodulus and Gelasius, the architects, the "brothers in the flesh" from Isauria, and with the above-mentioned Paul and others. He

[34] In *V. Sab.* (37, 126–27), the distance mentioned between the Great Laura and the Cave is 15 *stadia*, while in *V. John Hes.* (9, 208) it is stated that the distance is 30 *stadia*. The aerial distance between the monastery of Mar Saba and Bir el-Qattar is more than 3.5 km, and along the pedestrian track it is close to 6 km, i.e., the correct distance is therefore 30 *stadia*.

[35] See the chronology of the life of John the Hesychast (below, Part V, Chap. 2). This was in the 8th year of the indiction, and not in the 6th year, as in *V. John Hes.* 8, 207.

[36] Vailhé 1899–1900a, 283 erroneously determined 509 as the year in which the monastery was established.

turned the cave into a church and on the slope established a coenobium, which he called the "Monastery of the Cave" (τὸ τοῦ Σπηλαίου κοινόβιον). He was aided in this enterprise by Marcianus, priest of the Anastasis and *hegoumenos* of the monks of Holy Zion Church,[37] who visited Sabas frequently, bringing with him many contributions. In addition to the financial aid, he and his sons Antony and John aided the monks with their own hands in the construction work.[38]

Initially Sabas settled only four monks there. As administrator of the monastery he appointed Paul the Elder, associating with him three brothers from the Laura: George, Cyriacus, and Eustathius. During the course of time the site filled up and expanded. After Paul's death the leadership (ἡγεμονία) of the monastery was transferred successively to Cyriacus, Eustathius, and Sergius (*V. Sab.* 37, 127), and ca. 557–559, upon Sergius' death, the position went to another Eustathius. Cyril knew the latter personally and cited things he had heard from him (*V. John Hes.* 22, 218). It is quite possible that this Eustathius still served as an abbot when John Moschus and Sophronius visited the coenobium (*Pratum* 186, 3061).[39] The above-mentioned George was appointed bishop of Pelusion by Zoilus, the patriarch of Alexandria (542–551).

The proximity of Kastellion and the Cave led to close relations between them, and they are mentioned together a few times. Sabas would occasionally meet with the administrators of these two monasteries in the hostelry of the Laura in Jericho (*V. Sab.* 46, 136–37). Cyril also mentions a contribution of two curtains by a woman from Scythopolis for Kastellion and the Cave (*V. Sab.* 80, 186).

The friction between the shepherds of the desert and the monks during the period of drought is indicated by an episode (*V. Sab.* 59, 160)[40] in which a few shepherds disturbed the monks of the coenobium by grazing their flocks within the bounds of the monastery (ἐν τοῖς τοῦ μοναστηρίου τόποις), bothering them with repeated demands for food and disturbing their rest. This harassment stopped only after the flocks fell into

---

[37] Passarion established his monastery at the beginning of the 5th century for the *spoudaioi* of the Zion Church. It is possible that because of the adherence of some of his monks to the anti-Chalcedonian party, a change took place and another monastery was established next to the Zion Church, and Marcianus served as *hegoumenos* of this second monastery. The Zion Church and the church of the Holy Sepulcher were the two most important pilgrim churches in Jerusalem, and therefore it is clear that a central position was held by Marcianus in the clerical administration that then directed the liturgical rites in Jerusalem, if he served in both offices at the same time.

[38] Marcianus therefore began an ecclesiastical career and monastic life after previously having had a family. He was close to Archbishop Elias, who would later appoint him as the bishop of Sebasteia. His son Antony was appointed deacon of the church of Ascalon, an act that strengthened the position of Patriarch Elias' supporters in that city, the territory of Theodore of Ascalon, a close supporter of Peter the Iberian and later abbot of his monastery near Gaza (Chitty 1966, 103–4, 113; Perrone 1980, 136, 139, 148, 150, 153). John, Marcianus' second son, was appointed deacon of the Anastasis, and eventually, after the exile of Elias, would become the patriarch of Jerusalem (516–524).

[39] John Moschus started his monastic career in Palestine in ca. 565. Sometime during the reign of Tiberius (578–582), while on tour in Egypt, Sophronius joined him. During the years 580–590 they lived in the laura of the Ailiotes, which should be located in the Judean desert rather than in Sinai (Hirschfeld 1990, 55–56). Later, until leaving Palestine in 604, Moschus lived in the New Laura (Chadwick 1974, 55–58).

[40] In terms of the chronological sequence in Cyril's writings, this chapter is to be dated between the years 516 and 518, i.e., between the exile of Elias and the death of Emperor Anastasius. This was therefore during the drought, and this reality is apparently in the background of the monks' harassment by the shepherds in their search for food.

decline and stopped giving milk, so that the young kids and lambs died from starvation. This occurrence, which was caused by the drought, was perceived as a punishment for the harassment of the monastery and not obeying Sabas' orders. The shepherds promised to stop coming not only near this monastery but also near all the other monasteries, and then the flow of milk was restored.

At the end of May in the fourth year of the drought (520), the water in the cisterns of the monastery gave out, and the monks turned to Sabas, with the intent of abandoning the monastery. A wisp of cloud from which rain fell only on the monastery was perceived as a miracle, the answer to the prayers of the elderly Sabas (*V. Sab.* 66, 167). Incidental to this story, mention is made of the water reservoirs (δοχεῖα: cf. ibid. 32, 117) and the aqueducts of the monastery.

The monastery of the Cave was a coenobium surrounded by a wall. The concept of the "bounds of the monastery" mentioned in the story of the shepherds' harassment is to be understood as a bounded and fenced area outside the coenobium itself, which nevertheless was regarded as being within its boundaries. The traces of walls, preserved around the monastery at a distance of several hundred meters presumably are the remains of these fencing walls (see the map, Fig. 65).

John Moschus mentions an elderly hesychast named Abba Elias, who lived in the monastery of the Cave and who complained to him about the moral decline that had set in in his time: "In the days of our fathers three virtues were beloved [by the monks]: poverty, mildness, and temperance; while now avarice, gluttony, and insolence rule the monks." (*Pratum* 52, 2908). Incidentally, we learn from this that recluses also lived in the coenobium.

The coenobium continued to exist for many years after the Muslim conquest of Palestine. In 749 Zacharias, the uncle of Stephen the Sabaite, was appointed *hegoumenos* of Kastellion and the Cave, an office he held for only a short time before he died. During this period the monastery was also known as the Mar Georgii Cave (*V. Steph. Sab.* IX.1–3, 352–53, ed. Garitte), indicating perhaps that the monastery church was dedicated then to St. George.

Previous Research

According to Cyril's writings, the monastery of the Cave was located west of Kastellion, northeast of the Great Laura, and five *stadia* east of the Scholarius monastery (*V. Sab.* 66, 167). These data fit Bir el-Qattar (ref. point 1842.1258), which means "the well of drops" (Palmer 1881, 341). On the map this name denotes the upper cistern of the monastery (see below), which is used to the present day by the shepherds of the desert.

The cistern was marked on the map of the English survey but was not designated as an archaeological site. Palmer (1881, 341) comments that the cistern was fed by a conduit. The first description of the ruins and attempt to identify them as the ruins of a monastery were made by Schick, who apparently looked at the site only from afar while on his way west from Khirbet al-Mird. He mentions on the north bank of Wadi Abu Shu'la ruins of buildings called Qattar by the Arabs, under which there are, according to them, caves, a small room, and cisterns. Since he claimed that Khirbet al-Mird was the monastery of Euthymius, he was also of the opinion that this was to be identified as the monastery of

Martyrius. Marti (1880, 24) objected to these identifications but offered no alternative proposal. Furrer (1880, 235), in his comments on the survey of Schick and the article by Marti, correctly proposed identifying it with the monastery of the Cave, an identification universally accepted since then. Vailhé (1899–1900a, 283–84) provides a short survey of the history of the monastery. The ruins were described by Kasteren (1890, 110–12), Pierri (1947, 13), and Compagnoni (1978, 66–67). Corbo (1958a, 250) notes that the site is too ruined to be the focus of detailed research.

The Archaeological Remains (Patrich 1991)
During the course of the survey for the "Mar Saba Map," I conducted in 1981–82 a thorough measurement survey of all the ruins. In March–April 1983 a limited archaeological excavation was also conducted at the site, during the course of which the mosaic floor of the church (see below) was discovered. The monastery of the Cave is built on the north bank of Nahal Sakekah (Wadi Abu Shu'la), which begins on the east slopes of Jebel Muntar and is one of the main tributaries of Nahal Qumran.

Ruins related to the monastery are visible already at a distance of 400–600 m from the center. These include constructed paths, aqueducts, water reservoirs (harabeh in Arabic), boundary walls, an isolated building, a lime kiln, and quarries (Fig. 65).

The path leading to the monastery split off from the "Road of the Monasteries." The road connecting the monastery of the Cave and Kastellion passed along the ancient aqueduct, which began at the dam across Wadi Abu Shu'la. A third path connected the

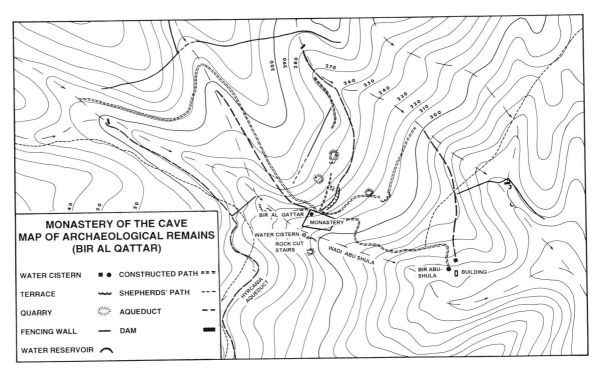

65. Monastery of the Cave. Map of the archaeological remains.

monastery to the Hyrcania valley. Two additional paths, leading to the quarries, go out from the monastery to the north and northeast.

Below the route of the main path leading to the monastery from the northwest, there is a ca. 350 m long aqueduct built of fieldstones, which fed the upper cistern of the monastery. A second aqueduct, ca. 500 m long, which came from the north, began in a dam across a tributary bounding on the northeast the spur on which the monastery is built. A cistern opposite the monastery apparently was used to irrigate its garden, which was built below in the streambed, as is indicated by the traces of several terraces.

In order to mark the bounds of the monastery to the east, a tower-like, two-storey building was erected at the top of an isolated, north-south elongated hillock overlooking the outlet of Wadi Abu Shu'la, at a distance of ca. 500 m. This is a rectangular structure with external dimensions of 5.3 × 9 m. Its outer walls are 0.8 m thick, and it is divided into three rooms. It has a white mosaic floor, and its entrance faces south.

The Ruins of the Monastery

The monastery of the Cave is a cliff coenobium similar to the present-day Mar Saba monastery (Fig. 66). There is a vertical differential of more than 38 m between its top and its bottom. To this group of cliff monasteries also belong the monastery of Theoctistus, the monastery of Choziba (Corbo 1958a, 250), and Khirbet ed-Deir (Hirschfeld 1992, 34–42). Three levels can be defined: upper, middle, and lower.

In the upper level are the wall, the opening of the upper cistern, and the remains of the dwellings. The north wall of the monastery encloses on this level a strip 90 m long and 20–25 m wide which slopes to the east and to the south. Two towers were erected at each of its ends.

In the middle level, which is the main one, there are cisterns, three dwelling caves, the church of the monastery, and the central structure. On the cliff dividing the middle and upper levels are the openings of two caves. The west one is "Sabas' Cave," the source of the name of the monastery. The approach is through a steep L-shaped tunnel, whose lower entrance opens in the cliff ca. 4 m below the floor of the cave.

The cave was transformed into a chapel by Sabas when the monastery was established. On the rock wall, to the right of the lower entrance of the tunnel, one can discern the remains of a molded Corinthian capital—a unique find in the monasteries of the desert. Seemingly, here was a plastered rock surface upon which was written the story of the holiness of the cave. The inscription was flanked on both sides by molded pilasters with capitals. Access to the inscription was almost certainly from the porch on top of the church (see below). Drawings of crosses and a few indecipherable inscriptions, painted in red paint on the rock, have also been preserved nearby. These inscriptions are the work of pilgrims or of the monks themselves. The lower opening of the tunnel that leads to "Sabas' Cave" also opened onto this porch.

A larger and more comfortable church was built below the cave. The church had a white mosaic floor with a geometric pattern of black squares standing on their corners. An analysis of the plan leaves room for a church 12 m long and 5–6 m wide. Fragments of an altar post and of a rounded altar plate, both of gray marble, were also found in the excavation.

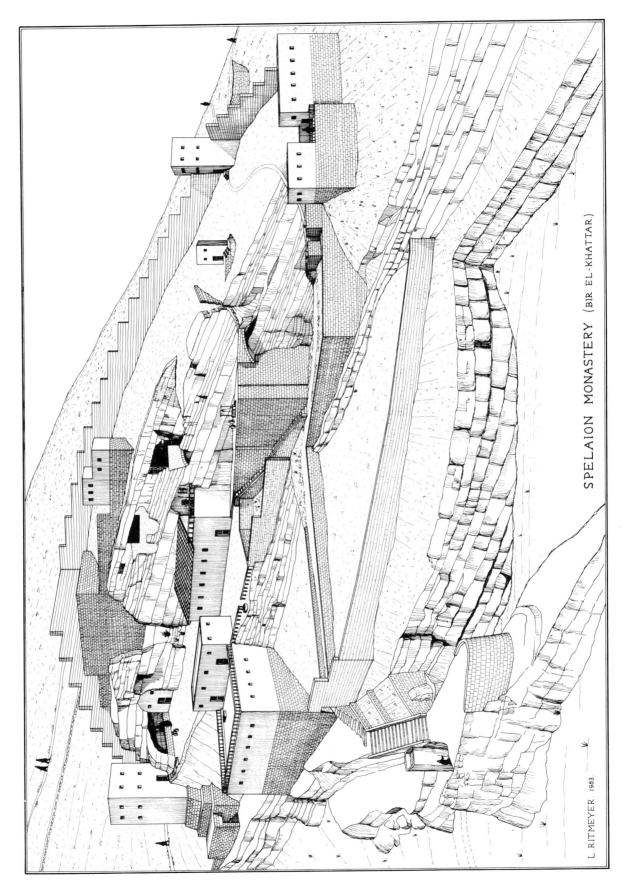

SPELAION MONASTERY (BIR EL-KHATTAR)

L. RITMEYER 1983

66. Monastery of the Cave, reconstruction.

To the south of the church, but on a lower level, were erected the foundations of a large structure 14 × 14 m. Close to its southeast corner is the lower entrance gate of the monastery. Since it was not excavated, it can only be conjectured that this structure served as the main service structure of the monastery—the site of the kitchen, bakery, food storeroom, dining room, and so on.

The lower level includes the entrance gate, the network of paths, and the buildings located in the east end of the monastery, which served as dwelling quarters. The garden of the monastery was located in the streambed. A rock staircase leads from the wadi to a leveled, open space and, after a turn of 160 degrees, to a flight of constructed stairs ca. 3.5 m wide which lead up to the lower gate. On the other side of the streambed, opposite the lower stairs, within an overhang of the rock, are the ruins of a rectangular structure 14.5 m long and ca. 5 m wide that could provide a shelter for guests.

D. The Monastery of the Scholarius (509)

History of the Monastery

The monastery of the Scholarius was the largest and most important of Sabas' coenobia. It was established on the site of the Tower of Eudocia.

The Tower of Eudocia

Eudocia was among the opponents of the Council of Chalcedon and supported the rebels against Patriarch Juvenal. These included almost all the laity and monks of the desert (excluding Euthymius and his followers), headed by the monk Theodosius, who seized the office of patriarch and held it for twenty months. Juvenal regained control of it only after receiving from Emperor Marcian a military force headed by the *comes* Dorotheus, the military commander (*dux*) of Palestine (*V. Euth.* 30, 47–48; Dan 1982, 278–82). Despite this, however, Eudocia continued to support the separatists (Aposchists), and the heresy grew even stronger among the monks of the Holy City and the desert. The letters she received from her brother Valerius and from her son-in-law Olybrius and others called upon her to return to the Catholic Church. Because of these entreaties, and as a result of the troubles she suffered with the killing of her son-in-law in Rome and her daughter and granddaughters being taken in captivity from Rome to Africa, she began to be assailed with doubts that perhaps the cause of her troubles lay in her erroneous beliefs (Frend 1972, 153). Therefore, out of concern for her family and to be at peace with her conscience, she decided to seek the counsel of the renowned saint, Symeon Stylites. To this end she dispatched to him the *chorepiskopos* Anastasius, together with several of her people. Symeon encouraged her and advised her to turn for guidance to a closer source, Euthymius, who was staying in the desert of Jerusalem.

Since Euthymius refrained from coming to the city, she went forth to the desert (455 CE), and, as was befitting her status, she ordered that a tower be built for her on the highest peak in the desert, ca. 30 *stadia* (6 km) south of the laura of the saint. These topographical details match the accepted identification of the site with the summit of Jebel Muntar, the highest peak in the Judean desert. Eudocia there hoped to benefit from the frequent instruction of the saint. Euthymius, however, upon hearing of her intent, retired to Rouba, and only under pressure from her emissaries—Cosmas, the cross warden, the old monk's former disciple, and Anastasius the *chorepiskopos*, who took with them Theoctistus as well—did he finally agree to come to her at the tower. The saint instructed her to abandon the evil teachings of Theodosius and Dioscorus, the patriarch of Alexandria, to accept the Chalcedonian confession of faith, and to join Juvenal. This was the one and only encounter of Eudocia with the old saint. Afterwards she returned to Jerusalem, and under her influence the "First Union" was implemented (456).

Eudocia did not return to the tower thereafter, and it was occupied by two Monophysite monks (*V. Sab.* 38, 127). They were driven out only in the wake of the "Second Union" between Marcianus and Patriarch Martyrius (478–486), twenty-three years later (479).[41]

In 478, that is, while the site was still occupied by the Monophysite monks, Sabas came to this hill after four years of wandering in the desert (*V. Sab.* 15, 97). Chitty (1966, 106) correctly wonders what Sabas was doing there in the company of these opponents of Chalcedon.[42] It is possible that he found himself there for only one night and did not go into the tower itself to spend the night (see also below, Part IV, Chap. 3). According to Cyril, from here, during night prayer, an angel pointed out to him the streambed of the Kidron—"a ravine which descends from Siloam"—and instructed him to settle in a cave on its east bank.

The Scholarius Monastery

About thirty years after the expulsion of the two Monophysites, the tower was occupied by two Nestorian monks (*V. Sab.* 38, 127). Their dwelling in a place that looked out on the three monasteries of Sabas—the Great Laura, Kastellion, and the Cave (which was only 5 *stadia* [900 m] distant: *V. Sab.* 66, 167)—vexed the elderly Sabas. With preaching and warnings he succeeded in persuading them to abandon the Nestorian heresy and join the Catholic Church, entrusting them to Theodosius for their reeducation. This took place in 509 (see below).

At the beginning Sabas settled three monks in the tower. As administrator and abbot of the monastery (διοικητὴς καὶ ἡγούμενος), he appointed his disciple John, of Byzantium, who had previously belonged to the first regiment of the *scholarii* (the guards of the imperial palace),[43] accompanied by two elder monks from the Laura, John and Gregory.[44] John, the former Scholarius, administered the coenobium for thirty-five years (509–544; see below for this chronology). After his death a monk named Cyriacus served

[41] This is the date proposed by Schwartz (1939, 370) for the "Second Union," and it is accepted also by Chitty (1966, 212) and Perrone (1980, 131). Festugière (1962a, 19) gives a general date, before 486.

[42] Perhaps this was one of the arguments raised against him by the rebels in his Laura. There is no hint of this in Cyril's writings.

[43] In the eastern part of the empire there were seven regiments (*scholae*), each of which was headed by a tribune, and they were directly subordinate to the emperor. In Justinian's time, each *schola* numbered 500 men. From these *scholae*, 40 soldiers (*candidati*), dressed in white uniforms, were selected to serve as the emperor's personal bodyguard. See Jones 1964, 613–14; Festugière 1962b, 54 n. 83.

[44] A distinction is to be made between him and a monk by this name, who was the priest of the monastery of the Scholarii, mentioned in *Pratum* 25, 2869; 178, 3048. If it is correct to identify the coenobium of the Scholarii (κοινόβιον τῶν Σχολαρίων) with the coenobium under discussion here (so de Journel, 64; Vailhé 1899–1900a, 22), this shows that later on additional Scholarii would join it. Another Scholarius named John, who was appointed by Patriarch Eustochius as the first *hegoumenos* of the New Laura after the expulsion of the Origenists (555), was a monk from the Great Laura (*V. Sab.* 90, 199).

as *hegoumenos,* until he resigned his office. Sabas cared for all its needs, taking care to visit it regularly (*V. Sab.* 38, 128). During the great drought (516–521), there was sufficient water in the cisterns of the monastery (*V. Sab.* 66, 167).

Abraamius, the Bishop of Cratea

The most renowned monk of the monastery was Abraamius. Like John the Hesychast, he was a bishop in Asia Minor who had relinquished the honor and glory of his office in preference to the monastic life in the Judean desert in the community of Sabas. The *Vita Abraamii* is one of Cyril of Scythopolis' short works.[45]

Abraamius (Ἀβραάμιος) was of Syrian origin, a native of Emesa (Homs) on the Orontes, the capital of Phoenicia Libanensis. He was born at the beginning of the reign of Zeno (474 CE). While still a child he joined the monastery near his city, where he stayed and was instructed in monastic discipline until he reached the age of eighteen (491–492 CE). Then, due to an attack by Saracens on his monastery, he moved to Constantinople, together with the abbot of the monastery. The latter was soon elected to head one of the monasteries of the city, and Abraamius joined him. John, one of the emperor's senior ministers, chose him to be priest and *hegoumenos* of the monastery he sought to establish in his native city of Cratea, in the province of Honorias,[46] on the site where his parents were buried. John bore the title *comes sacrarum largitionum* (= κόμης θησαυρῶν χρηματίζων), that is, he was in charge of the coin mints and of the gold (and apparently also the silver) mines throughout the empire and of the imperial factories in which weapons and shields, which were ornamented with the precious metals, were produced. He was also responsible for a number of taxes collected in precious metal, the payment of the donatives in gold and silver to the army and the civil service, and apparently also the payment of living allowances (*stipendia*), as long as these payments existed, to soldiers and government officials. In addition to these, he was also in charge of the production of uniforms and their distribution to the members of the imperial court, the army, and the civil service (Jones 1964; 369–70, 427–38).

Aplaton, the bishop of Cratea, was the brother of this government minister. In the course of the ten years of Abraamius' office as *hegoumenos,* the monastery acquired fame

---

[45] Besides the Greek text, which was published by Schwartz (1939, 243–47), the end of which is fragmentary, we also possess a complete Arabic translation. This, together with a German translation, has been published by Graf (*BZ* 14 [1905], 509–17). A Latin translation of this Arabic manuscript has been published as well (Peeters 1905, 349–56). These two publications therefore preceded the publication of the Greek original of *V. Ab.* by Schwartz. Festugière used the translation of Peeters, beginning from the place where the Greek manuscript is fragmentary. The Arabic translation is not a literal translation, but rather an abstract, which was made by a translator whose mastery of Arabic was imperfect, and the original meaning of several terms was unclear to him. Among the flaws in the translation: it does not distinguish between a coenobium and a laura, and Abraamius' office as *hegoumenos* of the monastery in Cratea it defines: "coenobiarch of the laura that he built." The *comes* Iohannes is defined as a *dux,* and the Laura of Sabas is identified with the laura of Souka.

[46] The province of Honorias was located in northern Asia Minor, along the coast of the Black Sea, between Bithynia in the west and Paphlagonia in the east, with Claudiopolis (today Bolu) as its capital. In terms of ecclesiastical administration, it was within the realm of the Diocese of Pontus. In the year 535/6, within the context of the changes made by Justinian in the organization of the provinces, it was united with Paphlagonia. See Jones 1964, maps II, VII. Cratea was a Paphlagonian city, which during the Hellenistic period became a colony of the kingdom of Bithynia. It is identified with the present-day city of Gerede.

and was expanded. Finally, after too many people gathered and came there—laity, monks, and bishops—Abraamius, who from his youth had preferred a solitary life, decided to leave secretly and flee to the Holy City. In the thirty-seventh year of his life (510–511) he arrived in Jerusalem, where he was invited to the hostelry of the Great Laura by John the Scholarius, who had met him while he was visiting the church of the Holy Sepulcher. John brought him to the Tower of Eudocia and added him to his community, after presenting him to Sabas and receiving his consent. This story is an example of the manner in which new monks were recruited for newly established monasteries and of one of the functions of the hostelry of the Laura in Jerusalem.

In the first stage, the small community still lived in the Tower of Eudocia, while in the second stage Sabas transformed the tower into a coenobium. During this same period another person from the province of Honorias joined the community. This was Olympius,[47] Abraamius' friend, a layman who came from the city of Claudiopolis, the capital of the province. Olympius came as an emissary of Aplaton, the bishop of Cratea, to find Abraamius and bring him back. Instead of this, however, Abraamius succeeded in persuading him to become a monk and join his monastery. Cyril notes that in no small measure this was also the result of Olympius' meeting Sabas (who at that time was occupied with the transformation of the tower into a coenobium). Within a short time Olympius had been elected deacon and priest, and was the second in command in the administration of the monastery.

When Abraamius had been there for four years (515), after Olympius' mission to return Abraamius to his monastery had not been successful, Bishop Aplaton removed him from his position as *hegoumenos* and even placed a ban on him. John the Scholarius and Sabas appealed to Elias, the patriarch of Jerusalem, in order to have the ban cancelled, but he ruled that it was not legal for one bishop to cancel a ban imposed by another bishop, especially if the one who imposed the ban was still alive. As a result, Sabas and John advised Abraamius to return to his city and obtain there from his bishop the cancellation of the ban, which he did. Only after an absence of twenty-one years did he return to the monastery of the Scholarius (see below).

Abraamius returned to his monastery in Cratea, and after the death of Bishop Aplaton he was elected in his place, at the request of all the inhabitants, who appealed to the metropolitan in the matter. Bishop Abraamius acted in the spirit of the Basilian ideal of activity for the welfare of the community: he established orphanages, hostelries, and hospitals; he gave alms to the needy, built churches, and, as was fitting for a saint, drove out demons and performed other miracles. In 531 he was in Byzantium regarding a legal matter pertaining to his community.[48] Here he learned that Sabas, who had come to the city on a mission to Justinian, had left three days before his arrival and had returned to Jerusalem.

Cyril attributes to this incident and his disappointment at not being able to meet with Sabas the final reason behind Abraamius' decision to abandon all and go a second

---

[47] In the Arabic translation of *V. Ab.*, the name appears in a distorted form: Albinius; Peeters 1905, 352.23.

[48] In this place the Greek text ends. The continuation is preserved only in the Arabic translation. See above, n. 45.

time to Jerusalem and the monastery of the Scholarius, since he was tired of the material affairs his office entailed. From another source, however, we learn that Abraamius, the bishop of Cratea, was present at all five sessions of the "home synod" (σύνοδος ἐν-δημοῦσα)[49] which convened in Constantinople between May 2 and July 4, 536, and therefore he could not have arrived in Jerusalem before the second half of that year (Schwartz 1939, 247–49; Festugière 1963a, 77 n. 14; *ACO* III 28.34; 116.20).

Upon his arrival in Jerusalem he joined his friend Olympius and John the Scholarius in their monastery. The three of them would go forth together to the desert of Rouba during Lent. There, influenced by anchorites, they began to follow their life-style, which they maintained for eight years. At the end of this period Olympius died, and John the Scholarius not long after him (*V. Ab.* 355.1–12).[50]

Abraamius, like the other monks about whom Cyril writes, was faithful to Orthodoxy. During the years of his stay in the coenobium he was famous as a miracle worker, exorcist, and healer of the sick, as well as a teacher and guide. One of his disciples was a monk named Leontius. Cyril mentions December 6 as the date of Abraamius' death, without mentioning the year (at any rate, this does not appear in the Arabic translation). It is obvious that this preceded the writing of the hagiography in 558 or 559 (Flusin 1983, 33–35).

A monastery of the Scholarii is mentioned by John Moschus, who stayed there for a while (*Pratum* 25, 2869; 178, 3048).

The Archaeological Remains
The identification of the monastery with the ruins located on the summit of Jebel Muntar (ref. point 1827.1269), the highest peak of the Judean desert (524 m above sea level), is universally accepted. From the peak the ground slopes steeply to the east. Moderate spurs extend to the north and to the south, while to the west the land slopes down moderately, forming a broad hill. The main route comes from Jerusalem along the local watershed, where the motor vehicle road currently passes as well. Two branches from this road go south to the Heptastomos laura and to the Great Laura, and another goes north to the monastery of Euthymius. A quite convenient shepherds' path descends from the monastery to the east, toward the "Road of the Monasteries," running east of Jebel Muntar. There are no remains of a paved path in this direction.

---

[49] A council attended by bishops and metropolitans who happened to be in the capital on church business. The patriarch of Constantinople was authorized to convene such a council at any time in order to discuss any ecclesiastical matter and to give his authority to its decisions. Such councils became a fixed institution in Constantinople. See Jones 1964, 890–91.

[50] His death is dated by Cyril to January in the 68th year of Abraamius' life, i.e., 541/2. If, however, we accept that Abraamius came to the monastery not before the second half of 536, then it transpires that John the Scholarius did not die before 544, after 35 years of service as the *hegoumenos* of the coenobium. And so the monastery was established not before 509. It should be remembered that the monastery of the Scholarius was established shortly after the monastery of the Cave (508). Therefore 509 is a proper date for the beginnings of the monastery of the Scholarius, and the date of the Scholarius' death is 544. The death date in 541/2 cannot be resolved with the 35 years in office of John as *hegoumenos*. It follows from this that the date of John's death was in the 70th year of Abraamius' life, and not as Cyril writes.

The monastery was encompassed by a rectangular wall bounding an area of ca. 44 × 58 m (Fig. 67). The east wall has mostly collapsed. Two or three courses of the 1.3–1.5 m thick wall have been preserved elsewhere. The internal walls, only the tops of which protrude above ground level, divide the area into subunits. The south side was apparently the residential wing of the monastery. The thickness of the walls is likely to indicate the existence of more than one storey here.

The west wing, with an area of 18 × 34 m, is divided by internal walls, thinner than those of the south wing, into three elongated chambers with a south-north orientation. This wing may have included storerooms, workrooms, stables, and so on.

The remaining area encompassed, according to our hypothesis, the church, and to the north of it a wide courtyard. The church was thus located on the highest point of the summit. All that has survived of it is a small cistern built of large hewn blocks ca. 1.2 m long, roofed by two east-west arches. All the other parts of the church were intentionally destroyed and cast down the steep east slope. Deep below the hill, in the wadi, running eastward, column drums 0.60 m in diameter and paving panels made of local limestone were found by us. Fragments of marble plates, clay tiles, mosaic stones, and of course potsherds were collected on the summit.

To the north of the main compound there is an elongated auxiliary building with a cistern near its west end. It is possible that this was the hostelry. The ruins of other secondary buildings lean against the west wall of the monastery. The main entrance to the monastery was presumably from the south terrace.

Typologically, the monastery of the Scholarius was a level coenobium. In terms of its dimensions, it is close to the coenobium of Euthymius. Its area, without the auxiliary buildings to the north and to the west, is 2,550 m². It therefore belongs to the group of large monasteries in the Judean desert (Hirschfeld 1987, 146–51; 1992, 49, table 3). Without archaeological excavation, it cannot be determined in which part of the structure the Tower of Eudocia was located and how it was integrated into the later monastery. Low boundary walls that surrounded the area of the monastery, to prevent the intrusion of the desert shepherds, are discernable to the south, west, and north. Something similar has also been found in other monasteries.

E. The Monastery of Zannos (511?)

In the writings of Cyril there is no explicit chronological data regarding the date of the establishment of this monastery. The fact that its story (*V. Sab.* 42, 132–33) is related before Sabas' first journey to Constantinople (ibid. 50, 139–41) may possibly indicate that this was before September 511, apparently as a continuation to the establishment of the other monasteries described above.[51]

Zannos and Benjamin, two "brothers in the flesh" (i.e., brothers by birth) who came from the Hebron area, were monks in the Laura and asked Sabas for the anchorite cell (κελλίον ἀναχωρητικόν) that he had built for himself at some distance southwest of the Laura. Their request was granted, and they began to spend part of their time in their

---

[51] Vailhé (1899–1900a, 292) dates the establishment of the coenobium of Zannos to 513, one year after the establishment of the Heptastomos laura, according to his opinion. This laura, however, was established in 510, and not in 512, as he assumed.

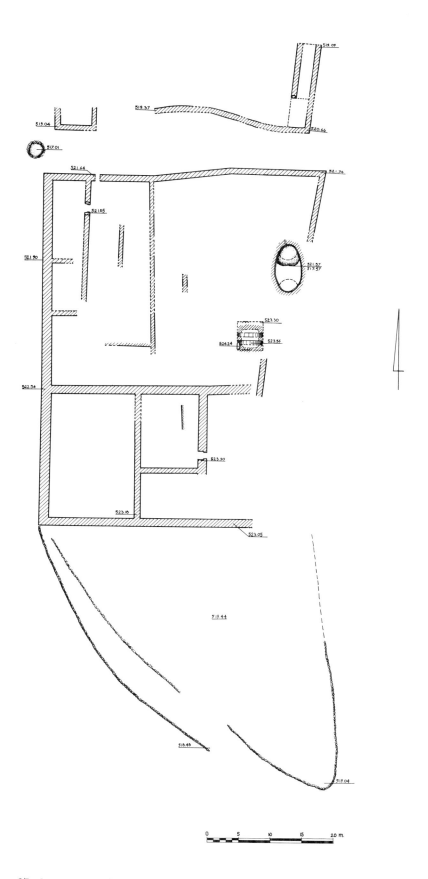

67. Monastery of the Scholarius, plan.

cells in the Laura and the rest of their time in this anchorite cell. Afterwards, with the aid of Sabas and with much effort, they transformed the cell into a coenobium, which was named after Zannos. After additional monks gathered there, Sabas established a church for them, dedicated it, and gave to the members of the community the monastic rules of his other coenobia (ibid. 42, 133.3–4).

The Archaeological Remains

Sabas' anchorite cell was located at a distance of 15 *stadia* (ca. 3 km) south, west, or southwest (πρὸς λίβα) of the Laura. In two of the manuscripts, the distance is given as only 5 *stadia* (900 m).

In the surveys conducted in recent years or earlier, no remains of a monastery were discovered within a radius of 3 km or more from the Laura, neither in the south nor in the southwest sectors. Corbo (1958c, 109–10) proposed identifying the coenobium of Zannos with the ruins of cells located on the east bank of the Kidron at a distance of 250–300 m from Mar Saba, cells that simply constituted hermitages of the Laura itself (nos. 42–43 on the map of the Laura, Fig. 26). These are not ruins of a coenobium. Complex 49, in contrast, one of the largest complexes of the Laura, was almost certainly intended for a group of monks, and its ruins could certainly be construed as a small coenobium (see the reconstruction, Fig. 41). In terms of the direction, it is located in the southern part of the Laura, ca. 500 m distant in an aerial line from Mar Saba and ca. 800–900 m (i.e., 5 *stadia*, a distance matching the shorter version of the manuscripts) along the path. Although this is the farthest complex south of the Laura, it is difficult to conceive of it as a separate coenobium. It contains only dwelling rooms, and there is neither an inner courtyard nor a church, nor any other communal building typical of a coenobium. It is merely an integral part of the Laura, and therefore I hesitate to identify it with the coenobium of Zannos.

Hirschfeld (1990, 41–43) proposed identifying the coenobium of Zannos with el-Burj, a ruin whose plan is that of a courtyard building and whose dimensions are ca. 30 × 30 m, in which marble fragments and colored mosaic stones, presumably of a chapel, were discovered. The site is ca. 2.3 km distant in an aerial line from Mar Saba, or ca. 3 km (15 *stadia*) along the path. The distance is right, but the ruins are located northwest of Mar Saba, and not as Cyril writes. An additional difficulty is the proximity of the site to the main route connecting the Laura of Sabas with the monastery of Theodosius and Bethlehem, a location not exactly suitable for the establishment of an anchorite cell. Meanwhile, however, we cannot provide a better proposal. Hirschfeld's proposal can be adopted if we assume that Cyril was not accurate about the direction, referring to the northwest as west. In this case the anchorite cell of Sabas was originally constructed at such a distance in order to mark the limits of its boundaries and thus to claim possession of areas far to the west of the Laura. Accordingly, it seems that seclusion for extended periods of time in this particular cell was not Sabas' main intention when he constructed it near the main route. An examination of the ruin only in a survey, without an excavation, did not make it possible to discern which portion of it served as the original anchorite cell.

F. The Monasteries near the River of Gadara and near Nicopolis (Emmaus)

These two monasteries were established during the period of Sabas' voluntary exile from his Laura (503–506). The monastery near the river of Gadara (παρὰ τὸν λεγόμενον ποταμὸν Γαδάρων), the Yarmuk, which was later known as the coenobium of Eumathius, developed from the cell that Sabas built next to the cave in which he first settled in 503, when he went into exile from the Great Laura (*V. Sab.* 33–34, 118–20; see below, Part III, Chap. 2). Cyril's testimony indicates that during the Byzantine period lions roamed in this area as in others along the Jordan and the shores of the Dead Sea. The cave in which Sabas settled was, according to Cyril, the cave of a lion.

Initially he was joined by one disciple, Basil, a relative of Severus and Sophronius, distinguished residents of Scythopolis. Within a short time he constructed a cell, probably with the financial means at Basil's disposal, and then two additional brothers joined. According to Cyril, Sabas left the place because of the troublesome number of lay people in the area. He returned to his Laura, hoping that the opposition to him had subsided.

After the death or dispersion of his three disciples, the cell was inherited by Eumathius the Isaurian, who turned it into a coenobium with a community of monks. After him, during the time of Cyril's writing, Tarasius, also an Isaurian, served as abbot.

Sabas discovered that during his absence the number of rebels had risen from forty to sixty, and he retired to the Nicopolis region. From the cell that had been erected for him there (504), a coenobium headed by him developed within a short time (*V. Sab.* 35, 120–22). After Sabas was reestablished at the head of his Laura, upon the intervention of Patriarch Elias, he appointed his disciple Severus of Nicopolis to head the monastery. After a number of years, when Severus died, he was succeeded by Domnus, who in turn was succeeded by Sabaron. Sabaron was extremely old at the time of Cyril's writing.

The sites of these two monasteries are not known (Vailhé 1899–1900a, 536, no. 45; 38, no. 86).

G. The Monastery of Severianus, Sabas' Disciple (ca. 514/15)

Severianus was one of Sabas' first disciples (*V. Sab.* 16, 99). In ca. 514/15[52] he established a coenobium near Caparbaricha (Καπαρβαριχά) in the Hebron hills (today Bani Naʿim). This was during the period of the struggle of Sabas and Theodosius against the religious policy of the Monophysite emperor Anastasius, who acted under the inspiration of Severus of Antioch. As proposed above (Part II, Chap. 1E), it cannot be ruled out that the laurae of Sabas' disciples were also established at the same time with the purpose of disseminating Orthodox monasticism throughout broader areas of the Judean desert and the desert of the Jordan and preventing any Monophysite monks or other heretics to gain ground there.

---

[52] This date is derived from what is related in *V. Sab.* 36, about the years in office of the first *hegoumenoi* of the New Laura, which was established in 507. The first of them, John, served for 7 years; the second, Paul, only 6 months. Afterwards he fled to Arabia, and returned from there to Severianus, in Caparbaricha, who at the same time was engaged in establishing his monastery there, and he died while he was with him. (A similar story, about flight to Arabia and return to Caparbaricha, is also related about Peter, the head of the Archontic heresy in Caparbaricha in the middle of the 4th century [Epiphanius, *Panarion* 40, 291–92].) The date given by Vailhé is prior to 516 (1899–1900a, 280–81, no. 115).

The Caparbaricha region was a Gnostic and Manichaean center in the fourth and fifth centuries (Stroumsa 1983; Stone 1984). This is where the ascetic monk (γέρων in Epiphanius; literally "elder," a technical term for an ascetic monk) Peter, the head of the Archontic heresy, lived in the middle of the fourth century. The Origenist monks who had been expelled from the New Laura by Agapetus in 514/15 were also accused of Manichaean tendencies (*V. Sab.* 36, 124). The monastery of Severianus was also established in the same period that these Origenists were expelled. Is this merely coincidental, or are these two different simultaneous facets of a struggle against various heresies? Cyril, at any rate, does not connect the two events.

According to tradition, it was here that Abraham, accompanied by the three angels, looked upon the ruins of Sodom. In 366 CE Paula visited the site (Jerome, *Epi.* 108.11). Euthymius established a coenobium in this region before the year 428 (*V. Euth.* 11, 22).

The monastery of Abba Severianus is also mentioned by John Moschus. At that time it was headed by Abba Menas (*Pratum* 159, 3028). The monks from there went on missions as far as Eleutheropolis, the district capital (*Pratum* 39, 2889).

Marcoff and Chitty (1929, 178) proposed identifying the monastery of Severianus with Khirbet ed-Deir in the upper Nahal Arugoth. Hirschfeld (1990, 43–44; 1992, 168–70) prefers identifying it with the ruin located ca. 2 km to the northeast of Bani Naʿim (ref. point 1676.1030). Among the ruins it is possible to discern a tower, halls, and dwelling cells arranged on three sides of an inner courtyard. An additional monastic site was discovered nearby.

H. Older Monasteries under the Supervision of Sabas: The Coenobia of Euthymius and Theoctistus

According to Cyril, Sabas cared for the monasteries of Euthymius and Theoctistus as much as for his own (*V. Sab.* 58, 159). This does not refer to building projects—these were older monasteries—but to their economic maintenance and organizational linkage. The laura of Euthymius became a coenobium between the years 482 and 485 (*V. Euth.* 43–44, 62–66), during the time of Euthymius' successor, Elias of Jericho, who headed the monastery for thirty-eight years (473–511). Afterwards Symeon of Apamea served as *hegoumenos* for three years (511–514); when he died, the monastery was headed by Stephen of Arabia, who received a considerable inheritance which he transferred to the monastery (*V. Euth.* 47–48, 68–69). Stephen was among Sabas' entourage in his journey to Aila in 518 to visit the exiled patriarch Elias of Arabia (*V. Sab.* 60, 161). He served as abbot for twenty-one years (514–535) and was succeeded by Thomas of Apamea, who found a flourishing community and decreased it (*V. Euth.* 48, 69). Eight years later (543) he was succeeded by his deputy, Leontius, who admitted Cyril to the monastery (ibid. 49, 72).

During this period the coenobium of Euthymius served as a place of novitiate for monks wishing to live in the Great Laura (see below, Part III, Chap. 5B). Thus, when the young Cyril came to John the Hesychast asking to be admitted to the Great Laura (543 CE), John directed him to the monastery of Euthymius to receive his novice training (*V. John Hes.* 20, 216; *V. Euth.* 49, 72). Cyril lived there about eleven years (544–555), until he was included among the monks chosen to repopulate the New Laura after the expulsion of all the Origenist monks (*V. Euth.* 60, 83). At the time of the writing of the *Vita*

Sabae (555–557), Gerontius was already abbot. The latter, a native of Medaba, was the grandson of Gerontius the elder, who had been healed by Sabas (*V. Sab.* 46, 137).

During the time of John Moschus, the monastery of Euthymius was still headed by this same Abba Gerontius (*Pratum* 21, 2868). Moschus also mentions an additional monk from this monastery (*Pratum* 124, 2985).

The coenobium of Theoctistus, which during the time of Euthymius shared a steward with the laura of Euthymius, afterwards split off from it. Already after the death of Theoctistus (466), Euthymius had ceased sending young candidates there, preferring to send them to Gerasimus, as he did with the young Cyriacus (*V. Cyr.* 4, 224). After Theoctistus, the monastery was headed by Maris for two years (466–468) and then by Longinus. The split came about in 485, when the monastery of Euthymius became a coenobium and Longinus was succeeded by Paul. The background to the split was a quarrel regarding an inheritance that had been given to both monasteries but was seized by Paul for his monastery alone (*V. Cyr.* 6, 226). Later on, during the sixth century, we do not hear of this monastery except for a report that Sabas cared for it and for the monastery of Euthymius. John Moschus does not mention it. In the eighth century it was abandoned, being inhabited by only one monk, Christophorus, with whom Stephen the Sabaite maintained a friendship (*V. Steph. Sab.* 24–27, ed. *AASS*).

I. Coenobia: Summary

The archaeological remains indicate that the coenobia built by Sabas were monasteries of moderate size, as was appropriate for a Basilian fraternity. These are not the Pachomian foundations of huge dimensions and enormous population. A similar picture is reflected in the literary sources as well. All the coenobia are located in the desert plateau. Three of them are located on the line of the Jebel Muntar-Mar Saba anticline and eastward, deeper in the desert than any of the coenobia that preceded them.

Typologically, the Small Coenobium, the monastery of the Scholarius, and the monastery of Zannos are level coenobia, although the first two are located at the top of a hillock and not on an actual plain. Kastellion, which was built on the ruins of the fortress of Hyrcania, may also be included in this category, while the monastery of the Cave is a clear example of a cliff coenobium (Fig. 66). As for his laurae, here as well Sabas did not adopt a single typological model for the architecture of his monasteries. Each coenobium was surrounded by walls. Only in Kastellion has a burial cave been discovered. The monasteries were supplied with water by means of cisterns that received their water from the drainage of the area of the monastery or by means of conduits.

The dwellings of the monks are of special interest. While we possess a great deal of knowledge regarding the anchorite cells in the laura monasteries, there are almost no substantial findings in Israel regarding the dwellings of the monks in the coenobia. The prevalent hypothesis is that in places such as the monastery of Martyrius or the monastery of Gabriel, the living quarters were on the second floor, which has not been preserved (Hirschfeld 1992, 176–90). It is difficult to assume that in the desert monasteries the monks slept together in dormitories, as is ordered by the Justinianic legislation (see above, Part I, Chap. 2E). In fact, in Khirbet et-Tina small dwelling cells were discovered which were part of the residential wing of the monastery (Hirschfeld 1992, 177–78, figs. 95–96). The ruins in the monastery of the Cave also indicate that the monks lived in separate cells, some of which were installed inside caves in a manner similar to that in which the monks of Mar Saba live today.

In the Egyptian coenobia, such as the monastery of Jeremias in Saqqara (Quibell 1912) or the monastery of Symeon in Aswan (Monneret de Villard 1927), the monks lived in cells and not in dormitories (Walters 1974, 105). Regarding northern Syria, Tchalenko (1953, 19–20, 152–59, 163–67) was hesitant to identify any of the large halls near the church in the magnificent sixth-century monasteries he explored as a common residential hall, or dormitory, and preferred the idea that in this phase the monks continued to dwell in their poor cells from the preceding phase, that of the *hîrtâ*. Others share this opinion.[53] Despite this, in light of the Justinianic legislation, we cannot totally rule out the possibility that also in sixth-century Syria, and possibly in Palestine as well, but not in the desert monasteries, the coenobitic monks shared a common dormitory; however, this requires further study (cf. Hirschfeld 1992, 177).

[53] Festugière 1959, 319–28; Canivet 1977, 213–15. Lassus, who initially held that the monks lived and slept in common dormitories (1947, 276), later changed his mind (*DACL* XV [1953], 1906–13).

3

Additional Building Projects

A. The Hostelries in Jericho and Jerusalem

The monks were forbidden to lodge in a lay hostelry when they were away from the monastery. They were permitted to stay only in a hostelry of a church or of a monastery.[54] When business affairs in Jericho increased—food, building materials, and weaving supplies were bought or collected there—Sabas established a hostelry there for his monks. This hostelry, like that near the Laura, was established in 491. Sabas thereby freed his monks from the need to go and search for a proper place to rest or spend the night when their affairs compelled them to spend the night in Jericho. The hostelry provided familiar surroundings, without worldly temptations, in which the monk continued to be subject to the regulations of his monastery and to the authority of Sabas. It also served as a branch that dealt with the worldly affairs of the Laura in the city: purchasing equipment or food, having work tools repaired, and so on.

Sabas also purchased gardens in Jericho and water rights for them, agricultural estates that were sources of income and that supplied fresh food to the Laura. At a later date he also established in one of the gardens a hostelry for the monastery of Kastellion (*V. Sab.* 31, 116.24). Sabas also used the hostelry in Jericho for occasional meetings with the heads of the coenobia of Kastellion and the Cave (ibid. 46, 136). Cyril found refuge in the hostelry of the coenobium of Euthymius in Jericho after having been ill for six months in the laura of Calamon (*V. John Hes.* 20, 217.4–10). The monastery of Choziba also had a hostelry in Jericho, where the monks found refuge after they abandoned their monastery during the Persian invasion (*V. Geor.* 35, 134).

The existence in Jerusalem of a hostelry belonging to a desert monastery was not exceptional. We know of hostelries there for the laura of Souka, the monastery of Euthymius, and the monastery of Theoctistus (*V. Cyr.* 6, 226). Sabas established four hostelries in Jerusalem, which hosted also non-Sabaitic monks and even lay people, and constituted a source of income.

In 494 he established in Jerusalem a hostelry (*xenodocheion*) for the Great Laura, a sort of urban branch. This was a short time after he had been elected archimandrite of

---

[54] Regarding the obligation of the monk, while staying outside his monastery, to lodge in a hostelry of a church or monastery, see *Koinonia* II, 155: *Pr.* 54; Vööbus 1960b, 27.3: the Regulations of Rabbula, bishop of Edessa in the 5th century; 80.2: the regulations attributed to Rabbula but dated to the 6th century. Monks would also lodge in the houses of laity who were known as admirers of holy men, lovers of monks, and followers of the customs of the Law. Sabas' monks used to lodge with the parents of Cyril (*V. John Hes.* 20, 217); the monks of the Laura would also lodge with the brothers in the village of Bouriron (*V. Sab.* 79, 185); there are also additional examples of this.

the monks, an office that undoubtedly required that he come and stay in Jerusalem more frequently than before. This strengthened his status, independence, and freedom of action in Jerusalem.

The Jerusalem hostelry of the Great Laura consisted of a number of cells in the vicinity of David's Citadel. The cells had been vacated in July 494, when Patriarch Elias assembled the *spoudaioi* of the church of the Holy Sepulcher from their scattered cells into a special monastery which he established for them near the patriarchate, close to the church.

Other cells, located farther north, were transformed by Sabas to serve as a hostelry for visiting monks, and he prepared a third hostelry for monks who were pilgrims to the Holy Land from beyond Palestine. Although this was a manifestation of concern for the welfare of the poor and those without means among them, they were nonetheless sources of income. They were also a first step for someone who desired to be admitted to one of Sabas' monasteries and become part of their community. The hostelries thus served as "recruitment centers."[55] The fourth hostelry in Jerusalem was established for the monastery of Kastellion (*V. Sab.* 31, 116).

The hostelry of the Laura was an important Sabaitic bastion in Jerusalem during the Origenist controversy, a place of refuge for the monks of Sabas and of the monastery of the Bessai who were pursued in the city streets (*V. Sab.* 86, 194.1–12). This hostelry, renowned as the *Metochia* (μετωχία) of Sabas, was an important stronghold of the monastery in Jerusalem for hundreds of years (see also below, Part III, Chap. 5D).

We do not possess any archaeological information about an urban hostelry of a desert monastery. Since the desert monasteries were of moderate size and population, each comprising only a few dozen monks, their hostelries were probably small. Each one undoubtedly included bedrooms, a dining hall, a kitchen, storerooms for food and equipment, and a chapel or church. Explicit mention is made only of a workshop in the hostelry of the Laura (*V. Sab.* 86, 194.1–12).

B. The Church in Moutalaska, the Birthplace of Sabas

During Sabas' first visit to the capital (511–512), he sent a sizeable sum of money to the village of Moutalaska in order to transform the house of his parents into a church in honor of Sts. Cosmas and Damian, which was done (*V. Sab.* 55, 147).

---

[55] Festugière 1962b, 42 n. 57. For the monastic quarter near the Tower of David, see Milik 1960–61, 187–88; for the hostelries and hospitals of Jerusalem, see ibid. 148–51. For the hostel of Sabas in Jerusalem, see Vincent and Abel 1914–26, vol. 2, 518, 911; Tsafrir 1975, 40–42.

Part III: Sabas as an Abbot and Monastic Legislator

1

The Administration of the Great Laura and the Other Sabaite Monasteries

A. The Abbot (ἡγούμενος), the Administrator (διοικητής), and the Relationship between the Sabaite Monasteries and the Great Laura

Sabas, as the founder and expander of the Great Laura, established the architectural framework within which the monks lived: each within his own cell, and within the laura as a community. The regulations he enacted for his monks regarding prayer, work, daily routine, and utensils fashioned the other aspects of daily life.

Cyril emphasizes that, as abbot, Sabas made sure that all the essential commodities needed by his monks would be within the monastery, so that those who wanted to withdraw from the tumult of the outside world would not have to leave its walls and return to the material world (*V Sab.* 18, 102). He took special care that all the elements required to celebrate the Eucharist at the proper times would always be present. To this end once he even permitted the custodian of the church to send some of its vessels to Jerusalem for sale (ibid. 58, 159–60). As founder, he was the one who received the first monks that constituted his community; and later he was also the one who decided who would be admitted to the laura. He determined when one would receive a cell and become a cell dweller, and who would undergo training in the Small Coenobium or in the coenobium of Theodosius. Like the heads of other monasteries, he was entitled to shave the head of a candidate and to dress him in the monastic habit as the first act of joining the monastic congregation (cf. *V. Cyr.* 4, 224; *V. Euth.* 49, 71; *V. Geor.* 4, 99; *V. Sym. Sali* 13, 1685–88).

Like other founders of monasteries, Sabas was the spiritual guide and supreme religious authority for his monks. His authority was not based on formal regulations but on his personality and the monks' admiration for him as a holy man. He therefore combined two roles: community leader in daily affairs and spiritual teacher. This was not the case with his successors. Like him, they carried the banner of the struggle against the Monophysites or against the Origenists; now, however, more than before, other figures gained prominence as spiritual fathers and were revered by pilgrims and the faithful. Thus we hear of John the Hesychast, the spiritual leader of the Great Laura after Sabas' death, who was renowned as a holy man. It was to him that Cyril's mother sent her young son; it was to him that Basilina, the deaconess of the Great Church of Constantinople, came from the capital. In the laura of Souka it was Cyriacus who was admired by all; he was the one who encouraged the fathers of the monastery during the Origenist struggle. In

Choziba, during a slightly later period, George was the venerated saint. None of these three was ever an abbot.[1]

Sabas was described by Cyril as a leader, guide, and shepherd (ἡγούμενος καὶ ὁδηγὸς καὶ ποιμήν) (*V. Sab.* 10, 100.6). The normal meaning of ἡγούμενος in Cyril's writings is father (abbot) of a monastery.[2]

Beyond the initial act of foundation, Sabas continued to care for and improve his monasteries, visiting them frequently and holding meetings with their heads, whom he himself had appointed from among his monks. They continued to regard him as their spiritual father and leader, to whom they turned in time of trouble, for reasons as varied as a lack of water or harassment by the desert shepherds.

Cyril chooses several terms to describe the other monastery heads, which almost certainly indicates the differences in status among them. The fact that those who headed most of the subsidiary Sabaitic monasteries are not called *hegoumenoi* by Cyril, who gives them a lower rank (see below), is of special significance. His writings seem to reflect the concrete reality and are not a literary attempt to aggrandize the more exalted reputation and standing of Sabas. His terminology also indicates the degree of dependence or independence gained by the various monasteries with regard to the Great Laura and to Sabas as founder.

The heads of the other monasteries are normally called administrators or supervisors (διοικηταί), but there are a few instances in which they are called *hegoumenoi*. The use of the first term (διοικητής) stresses the administrative role of the monastery head (Lampe 1961, 373) and a high degree of subordination to Sabas, while the term ἡγούμενος reflects a more autonomous status. The administration (διοίκησις) was mainly in those areas that normally were within the responsibility of the steward (οἰκονόμος) (cf. *V. Cyr.* 6, 226.3). In the prevalent terminology of ecclesiastical administration, *dioiketes* and *oikonomos* are identical, with both referring to the financial administrator of the church (as

---

[1] The difference between these two functions—a *hegoumenos* as the head of the community, as compared with a spiritual guide—can also be found in the monastery of Abba Seridos near Gaza at the end of the 6th century and in the Syrian monasteries. See Dorotheus of Gaza, *Vita Dosithei* 1, 122–23; Canivet 1977, 229 n. 3.

[2] Patrich 1989, 251 n. 2. Similarly in Theodore of Petra, in the Justinianic legislation (Granič 1929–30), in the *Pratum,* in the writings of Antony of Choziba, and in later writings. On the other hand, in Greek monastic literature this term is extremely rare in the 4th and 5th centuries; see Festugière, *HM* X.1, 67 n. 3 and XVIII.1, 53.2. Sarapion is defined as *hegoumenos*, not of a single monastery but of many communities in the district of Arsinoe, which together numbered ca. 10,000 monks, and who was also responsible for financial administration (οἰκονομία). In the Pachomian terminology, on the other hand, the *hegoumenos* is always an abbot of a single monastery (*Koinonia* I, 416 n. 1 to *G*[1] 79). The term is absent in the writings of Basil. The head of the Basilian brotherhood (ἀδελφότης) is called προεστώς—the one standing at the head, president (Amand de Mendieta 1957, 47 and n. 2). The leadership (προστασία) as the office of the abbot is mentioned also in *HPh* IV.5, and the abbot is at times called προστατεύων. See also *HPh* III.22; Canivet 1977, 227–29. The head of the Pachomian monastery is called *apa,* and in Syriac the head of the monastery is *rîšdayrâ.*

In Greek inscriptions from the Byzantine period in Palestine, the term *hegoumenos* appears with the meaning of "abbot of a monastery," in inscriptions dated to the second half of the 6th century (Meimaris 1986, 239–46; Di Segni, personal communication). This corresponds to the impression we receive from the literary sources described above. See also below, Part IV, Chap. 2.

an institution and not as an architectural structure) (Du Cange, *Glossarium*, s.v. οἰκονομία; Canivet and Leroy-Molinghen 1977, 472 n. 4).

We shall first survey Sabas' laurae and coenobia and then discuss the monasteries of his disciples. Of all the monasteries, the New Laura enjoyed the greatest amount of autonomy; as its history shows, a rebellious spirit was not foreign to its monks. Its abbots are all described as *hegoumenoi*—a phenomenon not found in any other Sabaitic monastery. The first abbot of the New Laura, John the Anchorite, a monk of Sabas' Laura, was appointed by him (*V. Sab.* 36, 124). Later abbots were chosen by the monks themselves, but their election also required Sabas' approval and confirmation (ibid.). Only in the case of Mamas does Cyril relate that the election was made without consulting Sabas (ibid. 125). However, in this case it seems that Cyril intentionally refrained from relating that Sabas confirmed the appointment of an abbot with Origenist tendencies. The autonomy that the New Laura enjoyed was undoubtedly a function of the circumstances of its establishment, the composition of its congregation (those rebelling against Sabas), their intellectual level, its geographic distance, and the fact that this was a large laura, apparently second in size only to the Great Laura. It had its beginnings with the 60 rebel monks, and when it was resettled in 555 CE, it had a population of 120 monks.

The heads of the Heptastomos laura, the brothers Paul and Andreas, are defined as "administrators" (διοικηταί). Řezáč (1958, 116) is of the opinion that being a laura it enjoyed autonomy, but the available sources indicate that there was a clear distinction between its status and that of the New Laura. Its high degree of dependence upon the Great Laura, which was only a short distance away, is reflected in the fact that even the food for the fraternal meal would be sent there by Sabas from the Great Laura (*V. Sab.* 39, 130).

Jeremias as well was appointed to administer (διοικεῖν) the laura named after him (ibid. 74, 179). It was founded during the last year of Sabas' life, so he was unable to care for it after its establishment, as he had done with his other monasteries. However, when it was founded he gave its monks the same set of regulations that the Great Laura had, and in this way their affiliation with the Great Laura continued even after his death.

The largest and most elaborate of Sabas' coenobia was that of the Scholarius. The relationship of this monastery to Sabas was not merely the result of a one-time act of establishment. Sabas continued to occupy himself with its construction and consolidation after the first phase, that of settling his monks in the Tower of Eudocia; according to Cyril, until his dying day he did not cease from visiting the place and showering an abundance of gifts on it (*V. Sab.* 38, 127).

John, who headed the coenobium for thirty-five years, enjoyed a great deal of autonomy. Cyril describes him as διοικητὴς καὶ ἡγούμενος (ibid.). It seems that the large community established there, the extended period of John's office, and his personal reputation brought about much more autonomy for this coenobium than for others founded by Sabas. It is not inconceivable that John attained his high status only after many years in office, possibly only after Sabas' death. It is also possible that the title *hegoumenos* was intended to emphasize the spiritual leadership of the community, in contrast to the administrative role reflected in the first title.

When Kastellion was founded, Sabas appointed an administrator (διοικητής) to head it, with his disciple as an assistant; both came from among the ranks of his monks. The assistant became the administrator of the monastery after the death of his predecessor, and he chose his two brothers as assistants. These would later head the monastery in succession (*V. Sab.* 27, 112.20–25; 46, 136). The administrators of Kastellion and the Cave would meet with Sabas in the hostelry of the Laura in Jericho, where they could consult him on various matters concerning the administration of their monasteries. The coenobium of Kastellion did possess property of its own: two hostelries, one in Jericho and the other in Jerusalem. Řezáč (1958, 116) interprets this as indicating some degree of autonomy, but it was Sabas who gave the property to Kastellion, and we should not overestimate the coenobium's degree of autonomy based on its ownership of property alone. Both Kastellion and the Cave were entitled to receive contributions directly from the faithful (*V. Sab.* 80, 186: the event is related after Sabas' death).

Sabas appointed one of the monks of the Laura as administrator (διοικητής) of the monks of the Cave. After the first one died, the leadership of the monastery (ἡγεμονία)[3] passed, in turn, to three of the monks there (*V. Sab.* 37, 126.20–27; 46, 136; *V. John Hes.* 22, 218). The last of these, Eustathius, filled this position when Cyril was engaged in writing the *Vita Ioanni Hesychastae* (559 CE).

The question arises: are there differences of meaning between ἡγεμονία and ἡγουμενία, or are these merely insignificant nuances? And if there are differences of meaning, are they the result of Cyril's literary tendency to give prominence thereby to Sabas as the head of the hierarchy, or do they reflect the actual reality? It is known that Cyril chose his words with care. It is therefore quite possible that the fact that Cyril defines the post of the heads of the monastery of the Cave, from the second one on, as ἡγεμονία, and refrains from explicitly applying to them the term ἡγούμενος, is not incidental and that

[3] This term, with the meaning of rule and leadership, is an ancient term, which already appears in early periods, and has no special connection to the role of monastery head. Theodoret, in *HPh*, generally uses the term ἡγεμονία with the meaning of the office of head of the monastery, while at the same time he uses the term in a secular sense to denote the authority of the emperor or of his representatives, and in one place it also denotes the office of bishopric. The word ἡγούμενος as a substantive, which is more prevalent in later monastic literature to denote the abbot (see above, n. 2), appears in *HPh* only once (III.22), while the form ἡγουμενία, derived from this term, does not appear in Theodoret at all (and according to Canivet, this word appears for the first time in the writings of Theodore of Petra; see below). In place of the term ἡγούμενος, which was prevalent to denote the heads of the philosophical schools, and in the New Testament to denote Christians possessing a certain degree of authority, but which in his time had not yet been accepted in monastic circles, Theodoret prefers the substantive of the verb ἡγεμονεύω, i.e., ἡγεμών. But this appears in his writings only once (XXVI.5), to denote the position of the head of the monastery of Teleda II. On the other hand, he also gives this title to Romulus (X.9), and Romulus was not an abbot but rather a civil officer. The common meaning of this word is military leader or governor. The monastic hierarchy, as described in the monastery of Teleda II, alongside Helidorus, the abbot of the monastery, are called προστατεύοντες and ἡγεμόνες (XXVI.5–6). See Canivet 1977, 227–30.

Cyril uses the term ἡγεμονία when speaking of monastery heads in two additional instances: (a) Gerasimus handed over the leadership of his coenobium to two brothers, Basil and Stephen (*V. Cyr.* 5, 225.21; *V. Ger.* 10); (b) in his reference to Gelasius, who succeeded to the leadership of the Great Laura (*V. Sab.* 84, 189.13–14). In contrast, the term ἡγουμενία, derived from ἡγούμενος, also appears in Cyril's writings. He uses it when speaking of the term of Maris as head of the monastery of Theoctistus (*V. Euth.* 36, 55.17; *V. Sab.* 10, 93.16) and of the term of Abraamius as head of his monastery in Cratea (*V. Ab.* 244.26 and 246.27). Theodore of Petra preceded Cyril in the use of this term (*V. Theod.* 6, 14).

its purpose is to emphasize their administrative rather than spiritual role and their subordination to Sabas. At the same time, however, it should be remembered that he uses the same term for the post of Gelasius at the head of the Great Laura, and this abbot was famous for his vigorous struggle against the Origenists; it is not clear why he refrained from defining him as ἡγούμενος.[4] It is possible, therefore, that there are no essential differences of meaning in Cyril's usage of ἡγεμονία and ἡγουμενία, and that in this case we are to conclude that in the course of time the degree of autonomy of the monastery of the Cave increased.

The title of Zannos—Sabas' disciple who founded a monastery—is not mentioned, but his status was probably the same as that of the heads of the other coenobia (Kastellion and the Cave). The proximity of this monastery to the Laura undoubtedly increased its dependency. The life of the monks here, as in the other Sabaitic monasteries, was regulated in accordance with the rules given them by Sabas (V. Sab. 42, 133).

In speaking of the monasteries of Sabas' disciples (ibid. 16, 99.20–25; 36, 124.18), Cyril refrained from giving them the title of *hegoumenos* and noted only the fact that they established monasteries. The author's tendentiousness seems to be conspicuous here.

Among all the coenobia, only the Small Coenobium did not have its own administrator. It apparently was perceived as an integral part of the Great Laura and was geographically the closest to it. It is possible that this is why it was not included in Cyril's concluding list of the monasteries under Sabas' supervision and care (ibid. 58, 158).

Cyril's list also includes the coenobium of Euthymius and that of Theoctistus. From the death of Euthymius on, the heads of his coenobium are defined by Cyril as *hegoumenoi* (V. Euth. 47–48, 68–70). Only Gerontius, whose term of office was later, during the time of Cyril's writing, is defined as a *dioiketes* of the coenobium (V. Sab. 46, 217). This probably reflects its dependency on and subordination to the Great Laura, whose novitiate it was at that time. This dependency is also implied by the list.

It is also possible to include the laura of Souka—the Old Laura established by Chariton—within the Sabaite monasteries. Its heads and monks supported the Great Laura during the entire Origenist controversy. Even before, when the 60 dissident monks withdrew from the Great Laura, the abbot of Souka refused to accept them in his monastery (V. Sab. 36, 122). Close relations were maintained between John the Hesychast and Cyriacus, the spiritual leaders of the two laurae, during the course of the Origenist controversy. The close ties between these two important laurae was so intensive that Cassianus, priest of the Great Laura, became the abbot of Souka for eight years and afterwards headed the Great Laura (V. Sab. 88, 196). Another monastery that may be included among Sabas' monasteries is that of the Eunuchs near Jericho (ibid. 69, 171), which occupied one of the two coenobia of Elias. It was established ca. 530 by the eunuchs of

---

[4] Cyril generally precedes his name with the title ἀββᾶς (V. Sab. 87, 195.2; 84, 190.6; 85, 191.9; 87, 194.13–15). He also gives this title to Eustathius, the head of the monastery of the Cave (V. John Hes. 22, 218), but Cyril does not reserve this exclusively for monastery heads, and he also uses it for John the Hesychast (ibid. 218.15). In the Byzantine literature, the title ἀββᾶς is an honorific title and does not necessarily refer to the abbot of a monastery. See Dorotheus of Gaza, 124 n. 1. Jerome opposed the usage of this title, which was introduced by the end of the 4th century through Syrian influence. See *Commentarium in Epistolam ad Galatas* 4, 6 (PL 26, 400). The Coptic *apa*, similar to the Greek ἀββᾶς, is derived from the Aramaic Syriac.

the patrician Anicia Juliana, an admirer of Sabas in Constantinople (see below, Part IV, Chap. 1).

The Sabaite monasteries never constituted a centralist union, like the Pachomian federation, where there was a clear hierarchy and a well-defined link to Pachomius as the founder and to the chief monastery of Phbow. The subordination of Sabas, which originated in the act of foundation, continued with his constant care for their existence and prosperity and in the regulations he gave them. These ensured the continuance after his death of the relationship between the monasteries and the largest and most important one, the Great Laura. The relative status of the heads of the other monasteries was determined, to a great extent, by their personal attributes and by the duration of their service; it was not the result of a written, defined hierarchy. Some were totally subordinate to the Great Laura, while others enjoyed some degree—at times a very great degree—of autonomy. These differences of status indicate that Cyril's writings do indeed reflect an actual reality, even though his tendentiousness is reflected in some passages.

B. The Steward (οἰκονόμος) and the Deputy (δευτεράριος)

Sabas was aided in the daily administration of the Laura by the steward (οἰκονόμος), who was second to Sabas in its administrative hierarchy. The steward of the Laura would impose various tasks upon the monks and the novices (*V. John Hes.* 5, 205; cf. *V. Euth.* 18, 28), and when tasks were changed (see below), he was entitled to select the monks with whom he desired to work. This selection was probably conditional upon Sabas' approval and confirmation. Thus it is related that it was the steward who chose John the Hesychast to be head of the hostelry and cook (*V. John Hes.* 6, 206). The steward supplied the monks with palm fronds (βάϊα) for work in their cells, and he gave the completed baskets to the head of the hostelry (*V. Sab.* 44, 135). The steward was responsible for all the food and water necessary for the common meal being in the food storerooms, which were under his authority (*V. Sab.* 58, 160; cf. *V. Euth.* 17, 27; 18, 28). Food supplies were brought to him, and he stored them in the *oikonomeion* (*V. Sab.* ibid.), a structure that included the food storerooms and probably also the dwelling cell of the steward (Hirschfeld 1987, 213; 1992, 19 n. 6). The steward was also responsible for the purchase of wheat from Macherontes and its transport from the Dead Sea to the Laura, for which he hired she-camels from the Saracens. Donations given to the monastery could be entrusted to him (*V. Sab.* 81, 187). He therefore was charged with the economic management of the Laura, and he dealt with the necessary funds. Rule 14 of the Sinai *Typikon* (Part III, Chap. 5D, below), from the twelfth to thirteenth century, states that the *oikonomos* had to be chosen from among the Syrian monks of the Laura, while the position of *hegoumenos* was re-served for a Greek-speaking monk.

The tasks of accommodating and feeding pilgrims, which in the laura of Euthymius were under the responsibility of the steward (*V. Euth.* 17, 22), were within the purview of the head of the hostelry in the Great Laura. We also hear that the tasks of the steward in the laura of the Towers, established by James, Sabas' disciple, included bringing the belongings of the dead to the *oikonomeion* (*Pratum* 5, 2856–57). The sources similarly mention a steward in the Old Laura (*V. Cyr.* 7, 227) and in Sinai (*Pratum* 125, 2988), where the archaeological ruins indicate that laurae, rather than coenobia, were prevalent. The only instance in the writings of Cyril of a steward in a coenobium is from the monastery of Theoctistus (*V. Euth.* 39, 59); the other references are to laurae. But this function is also attested by John Cassian (*Inst.* IV.20, 148) in a passage concerning his coenobium near Bethlehem, which he left ca. 385.

An experienced monk would be appointed steward after he had already lived in a cell for a few years. John the Hesychast was chosen for this office after he had lived in the Laura for more than five years, three of which were as a cell dweller (*V. John Hes.* 7, 207).

How long was the steward's term of office? We shall first examine the situation in the laurae, to which most of the available information refers, and then in the coenobia. In contrast to the abbot of the monastery, who was appointed for life, the steward would be replaced from time to time (*V. Sab.* 81, 187). In a laura there was a clear conflict between the community's need for this position and the fact that the appointment removed the monk from the silence of his cell and prevented him from living as a cell dweller. Therefore, in a laura, more than in a coenobium, it was imperative to specify the period of service to the community required of the steward and those performing other services which will be mentioned below.

How long was the steward's term of office? A fixed date was established for all appointments, namely, the beginning of the indiction year, September 1 (Schwartz 1939, 299, s.v. διακονία). Consequently, the minimum term of office for each position was one year. This apparently was the length of time served by Cyriacus in the Old Laura (*V. Cyr.* 7, 227). It is also possible that Domitian, the first steward in the laura of Euthymius, did not serve in this position for a longer period of time (*V. Euth.* 17, 22). John the Hesychast, however, served as steward in the Great Laura for three years, and during the period of his term of office (ἐπὶ τῆς διακονίας αὐτοῦ) the Laura flourished and was fully inhabited (*V. John Hes.* 7, 207.5).[5] Consequently, a monk's term of office in this important position, essential to the administration of the Laura, was likely to be renewed each year at the changeover date. Thus the monk filling the position would continue to hold it for a number of years on condition that his service was satisfactory to the abbot and the community. The complexity of the tasks and the skills needed to execute them properly required that a steward hold the post for a number of years for the community's benefit. A term of office, even of three years, did not entail for the monk an excessively prolonged period of absence from the laura's way of life that he had chosen. Although only the case of John the Hesychast is mentioned in the sources, it is possible that a three-year term of service (*diakonia*) was the accepted one for a steward, even if the extension of this term required yearly confirmation.

In the Heptastomos laura, as well as in most of the Sabaitic coenobia, the post of steward was combined with that of the head of the monastery, as we learn from the title διοικητής, administrator (Du Cange, *Glossarium*, s.v. οἰκονομία). It is clear therefore that in this case the holder of the post changed only when the abbot changed.[6]

---

[5] For the chronological reconstruction of the history and offices of John the Hesychast, see below, Part V, Chap. 2.

[6] Palladius (*HL* X.3, 30.11; 6, 31.11) mentions an *oikonomos* in the anchorite community of Pambo in Nitria, where a way of life similar to that of the Judean desert laurae was maintained (see Part A, Chap. 3, above). The *oikonomos* there administered the financial affairs of the community. One of the papyri from the 6th century discovered in Egypt is a receipt written by the διοικητής of a monastery to the sons of a person

In a coenobium, the term of the *oikonomos* was likely to be of longer duration than in a laura, due to the different way of life of its monks. The only information in Cyril's writings about a steward in a coenobium refers, as noted above, to the coenobium of Theoctistus at the time close to Euthymius' death (472). Cyril does not, however, state the duration of Elias of Jericho's term as steward before he was selected to serve as Euthymius' successor at the head of his laura (*V. Euth.* 39, 59). John Cassian's testimony refers to coenobitic practice about a century earlier.

We hear of a steward in the monastery of Euthymius as long as it was a laura. Later on, during Thomas' abbacy (534–542), we hear about his deputy (δευτεράριος) Leontius, who succeeded Thomas as abbot after the latter's death (*V. Euth.* 48, 70.13). At this time the monastery had already been a coenobium for many years. In the coenobium of Theodosius as well, we do not hear of a steward alongside the abbot of the monastery, but rather of a deputy (δευτεράριος). The Armenian Sophronius served for fifteen years (515–529) in this post before succeeding Theodosius as head of the monastery. Before this he had performed many different tasks, to the satisfaction of all (*V. Theod.* 240). If in this coenobium, the largest of the Judean desert coenobia, there had been a steward in addition to the deputy, then it would have had an administrative hierarchy more complex than that of the Great Laura or of the laurae in general. However, there is no information in the desert sources regarding this post in the monastery of Theodosius. Mention is made there of those responsible (οἱ διακονοῦντες) for the accommodation and feeding of pilgrims (Theod. Petr., *V. Theod.* 36–39) and of those responsible for the purchase of new garments for the monks (ibid. 81). We would expect that the latter task would be entrusted to the *oikonomos*, for the possessions of the monks who had died, including their garments, were kept in the *oikonomeion* (cf. *Pratum* 5, 2856–57).

In the writings of Antony of Choziba mention is made of a great number of service tasks in the Choziba coenobium; the stewardship is not one of them. Furthermore, a study of this source indicates that tasks that presumably should have been under his responsibility were divided among other functionaries: the abbot was the one who appointed the young George as an assistant to the gardener (*V. Geor.* 4, 99), and it was he who, with the aid of a lay purchasing agent (προαγοραστής), dealt with the purchase of wheat for the monastery (ibid. 25, 124), tasks that in the Great Laura were entrusted to the steward. Other tasks were entrusted to the storekeeper (κελλαρίτης), a service filled by the monks in turn. The storekeeper would supervise the baking of bread, in which a few monks were engaged, and he was responsible, of course, for the monastery's food stores (ibid. 37, 136). Antony, who was storekeeper at the hostelry in Jericho, where the fathers found refuge after the Persian conquest, had to bargain with laymen and even with women as part of his duties (ibid. 35, 134). A storekeeper is also mentioned in one of the inscriptions found in the monastery burial cave (Schneider 1931, 328, inscr. 210);[7]

---

mentioned there, for the lease of land (Bell 1917, 109, pap. no. 1704). This *dioiketes* was none other than the *oikonomos* of the monastery.

An *oikonomos* is mentioned in a number of Greek inscriptions discovered in the Holy Land and in Transjordan; however, as far as can be learned from their content and place of discovery, the reference is to the *oikonomos* of a church and not to that of a monastery (Meimaris 1986, 256–59).

[7] It is possible that the monk from the coenobium of Martyrius mentioned in *V. Euth.* (50, 72), who at the time of his appointment to a certain service received the keys from the altar, was also a cellarer.

a steward is not mentioned in them. In Choziba and in other coenobia, it was the abbot who dealt with financial matters. In the coenobium of Theoctistus as well, Sabas gave the coins he had brought with him from Egypt to the abbot of the monastery (*V. Sab.* 9, 93), and in the coenobium of Penthucla near the Jordan mention is made of the handing over of silver and gold to the abbot (*Pratum*, add. Nissen 13, 368). In the Great Laura contributions were given to the *oikonomos*, as was mentioned above, not to the abbot.

Also in the Justinianic legislation, which deals only with coenobitic monasteries, no mention is made of an *oikonomos* of a monastery (cf. Granič 1929–30, 29).[8] On the other hand, it is stated there that the legal responsibility for the financial administration of the monastery's property is imposed on the *hegoumenos* and, in the case of a church, on the *oikonomos* (*Cod. Iust.* I 3, 55, 2; *Nov.* 7, chap. 12).

It is possible, therefore, that over time a change took place in the administrative organization of the coenobia. In Euthymius' time, the monastery of Theoctistus had a steward (*V. Euth.* 39, 58), as did the monastery of John Cassian near Bethlehem at the end of the fourth century. After Euthymius' death his laura turned into a coenobium, and, according to his orders, the two monasteries—his and that of Theoctistus—came under one administration conducted by one steward: μίαν διοίκησιν ὑπὸ ἕνα ὄντα οἰκονό-μον (*V. Cyr.* 6, 226.3). This joint administration was cancelled by a rift in the relations between the two monasteries in 485, only a short time after the conversion of the laura of Euthymius into a coenobium. In the new situation, did each coenobium have a steward, or had another form of organization already been instituted? As noted earlier, from this period on there is no mention in the extant sources of a steward in the coenobia. Regarding the coenobium of Euthymius, there is an allusion from 535 in which a *hegoumenos* and his deputy are mentioned (*V. Euth.* 48, 70.13); a similar structure existed in the coenobium of Theodosius. It seems that from the beginning of the sixth century, and perhaps even earlier, this had become the common form of administration in the coenobia. This is evidenced by a mid-sixth-century inscription from the Kyra Maria monastery in Beth Shean (Scythopolis), which mentions a *hegoumenos* and a deputy, *deuterarios* (Fitzgerald 1939, 16, inscr. 7), and by an inscription of approximately the same date from the monastery of St. Catherine on Mount Sinai (Meimaris 1986, 249–51).[9]

This dual administration, in pairs, is to be found also in the secondary Sabaitic monasteries. In the coenobium of the Scholarius, Olympius received the second place in the administration of the monastery: τὰ δεύτερα τῆς τοῦ μοναστηρίου κυβερνήσεως (*V. Ab.* 245–46). Theodosius served as an assistant to Paul, the administrator of Kastellion, and when he became the administrator, he chose two assistants for himself (*V. Sab.* 27, 112.20–25). It is possible that the coenobium of Zannos was also administered jointly by the brothers Zannos and Benjamin.

[8] The *oikonomos* or *dioiketes* of a monastery is not mentioned in *HPh*. On the other hand, in the Regulations of the Syrian monasteries he is called *rabbaytâ* (or *rabbaita*, pl. *rabbay bate*), a term parallel to the Greek οἰκονόμος, which is frequently mentioned. See the index in Vööbus 1960a, entry *rabbaita*. The picture in the coenobia of Syria is therefore different from that revealed by the sources and inscriptions dealing with the monasteries of Palestine (on this see also above, Part I, Chap. 2C). In the Pachomian monasteries, divided into houses, each house was headed by a housemaster (οἰκιακός) and there was an *oikonomos* for the entire Pachomian federation.

[9] *Deuterarios* appears in the list of signatures of monks on the *libellus* sent to Pope Agapetus in 536. See Granič 1929–30, 26. For more on the office of the *deuterarios*, see Festugière 1962a, 125 n. 157; Lampe 1961, 339.

This arrangement was not limited to coenobia. In the Heptastomos laura, Sabas appointed from the outset two administrators, Paul and Andreas, "brothers in the flesh," of Greek origin (*V. Sab.* 39, 130.20–22). But the first instance in which we hear of administration in pairs is in the laura of Gerasimus, a combination of laura and coenobium, in which, after his death in 475, the "brothers in the flesh" Basil and Stephen served in the administration (ἡγεμονία) for six years (*V. Ger.* 10; *V. Cyr.* 5, 225.21). After them, however, the fathers of the monastery elected a single *hegoumenos,* Eugenius, who had been the deputy of Sabas as archimandrite of the monks (*V. Theod.* 239.12), and who headed the monastery for forty-five years until his death in 526 (*V. Ger.* 10).

Basil of Caesarea (*Reg. fus.* 45, 1032–33) had already established that each monastery must appoint a deputy for the abbot, who would administer the institution and supervise the brotherhood when the abbot was unable to do so because of travel, illness, or for any other reason. The candidate for this position had to be found worthy by the abbot and by the community. He was not necessarily the most elderly or senior among the community of monks. Basil emphasized that this arrangement was meant to prevent a democratic form of administration (σχῆμα δημοκρατικόν) in the absence of the abbot of the monastery, which had led in the past to violations of rules and breaches of discipline. The deputy had to supervise the community and guide it spiritually; he was the sole recipient of the queries and requests of guests, and other monks were forbidden to engage in this. He had to excel in judgment, be of exemplary conduct and faith, and be a wise administrator.

Faithful to Basil's teachings, we find in Theodosius' community, from its beginnings, those who held the position of his deputy (οἱ αὐτοῦ τὰ δεύτερα φέροντες), who cared for the material needs of the community when it seemed to them that Theodosius did not pay attention to this (Theod. Petr., *V. Theod.* 25). When the monastery became a large coenobium, the Armenian Sophronius served as Theodosius' deputy, *deuterarios.*

A sixth-century (rather than a fourth-century) reality is reflected, most probably, from the narrative about Chariton stating that upon leaving Douka he handed over the leadership to the one after him (τῷ εὐθὺς μετ᾽ αὐτὸν) (*V. Char.* 22, 32; Di Segni 1990a, 78 n. 33).

The importance of the position of steward and the skills needed to fill it apparently led in the course of time, in the coenobitic monasteries, to an additional permanent position being created alongside that of the abbot, in place of the temporary post of the steward, namely, the position of the deputy, who generally succeeded the abbot as the head of the monastery upon the latter's death. The deputy and the abbot carried out most of the economic tasks that previously had been imposed upon the steward. The different ways of life maintained in the coenobia and in the laurae led to a different development in their administrative organization. A permanent administrative position would prevent the laura monk from maintaining the life of a cell dweller, while in the coenobium, the installation of a deputy, as a permanent position, was less problematic in terms of disturbance to the maintenance of the routine way of life by the monk who held this position.

In the laurae the steward held a senior administrative position, second in rank to the abbot, but the limited term of office and the frequent changes prevented him from becoming also second in the hierarchy in terms of authority. The priests were superior to him (cf. *V. Euth.* 18, 28) and of course also the monks who excelled in their way of life, such as John the Hesychast, Cyriacus, or Abraamius, even if the latter did not fill any formal position in the administration of the community. The extant sixth-century sources therefore provide us with a diverse picture of the monastic administration, with differences between laurae and coenobia.

The term *deuterarios* is not mentioned in the Codex of Justinian (Granič 1929–30, 26), but there is reference to the second in rank (δεύτερος)—the next in line (ἐφεξεστός)—or to the third in rank (τρίτος). It is also stated that this (ecclesiastical?) hierarchy is not decisive when a successor for the abbot is to be elected (above, Part I, Chap. 2E).[10] In the monasteries of the Judean desert, as a general rule, it was the deputy (ὁ δευτεράριος) who succeeded the abbot in his post. This position was not just an honorary title, and from the outset a person suited for leadership and administration was elected or appointed to fill it.

In Syrian monasticism as well we hear of the "third in the monastery" (τρίτος τῆς μονῆς) (*HPh* III.22, 288; see also Canivet 1977, 230), but mention is also made there of "the second in the administration of the monastery" (τῆς ἡγεμονίας ἐκείνης τὰ δεύτερα διέπων) and many other ranks (cf. Part I, Chap. 2C, above).

The hierarchy in the Pachomian coenobia was more complex than that which we find in the monasteries in Palestine, Cappadocia, or Syria. The monastery, which was composed of a number of houses, was headed by the abbot of the monastery, the *apa*, to whom the deputy (δεύτερος) was subordinate. The duties of the deputy included reporting to the *apa* everything that happened in each of the houses, as well as selling the monastery's products in Alexandria and purchasing there what was necessary for its needs (*HL* XXXII.4, 90.7; 8, 94.2)—economic tasks, which in Nitria had been under the purview of the *oikonomos*. Each house (οἶκος) in a Pachomian monastery was headed by a housemaster (οἰκιακός), under whom there was also a deputy. The entire Pachomian federation had an *oikonomos*, to whom a biennial report was given by the monastery heads (see Part I, Chap. 2B, above).

The hierarchy in the Judean desert coenobia was much simpler than that of the Egyptian or Syrian coenobia. It consisted of an abbot and his deputy, recommended by Basil the Great. This simple administrative structure was appropriate for monasteries of moderate population, in the spirit of the Basilian brotherhood. Such was the size of most of the Judean desert coenobia.

C. Other Tasks

According to John Cassian, in Mesopotamia, Palestine, Cappadocia, and the entire East the service tasks, which included cleaning the monastery, collecting firewood, carrying water, washing lentils and legumes, and cooking, were performed in a cycle of weekly rotation. Such was the situation in his monastery near Bethlehem. The number of serving monks in each coenobium was determined in accordance with its size. The term of service lasted until the Sunday dinner, when the rotation of offices was done in a cere-

---

[10] It is possible that the "second in rank" or the "third in rank" mentioned in the Codex of Justinian are merely honorary titles taken from the order of seating in the church (regarding the permanent seats in the monastery church, cf. *V. Ab.* 9, 235).

mony in the church. Those finishing their term washed the legs of all the rest, who were praying for them, and on Monday, after matins, they delivered to their successors all the vessels and utensils required for their ministry. This change of offices was done under the supervision of the steward. In Egypt, on the other hand, the care for the cellar and the kitchen was assigned to an approved monk, who served as cook as long as his strength and age permitted. There was no weekly rotation of this task (*Inst.* IV.19–22, 146–53). It is mainly with Scetis that John Cassian was familiar.[11] In the later Palestinian sources, which refer to the monasteries of the Judean desert, there is no allusion to weekly offices. The tasks were assigned for an entire year. It seems that under Egyptian influence a change took place in Palestine.

All the officials (οἱ διακονήται: *V. Geor.* 20, 119) were of course required to fulfill their duties faithfully, for the welfare of the monks and to the satisfaction of the abbot. It seems that when each individual was appointed to his position, there was a sort of loyalty oath ceremony. An allusion to this is provided by what is told about a monk who held a position (διακονία) in the coenobium of Martyrius, who at the time of his appointment received the keys from the altar, as a pledge of faithful service, and at the end of his term had to return the keys there (*V. Euth.* 50, 72).

Guest Master and Cook

In Palestine, both the coenobia and laurae possessed hostelries. The care and feeding of pilgrims was entrusted in the laura of Euthymius, at least during its early phase, to the steward (*V. Euth.* 17, 27; 22, 35). In the Great Laura the task was entrusted, from the beginning, to a special official, the hosteler (ξενοδόχος). The standard period of service was one year (*V. John Hes.* 6, 206; *V. Sab.* 40, 131). The hostelry of the Laura was built in 491 (*V. Sab.* 25–26). In the beginning, the task of hosteler was imposed upon the cook (μάγειρος), a post whose existence was essential in the Laura from the outset. John the Hesychast served in this office during his first year in the Laura, when the hostelry was under construction and had not yet begun to function; he would cook for the builders (*V. John Hes.* 5, 205). At the beginning of the second year of his stay in the Laura, on September 1, 492, John was also appointed as guest master, thereby becoming the first monk to fill both positions. As part of his double office, he cooked food twice a day for the workers engaged in building the Small Coenobium and even carried the food to them, a distance of 10 *stadia* (ca. 2 km). He did this in addition to his other office as hosteler, responsible for the accommodation of the guests (*V. John Hes.* 6, 206). It is quite conceivable that the masons slept in the hostelry during the period of construction.

John the Hesychast was not the only monk to serve in this double capacity. Something similar is related about the monk James; as part of his duties, he was required to cook for those going out to the desert to harvest the *mannouthion* (*V. Sab.* 40, 131), a brief, seasonal task for which many monks, including cell dwellers, were mobilized (*V. Geor.* 14, 100–111). During regular periods, however, cooking for the monks was limited to the communal Saturday and Sunday meals, because the cell dwellers would take with them

---

[11] Cassian's reason for this is the importance attributed by the Egyptians to the work, which might be disturbed by frequent terms of weekly service. In the Pachomian monasteries a weekly rotation of services did exist between the various houses. The communities of Scetis were laurae. Service tasks were necessary in laurae as well as in coenobia.

to their cells enough food for the other days of the week. We should not ignore the fact, however, that there were also in the Laura monks who, due to the positions they filled, were not cell dwellers. These monks engaged in quite strenuous labor, and it is possible that a cooked meal had to be prepared daily for them, as was the case during the time of the *mannouthion* harvest. At any rate, the work load imposed upon the cook in cooking for the monks of the Laura was not uniform during all days of the week: most of the burden was toward the weekend.

In contrast, it was necessary to cook every day for the guests and pilgrims (and for the workers). It therefore was logical to establish a single kitchen in the Laura, locating it in the hostelry. This apparently was the reason why the two tasks were initially imposed upon a single monk. It seems, however, that in later stages, after the Great Laura had become a center attracting many visitors and pilgrims, as well as having a large population of monks, the positions of hosteler and cook were split, especially since the construction work continued simultaneously and it was necessary to continue cooking for the workers as well. Indeed, in a period later than the story about James, we hear about the Laura cook (ὁ μάγειρος τῆς λαύρας), who is not the hosteler (*V. Sab.* 48, 138).

A hostelry is also mentioned in the laura of Souka, where Cyriacus served for one year as hosteler (*V. Cyr.* 7, 226). It may reasonably be assumed that in other laurae as well there were arrangements for the accommodation of visitors, either in a separate building or in special cells set aside for them, and that a monk was appointed whose task it was to care for their needs.

In the coenobium of Theodosius, where there were three hostelries, one for important pilgrims, one for monks, and the third for the poor, there almost certainly were separate officials for each of the hostelries, although these are not mentioned in the sources. In contrast, mention is made, in the plural, of those responsible for the accommodation of pilgrims during the public celebrations held in the monastery on Palm Sunday and on the commemoration day of the Theotokos (feast of the Dormition), when many tables were prepared for them at the festive meal (Theod. Petr., *V. Theod.* 14–15, 36–39). Mention is also made of a guest master in the coenobium of Euthymius (*V. Euth.* 48, 70) and in Choziba (*V. Geor.* 4, 99; 23, 122; 57, 356). In both cases it would seem that he was working within the coenobium itself, and not in a separate building outside its walls, such as the one discovered in the excavations outside the monastery of Martyrius (Magen and Talgam 1990).

It may reasonably be assumed that in the Sabaitic coenobia—certainly in the largest of them, the monastery of the Scholarius—there was a monk in charge of this service. Even if there was no separate building that served as a hostelry, it could have been installed in a separate wing intended for this purpose. Olympius, for example, during the first period of his stay there, was regarded as a guest. In the smaller, secondary Sabaite monasteries as well, a duty roster was probably established for the care of guests, such as John Moschus and Sophronius, who went from one monastery to another, or Marcianus, who aided Sabas in the construction of the monastery of the Cave.

In the Great Laura the guest master was entrusted with an additional task: the baskets (τὰ μαλάκια) that each of the monks had woven in his cell were given to him (*V. Sab.* 44, 135). This may indicate that the hostelry of the Laura also served as a center for marketing local products to the outside world. Agents apparently came there to purchase the products and market them in the cities and villages.

We do not hear of *apokrisiarioi* (ἀποκρισιάριοι), emissary monks who took care of the material affairs of the monastery in the outside world, for example, matters concerning inheritances and the payment of taxes.[12] At the same time, however, we hear that the Laura monks reached distant places such as Scythopolis (*V. John Hes.* 20, 217), Bouriron (*V. Sab.* 79, 185), and of course Jerusalem and Jericho, to collect donations, make purchases, and carry out various missions not listed in detail. None of them was defined as an *apokrisiarios*. In each of these places the Laura monks had a definite place of lodging in the house of the faithful who were admirers of the monks (cf. *Pratum*, add. Nau 1905, 1.1).

Shipments of wheat that arrived from Transjordan would be unloaded next to the hostelry of the Laura (*V. Sab.* 81, 186). It appears that the wheat granaries and the mill installations were also located here.

The operation of a hostelry, as well as a hospital, alongside a monastery, was an integral part of the Basilian concept (*Reg. brev.* 155, 1184). The hostelry also served as a soup kitchen in which food was distributed to the poor. In the first year of his term as bishop, Basil established at the gates of Caesarea in Cappadocia an entire complex of buildings known as the Basiliada. These included a large church; dormitories for the monks; a large hospital in which medicines were distributed; an elaborate, well-equipped hostelry for the accommodation of strangers, the homeless, and lepers; workshops in which everything needed for the community was made; cattle sheds, and other installations (Amand de Mendieta 1957, 64; Giet 1941, 419–23). It is clear, therefore, just how closely the Cappadocian Theodosius adhered to the teachings of Basil, his venerated teacher. The hostelry was perceived not only as a building that would solve the monastery's accommodation problems, but also as a manifestation of good deeds by the monks on behalf of the society outside the monastery.

The *Historia Philotheos* does not contain any term denoting a hostelry or accommodations, such as ξενοδοχεῖον or ξενία; not even the verb ξενοδοχεῖν appears in this work by Theodoret. Despite this, however, there undoubtedly were hostelries next to many monasteries in Syria (cf. *HPh* iv.10, 312–16; x.4, 442; *V. Dan. Styl.* vii, 11–12), especially those that were located along main routes; there certainly were hostelries next to the important pilgrim centers. This is also evident from the archaeological finds in the Syrian monasteries (Festugière 1959, 320 n. 6; Tchalenko 1953–58, 19–20; Canivet 1977, 219). The commandment of hospitality is mentioned frequently in the regulations of the Syrian monasteries, but the technical term "hosteler" of the monastery is not mentioned in them (Vööbus 1960b, 219, hospitality).

The manner of accommodation in Nitria near the end of the fourth century was complex. Palladius, who stayed there for an entire year (391–392), tells of a hostelry located next to the church in which it was possible to stay for even two or three years (*HL* vii.4, 251.21). Twenty years earlier, when Rufinus visited the site (ca. 373–374), visitors were first received in the church by all the monks, who came out of their cells to greet them; each monk offered to take a visitor to his cell, which he temporarily placed

---

[12] For the *apokrisiarioi* of a monastery and their role, as indicated by the Justinianic legislation, see Granič 1929–30, 27–28. The Justinianic legislation speaks only of coenobium monasteries. See also above, Part I, Chap. 2E.

at the visitor's disposal. He does not mention either a hostelry or a hosteler (Rufinus, *HM* xx.6, 443; xxi, 356–57, ed. Schulz-Flügel). The original author of this work—an anonymous monk from the Mount of Olives who describes a journey to the monks of Egypt conducted in 394/5—similarly speaks of the accommodation of newcomers in the cells of the monks in Nitria, where, as was mentioned above, Palladius had seen a hostelry three years previously. It seems, therefore, that the practice of accommodation in the cells of monks continued even when a hostelry already existed.

There were also guest houses in the Pachomian monasteries. They were located near the gate, cut off from the rest of the monastery area, and the gatekeeper was responsible for their administration. They were intended mainly for the accommodation of candidates wishing to be admitted to the monastery and of relatives arriving to visit the monks (*Koinonia* i, 63–64; *Pr.* 51–52: *Koinonia* ii, 153–54). Similarly, there was a small guest house (μικρὸν καταγώγιον) for those wishing to join the monastery next to the gate of the monastery of Isidore in the Thebais, which was administered by the gatekeeper (*HM* xvii.8, 103). The hostelry of the Pachomian coenobium was not perceived as a vehicle for monastic charity, as was the case with Basilian monasticism.

The Monastery's Beasts of Burden and Their Drivers

The wheat purchased in Macherontes was transported from the Dead Sea to the Laura on the backs of she-camels hired by the steward for this purpose from the Saracens. As a general rule, however, the loads were transported by the monastery's animals—mules or donkeys—and not by hired camels. Beasts of burden were needed for construction and routine maintenance work, and therefore animals and their drivers were to be found in all types of monasteries, both in coenobia (*V. Euth.* 44, 65; 59, 71; *V. Sab.* 8, 92; 27, 112; 44, 134; *V. Geor.* 26, 125; 27, 126; *Miracula* 2, 363; 4, 364–65) and in the laurae (*V. Euth.* 18, 28 and below). The mules were used for transport and the donkeys for riding (Paul. El., *V. Theog.* 15, 95–96) and carrying water (*V. Ger.* 7, 7; *Pratum* 107, 2965), vegetables (ibid. 158, 3025), and other food (*V. Theod.* 238).

Sabas, who served for a time as a mule driver (βουρδωνάριος) while in the monastery of Theoctistus (*V. Sab.* 8, 92), had purchased beasts of burden in the first phase of the Laura's existence for use in construction work and to serve its inhabitants (ibid. 18, 102). The animals of the Great Laura and those of the coenobium of Kastellion were mobilized by Sabas for transporting food to the dissident monks who had settled in the ravine near Thekoa, where the New Laura would later be erected (ibid. 36, 123). In the desert of Rouba, where Sabas was accustomed to stay, he kept a donkey for his needs, which was tended by a monk named Phlais (ibid. 49, 139).

In the large monasteries there were a number of monks who served as drivers under an appointed supervisor (*V. Sab.* 44, 134; *Pratum* 125, 2988). This probably was the state of affairs in the Great Laura as well. This office entailed going out from the bounds of the monastery and negotiating with lay people. Knowledge of the local language, Syriac, was also useful (*V. Euth.* 18, 28). At times this task also entailed remaining outside the monastery overnight (*Miracula* 2, 363; 4, 364–66).

The Hospital and the Care of the Sick

In the second phase of construction, Sabas established an infirmary (νοσοκομεῖον) in the

Laura (*V. Sab.* 32, 117). The team of those treating the sick included a doctor (ibid. 41, 131). However, when Sabas fell ill, an illness from which he eventually died, he lay in his cell and not in the hospital, which was probably intended for the regular monks. Patriarch Peter took Sabas from his cell to his house in Jerusalem, where he treated him himself (ibid. 76, 182). In Jerusalem there was also the hospital of the patriarch, an institution mentioned by John Moschus, who tells of a monk from the laura of Pharan who fell ill with a stomach disorder and was sent there (*Pratum* 42, 2896). The monk Anthimus, when he was old and sick, also preferred, like Sabas, to remain in his own cell (*V. Sab.* 43, 133).

Services for the treatment of the sick also existed in the Old Laura, although it is not known whether there was a separate building there that served as a hospital or whether several cells were intended for this purpose. Cyriacus served there for one year as an attendant for the sick (*V. Cyr.* 7, 226). In the laura of the Towers, a sick monk would continue to remain in his cell or tower, where he received medical aid (*Pratum* 8, 2857; 10, 2860). In the laura of Calamon, on the other hand, there apparently was a hospital or rooms for the sick. Cyril, although he was not one of its monks, probably stayed there during the six months of his illness (*V. John Hes.* 20, 216–17; cf. Paul El., *V. Theog.* 7). The hospital of the Great Laura probably served the nearby secondary monasteries as well: Kastellion, the Cave, the coenobium of the Scholarius, the Small Coenobium, the laura of Heptastomos, and the monastery of Zannos.

Sabas' monks therefore did not need to receive medical treatment in the coenobium of Theodosius, where there were three hospitals: one for the monks, within the monastery; a second building, solely for lay people, apparently the wealthy classes who were likely to recompense the monastery in return for treatment; and a third for the poor—beggars (*Pratum* 9, 2860) and the homeless, who were not able to pay (Dan 1984, 149–54, 222–26; Patlagean 1977). Each of the three hospitals had its own medical staff, which cared for the sick in accordance with the directives of Theodosius, with medicines he mixed himself. Theodosius also established an old age home for the elderly and infirm fathers (Theod. Petr., *V. Theod.* 16, 41); there was also a separate building—a kind of monastery within a monastery—for monks who were mentally ill or senile (ibid. 17, 41–43). This coenobium also had a hospital in Jericho (ibid. 16, 41; *Pratum* 6, 2857). A renowned hospital was that of the Abba Seridos monastery near Gaza, which was established and managed by Dorotheus (Dorotheus of Gaza, *Vita Dosithei* 1, 122; Discourse XI para. 121, 372).

The care of the sick—not just sick monks but also lay people from outside the monastery—was an important principle of Basilian monasticism. The buildings of the Basiliada, built at the gates of Caesarea in Cappadocia, included a large hospital and clinics that provided medicines (Giet 1941, 419–23; Amand de Mendieta 1957, 64). Although he founded these institutions in the capacity of bishop and not abbot, he also imparted to his monks the importance of caring for the sick. Sick people from outside came to the monastery of Theodosius, which was located at the edge of the desert. It can be assumed that sick laymen, especially from among the desert shepherds, came to the hospital of the Great Laura as well, since the institution functioned under the aegis of Sabas, who was a holy man blessed with healing powers. At any rate, there are reports of two instances in which Sabas was summoned from the Laura to Jerusalem to heal bedridden patients (*V. Sab.* 45, 136; 68, 170–71). It may be assumed that there were many more instances in which the sick were brought to the Laura (cf. *V. John Hes.* 21, 218).

The Syrian regulations deal with the care of sick monks: they were permitted food somewhat better than that of the others, they were not required to fast, and they could sleep on beds, while the other monks were expected to sleep on the floor. A hospital alongside a monastery is not mentioned in these regulations (Vööbus 1960b, 222, sickness). In the large monastery of Izla there was a weekly duty roster for the care of the sick (Dadishoa's Rules 27, 175). In the regulations of Maruta, the care of the sick was the responsibility of the *rabbaytâ* (Maruta's Rules L.5, 92).

Palladius relates that there were doctors in Nitria, but does not mention a hospital (*HL* VII.4, 26.3). In Kellia, according to the testimony of Rufinus, the sick monks remained in their cells (*HM* xx.8, 444–45).

The regulations of Pachomius dealing with sick monks speak mainly of a special diet permitted them, in contrast to the monk's usual food. The hospital is the place in which the sick monk eats this special food and also receives additional clothing or blankets if necessary. Although there are officials in charge of the hospital, the housemaster also deals with this; the impression gained from the sources is that the sick monk continued to stay in the house to which he belonged and did not go to the hospital. Thus, for example, rule 43 states that the patient is forbidden to take with him to the house the food he received in the patients' room, not even fruit (*Koinonia* II, 143 no. 5; p. 184 n. 11; p. 165: *Pr.* 129; p. 207: Hors. *Reg.* 24; pp. 151–52: *Pr.* 40–47; p. 161: *Pr.* 92; p. 162: *Pr.* 105). The hospital in the Pachomian *Koinonia* was not an institution of social charity and welfare for the sake of the people outside the monastery, as we have found in Basil's teachings. In this as well, the monasteries of the Judean desert are more related to the Basilian system.

The Bakery and the Baking of Bread

A bakery (μαγκιπεῖον) was established in the Laura only in the second construction phase (*V. Sab.* 32, 117). Previously the supply of bread had probably been brought from outside, along with other foodstuffs. This was also the case with the sacred bread required for the liturgy. In the New Laura Sabas built a bakery (ἀρτοκοπεῖον) right from the start, when the monks' cells and the church were built (ibid. 36, 123). In the laura of Euthymius, the bakery (μαγκιπεῖον) was one of the first buildings built (426 CE) by Peter Aspebetus (*V. Euth.* 15, 24). This, therefore, was an essential element.

The bakery supplied not only the food needed to feed the monks but also the holy bread needed for the liturgy. Baking bread was one of the service tasks of the monks, with a usual term of service of one year (*V. Cyr.* 7, 226). Several brothers were occupied at the same time with the work of baking. The task of heating the furnace was especially difficult, for at times it was necessary to heat it twice and even three times in one day (*V. Geor.* 23, 122–23; *Pratum* 92, 2949). We do not know how often bread was baked in the Great Laura and in the other desert monasteries. In the monastery of Shenoute, in Egypt, for example, baking was done only twice a year. The bread was therefore eaten only after being soaked in water, and was stored during the year in suitable cupboards. But even if they baked every week, the intensity of the work of baking in the Laura was not the same all week long. The major effort was made before the weekend meals and ceremonies, after which the cell dwellers would be supplied with loaves of bread and other foodstuffs, which they took with them to their cells for the rest of the week. In addition, it was also necessary to supply the needs of the hostelry and the masons (as long as construction work continued in the Laura). It is possible that for these needs bread was baked on other days of the week as well, and not just in a concentrated manner before the weekend rites and meals.

There possibly were bakeries in all the secondary Sabaite monasteries, except for the laura of Heptastomos, to which cooked food was sent from the Great Laura. During our work in the laura of Jeremias in Wadi ez-Zaraniq, we found several brick fragments characteristic of a baking oven.

In the Byzantine monastery on top of Herodium, a bakery was constructed inside the caldarium of the Herodian palace. An elaborate baking oven was discovered also in Khirbet ed-Deir and in St. Catherine's monastery in Sinai (Corbo 1989, 84, pl. 130 and plan IV; Hirschfeld 1992, 85–87).

When Palladius visited Nitria (389–390), there were seven bakeries for the 5,000 monks there and for the 600 anchorites who were living deeper in the desert at Kellia (*HL* VII.2, 25). In the Pachomian monasteries, special regulations were in place for those working in the bakery (*Koinonia* II, 163: *Pr.* 116; 210–14: Hors. *Reg.* 39–47).

Simple Tasks
The simplest tasks were done by the novices (οἱ ἀρχάριοι). There was no allotted period of service for these duties, and several of them could have been done by one monk at the same time. The following tasks should be listed here:

(1) Carrying water from the spring (*V. John Hes.* 5, 205; cf. *V. Sab.* 8, 92; *V. Ger.* 7, 7; *V. Cyr.* 4, 225; *V. Geor.* 4, 99–100). The monk could be assisted by a donkey, upon which four water jugs could be loaded at a time (*Pratum* 107, 2965–69).

(2) Assisting the cook in his work (*V. John Hes.* ibid.; *V. Cyr.* ibid.).

(3) Assisting the construction workers (*V. John Hes.* ibid.).

(4) Collecting firewood (*V. Sab.* ibid.; *V. Cyr.* ibid.).

(5) Cleaning and trash disposal. There is no direct information about this in the sources referring to the Judean desert, but it is self-evident that this was an essential task. In the *Vita Georgii*, mention is made of a refuse dump from which George would collect pieces of cloth from which his clothing would be made. The refuse dump was probably located at the bottom of the cliff, under the center of the Laura, or under a cliff coenobium, as it is at present. Layers of refuse could have been burned when necessary.

(6) Serving as attendants for elderly and experienced monks, the fathers of the monastery (*V. Sab.* 43, 133; *V. Ger.* 5, 5). Fathers who were famous as exemplars had disciples who served them for long periods of time, in accordance with the relationship forged between the teacher and his disciple. This was not one of the regular service tasks in the monastery, which lasted for a specified period of time. According to the Justinianic legislation, an anchorite was entitled to have an attendant or two (*Nov.*

133.1). Several hermitages of the Great Laura as well as of anchorite settlements in Egypt indicate that the pattern of an elderly monk living with his disciple or attendant was quite common.

There was no gardener in the Laura. As was stated above (Part II, Chap. 1A), it had no fruit orchard because of the harsh climatic conditions.

D. Sacred Duties in the Monastery Church

The religious functionaries (οἱ κληρικοί) of the Laura included the priest (πρεσβύτερος) (V. Sab. 44, 135; 88, 196), deacon (διάκονος) (ibid. 73, 178), and the precentor (κανονάρχης) (ibid. 43, 134), who was also responsible for knocking on a sounding board which announced to the monks the times of prayer and funerals (ibid.; Pratum 11, 2860). The precentor also served as the guardian of the church treasures (κειμηλιάρχης) and was responsible for the sacred vessels and the ritual vestments (V. Sab. 58, 159). Cyriacus performed these two latter tasks for thirty-one years in the Old Laura (V. Cyr. 7, 226–27). The monk who performed these two tasks had to hold at least the rank of deacon (V. Sab. 84, 189). Cyriacus had already been ordained as deacon in the coenobium of Euthymius before arriving at the Old Laura. After holding these two posts for thirteen years, he was ordained as a priest and continued to fill them for an additional eighteen years (V. Cyr. ibid.). Thus it was possible to serve in these positions, which entailed a clerical rank, for an extended period of time. These ranks (priest, deacon, etc.), in contrast to the service positions, were given for life in an ordination ceremony.

In the Great Laura there was also an official in charge of the offering (προσφοράριος), who was responsible for the provision of the proper amounts of the sacred elements—bread and wine—necessary for the liturgy. In an emergency, Sabas permitted this official to take one of the church treasures to Jerusalem in order to sell it and then purchase with the proceeds a sufficient quantity of bread and wine for the Eucharist (V. Sab. 58, 159). It is possible that there were also certain monks whose task it was to carry the incense burners, to light the candles for illumination or for rituals and to carry them, both in the prayer rites in the church and at funerals (V. Sab. 43, 134). We hear of the candle lighter (κανδηλάπτηρ) in the coenobium of Choziba, where Antony also filled this position for a while (V. Geor. 34, 133–34; Miracula 6, 368–69). In the inscriptions found in the burial cave of this monastery, priests are mentioned sixteen times, deacons twenty-one times, and archdeacons twice (Schneider 1931, 332). Many of the anecdotes of John Moschus he had heard from priests in the various monasteries that he visited.[13]

If the abbot of the monastery was also a priest, he could celebrate the liturgy for the members of his community (see, e.g., V. Euth. 28, 45).[14] However, the abbot was not always

---

[13] Thus mention is made of a priest of the Great Laura (Pratum 59, 2912) and of the New Laura (ibid. 5, 2856); of priests in the laura of the Towers (ibid. 7, 2857); of a priest in the laura of Gerasimus (ibid. 12, 2861); and in the monastery of the Eunuchs (ibid. 135, 2997; 136, 3000). There is also a report of two priests and a deacon in Choziba (V. Geor. 35, 134; cf. Miracula 1, 362, where there is a general reference to the clergy, οἱ κληρικοί).

[14] An abbot and priest is also mentioned in an inscription from Jericho dated 566. See RB (1911), 288–90. It was also related of John of Choziba that he was a priest and administered the Eucharist to his monks (Pratum 25, 2869).

a priest. And if he was a priest, it must not be assumed that he normally conducted the rite and served as the celebrant during the liturgy. After Sabas was ordained a priest (490 CE; see below), he allowed other monks of the Laura to be ordained, and a priest was chosen from among them to conduct the rites. The following monks of the Great Laura were priests: Theodulus (*V. Sab.* 44, 135); John the Hesychast (*V. John Hes.* 8, 207); Cassianus (*V. Sab.* 88, 196, after Sabas' death); Thallelaeus, one of the sources of Cyril (*V. Euth.* 26, 39.18; 38, 56.20); and Peter, one of the sources of John Moschus (*Pratum* 11, 2860; 59, 2912).

The monks did not always willingly accept an appointment to the priesthood, and the example of Sabas (see below) is not the only one in the sources that refer to the Judean desert. An additional example is that of Olympius, the deputy in the coenobium of the Scholarius, upon whom the offices of deacon and priest were imposed (*V. Ab.* 245–46).

The monks of clergy rank (οἱ κληρικοί), and especially priests, constituted a defined group in the monastic community, distinct from the elders (οἱ γέροντες) (*Miracula* 1, 362) or the other brothers (*Pratum* 7, 2857). The priests of the Great Laura were buried together, separated from the burial place of the ordinary monks (*V. Sab.* 44, 135; see also *V. Euth.* 42, 61; John Rufus, *Plerophoria* 39, 90). The finds in the monastery of Khirbet ed-Deir accord with this (Di Segni and Hirschfeld 1987, 383–85). Their authority vis-à-vis the other monks was greater than that of the *oikonomos* in the Laura (cf. *V. Euth.* 18, 28). Various missions outside the Laura were imposed upon them (*V. Sab.* 44, 135; cf. *V. Geor.* 35, 134). The deacon Jeremias was included among Sabas' retinue on his mission to the court of Emperor Justinian (*V. Sab.* 73, 178). Many of the monks who participated in the Council of Constantinople in 536 were priests or deacons (see Part IV, Chap. 2, below).

Flusin (1983, 150) is of the opinion that the number of priests in the Laura was not limited. Not every priest, however, actually served the community at the altar. John the Hesychast, for example, was a priest but lived most of his life in the Laura as an anchorite in his cell. Ordination to holy orders (τὸ ἱερατεῖον) was regarded by Cyril, himself a priest (*V. Sab.*, title), as an exalted stage in the monk's career (cf. *V. Cyr.* 7, 226–27), an essential step in the grades of holiness. There were those who believed that the priests, after their death, possessed a "boldness of speech" (παρρησία) before the Lord, and requested that the latter intervene on their behalf in Heaven. This is indicated by an inscription found in a burial chapel in the monastery of Khirbet ed-Deir mentioned above.

During the early years of the Laura, Sabas' attitude toward holy orders was diametrically opposed to that of Euthymius, who had served as a priest while still in Armenia (*V. Euth.* 5, 13) and who at times conducted the rites by himself in his own laura, assisted by his disciple, the deacon Domitian (ibid. 28, 45). In his laura, there were, from the beginning, two priests besides himself and another deacon besides Domitian. The two priests and two deacons were nominated to serve in the church of the laura upon its consecration by Juvenal on May 7, 428, when the laura was inaugurated. In contrast, Sabas refused to accept ordination to the priesthood for seven years (483–490), and denied it to his monks as well (*V. Sab.* 18–19, 102–4). During these years the liturgy was celebrated by an itinerant priest who happened to be present but who was not a member of his community. In this regard—the appointment of religious functionaries—the

68. Calligrapher, illuminated manuscript, ninth century.

Laura established by Sabas was completely different from that of Euthymius, which was established according to the model of Pharan (more about this below, Chap. 4B).

E. The Calligrapher (καλλιγράφος) and the Library of the Laura

Among the monks of the Great Laura mention is also made of a calligrapher, a monk of Galatian origin named Eustathius, who was one of the Laura's anti-Origenist leaders (*V. Sab.* 84, 189). Copying manuscripts (Fig. 68) had always been one of the labors common among the monks, who found books to be faithful companions in their spiritual struggles, physical asceticism, isolation, and suffering. They therefore took upon themselves the laborious task of producing more books by copying them; the task was perceived as a sacred obligation (Vööbus 1960a, 389). This labor was prevalent in the Egyptian monasteries (*HL* XIII, 36–37, in Mount Nitria; XXXII.12, 96, in a Pachomian monastery; Evelyn-White 1932, 184–85; Chadwick 1968, 67) as well as in Syria (Vööbus 1960a, 389–93). Isaac of Antioch speaks of the obligations of the copyists: not to be negligent in their work; to write as if they were painting miniatures; to look carefully at the original codex, examining their copy and comparing it with the original diligently; to remove the errors that had slipped in and to correct the text accurately (Vööbus, ibid. 391 n. 16). Seemingly, all calligraphers were expected to maintain such a conduct and attitude. Not every monk who could write was considered a calligrapher, but only those who excelled in a clear script and respectful attitude to the original manuscript and to the task of copying, which had to be performed with the utmost precision and care.

Colophons are an important source of information regarding the work of calligraphy, and they illuminate the central role played by the monks in copying ancient manuscripts (although most of the extant manuscripts are from periods much later than that under discussion). In some cases the calligraphers were anchorites, while in other instances the task was performed in a coenobium on a large scale. Some monks were engaged in copying, others in binding, and yet others in illumination. Some mentioned their names, while others preferred anonymity, noting that only God knows their name.

Since the monasteries were centers of copying, they became not only production centers for new books, but also repositories in which manuscripts were collected and preserved. Books were received both from monks who died and from the faithful. The "Nag Hammadi Library" provides an example of a collection of thirteen bound books (*codices*) from the fourth century, which belonged to the Pachomian community of Chenoboskion.

The abbot of the Laura was responsible for its books, and they were given to the monks only by his permission (*Pratum* 55, 2909, in a laura near Gaza). Reading the scriptures was one of the recommended activities for a monk in his cell. Even Epiphanius, the strict monk, spoke in favor of the purchase of books (*Apoph. Pat.,* Epiphanius 8).

The monks of Gerasimus, complaining, asked for his permission to light a lamp in their cells at night to enable them to read (*V. Ger.* 4, 4). There are many mentions of books in monks' cells in the anecdotes of John Moschus (*Pratum* 46, 2901; 63, 2916; see also Chap. 3B, sec. 5, below). In the story about the senator's daughter who lived in the Jordan desert, mention is made of a holy elder, in the laura of the Egyptians, near the caves of Kopratha, who possessed the scriptures in two volumes (*De sync.* 7, 311; 11, 314). A book containing the entire New Testament in one volume was apparently rare (*Pratum* 134, 2997). The Justinianic legislation states that in each monastery there must be many books for the use of the monks (*Nov.* 133.2).

The library of the Great Laura undoubtedly contained a large collection of scriptures and patristic literature—writings essential to the Christological and Origenist disputes that occupied the Christian Church in the fifth and sixth centuries and in which the monks of the Laura took an active part (see below, Part IV, Chap. 3; Part V, Chap. 2). For example, among the Laura's books was a treatise of Antipatrus of Bostra against Origen, which was read by the anti-Origenists in front of all the monks who were gathered for this purpose in the Laura church (*V. Sab.* 84, 189).

The fact that the Great Laura was an important center for producing and copying texts of the scriptures is illustrated by the letter of the Sabaite monk Antiochus to Eustathius of Ancyra in Galatia. This letter, which goes on to relate the martyrdom of 44 of the Laura's monks during the Persian invasion, informs us that Eustathius had asked Antiochus to send him a copy of the holy scriptures in a single small volume, since in the exile imposed upon him by the Persian conquest he found it difficult to wander from place to place while carrying large volumes (Ant. mon., *Ep. ad Eust.*).

Cyril of Scythopolis included in his writings citations from many books. He had already collected the material for his compositions when still living in the coenobium of Euthymius; the final writing was done in the New Laura (555–556 CE) and in the Great Laura, to which he was summoned in order to finish his work (*V. Euth.* 60, 83.15–84.25; *V. Sab.* 75, 181.2–14; *V. John Hes.* 20, 217.21–24). The books that he used when writing were probably those of the monasteries in which he was staying; he used them in his cell, with the permission of the abbot of each monastery. It stands to reason that the library of the Great Laura was the largest and most developed of those in all the monasteries in which he was living, and that the books to be found in them were certainly to be found in the Great Laura as well. In his writings Cyril also made use of letters and archival documents that could have been found only in the library of the Great Laura.

Scholars mention the following works from which Cyril derived his material, incorporating it into his hagiographies: 216 citations from the scriptures (the Old and New Testaments);[15] 3 certain passages from the *Historia Lausiaca;* 2 passages from the *Vita Antonii;* 6 passages from the *Vita Pachomii* and more general parallels; 5 passages from the *Vita Theclae* and from the *Miracula;* 15 passages from the *Apophthegmata Patrum;* 7 passages from the *Historia Philotheos,* as well as literary and stylistic influences (this work constituted a model for him; he wanted to do for Palestinian monasticism what Theodoret had done for Syrian monasticism); 4 passages from Nilus of Ancyra's *Liber de monastica exercitatione;* 3 passages from Gregory of Nazianzus' *Eulogy for Saint Basil;* a passage from Cyril of Alexandria. There is also a noticeable influence from contemporary hagiography: the *Vita Theodosii* by Theodore of Petra and the *Vita Theognii* by Paul of Elousa (Schwartz 1939, 254–56; Festugière 1962a, 43; Chitty 1966, 131; Flusin 1983, 43–73).

Cyril derived thirteen theological passages in his writings directly from five different treatises of Emperor Justinian, thus presenting the Jerusalem theology as that of the imperial court. There are also parallels between the writings of Cyril and contemporary anti-Origenist writings, including Justinian's excommunications (*Anathemata*), the *Acts* of the Constantinople Synod of 553, and an unknown Sabaite composition (Flusin 1983, 73–83). Cyril also made use of various chronological lists attributed to Hippolytus, to Epiphanius of Salamis, and to the philosopher Heron; and of the *Consularia,* annals arranged according to the consuls' names (Schwartz 1939, 347, 350; Stein 1944, 173 n. 1; Jones 1964, 532–33). Cyril also faithfully copied letters and archival documents that he could find only in the archives of the Laura or in those of the Jerusalem Patriarchate. These include the letter of the archimandrites to Anastasius, the letter of Patriarch Elias to Anastasius, the letter of Elias to the monks rebelling against Sabas, and Justinian's edicts in response to Sabas' requests (Festugière 1962a, 43; Flusin 1983, 42). This list provides some idea of the scope of the library of the Great Laura.[16]

---

[15] So Flusin 1983, 42. In the Italian translation of Cyril's writings (Baldelli and Mortari 1990, 409–17), 216 citations are counted from the Old Testament and 364 more from the New Testament.

[16] Scholars (Nasrallah 1950, 95) counted no fewer than 738 citations of 258 works by 48 authors in the writings of John of Damascus. This gives some idea not only of the scope of his scholarship but also of the content of the Laura's library in this later period, although the library of the patriarch of Jerusalem was available for him as well.

The tradition of copying old manuscripts continued in the Laura in the following generations as well. The library of the Laura is also mentioned in the *Vita Stephani Sabaitae* (10, 354, ed. Garitte), in which it is related that Stephen was appointed to care for the library when he became a cell dweller. This task—apparently consisting of the repair, registration, classification, etc., of books—he performed, therefore, in his cell. During the period of Muslim rule, many works were translated into Arabic (for the benefit of the Arabic-speaking population of Palestine and beyond), and also into Georgian (for the benefit of the Georgian monks, whose numbers in Palestine increased, as well as for the use of the residents of Georgia). Thus the Laura became an important center of ancient and rare manuscripts (Ehrhard 1893; Blake 1965; Griffith 1986; Linder 1987b, 112–13).[17]

In addition, there was also the original literary activity of the Laura monks. This includes the monastic rule of St. Sabas, the hagiographies of Cyril of Scythopolis, and theological treatises composed in conjunction to the Monophysite and Origenist controversies (see below, Part IV, Chap. 3; Part V, Chap. 2). John Moschus and Sophronius settled the New Laura for a long period and visited the Great Laura frequently. He and Antiochus Monachus, the author of the *Pandectes,* are further examples of the intellectual level of the monks that lived there. Later authors included, among others, John of Damascus and Theodore Abu Qurrah (see below, Part V, Chap. 1). A rich library and a society of educated and intellectual monks were essential conditions for such literary creativity (Vailhé 1898a; Blake 1965; Griffith 1986). The sources mention other desert monasteries in which the monks were occupied with literary activity and the copying of manuscripts, especially those of Calamon and Gerasimus (Vailhé 1898c, 116–19) and the laura of Souka (Blake 1965; Griffith 1986; Linder 1987b, 112–13).

F. The Way of Life of the Monks Fulfilling Service Tasks in the Laura

Most of the tasks mentioned in the sources were common to the coenobia and the laurae. Almost every institution or communal structure found in the coenobium also existed in the Great Laura: church, bakery, kitchen, food storerooms, stables, hospital, hostelry. It may reasonably be assumed that it also contained a workshop, like those mentioned in the coenobium of Theodosius (Theod. Petr., *V. Theod.* 13, 34) and that of the Laura's hostelry in Jerusalem (*V. Sab.* 86, 194). An *oikonomeion* is mentioned only twice in the sources, referring in both cases to laurae: the Great Laura (*V. Sab.* 58, 160.6) and the Laura of the Towers (*Pratum* 5, 2857).

The core of the Laura was not enclosed by a wall, and therefore there was no need for a gatekeeper. Dining rooms are mentioned only in sources referring to coenobitic

---

[17] The copying of manuscripts continued at its scriptorium as late as the 11th–12th century, some illustrated (dated to the 11th–12th century; see A. Cutler, "A Psalter from Mar Saba and the Evolution of the Byzantine David Cycle," *Journal of Jewish Art* 6 [1979], 39–63, esp. p. 63). R. Curzon (*Visit to Monasteries in the Levant,* 5th ed., 1865, p. 225), who visited Mar Saba in 1834, saw there about a thousand manuscripts, stored in three different locations: in an upper chamber annexed to the main church, in the church's apse and in the "Tower of Justinian." Some of them later found their way to many European libraries. Papadopoulos-Kerameus (Ἱεροσολυμιτικὴ Βιβλιοθήκη II, St. Petersburg 1894) listed 706 manuscripts from Mar Saba in the library of the Greek Orthodox Patriarchate in Jerusalem, to which they were transferred in order to prevent the continuous looting. Only some 200 among them are earlier than the 16th century (*ODB* 1823; Ehrhard 1893, 67).

monasteries, and current archaeological findings also indicate that they existed only in coenobia (Hirschfeld 1992, 190–96). But no comprehensive archaeological excavations have yet been conducted in the core of any laura, so that at present it is impossible to determine categorically that there were no dining halls in laura monasteries. However, the sources relate that when it was necessary to assemble the entire community of monks, such as during the Origenist controversy, they were assembled in the Laura church (*V. Sab.* 84, 189). This may imply that there was not another suitable hall for this purpose.

There were also laurae with a genuine coenobium at their center, for example, the laura of Gerasimus. In the center of the laura of Calamon there also was a structure surrounded by a wall, a *kastron* with a gatekeeper (*V. Geor.* 6, 101). In Choziba the coenobium was the main section of the monastery, but outside its walls lived about 15 cell dwellers (Patrich 1990a).

In the Great Laura there was a group of monks whose everyday activity in the core of the Laura prevented them from maintaining the way of life of cell dwellers. Socially, the core was composed not only of novices who had just been admitted but also of veteran monks who held responsible positions, such as the steward and the hosteler. The precentor, who seemingly lived close to the church, was occupied with his task in the church mainly on the weekend, and there was no reason why he could not maintain the general way of life of a cell dweller on weekdays. But the monks appointed to service tasks, who did not engage in clerical activity, could not be cloistered in their cells during the week, and some of them even left the confines of the Laura on various missions. Did these monks practice a coenobitic way of life?

As for the prescribed prayers, they probably meticulously recited them seven times each day. But where did they pray on these occasions? We do not possess any explicit information on this, except for the night prayer: on weekdays there was no common night prayer in the church of the Great Laura (*V. Sab.* 43, 133), not even for those holding service positions. This coenobitic practice did not prevail there. It seems that the other daily prayers were also recited privately by each of the monks under discussion at the place of his service or in his own cell.

What were the eating habits of these monks? In the coenobia a daily meal was held at a fixed hour (*V. Geor.* 4, 99); in the Great Laura the monks who were mobilized for the *mannouthion* harvest received a daily cooked meal. Was this a regular arrangement valid for all the monks holding service tasks, whose occupation required more strenuous physical activity than that of a cell dweller? And if cooked food was indeed prepared for them daily, where was this meal served—in a dining room (which seemingly did not exist at all in the Laura) or in another room, close to the kitchen, which according to our proposal was located within the hostelry?[18] The extant sources do not provide answers to these questions. It may be assumed, however, that monks whose tasks involved greater physical exertion were provided with more food and better-quality food than were the regular monks, so that they would be able to function properly throughout their period of service. If this was cooked food, the meal almost certainly was served in a special room.

---

[18] In the Mar Saba monastery there currently is a small dining room in addition to the *trapeza*, or refectory, in which the daily communal meal is held. In the small dining room the monks can prepare food or hot drinks for themselves between the common meals.

If, however, this was food distributed to the monk on Sunday afternoon for the entire week, he undoubtedly consumed his rations alone in his cell, as did the other cell dwellers. When he was on duty outside his cell, he could take food with him in his satchel. All this indicates that one cannot speak of a coenobitic core at the center of the Great Laura.

G. The Economy of the Sabaite Monasteries and Their Means of Support

The Sabaite monasteries were not centers for the production of handicrafts or agriculture as were the Pachomian monasteries or some of the Syrian ones. The income from the sale of baskets woven by the monks in their cells was only marginal. It was not sufficient to sustain the Laura during periods of famine, when regular contributions also decreased. In that case the monastery's salvation came from the charity of its admirers: a caravan of thirty beasts of burden carrying food sent by the "sons of Sheshan" (Jerusalemite innkeepers) arrived at the Laura (*V. Sab.* 58, 160). A similar approach—reliance upon donations—prevailed in Syria (along with another approach that emphasized the economic role of the monasteries as centers for the production of agricultural and craft products) (Vööbus 1960a, 150–58).

Donations were given in kind or as silver and gold coins. The economic existence of the Sabaite monasteries was based on occasional or steady contributions by admirers or pilgrims and on bequests. This was also the case with the other monasteries of the desert (Hirschfeld 1992, 102–11). From the very inception of the Laura, admirers were wont to bring with them donations and contributions, which Sabas used for constructing and organizing the place (*V. Sab.* 18, 103). In about 490 Sabas' father died in Alexandria, and shortly afterwards his mother too. The family inheritance, which included a considerable amount of gold, was bequeathed to the Laura. With these monies Sabas purchased and established the hostelry in Jericho, with its gardens and irrigation rights, as well as the hostelry in the Laura. With money from an anonymous donation, amounting to 170 gold coins, he purchased the hostelries in Jerusalem.

The New Laura was founded with financial aid (one *litra* of gold) from Patriarch Elias. In establishing the monastery of the Cave, Sabas was aided by the work and many contributions donated by Marcianus, the priest of the Anastasis and the head of the church of Holy Zion, and by his sons Antony and John. Sabas was therefore successful in mobilizing assistance from the patriarch and from other distinguished church officials for the construction of various projects.

Admirers would contribute to the monastery yearly as an expression of indebtedness and appreciation to Sabas, both during his lifetime and after his death: a Saracen, who had been miraculously saved, contributed each year to the Laura one *tremissis* (= one-third of a gold coin) (*V. Sab.* 81, 187); a woman from Scythopolis donated two woven curtains to the Kastellion and the Cave monastery (ibid. 80, 186); Cyril's parents would give a yearly donation to the monks of the Laura (*V. John Hes.* 20, 217). There were also regular donations of food: Sabas' admirers in Medaba would send contributions of wheat and legumes to the Sabaitic coenobia and laurae (ibid. 45, 136). However, the main supply of wheat was purchased with money in Macherontes of Transjordan and, as mentioned, was brought across the Dead Sea and from there came by camel caravan to the hostelry of the Laura (ibid. 81, 186).

The monks would collect food that could be found in their desert environment, such as *mannouthion*, wild orache, or capers; all the cell dwellers were mobilized for harvesting the *mannouthion* (Hirschfeld 1992, 89). As noted earlier, there was no fruit orchard in the Great Laura, but there was one located near the Small Coenobium. If its trees provided a sufficient harvest, it possibly also supplied a portion of the Laura's needs.

Sabas resolutely refused to secure a steady income (πρόσοδος) for his monasteries, as in the years of severe famine (516–521) (*V. Sab.* 58, 159) and also later (531), when Justinian proposed ensuring the monasteries' economic survival by providing such an allotment (ibid. 72, 175). On the other hand, Sabas did not refuse to accept sizeable contributions from Justinian (ibid. 73, 178: 1,000 gold coins for the construction of a fortress; 74, 170: an unspecified amount), as he had previously received from Anastasius (ibid. 51, 143; 54, 146: a total of 2,000 gold coins). It was Sabas who decided how the money received from contributions would be divided (ibid. 55, 147–48; 74, 179).[19] However, he feared that the acceptance of a steady allotment would bring with it, in the course of time, enslavement to the donor as well as a change in the monks' way of life if their economic existence became orderly and assured.

Sabas was not unversed in financial matters. On the two occasions on which he was sent to the imperial court, the patriarch of Jerusalem entrusted him, among other matters, with important economic missions: on his first trip, he was requested to obtain an exemption from the *superflua discriptio* (περισσοπρακτία), which had been a burden upon the landowners, including the Church of Jerusalem, and possibly including his monasteries as well. He continued to deal with this later when he, together with other desert fathers, sent an appeal in this matter to Emperor Justin I. During his second trip he presented a detailed request for support for the repair of the damages caused by the Samaritan revolt (for a detailed discussion of these two matters, see below, Part IV, Chap. 4). Sabas therefore was quite familiar with financial matters. But generally funds came to the Laura as donations and bequests, not as regular allotments.

---

[19] By receiving these donations, his monasteries did not come under imperial jurisdiction. They continued to be subordinate to the jurisdiction of the local bishop, the patriarch of Jerusalem. See below, n. 42 of Part IV.

2

The Uprisings of the Monks against Sabas

Introduction

Life in a monastic community entails the acceptance of discipline. It is only natural, however, that in such a human environment there will occur violations of discipline and
occasional rebellion against the abbot. One of the early manifestations of such behavior
known in the monastic literature is the story of the breach between Pachomius and the
first hermits who joined him. They derided his humility, his modest ways, and the trouble
to which he went on their behalf; when peaceful measures such as personal persuasion
were of no avail, he expelled them from his community. When the expelled monks
turned to the bishop of the district for help, the latter also rebuked them for their actions
(Rousseau 1985, 90–91 and n. 17). There is also the well-known episode of the revolt
against Horsiesius, Pachomius' successor after the short term of Petronius (May 9–July
21, 346). Horsiesius rebuked the monks for the economic growth stressed by the monastery heads at the time: the expansion of plots of land, the increase in the number of work
animals, the establishment of a fleet of boats for marketing their agricultural produce
more efficiently. There was also an open clash with Apollonius of Thmošons. When Horsiesius rebuked him for his actions, Apollonius wanted to withdraw from the Pachomian
Koinonia and also urged other monasteries to do so. In the background of the split and
threat of dissolution of the *Koinonia* was included the tension between the veteran monks
and those who had joined the community of Pachomius at a later time, including Petronius, whom Pachomius had chosen as his successor, and Horsiesius. Because of the ensu-
ing tumult, Horsiesius decided, after a term of service of four years at the head of the
Koinonia, to resign his position, giving it to Theodore, one of Pachomius' veteran disciples, who had been more successful than Horsiesius in withstanding the opposition of
the monks. He himself withdrew to the monastery of Šeneset (Chenoboskion) (350 CE)
(Rousseau 1985, 157–58, 186–89; *Koinonia* I, 187–88, 195–97, 387–90 = G^1 127–30; *VBo*
130–31, 139–40). Horsiesius returned to head the Pachomian *Koinonia* only after Theodore's death (April 27, 387), holding this post for an unknown period after that year.
From the literary aspect, there is a marked influence of the Pachomian sources on the
manner in which Cyril describes the two phases in the revolt of the monks against Sabas
(Flusin 1983, 52).

We also hear in Egyptian monasticism of rebellions against the mighty Shenoute
and his successor Besa (Leipoldt 1903, 50–52, 149–55; Bell 1983, 29 and n. 60). Such
phenomena were not, however, unique to Egyptian monasticism. There are also reports
of revolts against Basil by some of his monks. This happened as a consequence of Basil's
appointment as bishop, thereby becoming fully integrated into the Church establish-

ment. One of the rebels was a monk and priest named Palladius, who went into exile in protest, joining Innocentius on the Mount of Olives (PG 26, 1167; Chitty 1966, 49–50). Some of Eustathius' admirers left him for the same reason when he was appointed bishop of Sebasteia.

The First Uprising (486–490)

Let us return to Palestine and the monks' revolt against Sabas. In 486, the forty-eighth year of his life, after the death of his friend Patriarch Martyrius and the beginning of the term of Patriarch Sallustius (486–494), certain monks in the Laura opposed his leadership and refused to obey him. That Sabas was the founder of the Laura and had admitted them into it were not reasons enough for them to acknowledge him as the head of the community and abbot of the monastery. This period, which lasted for five years (486–490), is congruent with the period of anarchy in the office of the archimandrites appointed by the patriarch to supervise the monasteries (see below, Part IV, Chap. 2), an anarchy that ended only upon the patriarch's intervention.

According to Cyril, the rebels were materialistic people (V. Sab. 19, 103). While speaking, however, of the second revolt, several years later, which was a continuation of the first, he calls the dissidents "nobles" (οἱ γεννάδες) (V. Sab. 35, 121). The opposition to Sabas eventually reached a climax when the dissidents (fewer than 40 monks) went to Jerusalem and complained to Patriarch Sallustius about Sabas' leadership and asked him to appoint another abbot over them in his stead. Two arguments were raised against Sabas: (1) that he refused to be ordained as a priest and would not permit any monks of his community, which at that time already numbered 150, to be ordained; and (2) that he was not capable of directing such a large community because of his rustic nature.[20]

The charges were therefore not of a theological-doctrinal nature. The charge of his rusticity was raised by those termed by Cyril as the "nobles." Scholars have noted the somewhat aristocratic nature of Palestinian monasticism (Chitty 1966, 88; Flusin 1983, 90–91); this is also the mentality reflected in the writings of both Cyril and Theodore of Petra (in his V. Theod.). Seemingly, both reflect in their style the views prevalent among their readers, a preference for the city over the country.

Cyril's writings contain a certain apologetic undertone when describing Moutalaska, Sabas' village, as a small, poor, unknown village in the district of Caesarea that would later be renowned on account of Sabas. The same undertone appears when he writes about Theodosius and emphasizes that, despite the latter's rural origins from Mogarissos in the district of Caesarea of Cappadocia, he was educated and served as a church cantor in the nearby city of Comana, also known as the "Golden City" (V. Theod. 235.27–236.7). Theodore of Petra is blunter, representing Theodosius' rural origins as something shameful (Theod. Petr., V. Theod. 6.8–23).

Cappadocia, Sabas' birthplace, was a province consisting mainly of villages and but a small number of cities. In the fourth century, when its territory encompassed ca. 80,000 km², the number of its bishops was small in comparison to the greater number of *chore-*

---

[20] V. Sab. 103.25–26: ἀνίκανός ἐστιν διοικῆσαι τὸν τὸπον διὰ τὴν πολλὴν ἀγροικότητα αὐτοῦ. 104.6: ἀγροικότερος δὲ ὢν κυβερνῆσαι ἡμᾶς ἀδυνατεῖ.

piskopoi—about fifty in the metropolis of Caesarea alone (Jones 1971, 174–90; Janin 1949).

This background makes it easier to understand the complaints of the dissidents regarding Sabas' rural nature. This was undoubtedly evident both in his appearance and his way of life. He was cross-eyed (στραβός) (*V. Sab.* 36, 123), sturdy, and of great physical strength (ibid. 8, 92). The thirty-four years that had elapsed since his arrival in the Holy Land he had spent in asceticism and struggle against the rigors of existence in the desert; this way of life undoubtedly hardened his nature. The dissidents are described as people of a materialistic spirit, in contrast to the virtues of asceticism, modesty, and frugality preached by Sabas. Thus, while instructing the laity who wished to withdraw from the world and become monks, he would say to them: "The cell-dwelling monk must be discriminating and zealous, a fighter, sober, temperate, orderly, apt for teaching and not in need of teaching, capable of harnessing all the members of his body and of keeping unfailing watch over his mind" (*V. Sab.* 28, 113). His avoidance of ordination to the priesthood and the prohibition against receiving it that he imposed on his monks are consistent with his strict approach, keeping himself until then away from any administration. His opponents were undoubtedly of urban origin and of Hellenistic upbringing and education, which was therefore of much broader scope than that of the countryman Sabas. This social background would later prove to be fertile ground for the absorption of the somewhat abstract Origenist ideas, specifically in the New Laura, where the exiled rebels settled (see below).

It is reasonable to assume that this social and educational gap was one of the important factors in the revolt. Thus we also find in Egypt, at the end of the fourth century, a confrontation between the local Egyptian monks, of simple village origin, and the foreign, educated monks such as Evagrius of Pontus or Arsenius, the former tutor of the princes Honorius and Arcadius at the court of Theodosius I (Hunt 1973, 469). In Syria there was also a polarization between the Antiochian, Greek-speaking monasticism and Church and the Syriac-speaking monks of eastern Syria and even of the environs of Antioch (Festugière 1959, 291–92; Vööbus 1960a, 18–19). It seems that when the rebels appealed to Sallustius, the patriarch was not yet acquainted with Sabas, however, upon the intervention of Cyriacus, priest and *hegoumenos* of the Anastasis and cross warden ("Guardian of the Cross"), he rejected the petition of Sabas' accusers, summoned him, and ordained him to the priesthood before their very eyes. Afterwards they all went down to the Laura, and Sallustius consecrated the Theoktistos Church, which Sabas had previously refrained from consecrating (Dec. 12, 490).

Sallustius' unequivocal action against the dissident monks, who were "of a materialistic mind," can also be seen as an expression of the strict stand adopted by the archbishop against the materialistic tendency prevailing among the monks. This stand is also revealed in his deposing the corrupt archimandrites Lazarus and Anastasius and appointing Marcianus as sole archimandrite in their place (see below, Part IV, Chap. 2). It is possible that this complaint against Sabas later indirectly became one of the reasons for his appointment by the patriarch as the archimandrite of the desert monks. From the accusations raised against him Sallustius learned that Sabas' character, way of life, and leadership were the opposite of those of the deposed archimandrites.

The intervention of the patriarch brought the first revolt to a conclusion and led to a period of tranquility that lasted about thirteen years, during which the Laura expanded and became firmly based. But finally the disagreement, which had been simmering below the surface, once again burst forth with renewed force, causing Sabas to leave the Laura that he had founded (503).

The Second Uprising and Voluntary Exile (503–506)

The grievances and criticism of Sabas' opponents in the Laura did not disappear, even after his appointment as archimandrite of the monks (before July 23, 494) and the physical growth and development of the Laura. His accusers, who also looked unfavorably on the establishment of Kastellion (492)—a monastery that could serve as a place of punishment for monks who sinned (*V. Sab.* 47, 137–38)—incited others, and when their number reached 40, they started an open revolt. Instead of turning for assistance to Patriarch Elias, who had recently dedicated the Great Church (the Theotokos Church) in the Laura (July 1, 501), Sabas preferred to leave his Laura and go into voluntary exile (*V. Sab.* 33–36, 119–25), thereby acting similarly to Horsiesius in the Pachomian *Koinonia*.

John the Hesychast also left the Laura as a result of Sabas' exile and went to live as an anchorite in the desert of Rouba. This took place between April 11 and September 1, 503 (*V. John Hes.* 11, 209; 28, 222). Sabas' exile came to an end in 506, when he was identified by Patriarch Elias among his visitors at Jerusalem at the Dedication feast (ἡμέρα τῶν ἐγκαινίων) of the church of the Holy Sepulcher and Golgotha (Sept. 13–20)[21] (Festugière 1962b, 47 n. 69). The exile therefore lasted more than three years, which can be divided into two sections, a short period spent in the region of the Yarmuk, near Scythopolis and Gadara, and a longer period spent in the area of Nicopolis (Emmaus).[22]

At first he settled in a cave near the River of Gadara (the Yarmuk). After a few days this became known, and some people from Scythopolis and Gadara came to him, including a young Scythopolitan named Basil, a relative of two of the city's notables (Severus and Sophronius), who began to live as a monk together with Sabas. The miracles performed by the saint attracted more people. Within a short time he had built a cell for himself, and two additional monks joined him. When, however, the stream of lay people coming to the place increased, he entrusted the cell to others and secretly left, returning

[21] For the yearly dedication festival of the church of the Holy Sepulcher and Golgotha, which lasted eight days beginning on Sept. 13, the date of the dedication of that church in 335 by Constantine the Great, see *Itin. Eger.* 48, ed. Maraval, 316–19.

[22] Leah Di Segni is of the opinion that the stay near the Yarmuk was of longer duration, and that the fact that Sabas was revealed to the patriarch only during the feast of the Dedication of 506, and not previously, indicates that on the Dedication feast of the preceding year he was still staying in the north and not near Nicopolis (Di Segni and Hirschfeld 1986, 266–67). It need not necessarily be assumed, however, that each year all the monastery heads came to the patriarch. According to Cyril (below), this was a common practice among the abbots, but not an obligation that each had to fulfill every year. Sabas' absence from the meetings during the Dedication feasts of the years 503–505 does not, in my opinion, mean that in those years he had not yet established the monastery near Nicopolis. Also the fact that near the Yarmuk Sabas managed to establish only a cell, while near Nicopolis he established a coenobium, indicates that the second period of absence was longer. Similarly, the impression gained from the story is that initially Sabas still hoped to return to the Laura, and only when he realized that his exile was not accompanied by a large wave of protest, but rather the opposite—the number of his opponents grew—did he reconcile himself to the new situation and agree to head a new monastery, this time a coenobium.

to his Laura, where he found that the number of rebels had increased to 60 monks. At first he treated them leniently; when, however, they raised false accusations against him (the details of which are not provided by Cyril) instead of begging his forgiveness for their breach of discipline, he left the Laura and went into a second exile in the region of Nicopolis. Here he secluded himself as a hesychast in the heart of the rural area, under a carob tree from the fruits of which he nourished himself. The local supervisor (ὁ τοῦ τόπου ἐπίτροπος) heard about the saint's presence and built a cell for him there. This cell soon developed into a coenobium under Sabas' direction (see Part II, Chap. 2F, above).

This time the rebelling "nobles" (οἱ γεννάδες) did not go to Jerusalem to present their claims against Sabas to the patriarch, because this would be perceived as a violation of monastic discipline. After a prolonged absence, they spread the rumor that Sabas had fallen prey to wild beasts in the desert, and they, with additional monks, therefore came to Jerusalem to request that the patriarch appoint another abbot in his stead. Elias, who had known Sabas from the days of his stay with Euthymius and their wanderings with him in the desert during Lent, and who on July 1, 501 had dedicated the Great Church of the Laura, rejected their request, but he did not send to look for Sabas. This is embarrassing since by that time Sabas was already serving as an archimandrite on behalf of the patriarch (although it was his predecessor, Patriarch Sallustius, who had nominated Sabas to this post). It therefore seems that by that time a certain discord had arisen between the patriarch and Sabas; otherwise the lengthy period during which he refrained from intervening is inexplicable. Perhaps this is why Sabas went into exile beyond the borders of the bishopric of Jerusalem. Cyril leaves this point mute. Elias, in any case, refused to depose Sabas.

In 506, when the feast of Dedication began, in accordance with the prevalent practice of the monastery heads, Sabas came to Jerusalem accompanied by several monks from the monastery near Nicopolis and was received by the patriarch together with the other monastery heads. Elias identified Sabas and urged him to return to his Laura, entrusting him with a letter ordering his monks either to obey him or leave the Laura.

The letter was read in the church in front of all the monks. The "nobles" and the other rebels, 60 in number, reacting violently, decided to leave the Laura. While some were occupied in packing their possessions, others took anything that came to hand—axes, hoes, shovels, and clubs—and assaulted Sabas' tower, destroying it completely by throwing down into the riverbed the wooden beams and blocks of stone. Afterwards they left and went to the laura of Souka, requesting to stay there. But the abbot of the monastery, Aquilinus, refused to receive them, and they eventually settled in the ruins of the cells that had once been built by the Aposchists in a ravine south of Thekoa, where they also found water.

When Sabas was restored to his position upon the intervention of Patriarch Elias, he did not pursue the seceders, who had destroyed his tower, but rather extended his aegis over them, manifesting his responsibility and expressing his authority as head of the Laura and as archimandrite, and continued to view them as his monks. He first conveyed to them a caravan of food supplies, and afterwards set about building the laura, with the backing of the patriarch, from whom he also received a sum of money for this purpose.

Thus the collective uprising against Sabas came to an end; however, there were also instances of violation of discipline by individuals. Such was the attempt of the monk

James to establish a new laura near the Heptastomos water cistern (see above, Part II, Chap. 1c). Of a different sort was the protest by the monk Jeremias against Sabas, regarding the manner of distribution of the funds he had brought with him from his second mission to Constantinople. Jeremias left the Laura, going to a distant ravine, where the laura named after him would be established (ibid., Chap. 1d).

The first uprising, which came to an end in 490, preceded the intensive building activity in the core of the Laura, and the foundation of Kastellion and the Small Coenobium. The second uprising preceded the erection of the other Sabaite monasteries. Therefore, Sabas' building projects, which brought a change in the primitive, peaceful, way of life, cannot be conceived as causing the riots. Such a cause is not referred to at all by Cyril.

Cyril's description of the uprisings of the monks against Sabas, a result of social causes, is a good example of the high degree of credibility that should be assigned to his writings. Unlike many hagiographers, his style is not laudatory and generic, but rather detailed and concrete. He does not curse the rebelling monks but rather gives the reasons for their opposition, including details that are not favorable to Sabas. His opponents are described as of noble descent and intellectuals, while Sabas is described as a rural person who opposes clerical ordination. In Cyril's writings there is a decisive preference of the *polis* over the village; nevertheless he does not refrain from mentioning Sabas' rustic origin. He does not conceal Sabas' early opposition to ordination, although this was in contrast to Cyril's values as well as to the approach of Euthymius.

Therefore, in spite of features resembling those in the story of the uprising of the monks against Pachomius, Cyril's narrative should be considered trustworthy on other points as well: he depicts Sabas as a chaste person who is able to forego the honor due to him, and prefers voluntary exile over an open war against the rebelling monks. One would also tend to accept at face value Cyril's statement, according to which Sabas followed the rebellious monks to Thekoa because he cared for their welfare and not in order to take revenge on their leaders.

3

Sabas as Founder and Disseminator
of Lauritic Monasticism

Introduction

Sabas contributed more than any other monk to the dissemination of lauritic monasticism in Palestine. Besides "the Greatest Laura" (ἡ Μεγίστη Λαύρα) which "stands at the head of all the laurae of Palestine" (*V. Sab.* 58, 158.19–20), he established three others, and his disciples established an additional three. Sabas' laurae were preceded by the laura of Gerasimus and that of Calamon near the Jordan River, which were close to each other and which had been founded about the middle of the fifth century, by the three laurae of Chariton, which had already been established in the first half of the fourth century—Pharan, Douka, and Souka—and by the laura of Euthymius, established according to the type of Pharan, which was consecrated in 428. Souka, now called the Old Laura (to be distinguished from the New Laura, which was established in 507), was associated in the sixth century with the Sabaitic institutions. Cassianus, previously a priest in the Great Laura, was its abbot from September 547 to July 548, after which he was elected to head the Great Laura. Euthymius' disciples founded only coenobia. Sabas was an exception in this regard. His activity gave new impetus to the lauritic life after a diminution of some thirty years in the foundation of laurae and just after the laura of Euthymius had been transformed into a coenobium (482 CE).

At the end of the fifth century, the Laura of Sabas stood at the head of all the laurae of the Judean desert, and that of Gerasimus headed the laurae of the Jordan desert (see below, Part IV, Chap. 2). A change occurred later: monks of Palestinian laurae who participated in the Council of Constantinople in 536 all came from Sabaitic laurae: the Great Laura, the laura of the Towers near the Jordan, the New Laura, and the laura of Firminus. During this period there was an especially strong Origenist influence in the latter two (see below, Part V, Chap. 2A). In the list of signatories to the decisions of the council and the documents connected with it, the representatives of the laura of the Towers were the only ones who signed in the name of all the Jordan River monks (*ACO* III.1, 36.70; 50.112; 130.73; 145.70; 158.73; 174.79; see also below, Part IV, Chap. 2). This laura now took the place of the laura of Gerasimus and attained senior status among the laurae of the Jordan desert.

Only a few laurae in the Judean desert and along the Jordan River were added later to those that had been founded by Sabas and his disciples. Cyril briefly mentions the laura of the Spring (πηγῆς): Cyriacus, its abbot, was one of the delegates sent by the patriarch of Jerusalem to participate in the Fifth Ecumenical Council held in Constantinople in 553 (*V. Sab.* 90, 198.28). Apart from this, we possess no other information regarding the laura of the Spring.[23]

John Moschus mentions the following laurae, which are not mentioned in earlier sources:

(1) The laura on Mount Mardas, identified with Masada. This was a settlement of anchorites who possessed a vegetable garden down below, near the Dead Sea (*Pratum* 158, 3025). The archaeological remains discovered at the site by Yadin indicate that indeed there was a laura there (Hirschfeld 1990, 53–55; 1992, 49–52). It began as a church established by Euthymius and his disciple Domitian ca. 425 (*V. Euth.* 11, 22). Euthymius stayed there for a short while, renovating a water cistern and undoubtedly living within the ruins of the fortress. He left this distant, isolated place before a community had sprung up there. This same church still existed in Cyril's time; he does not speak of a monastery. It therefore seems that the laura was established in a later period, between the time of Cyril's writing and the testimony of John Moschus.

(2) The laura of Peter near the Jordan (*Pratum* 16–18, 2863–65). Vailhé (1899–1900a, 43–44, no. 98) suggested that it may have been established by Peter, known as "Gyrnites," a colleague of Gerasimus, who, after Chalcedon, returned to Orthodoxy under Euthymius' influence (*V. Euth.* 27, 45). However, since Cyril does not refer to him as a founder of a monastery, this hypothesis is baseless. It has been proposed to locate it north of the laura of Calamon and south of the outlet of Wadi el-Qilt (Hirschfeld 1990, 55), a region with which Cyril was quite familiar. Therefore, it is almost certain that the laura was established only in the second half of the sixth century, even if it may have been named after the above-mentioned Peter Gyrnites.

(3) The laura Kopratha in the Jordan valley (*Pratum* 20, 2868; 91, 2949), which is the laura of the Egyptians (*De. Sync.* 7, 311). It has been proposed to identify it with el-Kefrein, ca. 10 km east of the Jordan River (Hirschfeld 1990, 79), but according to the sources it should be located west of the river.

(4) The laura of the Ailiotes, where John Moschus lived for ten years and whose founder he met (*Pratum* 66–68, 2917–19; 134, 2985–88). It was most probably located near the Jordan, and not in Sinai, which is the prevalent opinion.[24] It has been proposed to locate it near Jericho (Hirschfeld 1990, 55–56).

(5) Sapsas. This monastery was established beyond the Jordan, around the traditional location of the dwelling cave of John the Baptist, visited by Jesus himself. A nearby site was identified as the brook Cherith (*Pratum* 1–2, 2852–53), where the ravens fed the prophet Elijah (1 Kings 17:5). The monastery has been identified by Federlin (1902,

---

[23] It is not mentioned in Vailhé's "Répertoire" (1899–1900a). It is possible that John Moschus mentions it under another name. Leah Di Segni (personal communication) is of the opinion that this is the laura of Sapsas (see below), whose spring is mentioned in the sources. Hirschfeld (1990, 49–50) proposed identifying it with the scattered ruins near 'Ein el-Fawwar (ref. pt. 1831.1386), but these are not remains of a large laura.

[24] Leah Di Segni drew my attention to the fact that according to a *Prologos* to the *Pratum* (H. Usener, *Sonderbare Heilige I.*, *Der Heilige Tychon* [Leipzig 1907], 91–93), John Moschus lived for quite a long time in the desert near the Jordan, while on the other hand no mention is made there of his stay in Sinai. Placing the unidentified laura of the Ailiotes (in which John Moschus stayed for 10 years) near the Jordan, rather than in Sinai, would be in accord with this *Prologos*. For a French translation of the *Prologos*, see Schönborn 1972, 243–44. See also Flusin 1992, 16–17, n. 2.

152–55) with the remains traced at Bassat el-Kharrar, east of the Jordan (ref. pt. 2037.1387), which include a cave church. Abel interpreted these ruins, which are scattered over a large area, as a laura, and its name to mean *tzaftzafah* (willow), a tree growing there. This name is mentioned in the Medaba mosaic map, and therefore the monastery should be located on the map in the spot with a drawing of a tree beside which is the inscription: Αἰνων ἔνθα νῦν Σαπσαφάς, "Aenon, now (called) Sapsaphas" (Hirschfeld and Schmutz 1987, 49–50; Vailhé 1899–1900a, 278, no. 111). The Piacenza pilgrim mentions, at a distance of 3.2 km from the Jordan, the spring in which John baptized, and nearby the wadi in which Elijah was fed by the ravens, a wadi that was full of monks in his time (ca. 570). The monk Epiphanius (8th century) mentions that there was a spring in the cave of John the Baptist, which is located 1.6–5 km beyond the Jordan (Wilkinson 1977, 163). It is quite possible that this spring is the origin of the name "Laura of the Spring" mentioned by Cyril of Scythopolis (see above), and therefore Moschus' "Sapsas Monastery" should be identified with this laura (Di Segni, personal communication).

Moschus mentions two additional laurae. The first is the laura of Elusa (*Pratum* 164, 3032), possibly the place of seclusion of Paul, the author of *Vita Theognii* (Van den Gheyn 1891, 561–62), and it is quite possible that its origin goes back to the time of St. Hilarion (Vailhé 1899–1900a, 530, no. 34). The second is the laura near Gaza (*Pratum* 55, 2909). Both are located beyond the bounds of the Judean desert, and our information on them is meager. The laura of Peter the Iberian near Gaza was transformed after his death (Dec. 1, 489) into a magnificent coenobium by his disciple, Theodore of Ascalon (*V. Petr. Ib.* 143.18–144.23 [pp. 130–31 in the German trans.]).

In order to evaluate properly Sabas' contribution to the consolidation and dissemination of lauritic monasticism, we should examine the question: did he establish a new way of life for the cell dwellers, or did he adopt a pattern already prevalent in the laurae existing during his time? What are the similarities and differences between the way of life in the Sabaitic laurae and that prevalent in others, especially in the laurae of Euthymius and Pharan, on the one hand, and in the laura of Gerasimus, on the other, laurae about which we possess a great deal of information?

A. Gerasimus' Rules for the Cell Dwellers

For the sake of comparison, we shall first examine the way of life in the laura of Gerasimus. The author of the *Vita Gerasimi*, identified by some scholars with Cyril himself, and who in any event drew upon the latter's writings (Flusin 1983, 35–40; Grégoire 1904), refers to Gerasimus as "the founder and patron of the Jordan desert" and provides orderly and detailed information regarding this (*V. Ger.* 2–3, 2–4):

> 2. . . . after he founded there [in the desert of the Jordan] a very famous laura, he established in its center a coenobium and enacted a regulation (ἐνομοθέτησε) that the novices would dwell in the coenobium and would learn the monastic way of life, while those perfect in God's eyes, who are noted for their willing exertions, who have surpassed the majority in their ascent in the spirit of God, they shall dwell in the cells, and to them he gave such a rule (οὗτως . . . κανονίσας) that each one of them shall dwell in seclusion in his own cell five days of the week, eating nothing except bread, water, and dates, while on Saturday and

Sunday they [all the anchorites] would come to the church, and after having participated in the Divine Mysteries, they would partake of cooked food accompanied by a little wine in the coenobium—all [the monks, i.e., both anchorites and coenobites] used to perform the office of the psalm-singing together on Saturday and on Sunday—while on the other five days [the cell dwellers] had to seclude themselves, as was stated.

3. They were forbidden to light a lamp in the cell at all, or to make a hot drink, or to eat cooked food; nay, they were absolutely poor, humble of spirit, and complete master of the urges of the flesh. They controlled the stomach and all bodily pleasure; and not only this, they also became free from the passions of the soul, from pain and from anger and from cowardice and from lethargy. . . . In their cells they made rope and baskets; and each one of them would bring on Saturday to the coenobium the fruits of his weekly labor, and on Sunday afternoon he would take the weekly supplies, loaves of bread and dates and one waterskin, and so he would return to his cell. . . . None of them would have in his cell any material possessions, except for these essential things, one tunic and a cloak and a hood; and for bedding each one had one reed mat, and a patchwork blanket, and a cushion, and one clay bowl, in which he both ate and also moistened the palm fronds.

Each monk was to conduct the evening prayer in his cell; however, he was forbidden to light a lamp to read by its light after the prayer (*V. Ger.* 4, 4–5). No one had possessions of his own, and everything was communal property (ibid.).

The set of rules that Gerasimus gave to the cell dwellers therefore relates to the following aspects: (1) the division of the week between weekdays in the cell and the weekend in the church; (2) the food: during the week in the cell, and on the weekend in the coenobium; (3) prayer in the cell and weekend ceremonies in the church; (4) the work of the monk in his cell; (5) the monk's utensils and garments.

B. The Way of Life in the Great Laura

What information do we possess regarding the way of life in the Great Laura, in each of these aspects?

The Division of the Week between Weekdays in the Cell and the Weekend in the Church
The monks in the Great Laura also stayed in their cells five days a week and gathered in the church of the laura on Saturday and Sunday (*V. Sab.* 18, 102; 20, 105; 58, 159; *V. John Hes.* 7, 206). Such already was Sabas' weekly regime when he lived for five years (469–473) in a cell outside the coenobium of Theoctistus, about fourteen years after the establishment of the laura of Gerasimus. He was accustomed to leave his cell and come to the coenobium early Saturday morning, and to return to his cell toward evening on Sunday. In Choziba, in contrast, the cell dwellers would come to the coenobium only toward evening on Saturday, before the evening prayer (*V. Geor.* 12, 107–9; 42, 143–44).

Food and Drink

Food

The food Gerasimus permitted his monks on weekdays was very basic: bread, water, and dates. In the Great Laura, we also hear, in addition to dates, of carobs: in Sabas' cell, during his last illness, Patriarch Peter found a small quantity of dates and carobs (*V. Sab.* 76, 182). Sabas also ate carobs in his place of exile near Nicopolis. John the Hesychast was successful in having a carob tree take root in the rock against which his cell was built (*V. John Hes.* 25, 220). Dry slices of bread served as food for the monks during Lent as well (*V. Sab.* 24, 107).

It was a measure of asceticism to eat the leftovers of cooked dishes.[25] Aphrodisius, who would leave his cell only once a month, would take on his return to his cell the remnants of cooked dishes and would eat small amounts of them during the entire month (*V. Sab.* 44, 135). We also hear of a similar practice in the laura of Calamon and in the cells of Choziba. George and his brother would receive from the gatekeeper of the *kastron* of Calamon the scraps of cooked food once a week and would eat them during the entire week (*V. Geor.* 6, 101). In his cell in Choziba, George would crush the food remnants and make them into balls which were put in the sun to dry and were eaten after being moistened with water. This was his only food during the week. In his cell he abstained from wine, oil, and bread (*V. Geor.* 12, 107–9). Previously, when he lived with his brother in the laura of Calamon, they both abstained from wine (ibid. 6, 102). Such foodstuffs apparently were to be found in the cells of less strict monks. Anchorites who did not belong to a monastic community and did not receive nourishing meals on the weekends might eat fresh vegetables from their tiny gardens (*V. Cyr.* 16, 232) or legumes soaked in water (ibid. 19, 234).

A more stringent regime of asceticism was to fast in the cell during weekdays, as did Sabas, in his cell outside the monastery of Theoctistus (*V. Sab.* 10, 94); Gerasimus, during his entire life in Palestine (*V. Ger.* 4, 4–5); John the Hesychast, during the first three years of his life as a "cell dweller" (*V. John Hes.* 7, 206) and also at a later period, when he lived for six years secluded in the desert of Rouba, where he would eat only once every two or three days (ibid. 11, 209); and Heraclides, the brother of George of Choziba, in the laura of Calamon (*V. Geor.* 9, 104). Cyriacus, despite the fact that he was living in the coenobium of Gerasimus, behaved as an anchorite, eating only bread and water every two days, abstaining from oil, wine, or *eukration* (see below), which were permitted to coenobites (*V. Cyr.* 5, 225).

In a later phase of his life, John for many years ate only porridge (ῥοφή), into which he would mix ashes from the censer (*V. John Hes.* 19, 215). It is possible that this porridge was permitted only to the elderly monks. Thus, for example, Antony would prepare for the elderly George semolina porridge (σεμίδαλιν) when he served as his disciple and

---

[25] I heard from the monk Chrisantos in the monastery of Mar Saba about the current custom of burning the remains of the meal after the Eucharist, for fear that a bit of the holy wafer might have been mixed with them. It is possible that for the same reason eating leftovers from the dishes served at this meal was regarded during the Byzantine period as an expression of extra piety. In all the sources that mention this it is stated that the food was collected from the remains of this meal and not from the weekday meals.

attendant in the coenobium of Choziba after the Persian conquest (*V. Geor.* 43, 336).[26] In one instance it is related that Sabas cooked in his cell a dish containing beans for one of his monks (*V. Sab.* 40, 131). It is possible that the monk's food also included legumes and vegetables. In any event, as was described above (Part II, Chap 1A), we have not found cooking facilities in any cell of the Great Laura.

Drink

In addition to water, two other drinks are mentioned in the sources dealing with the life of the monks.

Eukration. John would drink *eukration* (εὐκράτιον) in his cell (*V. John Hes.* 19, 216.1). *Eukration, eukraton* (εὔκρατον), or *eukras* (εὔκρας) (*V. Sab.* 44, 135.2; 60, 161.25; *V. Cyr.* 5, 225.7; *Pratum* 184, 3057B-C, in the Thebaid, Upper Egypt) was a hot drink brewed from pepper, cumin, and anise, and which was common among the monks, especially in Palestine (Festugière 1962b, 61 n. 99, which refers to the Greek Du Cange *Glossarium,* 445 ff). Aphrodisius' abstention from wine and *eukras* implies that the norm in the Great Laura was to consume them, and the example from John the Hesychast indicates that this refers to a drink that the monk took in his cell, not to a drink served only in communal meals. Gerasimus prohibited his monks from drinking *eukration* in their cells; according to him, this was a drink suitable for coenobites (*V. Ger.* 4, 4).[27]

Wine. In Nitria the monks drank wine (mixed, of course, with water, as was the custom in ancient times), which was sold there (*HL* VII.4, 26). In Scetis it was accepted on the holidays; however, abstention from it was a common ascetic virtue. Pachomius, in contrast, allowed wine to be drunk only by monks who were sick (*Pr.* 45, 54: *Koinonia* II, 152, 155, 187 n. 1; see also Chitty 1966, 31, 44 n. 129).

In Syria there were various practices. During the fourth century and the first half of the fifth, wine was not prohibited in Syria (Canivet 1977, 217), although abstention from it was regarded as an ascetic virtue (*HPh* V.9, 342). Maruta did not forbid it and ruled that the monks should conduct themselves according to what is beneficial for the body, that is, they should not indulge excessively in it. On holidays a *hemina* (ἡμίνα = *hin*) was distributed to each monk, and on memorial days as well a portion was set aside for them (Vööbus 1960b, 143.25). Rabbula, in his regulations, on the other hand, prohibited wine drinking both by monks and by *benai qeiāmā* (Vööbus 1960b, 27.4, 42.23, 47.46,

---

[26] For modifications in diet due to age, see also Jerome, *V. Hil.* 11, 32–33; *HL* XXXVIII, 122, Evagrius. Between the ages of 21 and 26, Hilarion first lived (for 2½ years) on a half-pint of lentils a day, soaked in cold water, and then on dry bread with salt and water. Then, from his 27th to his 30th year, he kept himself alive on wild herbs and the raw roots of some shrubs. From age 31 to 35, each day he had six ounces of barley bread and a slightly cooked green vegetable without oil. Later, when he became weak, he added oil to his diet, and so until his 63rd year. From 64 to 80 he abstained from bread, and a meal of crushed vegetables was made for him. His food and drink together weighed scarcely five ounces. As for Evagrius: after living for 16 years without eating any vegetables, fruit, or cooked food, "his body required food prepared over fire, because of his weak stomach. He did not take bread, but partook of herbs or barley gruel or porridge for two years" (trans. Meyer 1965, 114).

[27] The name of John Moschus in many manuscripts is Eukratas. He and his disciple and colleague Sophronius are referred to as Eukratades. An abbot of the monastery of the Eukratades appears among the signatories of the Council of Constantinople in 536. A monastery of this name existed a century later in Carthage. It has been suggested that this term designates monks who perpetually abstained from drinking wine; see Schönborn 1972, 56 n. 13.

80.3; the last reference is to the rules from the 6th century attributed to Rabbula). The rules of Babai (end of 6th–beginning of 7th century) prohibit the monk from drinking wine when staying occasionally outside the monastery (ibid. 180.10). According to anonymous coenobitic rules from the seventh to eighth century, it was proper for monks to abstain from food and wine on Wednesdays and Fridays, the stationary days (ibid. 73.12); on other days, therefore, drinking wine was permitted.

Basil maintained that, just as it is incumbent upon a monk to refrain from the company of women, so too is it incumbent upon him to abstain from wine; he is permitted to consume it only for medicinal purposes and not more than is necessary (*Ascetica*, 652, 877).

As mentioned above, it seems that wine drinking was prevalent among the cell dwellers in the Great Laura, unless they were strict with themselves, as was Aphrodisius. Gerasimus permitted his monks a little wine only in the fraternal meals on Saturday and Sunday; on these occasions it was also served in the Great Laura (*V. Sab.* 58, 159). Sabas and the administrators of Kastellion and the Cave drank wine during their meal in the laura hostelry in Jericho (ibid. 46, 136). The fact that Antony emphasizes that George of Choziba and his brother abstained from wine in the laura Calamon and in Choziba (*V. Geor.* 6, 101; 12, 108) indicates that other cell dwellers in these two monasteries, adjacent to the laura of Gerasimus, did consume it.

In the Great Laura, the diet of the monks in their cells included, in addition to water, bread and dates, vegetables, legumes, carobs, porridge (for the old monks), *eukration*, and wine. This diet was different from that which Gerasimus had appointed for the monks of his laura. However, from what is related in the *Vita Gerasimi* 4, we learn that Gerasimus' monks had difficulty observing these norms strictly and asked him to be allowed *eukration* and cooked foods. It is therefore possible that the actual differences in diet between the two laurae were not so marked. After all, we should note that the information we possess regarding the diet of the cell dwellers in the Great Laura is collected from narratives scattered throughout Cyril's writings, and was not preserved in a collection of regulations, as in the *Vita Gerasimi*.

In Choziba the cell dwellers would also keep oil for consumption in their cells (*V. Geor.* 12, 107–9). There are no allusions to this being permitted or common in the Great Laura where it was part of the fraternal meals on Saturday and Sunday (see below). The use of oil in Choziba may reflect a deterioration of discipline between the time of Cyril and that of Antony in the first half of the seventh century. The cell dwellers of Choziba would also pick caper buds and pods, in the proper season, and take them to their cells on their way back from the coenobium (ibid. 42, 143–44). Other wild plants that were collected in the desert include the *maloa* (μαλῶα)—saltbush, whose leaves are edible—and the *mannouthion* (μαννούθιον) (*V. Euth.* 50, 72; 56, 77; *V. Sab.* 8, 92; 40, 130; *V. Geor.* 14, 110, and elsewhere; Hirschfeld 1992, 89–90, but see Mayerson 1993).

The Food Served at the Weekend Common Meals

Regarding the "love feast" (*agape*), the *Vita Gerasimi* talks generally about cooked food and a little wine. Cyriacus, when he served as the kitchen attendant in the coenobium that formed the center of this laura, was cleaning vegetables on Friday night for the common meal of the fathers on the next day (*V. Ger.* 5, 5–6). In contrast to this sparse information about the laura of Gerasimus, our knowledge is greater regarding the monks' menu for the Great Laura's fraternal meal. Included were vegetable dishes (λάχ-ανον), legumes (ὄσπριον), or *pseudotrophion* (ψευδοτρόφιον) (*V. Sab.* 44, 135). The legume dishes included a bean dish (φάβα) called *pissarion* (πισάριον) (*V. Sab.* 40, 130), and there were also squash dishes (κολοκύνθια). We do not know what *pseudotrophion* was (Festu-gière 1962b, 61 n. 101). These meals also included wine, bread, oil, cheese, and honey (*V. Sab.* 58, 159). The bread was fresh, if we assume that baking was done every week before the common weekend meals. On Sunday afternoon the loaves of bread and other foodstuffs were distributed to the cell dwellers. In the festive Easter meals, white bread and eggs were served along with the above-mentioned foods (*V. John Hes.* 12, 211).

In Choziba the meal also included, besides vegetable and legume dishes (λάχανα καὶ ὄσπρια), food with stones (ὄστρακα), probably dates or olives (*V. Geor.* 12, 107–9). Meat was permitted only to the sick (*Pratum* 65, 2916). We do not hear of fish in the sources from this period.

The Monk's Work in His Cell

Weaving baskets, mattresses, mats, or ropes was prevalent among monks everywhere (Warren 1937). In the Great Laura, the only work of the monk in his cell that Cyril mentions is basket weaving, which obviously was the predominant work. The steward was responsible for supplying the raw materials needed—palm fronds and branches—while the finished baskets were given to the head of the hostel (*V. Sab.* 44, 135). Sabas himself engaged in this work when he lived in a cell outside the coenobium of Theoctistus (*V. Sab.* 10, 94). It may reasonably be assumed that the monks also wove ropes, as in the laurae of Gerasimus and Pharan (*V. Euth.* 6, 14), since the palm fibers needed could be obtained together with the palm fronds used for weaving baskets.

Cyril engaged in writing in his cell in the New Laura and later in the Great Laura. There is also mention of a calligrapher (καλλιγράφος) (*V. Sab.* 84, 189) who was copying manuscripts. Literary work, including the copying of books, was also done in the laura of Gerasimus (on this see above, Part III, Chap. 1E).

Monastic Garments and Furnishings

1. *Garments*

The items the monk kept in his cell answered his most essential needs: clothing, bedding, and eating utensils. Information on this in the sources relating to the Judean desert is generally incidental and scattered. The list mentioned in Gerasimus' regulations is exceptional, but even it does not mention all articles of clothing. Therefore it is necessary to consult the sources regarding the monk's clothing in other monastic centers in order to learn if it was similar in all regions and what amount of clothing a monk was permitted to keep in his cell. We shall therefore examine the garb of the monk in Egypt, in Syria, and in Basil's teachings. Although the comparison is not always in the same chronological context, it will increase our scope and understanding.

In discussing the monk's habit, we shall focus on the following: the clothing itself, the materials from which it was made, and its quantity—were the monks supplied with only one habit, or did regulations permit more than one set of clothes? We must also distinguish between the norm and asceticism in clothing, which was a deviation from the norm, for example, prolonged wearing of the same clothes until they wore out or wearing clothes that were harder on the body.

Egypt. A detailed list of a monk's articles of clothing in Egypt is provided by John Cassian (*Inst.* I.3–9, 43–51).[28] They include:

(1) A hood or cowl (κουκούλιον, *cuculla*), which covered only the monk's head and the nape of his neck down to the shoulders. It was to be worn constantly, day and night.

(2) A linen tunic (κολόβιον, *colobium*) with sleeves that scarcely reached below the elbow, leaving the rest of the arm bare. Jerome, who calls the tunic *lebito* (λεβιτών), describes it as sleeveless (Fig. 69). Despite some possible differences in shape between the two, as monastic garb they are synonymous (Draguet 1944, 95).

(3) Double shoulder cords or straps, woven of linen yarn, tied together on the back of the neck, descending from there along both sides of the neck to beneath the armpits, and then tied on the body around the hips to tighten the tunic to the body (cf. Fig. 70). John Cassian calls them *rebracchiatoria, subcinctoria,* or *redimicula.* In Greek they were called ἀνάλαβοι. Figure 71 depicts shoulder straps made of leather rather than linen.

(4) A small cape (*palliolum*),[29] which covered the neck and shoulders and is called *mafort* (μαφόριον). In Jerome's translation of the regulations of Pachomius it is called *amictus* (a loose upper garment) or *sabanum* (a linen cloth). This was the outer wear of the Egyptian monks. John Cassian emphasized that by wearing this they avoided both the expense and the display of (the larger) cloaks (*planeta/paenula*) and coats (*byrrus*) (see also Draguet, 1944, 103–8).

(5) A goatskin, called *melote* (μηλωτή) or *pera* (= satchel). This was an essential item for the monk going on a journey. In his cell he could take it off and set it aside.

(6) A staff or walking stick (*baculum*).

(7) Sandals (*calciamenta*). These were not obligatory daily, but were used when necessary (Figs. 70, 71).

[28] For the clothing of the monks of Egypt, see also Evagrius Ponticus, *Capita Practica*, the introductory letter to Anatolius (PG 40, 1220–21; SC 171, 484–91; CS 4, 13–14). For the clothing of the monks in the region of Gaza in the 6th century, see Dorotheus of Gaza, *First Discourse* (SC 92, 168–77; CS 33, 86–90). In speaking of the symbolism of the monastic habit (τὸ σχῆμα), Dorotheus mentions a sleeveless tunic (κολόβιον), upon which was a purple mark denoting it as a tunic of monks, a leather belt (ζώνη δερματίνη), a shoulder strap (ἀνάλαβος), and a cowl (κουκούλλιον). The ἀνάλαβος is translated as "scapular" in both the French and the English translations. In my opinion this rendering is incorrect. For a definition of scapular see *DACL* XV.1, 986. In another place Dorotheus mentions undergarments (τὰ ἱμάτια) in general and a cape (μαφόριον) (SC 92, 180–81). He does not mention a goatskin, but otherwise this habit resembles that of the Egyptians. Some fine 11th-century illustrations of monastic garb, including the shoulder straps, the cape or himation, the scapular, and the sandals are found in the Princeton MS of the Heavenly Ladder. See J. R. Martin, *The Heavenly Ladder* (Princeton 1954), especially pl. XV, illus. 66, which is reproduced here as Fig. 70. I am indebted to Prof. Henry Maguire for calling my attention to these illustrations.

[29] This is the diminutive of *pallium*, the Latin term for the large rectangular monastic cloak, called ἱμάτιον in Greek. This Greek word is used frequently by Cyril of Scythopolis and other hagiographers. The Latin word should not be confused with the ecclesiastical woolen vestment conferred upon archbishops in the Latin Church, or with the longer and wider sash-like cloth, given by the Oriental patriarchs to their metropolitans or other distinguished bishops. This is an episcopal vestment, not a monastic one. See under "Pallium" in *The Oxford English Dictionary* XI; *New Catholic Encyclopedia* X; *ODB*, "Himation" and "Pallium." For the monastic garb see also N. P. Ševčenko, *ODB*, "Colobium"; "Costume—monastic and ecclesiastical"; "Mandyas"; "Schema." I am indebted to Dr. N. P. Ševčenko for discussing with me matters of monastic garb.

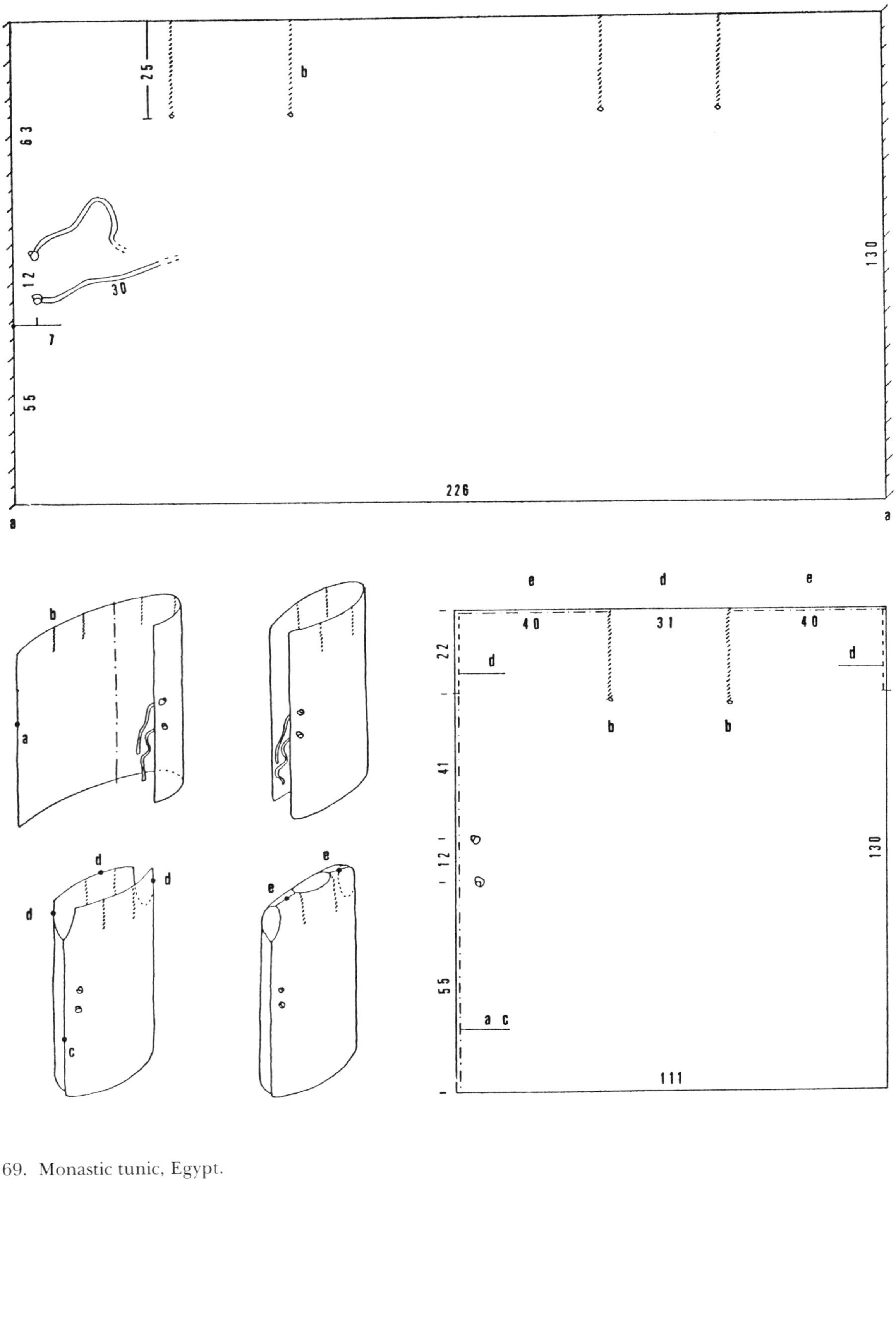
25
b
63
12
30
7
55
130
226
a
a
e
d
e
40
31
40
22
d
d
b
b
41
12
130
55
a c
111
b
a
d
d
d
c
e
e

69. Monastic tunic, Egypt.

70. The monk's garb. Scene from an eleventh-century illuminated manuscript.

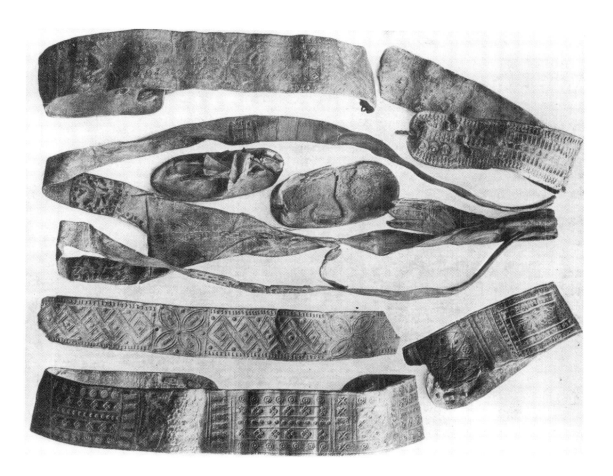

71. Monastic garb from Egypt: leather belts, sandals, and ἀνάλαβοι.

(8) A belt, called *cingulo* or *zona* (ζώνη) (*Inst.* 1.1.2–5, 34–39), was obligatory for monks everywhere. It was wound around the hips and was a separate item from the above-mentioned shoulder straps (Fig. 71). It was to be made of leather (ibid. 1.11.2, 52) or linen (*Jer. Praef.* 4: *Koinonia* II, 142).

All these items are also mentioned in the Pachomian sources (Besse 1900, 249–54; Evelyn-White 1932, 194–96; Draguet 1944, 95–111; *Koinonia* II, 184 n. 10). The Pachomian monks were expressly forbidden to wear a woolen tunic or mantle, or a soft sheepskin with unshorn wool (*Pr.* 81: *Koinonia* II, 159–60). John Cassian emphasizes (ibid. 1.10, 50–53) that these garments are not obligatory in every place, and may change from one province to another, depending on weather conditions and the customs of the district. In fact, this was not the standard garb of monks in all Egyptian monasteries. According to Copres, the abbot of a monastery in the region of Bawit, Middle Egypt, Patermuthius, the founder of his monastery, was the first to introduce a habit for the monks (*HM* x.3, 76). Although this is not known from any other source, it is clear that in the second half of the fourth century monastic habits were customary and common in Egypt. Patermuthius gave a young man who joined him a sleeveless tunic (λεβιτών), a hood (κουκούλιον) for his head, a goatskin (μηλωτή) on his shoulders, and a linen cloth (λέντιον) around his waist (*HM* x.9, 79). The shoulder straps and cape are not mentioned, and the belt was linen.

Apollo, the founder of the Bawit monastery in the Thebaid, wore, when he lived in the desert, a tunic (κολόβιον) and a small linen cloth (λέντιον) wrapped around his head (*HM* VIII.6, 49) that looked more like a sash than a hood. The color of his habit was white (*HM* 19, 54).

The shape of the cowl, tunic, goatskin, and shoulder straps is known from the garments that enwrapped several embalmed monks found in the excavations of the "Epiphanius Monastery" and at Qurnat Mar'y in Egypt (Winlock and Crum 1926, 150; Castel 1979). The tunic (Fig. 69), which measures 1.30 × 1.11 m, is sleeveless (unlike that described by John Cassian, but in accord with Jerome's and Dorotheus' descriptions). It was made of a 1.30 × 2.26 m linen sheet folded in half with its ends sewn together on three sides, leaving an opening for the head and arms. The cowl was made of a 45 × 73 cm piece of soft wool cloth with embroidered edges. The rectangular cloth was folded in half, one corner was sewn up, and the other two were left open. Loops were sewn in the two open corners, and two crosses of green wool thread were embroidered at their edges. It has been suggested that the "goatskin" was the wide leather apron forming the outer covering of the embalmed bodies (Fig. 72). This apron, 1.20 m. long, was made of tanned goat or sheep skin. Its upper edges were tied to each other and placed around the neck, and the bottom edges, at knee height, were cut into parallel strips 3.5 cm wide and 31 cm long, so that this section of the garment looked like leather fringes hanging from the bottom edge of the apron. It was tightened around the hips with a leather belt 73 cm long, 3.6 cm wide, and 2 mm thick. The shrouds, ten layers of sheets of identical size, were held tight around the body by means of woven linen strips 2.5 cm wide (Fig. 73) sewn together to form a string with a total length of 60 m. The separate strips from which this string was made are probably the shoulder cords or straps—a suggestion not mentioned by Castel.

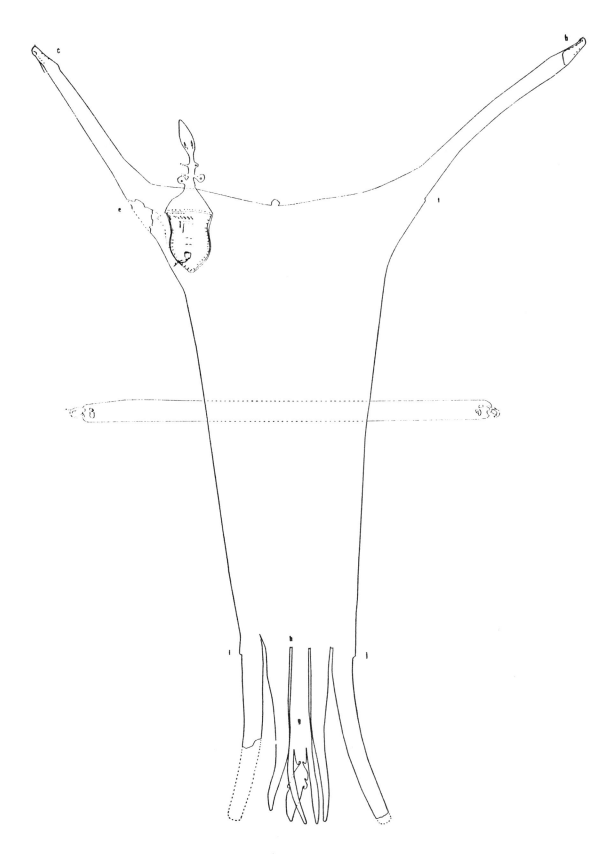

72. Leather apron (μηλωτή) of a monk, with a leather belt and a pocket. Egypt, Qurnat Marʿy.

73. Embalmed monk wrapped in shrouds
tightened by woven linen strips. "Monastery of
Epiphanius," Upper Egypt.

All the monk's garments, except for the goatskin, which was made of tanned leather
with no hair, and the cowl, which might have been wool, were made of linen (Draguet
1944, 109 n. 143) and therefore were light-colored garments. In the church, without
their goatskins on, the monks were conspicuous in their whiteness (*HM* II.12, 39; x.9,
79; *Apoph. Pat.*, Cronius 5: CS 59, 99).

Regarding the amount of clothing, the regulations of Pachomius specified that each
monk have two linen tunics in addition to the one he wore; two hoods—one for day and
one for night (Draguet 1944, 103); and only one each of the other items (*Jer. Praef.* 4; *Pr.*
81: *Koinonia* II, 142 and 159–60, respectively).[30] If anyone had more clothes than were
allowed him by the regulations, he was obliged to bring them to the storeroom keeper
(*Leg.* 15; *Pr.* 81: *Koinonia* II, 183 and 159–60, respectively; cf. *HM* II.12, 39).

[30] Draguet (1944, 95), in contrast to Veilleux (*Koinonia* II, 184 n. 10), is of the opinion that the Pachomian regulations speak of only two tunics, one for everyday and the other for the Eucharistic ceremony, and
not of three tunics.

In the *Apophthegmata Patrum* there is a story related by Abba Phocas of the Theognius monastery near Jerusalem about his earlier days in Scetis. Phocas mentions the practice of the Egyptian monks to preserve the first habit (*schema*/σχῆμα) given them when they entered upon the monastic life and were consecrated as monks. They used this habit only on Sundays in the coenobium, wore it on their deathbeds, and were interred in it (*Apoph. Pat.*, Phocas 1: CS 59, 201; cf. ibid., Dioscurus 3: CS 59, 46). This information indicates that the garments worn by the embalmed monks mentioned above were actually worn by them during their lifetime.

In the *Apophthegmata Patrum* and the *Pratum* there are two episodes about a monk from Sinai who brought from his cell a new tunic (λεβήτων) and everything necessary for another monk who wore only a worn-out goatskin (*Apoph. Pat.*) or a worn-out tunic and an old, small cape (πολύραφον χιτῶνα καὶ μικρὸν μαφόριον παλαίον) (*Pratum*). This implies that he had in his cell at least one tunic in addition to the one he wore in church—a white tunic like those of the other brothers, who looked like a band of angels (*Apoph. Pat.*, Cronius 5: CS 59, 99; *Pratum* 5.1, ed. Nau 1905, 46). The Sinai monks therefore followed the Egyptian practice: they had more than one set of garments in their cells.

Syria. The information about the monastic habit (*'askema*) of the Syrian monks is quite scanty and not as great or detailed as that pertaining to the Egyptian monks. In the fourth century there was no uniform habit: disciples received the clothing designated by their master. But by the sixth century the monastic habit is already well established (Vööbus 1960a, 265–69).

A detailed list of monastic garb is provided by John of Ephesus (*Eastern Saints* 20, 282), who describes Syrian practices almost contemporaneous with those of Palestine encountered by Cyril of Scythopolis. John's list includes the cowl (*kwsyoto*), tunic (*kwtnt'*), girdle ('*rqto*),[31] *m'alyono*, and *galo*. The last two items are interpreted similarly as a cloak or outer coat, but it is clear that there must have been some difference between them. The *galo* may have been the equivalent of the Palestinian cloak—the ἱμάτιον or πάλλιον— and the *m'alyono* may have been the equivalent of the Palestinian ἐπιρριπτάριον (= scapular).[32] As we have seen above, Egyptian monastic garb did not include a long, wide cloak.

The monk's clothing had to be simple and cheap, not new but used and somewhat worn. Wearing the same garment until it disintegrated was regarded as a manifestation of piety. The Syrian monk's garments were made of wool, not linen, since linen garments were regarded as luxury items. Though abundant in Egypt, linen was scarce in Syria (Vööbus 1960b, 59.10). The only proper color was black (see also Chitty 1966, 55, citing Eunapius, a 4th-century pagan author, according to which the monks' garments were black). White garments and mantles were prohibited (ibid. 148.3, regulations attributed to Maruta). Hair tunics (χιτών), made of goat hair (*HPh* v.8, 240–41 n. 2; Vööbus 1960b, 28.6, 58.7), were an expression of asceticism, since they were harsh on the skin. Anyone

---

[31] See also Vööbus 1960b, 75.18: cowl; 58.7: tunic; 148.6: girdle; and J. S. Assemani, *BO* III.2, 898. Theodoret also mentions an apron of sheepskin (μηλωτή) (*HPh* III.1, 247 n. 3) or goatskin (σισύρα) (*HPh* V. 8, 240 n. 2; IX.9, 424; XIV.2, 10; Vööbus 1960a, 259, 267). Shoes were prohibited; only sandals or other light footwear were permitted (Vööbus 1960b, 148.4; Palmer 1990, 84 n. 66). In many instances the monks preferred to go barefoot.

[32] See below, the discussion on the monastic garb in the Judean desert. For the meaning of these Syriac words, see R. Payne Smith, *Thesaurus Syriacus* (Oxford 1901). Cf. also Palmer 1990, 84 n. 66; 86.

wishing to be even more strict with himself preferred rougher garments, made of coarse leather (*HPh* XVIII.1, 54; XXVI.12, 184; XXVII.3, 220), straw or palm weavings, or rags (*HP* VI.9, 312; XII.2, 462; XIV.2, 10). There were even those who lived naked, with a cowl on their heads, their long beards being the only covering for their bodies (Vööbus 1960a, 267–69; cf. *Pratum* 91, 2948–49; 122, 2983–86, naked monks). Rough garments such as these, which were an expression of extreme asceticism and not a monk's normal clothing, were also known in Egypt (*Pratum* 124, 2985, tunics of buffalo leather in Egypt; 120, 2934; 123, 2935, tunics of palm fibers in Sinai).

The norm was a single habit (Vööbus 1960a, 259): Aphrahat lived his entire life wearing the same tunic and refused to receive another in its place (*HPh* VIII.4, 380). It was forbidden to sleep without clothes or to loosen one's girdle when going to sleep (Vööbus 1960b, 141.19). In these rules, which may date from the first half of the fifth century, there is information regarding winter clothing that the coenobites received at the end of the month of Teshri (November), which replaced their summer garments. On this occasion each monk marked his name on his summer clothes and placed them in the community house until the next time for exchange, when he once again received his stored clothing (Vööbus 1960b, 142.22). There is no mention of such an arrangement in the Egyptian monasteries, presumably because the climatic differences between summer and winter are not so great in Egypt as they are in Syria.

The Writings of Basil. Sozomen relates that the rules established by Eustathius for his monks in Armenia, Paphlagonia, and Pontus dealt with matters of conduct, food, and clothing (*HE* III.14.31, 123). Basil also included the subject of the monk's dress in his teachings. He attributed a didactic effect to the habit worn by monks: just as soldiers, government officials, and the like have uniforms, so too it was proper for monks to have uniforms, including standard footwear. Their clothing should fulfill the requirements of modesty and provide the warmth necessary for the body. On the other hand, the principle of poverty dictated humble, simple, and practical clothing. There was no need for different clothing to be worn at home or outside, in daytime or at night. The monk's clothing should be suitable for all occasions, meeting the needs of the day and providing sufficient warmth at night. Basil does not list individual items except for the belt, which was essential, especially for anyone engaged in labor, because it fastens the monk's tunic to his body, thereby preventing him from becoming entangled in his clothes as he moves about. On the basis of Luke 3:11 ("He [Jesus] answereth and saith unto them, He that hath two coats, let him impart to him that hath none"), Basil argued that owning more than one habit was prohibited (*Reg. fus.* 22–23, 993–1000).

Basil stated that a monk's clothing was the property of his monastery. It should be kept in a special storeroom and distributed to each monk according to his needs and the instructions of the abbot (*Ascetica* 877–79).

The Great Laura. Gerasimus permitted his monks one tunic, a cloak, and a hood (ἓν κολόβιον καὶ πάλλιον καὶ κουκούλλιον). The monks of his coenobium also had sandals (σανδάλια) (*V. Ger.* 5, 6). These were less essential for the cell dwellers, who came to the church only on weekends.

A tunic, a cloak, and a cowl were the common clothing of the Judean desert monks. Thus Euthymius appeared in a dream wearing a black cloak or mantle (μαντίν) above his tunic (κολόβιον), which was longer than the mantle, and holding a staff (*V. Euth.* 50, 74; Festugière 1962a, 129 n. 166).

The staff, used by Egyptian monks, is also mentioned in the sources referring to the Judean desert (*V. Euth.* 50, 73; *Miracula* 4, 365; *Pratum* 19, 2865). A goatskin, a belt, or shoulder straps are not mentioned in Cyril's writings. The cloak, which was the outer garment, and the cowl were black, as for the Syrian monks. We have no information regarding the color of the tunic (Festugière 1962a, 129 n. 166; Hirschfeld 1992, 91–93).

There were no major differences between the dress of Sabas' monks and those of Gerasimus. The monks rebelling against Sabas took with them their clothes or their cloaks (τὰ ἱμάτια) when they left the Great Laura (*V. Sab.* 36, 122). Aphrodisius, in the Great Laura (*V. Sab.* 44, 135), had only one tunic (χιτών), which implies that the norm in the Laura was two tunics per monk. As we have seen, two or three tunics was the norm in the Pachomian monasteries as well as in Sinai. It may reasonably be assumed that Aphrodisius also had a cowl and a cloak, as did the other monks in the Laura (*V. Sab.* 36, 122), and so no special mention was made of them. If the norm in the Laura was two cowls, as in the Pachomian monasteries, it is possible that Cyril would have mentioned that one cowl was sufficient for Aphrodisius. Regarding the amount of clothing, therefore, there were differences between the actual situation in the Laura of Sabas and the formal regulations of Gerasimus, which were stricter. But in terms of clothing as well there were also more extreme practices.

Sabas' ideal was a patchwork cloak (κεντώνιον, κεντονάριον) as an outer garment. According to Cyril, this is how Sabas dressed, even when standing before Emperor Anastasius in his palace (*V. Sab.* 51, 142.8; see also ibid. 33, 119.2, and Festugière 1962b, 61 n. 100). Such also were the cloaks of Heraclides and his brother George of Choziba, who were distinguished as monks extremely strict with themselves (*V. Geor.* 9, 105; 12, 108; 13, 109). However, the lack of a cloak (ἱμάτιον) was considered to be a result of poverty, not asceticism (cf. *Pratum* 68, 2917).

It cannot be determined if it was the custom in the laurae to purchase new habits for the monks from time to time, as was the practice in the coenobium of Theodosius (Theod. Petr., *V. Theod.* 81). Nor is there any information regarding the time set aside for washing clothes, as was the practice on Sundays in the Pachomian monasteries (*Pr.* 67: *Koinonia* II, 157).

To sum up, according to the literary sources to ca. 560 CE, monastic dress in the Judean desert consisted of a cowl, a tunic, a cloak, sandals, and a staff. We may assume that a belt was included as well, although it is not mentioned. In the later sources, from the beginning of the seventh century, we encounter another item, the ἐπιρριπτάριον. It normally covered the shoulders and upper arms (*Pratum* 92, 2949), but if necessary, it could be wound around the hips, as George used it when his clothes were stolen (*V. Geor.* 4, 99). In the *Vita Georgii*, it is mentioned in addition to the cloak (ἱμάτιον); so it was not an outer garment such as a cape (cf. Hirschfeld 1992, 91–92). In another place (see below), it is mentioned separately from the cowl. It should probably be conceived of as a scapular, thrown over the head and resting on the shoulders, covering the front and back. Such an item is depicted in many works of art (of later date), under the cloak (see Figs. 70 and 74). But it cannot be ruled out that it was a scarf-like piece worn over the cloak as in the two icons of St. Catherine's monastery in Sinai, dated to the eighth–ninth century, depicting St. Chariton and St. Theodosius.

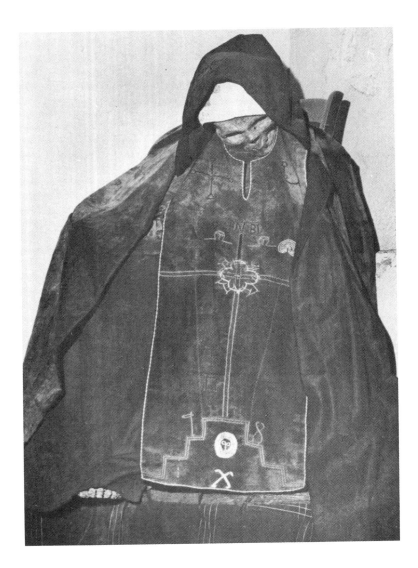

74. Skeleton of the sixth-century monk Stephen, who died in this position while on guard at the ascent to Mount Sinai. The skeleton is clad in the traditional monastic garb: tunic, cowl, scapular, and cloak.

A detailed list of Sabaitic garb is found in a late eighth-century source (*V. Steph. Sab.* 15.1, 262). Stephen would withdraw to the desert wearing a cowl, a tunic, and an *epirrhiptarion*, all made of hair, a material hard on the body; he wore sandals on his feet and was girdled with a leather belt. In his hand he held a staff with an iron cross attached to its end. The long cloak (ἱμάτιον) is not mentioned here due to his asceticism.

Functionally, the Palestinian ἐπιῤῥιπτάριον and the Syrian *m'alyono* are equivalent to the Egyptian goatskin (μηλωτή). Frontally they all look like an apron worn over the tunic. In terms of the components of the monastic habit, its color and materials, there is a similarity between Palestine and Syria rather than Egypt.

2. *Furnishings*

The sources relating to the Judean desert include a small amount of information on this subject as well. For comparison we shall first examine the information available on monks' furnishings in the monastic centers of Egypt and Syria and then discuss the situation in the Great Laura.

Bedding

(a) *Egypt*. Pachomius' monks were forbidden to sleep in a prone or supine position, but had to sleep sitting on an inclined seat. According to Palladius, the seat was made of stone and covered with a sheet (*HL* XXXII.3: *Koinonia* II, 126). However, according to the regulations of Pachomius, this was a movable piece of furniture, which could be placed on the roof of the cell, where the monks slept on excessively hot nights, or could be taken to the fields when the monk's work required him to sleep outside his cell. The only thing permitted to be placed upon it was a mattress (*Pr.* 87–88: *Koinonia* II, 160, 188; see also *G*[1] 14, 79: *Koinonia* I, 307 and 351; *Paral.* 30: *Koinonia* II, 54; John Cassian, *Con.* I.23.4, 108; Draguet 1944, 87–90). It was forbidden for a monk to have a pillow in his cell (*Pr.* 81: *Koinonia* II, 159–60).

   (b) *Syria*. The rules for the monks of Persia, a Monophysite source, and the regulations of Maruta (early 5th century) required monks to sleep on mats and carpets stretched on the ground; only the abbot and the weak were permitted to sleep on beds (Vööbus 1960b, 90.8, 141.19). Sleeping on a pile of straw was regarded as a special measure of asceticism, not the normal practice. Zenon, who lived in a burial cave near Antioch, slept on straw. Theodoret, praising his asceticism, relates that he did not have a bed (κλίνη) there (*HPh* XII.2, 462; 5, 468), thus implying that this probably was to be found in the cells of ordinary monks. On the other hand, the anonymous Monophysite rules for coenobium monks dating from the eighth–ninth century—a unique composition in this literary genre, distinguished by its orderly structure, its reference to the conduct of the monk in his cell, and its establishment of norms for daily life—forbade monks to sleep in a prone or supine position. They were required to sleep in a sitting position with the back leaning against the wall or sitting on a seat made of stone or wood, facing the east (Vööbus 1960b, 106.3–4). These regulations, originating from an unknown coenobium, therefore preserved the practices of the Egyptian monks.

The Syrian monks were renowned for developing special methods for prolonging vigilance and depriving the body of rest (Vööbus 1960a, 264–65; *HPh*, ed. Price, 220: index entries: "ascetic practices—sleeping on the ground, standing ceaselessly, vigils"). These practices persisted in the sixth century (*Eastern Saints* 35, 612) and are also attested in the architecture of some monastic cells, where narrow, vertical recesses were constructed for this purpose (Palmer 1990, 97–107, figs. 29, 32; see also above, Part II, Chap. 1F).

3. *Personal Items and Other Utensils in the Monk's Cell*

   (a) *Egypt*. The regulations did not permit the Pachomian monks to keep in their cells any items other than bedding and the approved garments. If any other object was found, it was taken away without warning. The possession of coins was expressly prohibited (*Jer. Praef.* 4: *Koinonia* II, 142; *Pr.* 81, ibid. 159–60), but books were permitted (Evelyn-White 1932–33, 215; Chadwick 1968, 24). Being coenobites, they did not need any cooking vessels in their cells.

   (b) *Syria*. The commandment of poverty scrupulously obeyed by Syrian monks allowed them to possess only a basic eating vessel (*rabu'a*) in addition to their clothing and bedding (Vööbus 1960a, 259). In reality, however, in the region of Antioch, the monks had more utensils. Theodoret, emphasizing the piety of Zenon, who lived in seclusion in a nearby burial cave, mentions that he did not have a bed (κλίνη), lamp (λύχνος), hearth (ἐσχάρα), pot (χύθρα), oil flask (ληκύθιον), chest (κιβώτιον), or book (βιβλίον). If he wanted to read, he would borrow a book from his fellow monks and return it when he finished reading it before borrowing another. He slept on a pile of chipped straw (φορυτόν) and had no key (κλειδίον) or bar (κλεῖθρον) to lock the door of his cell (*HPh* XII.2, 462; 3, 464; 5, 468).[33] Consequently, all these items were probably to be found in the cells of less strict monks. Zenon did have two jugs (σταμνία) in which he would bring water to his cave from a nearby spring. We learn from this and other sources that the monks kept their few belongings—clothing and books—in a wooden chest. Eating utensils included containers for wheat, oil, and water, a pot that could be placed on the fire, and a drinking cup. Glass vessels, which were inexpensive in Syria, were also commonly used by the monks (Canivet 1977, 215–16).

(c) *The Monk's Utensils in the Great Laura.* The monks who rebelled against Sabas took their movable property with them when they left the Laura (*V. Sab.* 36, 122). Cyril does not specify what these included, but it is clear that the monks kept utensils and personal items in their cells. Let us first return, however, to the regulations of Gerasimus. For bedding, he permitted one straw mat (ψιάθιον), a patchwork blanket (κεντώνιον), and a pillow (ἐμβρίμιον); for eating utensils, a clay vessel (σκεῦος ὀστράκιον); the permitted food—bread, dates, and water—did not require more than this. The clay vessel served for drinking water and for soaking palm fronds; it therefore was not a jar with a narrow opening, but rather a more open vessel in the form of a small bowl or krater. Drinking water was brought once a week in a waterskin (κιλικήσιον), unless the monk had a water cistern next to his cell, as we have found in many instances in the Great Laura and in other monasteries.

Cooking Implements
The eating utensils in the cell of Aphrodisius included a bowl (λεκάνη) in which he kept his food; it may be assumed that he also had a drinking vessel for water (cf. *Pratum* 19, 2865). His cell did not contain an earthen pot (χύθρα), copper cooking vessel (χαλκίον), stove (μαγειρεῖον), or mattress (χαλάδριον). All these were to be found in the cells of the regular monks in the Great Laura, but Aphrodisius, as was mentioned above, did not cook. It follows from this that normally the monks of the Laura did cook in their cells, and even warmed *eukration,* as the sources indicate. Thus we hear of a bowl (καυκίον) in the cell of John the Hesychast, from which he would eat porridge (*V. John Hes.* 19, 216). It is also related that Sabas cooked in his cell (*V. Sab.* 40, 131). As was mentioned above, Gerasimus' monks also had difficulty observing the prohibition against heating drinks and cooking food, and these cooking utensils were probably to be found in their cells as well. In hermitage 3 near 'Ein Abu Mahmud a good example of a cooking stove with a rock-cut flue above it was preserved (Fig. 58).

---

[33] An elaborate locking system with a bar was found in hermitage 3 near 'Ein Abu Mahmud. See Part II, Chap. 1F and Fig. 59.

Stoves found in almost all the cells of Choziba indicate that the anchorites there cooked their food and perhaps also baked bread for themselves. However, we did not find stoves such as these, or such as the elaborate cooking installations in the cells of Esna or Kellia, in the cells of the Great Laura, where there apparently were small stoves and not large ovens.

Bedding and Other Monastic Furnishings

The bedding used by Aphrodisius included a mat on piles of straw (στιβάδιον ἐπὶ ψιάθιον) and a patchwork blanket (κεντώνιον). Regular monks of the Laura would sleep on a mattress (χαλάδριον). A bed was apparently reserved for the sick (*V. Theog.* 15, 96; *Pratum* 182, 3053), as in the Syrian monasteries.

In the laura of the Ailiotes, it was the practice to sleep on a chair or on a wicker armchair, as did the Egyptian monks (*Pratum* 63, 2916; 68, 2917). Cyril had in his cell in the New Laura a seat (καθέδρα) on which he sat while writing (*V. Euth.* 60, 84), but he did not sleep in it. Sleeping on a pile of hay with or without a mat (*V. Geor.* 40, 142), and especially on the bare earth, were measures of asceticism.

The accoutrements of an anchorite or of a wandering monk also included a leather bag (μηλωτάριον) in which he would carry his food during his wanderings in the desert, and a small hoe (μικρὸν σκαλίδιον) with which he could dig up *melagrion* roots or onions (*V. Sab.* 13, 96; 24, 108; *Pratum* 3, 2854; *V. Euth.* 38, 56–57). In the *Vita Stephani* (*V. Steph. Sab.* 15.1, 262), mention is made of a satchel made of hair and containing a small Bible and a small knife used to cut the soft ends of the reeds and date hearts.

The Living Conditions of George of Choziba

Relatively ample information for comparison is found in the *Vita Georgii*. George of Choziba, a cell dweller who maintained an ascetic way of life, had besides clothing the following items in his cell (*V. Geor.* 12, 108; 13, 109): as bedding, a patchwork mat (στρῶσις ῥακίων); for eating and food preparation, a clay vessel (κέραμος), a stone mortar (ἴγδη λιθίνη) for grinding food scraps, and probably also a bowl for soaking the dry food balls before eating them.

Thus, regarding clothing and bedding, George's standards were similar to those of Gerasimus, although George practiced an additional degree of poverty and asceticism. Instead of a regular mat, presumably made of reeds or palms, he slept on a patchwork mat, and he had a patchwork cloak, which possibly also served as his blanket. He possessed a jug and a sheet only toward the end of his life, when he lived within the coenobium (*V. Geor.* 36, 135).

Conclusion

It is clear from the preceding survey that there were differences in monastic regulations and their application within the various monasteries in both Palestine and the other monastic centers. As we have seen, there was a similarity between Gerasimus' standards and Aphrodisius' conduct. In the Great Laura, Gerasimus' norm was one of asceticism and strictness. However, even in the laura of Gerasimus there apparently was a difference in the areas of diet and cooking between regulations and actual practice. Nevertheless, the differences noted between the rules of Gerasimus (a legal standard difficult to maintain) and the practical reality in the Great Laura (cooked food and sleeping on a mattress) may have their source in the gap of approximately a hundred years between Gerasimus' rules and the time of Cyril's writing. Nor should we ignore the possibility that the author of the *Vita Gerasimi*, apparently a monk in his laura (Flusin 1983, 36–40), wanted to enhance the founder's reputation by exaggerating the strictness of his rules. At any rate, in no area were Sabas' regulations for the cell dwellers stricter than those laid down by Gerasimus for his monks.

The prohibition against monks' owning private property (*V. Ger.* 4, 5) is revealed in Sabas' conduct when he came to the coenobium of Theoctistus. He handed over to Theoctistus everything he had brought with him, and again upon his return from the encounter with his parents in Alexandria, when he gave Theoctistus the three gold coins he had received from them. This was a common practice, included in the regulations of the Syrian monasteries as well (Vööbus 1960b, index entry: "possessions, private") and in those of Pachomius (*Jer. Praef.* 4: *Koinonia* II, 142; *Pr.* 81, ibid. 159–60). Basil also forbade monks to have private property (*Ascetica* 877–79). It may reasonably be assumed that Sabas' regulations were in accord with these rules. An echo of this is the prohibition against transferring a cell or giving it as an inheritance to another, which is included in a set of regulations from Sinai attributed to Sabas (see below, Chap. 5D, Regulation 8). As for the bequeathing of property to a monastery, it was only the Justinianic legislation that gave legal validity in civil law to such monastic regulations by establishing legal procedures for transferring private property to the monastery (Orestano 1956).

C. The Way of Life in the Laurae of Chariton and in the Laura of Euthymius

For comparison we shall now turn to the earlier laurae of Chariton—Pharan, Douka, and Souka—and the laura of Euthymius, which according to Cyril was established "according to the type of Pharan" (κατὰ τὸν τύπον Φαράν) (*V. Euth.* 16, 26.17; see also ibid. 9, 16). It is clear that by this Cyril was not referring to the physical layout of the laura but rather to the way of life maintained within it: Pharan was built along a ravine, at the foot of high cliffs, while the cells of the laura of Euthymius were dispersed over a flat area (*V. Euth.* 43, 64–65; 14, 24). The prevalent opinion among scholars is that Pharan, established by Chariton at the beginning of the fourth century, was a prototype that was adopted by Euthymius and later by his disciple Sabas as well (Rubin 1982, 25–26). This opinion needs to be examined, especially since Cyril never defines the Great Laura as a laura of the Pharan type.

The *Vita Charitonis* was written in the sixth century, apparently by a monk of Souka, who was inspired by the writings of Cyril (Di Segni 1990a, 11–12). Therefore it may be argued whether the life of the monks described in the *Vita* faithfully reflects the reality in the time of Chariton. It seems rather that the practices prevalent in Pharan during the author's time are reinforced by attributing them to Chariton and his regulations (Garitte 1941, 6–15). Chariton left instructions for his monks in Pharan before he moved to Douka (*V. Char.* 16–17, 28–29), but these were not written regulations, nor did Euthymius leave any written rules. Therefore, in order to learn of the way of life in these laurae, we must collect details that are scattered throughout various sources. This information will be examined in the same order as above: (1) the weekly schedule; (2) food and drink;

(3) prayer practices; (4) the manual work of the monk in his cell; (5) the monk's garments and utensils.

(1) Chariton laid down the precept that monks must not emerge frequently from their cells, but rather stay inside as much as possible (*V. Char.* 17, 29). This clearly refers to weekdays. In the laura of Pharan the rule of remaining in one's cell continuously during the week was probably not rigorously followed, and the monks apparently were accustomed to leave their cells and associate with one another.

On the other hand, while discussing the Eucharistic rite in the desert monasteries (see below), it will be seen that it was held in Pharan only on Sundays. Thus the monks could remain in their cells six days a week, and not five, as Gerasimus had instructed his monks and as was the practice, at a later period, in the Great Laura.

Also in Sinai, where the lauritic way of life was prevalent, the monks would come to the church only on Sundays (*Pratum* 126, 2988). The monk Nilus (ca. 400) speaks of anchorites in Sinai who lived in cells 20 *stadia* (ca. 4 km) or more from one another and who would gather on Sundays in church. During the week they sometimes visited each other, in order to maintain proper relations among themselves (Nili, *Narr.* 3, 619–22). This, therefore, was a practice similar to that in the laura of Pharan.

(2) Chariton established that it was necessary to eat only once, at the end of the day, a small amount of food that must be unprocessed and simple: bread with salt and spring or rainwater (*V. Char.* 16, 28). If the food did indeed include only bread and water, then this was even less than what Gerasimus had permitted his monks. Such a diet was prevalent among the Syrian anchorites (cf. *HPh* II.2, 196, Juliana Saba; XI.1, 454, Romanus: only bread and water, with no mention of salt; ibid. IX.3, 412, Peter the Galatian; XII.3, 462, Zenon). Palamon, Pachomius' teacher, lived on bread and salt (*G*[1] 6: *Koinonia* I, 301). Euthymius regarded it as self-evident that bread was to be consumed with salt (*V. Euth.* 39, 58), but in the pantry of his laura there were also wine and oil (ibid. 17, 27). These presumably were served only at the festive communal meals.

(3) Chariton instructed his monks to pray and chant psalms seven times a day at prescribed hours and with great concentration (*V. Char.* 16–17, 28–29). He placed special emphasis on rising for night prayer and required that the monks stay awake six hours during the night, which was the accepted quota (see below, Chap. 4A). Psalms could also be recited between the hours of prayer while the monks were engaged in labor. He also recommended that his monks study the scriptures in their cells.

There is no mention in the writings dealing with Chariton of the weekend rites, but we read in the *Vita Euthymii* of the need to come at night to the church, and below (Chap. 4B) we shall see that this was a reference to the night between Saturday and Sunday, when they came to the church for a night vigil and remained there until the Eucharistic rite which took place only on Sunday. Regarding weekend prayers, therefore, there is a decisive difference between Pharan and what Gerasimus and Sabas established for their monks.

(4) Chariton ordered that a monk in his cell should be engaged in labor while reciting psalms (*V. Char.* 16, 28). Euthymius wove ropes in his cell in Pharan, thus earning his livelihood and giving the excess income to the needy (*V. Euth.* 6, 14). This routine of a monk working in his cell was common to all the laurae. The impression gained from this text, however, is that the income from the work went directly to the monk who used it

to purchase his food and distributed the rest to the needy. Such an individualistic pattern of earning is also attested in the early stages of the anchorite colonies in Lower Egypt (see Part I, Chap. 2A). If this formulation by Cyril is not a figurative but rather a realistic description, then there was a considerable difference in the administrative and economic organization of Pharan at the beginning of the fifth century and that of the later laurae. In the later ones, caring for the livelihood of each monk was the responsibility of the central administration of the monastery, and the monk did not receive any income for his labor that could be distributed to the needy. The structure in Pharan reflects a looser monastic administration than that known to us from the Great Laura and even from that of Euthymius.[34]

It is possible, however, that the status of Euthymius, who settled in a cell outside Pharan, and not within the laura itself, was different from that of monks who lived in cells within the laura. Cyril states about Euthymius: "Since he loved quietness, he stayed in a monastic cell outside the laura" (φιλήσυχος ὢν ἔμεινεν εἰς ἀναχωρητικὸν κελλίον ἔξω τῆς λαύρας) (V. Euth. 6, 14.10–11). Perhaps he was not considered as one of the laura monks and preserved a certain independence.

During Chariton's time, a multitude of men, women, and children flocked to the monastery, distracting and disturbing the monks to such an extent that Chariton decided to leave the laura and go to Douka (V. Char. 18, 29–30). Did this situation continue in Pharan, and did it also exist when Euthymius was living there? Perhaps the tumult from which Euthymius wanted to distance himself had its source in the fact mentioned above: the monks of the laura were not obliged to remain in their cells during weekdays, and therefore Euthymius did not find within its bounds the tranquility he sought. In addition, Euthymius was not alone in the place where his cell was located: Theoctistus was his neighbor, and a friendship developed between them.

In Cyril's statement, what is the meaning of "outside the laura"? There was no wall separating the area inside the laura from that outside. It is possible that some topographic marking, perhaps a tower, determined its bounds. Or possibly it was the density of the cells that determined this, with Euthymius' cell being several hundred meters distant from the others which were grouped around the core of the laura, and therefore his cell was perceived as being "outside." An examination of the archaeological remains does reveal a concentration of cells around the center and a number of additional cells ca. 1200 m distant from them to the west (Patrich 1989, fig. 160; Hirschfeld 1990, 7, fig. 4; 1992, 22, fig. 2). Other building remains located farther east are possibly connected to the laura as well.

It is clear that the hierarchy and rules of discipline familiar to us from later periods did not exist in the laura of Pharan during the period under discussion. We do not hear of an abbot of the monastery. Similarly, the author of the Vita Charitonis does not mention the names of Chariton's successors in the leadership of the laura. Is this only because they did not leave their mark on its history? Moschus, however, who lived in Pharan for

---

[34] Allusions to private incomes of monks in the Great Laura are to be found only in a later period, in the 7th and 8th centuries under the Muslim regime, when a monk would send his disciple to Jerusalem or Damascus to sell his baskets and wares, rather than use an agent appointed for this task by the abbot, whose duty was to market the products of all the monks (Pass. Mich. Sab. 3, 67–68; V. Jo. Damas. 26: PG 94, 465–67).

a period of ten years (568–578), does mention several of the monastery's abbots (Chadwick 1974, 55–56).

Apparently during the time of Euthymius each monk still had a great deal of free choice regarding the way of life he wished to follow, similar to the situation in Nitria during the lifetime of Palladius. There is no mention that Euthymius asked the abbot of Pharan for his farewell blessing when he went forth from his cell into the heart of the desert with Theoctistus. Furthermore, it was the fathers of Pharan, not the abbot, who searched for the missing Euthymius and Theoctistus, and it was their decision to move from the laura and establish a new monastery. Their action was apparently not conditional upon the consent of the abbot since there is no evidence even of his existence. It is quite possible that the laura was directed by the fathers of Pharan, a group of elderly monks. Also in Mount Nitria there was no abbot at about this time. The settlement was directed by a group of eight priests led by a senior priest (see Part I, Chap. 2A, above).

Cyril's descriptions, written during the early second half of the sixth century, refer to monasteries with a consolidated internal hierarchy. This was the result of a long period of development during the fifth and sixth centuries after the formulation of the fourth canon of the Council of Chalcedon, which deals with the integration of the monastic movement within the Church, and after the legislation of Justinian regarding monks (Granić 1929–30). We therefore should not draw erroneous conclusions from Cyril's writings regarding the internal organization of the monasteries at the beginning of the fifth century, especially regarding those of the laura type, which had a looser administrative framework than that of the coenobia. In fact, the discussion above has pointed out several differences in the way of life and the administrative structure between the older laurae and the Great Laura of Cyril's time.

(5) As regards clothing, Chariton was accustomed to wear a tunic of hair (τρίχινον ἔνδυμα: V. Char. 15, 27), not necessarily a figurative phrase (cf. Matt. 3:4), and to lie down—only for a short while—on the ground, passing most of the night in prayer. This, however, was an exceptional ascetic practice, not the norm.

More information from the end of the fourth century (ca. 388) regarding the way of life in another laura of Chariton, that of Douka, is provided by Palladius (HL XLVIII, 142–43), who mentions that one could see various ways of life there. However, he provides details only regarding the way of life of Elpidius, the abbot of the monastery, who, according to Palladius, turned the mountain into a city. Elpidius, a Cappadocian by origin, was noted for his asceticism. Palladius writes at length about the night vigils that he kept. This practice, of course, was in accordance with the spirit of Chariton's teachings, and Euthymius also attributed great importance to night vigils (V. Euth. 21, 34). A disciple of Elpidius named Sisinius, also of Cappadocian origin, secluded himself in a cave after having lived in Douka for six or seven years, and for three years he refrained from sitting or lying down and did not go out. Such extreme asceticism, which undoubtedly had its origins in Syrian or Eustathian influences upon these Cappadocians, disappeared during a later period, when the influence of Basil's teachings increased. Euthymius himself declared that a monk should not perform extreme acts of asceticism and that a young man who did so was guilty of arrogance (V. Euth. 9, 17).

Our information about the third laura of Chariton, Souka, dates from the end of the fifth and the first half of the sixth century, the period when Cyriacus lived and was

active there. This was a time in which an orderly lauritic life-style had already been established in the monasteries of Gerasimus and Sabas, a reality different from that prevalent
during the fourth and the beginning of the fifth century.

This survey therefore indicates that in many aspects the laura of Pharan was distinguished from the laurae of Gerasimus and Sabas (see also below, Chap. 4). It is clear that
Sabas did not establish his Laura on the model of Euthymius (the model of Pharan), but
rather according to a model closer to the laura of Gerasimus. In contrast to Gerasimus,
however, Sabas did not establish it around a coenobium. Sabas placed the novitiate, the
Small Coenobium, outside the bounds of the Great Laura or sent those turning to him
to Theodosius. His laura, therefore, was a settlement solely of anchorites.

4

The Weekly Liturgy in the Monasteries of Sabas
and in the Other Desert Monasteries

A. The Daily *Cursus* of Prayers and the Weekly Cycle

Introduction

Prayer was an important component in the spiritual life of the monks and in their daily routine. In order to understand their life properly, we must become familiar with their prayer practices, especially the daily schedule (*cursus*) of their regular weekday prayers, rather than the content or inner order (*ordo*) of each office.[35] This study will enable us to understand several unclear matters in Cyril's writings. Thus, for example, the requirement that the monks come to the church at night is the only explicit characteristic given by Cyril for a laura of the Pharan type. Studying the prayer practices of the monks will enable us to determine to which nocturnal office Cyril is alluding and to compare such a laura with those founded by Sabas.

The monk's prayer routine and the rituals performed in the church were among the most important matters determined by the abbot of each monastery, and he took pains to impart them to his monks (*V. Char.* 16, 28; *V. Euth.* 39, 57–59; *V. Ger.* 2, 2–3; Theod. Petr., *V. Theod.* 18–19, 44–49; *V. Sab.* 32, 118; 43, 133–34). Familiarity with the monastic Book of Psalms, which made up the monk's daily prayers, was one of the basic requirements of a novice. Sabas had already learned the Psalms at the age of eight when he started out in the Flaviana monastery in Cappadocia (*V. Sab.* 2, 88). He demanded this knowledge and familiarity with the order of prayer from the novices who came to him at the Laura (*V. Sab.* 28, 113; cf. *Pratum* 166, 3033), and it was he who determined the routines of prayer in the Laura's two churches (*V. Sab.* 18, 102; 32, 118). The prohibition against talking in church during the prayers, which is also included in the Regula of Pachomius (*Pr.* 81: *Koinonia* II, 146) and those of the Syrian monasteries (Vööbus 1960b, 84.25, regulations attributed to Rabbula), is also mentioned in Cyril's writings (*V. Euth.* 9, 18). Euthymius did not create something new, but rather reiterated the essential rules of conduct for the monks.

Cyril's "heroes" were all ordained as priests at some point in their lives. It seems, however, that Theodosius excelled more than everyone in his acquaintance with the fine details of church services. When he was still a child, he served as a reader (Theod. Petr.,

---

[35] The earliest *horologion* of Mar Saba is the 9th-century Sin. gr. 863, published by J. Mateos, *Studi e Testi* 233 (Vatican City 1964), 47–76.

V. Theod. 2, 7) or cantor (ψάλτης) in the church of Comana in Cappadocia, where he received painstaking instruction in the order of prayers of the church and learned by heart the Book of Psalms and the other scriptures (*V. Theod.* 236). With this training, after coming to the Holy Land, he was a welcome recruit to the Cathisma church, which had been established by Hicelia, a noble Roman matron. She was the first to institute a candle-light procession for the feast of the Presentation of Jesus in the Temple and his encounter (ὑπαπάντησις) with Symeon of Jerusalem, who foresaw him as the Messiah (Luke 2:21–32). This feast was celebrated on February 14, forty days after Christmas (today the feast of the Purification of the Virgin, celebrated on Feb. 2; see Festugière 1963a, 58 n. 5). Theodosius served as a cantor in her church and was one of its staff of monks; after her death he administered the church. Theodosius determined the order of prayer in each of the four churches in his coenobium (Theod. Petr., *V. Theod.* 18, 44–45). Even on his deathbed he took care to appoint in each of his churches the monks who would chant psalms in pairs (an important remark in itself) and those responsible for the readings and the spiritual management of the ritual. He sought to ensure that even after his death the order of divine services would continue uninterrupted (ibid. 19, 49; see also *V. Theod.* 238). As was mentioned above, it was Sabas' concern as well to formulate the order and content of the liturgy in his monasteries, the celebration of the Eucharist, and the establishment of a monastic liturgical calender (see below, sec. B and Chap. 5c, para. 4).

Our information regarding the daily prayer schedule in the monasteries of the Judean desert is quite scanty. Most of it is derived from sixth- and early seventh-century sources, but the earliest evidence for monastic prayer in Palestine is that of John Cassian, which refers to the end of the fourth century (see below). Only if we assume a uniform practice in both laurae and coenobia and in urban and desert monasteries can we reconstruct the *cursus* of the daily liturgy, and even then the available sources do not give a complete picture. We must therefore examine the question on the broader background of the prevailing practices in other eastern monastic centers. This approach will also enable us to trace sources of influence on the Palestinian monastic liturgy. The following survey is based mainly on the work of Taft (1986).

The "pure" monastic Egyptian *cursus* by the end of the fourth century, both in Scetis and in the Pachomian monasteries, consisted of only two daily offices, one on rising and the other in the evening before retiring (such were also the cathedral offices at this period). In Scetis the morning office began at cockcrow, while in the Pachomian system, it seems, it was held at dawn, as in the cathedral *horarium*. In the Antonian colonies of Lower Egypt, these offices were held by each monk in his cell, while in the Pachomian monasteries they were held in common, in the church (morning) or in the houses/dormitories (evening). Earlier, in the third and early fourth centuries we encounter a continuous, ceaseless monastic prayer, interpreting literally 1 Thessalonians 5:17: "Pray without ceasing" (Hausherr 1956b). This was the practice of Antony and Palamon, Pachomius' teacher. During this period it was the practice to chant psalms aloud, constantly, uninterruptedly throughout the day. This practice prevailed as a private devotion even after fixed prayer hours were established, and it remained the spirit of the Egyptian monastic daily liturgy (Taft 1986, 66–73).

A different type of monastic office evolved during the fourth century in the urban monasteries. John Cassian (*Inst.* II.1–2, 59–61; III.3–4.2, 94–107), writing while already in Gaul, during the years 417–425, but referring to his monastery in Bethlehem, where he lived from ca. 382/3 to 385/6, describes a *cursus* of six prayer hours: at cockcrow, sunrise, at the third, sixth, and ninth hours, and vespers (at the eleventh hour).[36] He omits all mention of a formal office of compline (Taft 1986, 79).[37] He claims that an office of terce, sext, and none was the rule of the monasteries of Palestine, Mesopotamia, and the entire Orient, that is, the Diocese of Antioch. According to him, the office at sunrise was an innovation of his monastery in Bethlehem, where it was introduced in order to prevent the monks from going back to bed after nocturns and sleeping through until terce. Taft (1986, 78) suggests two stages of development in the Palestinian liturgy. First the "little hours" were added to the original Egyptian two-synaxis *cursus* and then, ca. 380, came the "new service" of matins at sunrise. Terce, sext, and none were recognized hours of private prayer already in the third century.

The time of the nocturnal vigil (nocturns) at cockcrow and its completion before dawn are also alluded to by Palladius' narrative about the ascetic monk Adolius on the Mount of Olives at about the same period. From the evening until the vigil prayer he would stand outside, exposed to the ravages of the weather, reciting psalms and prayers. When the knocking time arrived, he would pass between the cells and bang with a clapper on the doors, awakening the monks for the night prayer. It was only when this was finished, before dawn, that he would hasten to his cell for a short two hours' rest, until the next time of psalms, that is, the morning prayer which began with sunrise. Then, after praying, he would continue with the daily schedule until the evening (*HL* XLIII, 130). But there were also circles that recommended adherence to the earlier private devotion of continuous prayer (*Apoph. Pat.*, Epiphanius 3).

John Chrysostom refers to offices in Antioch at about the same period that resemble the usage of Bethlehem, including a morning office at daybreak. Maruta, however, in his regulations (early 5th century), specified seven times a day for prayer: morning, the third hour, the sixth, the ninth, the table hour, evening, and night (LIV.20: Vööbus 1982, 98.20–23). Seven times for prayer are recommended by the Nestorian Abraham of Kashkar in the late sixth century in the rules referring to his monastery at Mount Izla near Nisibis (Vööbus 1960b, 157–58). On the other hand, John of Ephesus, a Monophysite who wrote at about the same time, speaks of four times for common prayer in the monasteries in the region of Amida: nocturns, matins, sext, and vespers. Terce, none, and compline were private prayers, and continuous prayers between these hours were expressions of extreme devotion (see Brooks' commentary on *Eastern Saints* 35, 610; cf. Vööbus 1960a, 287 n. 52). Thus in eastern Syria and among ascetic circles we find a diverse range of prayer practices.

In the community of Juliana Saba in the province of Osrhoene, the monks would assemble for communal vespers that included the chanting of psalms. During the day, however, the disciples would walk in pairs in the desert and recite in turn fifteen psalms in succession while standing or recite prayers while genuflecting, from the early morning

---

[36] Jerome, who is in favor of fixed prayer times, mentions only five prayer hours per day, as a private devotion: at dawn, at the third, sixth, and ninth hours, and vespers. At night one should wake up two or three times for prayer (*Ep.* 22.37, 153). A prayer should also be said before and after each meal.

[37] Cf. the note of the editor, Guy, on *Inst.* III.4.3, 105, referring to *Inst.* IV.19.2, 146.

hours until late in the afternoon. The practice here, therefore, was continual daily prayer, similar to the early Egyptian practice (*HPh* II.5, 204–6). In the bilingual community of Publius in Zeugma in Euphratensis, all the members of the community met for the chanting of psalms in the morning and in the evening (*HPh* v.5, 334–36), similar to the "pure" monastic practice in Egypt by the end of the fourth century. Alexander Akoimetos (ca. 350–400) first arranged four service hours: the third, sixth, ninth, and nocturns. Later he developed this into seven times for prayer during the day and seven times during the night (*V. Alex.* 28, 678–79).

It was in Cappadocia that a full monastic *cursus* of seven prayer hours was developed. St. Basil, inspired by the private practice recommended to pious believers at least from the second and third centuries, maintained seven daily prayer times. This teaching was in accordance with his basic philosophy that monasticism is nothing but the complete and faithful fulfillment of all the commandments of Christianity. Thus he added five prayer times to the two customary prayer hours in the urban churches: morning prayer (ὄρθρος) at dawn and vespers. The five added prayer hours were at the third, sixth, and ninth hours, a concluding prayer (compline), and a midnight prayer. He established that the monk must punctiliously observe these hours, wherever he is, even if his labors take him far from the church or his monastery (Basil, *Reg. fus.* 37, 1009–16; Mateos 1963, 69–87; Taft 1986, 84–89).

The Daily *Cursus* of Prayers in the Monasteries of the Judean Desert

A *cursus* of seven times for prayer also prevailed in the desert monasteries of Jerusalem in the sixth century. This is explicitly attested for the monastery of Theodosius (Theod. Petr., *V. Theod.* 18, 45) and the laurae of Chariton (*V. Char.* 16, 28). The author of the *Vita Charitonis* ascribed this regulation to Chariton, who lived in the first half of the fourth century, but this is an anachronistic statement. However, it is clear that the author, a monk of Souka in the second half of the sixth century, was familiar with this practice. It seems, therefore, that at that time such was the *cursus* in coenobia, in laurae, and among anchorites (cf. *Pratum* 136, 3000).

According to the same author, Chariton also instructed his monks to remain awake for six hours[38] each night. In addition to the psalms recited at prayer times, he also recommended that each monk recite psalms while working in his cell on craftwork that did not divert his attention or read the scriptures (*V. Char.* 16, 28). The continuous repetition of psalms all day long indicates an Egyptian influence. An anecdote of John Moschus tells of a monk reciting psalms in his cell in the coenobium of Theognius while engaged in basket weaving, and another mentions a monk reciting psalms during the course of the day, not necessarily at the times fixed for prayer, in the coenobium of Theodosius (ibid. 105, 2965; 160, 3028).

A nightly vigil of six hours, recommended by Chariton, was probably the prevalent practice, as we learn from the Egyptian sources.[39] In connection with Chariton's recom-

---

[38] In ancient times, night and day, whose lengths change according to the seasons of the year, were divided into 12 hours each. The length of a daytime hour was accordingly different from that of a nighttime hour, and both of them changed with the seasons.

[39] Regarding the night prayers, we find in the earliest period in Egypt four alternatives, in each of which the night is divided equally between 6 hours of sleep and 6 hours of prayer (Mensbrugghe 1957).

mendation to his monks in Pharan to read the scriptures in their cells between the times of prayer, one should note that John Moschus relates the following sixth-century story about a monk of Pharan. The monk was so stricken by thoughts about the profound significance of a saying of Jesus to the Apostles that he could not restrain himself. He left his cell in the middle of the day to go to a learned monk in the laura of the Towers near Jericho in order to have it interpreted for him (*Pratum* 40, 2893).

Information on any specific office in the desert monasteries is very meager. John Moschus mentions the psalms of the third hour recited by an anchorite who lived in a cave near the Jordan River (*Pratum* 40, 2893). The "little hours" were not held on Sunday (cf. ibid. 2896). At vespers (ἑσπερινόν), as at other prayer times, all the monks of the coenobium would assemble in the church (*Miracula* 1, 362). In the first part of this prayer (τὰ λυχνικά), the lamps would be lit (*V. Sab.* 60, 161; Festugière 1962b, 89 n. 182). According to Egeria, the lighting of the lamps was held at the tenth hour, two hours before sunset (*Itin. Eger.* 4.24, 238–39). It may be assumed that there was no difference between this practice in the Jerusalem churches and in the desert monasteries, for it was the falling darkness that dictated the time. The sources mention a lamplighter (κανδηλάνπτης) in the monastery of Choziba (*Miracula* 6, 368–69), a task held for a period of time by Antony of Choziba (*V. Geor.* 34, 133).

There are more details about the rising office—the nocturnal vigil—in the desert monasteries. The time for the night prayer was announced to the monks by knocking on a wooden beam or a sounding board (τὸ ξύλον) (cf. Fig. 75);[40] it is reasonable to assume that they were informed in a similar manner of the other daily prayer times (and meal times as well). This was the task of the precentor (κανονάρχης), who consulted a sundial (Fig. 76). Such was the practice both in the coenobia (*Miracula* 1, 362; *Pratum* 104, 2961, in the monastery of Theodosius) and in the laurae (*V. Cyr.* 7, 227; *V. Sab.* 43, 134). The call for the night vigil prayer obviously was of special importance. When Cyriacus served as precentor, he would not cease knocking until he had finished reciting to himself the entire Psalm 118 (119), the longest chapter in the Psalter, containing 176 verses (*V. Cyr.* 7, 227).

Antony preferred to divide the night into three parts, the first and the third of which he would pass in prayer, sleeping in the middle part. This practice did not completely disappear in later periods. It was followed by Varsanuphius, who went into seclusion near Gaza in the 6th century (becoming a complete recluse in 543), and who recommended 6 hours of sleep (response to question 146 [75], p. 130, ed. Régnault-Lemaire).

Palamon knew of three alternative approaches: ceaseless prayer until midnight, followed by sleep until the morning, the practice of Abba Isaiah in the 5th century in Scetis (*Discourse* 4, para. 45, p. 61, ed. Régnault-de Broc); the reverse order: sleep until midnight and ceaseless prayer from midnight until morning; and the division of the night into alternating short periods of prayer and sleep, from the evening until the morning.

[40] The metal mallet with which they would beat on a wooden board in the Greek monasteries is currently called τὸ σήμαντρον or τὸ σημαντῆρι. This term is not mentioned in Cyril's writings. See Festugière 1962a, 119–20 n. 145. According to Jerome, the call to the synaxis in the Pachomian monasteries at the end of the 4th century was done with a horn or trumpet (*vox tubae*), (*Koinonia* II, 145: *Pr.* 3), but see Veilleux's note (ibid. 185), who is of the opinion that this is a paraphrase by Jerome, made during the course of his translation of the *Regula* of Pachomius.

75. Mar Saba monk knocking on a sounding board, calling for prayer.

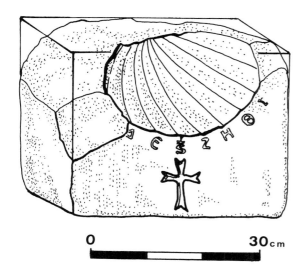

76. Sundial from Kastellion.

In the coenobium all the monks would hurry to the church for the night prayer (νυκτερινή) (*Miracula* 1, 362; *V. Euth.* 50; 72), while each cell dweller or anchorite would recite the night psalms in his own cell or cave (*V. Geor.* 13, 109; regarding Sabas, see below). Gerasimus forbade his monks to light a lamp at this hour in order to read by its light after the prayer; according to him, this practice was appropriate for the coenobites, not for the cell dwellers (*V. Ger.* 4, 4; cf. Theod. Petr., *V. Theod.* 18, 48). These episodes indicate that the office was concluded when it was still night.

The story of Sabas and the lion in a cave near the river of Gadara (*V. Sab.* 33, 119) informs us about the practice of the anchorite in the recitation of the night psalms and its time—after midnight—in accordance with the Palestinian tradition and not the Cappadocian one. The lion, in whose cave Sabas established his dwelling, returned to the cave around midnight and found Sabas sound asleep. Afterwards Sabas arose and began to recite the night psalms, and upon completion of his recitation he went back to sleep.

In the Great Laura, in addition to the private night prayer in the cells, was there also a communal night prayer in the great church? Incidental to the story of the death of the monk Anthimus (*V. Sab.* 43, 133), it is related that Sabas awoke during the night before the knocking time, and the sound of a multitude of people chanting psalms filled his ears. He wondered, left his cell for the church, and found it locked; he then understood that the voices were those of the angels accompanying the soul of Anthimius on its way to heaven. Sabas wondered whether a prayer was being conducted in the church, in contrast to the accepted practice and in opposition to his opinion.[41] It is evident therefore that no night prayer was conducted in the church during weekdays.

From the continuation of this narrative we learn that when Sabas summoned the precentor and ordered him to strike the knocking board, monks were found who joined Sabas; accompanied by candles and incense, they made their way to Anthimus' cave.

---

[41] According to Festugière's translation of this passage, Sabas wondered *whether the prayer in the church had already begun,* for the hour of knocking, calling all to prayer, had not yet arrived. Such a night prayer was held in coenobia. But Festugière erred in his translation. I am indebted to Leah Di Segni, with whom I consulted regarding this point.

Upon hearing the sounding board, each monk was to awaken from sleep but remain in his cell. Cyril does not list which monks joined Sabas and how they assembled around him. It is possible that these were the monks who held service positions in the maintenance and administration of the Laura, who due to their daily occupations were not cell dwellers and probably lived in the center of the Laura close to the church, and therefore it was a simple matter to summon them from their cells. But despite the fact that they were not cell dwellers, each of them recited the night vigil alone in his cell. They did not gather at this hour in the church, as did the coenobites, although Sabas would at times spend the night alone in private prayer in the church (*V. Sab.* 17, 101).

Nocturnal Vigilance

Remaining awake the entire night was considered to be an expression of asceticism and excellence in the battle against the Evil One. In Palestine there was no monastery of *akoimetoi* (ἀκοίμητοι) like the famous monastery near Constantinople founded by the monk Alexander (Pargoire 1907; Vailhé 1912; Grumel 1937),[42] but it is almost certain that many of the monks adopted this practice for some period or other during their monastic career. There are many reports of nocturnal vigils; Chariton was known for them. For his monks, however, he established the accepted norm of nocturnal vigilance of only six hours (*V. Char.* 15, 27; 16, 28) (a rising office at cockcrow actually meant a six-hour sleep after compline). In the laura of Douka, Elpidius, a Cappadocian who expanded and consolidated this monastery, was also noted for his nocturnal vigilance. Palladius, an eyewitness, describes how Elpidius would recite psalms at night while standing; he continued this practice for twenty-five years. The presence of Palladius and others apparently indicates that this refers to a vigil in the church and not in Elpidius' cell (*HL* xlviii, 142–43). During this same period the monk Adolius, from Tarsus in Cilicia, that is, a monk of Syrian origin, living on the Mount of Olives, adopted an extreme manner of vigilance (described above).[43]

Sabas, during the eleven years that he lived in the coenobium of Theoctistus, when still young, would spend his days in physical labor and his nights without sleep, reciting psalms (*V. Sab.* 8, 92). The night that a pillar of fire pointed out to him the location of the cave in which he established the Theoktistos Church, he was outside his cave wandering along the gorge while reciting psalms. After the revelation, he remained awake outside his cave the entire night, reciting psalms and praying (*V. Sab.* 18, 101). By way of contrast, in the story about Sabas and the lion, he awoke for the vigil prayer and did not maintain vigilance the entire night, and such was also the case in the story of Anthimus' death.

Such asceticism was maintained not only by the laurites and anchorites. John Moschus relates an episode about a monk from the monastery of Theodosius who kept night vigils for ten years, reciting psalms and prostrating himself on the steps of Theodosius' cave, after which he would remain there until the knocking hour, when he would

---

[42] In the church of this monastery, psalms were chanted without interruption, all day and all night, by alternating choirs of monks.

[43] On the extreme vigilance practiced by Syrian monks near Amida in the 6th century, see Vööbus 1960a, 264–65; *HPh*, ed. Price, 220. See also the following note.

go up to the church and participate in the night prayer with all the fathers (*Pratum* 105, 2965). Moschus similarly tells the story of another monk from the same monastery who would come to the church early, before the knocking time, and then recite the *Kyrie eleison* in the church in addition to the usual psalms, or he would pray outside raising his hands to heaven (*Pratum* 104, 2961). Cyriacus also would pass the nights in prayer when he was in the coenobium of Gerasimus (*V. Cyr.* 4, 225). It is also related that there was a monk in Choziba, a former boxer, who exhausted himself during the day in his work and during the night would engage in lengthy prayer in front of the tomb of the five holy fathers, and afterwards, before the knocking hour, would take a short nap while sitting on a stone bench; after the vigil prayer he never slept but would go out to gather *mannouthion*, even before dawn (*V. Geor.* 19, 118).

Vigilance was kept while reciting prayers by maintaining a standing position. In order to make it easier for the monks to remain erect in their cells, or prevent them from sleeping on their side, supports for the body were installed, intended to prevent the exhausted monks from keeling over (*V. Euth.* 21, 34; Theod. Petr., *V. Theod.* 7, 18).[44]

Remaining awake the entire night was an ascetic practice, and like any other type of asceticism, it was an effort beyond the norm, an expression of excellence. This demand is not included among the normative instructions Gerasimus gave to his monks (*V. Ger.* 2–3, 2–4) and, as noted above, Chariton did not demand this of his monks either. On the other hand, the night vigil held between Saturday and Sunday was not regarded as a special act of asceticism but rather as the norm. Its observance was mandatory for all the monks in the monasteries in which it was practiced.

The All-Night Vigil between Saturday and Sunday

1. *In the Great Laura*

Sabas instructed that at the Laura "an all-night vigil (ἀγρυπνία) be held, uninterruptedly from evening until the morning, in both the churches on Sundays and dominical feasts" (*V. Sab.* 32, 118).[45] These vigils were initiated by Sabas upon the dedication of the Theotokos Church (July 1, 501). If it had been the practice before then to conduct the Eucharistic rite not only on Sunday but on Saturday as well, then the night between the two ceremonies was probably also a vigil (see below, sec. B, regarding the Eucharistic rites in the Laura).

2. *In the Laura of Euthymius and in the Laura of Pharan*

Such a practice did not exist in the laura of Euthymius (cf. Arranz 1980, 106). Cyril tells of an altercation between Euthymius and another monk when the two hastened to the church for the night prayer (*V. Euth.* 24, 36). Cyril took the trouble to mention that

---

[44] Cf. John of Ephesus, *Eastern Saints* 35, 612: "[There were] others, ranged in rows and standing on standing posts, and others who were tied to the ceiling of the room by ropes and vine branches, and were suspending themselves by them in a standing posture all night, having put them under their armpits, and others who were sitting on seats and never falling on their sides."

[45] For the night-long vigil in the monastery of Theodosius on Easter, see Theod. Petr., *V. Theod.* 20, 50–53.

this happened on Saturday night, implying that the night prayer was not held in the laura church on the other days of the week. The holding of a night prayer between Saturday and Sunday, and not of an all-night vigil in the church, is a significant difference between the prayer practices of the laura of Euthymius (a laura of the type of Pharan) and the Sabaite laurae.

Additional evidence, from the end of the sixth century, that a vigil was not held in the church of Pharan on the night between Saturday and Sunday is adduced by Moschus (who lived there during the years 568–578) in a story about the monk Cosmas, whom he knew personally. On this night Cosmas used to stand, from evening to dawn, reciting psalms and reading in his cell and in the church (*Pratum* 40, 2896). This implies that he began his night vigil in his cell and completed it in the church, where he undoubtedly arrived after the night knocking. These two stories prove that in laurae of the Pharan type it was not customary to gather in the church on Saturday for the Sunday Eucharistic rite. Nor was it held in these laurae on Saturday, as we shall see below. The gathering in the church was for the purpose of reciting the night prayer. This was followed by the morning prayer (*matutinale*/ὄρθρος) at sunrise, as was the accepted practice, and it was only at a later hour that the Sunday liturgy was held.

Now we can properly understand the reasoning that prevented Euthymius and Theoctistus from establishing a laura around the cave at Nahal Og (Wadi Mukellik): "At first (Euthymius and Theoctistus) did not want to make the place into a coenobium, but into a laura after the type of Pharan; but, when they realized that nobody would be able to come to the church by night, on account of the inaccessible nature of the site—as I said above—step by step they built the place into a coenobium, keeping the cave as church" (*V. Euth.* 9, 16–17). In the Sabaite laurae there was no need for the monks to go from their cells to the church at night, and therefore no obstacle to their cells being located in rocky ravines or cliff formations, such as the channel of Nahal Og. Sabas and his disciples established in such ravines the Great Laura, the New Laura, the laura of Firminus, and the laura of Jeremias, whose layout and remains were explored and are known today. Pharan and Souka were also established in similar ravines, but there the monks would make their way to the church on Saturday nights. When Euthymius learned of the topographical limitations of the banks of Nahal Og in which he settled, and the resulting difficulties of holding this night prayer, he refrained from establishing a laura there. As for his laura, he preferred to locate it in a flat area, which would enable his monks to make their way safely at night from their cells to the laura church.

Apparently there was no Saturday night vigil in the coenobium of Theoctistus either. Therefore, on Saturdays Euthymius saw no need to leave his anchorite cave in his laura (in the years 426–428, before a community had come into being there) and go to the coenobium. This was a later practice of George and the other cell dwellers in Choziba, who would come to the coenobium late on Saturday in order to hold an all-night vigil in the church before the Sunday liturgy (see below).

3. *In the Laura of Gerasimus*

Was it indeed Sabas who began the new practice of the laura monks assembling from their cells on Saturday and remaining in the center of the laura until after the Sunday liturgy? Gerasimus' regulations, which preceded Sabas' activity as an abbot by about thirty years, determined that each monk of his laura would remain in his cell on week-days and come to the church on Saturday and Sunday. The Saturday and Sunday prayers were communal, with all the monks—both cell dwellers and coenobites—participating. It is not stated, however, that the night between Saturday and Sunday should be held in communal vigil; and since it would have been very difficult to arrange sleeping accommodations for 70 monks in the heart of the coenobium, in conditions appropriate for the laurites, we should assume that the laurites returned to their cells sometime after the Saturday communal meal and then came again to the church for the Sunday office. If the people of Jericho crowded the place, bringing donations for the monastery, they would leave the coenobium and return to their cells more promptly.

4. *In Choziba*

Observing an all-night vigil between Saturday and Sunday was practiced by the cell dwellers of Choziba at the end of the sixth and the beginning of the seventh century during the time of George of Choziba. They would come to the coenobium late on Saturday toward the evening prayer and stay until the afternoon of the following day (*V. Geor.* 12, 107–9; 20, 119–20; 42, 143–44). His disciple Antony states that George refrained from sleeping in the coenobium (ibid. 20, 119–20), implying that he and the other cell dwellers observed an all-night vigil in the church between Saturday and Sunday. It is quite possible that all the inhabitants of the coenobium (and not only Antony, of his own volition) joined the cell dwellers there.

5. *Conclusions*

The Sunday *agrypnia* was an important innovation that Sabas introduced into the Palestinian monastic rite. There was nothing like it either in Pharan or in the laurae of Euthymius and Gerasimus. During the sixth century it spread to other monasteries, and by the end of that century it was practiced in Choziba. At about the same time it is also attested in Sinai (Longo 1965–66, 251–52; Taft 1986, 198–99). Yet the older Palestinian tradition was still preserved in Pharan.

Cyril of Scythopolis does not give any details about the *ordo* of this office. But our earliest source about the liturgical materials included in this *agrypnia* is the not much later narration of John and Sophronius on Nilus of Sinai, mentioned above (although this material, at least in its entirety, is not necessarily as old as the rest of the account; see Arranz 1976, 48; Taft 1986, 199). This office became the most recognizable feature of the Sabaitic *Typika* of later generations, being located at the very beginning of these texts and forming the centerpiece of the Byzantine monastic liturgy. The Athonite redaction of the new Sabaitic *Typika* of the eleventh and twelfth centuries constitutes the Byzantine rite of the present day (Arranz 1980, 174–78; Taft 1988, 187).

B. The Celebration of the Eucharist

Introduction

How frequently was the Eucharist celebrated in the various monasteries of the Judean desert throughout the Byzantine period? This is an important factor in the life of any monastic community. When speaking about the frequency of the Eucharist, some distinctions must first be made: "There are community Eucharists and Eucharists of a more private nature. There is the eucharistic liturgy or mass; and the eucharistic communion, whether during mass or not; and the relative frequency of each. Finally, each of these 'Eucharists' has its own rhythms and demands its own separate answer to the question, 'How often?'" (Taft 1984, 61). We must also distinguish between the "community" Eucharist and the monastic practice.

The Eucharist was not celebrated everywhere throughout the Christian world with the same frequency; there were also changes and developments during the course of the first centuries of Christianity. The theological basis for this rite is Jesus' speech in the Capernaum synagogue (John 6:32–35, 53–56). Breaking and eating the sacred bread and drinking the consecrated wine (cf. Matt. 26:26–28 and parallels) constitute a form of joining (communion) with the body of Jesus and recalling his memory and are the key to personal redemption (1 Cor. 10:16; 11:23–25), but the New Testament does not specify with what frequency the Communion rite is to be celebrated. On the basis of a comparison with the manna that the Children of Israel gathered in the desert each day, except for the Sabbath, it can be interpreted that this should be done frequently, and thus many viewed it as man's daily food, similar to regular bread. In this spirit, the *Pater Noster* (Matt. 6:9–11; Luke 11:2–3) is interpreted as referring to the bread of the Eucharist. However, there is no unequivocal proof in the New Testament supporting this interpretation of a daily Eucharist. The Acts of the Apostles (20:7) speak of the rite on Sunday.

The second-century sources are already clear, speaking of a weekly rite on Sunday in which all members of the community participated. Starting from the third century we encounter a different reality: the sources speak of frequent Communion—several times per week. Many of the church fathers in both East and West recommended celebrating the Eucharist daily. But the faithful, and even the monks (for different reasons), mainly in the East, did not carry out this recommended practice (Dublanchy 1911; Duhr 1953; Taft 1984, 63).

According to Taft (1984, 64–65), during the fourth century, as a result of the triumph of the Church, an evolution took place: "We see the Eucharist spreading from Sunday, to Saturday and Sunday in Alexandria, North Syria, Asia Minor and Constantinople; to Wednesday, Friday, Sunday in Palestine (including Jerusalem), Cyprus and Mesopotamia; to Friday, Saturday, Sunday in Antioch; to Wednesday, Friday, Saturday and Sunday in Caesarea; and finally to 'every day' in fifth-century Alexandria." Daily Mass was instituted in Rome and Constantinople only later.[46]

The following survey will focus mainly on monastic circles in the East, and only to a lesser extent will it include information on the "community" practice in each region.

---

[46] According to Gorce (*V. Mel. Jun.* 99 n. 1), prior to the 4th century, two different types of liturgical week were in practice in the Christian world: in one the Eucharist was held on Wednesday and Friday, which were fastdays, and the rite marked the conclusion of the fast, which lasted until the ninth hour. According to this model, Saturday was a non-liturgical day, i.e., the Eucharist was not celebrated on it. This practice is mentioned as early as the 3rd century in North Africa by Tertullian. The second system is the one that developed in Egypt; according to it, the fastdays Wednesday and Friday are non-liturgical days, and the Eucharist is celebrated only on Saturday and Sunday. It appears that Basil, who speaks of four weekly Eucharists, on Wednesday, Friday, Saturday, and Sunday (see below), combined both traditions. Melania was influenced by the first method, which was quite rare in the East.

Eucharistic services held on feast days or on special occasions are excluded. The purpose is to point out diversity and evolution and possible sources of influence on the Palestinian monastic practice and the significance of the Sabaitic system within it.

1. *The Eucharistic Rite in Egypt*

Although the *Vita Antonii* by Athanasius does not contain any specific mention of the Eucharistic rite, the prevalent scholarly opinion is that Antony did not maintain that the monk is exempt from taking part in this basic sacrament of Christianity, and that he himself did not refrain from participating in the rite whenever possible. The hagiographies of Jerome as well do not refer to this subject (Dekkers 1957). There were monks, such as the Messalians in Asia Minor, who wished to refrain from the Eucharist, believing that they no longer had any need for it. Such was also the case with the Egyptian monks Valens and Heron, who are mentioned by Palladius (*HL* xxv.5, 80; xxvi.2, 81; see also xvii.9, 46; xxvii.2, 83; lix.2, 153–54). John Cassian, who was quite familiar with the practice in Lower Egypt as well as in Palestine, rebukes monks who refrained from participating in the liturgy more than once a year, since they believed that only saints were worthy of it. He charges that in doing so they are guilty of the sin of excessive pride, which they wanted to avoid. He emphasizes the need to participate in the rite, at least on Sundays (*Con.* xxiii.21.1–2, 167–68). There were not many such extreme anchorites, however, and in general even those in seclusion attempted to participate regularly in the Eucharist in a village or community near their place of seclusion.

There are stories about a priest who came on a regular basis to monks in their place of seclusion, bringing with him the sacred elements or performing the rite in a place where they assembled for the purpose.[47] Again, an ascetic anchorite in the Achoris region named John received Communion every Sunday from a priest whom he met at a predetermined place (*HM* xiii.4, 99; 8, 100). There is also a story about Helle and the village priest, who would come every Sunday to the monastery beyond the river in order to conduct the Eucharistic rite for the brothers. He ceased doing so, stricken by fear, after a large crocodile had torn to pieces several people who had tried to cross the Nile at that same place (*HM* xii.6–9, 94–95).

In fact, the anchorites and monks who lived in communities, in both Lower and Upper Egypt, followed the practice of the local church. The general practice in Egypt in the fourth century was to celebrate the Eucharist twice a week, on Saturday and Sunday. Thus Socrates Scholasticus, referring to a period ca. 380 (Taft 1984, 63), relates that in Egypt, apart from Alexandria and its environs, the Communion rite was held on Saturday and Sunday (*HE* v.22, 636). But, at a shortly later period, the rite was celebrated in Alexandria on Saturdays also.

According to Palladius, the monks of Nitria would come to the church only on Saturday and Sunday, not on the other days of the week (*HL* vii.5, 26). We also learn this from the description of Nitria in the *Historia Monachorum* (xx.5–8, 120–21). In his Latin

---

[47] The verb used in Coptic to describe the gathering of the monks by the priest for the conducting of the Eucharist has its source in the Greek verb συνάγειν, "to assemble," which is the source of the word σύναξις, with the meaning of Eucharistic rite (Veilleux 1968, 228; Festugière, *HM* 82 n. on para. 34; Ward's trans., 133 n. 2 on chap. 12; Lampe 1961, 1302, meaning B).

translation, Rufinus adds that this was the practice in Kellia (Rufinus, *HM* xx.8-PL 21, 444–45; ed. Schulz-Flügel, xxii, 358–59). There is also a teaching by Poemen, a monk of Scetis, regarding the consecration of the bread and wine on Saturday and Sunday (*Apoph. Pat.*, Poemen 30). John Cassian also supplies evidence for this practice in Scetis (*Inst.* iii.2, 92–4; *Con.* iii.1, 139; Chadwick 1968, 67–69).

Such was the practice in the Pachomian monasteries as well (Veilleux 1968, 230–35, 248). During the earliest stage in Pachomius' first monastery, the rites were conducted in the church of the nearby village, to which the monks marched with Pachomius at their head. When the community grew, he established a church within the monastery itself. However, as long as there was no priest within his community, the monks continued to attend the village church for the rite on Saturday evening, while the village priests came to the monastery for the Sunday rite (Veilleux 1968, 230–31).

According to Socrates, in Egypt beyond Alexandria, and especially in the Thebaid, the Saturday rite was special, different from the accepted Christian rite in other places, in that it was held toward evening after a festive meal. A short while later John Cassian, who was quite familiar with the Egyptian customs in Scetis during the years 385–399, attests to the practice of assembling on Saturday and on Sunday at the third hour (*Inst.* ii.2.2, 60; iii.2, 93–95).

In the Apollo monastery in Bawit (in the Thebaid), there was a daily Communion service at the ninth hour. There were also monks who lived on the mountain outside the monastery who came there each day in order to communicate, after which they would go home until the rite on the following day (*HM* viii.50–51, 66–67). But there is no evidence of a daily Eucharistic liturgy in any coenobitic community in Egypt (Taft 1984, 69 and n. 73).

2. *The Eucharistic Rite in Syria*

Chapter 14 of the *Didache*, a Syrian source of the second century, mentions one Eucharistic rite per week, on Sunday. Later sources, for example, the *Apostolic Constitution* and Socrates Scholasticus (*HE* v.22, 636), both referring to a period ca. 380, and John Malalas in the sixth century (*Frag.* no. 44, ed. de Boor, 171; Di Segni 1988, 219) indicate that the practice throughout the entire East was to celebrate the Eucharist twice a week, on Saturday and Sunday. Other sources from the end of the fourth century on add Wednesday and Friday (ref. in Taft 1984).

What information is available concerning the frequency of this rite in monastic circles? The sources are meager regarding the Eucharist in the Syrian monasteries in the fourth and fifth centuries and regarding its place in the ritual along with the psalms, prayer, and scripture reading. Only two of the monks about whom Theodoret speaks also served as priests in monasteries of the coenobium type, and churches are mentioned in only two monasteries. The archaeological findings, on the other hand, indicate the existence of a church in every monastery. Despite the meager direct evidence, it is clear that the Syrian monks highly regarded the Eucharist and its celebration. Some early Syriac writings developed the theme that the hermit, as a dwelling place of the Holy Spirit, offered in his life a spiritual sacrifice equivalent to the Eucharist; or that, despite the monk's bodily distance from the divine service conducted in the church, he were spiritually present (*HPh*, ed. Price 1985, 99 n. 6; Beck 1958, 259–60). Indeed, due to their special way of life, anchorites did not attend divine service regularly (e.g., *HPh* XIII.4, 480–82).

There were instances in which special arrangements were made in order to enable the anchorite to communicate. Bassus, in his capacity as *periodeutes* (περιοδευτης), used to bring the sacred elements to Symeon when the latter lived as an anchorite before ascending his pillar (*HPh* XXVI.7, 172), and Theodoret held a special liturgy for the anchorite Maris when he visited him (*HPh* XX.4, 66–68). On the other hand, the anchorite Zenon took care to participate every Sunday in the Eucharistic liturgy in the church near the place of his seclusion (*HPh* XII.5, 468), and similarly the anchoress Domnina (*HPh* XXX.1, 240; Canivet 1977, 230–32). However, the regular participation of anchorites in the liturgy was exceptional, and it should be noted that Zenon and Domnina did not participate in the Saturday service which, according to the above-mentioned testimony of Socrates and Malalas, was held in Syria as well. The monks therefore did not take part in this rite as frequently as ordinary believers.

The monastic regulations also mention a communal Eucharist held only on Sunday, and it was recommended that the monks maintain vigilance during the preceding night (Vööbus 1960b, 91.12, Rules for the Persians). Similarly, the regulations of the Izla monastery mention a communal prayer for the cell dwellers only on Sundays or on feasts, attendance at which was mandatory (ibid., Abraham's Rules 8, 161; Dadishoa's Rules 4, 168–69).

3. *The Eucharistic Rite in Cappadocia in the Teachings of Basil*

Basil attributed more importance to the divine liturgy and its inclusion in the monastic life than did other leaders of the movement (Dekkers 1957, 46). Like the church fathers in the West (see below) and John Chrysostom in Constantinople, he was in favor of daily Communion. He himself, however, received it only four times a week—Wednesday, Friday, Saturday, and Sunday—and on other days of the week only if this was a memorial day for a saint (Basil, *Ep.* 93, 203 ff, ed. Courtonne). This was the frequency with which the Eucharist was celebrated in Caesarea.

Basil also mentions the practice of taking the sacred elements home, after they had been consecrated by the priest, and partaking of them each day, or a number of times during the week, as an act of participation in Communion. He approved of this practice only in cases when there was no priest available from whom the monk could receive the sacrament. He states that this was practiced not only during periods of religious persecution but also among the anchorites in places where there was no priest, so that the monks used to partake of Communion by themselves in their cells. Similarly in Alexandria and in Egypt, every person, even among the laity, would keep the sacred elements at home and take Communion at will. It was sufficient that the elements had been consecrated once, so that small portions of them could be taken periodically, as if consecrated and given by the priest's very hands each day (Basil, *Ep.* 93, 204). Gregory of Nazianzus also mentions this practice, but Shenoute of Atripe prohibited it to his monks (Dühr 1953, 1240). Moschus tells of a similar practice in the sixth century in Seleucia near Antioch: receiving Communion on Holy Thursday and carrying it home in a box for private use (*Pratum* 79, 2935–38). He states that this was the local custom; however, this refers only to the consecration of the elements on Holy Thursday and not to a weekly practice. At any rate, it is clear that these practices fell within the category of a private, rather than a communal, rite.

4. *The Eucharistic Rite in the West*

In the West, already in the third century, in the writings of Tertullian and Cyprian there is mention of the practice of taking home the consecrated elements in order to partake of them privately. In the fourth and fifth centuries Ambrose of Milan, Jerome, Augustine, and Zenon of Verona also speak of this practice. It was prohibited by the Council of Toledo in 400, which required communicants to consume the sacred elements in church immediately after receiving them from the priest (Dühr 1953).

In the West, more than in other places, the practice of celebrating daily Mass prevailed. Tertullian and Cyprian preached in favor of this in the third century, as well as Ambrose of Milan, Chromatius of Aquileia, Zenon of Verona, Hilary of Poitiers, and Augustine of Hippo in the fourth and fifth centuries. It was, however, an expression of excessive piety, and church fathers complained about the faithful who neglected to observe it. According to Ambrose, indifference to the daily celebration of the Mass was characteristic of the East.

Augustine was aware of the existence of other practices and refrained from censuring them: some held the rite on Saturday and Sunday and others only on Sunday. According to him, the proper method was to follow the practice of the local church (Epistle 54.2, 3, Response to the questions of Januarius: PL 33, 200–201). According to Socrates (ibid.), in Rome (and in Alexandria), in contrast to the entire Christian world, the Eucharistic rite was not celebrated on Saturday (Dühr, 1953; Dublanchy 1911; Testore 1950, 135).

Gerontius held a private Mass every day on the Mount of Olives for Melania, who came from the West. John Rufus states that this was a Roman practice (*V. Petr. Ib.* 31 [36]), a statement also included in the Latin version of the *Vita* (*V. Mel. Jun.*, ed. Gorce, 99 n. 13). In contrast to her private practice, Melania designated for her nuns on the Mount of Olives only two Eucharistic rites per week, on Friday and on Sunday, in addition to feast days (*V. Mel. Jun.* 48, 218–19 and Gorce's introduction, ibid. 98–101). The Eucharist was not celebrated there on Saturday.

In the early sixth-century pre-Benedictine *Rule of the Master,* Mass was celebrated only on Sundays, though Communion was distributed daily. John Cassian, in the early fifth century, also recommended to his monks at Provence to take Communion each day if possible (*Con.* VII.30, 271). Benedict's *Rule* barely mentions the Eucharist, and except for Sunday Mass in the monastery church, it is not clear that there was even daily Communion (Taft 1984, 69).

5. *The Eucharistic Rite in Palestine*

Evidence that the Eucharist was celebrated on Saturday in Palestine (and in the entire East) is found in the above-mentioned passages in Socrates and Malalas.

According to Egeria (*Itin. Eger.* 24.1–25.6, 235–51), who visited Jerusalem in 381 and 384, the Eucharist was celebrated there four times a week—on Wednesday, Friday, Saturday, and Sunday—similar to the Cappadocian practice (ibid. 27.5–6, 238 n. 2; Wilkinson's trans., 70; Gorce, *V. Mel. Jun.* 114–15; cf. Taft 1984, 64, who excludes Saturday).

In most churches, the Sunday liturgy was celebrated before the fourth hour, and it was only in the church of the Holy Sepulcher, because of the length of the sermons, that the rite began only after the fourth or fifth hour.

As in other places, the monks celebrated the Eucharist less frequently than did ordinary believers (see Dekkers 1957, 41). Information concerning monasteries in Palestine, not those of the Judean desert discussed below, is quite meager. It is known that at the end of the fourth and the beginning of the fifth century Paula's nuns, who also came from the West, would participate in Sunday Mass in the church of the Nativity, which was close to their nunnery (Jerome, *Ep.* 108.20, 186). On weekdays prayers were held within the nunnery. These prayers did not include the Eucharistic rite (Gorce, *V. Mel. Jun.* 98 n. 2).

The anchorites in Sinai mentioned by Nilus in his *Narrationes* (3, 620) ca. 400 CE lived in cells 20 *stadia* or more from each other and visited each other during the week, but assembled in the church only on Sundays. Varsanuphius, in the sixth century, in contrast, recommended celebrating the Eucharist more frequently. In fact, in the nearby monastery of Abba Seridos, in the region of Gaza, the Eucharist was celebrated on Wednesday and Friday as well (Perrone 1988, 471 n. 18; Barsanuphius and John, Question 32, 34–35, ed. Régnault-Lemaire).

In 507 the rebellious monks who left the Great Laura, settling in the ravine where the New Laura would later be established, made their way to Thekoa every Sunday in order to participate in the consecration of the sacred bread in the prayerhouse of the prophet Amos (*V. Sab.* 36, 123). These monks attributed great importance to the celebration of the Eucharist regularly—one of the reasons for their rebellion against Sabas was that he kept himself, and even prevented his monks, from being ordained as priests. It may be assumed that in Thekoa the Eucharist was celebrated on Saturday as well, as it was in all of Palestine, the East, and in Egypt. Consequently, the above-mentioned passage of Cyril may be so interpreted, that monks would celebrate the Mass only on Sunday. It is also possible, however, that they intentionally refrained from coming twice a week to the community church, which women and children also attended, in order not to mingle with them too frequently. As we have seen, the anchorite Zenon near Antioch would also come for prayer and the divine liturgy in the church only on Sundays, although this rite was held in that region also on Saturday.

6. *The Eucharistic Rites in the Monasteries of the Judean Desert*

A monk who had been ordained was also authorized to celebrate the Eucharist in his cell, either for himself or together with others, in their honor or at their request. Such a rite could be celebrated on any day of the week and was an act of communion among the participants, expressing a mutual recognition of each other's orthodoxy. John the Hesychast celebrated the liturgy in his cell for the nephew of the deaconess Basilina, thereby uniting him with the Orthodox Church (*V. John Hes.* 23, 219). There are scattered allusions throughout the sources to altars, icons, and other liturgical furnishings connected with the monk's private chapel in his cell (see above, Part II, Chap. 1A).

Moschus tells of an elderly monk from the laura of Abba Petrus near the Jordan River who, during his fifty years of seclusion, ate bran (πίτυρα), drank no wine, and ate no bread other than the sacred bread, which he partook of three times a week (*Pratum*

17, 2864–65). It is extremely doubtful whether we can conclude from this that on these days he consecrated the sacred elements privately in his cell (which he did not leave), since Moschus does not refer to him as a priest. It is more likely that he followed the practice mentioned by Basil (*Ep.* 93, etc.), in which the sacred bread of which he partook was brought to his cave together with his food. In the coenobium it was also possible to celebrate a special liturgy on a regular weekday in honor of a distinguished guest or a generous pilgrim, such as the rite celebrated by the monks of Choziba for the matron from Byzantium who sought a cure in their monastery. In this case as well, the rite served as an act of communion (*Miracula* 1, 362–63).

More important for our discussion, however, are the routine services and the Eucharistic rites in which all the monks of the community took part, and not the special ceremonies or the private ceremonies conducted by monks in their cells. Our question again is: how many times per week was the Eucharist celebrated in the desert monasteries of Jerusalem? Was this done only on Sunday—as in the nunnery of Paula in Bethlehem and as in the practice of the Sinai monks of whom Nilus speaks—or was the rite held also on Saturday, as was the practice in the Egyptian monasteries? The available information is meager and scattered; nevertheless, it is possible to draw unequivocal conclusions regarding the practice in each individual monastery and to determine that the practices were not uniform. When speaking of laura monks, one should note that even if the general practice was that on Saturday they left their cells and went to the church for prayer, this does not necessarily mean that on that day the Eucharistic rite was also held there.

(a) *The Eucharistic Rite in the Monasteries of Euthymius and in the Laura of Pharan*
In the period in which Euthymius lived in the monastery of Theoctistus, he would receive food and meet with people requesting interviews only on Saturdays and Sundays (*V. Euth.* 10, 19; 18, 28; 21, 34). The other days of the week he would live as an anchorite in his cell. He would go to the church not only on Sunday but also on Saturday (*V. Sab.* 7, 91). On these days he would join the monks of the coenobium, who also conducted their prayers in the coenobium church on weekdays while he prayed daily in his cell. But the Eucharistic rite was conducted in the monastery of Theoctistus only on Sunday, as we learn from an episode from the time of Euthymius' return from his wanderings in the deserts of Marda and Ziph (426 CE), before a community of monks had formed around him. He agreed to come to the coenobium of Theoctistus only on Sundays in order to celebrate the rite (σύναξις) together (*V. Euth.* 14, 24).[48] It may reasonably be assumed that if the Eucharist had been held in the coenobium on Saturdays as well, Euthymius would not have refrained from participating in it, celebrating together with his monks.

Also during his Lenten sallies into the desert, Euthymius would celebrate the liturgy only on Sundays, distributing the sacred bread to the disciples and monks that were with him, including Gerasimus (*V. Euth.* 32, 51; *V. Cyr.* 5, 225). Celebrating the Eucharist only on Sundays during Lent enabled him to maintain his fast during the rest of the week, including Saturday. But the Lenten practice does not necessarily bear evidence for a single, Sunday Eucharist in regular weeks.

We have seen that in the coenobium of Theoctistus the liturgy was celebrated once a week on Sundays. This was certainly also the practice in the laura of Euthymius and seemingly also in the laura of Pharan. It is possible that such was the prevalent practice during the fourth and fifth centuries among monks throughout Palestine, like that of the Syrian monks but in contrast to the practice in Egypt.[49] It seems that on Saturday the monks of the laura of Euthymius would come out from their cells and go to the church, as Euthymius himself had done when he lived in the coenobium of Theoctistus and later in his laura (cf. *V. Sab.* 7, 91). In any case, the Saturday prayer did not include the Eucharistic rite and the night between Saturday and Sunday was not spent in a vigil, neither in the laura of Pharan nor in the laura of Euthymius. On Saturday evening the monks would return to their cells and leave them for the church again only for the vigil prayer, at cockcrow, before dawn on Sunday (see above, Chap. 4A).

(b) *The Eucharistic Rite in the Coenobium of Choziba*

An episode from the early phase in Choziba, the period of the Syrian anchorites, recounts that the Eucharist was celebrated there only on Sundays. The sacred elements were brought from Jericho after the morning prayer (the third, sixth, and ninth hour prayers were not recited on Sundays). Lay people or other monks used to join Aias, an elderly monk, and his disciple Zenon—the fifth in the series of Syrian monks—and celebrate the Eucharist with them (*Miracula* 5, 366).[50]

There is ample information about the Sunday liturgy in the coenobium of Choziba during the time of George, the end of the sixth and the beginning of the seventh century. The cell dwellers, including George, used to assemble and join the other monks in the coenobium. Several passages in the *Vita Georgii* allude generally to the custom of coming to the coenobium every Sunday (*V. Geor.* 16, 115; 20, 119–20; 33, 131–32; 34, 133), while others mention the coming of the cell dwellers to the coenobium already on Saturday: "For on Saturday, late in the day, the cell dwellers used to ascend to the coenobium, to take part in the divine office and in the liturgy of the immaculate mysteries, then to eat with the fathers who lived within the monastery" (ibid. 12, 108).[51] In another chapter the duration of their stay is better defined: "we, the cell dwellers, used to come to the coenobium for the Saturday night vespers . . . on the following day, in the afternoon, . . . we went out to the cells" (ibid. 42, 143–44).[52] This implies that the cell dwellers, who arrived for the evening prayer on Saturday evening, returned to their cells only the following

---

[48] In *V. Euth.* 28, 45 there is a detailed description of the consecration of the holy elements in the Eucharistic rite in the laura, which was conducted by Euthymius, assisted by Domitian. See also *Pratum* 219, 3109–12 regarding the distribution of the holy wafer from the holy cup by the deacon in the church of the laura of Gerasimus.

[49] The special importance Euthymius attributed to Lenten sallies into the desert, as well as his wanderings in the desert for several years, accompanied by his disciple Domitian, were also in the spirit of Syrian, rather than Egyptian, monasticism.

[50] John Moschus, who recounts a similar anecdote (*Pratum* 25, 2869–72), attributes it to the time of John of Choziba.

[51] ὄψε γὰρ σαββάτου εἰώθησαν κελλιῶται ἐν τῷ κοινοβίῳ ἀνέρχεσθαι καὶ συγκοινωνεῖν τῷ τε κανόνι καὶ τῇ λειτουργίᾳ τῶν ἀχράντων μυστηρίων καὶ τῇ ἑστιάσει τοῖς ἐν τῷ μοναστηρίῳ πατράσι.

[52] . . . ἐρχομένων ἡμῶν τῶν κελλιωτῶν εἰς τὸ κοινόβιον εἰς τὰ ἑσπερινὰ τῆς Κυριακῆς. . . . καὶ πάλιν ἐπὶ τῇ δείλῃ ἐξελθόντων ἡμῶν ἐπὶ τὰ κελλία. . . .

afternoon. George would stay in the church the entire time, accompanied by his disciple Antony (ibid. 34, 133). (This passage should be thus understood, for if the old monk had come to the coenobium only on Sunday and returned to his cell the afternoon of the same day, Antony would not have been able to spend an entire day and night in his presence as he states.) George refrained from sleeping in the coenobium (ibid. 20, 119–20), that is, the night between Saturday and Sunday was a vigil for him. The practice was to celebrate the Sunday Eucharist after the morning prayer (*Miracula* 5, 366; cf. *Pratum* 40, 2896, regarding Pharan).

Was the Eucharist also held in the coenobium later on Saturday, after the evening prayer and before the vigil? There is no proof of this, and it is highly doubtful whether this is the correct interpretation of the sentence from chapter 12 cited above. In the monasteries of Lower Egypt, the practice was to celebrate the Eucharist twice a week, on Saturday and Sunday. The monks would assemble in the church at the third hour to perform the rite (John Cassian, *Inst.* III.2, 92–93). On each occasion, after the rite, a meal would be served to the monks in the church (ibid. V.26, 234), and the night between Saturday and Sunday was a vigil (ibid. II.18, 88). In the Pachomian monasteries, in contrast, the first Eucharistic rite was celebrated on Saturday evening (Veilleux, Koinonia II, 186 n. 1, on *Pr.* 15; 271 n. 4, on *SBo* 25); Socrates Scholasticus states, as mentioned above, that in the Thebaid it was preceded by a festive meal. Although this was the district of origin of John of Choziba, the founder of the coenobium of Choziba, there is no proof in the sources relating to Choziba of a late Saturday Eucharistic rite. According to the *narratio* of John and Sophronius mentioned above (Longo 1965–66, 251–52), the Saturday *agrypnia*, which started with vespers, was followed by an evening meal and then the vigil service began. We may assume that such was also the case in Choziba.

It is clear from what has been stated above that in the time of George the practice in Choziba was that the cell dwellers would gather in the coenobium for the Saturday evening prayer. The night between Saturday and Sunday was a vigil, at least for the cell dwellers and the stricter coenobites. On the following day the sacred elements were consecrated, followed by a festive meal. The afternoon hours, after the meal, were devoted to socializing. George would interview new candidates (*V. Geor.* 12, 108; 16, 115; 33, 131–32; 34, 133) and advise and instruct monks and the various functionaries in the administration of the monastery and in the fulfillment of their tasks (ibid. 20, 119–20).[53]

Therefore, in the coenobium of Choziba the divine liturgy was celebrated only on Sunday. This practice, already in effect in the monastery since the time of the Syrian monks, the middle of the fifth century, was preserved in later centuries. As mentioned earlier, in the laura of Euthymius, the coenobium of Theoctistus, and the laura of Pharan, the liturgy was also celebrated only on Sunday. In these latter monasteries, however, the night between Saturday and Sunday was not kept as a vigil in the church (on this see Chap. 4A, above). This was not the case in the coenobium of Choziba.

---

[53] Saturday was not devoted to mundane conversations, but rather Sunday afternoon; this apparently is the reason why in the chapters in which Antony speaks of the interviews George held with the monks, he mentions only Sunday as the day in which the cell dwellers, including George, would come to the coenobium. The fact that George already came to the coenobium on Saturday evening is irrelevant in the context of these chapters. It may also be possible to resolve these presumably contradictory data by what is said in chap. 42, 143–44, that "Sunday" already started with the Saturday evening service.

(c) *The Eucharistic Rite in the Laura and Coenobium of Gerasimus*

The regulation on this matter established by Gerasimus for his monks states: "On Saturday and Sunday they [all the anchorites] would come to the church, and after having participated in the Divine Mysteries, they would partake of cooked food, accompanied by a little wine, in the coenobium. All [the monks, i.e., both anchorites and coenobites] used to perform the office of the psalm singing together on Saturday and on Sunday" (*V. Ger.* 2, 2–3; cf. ibid. 3, 3–4).[54]

This implies the existence of two Eucharistic rites, on Saturday and on Sunday, like the practice prevalent in Egypt to which John Cassian alludes. No vigil between Saturday and Sunday is mentioned, and therefore it seems that after each ceremony the monks returned to their cells. During Lent Gerasimus partook of the sacred bread only on Sundays (ibid. 4, 5; *V. Cyr.* 5, 225), as was Euthymius' practice during the fast. As mentioned above, during this period of the year they refrained from celebrating two weekly liturgies, so that they would not break the fast on Saturday by partaking of the sacred elements.

It is known that in the laura of Calamon the liturgy was regularly celebrated in the church, with all the inhabitants of the laura participating. It is not mentioned on what day and with what frequency it was celebrated, that is, whether an additional weekly ceremony was held there besides the usual one on Sundays (*V. Geor.* 9, 105).

(d) *The Eucharistic Rite in the Great Laura*

What was the practice in the Great Laura of Sabas? We can trace a change in Sabas' attitude toward the Eucharistic rite in the Laura and the importance of its regular celebration. Initially, when the Laura was first established in 483, the rite was conducted by an itinerant priest in the little oratory erected on the east bank (*V. Sab.* 16, 100). Not only did Sabas refuse to accept ordination, but he did not permit any of his monks to be ordained, perceiving this as a first manifestation of aspiration for power and the source of all evil.[55] It seems that during this first stage the rite was performed only in a completely random manner, when an itinerant priest happened to come along.[56]

From the time that the Cave Church (Theoktistos Church) had been constructed, in the first years of the Laura's existence (prior to 486, the year of Martyrius' death; see *V. Sab.* 18, 103), Sabas established that the Saturday and Sunday prayers would be held there and not in the little oratory as before (ibid. 102). It is clear, therefore, that during this phase the monks assembled for communal prayer on these days. Sabas still withheld the priesthood from himself and from his monks, and the consecration of the elements

---

[54] τὸ δὲ Σαββάτον καὶ τὴν Κυριακὴν εἰς τὴν ἐκκλησίαν ἐρχόμενοι καὶ τῶν θείων μετασχόντες μυστηρίων εἰς τὸ κοινόβιον μετελάμβανον ἐψητοῦ ὀλίγῳ οἴνῳ χρώμενοι. ὁμοῦ δὲ ἅπαντας τὸν κανόνα ἐπετέλουν τῆς ψαλμῳδίας τῷ τε Σαββάτῳ καὶ τῇ Κυριακῇ (ed. Koikylides 1902). The last phrase does not appear in the manuscript published by Flusin (1983, 228).

[55] In Scetis as well there was no priest during the first 10 years of its existence (Chitty 1966, 33). According to the early 6th-century pre-Benedictine *Rule of the Master*, there were no priest-monks in the brotherhood, and the monks went to the local church for the Sunday Eucharist, or perhaps occasionally made use of visiting priests (Taft 1984, 69).

[56] Cf. the above-mentioned story of the monk Helle in Egypt, who troubled himself to bring a priest from the village to the monastery, which was located on the other side of the Nile, to conduct the Eucharist there (*HM* XII.6–9, 94–95).

continued to be performed by a priest from outside who was not a member of his community. This position roused his monks against him and was one of the complaints they raised before Patriarch Sallustius in 490.

During the lengthy period from the establishment of the Laura until the year 490, a period in which the Eucharistic rite possibly was not held on a regular basis and, at any rate, was not conducted by a priest from the Laura, another regulation was in force, namely, that the laurites would be secluded in their cells only five days a week. On Saturday and Sunday they gathered in the church, even if the prayer did not include the consecration of the bread and wine.[57]

As a result of Sallustius' intervention, Sabas was ordained as a priest for the needs of his monks. Now for the first time, about five years after the construction of the Theoktistos Church, it was inaugurated and consecrated by placing under the altar numerous relics of martyrs, which was required for the celebration of the Eucharist. This took place on December 12, 490 (*V. Sab.* 19, 104).[58]

In this second phase, which lasted until the inauguration of the larger Theotokos Church, the rites held in the Cave Church both on Saturday and Sunday probably also included the consecration of the bread and the wine. Explicit evidence of this exists only for the third phase, but this matter had been at the center of the grievances against Sabas presented to Sallustius, and it probably was resolved then.

When several monks of Armenian origin—Jeremias, accompanied by his two disciples, Peter and Paul—came to the Laura shortly after the consecration of the Cave Church, Sabas permitted them to conduct the office of psalmody in Armenian in the little oratory on Saturdays and Sundays (*V. Sab.* 20, 105.10–11).[59]

In the third phase, with the dedication of the Great Church, the Theotokos Church, in July 501, Sabas instituted new orders of prayer in the Laura, in whose center there were now two churches (*V. Sab.* 32, 117–18). In this phase he moved the Armenians from the little oratory on the east side of the Kidron, which had already been in their hands for about eleven years, to the Theoktistos Church, permitting them to hold services there in Armenian—reciting psalms, reading the New Testament, and reciting other prayers in the synaxis (τὸν τῆς ψαλμῳδίας κανόνα . . . . τὸ μεγαλεῖον καὶ τὴν λοιπὴν ἀκολουθίαν ἐν ταῖς συνάξεσιν (*V. Sab.* 117.21–23)—but during the offering of the divine elements (ἐν τῷ καιρῷ τῆς θείας προσκομιδῆς) he ordered them to go and join the Greek-speaking monks.

When he learned that the Armenian monks added the phrase "Who was crucified for us" to the *Trisagion* hymn, which is recited in the liturgy prior to the offering of the elements—a part that he had allowed them to pray in their own tongue—he ordered them to recite this hymn in Greek, according to the early version of the Orthodox Church and not according to this innovation of Peter the Fuller.[60]

---

[57] According to the monk Chrisantos from the monastery of Mar Saba, a common Eucharistic service for all the monks is held there at present only once every two weeks, on Sunday.

[58] A priest could celebrate the Eucharist even if there were no sacred relics beneath the altar stone, if he spread a consecrated tablecloth (ἀντιμίσιον, εἰλητός) over it (Sophronius, *Commentarius liturgicus* 5: PG 87.3, 3985).

[59] 105.10–11: καὶ ἐπέτρεψεν αὐτοῖς ἐν τῷ μικρῷ εὐκτηρίῳ Ἀρμενιστὶ ἐπιτελεῖν τὸν κανόνα τῆς ψαλμῳδίας τῷ τε Σαββάτῳ καὶ τῇ Κυριακῇ.

[60] Peter the Fuller was the patriarch of Antioch three times between the years 469 and 488, being

Further, "He [Sabas] prescribed that on Saturday the office (σύναξις) should be held in the church built by God (*Theoktistos*), while on Sunday it would take place in the Church of the Mother of God (*Theotokos*), and an all-night vigil (*agrypnia*) should be held, uninterruptedly from evening until the morning, in both the churches on Sundays and dominical feasts" (*V. Sab.* 32, 118.17).[61]

How are we to understand this passage? For whom was this order established—for the Armenians or for the entire community? It seems that the first part of the sentence, which speaks of the division between the two churches, is addressed to the Armenians, while the second part, which speaks of the vigil, is addressed to all members of the community. On Saturday the Armenians would assemble for prayer in the Cave Church (Theoktistos Church), but for the consecration of the sacred elements they would cross the courtyard and join the Greeks in the large church, as the Armenians and the Bessoi would do in the monastery of Theodosius (see below). As regards Sunday, Sabas ordered the Armenians to gather, for the entire course of the rite, with the Greeks in the large church. It is clear that this refers to two Eucharists in the Great Laura, one on Saturday and one on Sunday. For the all-night vigil between Saturday and Sunday, each congregation would stay in its own church, and so also for the evening prayer on Saturday and the Sunday morning prayer. On Sunday afternoon the cell dwellers returned to their regular places.

Therefore, regarding the frequency of the Eucharist, Sabas adopted the regulation that Gerasimus had already established for his monks many years before, which had its source in Egyptian monasticism. However, in addition to the two Eucharists established by Gerasimus on Saturday and Sunday, Sabas added a communal all-night vigil in the church between Saturday and Sunday, with all the monks participating.

(e) The Eucharistic Rite in the Monastery of Theodosius

Theodosius' community was also multinational. In his coenobium there were separate churches for Greek-, Armenian- and Bessic-speakers (presumably Georgians, rather than members of a Thracian tribe; see Part v, below). In each church the daily liturgy—psalms, prayers, and scripture reading—was held in the appropriate language. During the Eucharist, however, they all joined the Greeks in the large church, where a common ceremony was held in Greek (Theod. Petr., *V. Theod.* 18, 45–46).[62] We do not know whether this rite was held there on Saturday as well, as was the practice in the Great Laura, or whether they adhered to the earlier Palestinian practice, which was maintained in the laurae of Euthymius and Pharan. Nor do we have any knowledge of a vigil between Saturday and Sunday in this monastery.

---

deposed twice. For the place of the *Trisagion* hymn in the liturgy preceding the offering of the sacrifice, see Mateos 1971, 99–107.

[61] The meaning of the word σύναξις here is that of assembling for prayer together, and not of the Eucharistic rite, similar to the meaning this word has several lines previously (*V. Sab.* 117.23). See commentary in Festugière 1962b, 44 n. 61.

[62] Also in the monastery of Publius in Zeugma in Euphratensis (second half of the 4th century) there was a bilingual community, Greek- and Syriac-speakers. The two communities met twice a day, morning and evening, in the chapel of the monastery for a common ceremony of reciting psalms, each community in turn in its own language (*HPh* V.5, 334–36).

7. *The Weekend Meals*

In the laura of Gerasimus communal meals were held both on Saturdays and Sundays. The coenobites also participated in these meals, which were served in the dining room of the coenobium. The people of Jericho, who venerated them, would bring them food from their homes on these two days (*V. Ger.* 2, 2–3; 4, 5).

In the Great Laura also it was the practice to serve a meal to the assembled brothers both on Saturday and on Sunday. The brothers would assemble in the center of the Laura when the signal was given by knocking the sounding board (*V. Sab.* 58, 159); Cyril does not state at what hour this took place. Preparations for the meal were made under the direction of the steward, who purchased the supplies and was responsible for ensuring that all the necessary items were in the pantry and food storerooms. Food supplies were supposed to arrive at the Laura not later than Friday. Once, during a time of famine (during the protracted drought of the years 516–521), a caravan of thirty pack animals arrived on Friday—the donation of the "sons of Sheshan," innkeepers from Jerusalem—with supplies for the meal: wine, bread, wheat, oil, honey, and cheese (ibid.). It is possible that these meals were held in a suitable hall arranged for the occasion to serve as a dining room, rather than in the church or the courtyard. However, the existence of such a dining room in the Laura is not mentioned in the sources.

The cell dwellers of Choziba would come to the coenobium only late on Saturday (*V. Geor.* 12, 107–9), before vespers (ibid. 42, 143–44). They also would bring with them the products of their weekly labors in their cells—wicker baskets, ropes, mats—as the monks of Gerasimus' laura and the Great Laura were accustomed to do. They probably took care to arrive at the coenobium sufficiently early to hand over their loads and prepare themselves for the prayer service. As mentioned earlier, it seems that after vespers a communal meal was served for both the coenobites and the cell dwellers and then the all-night vigil began. In regular days the daily meal was served at the ninth hour (*Pratum* 153, 3021),[63] while vespers started with the lighting of the candles at the tenth hour. The Sunday meal, which was held after the Eucharist, according to the accepted custom, was shared by all. We possess no information regarding the weekend meals in other monasteries.

Conclusion

Gerasimus began a new practice for the laurites, different from what had been the standard practice in the earlier laurae, Pharan and probably Chariton's other laurae and the laura of Euthymius. He established for his monks two weekly Eucharistic services, one on Saturday and one on Sunday. Sabas adopted these two services and added an all-night vigil in the church between Saturday and Sunday. In the laura of Euthymius the Eucharistic service was held only on Sunday, and the night between Saturday and Sunday was not a vigil in the church. This practice of the laurae of the Pharan type was the early practice of the laura monks in the Holy Land. A single Eucharistic service per week on Sunday was not in accordance with the non-monastic, community practice of the Church of Palestine, in which the divine liturgy, to the best of our knowledge, was held

---

[63] The meal prepared by Antony for George after the evening prayer (*V. Geor.* 43, 336) was a private meal for an elderly monk and not a communal meal for all the brothers.

both on Saturday and Sunday. The early monks probably adhered to the principle according to which the celebration of two liturgies per week was not proper for monks.

Information about this in the coenobium of Choziba dates from a slightly later period than the time of Cyril's writing. There as well the Eucharist was held only on Sunday, but the night preceding it was held in vigil by the cell dwellers and probably also by the coenobites.

The overall picture, therefore, is diverse rather than uniform. We cannot speak of a single, common practice of all the cell dwellers and laura monks. There were differences between one monastery and another, and there was a process of development throughout the period. In scheduling two Eucharistic services per week and insisting on not admitting young boys to the laura (see Chap. 5B, below), Gerasimus, and later Sabas, adhered to the rules prevalent in the Egyptian monasteries. The early Palestinian practice, as revealed in the laura of Pharan, was different.

Regarding weekend prayers, which dictated the way of life of the laura monks on these days, there were differences between Sabas' practice and that of Euthymius, whose laura was of the Pharan type. It was Gerasimus' practice—celebrating the Eucharist on Saturday and Sunday—that was adopted thirty-five years later in the Great Laura. Nevertheless, Cyril did not regard Sabas as a disciple of Gerasimus, and we may assume that neither did Sabas and the monks around him. Sabas knew Gerasimus from the time when he joined Euthymius in his sallies into the desert during Lent. However, Sabas' biography is connected with Euthymius and not with Gerasimus. It was Euthymius who received him as a monk and guided him in the desert life. His being Euthymius' disciple is expressed most clearly in Sabas' religious doctrine: total loyalty to Chalcedonian Orthodoxy and hostility to Monophysite or Origenist ideas. His establishing a different monastic organization—a way of life for the laura monks different from that of Euthymius' and a different order of weekend services—is not sufficient for considering Sabas a disciple of Gerasimus. The theological foundations of Gerasimus' religious life were not consolidated and firm enough, and, without Euthymius' influence, he might have continued his opposition to the Council of Chalcedon, whose opponents he joined during the revolt against Patriarch Juvenal in 451.

However, Gerasimus' innovations clarify why the authors of the *Vita Gerasimi* refers to him as the "founder and patron" (πολιστὴς καὶ πολιοῦχος) of the Jordan desert (*V. Ger.* 2, 2; Flusin 1983, 228.2). This same title, referring to the entire desert and not just to the Jordan desert, was bestowed upon Sabas by Patriarch Elias in his letter to Emperor Anastasius (*V. Sab.* 50, 141.9–10). The author of the *Vita Gerasimi* (ibid.) also describes Gerasimus as the enactor of regulations for his monks (αὐτοῖς κανονίσας) (Flusin 1983, 228.8; see also Chap. 3A, above). With this background, it can easily be understood why the abbot of the laura of Gerasimus was chosen to serve as Sabas' deputy as archimandrite for the cell dwellers and the anchorites; senior status had already passed during this period (ca. 494) to the Laura of Sabas.

5

Sabas as a Monastic Legislator

A. The Rule of St. Sabas

Cyril describes Sabas not only as a leader but also as a legislator for all the anchorites and cell dwellers: ἄρχων ὑπῆρχεν καὶ νομοθέτης παντὸς τοῦ ἀναχωρητικοῦ βίου καὶ πάντων τῶν ἐν ταῖς κέλλαις ζῆν προῃρημένων (*V. Sab.* 65, 166.15–16).[64] Neither Euthymius, Theodosius, nor even Chariton were described in this manner. Only the author of the *Vita Gerasimi* states that Gerasimus established a rule for the cell dwellers (discussed above, Part III, Chap 3A).[65]

The very existence of a written rule for a community of cell dwellers is an exceptional phenomenon. No such rule developed in the Antonian colonies of Lower Egypt, and all monastic rules in the East and the West were formulated for coenobites. Sabas' regulations were an important innovation of Palestinian monasticism and no doubt contributed to the intrinsic strength of the Sabaitic system, the self-awareness of the monks, and their sense of community.

We know of several early Byzantine rules for monks in the East. Such are the *Regula* of Pachomius (*Koinonia* II),[66] those of Basil the Great (Gribomont 1953; PL 103, 483–554; PG 31, 889–1305), and the canons of the Syrian monasteries (Vööbus 1960b, 1982, 1988). Cyril mentions in several places in the *Vita Sabae* a written set of regulations composed

---

[64] Cf. also *V. Sab.* 7, 91.23 (Euthymius' vision of the future of Sabas): καὶ ἔσεσθαι αὐτὸν ἀρχηγέτην τε καὶ νομοθέτην πάντων τῶν καθ' ἑαυτοὺς ἀναχωρούντων. ("And he will be the founding father and legislator of all the anchorites living by themselves").

[65] Three different sources of rules referring to monks can be defined: monastic rules such as that of Pachomius, Basil, Sabas, Benedict, the Syrian Conons, and the later Byzantine *ktetorika typika* (Galatariotou 1987); ecclesiastical legislation such as canons 4, 8, 16, 24 of the Council of Chalcedon; and imperial legislation such as that of Justinian. The Rule of St. Benedict was composed in ca. 540, while he was living on Monte Cassino. The monastic legislation of Justinian is also posterior to that of Sabas. However, it is interesting that both in the East and in the West there was intensive monastic legislation in the first half of the 6th century.

[66] The treatise known as "The Rules of Saint Pachomius" is not that written by Pachomius himself for his disciples but rather a collection that developed and reached its final formulation at the end of the 4th century (*Koinonia* II, 7–13). The original composition was written in Sahidic, and was translated into Greek for the Greek-speakers in the *Koinonia*, such as the monks of the monastery of Metanoia (Canopus). Jerome received a copy from them, which he translated into Latin in 404, adding an introduction (*Praefatio*) describing Pachomian monasticism.

The Latin version has been preserved in its entirety, and lengthy passages also exist in Greek and in Coptic. Similarly there are the regulations of Horsiesius, which have been preserved only in Coptic (*Koinonia* II, 141–223).

According to Palladius, Pachomius received his Rule engraved on a bronze tablet from an angel (*HL* XXXII.1, 88). According to Sozomen (*HE* III.14.9, 119), this tablet was still preserved during his time (beginning of the 5th century). The monks of Pachomius therefore attributed to the Rule the validity of the words of God, descending from Heaven.

by Sabas for his monks. Although it is not extant, the contents of several of these regulations can be deduced from Cyril's text.

In chapter 42 (133.3–4), it is stated that Sabas gave the dwellers of the coenobium established by the brothers Zannos and Benjamin the canons of his other coenobia.[67] In chapter 74 (179.22), we learn that Sabas gave the monks of the laura of Jeremias the canons of his Great Laura.[68] In chapter 76 (182.21–23), mention is made of written laws (παραδώσεις) that he established for his monasteries (μοναστηρίοις), which he handed over on his deathbed to his successor Melitas, ordering him to preserve them intact.[69]

In all these passages, Cyril takes care to mention that the regulations were valid and intended only for Sabas' monasteries, and not for all the desert monasteries. Sabas therefore composed them by virtue of his position as abbot and founder of the monasteries, not as archimandrite of the desert monks. We further learn from these texts that there were two different sets of regulations, one for the coenobia and another for the Great Laura and Sabas' other laurae. Both sets were given to his successor Melitas, and therefore Cyril uses in the last passage the general term μοναστηρίοις.

These regulations have not come down to us in their original form. However, in the monastery of St. Catherine in Sinai are preserved two Greek manuscripts (Sin. gr. 1096, of the 12th–13th century, and Sin. gr. 531, of the 15th) that contain a *typikon* (τυπικόν) of Sabas' monastery. A *typikon* is a liturgical manual dealing with the order and content of the prayers for the liturgical year of the church, listing the dates of holidays, commemoration days, and the order of prayer for each of them. A monastic *typikon* also includes regulations for the life of the monks.[70] Accordingly, the Sabaitic *Typikon* from Sinai (reproduced by Dmitrievskij 1917, 20–65) consists mainly of regulations concerning the order of the church services and special feasts celebrated in the monastery. The Sabaitic contribution to the canonization of the Byzantine rite attested by such Sabaitic *typika* will be discussed below (sec. c4). On folios 145–146 of Sin. gr. 1096, there is a set of monastic regulations and practices concerning the way of life of the monks of the Laura of Sabas. The title of the collection is: "Rule, Tradition, and Law of the Venerable Laura of St. Sabas."[71] This collection of regulations was published in 1890 with a Russian translation and a discussion, by Dmitrievskij,[72] and again by Kurtz (1894) in a review article of Dmitrievskij's work, accompanied by a short discussion and minor alterations from the first reading.

From the title and contents, there is an evident affiliation to Sabas' regulations mentioned by Cyril, who explicitly states the content of several of them in the course of his

---

[67] τοὺς κανόνας τῶν ἄλλων αὐτοῦ κοινοβίων παρέδωκεν ἐκεῖσε.

[68] τῆς ἑαυτοῦ Μεγίστης Λαύρας κανόνας.

[69] παραγγείλας αὐτῷ τὰς παραδόσεις τὰς παραδοθείσας ἐν τοῖς ὑπ᾽ αὐτὸν μοναστηρίοις ἀτρώτους διαφυλάξαι δοὺς αὐτῷ ταύτας ἐγγράφως. ("He instructed him to preserve intact the regulations he had set forth to his monasteries, giving them to him in writing").

[70] For the definition see *Enc. Catt.* XII, 123; *ODCC* 1401; *ODB* 2131–32. A set of rules of a monastery is also mentioned in *Pratum*, add. Nissen, no. 13. The existence of many sets of regulations indicates the various nuances in the ways of life of the monks in different monasteries.

[71] τύπος καὶ παράδοσις καὶ νόμος τῆς σεβασμίας λαύρας τοῦ (ἁγίου) Σάββα.

[72] A. Dmitrievskij, "The Rules of St. Sabbas Monastery," *Works (Trudy) of the Kiev Academy* (Kiev 1890), 170–92 (Russian). I have not seen this article. The text alone was republished by Dmitrievskij (1895, 222–24). See also Chitty 1966, 117 and n. 166 on p. 122.

narrative. At the same time, however, we can clearly recognize several additions, which reflect life in the Mar Saba monastery during later generations.[73] Although continually referred to as a laura, after the Arab conquest of Palestine it was gradually transformed into a coenobium. Given this new situation, the rules Sabas formulated for his coenobia may have been found to be appropriate, and they replaced the former lauritic rules.[74]

The Rule from Sinai attributed to Sabas, which in its present form is dated to about the eleventh century, can be perceived, according to Kurtz (1894, 168), as an archetype of τυπικὰ κτητορικά—rules established by founders for regulating the daily conduct of the monks, the administration of the monasteries, and their liturgies (Meester 1940; Galatariotou 1987). It is counted among the forty extant Greek *ktetorika typika* listed by Galatariotou, dated between ca. 800 and 1400.[75] Yet a large number of monasteries existed without ever acquiring a written *typikon*, living simply according to the oral tradition of the monastery. In its composition and content, the Rule attributed to Sabas is in accord with a large number of *typika*, classified as "non-aristocratic" by Galatariotou. These differ greatly in their literary style and morphology (Galatariotou 1987, 80). A similar stylistic diversity is encountered in the Syrian Rules (Vööbus 1960b, 1982, 1988), most of which also belong to the same literary genre and are earlier than the Greek *typika*. The Pachomian Rules are the earliest in this genre (end of the 4th century). Stylistically it is impossible to tell to what extent the present Rule preserves the exact phrasing of the original Rule

[73] Thus it is clear, for example, that the date of the composition in its current format is later than the death of Sabas; along with the Greek-speakers, mention is made of monks of Iberian origin, i.e., Georgian-speakers, instead of the Armenian monks who lived in the Laura during Sabas' time; Frankish monks are mentioned only in MS 1096, which reflects the reality of the period of the Crusades, but not in the later MS 531. Below (sec. D) is given a translation of this set of rules, prepared by Leah Di Segni. For convenience' sake, the translated rules have been numbered, even though they are written in a continuum in the original. The reality reflected in regulation 12 is that of a coenobium, only a few of whose monks—those who chose and received permission for it—live a laurite form of life, being secluded in their cells and exempt from coming to the church except for the vigil. We learn from regulation 6 that this rite was conducted each week, in the night between Saturday and Sunday. On the other nights of the week they were exempt from coming to the church. This was not so for the other brothers: for them being prohibited from leaving their cells was a means of punishment (regulation 11). I.e., although in the *titulus*, as well as in several of the regulations (nos. 1, 2, 3, 6, 8, 13), the monastery is defined as a laura, this is not reflected at all in the contents of the regulations. On the contrary, these reflect a coenobite reality, in which members of different linguistic communities—Greeks, Syrians, Georgians, (and Franks)—live together, each gathering in its own church, conducting the daily prayers in its own tongue at the proper time (regulation 4). Only the Eucharist was celebrated in the Great Church, in Greek, for the entire community.

[74] To Sabas (and to Theodosius) is also attributed another work, entitled *Constitutio Sabae et Theodosii de vita monachorum coenobitarum et celliotarum*, included in MS Coislin, 295 (Vailhé 1898a, 2; Leclercq 1950, 201). This composition is preserved in a 14th-century manuscript from Mount Athos. The reality reflected in it is coenobitic, so it may originate from an amalgamation of Sabas' coenobitic Rule with that of Theodosius. The cell-dwellers meet daily in the common church for the morning prayer and for vespers as well as for the Eucharist, whenever it is held. This common church is located in the midst of their cells or in the coenobium on which they are dependent. Each hermitage has, besides, its own chapel; each monk or group of 2–3 monks dwelling in it have to maintain their livelihood and work for their own income. This composition demonstrates the Palestinian monastic influence on Athonite monasticism, which was also evident in the development of the Athonite rite. For the French translation of the *Constitutio* and introduction, see Meester 1937. The διατύπωσις attributed to Theodosius the Coinobiarch referred to by Theodore of Stoudios may allude to this set of rules. See Leroy 1958, 209.

[75] A critical edition with a French translation of five 11th–12th-century *typika* was published by P. Gautier, *REB* 32 (1974); 39 (1981); 40 (1982); 42 (1984); 43 (1985).

of Sabas. The approach here will be to examine the content of the regulations in order to find possible allusions to them in Cyril's writings and thus to reconstruct Sabas' original Rule.

The way of life in the Great Laura—the weekly schedule, the monk's diet, his manual work, his garb (both the items of clothing and their quantity), his utensils, the weekly liturgy, and the weekend rites—was probably established in the lauritic regulations, which I have attempted to trace and reconstruct above (Part III, Chaps. 3–4), making use of every possible piece of information found in Cyril's works. I will now attempt to draw from Cyril's writings several additional regulations, which Sabas established for the Great Laura and his other monasteries. The discussion will begin with the regulation parallel to law 1 in the set of regulations from Sinai (see sec. D below), which shall be examined within the broader context of the training program for the monks.

B. The Novitiate

1. Introduction

The novitiate was the period of probation and training at the beginning of the monastic life. In this regard, one should distinguish between three different phases:

(a) The candidacy, in which the candidate (*postulant*) was questioned about his origin and motives. This stage could conclude with a short interview with the abbot, following which he would decide whether to reject or accept the candidate.

(b) The novice phase (*novitiatum*), preparation and training before joining the class of monks and receiving the monastic habit. In this phase the admitted candidate learned the monastic rule, in both theory and practice, and was examined for his adjustment to and suitability for this way of life. The length of this phase differed from one place to another and in different periods. The candidate who completed this phase received the monastic habit (σχῆμα) (either privately or in a public ceremony; in this matter as well there was no uniformity), and was regarded as a full-fledged monk. This phase was meant not only for the young but for anyone desiring to become a monk.

(c) Novitiate and training in a coenobium, before the transition to a laura. Anyone who had completed the second phase and wished to become a laura monk was required to live for a quite extended period of time, about ten years or more (see Table 4 below, p. 265) in a coenobium, until becoming a mature adult and an experienced monk. Only then could he be admitted to a laura.

The first two phases were intended only for coenobium monks. At the same time, however, the abbot of a laura had the prerogative of admitting candidates to the laura immediately after the first phase, if they were not young and beardless and especially if they had already acquired proven experience as monks or as church functionaries with a reputation and a disposition for the ascetic life. The intent of the regulation forbidding the admission to the laura of beardless youths (see below) was not directed only to young candidates who had to pass the first two phases, but also to children who had been dedicated to the monastery or had been raised and educated in a coenobium from an early age.

A distinction must therefore be made between the novitiate for coenobite and laurite life. In coenobitic monasticism (Pachomian, that of Shenoute, Basilian, Syrian, or that to which the Justinianic legislation refers; see above, Part I, Chap. 2), it is possible to discern either the existence or absence of phase (b) of the novitiate. Phase (c) applied only to Antonian monasticism, as in the anchorite colonies of Kellia and Scetis, the Palestinian laurae, or the anchorite colonies founded by Abraham of Kashkar on Mount Izla near Nisibis (see Part I, Chap. 2c, above).

In order to evaluate properly the essence of this phase in Judean desert monasticism and in the Rule of Sabas, we must first survey the state of affairs in the other monastic centers. We will begin with the coenobitic centers, and follow by a discussion of the anchorite settlements.

2. The Novitiate in Coenobitic Monasticism

Egyptian, Pachomian coenobitism did not recognize the concept of a novitiate. It can be understood from the *Regula* (*Pr.* 49) and the *Vita Pachomii* that new candidates joined the community after an extremely short period of candidacy: the candidate was under the supervision of the official in charge of hospitality for a few days, living in the outer building, where his moral conduct was examined and where he learned the obligations to be fulfilled and regulations to be observed in the coenobium. If he was found to be suitable, he was stripped of his lay clothing, given the monastic habit, and presented by the gatekeeper to the community during the great synaxis (Amand de Mendieta 1957, 48–49). Two of the innovations introduced by Shenoute into Pachomian coenobitism were a period of novitiate one to three months long in the gatehouse of the community and the signing by new monks of a written covenant (διαθήκη) containing a commitment not to defile the body in any manner, steal, bear false witness, or commit any deceitful act in secret (Leipoldt 1903, 106–13; Winlock and Crum 1926, 139; Bell 1983, 29 n. 51, 109 n. 87).

Basil recognized the essential importance of the period of the novitiate (*Reg. fus.* 10, 944–48). Everyone was to be permitted to join and become a monk, and no one was to be categorically rejected. The candidate's past, however, had to be thoroughly investigated. Basil did not specify the duration of the training period. A person who had previously led a proper religious life would be accepted quickly; someone who had previously been apathetic to his religious obligations would be examined carefully in order to ascertain that he was not unstable and had not arrived at the decision to "withdraw from the world" without deep intent. Such a candidate had to be instructed and examined over a period of time. If he was found suitable, he was to be accepted; if not, he was to be rejected.

Basil's regulation 15 (ibid. 952–57) deals with the admission and education of young children and the manner of their integration into the life of the monastery without causing disturbance to all the monks. They would join the monks' community only after reaching maturity and being capable of making the decision themselves. The acts of decision and joining were to be public ceremonies, following which the youth became a regular member of the monastic community and its communal life. Whoever decided at that stage that he did not want to join the monastery could leave; this too would be a public ceremony, in the presence of witnesses.

The Syrian coenobitic rules also refer to the first two phases mentioned above. Maruta (Rules LIV.23–26: Vööbus 1982, 99–100) established that the candidate would be carefully questioned by the abbot regarding his place of origin, profession, and motives. He specified in which cases the candidate was to be accepted for training and in which he would be rejected, whether he was a free man or a slave. He also ruled that an unintentional murderer who asked for admission was to be accepted as a monk.

The novitiate lasted three years, during which the candidate was prohibited from leaving the bounds of the monastery (Rules attributed to Rabbula 21: Vööbus 1960b, 83; Rules for the Persians 14, ibid. 91). At the end of this period the candidate would receive the monastic habit. A trial year was to be added for the lay person who was unfamiliar with the religious obligations (ibid. 20, 92). At the beginning of the training period, the candidate's hair was cut and fashioned into the monastic tonsure (ibid.; see also Vööbus 1970b).

A very detailed process of this kind is described by John of Ephesus regarding one of the Amidene monasteries (*Eastern Saints* 20, 278–83), while commenting that this was not the prevalent practice in his time for accepting lay people into a monastery. A layman who wishes to become a monk is first questioned about his place of origin, family, and motives. Then he is allowed to stay for thirty days at the gate with the poor, enabling him to give up his intention of becoming a monk. If he is still resolute in his decision after thirty days, he is allowed to enter the enclosure and participate in the vigils and all the menial labors with all the brothers for three months. Only then is there a ceremony before the altar, cutting a small round piece of hair from the crown of his head, and he becomes a penitent, not yet a monk. This status lasts three more years. Then he is awarded the monastic *schema* in a ceremony at the altar.[76]

Half of the head was shaved three months after the start of the penitence period, and the tonsure was completed only after a year, when the candidate also received a tunic and a cape, both made of straw, and a string for a belt. This process may reflect the three grades of *archarios* = *rasophoros* = novice, *mikroschemos* and *megaloschemos* (Assemani, *BO* III.2, 898). In the Greek sources a distinction between *mikroschemoi* and *megaloschemoi* monks, the latter being awarded also the cowl and *analabos,* is first mentioned by Theodore of Stoudios at the beginning of the ninth century. He disapproved of this hierarchical structure (*ODB* 1499, 1849; Meester 1942, 5, 82–86).

The Justinianic legislation, which is concerned with coenobitic monasticism, also deals with this subject. An unknown person who wished to join a monastery was required to undergo a three-year candidacy period. During this time the abbot was to examine his motives and conduct and to investigate his origins and civil status: whether he had commitments as a *curialis* or was known to be exempt from civil obligations; whether he was a free man or an escaped slave, a tenant, a serf, or a fugitive criminal. After three years, the candidate enjoyed immunity and could not be bothered because of his former status or deeds. During this period he had to learn the monastic discipline, but his hairstyle and garb were those of the laity. If at the end of the candidacy period he was found

---

[76] A public ceremony of the awarding of the habit and the adoption of monastic life is described by Pseudo-Dionysius the Areopagite, *De Ecclesiastica Hierarchia* VI.2 (ca. 500 CE), apparently reflecting the practice in Syria. According to this description, the ceremony was conducted by a priest delivering a special prayer. Afterwards he called upon the candidate to cast behind him all the sins of the past and asked him about his intent to adopt the perfect way of life as a monk. After confirmation by the candidate, he cut his hair in the monastic tonsure, made the sign of the cross over him, removed his secular clothes and gave him the habit, and embraced him—as did the other fathers present at the ceremony—following which the Eucharist was conducted.

fit to live in the monastery, he would receive the monastic habit (στολή) from the abbot (*Nov.* 5.2 [535 CE]; *Nov.* 123.35 [546 CE]). In the earlier novel the community's consent was required for the admission of the candidate; later on, however, it was established that this decision lay with the abbot alone. In the later Greek *ktetorika typika* we find diverse customs. Theodore of Stoudios prescribed an entry procedure that lasted only two or three weeks, while in other *typika* the period of probation might last three years (Galatariotou 1987, 116–20).

3. The Novitiate in the Laurite System: Egypt

We will now survey the information regarding the manner of admission to the anchorite settlements in Egypt (Evelyn-White 1932, 191–94). We learn from the sources that at the beginning of the monastic movement any monk of repute could impart monastic status to a person by investing him with the monastic habit. Afterwards the practice or regulation was adopted that it was the responsibility of the abbot to decide whether to accept or reject candidates.

The candidate was not required to take any formal vow. In Scetis candidates under the age of eighteen generally were not admitted; there are sources, however, that mention young children living there (Chitty 1966, 66–67). After the candidate was found to be fit for the monastic life, a simple private ceremony of receiving the habit was held. This was the case with Porphyrius of Gaza, who came to Scetis in 378 and was found worthy to receive the habit after a few days (*V. Porph.* 4, 4). In another, more detailed source we find the following stages of the private ceremony, which began the day after the candidate's arrival: introductory statements, shaving the head, placing the monastic habit on the ground, reciting prayers over it for three days and nights with the candidate, and at dawn of the fourth day dressing him in the habit.

Regarding the period and manner of trial and training, Evelyn-White (1932, 183) proposes for Scetis a system similar to that of the monastery of Gerasimus, that is, a coenobitic center on whose periphery, at some distance from the center, the anchorites lived. According to this reconstruction, the candidates who were found worthy and received the habit in a private ceremony following their arrival underwent a training period in the coenobium before being permitted to move to the cells.

Regarding Kellia and Mount Nitria, it was noted above (Part I, Chap. 2A) that at the end of the fourth century the latter was regarded as a semi-coenobitic novitiate before the anchorite's transition to Kellia. It may reasonably be assumed that the habit was awarded to the candidate only after completing a probation period in Nitria. He then remained there for a period of time, learned the monastic life, and only afterwards moved to Kellia. This was not an institutionalized procedure nor a formal obligation, but a useful prescription for proceeding in the monastic life. Thus, for example, Evagrius Ponticus, and after him Palladius, settled in Kellia only after a stay of one or two years in Mount Nitria (Evelyn-White 1932, 85, 169–71, 194). According to John Cassian (*Con.* III.1, 139–40; XVIII.4–6, 13–18), speaking of Paphnutius who would eventually succeed Macarius in Scetis, the coenobium was a training stage for him before assuming the life of an anchorite.

In the anchorite settlement established by Abraham of Kashkar at the end of the sixth century on Mount Izla near Nisibis (see above, Part I, Chap. 2C), a period of examination and novitiate in the coenobium was observed. The Rules of Dadishoa already speak of a three-year period in the coenobium before the novices were permitted to build cells for themselves, if found worthy to do so (Abraham's Rules 5: Vööbus 1960b, 160; 10, ibid. 161–62; Dadishoa's Rules 13, ibid. 170–71; Babai's Rules 7, ibid. 179). This was also the practice in the monastery of Beit Abbe in Mesopotamia during the sixth to eighth century, under the influence of the reforms instituted by Abraham of Kashkar in all of Mesopotamia (Butler 1898, 242). This preparation period was not, therefore, longer than that prescribed in the earlier Syrian rules for admittance to a coenobium.

4. The Novitiate in the Laurae of the Judean Desert and in Sabas' Rule

From the literary sources referring to Judean desert monasticism we learn that here as well attaining the status of monk was done in a simple, short act of awarding the monastic habit. An outstanding example is the story of the senator's daughter in the Jordan desert, who received the habit from an old monk who lived in the caves of Kopratha in the laura of the Egyptians (*De Sync.* 11, 313–14). After receiving it she began to live as an anchoress in a cave near the Jordan, outside of a communal framework, and therefore this example cannot be considered an act of joining a community.

Bestowing the habit on a new monk was generally done by the abbot, that is, a senior monk of recognized official status. Receiving the monastic habit on the spot, after expressing the wish to become a monk, is mentioned in one of John Moschus' anecdotes (*Pratum* 166, 3032–33) regarding a robber who asked to be admitted to the laura of Firminus. The abbot gave him a warning but awarded him the monastic habit. After this the novitiate period began in a coenobium, where he studied the Psalter and the monastic rules, which were the things required of a novice (see below). The phase of study and training therefore followed the awarding of the habit, which was not the practice in Syria.

Similar is the story of Symeon Salus (the Fool) (early 7th century), who immediately upon his arrival was admitted as a monk in the monastery of Gerasimus and received the holy habit (σχῆμα ἅγιον) from the abbot. An additional detail in this story is that the recipient was exempt from all work for seven days, during which he wore the awarded habit; only afterwards was he allowed to take off the ceremonial habit and wear simpler, everyday garb (σακκόμαχιν) (*V. Sym. Sali* 13, 1685–88; Rochcau 1978). In approximately the same period, Theodore of Sykeon (d. 613) received the habit from the abbot of Choziba immediately upon his arrival, after having previously toured the holy places and monasteries and having visited different monks in order to learn their way of life (*V. Theod. Syk.* 24, 24). The author adds that the abbot acted in this fashion after it was revealed to him in a heavenly vision that the person before him was worthy of receiving the monastic habit. This addition was intended to explain the awarding of the habit, even though the candidate did not intend to remain as a monk in Choziba. Indeed, immediately after this Theodore left the monastery and returned to his own country, Galatia. The addition was not meant as an excuse for the abbot's awarding the habit immediately upon Theodore's expressed wish to become a monk: the abbot's act was in accordance with the prevailing practice in the Judean desert. This was similar to the Egyptian practice and unlike that in Syria and in the Justinianic legislation.

Eighteen-year-olds also received the habit immediately after stating their wish to the abbot. This was the case with Cyriacus, who received the habit from Euthymius (*V. Cyr.*

4, 224). There is no mention of awarding the habit to a youth under the age of eighteen,[77] and Euthymius stated that it was forbidden for a beardless youth to be admitted to a laura (ibid.; *V. Sab.* 7, 91; *V. Euth.* 31, 50).

When Sabas had become an abbot, he acted as Euthymius had with him, and made a rule for himself (νομοθεσίαν αὐτῷ δίδωσιν) not to admit youths to the Laura, and also transmitted to the heads of the other laurae this regulation, which was an ancient law (νόμον παλαιόν) accepted by the early fathers. A eunuch with a face resembling a woman's was also prohibited from dwelling in it (*V. Sab.* 7, 91.24–28; 69, 171). This, as noted earlier, is the content of regulation 1 in the set of regulations from Sinai. According to Sabas (ibid. 29, 114), this particular rule originated with the fathers of the desert of Scetis. Euthymius was familiar with it but did not observe it strictly, at least not in special instances. Thus in about 428 he admitted to his laura, as his first disciples, the three brothers Cosmas, Chrysippus, and Gabriel despite their young age. He ordered that Gabriel, who was a eunuch and had a woman's face, live as a recluse, forbidding him to leave his cell (*V. Euth.* 16, 25–26). The young Sabas also had been initially admitted by Euthymius, who entrusted him to his disciple Domitian. But later he changed his mind and sent him to the coenobium of Theoctistus (*V. Euth.* 31, 50; cf. *V. Sab.* 7, 91). It seems that from then on (457 CE) this was a general rule that was followed. Indeed, the request of the young Cyriacus to be admitted to the laura in 468 was categorically rejected by Euthymius, even though Cyriacus had stayed there as a guest quite a long time before he was awarded the habit and before being interviewed by Euthymius. The latter dressed him in the monastic cowl and sent him to Gerasimus, since Theoctistus had already died. Gerasimus admitted him into the coenobium but not into his laura (*V. Ger.* 5, 5; *V. Cyr.* 4, 224–25).

In the second half of the sixth century, when the young George of Choziba had come from Cyprus and asked to join his brother in the laura of Calamon, his request was rejected and he was sent to the coenobium of Choziba, where he began the monastic life. Prior to this, while still in Cyprus, after he had been orphaned, he had grown up in a monastery headed by one of his uncles (*V. Geor.* 2, 2). This survey enables us to trace the introduction and application of an early monastic regulation, which had its source in the fathers of the desert of Scetis.[78] Sabas did not innovate but rather adopted as an obligatory rule in his monasteries an ancient regulation that had already been prevalent in the desert monasteries. Along with the rejection of youth wishing to be admitted to the laurae, an institutional framework was established for them: the coenobium functioned as a school in which they would prepare themselves for the lauritic life and also reach maturity, grow a beard, lose their youthful appearance, and therefore cease from being a temptation for the older monks of the laura.

Sabas was already well-versed in the regulations of coenobitic monasticism from the age of eight; he knew and observed them during the course of ten years in the monastery of

---

[77] About the legal significance of the age in civil and ecclesiastical contexts, see Part I, n. 39 above.

[78] In the background of this, of course, is the intent to remove from the anchorites the temptation to have homosexual relationships with the youths. See Chitty 1966, 66–67; Chadwick 1968, 11 n. 1. We also hear of the prohibition against admitting youths to the monastery in the Syrian Rules. See Vööbus 1960b, anonymous collection VIII.5, 72; Dadishoa's Rules 17, 171. The first reference speaks of a coenobium and the second of the large monastery of Izla, a coenobium with cell dwellers around it.

Flaviana in Cappadocia. Despite this, however, he had to begin his monastic life in the Judean desert as a novice in a coenobium. Monastic life was not a fixed, regulated framework but rather daily practice: the struggle with concupiscence, which is especially strong during early manhood and not during the adolescent years. During his years in the coenobium, the youth acquired experience, learned to control his body and thoughts, and when he reached the level of "perfect" (τέλειος) (Flusin 1983, 228.6), the laura was open to him.

The institutional pattern prevalent among the anchorite communities in Egypt, according to which the candidates underwent in the coenobium preparation and training for lauritic life, was first introduced into the Judean desert by Gerasimus. In about 455 he founded a laura with a coenobium at its center and enacted a regulation (ἐνομοθέτησε) that beginners (οἱ ἀρχάριοι) would live in the coenobium where they would be brought up in the monastic way of life (μοναχικὴ πολιτεία), while the perfect ones (οἱ τέλειοι) would live in the cells (V. Ger. 2, 2).

Faithful to the prevalent idea that preparation in the coenobium was essential before beginning the anchorite life, Sabas maintained that "as the flower precedes the growth of the fruit, so the coenobitic life must precede the solitary life" (V. John Hes. 6, 206.8–10). Sabas therefore sent youths and eunuchs who wished to be admitted into his laura to the coenobium of Theodosius for training and preparation (ibid. 29, 114; 69, 171). However, for adults who desired to withdraw from the world and join the Laura, Sabas erected the Small Coenobium north of the Laura, appointing for them austere and sober-minded monks to serve as their tutors (ibid. 28, 113). During the period of novitiate the novice had to learn the Psalter, the order of prayer, and monastic discipline (ibid. 113.8–10).[79] The separation between youth and adults was maintained in the novitiate phase as well.

Formal instruction was not sufficient, nor was a specified time determined for this period. Sabas maintained the following: "The cell-dwelling monk must be discriminating and zealous, a fighter, sober, temperate, orderly, apt for teaching and not in need of teaching, capable of harnessing all the members of his body and of keeping unfailing watch over his mind" (ibid. 113.10–14). The degree of self-control that the laura monk had to attain is expressed in the comment Sabas made to Theodosius: "Sir Abba, you are *hegoumenos* of children, while I am *hegoumenos* of *hegoumenoi*, for each of the monks under me is independent and *hegoumenos* of his own cell" (ibid. 65, 166.24–26). During the novitiate period, the candidate was therefore under supervision and probation, to see how he was adapting and how he fulfilled the monastic regulations.

An examination of all the extant literary sources referring to the Judean desert provides the following data regarding the relationship between the laurae and the coenobia, which served the former as a school:

The table indicates that the period of novitiate in the coenobium was likely to last about ten years or more, until the candidate reached maturity—roughly the age of thirty—and had become an experienced monk. Only afterward was the novice allowed to be admitted to the Laura, which was manifested by receiving a cell from Sabas. At this stage he permitted the rich to build their own cells (V. Sab. 28, 113). In Egypt and Syria

---

[79] τό τε ψαλτήριον μάθωσι καὶ τὸν τῆς ψαλμῳδίας κανόνα καὶ τὴν μοναχικὴν παιδευθῶσιν ἀκρίβειαν.

Table 4. Novitiate: The Coenobium-Laura Relationship

Coenobium	Laura	Date/period	Monk and duration of stay in the coenobium until attaining the degree of "perfect"
Gerasimus	Gerasimus	Founded ca. 455	
Theoctistus	Euthymius	Until the death of Theoctistus in 466	Sabas, from the beginning of 457 to 468
Gerasimus	Euthymius	After the death of Theoctistus	Cyriacus, from 466 until after March 475 (the death of Gerasimus)
Small Coenobium	Great Laura	Founded in 493	For adults
Theodosius	Great Laura	During the time of Sabas and Theodosius	For youths and eunuchs
Euthymius	Great Laura	Beginning of 544*	Cyril, from the beginning of 544 to 555 (when he moved to the New Laura)
Choziba	Calamon	Second half of 6th century	George of Choziba
Abba Dorotheus (near Gaza and Maiuma)	Firminus**	End of 6th century	9 years

*After the death of Sophronius the Armenian, the successor of Theodosius, who served as abbot for 14 years and 2 months.

**Pratum 166, 3032–33. In this case the removal was intended to protect the monk, who had previously been a robber and murderer, from the authorities of the Diospolis region.

the periods of novitiate, or stay in a coenobium prior to becoming a cell dweller, were much shorter.

Regarding the coenobium-laura relationship, an examination of the table reveals a dynamic picture: as long as Theoctistus was alive, his coenobium served as a novitiate for the laura of Euthymius; after his death, the coenobium in the center of the laura of Gerasimus began to serve as the novitiate for the laura of Euthymius as well. The coenobium of Theodosius served as a novitiate for the Great Laura during a long period of time; at the beginning of 544, however, the young Cyril was not sent there by John the Hesychast but rather to the coenobium of Euthymius, which was now a Sabaitic institution. It seems that during this period a schism occurred between the two monasteries, in contrast to the close relationship they had had during the time of Sabas and Theodosius. The basic principle that a youth wishing to live in a laura would begin in a coenobium had not changed, but the institution chosen to serve as a novitiate was undoubtedly chosen, during each period, according to the prominence of its head and the suitability of the coenobium to fill its educational function.

It seems that from the second half of the fifth century desert monasticism became more and more organized: the principle that youths were not to be allowed to live among the anchorites was strictly maintained, and a suitable framework was established in the coenobium for their training. Previously, this rule had not been strictly followed: Euthymius, as was stated, admitted to his laura three young brothers, one of whom was also a eunuch. We also hear that in Choziba—a monastery founded by five Syrian fathers who lived successively in the same cell—Aias, the fourth monk, received Zeno, the fifth monk, when he was still a beardless youth. This Zeno also died beardless, and was buried in the same tomb with the fathers who had preceded him there (*Miracula* 6, 368). These events took place close to the middle of the fifth century.

John Climacus tells of a Sabaite monk, also named John, who was besought by three young monks to serve as their teacher. John the Sabaite wanted to evade this task, and conceded only to advise them where each of them should go for training. One was sent to another monastery, to be instructed by an experienced abbot, the second was directed to a coenobium, and the third was ordered to lead an austere life, being entirely obedient to any supervising monk (*Scala Paradisi* 89: PG 88, 721–24). None of them was directed to the Small Coenobium. These events took place at the end of the sixth century. It seems that by that time the Small Coenobium ceased to function as a novitiate, and the prevailing training practice was different from that attested by Cyril. Each candidate was entrusted to an elderly, experienced monk, who decided upon the individual training appropriate for each. In any case, untrained youths were not admitted.

By the end of the eighth century Michael the Synkellos was a teacher and guide of the young brothers Theodore and Theophanes upon their arrival at the Laura (*V. Mich. Sync.* 5, 52–54). Changes obviously occurred under Muslim rule. The entire framework became loose, and thus at the beginning of the eighth century Zacharias brought his nine-year-old younger nephew, Stephen the Sabaite, to live with him in his cell (734 CE). Conscious of the ancient rule, however, Zacharias forbade him to be seen at the entrance (*V. Steph. Sab.* 7, 351, ed. Garitte).

The insistence on the rule not to admit into the Laura youths or adults who had not undergone prior preparation in a coenobium permitted candidates to be weeded out and ensured that only mature (thirty years of age or older) and outstanding monks would come to the Laura. This pattern, which had been established by Sabas and which was carefully maintained after his death, was one of the factors leading to the monastery becoming the center par excellence of spiritual life and literary creativity, since its monks were educated and well-versed in monastic life and in religious doctrine.

C. Other Regulations and Punishments in the Writings of Cyril of Scythopolis

1. Regulations

(a) A woman may not enter the Laura (*V. John Hes.* 23–24, 219). This law is included in regulation 2 in the set of regulations from Sinai (see below, sec. D). This prohibition was valid in every male monastery, Choziba being the only exception due to an event whose memory was preserved by local tradition.[80] Explicit rules on this subject were preserved

---

[80] *Miracula* 1, 360–63: a noblewoman from Byzantium, seeking to find a cure for her illness, came to Jerusalem and went among the monasteries, and afterwards went among the monasteries along the Jordan. When she was on her way back, passing by the monastery of Choziba, she asked her escorts to bring her to

in the Syrian monasteries,[81] and it is mentioned even earlier by Basil (*Ascetica*, 877). The Justinianic legislation also prohibited women from entering monasteries for any reason (*Nov.* 133.3). This interdiction is commonly repeated in the later *ktetorika typika* (Galatariotou 1987, 121–24).

(b) In the same spirit, Sabas demanded that his disciples take care to maintain modesty and to restrain their evil urges; he forbade them even to glance at a woman (*V. Sab.* 47, 137–38). An echo of this is preserved in rule 3 of the Sinai regulations. This rule was dictated by the monk's obligation to maintain modesty and to abstain from sexual intercourse and marriage—the most basic demand imposed upon anyone wishing to be a monk—and therefore contained nothing unique.

(c) Conduct during mealtimes and during the course of prayer: Euthymius ordered his first disciples in the coenobium he established together with Theoctistus not to talk in church during prayer nor in the dining room while the monks were eating (*V. Euth.* 9, 18). Sabas most probably adopted this basic rule in his monasteries as well; he was familiar with it from his stay in the coenobium of Theoctistus. A similar practice prevailed in the Pachomian monasteries (*HL* XXXII.6, 92).

2. Punishments

Discipline in any particular monastery was not the result of a system of punishments determined by the Rule, but rather issued from the free choice of each individual monk. Obedience to the regulations and subordination to the fathers in charge are essential principles in the entire monastic system. Nevertheless, at times the monks of the Laura rebelled against Sabas' leadership, and there were also instances of less severe violations of discipline.

Monastic life was full of struggles, along with failures, which required the intervention of the appointed fathers, either by preaching and rebuke or by punishment. We have not found in the Judean desert any whipping posts like those that were next to the church on Mount Nitria (*HL* VII.3, 25). The fathers of the monasteries in the Judean desert preferred rebuke, preaching, and instruction. At times, however, it was necessary to impose punishments. The holy men among them—Euthymius, Sabas, George of Choziba—also succeeded in establishing their authority by inflicting corporal punishment on violators of discipline by the force of their charisma, without any physical contact or violence. Such deeds were perceived as miraculous acts of heavenly intervention, as in the following examples.

(a) The monk Auxentius was asked by the steward of the laura of Euthymius to assume the post of mule driver, but he refused. The entreaties of the priests John and Kyrion were also of no avail; he even turned his back on Euthymius' words and stubbornly refused to obey. Immediately he was seized by trembling and fell to the ground—

---

the monastery, ignoring their protests that it was forbidden for a woman to enter there. When she arrived all the fathers were assembled in the church for the evening prayer, and the two gatekeepers left their post, leaving the gate open, thereby making it possible for the woman to enter into the courtyard. When the fathers went out from the prayer they were surprised to find her in their courtyard. The woman was healed, and from that incident on, women pilgrims were permitted to enter only the gates of the monastery of Choziba. See Patrich and Di Segni 1987, 275–77.

[81] Vööbus 1960b, Rabbula's Rules 1, 27; 15, 40; John of Tella's (Bar Qursos) Rules 6, 58; anonymous collection VIII.4, 71; Rules of Jacob of Edessa 11, 96.

characteristic signs of epilepsy. At the request of the fathers, Euthymius raised him up, made the sign of the cross over him, and restored him to health; Auxentius finally accepted the position (*V. Euth.* 18, 28–29).

(b) Maron and Klematios, two of Euthymius' monks, wanted to leave the laura at night, without requesting his permission or receiving his blessing (παράθεσις).[82] Euthymius summoned them and warned them, attempting to persuade them with his words. Klematios burst out laughing, thereby arousing the wrath of Euthymius, who sent him away. Klematios was immediately stricken with shaking and dizziness and fell on his face, clenching his teeth. Once again, upon the intercession of the fathers, Euthymius raised him up, and by making the sign of the cross over him, healed him (*V. Euth.* 19, 30–32).

(c) The monk James, who without Sabas' permission began to build a small prayer-house and cells near the Heptastomos cistern, and refused to heed the elder's rebuke, was stricken with a fever that lasted seven months, from which he was healed only when he requested pardon from the holy man (*V. Sab.* 39, 129–30).

(d) The hand of the monk who was appointed tutor for the young George, at the beginning of the latter's career in Choziba, withered after he slapped the young man's cheek (*V. Geor.* 4, 100). This episode also illustrates that occasionally veteran monks did not refrain from physical punishment (slaps and blows) of the youths subordinate to them.

(e) An impertinent and haughty monk, who acted in an unruly manner during the outdoor meal at the harvest of the *mannouthion* and refused to heed the reprimands of the aged George, was stricken by poisoning from a wound in his ankle caused by a colony of ants that burrowed around him when he fell asleep, thus fulfilling the curse placed upon him by George (*V. Geor.* 14, 110–11).

Sabas also chose the manner of personal example and lesson: the same monk James, who served as guest master, did not take care to be frugal and threw the remains of his cooked dish (beans, called *pissarion*) out of the window into the ravine. Sabas, who saw this, collected the beans, dried them, and at the end of James' year of service summoned him and served him the beans, after cooking them once again. James found the meal to be tasty; then Sabas told him the story. His moral: whoever does not know how to refrain from waste also will not know how to lead a community. This was an important lesson for James (*V. Sab.* 40, 131; cf. John Cassian, *Inst.* IV.19).

But in every human community in which rules have been established to maintain its way of life, along with obligations and prohibitions, there are also punishments. This was the case in the monasteries as well. Cyril mentions several of these punishments in his writings.

---

[82] Regarding the necessity of receiving permission from the head of the monastery (*rîšdayrâ*) to leave the monastery for private matters or for home visits, see Vööbus 1960b, 30.13; 83.20. It was also established in the Rule that if the monk had been in the monastery, "wearing the habit," for less than 3 years, then not even the permission of the *rîšdayrâ* was sufficient (ibid. 91.14). It was also established that the amount of time to be spent outside had to be predetermined (ibid. 206.2). In the Pachomian Rule as well it was established that a monk could go on a journey outside the monastery, if this proved to be necessary, only with the permission of the head of the monastery (*Koinonia* II, 157: *Pr.* 63), and if a monk goes out to visit a sick relative, or for any other reason, an additional monk who excels in his monastic qualities is to accompany him (ibid. 155: *Pr.* 54; 156: *Pr.* 56).

(a) A monk who was not particular about modesty in his regard, while walking along, cast his eyes upon a woman and was sent by Sabas from the Laura to Kastellion, until he learned to restrain his mind and his eyes (*V. Sab.* 47, 137–38).

(b) Secluding oneself within a cell as a recluse, which was perceived as the supreme degree of asceticism and a sublime way of life accompanied by *hesychia*, was at the same time a punishment for monks who stumbled in their behavior: this was the punishment imposed by Sabas upon the monk James for having castrated himself by cutting his testicles with a knife, in order to excise the evil urge, an act which was against "the rules of God and the ecclesiastical canons."[83] At first, after James had recovered, Sabas expelled him from the Laura as one who attempted suicide. Afterwards, upon the intervention of Theodosius, his punishment was mitigated, and he was sentenced to seclude himself in his cell without going out and without receiving anyone except his servant (*V. Sab.* 41, 131–32).

(c) Incidental to this story, we learn that the punishment for attempted suicide was banishment from the Laura.

(d) Expulsion from the monastery of Theodosius was decreed for Aphrodisius, who was the official in charge of the mule drivers in the coenobium. He did not succeed in controlling his anger and with his great strength killed one of the mules with a blow of his fist. When Aphrodisius came to him, Sabas, instead of the decree of expulsion, forbade the offender from leaving the Laura or visiting other cells. He was allowed to leave his cell only once a month (*V. Sab.* 44, 134–35). This was a very severe punishment for a coenobium monk, whose previous post required him to engage in many outside duties; he was compelled to maintain a life stricter than that of a regular laura monk, being forbidden to associate with others or leave the Laura, which was permitted to other monks from time to time.

(e) A disciple named Phlais, who performed various tasks in Sabas' mission, stumbled once and committed adultery, and disappeared out of his great shame and sorrow. Sabas searched for and found him, encouraged him, but also warned him; and in order that Phlais would not again fail in this manner, he forbade him to perform any tasks outside the monastery. From then on he secluded himself in a cell (*V. Sab.* 49, 139). Regulation 3 of the Sinai rules decrees for this sin the punishment of expulsion from the brotherhood.

(f) Patriarch Elias presented the rebels against Sabas (see above, Part III, Chap. 2) with two choices: to end the rebellion and be subservient to him in everything or to leave the Laura. The rebels chose to pack their things and leave. Sabas himself preferred to deal with the rebels by means of persuasion and even chose to go into voluntary exile rather than impose his will on the rebels. He also refrained from initiating an appeal to the patriarch to intervene. Regulation 9 of the Sinai rules similarly decrees expulsion from the monastery as the punishment for quarrelers who refuse to be reconciled.

(g) Expulsion from the Laura on theological and doctrinal grounds entailed the consent of the patriarch or a decision by the fathers of the Laura. The first Origenists in the New Laura—Nonnus and his fellows—were expelled in 514 by Agapetus, the head of the New Laura, only after he had obtained the opinion and consent of Patriarch Elias.

---

[83] We hear about this phenomenon also among the monks of Syria; see Vööbus 1960a, 257–58.

The patriarch was also allowed to order the abbot to get them back (*V. Sab.* 36, 124–25). During the time of Gelasius, forty Origenists were expelled from the Great Laura, upon the initiative of the abbot and upon the decision of the fathers of the Laura (*V. Sab.* 84, 189–90). And at the beginning of 540, under pressure by the priest (*papas*) Eusebius of Constantinople, the fathers of the Great Laura expelled the leaders of the Anti-Origenists (*V. Sab.* 85, 191). Finally, in 555, the expulsion of the Origenists from the New Laura was carried out by Patriarch Eustochius, relying upon the decrees of the emperor and assisted by a military force he received from the provincial governor (*V. Sab.* 90, 199).

We do not know whether punishments for deeds such as those mentioned above were listed in Sabas' original Rule; however, the set of regulations from Sinai does refer to some of these cases. It may be assumed that the various punishments did have a basis in the Rule and were not imposed in an arbitrary or spontaneous manner.

3. Attitude toward Mortification

Euthymius maintained that asceticism should not be indulged in to excess, which would be ostentation. As regards food, "the best kind of abstinence is to partake of food at the hour of the meal a little less than the body requires" (*V. Euth.* 9, 18). He thereby adhered to the Basilian ideal. Some of the extreme forms of mortification characteristic of Syrian monasticism (Vööbus 1960a, 256–78) were encountered by Palladius around 400 CE on the Mount of Olives (a monk with chains around his body; *HL* XLIV, 131–32) and in the Jordan region (a monk who secluded himself in a tomb and did not sit or lie down for three years; ibid. L, 144). These were extremely rare in Palestine and the Judean desert during the periods described in the writings of Cyril of Scythopolis. Nor did Sabas propose extreme, unnatural mortification. While in the monastery of Theoctistus he was known for possessing excellent manners and exhibiting rational behavior, and therefore Abbot Longinus approved his request to live in a cell outside the coenobium (*V. Sab.* 10, 94). His mortification was expressed in two ways: a fast during weekdays for the five years that he lived outside the coenobium (ibid.) and, in later periods, during Lent (ibid. 24, 109; 64, 165), and his patchwork cloak (ibid. 33, 119.2; 51, 142.8). The asceticism of Aphrodisius was outstanding in the Great Laura: he possessed only one tunic; his eating utensils consisted of only a bowl; he slept on a mat upon which was a straw bedding, without a mattress, and he covered himself with a patchwork blanket; he completely refrained from cooked food, eating the scraps of the fraternal meal; he abstained from wine and *eukras;* and he would leave his cell only once a month (*V. Sab.* 44, 134–35).

4. The Quadragesimal Fast, Feasts, and Prayer Rites

In the Early Church there was a development in the customs concerning the fast preceding Easter, and there were local differences. During the first three hundred years such a fast was not practiced. Indications of the existence of the "quadragesimal fast" are extant from the fourth century on. The fifth canon of the Council of Nicaea recommends that the bishops in each district hold two regional synods per year in order to arrange various ecclesiastical matters. The date established for the biannual synod was "before the period of the forty" (πρὸ τῆς τεσσαρακόστης). This source does not specify what characterizes this time of the year. The prevalent opinion is that the "period of the forty" was regarded at the beginning as a preparatory period preceding baptism and as a period of fast and inner improvement before Easter. Fasting played an important role in the religious life during this part of the year. In most locations, the fast period was less than forty days, and there were places in which it was no more than fifteen days. Socrates Scholasticus (*HE* v.22, 636) wondered about this, since people nevertheless spoke of the "quadragesimal fast."

In Antioch and in the East there was a distinction between the fast period—the "quadragesimal fast"—and the Easter week fast. Sozomen (*HE* vii.19, 331) and other sources state that from Constantinople to Phoenicia it was the practice to maintain seven weeks of fasting. In each week there were five fast days; the fast was interrupted on Saturdays and Sundays, excluding the Saturday preceding Holy Week. Thus the fast period included thirty-six fast days. In Jerusalem the practice was different: at the end of the fourth century Egeria speaks of eight weeks of fasting, with five fast days each week. Holy Saturday, which was also a fast day, was counted in the Easter fast. Thus the fast period included exactly forty fast days, analogous to Jesus' fast in the desert. It is possible that the Church of Jerusalem later restricted the duration of the fast to six weeks, as we learn from Sozomen (ibid.) and from the writings of Peter, the patriarch of Jerusalem (524–544) (PG 95, 71–78). Dorotheus of Gaza, on the other hand, also speaks of an eight-week fast which included exactly forty fast days (PG 88, 1788). Thus we cannot speak of a single uniform practice in the Holy Land.

In Alexandria as well a distinction was made between the "quadragesimal fast" and the Easter fast, but the two fasts together lasted only six weeks. According to Socrates Scholasticus (*HE* v.22, 636), the Roman Church fasted only during the last three weeks before Easter. Some scholars are of the opinion that these should be counted as three non-consecutive weeks: the entire fast period lasted six weeks, but the fast was maintained only during the first, fourth, and sixth weeks. At any rate, for fifth-century Rome there are sufficient sources indicating that the fast lasted six weeks and included Saturdays. This was also the pattern in Alexandria, Libya, Illyricum, and in all the churches of the West (Sozomen, *HE* vii.19, 331). Thus in most of the Christian world the fast included thirty-six fast days, and only in Jerusalem and Palestine was another practice recognized, a fast lasting eight weeks prior to Easter week and including forty fast days.

The daily fast ended with the concluding, or evening, meal. According to Basil, Epiphanius, Chrysostom, and others, it was forbidden to end the fast before the evening. However, according to Socrates Scholasticus (*HE* v.22, 636), there were places in which the fast already ceased at the ninth hour, about 3:00 P.M. The main meal was normally served at the fifth hour, about 11:00 A.M.; therefore, during the fast period, it was delayed by at least four hours.

During fast period, not all sorts of food were permitted during the concluding meal. Foods of animal origin—meat, eggs, and dairy products—were forbidden. Some refrained from fish and fowl. Permitted foods therefore included bread, vegetables, and salt. Wine was prohibited, and the main beverage was water (Vacandard 1910, 1724–34).

These were the fasting practices among ordinary believers; the monks obviously adopted more stringent fasting practices. During the fast period Euthymius and Gerasimus would refrain from all food during the six weekdays and only on Sunday would partake of the Eucharist (*V. Euth.* 32, 51; *V. Ger.* 4, 5; *V. Cyr.* 5, 225). Sabas refrained from food for five days during the week and partook of the Eucharist on Saturday and Sunday

(*V. Sab.* 24, 108). Less strict monks were not required to abstain completely from food during the weekdays. They could eat bread and roots of *melagrion*—fare more meager and simple than that eaten on regular days (*V. Sab.* ibid. 107–8; 38, 56–57).

Going forth to the desert during the fast period was apparently begun by Euthymius. He would go to the desert of Coutila with Theoctistus when they were still in the laura of Pharan, and continued to do so in his laura as well. The date of going into the desert was fixed: January 14, the eighth day of Epiphany (*V. Euth.* 7, 14–15; 25, 38–39; 39, 57; *V. Sab.* 11, 94; 22, 106). (This differs from the practice in Jerusalem related by Egeria, from whom we may deduce that the date changed according to the date of Easter.) They remained there until Palm Sunday, the beginning of Holy Week prior to Easter. During the Holy Week fast Euthymius remained in the laura. The duration of his Lenten fast therefore differed from year to year and could exceed eight weeks, depending on the changing date of Easter. According to the Alexandrian practice, which was accepted at the Council of Nicaea, this date was the Sunday following the vernal equinox (today, March 20).[84] Heavy rains in the desert could delay the date of departure (*V. Euth.* 25, 38–39). At times the young Sabas was invited to join Euthymius on this journey (*V. Euth.* 38, 56–57; *V. Sab.* 11, 94–95).

When Sabas became head of a monastery, he also adopted this practice. During this period he would go out to the desert "almost every year" (*V. Sab.* 22, 106). At times, instead of going forth to the desert, he would pay a visit to the holy places along the Jordan and the Sea of Galilee, going as far as Panias (ibid. 24, 107–8). He generally would go by himself (ibid. 22, 106; 27, 110; 39, 129), but at times was accompanied by a disciple (ibid. 24, 107–8; 37, 126).

Begun by Euthymius, the departure into the desert during Lent was a privilege reserved for the abbot, who could choose the monks who would accompany him. This was so with Euthymius, Gerasimus (*V. Ger.* 4, 5; *V. Cyr.* 5, 225), Sabas, and John the Scholarius (*V. Ab.* 7, 234). We do not hear of any individual monk going out to the desert during Lent unaccompanied by the abbot.

Sabas changed the date of departure that had been set by Euthymius. Since the annual memorial day for Euthymius was January 20, Sabas postponed the beginning of his fast by a week. Thus he would also be in the Laura for the memorial day honoring St. Antony the Great (Jan. 17). This commemorative day, which started with an all-night vigil, was instituted in the laura of Euthymius a few days before he died (*V. Euth.* 39, 57); previously it had been his custom to go out into the desert before that day. Sabas therefore was also adopting a rite established by Euthymius at the end of his life. His presence in the Great Laura at the memorial services for St. Antony, the founder of anchorite monasticism, and for St. Euthymius the Great undoubtedly added an important dimension to these feasts, which were certainly of special significance to the monastic communities.

Sabas also established for his monks that before the dominical feasts an all-night vigil should be held in the churches of the Laura (*V. Sab.* 32, 118). As noted, the memorial day for St. Antony began with an all-night vigil, and it may be assumed that this was so

---

[84] Regarding the difficult problem of determining the date of Easter and the disputes in the early Church on this issue, see A. Strubel, *Ursprung und Geschichte des frühchristlichen Osterkalenders,* TU 121 (Berlin 1977).

on the memorial day for Euthymius as well. Sabas thereby contributed to consolidating the calendar of holidays in his monasteries and to formulating their liturgy.

Sabas also changed from Euthymius' habit of fasting six days a week during Lent, and fasted only five days a week (as was the practice in Jerusalem during Egeria's time). This was obviously related to the fact that Sabas scheduled the celebration of the Eucharist on both Saturday and Sunday in the Great Laura, while in the laura of Euthymius, the monastery of Theoctistus, and the laura of Pharan, this rite had been held only on Sundays (see above, Part III, Chap. 4B).

The present-day *Sabaitic Typikon*, on which the Byzantine rite is based (Egender 1975; Arranz 1976, 1982; Taft 1986, 273–91), is a liturgical *typikon* of the Greek Orthodox Church and has no direct connection with the monastic Rule mentioned by Cyril of Scythopolis and discussed above. Symeon of Thessalonike (d. 1429) traces its transmission to the very beginning of Palestinian monasticism. He indicates that these liturgical orders, set down by Sabas, originated with Chariton, who (orally) transmitted them to Euthymius and to Theoctistus, from whom Sabas received them. Then, being lost when the monasteries were destroyed by the barbarians (during the Persian conquest; see below, Part V, Chap. 1), they were formulated again by Sophronius[85] and later on by John of Damascus (Symeon of Thessalonike, *De Sacra Precatione*, PG 155, 556). Sophronius lived for ten years in the post-Origenist New Laura, a Sabaite institution, and was well versed in the Sabaitic tradition, both regarding monastic life and Orthodox theology (see Schönborn 1972). John of Damascus was the most famous Sabaitic monk of the eighth century. It was mainly the Sabaitic monks who preserved the Palestinian monastic liturgy throughout the ages.

The early *Sabaitic Typikon* of the seventh and eighth centuries was adopted by Theodore of Stoudios for his monastery in Constantinople. Absorbing elements from the cathedral rite of the capital, the *Stoudite Typikon* was shaped later during the ninth century. The *Sabaitic Typikon* of the present is the final generation of liturgical *typika*, codifying the neo-Sabaitic rite formed in the eleventh and twelfth centuries, when the monasteries of Palestine adapted the *Stoudite Typika* of the ninth century. The final form of the *Sabaitic Typikon* is the Athonite redaction, which took shape under the hesychasts in the fourteenth century. This redaction became the definitive liturgical synthesis of the Byzantine rite, supplanting the earlier *Stoudite Typika* (Taft, *ODB* 1823 and 1961; 1986, 273–77; 1988).

The liturgical orders established by Sabas for his monasteries were the first step in a long process of evolution of the present Byzantine rite. Sabaite monks of later generations, who preserved, modified, and transmitted the Palestinian monastic rite, played a decisive role in this process.[86]

---

[85] Sophronius is considered editor of the 13th-century Sabaitic *Typikon*, Paris gr. 361 (Dmitrievskij 1917, 130): τυπικὸν . . . τῆς λαύρας τοῦ ὁσίου Σάβα συντεθὲν καὶ συγγραφὲν παρὰ τοῦ ἁγιωτάτου πατριάρχου πατρὸς καὶ ἱερομονάχου Ἱεροσολύμων κυρίου Σωφρονίου.

[86] Dmitrievskij (1917) collected five *typika* classified as of the Jerusalemite redaction, dated to the 12th–13th centuries, and 116 *typika* classified as of the Jerusalemite-Constantinopolitan redaction, dated to the 13th–16th centuries. The Jerusalemite *Typika* are identified by their titles as of the Laura of St. Sabas. Thus, for example, the title of *typikon* no. II (Sinai gr. 1096) is: Τυπικὸν τῆς ἐκκλησιαστικῆς ἀκολουθίας τῆς ἐν

D. The Sinai Monastic Rule of Mar Saba

"Rule, Tradition, and Law of the Venerable Laura of [St.] Sabas"
(trans. Leah Di Segni from E. Kurtz, *BZ* 3 [1894], 168–70; the square brackets indicate later additions to the original Rule of Sabas, as suggested by Kurtz).

1. [The commands given by our holy and blessed father Sabas must be observed, and] a eunuch or a beardless (youth) is never to be admitted into the Laura.
2. As to women, none is to be permitted to enter the Laura for the purpose of prayer, not even its satellite institutions—*metochia* (μετοχίοις), especially within the second gate of the Great *Metochion* (μεγάλου μετοχίου).[87]
3. If one of the monks of the Laura is caught entering a nunnery and eating and drinking and staying there, or storing up anything on the pretext of safekeeping, or cutting his hair, or entertaining (impure) thoughts, or writing to a woman and corresponding with her, or at all maintaining relations or sexual intercourse with women, he will be cut off from the brotherhood as a cause of scandal not only to Christians but also to the Gentiles.
4. The Iberians or the Syrians [or the Franks] shall not be permitted to conduct a complete prayer service in their churches, rather, they will gather in them to chant the liturgical hours and the daily canon (τὰς ὥρας καὶ τὰ τυπικά) and will read the (Epistles) of the Apostle and the Gospels in their own language, and afterwards they will come into the great church and participate in the pure, lifegiving Divine mysteries together with the entire brotherhood.
5. [The priest appointed for this will conduct an early prayer on the tomb of the saint].
6. No one, under any circumstances, will have permission to leave the Laura on Saturday, because of the forthcoming vigil, except for an unavoidable need and in the service of all. After the vigil he may go forth for his business, with the permission of the head of the monastery (προεστώς) or the director of the liturgy (ἐκκλησιάρχης). But if he is not present at the vigil rite held at that time, he will not at all receive (permission): because the entire preceding week ought to suffice for him to attend to his duties (διοικῆσαι τὰς δουλείας αὐτοῦ). And this, if possible (will be done only) once per month.
7. Those who go out to the desert and those who dwell in the deserts, if they do this with the permission and blessing of the head of the monastery (προεστώς), will take the supplies they need; but if they go out without permission, on their own accord, they will not be admitted upon their return.

Ἰερουσαλύμοις εὐαγοῦς λαύρας τοῦ ὁσίου θεοφόρου πατρὸς ἡμῶν Σάββα. In other *typika* it is added that it is of other monasteries of Jerusalem as well. The central role of the Sabaitic liturgical tradition in the transmission of the Byzantine rite is evident.

[87] The hostel of the monastery of Sabas in Jerusalem was called *Metochia* (Μετοχία) during the Middle Ages. See Vincent and Abel 1914–26, vol. 2, 518, 911. This apparently is the meaning of the "great estate (= metochion)." It is by this name that the "branch" (Deir Zerir) of the St. Catherine monastery in the oasis of Feiran is called, as I was informed by Prof. Yoram Tsafrir. The mention of estates, in the plural, possibly indicates that in the period reflected by the Rule, the monastery still had a number of hostels, as was the case during the Byzantine period.

8. If someone, under Divine Providence and the decision of the patriarch, will be appointed metropolitan or bishop or abbot (ἡγούμενος) in another monastery (μοναστήριον), or to any degree of the Great Church, he will no longer have control of his cells in the Laura and in the estate (τῷ μετοχίῳ), nor will he have authority to sell or give them away; rather (the cells) will be at the disposal of the holy monastery, and they will be given by the abbot of the monastery to other worthy and needy brothers. This rule is to be observed also upon the brothers' death, and without the consent and disposition of the abbot (ἡγούμενος), no one will have the right to bequeath his cell to his own disciple.

9. If there will be an altercation between brothers, and evil will prevail to the point that they strike each other and raise their hands (against each other)—if they will not be reconciled and live in peace and mutual love, they shall be expelled from the monastery as troublemakers, and alien to the commandments of the Messiah. Indeed, the servant of the Lord shall not quarrel, as the divine apostle says (2 Tim. 2:24).

10. If one of the brothers will be found intoxicated, and maltreating, or abusing anyone, or makes ties of friendship and closeness—either he shall mend his ways or he shall be expelled.

11. Similarly regarding the (holders of) positions: whoever shall be caught stealing shall be suspended from his post, while receiving punishment for his correction and repentance, and shall not go out from his cell, except at the set times of assemblies in the church and the prayers.

12. And those who wish to live in silence and have permission not to come to the church, but on the other hand not to completely shut themselves up—it is our wish that they assemble with the others if only during the vigil rites. But regarding the appearances in the cities and the villages and in the memorial services for saints and other processions, they will certainly remain in seclusion; indeed, silence may prosper more in labor than in speech.

13. The strangers who come from outside, if any of them want to make a start in the Laura, we shall accept them for a stay of seven days; but if they are (monks?) who dwell in the city or visitors who come in order to genuflect, a respite of three days is sufficient for them, because of the masses of the poor who arrive every day.

14. And since the destructive demons, on occasion of the appointment of the monastery leaders, are wont to cause dissensions and quarrels between the two nationalities, that is, the Greek-speakers and the Syriac-speakers, in order to remove this stumbling block, we establish that from now on none of the Syrians will be appointed to the post of abbot (ἡγούμενος), whereas for stewards (οἰκονόμοι), hostelers (δοχειάριοι), and the other jobs we order and agree that Syrians shall be given preference, because in their lands of origin people are more efficient and practical.

Part IV: Sabas as an Ecclesiastical Leader

1

Sabas, A Holy Man (*hosios*)

Sabas was revered as a holy man. Cyril adds to his name the title ὅσιος ("holy"). As a holy man, he was gifted, like Euthymius (*V. Euth.* 21, 34.25–30), with the grace (χάρισμα) of participation in the Holy Spirit, illumination by the divine light, clairvoyance, healing the sick and driving out unclean spirits, and the ability to perform various miracles. The date of his death, December 5, was kept in the calendar of saints.

Sabas' *Life* includes many miracles. Miracles were perceived as manifestations of divine grace, and the holy man merited having divine grace manifested through him, since he possessed a "boldness of speech" (παρρησία: *V. Euth.* 25, 38.16) before God. In this manner Cyril and his contemporaries explained the ability of the holy man to perform deeds that are beyond the capabilities of ordinary mortals (Flusin 1983, 155–82). It was the Christian belief in the supernatural powers of the holy man that gave him his special status in Byzantine society (Brown 1971).[1] At the same time, however, at least some of the miracles related in saints' lives consist of a literary *topos* with the clear intent of attributing Jesus' virtues to the holy man, but this is not the place to demonstrate these parallels (cf. Canivet 1977, 117–46; Cox 1983).

The process of Sabas' establishing his monastery near Nicopolis (see Part II, Chap. 2F, above) reveals the importance of the holy man in Byzantine society, especially the people's desire to "hold on" to him and cause him to dwell in their midst by erecting a cell and a monastery for him so they might benefit from his apotropaic power and his abilities as a miracle worker and healer of the sick. His blessing was considered more prophylactic than any amulet, since he was the *locus* of the "supernatural." In the fifth and sixth centuries the holy man took the place of the village patron (προστάτης) of the preceding period as a source of patronage, protection, and security for the villagers. In their eyes, his power (δύναμις) was supernatural, remaining in force even after his death; this is the reason for the veneration of saints' tombs and relics. The miracles performed by the saint or his relics were expressions and manifestations of this power (Brown 1971). Another example of a monastery established in the manner of that near Nicopolis is the monastery built for Euthymius by the villagers of Aristoboulias and the nearby villages between the years 421 and 425 so that he would remain living in their midst (*V. Euth.* 12, 22–23; 14, 23–24). Similar examples are known from Syria (Vööbus 1960a, 160).

---

[1] This aspect of monasticism—the veneration of the monk as a holy man—was not discussed by Vööbus 1958a, 1960a, 1988.

The first miracle of Sabas occurred while he was still in the monastery of Flaviana in Cappadocia: he entered a heated oven to remove the clothes of the baker which had been left there to dry, and emerged unscathed (*V. Sab.* 5, 89–90). Most of his miracles, however, were performed when he was already an abbot. The spring of the Laura was revealed to him in a miraculous manner (ibid. 17, 101). He turned vinegar to wine (ibid. 46, 136–37) and made a bitter pumpkin dish sweet (ibid. 48, 138). Like Gerasimus and the monk Zosimus mentioned in the *Life* of Mary the Egyptian,[2] Sabas succeeded in taming a lion to do his bidding (ibid. 33–34, 119). He also possessed the ability to drive out demons and to wrestle with them (ibid. 27, 110–11; 33, 118.28). He miraculously imposed punishments in cases of serious violations of discipline. The illness suffered by the monk James (ibid. 39, 130) and the sterility that befell the flocks of the desert shepherds who harassed his monasteries (ibid. 59, 160–61) were perceived in this light. As with Euthymius and many other holy men, several miraculous instances of causing dew and rain to fall were attributed to him: the miracle of the cloud in the desert (ibid. 26, 109); the rain in the coenobium of the Cave (ibid. 66, 167), and the rain in Jerusalem (ibid. 67, 167–69; cf. *V. Euth.* 25, 38–39). This last miracle occurred at the end of the severe drought that struck Palestine during the years 516–521, which was accompanied by an invasion of locusts. It was therefore of special importance and gave Sabas a high reputation among the inhabitants of Jerusalem. Cyril also mentions four healing miracles (*V. Sab.* 45, 136; 62, 163–64; 63, 164; 68, 170–71), which indicate that the believers, including Peter, the patriarch of Jerusalem, had confidence in his healing ability and turned to him for this purpose. Other miracles were attributed to his name and memory after his death (ibid. 78–82, 184–87).

Like other holy men, Sabas was also endowed with the gift of prophecy. Cyril attributes to him prophecies regarding the fate of Marinus the Syrian, a Monophysite who was the senior financial advisor of Emperor Anastasius (ibid. 54, 146–47), and that of Silvanus the Samaritan (ibid. 61, 163; 70, 172); the barrenness of Empress Theodora (ibid. 71, 174); and the conquests of Justinian (ibid. 72, 175–76; 74, 178). Sabas also predicted the date of his own death (ibid. 76, 182), as did other holy men.

Sabas' relations with the faithful who were not from monastic or church circles sheds light on his veneration as a holy man. The inhabitants of Medaba, in Arabia, often came to Sabas to consult him on various matters and to obtain spiritual guidance and physical healing (*V. Sab.* 45–46, 136–37). In return they sent wheat and legumes to the monastery. Especially close ties were formed with one of the families in Medaba after the father, Gerontius, fell from a beast on his way to pray in the church of the Ascension on the Mount of Olives and was healed by Sabas (ibid. 45, 136). His son Thomas brought to his house a gourd-bottle from the hostel of the Laura in Jericho, after Sabas had turned the vinegar it contained into wine. This gourd-bottle was preserved in Gerontius' house for many years, and when anyone fell ill, the members of the family filled it with water which they sprinkled on the sick person, causing him to be cured. Cyril heard these details

---

[2] We must distinguish between this Zosimus, who was active in the 5th century, and the Zosimus who was in contact with Dorotheus of Gaza and who headed a monastery near Caesarea. This Zosimus lived during the first half of the 6th century, and Evagrius Scholasticus also speaks of him (*HE* IV.6). See Vailhé 1900–1.

from Gerontius (grandson of the first Gerontius), who was at that time the administrator of the coenobium of Euthymius, where Cyril was staying. The gourd-bottle is an example of the veneration of objects sanctified by a holy man. About 250 years later the two brothers Theodore and Theophanes (the *Graptoi*) came to the Laura of Sabas from this region of Arabia, Moabitis.

Sabas' admirers in the village of Bouriron in the coastal plan, near Ascalon, continued to venerate and worship him even after his death. Two brothers from the village were accustomed to host his monks who came there occasionally on various missions. When the brothers were stricken with a serious illness during the grape harvest, they prayed to his spirit to heal them; they were cured after he appeared to each of them in a dream. From then on they kept an annual memorial celebration on the day the miracle had taken place (ibid. 79, 185–86). The cult of Sabas as a holy man was therefore widespread in the coastal plain as well. About two hundred years later, Stephen the Sabaite came to the Laura from the village of Julis, located in the same region.

There is an especially large amount of information regarding the veneration of Sabas in Scythopolis, the birthplace of Cyril. Ties between the inhabitants of this city and the desert monks had already begun during the time of Euthymius, whose first eleven disciples included Cyrion of Tiberias, who was a priest in the house of the holy martyr Basil in Scythopolis (*V. Euth.* 16, 26). Another of his disciples, Cosmas, became the bishop of the city (not before 466) (ibid. and 37, 55–56).

Sabas was staying in the region of Scythopolis during his first exile (503 CE), when he settled in a cave near the river of Gadara. A youth named Basil, who was a relative of two of the notables of Scythopolis, joined him and became a monk; many of the inhabitants of the city streamed to the place to gaze upon him and venerate him (*V. Sab.* 34, 119).

The great veneration given to Sabas in Scythopolis is revealed by the reception he received during his two visits to the city on behalf of the patriarchs of Jerusalem. He arrived there in 518 with other fathers of the desert monasteries in order to disseminate the contents of Emperor Justin's letter that put an end to the religious policy of Severus and Anastasius (*V. Sab.* 61–63, 162–64; see also below, Chap. 3). Sabas was staying in the house of the metropolitan, and when he went to visit the anchorite John in the monastery of Enthemaneith ('Ein Themaneit?), which was close to the city, he was accompanied by many admirers who followed him through the city streets. They also witnessed one of his miraculous cures: the healing, by the touch of his hand, of a woman suffering from a discharge, a miracle whose memory survived in Scythopolis until the time of Cyril. The report of this miracle led to a gathering of other people, and while he was in Enthemaneith he cured, with oil from the holy cross, a young girl possessed by a spirit, who had been brought to him by her father. Sabas anointed her entire body, from head to toe, with the oil. Cyril's father was an eyewitness to the miracle and from that day on did not leave Sabas, who visited in his home many times and also associated there with the dignitaries of the city.

Sabas visited Scythopolis a second time close to the time of his death, in 532, after his return from his second journey to Constantinople (ibid. 75, 180–81). This time his purpose was to convey Justinian's orders concerned with repairing the damage caused by the Samaritan revolt and to deal with the required arrangements (see below, Chap. 4). He received an enthusiastic welcome, for the city also had sustained damage during the revolt. Metropolitan Theodosius came out to receive him, along with all the inhabitants of the city, including of course Cyril's father who was now the administrative director of the patriarchate and who accompanied him everywhere. He also brought his wife to Sabas to receive the saint's blessing. It may reasonably be assumed that other admirers of Sabas in the city acted in a similar manner. This time as well Sabas visited the house of Cyril's parents, blessing them and their seven-year-old son.[3] From then on Cyril regarded himself as a disciple of Sabas, and his parents' house served as a guest house for the monks of the Laura whenever they came to the city, even after Sabas' death, which occurred shortly afterwards. His parents used to send a yearly contribution to the Laura.

Among the women who venerated Sabas' memory in Scythopolis was one named Genarous, who donated two woven altar curtains to the monastery of Kastellion and the monastery of the Cave (ibid. 80, 186). Another admirer of Sabas and of the other desert monks was Abba George the anchorite, the founder of a hermitage in a place called Beella near Scythopolis, who urged Cyril to write and to whom Cyril dedicated his saints' lives.

Sabas also had numerous admirers in Jerusalem, especially after his rain miracle there. Among them were Marcianus, the priest of the Anastasis and *hegoumenos* of the monks at the Holy Zion church, who, together with his two sons, assisted Sabas in the construction of the Cave monastery. Another Jerusalem family included the "sons of Sheshan," victualers of the Holy City, who sent a convoy of food to the Laura during the period of drought (*V. Sab.* 58, 160).

Sabas also had admirers at the imperial court in Constantinople. He served as advisor and spiritual father to Ariadne, Emperor Anastasius' wife, and to the noblewomen Anicia Juliana and Anastasia, who was the wife of the patrician Pompeius, a nephew of the emperor (ibid. 53, 145).[4] Anastasia would later become the mother superior (Ἀμμᾶς) of a nunnery on the Mount of Olives; she told Cyril of the details of Sabas' first journey to the capital. Anicia Juliana was, on her mother's side, the granddaughter of Valentinian III, the emperor of the West, and the great-granddaughter of Theodosius II. Her father Olybrius had been the emperor of the West for a number of months. She was a very wealthy woman, who erected in Constantinople the magnificent church of St. Polyeuktos.[5] After her death her eunuchs came to Sabas in 527/8 and asked to be accepted into the Laura as monks; they eventually founded the monastery of the Eunuchs near Jericho (ibid. 69, 171). This indicates that her encounter with Sabas in the capital in 511/12 was not a casual event of only momentary significance, but that she and her household remained admirers of Sabas in later years as well. The generous monetary contributions that Sabas received for the maintenance of his monasteries (above, Part III, Chap. 1G) were to a large extent a function of his personal reputation and veneration as a holy man.

---

[3] Cyril was born in ca. 525; see Flusin 1983, 13.

[4] Pompeius and Anastasia were loyal Chalcedonians and cared for the deposed patriarch Macedonius in his exile. See Stein-Palanque 1949, 216 and nn. 3, 7; Festugière 1962b, 72 n. 136. Anastasia's veneration of Sabas is evident from her words (ibid. 54, 147).

[5] About this matron and her church, discovered and excavated in the 1960s, see M. Harrison, *A Temple for Byzantium: The Discovery and Excavation of Anicia Juliana's Palace Church in Istanbul* (Austin 1989).

77. The larnax with the embalmed body of St. Sabas in the main church, Mar Saba.

When he died (Dec. 5, 532) Sabas was interred in a burial place under the courtyard between the two churches of the Laura (*V. Sab.* 76–77, 132–33). Cyril relates that fifteen years later, when he was descending to the tomb in order to venerate Sabas' remains, he saw his body incorrupt. An aedicula was erected in the middle of the courtyard at a later date (Fig. 13). His remains were translated to Venice in the thirteenth century, whence they were brought back to Jerusalem on October 26, 1965. On November 12 the body was solemnly reburied in a decorated wooden larnax inside the main church (Fig. 77).[6]

[6] There are several Venetian accounts concerning the translation of the relics of St. Sabas to Venice. According to the official version, as told by the cardinal of Venice, the Sabaite monks carried the relics to Constantinople at the time of the Persian invasion, and they remained there for several centuries. When Constantinople was threatened by massacre and disaster in the 13th century, the Venetian leader Lorenzo Tiepolo was persuaded to translate the relics to Venice, where they were placed in the church of St. Antonino. But attributing the initial translation to the Sabaite monks is clearly false, since the history of the Laura during the Persian invasion and its restoration thereafter are well known.

According to another Venetian tradition, the relics reached Venice in 911, after being bought in Constantinople by the Venetian merchant Pietro Barbolano Centranico. In Venice a church was built in honor of the saint in 1076. After being burnt and rebuilt, its name was altered to St. Basso. According to yet another tradition, the Venetians transferred Sabas' remains to Acre and shortly after, in 1256, Lorenzo Tiepolo sent them to Venice to avoid the risk of their being seized by the Genoese (see Salem 1966–67; G. Heydock, *Der Heilige Sabas und seine Reliquien* [Geisenheim 1970], 45–60). However, according to the monk Sophronius (1547), Sabas' relics were taken to Venice when the monastery was abandoned for a hundred years, until 1540 (Khitrovo 1889, 273–74). But it seems that the period of desertion was shorter, since in 1481 Perdikas,

Relics of his body are also preserved in the Kykko monastery in Troödos, Cyprus; Vatopedi monastery, Mount Athos; Meteora monastery in Meteora; and in the church of Zoodochou Peges in Koine, Chios (Meinardus 1970, 245).

His feast was celebrated by the Byzantine Church on December 5. His *Life* was widespread in the Byzantine world. It is preserved in many manuscripts in its entirety as well as in abbreviated forms: a redaction of the tenth century by Symeon Metaphrastes and two pre-Metaphrastic versions originating from *menologia*. The *Life* is also known in several ancient translations: an Arabic one preserved in many manuscripts, first prepared in Mar Saba between 885 and 890; a Georgian translation of the ninth to tenth century; and an old Slavonic one (Lafontaine 1973; Schwartz 1939, 319–39).

In works of art—icons, murals, and illuminated manuscripts—he is frequently depicted standing either alone or with other saintly desert monks. The earliest representations of him are in the frescoes of Sta. Maria Antiqua in Rome (757–767) and in a tenth-century manuscript (*Menologium Basilii*) (Lechner, *LCI* VIII, 296–98). In the eleventh-century frescoes at Asinou, Cyprus, he is depicted standing next to Sts. Euthymius and Antony. It is nearly certain that he was depicted among the saints in the burial chapel at Kastellion, although his name has not been preserved (see above, Part II, Chap. 2A). Several eleventh- to twelfth-century Byzantine lead seals of Mar Saba are known, depicting St. Sabas holding a scroll or a cross. The figure of the saint on the obverse is identified by an inscription; on the reverse is another Greek inscription mentioning the laura of St. Sabas. Two lead medallions from the Flagellation Museum in Jerusalem depict a scene of Sabas' death.[7]

An extraordinary relic of St. Sabas is a processional cross of gilded silver, 43 cm wide, now in the Cleveland Museum of Art (Figs. 78, 79).[8] At the center of its reverse a medallion in relief depicts the icon of St. Sabas. Each of the cross's four arms depicts a pair of ascetics incised in niello: on the upper arm, Sts. Antony and Euthymius; on the left arm, Sts. Ephraem the Syrian and Hilarion; on the right arm, Sts. Anastasius of Sinai and John Climacus; on the lower arm, now missing, Sts. Arsenius and Abramius. The lower arm also included a Greek inscription (the accuracy of which is not guaranteed), according to which the cross was dedicated to St. Sabas and was made at the orders of a certain Nicholas, a monk, priest, and founder of the monastery of Glaistine. The site (if copied correctly) is not known, but according to Cyril Mango it should be sought in one of the provinces in Asia Minor, not in Constantinople. It is believed to be of the eleventh century.

---

the metropolitan of Smyrna, visited a monastery that did not seem to be deserted (Vailhé 1899–1900b, 170). Further research is required in order to clarify these conflicting accounts of the translation of the relics.

[7] For the seals see V. Laurent, *Le corpus des sceaux de l'empire byzantin* V.2, Paris 1965, seals 1577–1578; F. Manns, "Les sceaux byzantins du musée de la Flagellation," *LA* 26 (1976), 234, seal 22. As for the medallions, see B. Bagatti, "Medaglie Ricordo della Laura di San Saba," *TS* 11–12 (1973), 368.

[8] I am indebted to Dr. Alice-Mary Talbot, of Dumbarton Oaks, for bringing this relic, which deserves a separate study, to my attention, and to Mr. Stephen Fliegel, curator of the department of medieval art of the Cleveland Museum of Art, for permission to reproduce its photograph here. For a short description and illustrations of both the obverse and the reverse, see C. Mango, "La croix dite de Michel le Cérulaire et la croix de Saint Michel de Sykéôn," *Cahiers archéologiques* 36 (1988), 43 and figs. 7–8 on p. 45.

78. St. Sabas processional cross, reverse, first half of the eleventh century, Asia Minor, gilded silver and niello.

79. St. Sabas processional cross, reverse, detail: medallion depicting St. Sabas in relief.

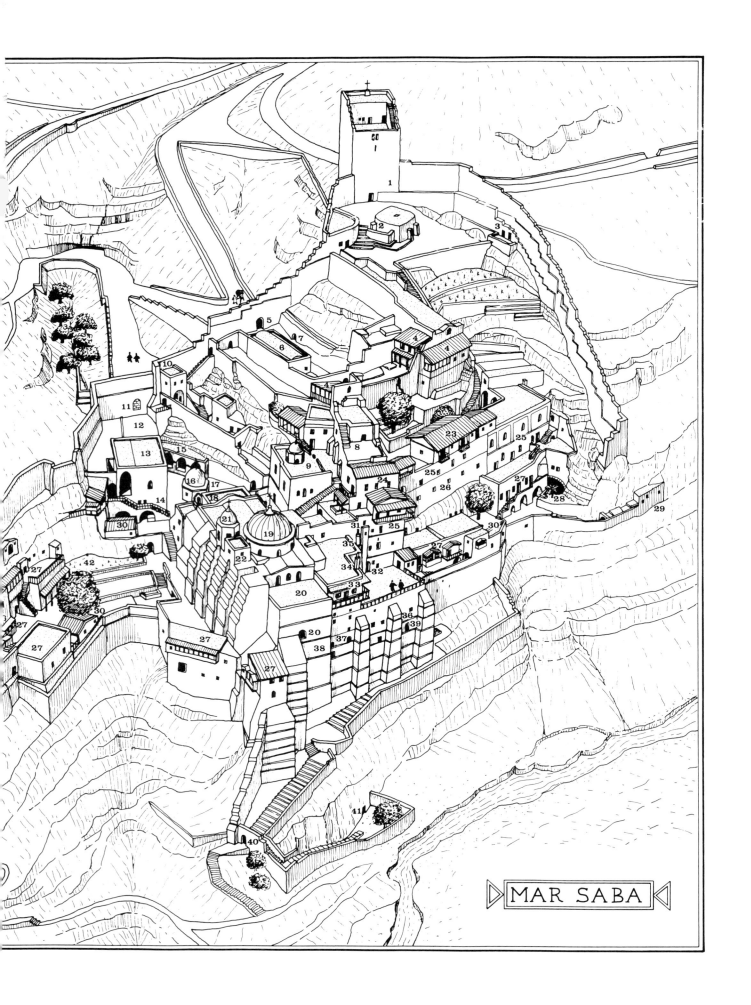

MAR SABA

80. Mar Saba. An aerial view.

Legend
1. "Tower of Justinian"
2. Upper water cistern
3. Water cistern
4. Deserted cells
5. Upper gate (not in use)
6. Stable
7. Storage area for straw
8. Chapel of St. John of Damascus
9. Chapel of the Archangels
10. Gatehouse
11. Blocked opening
12. Treshing floor for wine press (not in use)
13. Reading hall
14. Reception hall
15. Chapel of St. Nicholas of Myra
16. St. Sabas' tomb
17. Paved courtyard (cemetery underneath)
18. Western narthex of the main church
19. Dome of St. Mary Theotokos Church
20. Roof and window of the apse
21. Belfry
22. Clock room
23. Two apartments for visiting bishops
24. Guest rooms for priests
25. Hostel for visitors
26. Dwellings for monks (not occupied)
27. Dwellings for monks
28. "Palm tree of St. Sabas"
29. Chapel of St. John Chrysostom
30. Lavatory
31. Chapel of St. George
32. Dwelling place of Mar Saba abbot
33. Reception hall
34. Kitchen chimney
35. Bakery chimney
36. Refectory (*trapeza/aristeterion*)
37. Kitchen
38. Storeroom
39. Bakery
40. Lower gate
41. Sacred spring
42. Garden
43. Chapel of Anna and Joachim; Sabas' *hesychasterion*
44. "Women's Tower" and Chapel of St. Symeon Stylites

L. RITMEYER

2

Archimandrite of the Monks (before July 23, 494)

A. The Office of Archimandrite

An archimandrite (ἀρχιμανδρίτης) was the head of a *mandra* (μάνδρα), literally "sheep-fold." In the monastic context, however, a *mandra* referred to a monastery surrounded by a wall, that is, a coenobium. This is the meaning it assumed in Syriac as well. The use of the term for a monastery began in the fourth century in Mesopotamia, and is the source of the combination *archimandrites* (ἀρχιμανδρίτης), meaning "abbot of a monastery."[9]

From the end of the fourth century to the middle of the sixth, the official in charge of a group of monasteries is called in various sources *exarchos* (ἔξαρχος τῶν μοναστηρίων).[10] During this period the term *archimandrite* was widespread throughout all the monastic centers—in Asia Minor, Syria, and Egypt (Barison 1938, 36)—with the meaning of abbot of a monastery. Only in the course of the sixth century is a change evident: the prevalent term denoting the abbot becomes *hegoumenos* (ἡγούμενος) (see above, Part III, Chap. 1A), and the term *archimandrite* is reserved for the heads of important monasteries, assuming a significance parallel to that of *exarchos*.[11]

The archbishop of Jerusalem placed one or two *exarchoi/archimandritai* at the head of the desert monks. It seems that this organizational innovation, in which the monastic movement was integrated into the ecclesiastical establishment, was first instituted in Palestine by Juvenal (428–458), who brought the Jerusalem patriarchate to premier status

---

[9] It appears in southern Syria in a Greek inscription from Eitha in the Bashan, dated to 354 or 355. This word does not appear in Basil's writings, and it is also rare in the Greek literature dealing with the Egyptian monasteries.

[10] According to the Justinianic legislation, it was the duty of the patriarch, metropolitan, or bishop to ensure that discipline would be maintained in each monastery. To this end they had to send to the monasteries supervisors, whose task was to protect discipline, hence their title, ἐκδίκοι (defenders of the law). There were districts in which there was an *exarchos* (ἔξαρχος), who was appointed by the patriarch as supervisor over the monasteries. Such was the situation in Constantinople, where this office is first mentioned during the time of Patriarch Acacius (471–489). The *exarchos* also had a deputy (Granič 1929, 29). The task of the exarchos was to send his delegates (*apocrisiarii*/ἀποκρισιάριοι) to the monasteries, so that they would supervise discipline and report to him about what was happening. He had to punish transgressors properly (*Nov.* 133.4 [539 CE]).

[11] Cyril of Scythopolis uses it in this new meaning while speaking of Sabas and Theodosius, and while describing the history of the office. It is clear, therefore, that Passarion in his time, as well as Sabas and Theodosius afterwards, bore the title of *exarchos*. The title *archimandrites*, as used by Cyril regarding Passarion and his successors, is therefore anachronistic (Pargoire 1907). Nevertheless, for convenience' sake I shall use this term below, because our discussion is based on Cyril's terminology.

among the bishops of the three provinces of Palestine and who saw it become the fifth patriarchate in the Christian world, alongside Rome, Alexandria, Antioch, and Constantinople (Honigmann 1956). The office of archimandrite is first mentioned in 428: during the dedication ceremony of the church of the laura of Euthymius (May 7), Passarion the Great accompanied Juvenal and Hesychius, the priest and teacher of the church, on account of his function as *chorepiskopos* and *archimandrites* of the monks (χωρεπίσκοπος καὶ τῶν μοναχῶν ἀρχιμανδρίτης) (*V. Euth.* 16, 26.18–19).

A *chorepiskopos* was a bishop of a rural district or region subordinate to the district city and to the bishop heading it. The *chorepiskopoi* were permitted to supervise the churches within the bounds of their jurisdiction and to serve as priests. They were authorized to appoint only readers, subdeacons, and exorcists; however, they were forbidden to ordain deacons or priests without the approval of the bishop of the city to which they were subordinate and who had appointed them (Jones 1964, 879; Lampe 1961, 1536). But in the Syrian monastic Rules of Maruta (410 CE), a *chorepiscopa* is a supervisor of monasteries.[12] Such a supervisor was called an *exarchos* in Constantinople (see above, note 10). The second office held by Passarion, according to Cyril, was that of archimandrite, a term that, as noted above, underwent an interesting development during the Byzantine period.

Thus Passarion's office as archimandrite was not related to his famous monastery on Mount Zion (Vailhé 1899–1900a, 39–41, no. 90) but rather to the monasteries and monks (as opposed to the churches) in his district, over which he had been appointed by Bishop Juvenal. *Chorepiskopos* and *archimandrites* therefore were not two identical functions.

It seems that after the death of Passarion, shortly after the dedication of the church of the laura of Euthymius, his positions were divided among several church officials: Anastasius, a cleric of the Anastasis and guardian of the sacred vessels, who had been the disciple of Passarion and would later become the patriarch of Jerusalem (458–478), received the office of *chorepiskopos* (*V. Euth.* 22, 35),[13] while the office of archimandrite was divided among two persons. In the year 452 we hear of two archimandrites of the monks (*V. Euth.* 27, 42.10–14).[14]

---

[12] The Syriac monastic rules of Maruta, which were formulated from the perspective of a bishop seeking to integrate the monastic movement within the episcopal see, are quite detailed regarding the duties of the *chorepiscopa*. According to these rules, all the monasteries in each district were subordinate to a bishop (*episcopa* in Syriac), and a *chorepiscopa* (χωρεπίσκοπος) supervised them on his behalf. The *chorepiscopa* had to be elected from among the order (*tagma*/τάγμα) of the monks (Maruta's Rules XXV.1–5; Vööbus 1982, 74). One of his duties was to convene all the monks in his district into a general assembly once a year at a time he would determine (ibid. XXVII.2, 76.22–23). He was also responsible for reading the canons twice a year before the monks (ibid. LVIII.2, 102.12). It was the duty of the bishop to apportion the means of existence among the various monasteries: if some enjoyed plenty while others suffered from want, he had to take from the former and give to the latter (ibid. XXV.6, 75.3–6). There is no doubt that he was assisted in this by the *chorepiscopa*. On Maruta and his Rule, see above, Part I, nn. 20, 21.

[13] Anastasius the *chorepiskopos* was the confidant of Eudocia, and was sent on her behalf in 455 to Symeon Stylites, and afterwards to Euthymius, in order to consult with them regarding the validity of the Acts of the Council of Chalcedon. He and Cosmas, the cross warden, were authorized by her to give publicity in Jerusalem to her reconciliation and union with Patriarch Juvenal (*V. Euth.* 30, 47–49).

[14] Schwartz (1939, 376) is of the opinion that the basis for the division during this period did not lie in the distinction between the coenobia and the laurae, since there were too few laurae to merit their own special supervisor. I do not share this view.

These two archimandrites were Elpidius, the disciple and successor of Passarion in the office of abbot of the monastery on Mount Zion, and Gerontius, the successor of Melania the Younger in the administration of her monasteries on the Mount of Olives, an office that he began to fulfill after her death on December 31, 439. It is doubtful whether he had served as archimandrite previously when he was still subordinate to Melania, before he himself was the head of the male monastery established in 436 (cf. also Perrone 1980, 39 n. 9 and 135 n. 110).[15] Passarion died at the end of 429 (*V. Euth.* 16, 27). If Elpidius immediately succeeded him in the office of archimandrite as well, then he, like Passarion, was sole archimandrite for a period of more than six years. During this period most of the desert monasteries were still laurae. It is possible that the growth of large coenobia, such as the monastery of Romanus near Thekoa, alongside the earlier laurae, led Juvenal to appoint another archimandrite in addition to Elpidius. This second archimandrite was responsible for the desert and rural coenobia. The task was imposed upon Gerontius, who headed one of the most important monasteries in Jerusalem. This therefore did not take place before 436, and possibly not before the death of Melania, but certainly it occurred before the Council of Chalcedon. During this period Juvenal was occupied with the organization of the Church of Jerusalem, desiring to enhance its status and to place it at the head of the bishoprics of Palestine.

Elpidius' successors were Elias and then Lazarus, both abbots of the monastery of Passarion. Gerontius' successor was Anastasius. The terms in office of Lazarus and Anastasius (who began his term in 484),[16] according to Cyril (*V. Sab.* 30, 114.27–115.14), were marked by anarchy and polyarchy. The disorder and multiplicity of authorities led to revolt and chaos, concern for materialistic matters rather than for spiritual ones, the loosening of monastic discipline, and the misuse of their office and position. Nor did they remain vigilant in defending Orthodoxy, especially with the ascent to the throne of Emperor Anastasius in 491.[17] In that year Patriarch Sallustius decided to depose them and appointed in their stead a single archimandrite, Marcianus, the instigator of the "Second Union" of the Church of Jerusalem in 479. Marcianus died shortly after his appointment (Nov. 23, 492); after his death the office was once again divided among two archimandrites, Sabas and Theodosius. They were appointed before the death of Sallustius on July 23, 494 (Schwartz 1939, 290; Chitty 1966, 110; Perrone 1980, 38–39 and n. 9; Flusin 1983, 137–39).

Cyril is not clear regarding the exact date of their appointment. Between the death of Marcianus and that of Sallustius there is an interval of approximately twenty months.

---

[15] There is no allusion to this in *Vita Melaniae*, despite the fact that it was apparently written by him a short time after the Council of Chalcedon (Honigmann 1956, 228; Gorce, *V. Mel. Jun.* 54–62), during the period when he already served as archimandrite.

[16] Schwartz 1939, 290 and Festugière 1962b, 149 err in listing Anastasius among the successors of Passarion instead of as the successor of Gerontius. Gerontius was expelled from his monasteries as a consequence of his opposition to the "Second Union" between the bishops and Patriarch Martyrius, after having headed the monasteries of Melania for 45 years. There is no evidence that he was deposed from the office of archimandrite prior to this. Anastasius therefore began his office in 484 (for the chronology of Gerontius, see also Perrone 1980, 135 n. 110).

[17] The monasteries of Passarion and of Melania were bastions of opposition to the Council of Chalcedon. Gerontius was mentioned in the previous note. Elpidius did indeed join the supporters of the "First Union" between Eudocia and Juvenal, but other disciples of Passarion—Marcianus and Romanus— refused to be reconciled with Juvenal.

It is stated in the *Vita Sabae* (30, 115.16) and in the *Vita Theodosii* (4, 239.3) that after Marcianus' death the monks assembled in the house of the patriarch, who was ill, in order to choose Sabas and Theodosius as the archimandrites. At the beginning of chapter 30 (*V. Sab.* 114.23–25), however, Cyril relates that Sabas and Theodosius were appointed by Sallustius only when he was on the point of death. If both passages allude to the same time, when Sallustius was actually on his deathbed, then during the entire interval of some twenty months there was no archimandrite for the monks. If, however, the appointment had occurred immediately after Marcianus' death, then it did not take place when Sallustius was actually on his deathbed (see also Festugière 1962a, 20–21, chronological table).

The story of the election seems to indicate that the first possibility is more plausible, especially since this story is related by Cyril after that of the establishment of the Small Coenobium in 493. The special situation that arose upon the death of Marcianus, whose appointment had also constituted a change in several ways—the location of his monastery outside Jerusalem and his nomination as the sole archimandrite—compared to what had been the accepted practice, apparently led to a period of examination and search for suitable candidates. The illness of the patriarch certainly did not make the task of selection any easier. The delay may have been caused by doubts whether to entrust the office to a single person, as in the case of Marcianus, or to divide it between two people as before.

The delay in making a decision probably led to the formation of pressure groups. Therefore, in contrast to what had been the accepted practice—the archimandrites inheriting their office or being selected by the patriarch, as was Marcianus—Sabas and Theodosius were elected to the office by the monks themselves. Sallustius confirmed their election only because of the monks' insistence. The patriarch may not have immediately acquiesced to the wishes of the desert monks, and may have initially hesitated to appoint their candidates, since such an appointment was an innovation from several points of view: for the first time desert-dwelling monks, staunch supporters of the Council of Chalcedon, were appointed to these high church offices (Chitty 1952, 27). It should be recalled that Sallustius was aware of the opposition to Sabas in his Laura, for it was only upon his intervention that the first revolt of the monks had ended. This fact was likely to increase the patriarch's hesitations about giving Sabas the office of archimandrite. It was only pressure from the monks loyal to Sabas that finally led to his appointment.

B. The Electing Body and Areas of Authority

The demand to appoint Sabas and Theodosius as archimandrites came from "the entire class of monks" (παρὰ παντὸς τοῦ μοναχικοῦ σχήματος) (*V. Sab.* 30, 114.25–26; 65, 166.18).[18] The reference is not to all the monks of Palestine but to "all the desert monks" who gathered and came to the house of the patriarch (*V. Sab.* 30, 115.18; *V. Theod.* 239.2), unanimously choosing Sabas and Theodosius as archimandrites.

[18] In two other places Cyril uses similar terms: while speaking of the chaos that reigned among the monks during the office of Lazarus and Anastasius as archimandrites, he uses the term μοναχικόν, "the class of monks" (115.7), and in another place, while speaking of the leadership of Sabas and Theodosius, he uses the expression ἅπαν τὸ μοναχικόν as a description of the entire monastic community (166.12).

Their authority extended over all the monasteries and monks in the district of the Holy City (ibid. 239.5; *V. Sab.* 115.18; 166.14). Indeed, in one passage (*V. Theod.* 239.10–11) Sabas' office is described as extending to all the laurae and anchorites of Palestine. In another passage, however, the geographic area of his authority is defined in a more precise manner: in the letter sent by Patriarch Elias to Emperor Anastasius (*V. Sab.* 50, 141.9–10), Sabas is presented as "the colonizer and patron of our desert, and the light of all of Palestine." For example, Sabas' authority did not extend to the laurae in the district of Gaza or Elusa, and Theodosius' authority did not extend to the coenobia of the district of Eleutheropolis, where the Monophysites enjoyed a strong position. The archimandrite of the laurae in this district was Mamas, a successor of Romanus, whom Sabas had restored to Orthodoxy after their return from Constantinople in 512 (*V. Sab.* 55, 147.14). The office of Sabas and Theodosius as archimandrites therefore extended, according to Cyril, over the district of the city of Jerusalem, and not over all of Palestine, as Flusin suggested (1983, 137–39). But even within this district, it is highly doubtful whether the coenobia of the Holy City itself were subordinate to Theodosius. It can be assumed that they were directly subordinate to the patriarch. However, for the desert of the Holy City, which also belonged to the district of Jerusalem, a separate supervisor, who was also a *chorepiskopos*, had already been appointed during the time of Juvenal, and the desert monks were subordinate to him as the patriarch's representative. Theodosius and Sabas are not defined as *chorepiskopoi*, who had the right to make appointments to the lower ranking priestly offices and were responsible for the churches. They were only archimandrites, and their authority extended only to the monasteries and monks in the rural areas (χώρα) and, in our case, in the desert (ἔρημος), and not in the city (πόλις).

Sabas' deputy was the abbot of the monastery of Gerasimus; consequently the authority of the archimandrite also extended over the Jordan desert, located in the district of Jericho. Jericho was a bishopric, as we know from the lists of the signatories to the acts of the councils of Nicaea (325), Constantinople (381), Diospolis (415), and Jerusalem (518 and 536) (Bagatti 1971a, 94). During the Byzantine period, its district was regarded as a rural district—Ῥεγέων Ἰεριχώ—in the list of George of Cyprus (*Descriptio Orbis Romani*, line 1017, ed. Gelzer 1890). In terms of ecclesiastical hierarchy, the monasteries of the Jordan desert were subordinate to the bishop of Jericho, who undoubtedly was responsible for the ordination of their priests and deacons. From the organizational aspect, however, the monasteries of the Jordan were included in one large unit, together with the desert monasteries of Jerusalem, and constituted a distinct geographical entity within it. The office of Theodosius and Sabas as archimandrites therefore encompassed the monasteries and monks of the deserts of Jerusalem and the Jordan, and not the entire region of Palestine (similarly Schwartz 1939, 290).

C. Definition of the Office and Its Relation to the Organization of the Monastic Movement

Sabas and Theodosius were chosen to be archimandrites and *exarchoi* (ἀρχιμανδρῖται καὶ ἔξαρχοι) (*V. Sab.* 30, 115.17–18; 118.23–24). These are synonymous terms here. As noted above, the *exarchos* was a supervisor of monasteries directly subordinate to the patriarch

(Festugière 1962b, 41 n. 53; Lampe 1961, 493 sec. 5).[19] Archimandrite, in this case, refers to the head of a group of monasteries; he is not an abbot of a specific monastery (Lampe 1961, 240). According to Novel 133.4 of Justinian, which reflects a reality more fitting to the monasteries of Constantinople and its environs, the task of the *exarchos* was to maintain discipline in the monasteries. He had ambassadors (*apokrisiarioi*) who visited the monasteries and reported to him about what was happening in them. He himself was subordinate to the patriarch. It seems, however, that the task of the *exarchos* or archimandrite of the monasteries was also to supervise and ensure the economic well-being of the monks. This apparently is why Marcianus aided Sabas, supplying him with food during the foundation of Kastellion. Sabas distributed the gold he brought with him from his two visits to Constantinople among the monasteries, not necessarily among his own monasteries, which aroused the ire of his monks against him (see below, Chap. 4). Hypatius gave Sabas and Theodosius 100 pounds of gold to distribute to the monks (*V. Sab.* 56, 152).

The division of the office between Sabas and Theodosius reflects the basic structure of the monastic movement: Sabas was appointed archimandrite and legislator for all the anchorites and those choosing to dwell in cells,[20] while Theodosius was appointed as head and archimandrite of the coenobia dwellers.[21] A deputy was also appointed for each of them. Sabas' deputy was Eugenius, the abbot of the monastery of Gerasimus (*V. Theod.* 239.12); Paul, the abbot of the monastery of Martyrius, was chosen as the deputy and assistant of Theodosius (*V. Sab.* 30, 115.22–24; *V. Theod.* 239.6–7). This therefore was a balanced leadership, which also gave proper representation to the monasteries near the Jordan. Sabas, as the successor of Passarion and Elpidius (*V. Theod.* 239.8–9), was thus appointed as archimandrite over two groups of monks: the anchorites who lived by themselves, in seclusion, cut off from every framework of communal life, and the laura monks, the cell dwellers.[22]

The Anchorites
The anchorites lived by themselves, or with a disciple, in a cell or cave in the desert

---

[19] Cyril refers to Theodore Ascidas as the *exarchos* of the monks of the New Laura (*V. Sab.* 83, 188.26–27). This is not a title or office given him by the patriarch. We saw above that Cyril prefers to use the term *archimandrites* instead of *exarchos* of monasteries. The term *exarchos* in connection with Theodore Ascidas denotes his status as the head of the Origenists of the New Laura in the delegation that went to the capital to participate in the Council of 536. (Another leader of the Origenists who went there was Domitian, the *hegoumenos* of the monastery of Martyrius; he, however, is not defined as an *exarchos*). A similar meaning should be attributed to the definition of Severus as an *exarchos*—head of the *Akephaloi* and the *Aposchistai* (Schwartz 1939, 147.14; 148.21; 154.26; 155.6). It is of interest to note that in the list of participants in the council, this Theodore signed as deacon and monk of the New Laura, preceded by several places in the list by Terentius, priest of the same laura, i.e., a more senior representative in terms of church hierarchy, who appears in the list of priests, a list preceding that of the deacons. Cyril's terminology was not determined by this church hierarchy.

[20] *V. Theod.* 239.10–11: ἀρχιμανδρίτην τε καὶ νομοθέτην πάντων τῶν λαυρῶν τε καὶ ἀναχωρητῶν. *V. Sab.* 30, 115.24–26: ἄρχων καὶ νομοθέτης παντὸς τοῦ ἀναχωρητικοῦ βίου καὶ πάντων τῶν ἐν τοῖς κέλλαις ζῆν προαιρουμένων. Similarly in *V. Sab.* 65, 166.15–16.

[21] *V. Sab.* 30, 115.20–21: ἀρχηγὸς καὶ ἀρχιμανδρίτης παντὸς τοῦ κοινοβιακοῦ κανόνος ἔχων. Similarly in *V. Sab.* 166.13–14; and in *V. Theod.* 239.5.

[22] In Cyril's writings, "cell dwellers" is used to designate laura monks: *V. Sab.* 113.10; 115.24–26; 138.9; 166.15–16; *V. Theod.* 239.10–11. See also Flusin 1983, 141 n. 267.

without being part of a community. Some remained in the same cave for many years, while others wandered from place to place. Although the establishment of laurae in the desert attracted the desert anchorites to settle there in a fixed location—such was the initial core of the Great Laura, which was composed of anchorites and "grass-eaters" who gathered around Sabas (*V. Sab.* 16, 99.17–19)—there were still anchorites who adhered to the solitary mode of life. Thus it is related of Sabas and Agapetus that while on their way along the Jordan, to the north of Jericho, toward the holy places around the Sea of Galilee—Chorsia, Heptapegon, and Panias—they visited an anchorite in his cave and on their way back discovered that he had died, and buried him (*V. Sab.* 24, 107.23–108.26). The *Vita Cyriaci* includes the story of the anchoress Maria, a former harp player in the church of the Holy Sepulcher, who died a short time before Cyril wrote this *Vita* (*V. Cyr.* 18–19, 233.4–234.23). Sabas himself adopted the anchoritic life-style for four years (473–477) after the death of Euthymius (*V. Sab.* 15, 98–99), and for an additional five years when he lived alone in a cave in the Kidron, before the establishment of the Laura. John the Hesychast lived in this manner for six years (503–509) in the wake of Sabas' voluntary exile from the Laura (*V. John Hes.* 11–13, 209–12). Cyriacus used to go into seclusion for long periods of time in the deserts of Natoupha and Rouba and in Sousakim (*V. Cyr.* 20, 235), as did John the Scholarius and Abraamius (*V. Ab.* 7, 234). In the monastery of Theodosius there was a hospital for the anchorites who went insane as a result of the way of life they had chosen. During the Persian invasion, an anchorite named John is mentioned who lived alone with his disciple in the laura of Heptastomos (Strategios, *Expug. Hier.* 6). Anchorites were not wanting in the desert during the eighth and ninth centuries as well (see below, Part v, Chap. 1).

There were also monks who lived as recluses in monasteries near cities or even in the cities themselves, near urban churches. Such was Longinus the tutor of Theodosius, who secluded himself in a cell near the Tower of David (*V. Theod.* 236; Theod. Petr., *V. Theod.* 5, 13.11; Festugière 1963a, 109). It was similar with John, the anchorite from the monastery of Enthemaneith near Scythopolis, and Procopius the hesychast, whom Sabas went to visit during his journeys to Scythopolis, the first in 518 and the second in 532 (*V. Sab.* 62, 163.15; 75, 180.17). Sabas apparently was not appointed over them because they were not desert monks.

It seems, however, that the more numerous the laurae became, pure anchoritism became rarer and rarer, for the laura offered a way of life not fundamentally different from anchoritism: if a monk desired to be exempt from participating in communal life in order to maintain a strict life of mortification in total seclusion, this could also be done in a cell in the laura or near it (Flusin, 1983, 142). Similarly, Sabas permitted John the Hesychast to live as an anchorite in his cell in the laura (*V. John Hes.* 14, 212.15–26), and during Lent it was possible, with special permission, to leave the laura and wander deep in the heart of the desert. Against such a background, it can easily be understood why Cyril occasionally defines all the monks of the laura as "anchorites."[23]

During the period in which Sabas was an archimandrite, pure anchoritism was still a living, admired reality, to the extent that anchorites were listed as a separate category.

---

[23] *V. Euth.* 91.10: Euthymius refused to admit the young Sabas to his laura, because it was not proper for a young man to live among anchorites; *V. John Hes.* 205.2–4: when John joined the Laura, he found there a community of 150 anchorites.

However, for the reasons given above, they presumably constituted a very small portion of the total number of monks.

The Laurae
There is a resemblance between the laurae of the Judean desert and the monastic institutions of Mount Nitria, Kellia, and Scetis in Lower Egypt. Life in a laura was a combination of coenobitism and anchoritism: the monks of the laura were subordinate to the abbot and were obligated to perform various services for the community of monks; they assembled every weekend for common prayer in the church of the laura, while during the weekdays each monk would stay in his cell by himself or together with a disciple or servant (see above, Part III, Chap. 3). When Sabas was appointed archimandrite of the laurae monks, there existed in the Judean desert only the Great Laura, with more than 150 monks, and the three early laurae—Pharan, Douka, and Souka—which had been established by Chariton in the first half of the fourth century. The laura of Euthymius, erected according to the type of Pharan and dedicated in 428, had already become a coenobium (482 CE).

A second lauritic center existed near the Jordan River. It included the laura of Gerasimus, who had developed a well-formulated lauritic system different from the type of Pharan (see above, Part III, Chap. 3). Seventy anchorites lived in this laura, which had been established ca. 455 around a coenobium in which the novice monks underwent their preparatory period (Vailhé 1898c; 1899–1900a, 537–38, no. 50; Schneider 1938). The second laura near the Jordan was that of the Reedbed (Calamon), in which anchorites had already lived during the time of Chariton (V. Char. 13, 26); however, they apparently were organized into a laura only during the years 452–470, presumably under the influence of Gerasimus (Vailhé 1898c; 1899–1900a, 519–20, no. 16). It should come as no surprise, therefore, that a representative of this second center, Eugenius, the abbot of the laura of Gerasimus, was appointed as Sabas' deputy.

The Jordan monks are found as a distinct group with a separate representative among the list of signatories to the declaratory letters (libelli) of the monks of Palestine to Menas, the patriarch of Constantinople, and to Emperor Justinian, which were sent in 536. The first four representatives of the desert monks, who signed on behalf of the archimandrites of the monks and their deputies, were monks from the coenobia of Theodosius and Martyrius and from the laurae of Sabas and that of the Towers near the Jordan. The first three signed in the name of the monks of the desert of Jerusalem, while the latter signed at times also in the name of the monks of the Jordan (ACO III.1, 36.70; 50.112; cf. ibid. 145.70, where he also signs in the name of the monks of the desert of the Holy City; Flusin 1983, 139–40 n. 259). No other monastery along the Jordan is represented in the list of signatories. The signature of a monk from the laura of the Towers near the Jordan indicates the strengthening of the status of this Sabaitic laura (see below), relative to the decline of that of the laura of Gerasimus, among the Jordan monks.

The other laurae of the Judean desert were established only after the appointment of Sabas as archimandrite of the laurae. Three laurae were established by Sabas himself: the New Laura (507), the laura of Heptastomus (510), and the laura of Jeremias (531); and three others were founded by his disciples: the laura of Firminus near Mikhmas; the laura of the Towers founded by James near Jericho, which in 536 had already attained premier status among the laurae near the Jordan and whose abbot, a monk named Cyriacus, personally attended the Constantinople synod in the same year; and the laura of Neelkeraba near the Jordan, founded by Julian "the Hunchback." Additional laurae in the Jordan desert mentioned in the literary sources apparently came after Sabas' time, except for the laura of Sapsas, which was founded during the time of Patriarch Elias (494–516), that is, after Sabas' appointment as archimandrite (see above, Part III, Chap. 3, intro.); while the laurae in the region of Gaza, near Elusa (Part III, ibid.), and in Sinai (Finkelstein 1985; Dahari 1982) were not within the bounds of his authority as archimandrite.

The Coenobia

Coenobitism in Palestine was very close to the monastic system of Basil the Great and not to the Pachomian system (see above, Part I, Chap. 2). The Pachomian federation was a closed system distinct from the body of the Church. From the economic aspect, the Pachomian monasteries were production centers for agricultural and various handicraft products. Charitable activity was not essential in the life of the monks or in the organization of the monasteries. This was not so in the Basilian system. Basil posited a high degree of involvement in the life of the lay community in which the monasteries were located, willingness to become part of the ecclesiastical establishment, nonexcessive indulgence in fasts and mortification, and preference for community life over anchoritism.

Following the Basilian spirit, the heads of the large coenobia in Jerusalem at the beginning of the fifth century ascribed importance to charitable activity for the common good: Passarion established a large soup kitchen for the poor (beth miskena: πτωχοτροφεῖον, πτωχεῖον) outside the eastern gate of Jerusalem (Vincent and Abel 1926, 516–17; Chitty 1966, 86); and the nunnery of Melania the Younger on the Mount of Olives was occupied by 90 young women assembled by her husband, Pinianus, from "places of ill-repute" (V. Mel. Jun. 41, 206). Peter the Iberian, inspired by Passarion, and as long as he had sufficient resources, would accept pilgrims and the poor at the monastery he established in Jerusalem, to the left of the road leading from David's Tower to Zion, and would feed them, up to a daily quota of twenty tables (V. Petr. Ib. 45–46). Eudocia, the patroness of the monks, also engaged extensively in deeds of charity for the public good. Her enterprises included not only churches and monasteries but also hospitals and shelters for the poor and the old (V. Euth. 35, 53; V. John Hes. 4, 204; Dan 1982, 277–78; Vincent and Abel 1926, 909–11; Holum 1982, 219).

Theodosius viewed himself as a successor of Basil and would cite the latter's statements and regulations in his sermons (Theod. Petr., V. Theod. 20, 50–53). Like Basil, he attributed great importance to the love of one's fellow man, and the charitable acts deriving from it, along with the love of God (ibid. 13, 33). His monastery was noted for its hospitality and generosity to the needy. On holidays, when its gates were opened to masses of believers, up to a hundred tables of food were set in the courtyard, and the poor also received items of clothing (ibid. 13–17, 34–44).

Cyril defines the coenobium of Theodosius as "a great and populous coenobium . . . which surpassed all the others and presides over the coenobia all over Palestine" (V. Theod. 237). According to Theodore of Petra, the community numbered more than 400 monks at the end of Theodosius' life (Theod. Petr., *V. Theod.* 18, 46). According to Cyril, Sophronius the Armenian, Theodosius' successor (529–543), increased and expanded the monastery fourfold, enriching it with property and yearly incomes, and tripled the community living there (*V. Theod.* 240–41). The main growth therefore took place during the Justinianic era, a period of prosperity in the entire province.

As noted earlier, the coenobia under the authority of Theodosius were not those located within the city of Jerusalem itself, some of which were organized as a τάγμα or as σπουδαῖοι, and their heads were directly subordinate to the bishop of Jerusalem, as was the practice in every other bishopric. Theodosius' authority extended to the coenobia of the desert of Jerusalem and of the Jordan, and apparently also to those located on the fringes of the desert in the region close to the villages of Bethlehem and Thekoa, which were included in the district of Jerusalem (Avi-Yonah 1966, 155–56). It may reasonably be assumed that the monasteries located more to the south, in the region of Caparbaricha and the desert of Ziph, or those located farther north, in the region of Machmas, were also subordinate to him. These coenobia included the monasteries of Euthymius' disciples: Marinus (the founder of the monastery of Photinus) and Lucas, who founded their monasteries near Metopa; Martyrius, on the Jerusalem-Jericho road; Elias, near Jericho; Gabriel, east of the Mount of Olives; the monastery established by Euthymius near Caparbaricha; the monastery of Theognius; the coenobium of Choziba; and possibly other monasteries that were already in existence within these geographical limits but whose names have not been preserved. The second most important of these coenobia was the monastery of Martyrius, and Paul, its abbot, was therefore appointed as Theodosius' deputy.

It is highly doubtful, however, whether the coenobia formally subordinate to Theodosius actually included any Sabaitic foundation such as the coenobium of Kastellion, which had been established already in 492, and the Small Coenobium, founded in 493, before the appointments of Sabas and Theodosius as archimandrites. Also the coenobia later established by Sabas, such as the monastery of the Cave (508), the monastery of the Scholarius (509), the monastery of Zannos (511), or the coenobium established by Severianus, Sabas' disciple, near Caparbaricha (514/15) were most probably not subordinate to Theodosius but rather to Sabas. Sabas established a special Rule for his coenobia (see above, Part III, Chaps. 1A and 5A). Moreover, Sabas also supervised the coenobia of Theoctistus and of Euthymius, taking care of all their needs (*V. Sab.* 58, 158.22–159.2; Flusin 1983, 144).

Composite Institutions

The division of the desert monks into anchorites and laura dwellers on the one hand and coenobites on the other does not reflect the complex structure of the monastic movement. We know from Cyril's writings and from additional sources that there also existed composite institutions in the Judean desert. There were cell dwellers who were considered as coenobium members. They lived in cells outside the walls of the coenobium, not far from it, and led a laurite way of life. An example of a monk maintaining such a way of life is Sabas himself when he lived in a cell outside the coenobium of Theoctistus. A survey conducted along the streambed of Nahal Og around Deir Mukellik showed, however, that this was the only monastic cell located outside the coenobium (Fig. 54). A settlement of cell dwellers did not develop here; it is possible, however, that there were monks who lived in this fashion alongside other coenobia as well. The "cells" (τὰ κελλία) of Choziba (Figs. 53, 60, 61) are the most outstanding example of this. Although their description in the *Vita Georgii* and in the *Miracula* by Antony of Choziba refers to a later period—the end of the sixth and beginning of the seventh century—the example of Sabas indicates that such a pattern of monastic life already existed during the time of Sabas and Theodosius. Such cell dwellers were subordinate to the abbot of the coenobium and therefore were included among the monks subject to the supervision of Theodosius, although from the formal aspect, as cell dwellers, they should have been subordinate to Sabas.

The opposite framework was that of the laura of Gerasimus, which included 70 anchorites and in the center of which a coenobium was established as a novitiate. Only after the candidates had learned the regulations of monastic life and had proven themselves as excelling in their endeavors and as perfect, were they permitted by Gerasimus to move into the cells and live as monks of the laura. It is clear that this coenobium was subordinate to the abbot of the laura of Gerasimus, who was Sabas' deputy archimandrite, and not to Theodosius, the archimandrite of the coenobites.

Summary

The reality, therefore, was much more complex than a formal division of the monasteries between Theodosius and Sabas, since the sphere of Sabas' authority overlapped with that of Theodosius' defined authority and vice versa. This situation was likely to become a source of quarrels and disputes; understanding and cooperation between the two were necessary to prevent tensions, disagreements, or polyarchy—the multiplication of authorities (using Cyril's words, from another context)—if one archimandrite would attempt to enforce his authority on monks who were subordinate in practice to the other archimandrite. Although it seems that one can find, between the lines, allusions to tensions or mutual provocations, the general impression derived from Cyril's writings is that of friendship, understanding, mutual appreciation, and cooperation between Sabas and Theodosius during the course of the thirty-five years they jointly served as archimandrites (494–529) (*V. Sab.* 29, 114; 64, 165; 65, 166–67). The fact that Theodore of Petra does not mention Sabas in his work says more about the author and his approach than about a split that came about between the two. As for Cyril, Sabas' disciple and admirer, although at times he underestimates the part played by Theodosius in various events, he nevertheless devoted a separate composition to him as well.

At the same time, however, it seems that we should not exaggerate the validity of the formal division of authority. It seems that the office of archimandrite had greater importance within the framework of the church administration as a means for subordinating the monks to its authority than as a sharp, precise format dividing the monastic movement between those subordinate to Sabas and those subordinate to Theodosius.

The fact that at this time abbots of desert monasteries, rather than of monasteries located in Jerusalem or in its rural environs, were elected as archimandrites of the desert monks indicates the sizeable increase in the influence of the desert monks on the ecclesiastical establishment, since it was under their pressure that Sabas and Theodosius were chosen. Moreover, for the first time, an abbot of a laura was elected as archimandrite of the laurite monks and of the anchorites. Previously the holders of this office had been the abbots of the coenobium of Passarion on Mount Zion.

Sabas and Theodosius also differed from the archimandrites who preceded them in their clear stand in favor of the Council of Chalcedon. This would be of great significance in the future, in the organization of the monks for the struggle on behalf of Orthodoxy against Emperor Anastasius and the *synodikon* of Severus of Antioch (see below, Chap. 3). Their leadership as archimandrites was expressed mainly by their mobilization of all the monks in the struggle for the Chalcedonian doctrine, a struggle later continued by their successors, who represented the desert monks in the Council of Constantinople (536). Gelasius and Sophronius, the respective successors of Sabas and Theodosius, also acted as the representatives of the monks in the struggle against the Origenists, along with Patriarch Peter (*V. Sab.* 85, 191.27).

One other office of representation is mentioned in the literary sources, the τοποτηρη-τής. In the list of participants in the Council of Constantinople (536) and in the lists of signatories to various documents connected with it, mention is made of representatives from four laurae: the Great Laura, the laura of the Towers, the New Laura, and the laura of Firminus; and from two coenobia: the coenobium of Martyrius and that of Theodosius. The first four signatories in the lists of the monks of Palestine are, in order, the emissaries of the coenobia of Theodosius and Martyrius and those of the laurae of Sabas and of the Towers near the Jordan. None of them bears the title of archimandrite in the broad meaning of the term, as discussed above.[24] All the monks, and not just the first four, signed not only in the name of their monasteries but also in the name of all the monks of the Holy City or of the Jordan. An exception in these lists is Leontius, a monk and abbot (*hegoumenos*), who bears an additional, unique title: τοποτηρητὴς τῆς ἐρήμου πάσης (*ACO* III.1, 130.76; 145.73; 158.76; 174.82). A τοποτηρητής was a representative sent to a specific event (in contrast to the *apokrisiarios*, who was a permanent delegate). It is not known whether the post was awarded by the patriarch of Jerusalem or by Emperor Justinian, and it seems that the Leontius in the list is not Leontius of Byzantium but rather Leontius of Jerusalem (see below, Part v, end of Chap. 2A).

The list in document 14 (ibid. 50–51), like the other lists, is arranged according to the clerical rank of the signatories. First appear the priests (ibid. lines 109–16), followed by the deacons (lines 118–20), and finally the simple monks without priestly rank (lines 121–28). Leontius appears between the list of priests and that of the deacons (line 117); he signed in the name of all the holy fathers (ἁγίων πατέρων) of the desert and the Jordan. All the others signed only in the name of the monks (μοναχῶν) of the desert of the Holy City; Cyriacus and Trajan, from the laura of the Towers, and another monk from the Jordan, by the name of Basil, signed in the name of all the monks of the Jordan (lines 112, 115, 127). Leontius was therefore the only one signing in the name of senior monks (holy fathers) of both the desert and the Jordan. Therefore, despite his place in the list,

---

[24] The term archimandrite appears here with the limited meaning of "abbot of a monastery": Domitian is defined as priest and archimandrite of the monastery of Martyrius, and Cyriacus, the abbot of the laura of the Towers near the Jordan, is defined at times as a *hegoumenos* (*ACO* III.1, 130.73; 145.70; 158.73; 174.79), and at other times as an archimandrite (ibid. 36.70; 50.112). On p. 133 Sophronius the abbot of the monastery of Theodosius is defined as "the first" (πρῶτος) of the entire desert of Jerusalem, indicating its superiority at this period in Palestinian monasticism.

his function is not to be viewed as a clerical rank lesser than a priest and higher than a deacon, but rather as a representative role, which permits him to sign in the name of all the senior monks. However, Leontius did not have a special office or status in the monastic movement in the Holy Land per se. His title does not reflect a change in the organization of the monastic movement in the Holy Land and in the manner of its integration into the ecclesiastical establishment. Otherwise we should expect to find his signature at the very beginning of each list.

3

Sabas in the Struggle for Chalcedonian Orthodoxy

A. The First Two Generations: 457–508

From the very beginning of his monastic career, Sabas was a loyal pro-Chalcedonian. As soon as he came to the Holy Land, at the age of eighteen, he chose to join Euthymius. This was not only the choice of a way of life—the life of a monk dwelling in the desert—but also a declaration of devotion to the pro-Chalcedonian party a short time after the "First Union" (456), in which Empress Eudocia and many of the opponents of the Council of Chalcedon were reconciled with Patriarch Juvenal. It was Euthymius who influenced Eudocia to effect this reconciliation (*V. Euth.* 30, 47–49; Chitty 1952, 22–24; 1966, 90–92; Perrone 1980, 103–15). At about the same time (457), two monks who had left Nitria, as a result of the strengthening of the Monophysite party in Egypt after the death of Emperor Marcian, joined the laura of Euthymius. These were Martyrius, a Cappadocian, and Elias, an Arabian, who would later become the patriarchs of Jerusalem and the formulators of the religious policy of that diocese. Martyrius would initiate a compromise along the lines of the *Henotikon* of Zeno, and Elias would adopt a more emphasized pro-Chalcedonian doctrine during a more tempestuous period, that of the Monophysite Emperor Anastasius and Severus of Antioch (512–518), in which the thirty years of "cease-fire" between the Chalcedonian and Monophysite parties came to an end. When Sabas was accompanying Euthymius into the desert, he became acquainted with the two future patriarchs; fertile cooperation would blossom from this acquaintance.

The reign of Leo I (457–474) was marked by passivity and neutrality. The Monophysites in Egypt did not hesitate to flex their muscles and, under the leadership of Timothy Aelurus (the Cat), murdered Patriarch Proterius. During this entire period Sabas lived as a simple monk in the coenobium of Theoctistus and in a nearby cell outside its walls. The "neutrality" of the period was also evident in the policy of the Palestinian Church headed for twenty years (458–478) by Patriarch Anastasius, who sought balance and coexistence between the two parties (Perrone 1980, 116–27). Euthymius had reservations regarding this patriarch, despite the latter's attempts to draw closer to him (Chitty 1952, 25).

Anastasius and the bishops of Palestine signed the *Encyclical* of Basiliscus (475); however, the short-lived fame of this usurper marked the conclusion of this prominently anti-Chalcedonian trend. Due to his advanced age, Anastasius' status was not hurt, even though he did not recant from this signature during the time of Zeno. The centripetal forces, seeking compromise and coexistence, overcame the centrifugal ones that wished to deepen the rift caused by the Council of Chalcedon, such as Peter the Iberian, Isaiah the Egyptian, Theodore of Ascalon, and Romanus' monks. Such was the goal of Zeno's

Henotikon (482), which emphasized the declaration of faith of the Council of Nicaea, instead of that of the Council of Chalcedon, and rejected any formula contradicting this symbol. He was preceded in this formulation by Patriarch Martyrius (478–486), who by adopting this approach succeeded in bringing about the "Second Union" in the Church of Jerusalem (479) between him and the separatist monks headed by the abbot Marcianus (Chitty 1952, 26–27; Perrone 1980, 127–39). This same year Sabas settled in the Kidron, but a monastic community had not yet formed around him. He did not take an active part in this union. These formulations of compromise were an expression of the moods prevalent in the Chalcedonian party during the period.

Against this background it is easier to understand Sabas' presence in the Tower of Eudocia, where a number of Monophysite monks dwelled, at the end of his wanderings in the desert (478) before he established his residence in the Kidron (*V. Sab.* 15, 97; 38, 127; cf. Chitty 1966, 106). Although Sabas always remained loyal to Chalcedon, he probably supported the compromise proposed by Martyrius and that of the *Henotikon*, since we hear that Sabas received support from Martyrius during the first phase of the construction of the Laura (483–486).

Patriarch Sallustius (486–494) continued Martyrius' policy. Although he supported Athanasius II of Alexandria, who accepted the *Henotikon* while attacking and censuring Chalcedon, near the end of his life he exhibited a tendency toward renewed approval of the Chalcedonian dogma (Chitty 1952, 27; Perrone 1980, 141–45). Marcianus, formerly one of the leaders of the separatists and the instigator of the "Second Union," was appointed by him as the sole archimandrite of the desert monks (491–492). Sallustius intervened on behalf of Sabas during the first revolt against him by the monks of the Laura, ordained him as a priest, and afterwards, before his death (June 494), appointed him and Theodosius as archimandrites of the desert monks. This led the entire monastic movement to adopt loyalty and active commitment to Chalcedonian Orthodoxy.

Emperor Anastasius (491–518) possessed clear Monophysite tendencies (Charanis 1974; Stein-Palanque 1949, 157–76); however, for about twenty years, he refrained from adopting extreme measures against the supporters of Chalcedon in the Church of Palestine. The controversy between the two parties became more acute as a result of the activity of the fanatic monk Nephalius, who sought, ca. 508, to expel the Monophysites from their strongholds in the Gaza coastal plain. It was his activity that led to Severus' journey to the capital, where he succeeded in acquiring great influence at the court of Anastasius, formulating his *Typos,* an anti-Chalcedonian pamphlet that all the patriarchs were required to confirm (509/10).

Elias' succession to the office of patriarch (494–516) and the leadership of Theodosius and Sabas created a counterbalance to the strengthening of the pro-Monophysite policy of the emperor (Perrone 1980, 145–51). Sabas settled the desert with his monks, whose numbers grew (Chitty 1952, 32 n. 3). Many monks underwent preparation in the great coenobium of Theodosius, which also served as a school for novice monks. The strongholds of the heretics in the desert, such as the Tower of Eudocia, in which two Nestorian monks lived at the time, were uprooted, and a new monastery was established in its place (509). The desert of Thekoa, which in the past had been the territory of the monks of Romanus (one of the leaders of the uprising against Juvenal), became a territory of the Sabaitic monks upon the establishment of the New Laura. The numerical increase of the desert monks—a result of the policy and leadership of Sabas—transformed them into a concrete force, an army likely to fight back against the assaults of the Monophysites and to confront fearlessly the emperor's agents (Perrone 1980, 151–73). The patriarch and his archimandrites now had at their disposal "soldiers," zealous to defend their religious doctrine (see below).

The Great church in the Laura, which had been consecrated by Patriarch Elias in 501, was dedicated to Mary "the Bearer of God," *Theotokos*, whose worship was officially recognized by the Church in the first Council of Ephesus (431). This dedication constituted an anti-Nestorian act (Baldi 1952–53; Cameron 1978, 87–88). During the same period Sabas forbade conducting the Eucharist in the Laura in a language other than Greek, after he learned that the Armenian-speakers had added to the *Trisagion* the Monophysite formula of Peter the Fuller, "Who was crucified for us" (*V. Sab.* 32, 118).

The true critical moment in the struggle on behalf of Orthodoxy came when the emperor sought to harm the standing of the patriarch of Jerusalem, Elias.

B. Sabas' Defense of Patriarch Elias before Emperor Anastasius (Autumn 511–May 512)

Introduction

Sabas' first acquaintance with Elias was in the period in which they both were disciples of the great Euthymius. During a later period, when Elias had become the patriarch of Jerusalem and had assembled the *spoudaioi* of the church of the Holy Sepulcher, who lived dispersed in cells on Mount Zion, into a monastery close to the house of the patriarch, Sabas purchased from him some of the cells and turned them into hostels of the Laura in Jerusalem. The patriarch thereby was involved in the establishment of a Sabaite center in the city. It was Patriarch Elias who dedicated the Great church in the Laura of Sabas (July 1, 501), and he was the one who restored Sabas to his position as head of the Laura after the latter's voluntary exile (in which he did not intervene), afterwards helping him in the establishment of the New Laura (507).

In autumn 511 (Chitty 1966, 122 n. 153), when Sabas was seventy-three years old, Patriarch Elias asked him to go to the capital, together with other monastic fathers, in order to intercede there with Emperor Anastasius to deter him from taking punitive measures against the patriarch (*V. Sab.* 50–54, 139–47). In the background of this journey was the deposition of Patriarch Macedonius from his office in the capital by the emperor and the appointment of Timothy in his stead (after August 7, 511). Although Elias and Flavianus of Antioch did confirm the synodical letter of Timothy, they refused to recognize the deposition of Macedonius. This aroused the emperor's ire, and he intended to punish them for it. Elias wanted to forestall this by sending a delegation of monastery heads, including Sabas, to the emperor, presenting them in his letter to the emperor as "faithful servants of God, the rulers of the entire desert," and Sabas as "the colonizer and patron of our desert and the light of all Palestine."[25]

While the delegation was on its way to the capital, the emperor convened at Sidon a synod of bishops from Anatolia, Syria, and Palestine, with the intent of punishing Flavi-

---

[25] *V. Sab.* 50, 141.9–10: τὸν πολιστὴν καὶ πολιοῦχον τῆς καθ᾽ ἡμᾶς ἐρήμου καὶ ὅλης τῆς Παλαιστίνης φωστῆρα.

anus and Elias, but this intention failed (Festugière 1962b, 67 n. 120; 132–33; Schwartz 1939, 380).

1. Sabas and Anastasius: the First Encounter (*V. Sab.* 51, 141–43)

When the delegation arrived in the capital and informed the emperor of its arrival, all its members were summoned to the palace and were brought into the emperor's reception hall. At this point in his narration, Cyril finds occasion to praise Sabas excessively: all were dressed appropriately for the prestigious meeting, while Sabas, who was dressed in worn garments,[26] was refused entry by the court gatekeepers, who thought he was a beggar. It was the emperor who noted the absence of Sabas, of whose expected arrival he had been informed by the letter of Patriarch Elias. After a search, Sabas was discovered in a corner of the entrance hall, where he had remained by himself, reciting psalms. When Sabas was brought in "beyond the curtain," Anastasius rose to greet him, received him with great honor, and asked all the fathers to sit and present their requests. In this regard as well Cyril emphasizes the uniqueness of Sabas' conduct: each of the other fathers was concerned only for the welfare of his own monastery. One asked for the lands surrounding his monastery, and another requested another imperial edict on his behalf; only Sabas implored the emperor not to harm the Diocese of Jerusalem and its patriarch. The fact that Sabas received from the emperor 1,000 gold coins for his monasteries suggests that at the same time more prosaic matters did not escape his attention. The other fathers returned to Palestine, while Sabas requested from the emperor permission to spend the winter (511/12) in the capital. The emperor acceded to his request and even permitted him free entry to the palace.

2. The Second Encounter between Sabas and Anastasius (*V. Sab.* 52, 143–44)

In the meantime, reports from the synod of Sidon reached the capital: the emperor's intent to condemn the decisions of Chalcedon had been frustrated, at the instigation of Flavianus of Antioch and Elias of Jerusalem. However, after the synod adjourned, these two gave Eutropius, the emperor's representative at the synod, a letter in which they rejected the decisions of the Council of Chalcedon because of the scandals caused to the unity of the Church in its wake (Schwartz 1939, 380). Anastasius saw in this ambivalent position a harsh contempt for him and an act of deception. A few days after the meeting with the delegation from the Holy Land he again summoned Sabas, who had alone remained in the capital, and announced to him his intention to depose Elias from his see because of the above-mentioned deeds and because of Elias' opposition to the emperor's deposition of the two earlier patriarchs of Constantinople, Euphemius (490–496) and Macedonius (496–511).

The deposition of Elias would actually take place only four years later. Cyril attributes to Sabas the appeasement of the emperor and the cancellation of his plan to depose the patriarch immediately. Sabas defended Elias in the spirit of the *Henotikon*, responding that the latter was faithful to Orthodoxy and rejected the heresies of both Nestorius and Eutychius, choosing the median path of the Orthodox Church. He claimed that Elias

---

[26] According to what we know of other monks, such as Alexander Akoimetos and George of Choziba, it is not necessarily a false description.

adhered to the doctrines of Cyril of Alexandria, and imposed bans both on those opposed to him and on those to whom he was opposed. Therefore, Sabas implored the emperor, it was incumbent upon him to defend the Holy City against assaults and disturbances and not to harm the welfare of the Church of the Holy Land. Anastasius responded favorably to Sabas' arguments and refrained from acting against Elias at that time.

3. Sabas and the Noblewomen (*V. Sab.* 53, 145)

After leaving the emperor, Sabas went in to Ariadne, the emperor's wife and the daughter of Leo I. Sabas blessed her and encouraged her to remain loyal to the faith of her father (who had followed the pro-Chalcedonian policy of Marcian).

Sabas established his dwelling outside the city in the suburb of Rufinus near Chalcedon (Festugière 1962b, 71 n. 134). Two noblewomen came there to visit him, Anicia Juliana and Anastasia (see above, Chap. 1), and he served as a spiritual guide and father to these pious women, and strengthened them in their support of the Chalcedonian party in the capital.

4. The Episode of Mamas (May 512) (*V. Sab.* 55, 147)

On the ship, on his way back from the capital to the Holy Land (May 512), Sabas met Mamas, the archimandrite of the Aposchist (separatist) monks in the district of Eleutheropolis (Evagrius Scholasticus, *HE* III.33). In Constantinople a bitter dispute had erupted between Mamas and Severus, as a result of which Sabas succeeded, during the voyage, in persuading Mamas to abandon his erroneous belief and join the Catholic Church. Upon their arrival in the Holy Land, Sabas brought Mamas to Patriarch Elias, where Mamas embraced the decisions of the Council of Chalcedon and imposed a ban on Eutychius and Dioscorus. Cyril relates that this conversion had considerable effect in the Holy Land, with many people influenced by his deed and acting as he had done.

C. The Continuation of the Controversy over Patriarch Elias in Jerusalem (Nov. 512–Sept. 516)

After the failure of the Synod of Sidon (511 CE) convened by Anastasius, Philoxenus and Soterichus of Caesarea in Cappadocia searched for another way to attack the position of Flavianus and Elias. They eventually succeeded in compelling Flavianus to reject Chalcedon, deposing him from his office as patriarch of Antioch, and sending him into exile. In his stead the emperor appointed Severus, the head of the *Akephaloi* in Egypt (Duchesne 1925, 29–30; Stein-Palanque 1949, 173 and n. 1; Charanis 1974, 63–77). Elias refused to receive the synodical letters of Severus, sent after his consecration (Nov. 512), which included an explicit rejection of the Symbol of Chalcedon. In May 513 Severus once again sent the same synodical letters to Jerusalem, this time accompanied by a number of priests and an imperial force (*V. Sab.* 56, 148–49; Evagrius Scholasticus, *HE* III.33; Schwartz 1939, 383–87; Stein-Palanque 1949, 174–76; Charanis 1974, 98–101).

When the arrival of the delegation became known, Sabas hurried to Jerusalem with the other desert *hegoumenoi*. They expelled from the city the priests bearing the synodical letters of Severus, summoning masses of monks from everywhere and the Jerusalemites to assemble before the church of the Holy Sepulcher. The crowd began to shout to the *magistrates,*[27] to the commanders, and to the soldiers sent by the emperor: "A ban on Severus and on those in communion with him!"

It is possible that the establishment of the monastery of Severianus near Caparbaricha and the monasteries of his other disciples are to be dated to the following period, 514/15 CE, and that the motive behind these settlements was to prevent any possibility that the Monophysites would establish themselves, with the encouragement of Severus and Anastasius, in the Judean desert. Cyril, at any rate, makes no allusion to such a motive; it is possible, however, that this was not an overt intention (see above, Part II, Chaps. 2G, 1E).

In light of Elias' second refusal to accept the synodical letters of Severus, the emperor ordered Olympius, the *dux Palaestinae*, to travel from Caesarea to Jerusalem with a military force in order to drive Elias from office. In order to damage Elias' credibility in the eyes of the monks and his supporters, the emperor entrusted Olympius with a copy of the letter of remorse he had received from Elias upon the conclusion of the Synod of Sidon, in which he denied the Council of Chalcedon and almost accepted the *Typos* of Severus. This undoubtedly sowed confusion among the monastery heads and weakened their stand on behalf of the patriarch. This time the emperor was successful. Olympius presented the letter, Elias was deposed and exiled to Aila, and in his stead Olympius appointed John, the deacon of the Anastasis Church (Sept. 1, 516), who promised to come into communion with Severus and impose a ban on Chalcedon. The inhabitants of the city regarded John as a traitor.

D. The Uprising of the Monks against Emperor Anastasius and the Monks' Assembly in St. Stephen's Church (Sept. 516–July 518).

Elias' deposition did not lead to a calming of the atmosphere. The monks continued to defend the Chalcedonian doctrine vigorously, erupting in open revolt against the religious policy that the emperor sought to impose upon the See of Jerusalem (*V. Sab.* 56–57, 148–58; Charanis 1974, 101–2). The new patriarch John was well known to Sabas. He was the son of Marcianus, priest of the Anastasis, *hegoumenos* of the Holy Zion monastery, and later bishop of Samaria, who together with his two sons—this John and Antony, the future deacon and bishop of Ascalon, and one of the two assessors of the damages caused by the Samaritan revolt—came to aid Sabas in the construction of the monastery of the Cave. When Sabas and the other desert fathers learned of John's promise to come into communion with Severus, they gathered around him and obtained formal confirmation that he did not admit Severus to communion, but rather intended to struggle in the defense of Chalcedon, and that he viewed the monks as allies. This episode reveals the contrast between the conciliatory policy of the clergy and the uncompromising stand of the monks, who also won the support of the masses.

John therefore broke his promise to Olympius, who had died in the meantime. When the emperor learned of this, he ordered the new *dux Palaestinae*, Anastasius the

---

[27] τῶν μαγιστριανῶν. Regarding them, see Stein-Palanque 1959, 113–14 and elsewhere; Linder 1987a, 223–24 n. 4. This was a team of officials and letter-bearers on horses, organized in a military format. They were first so organized by Constantine, and they served many other purposes: protecting the imperial mail service, conducting arrests, accompanying official transports. They also served as undercover police, against both government officials and citizens.

son of Pamphilius, to go to Jerusalem and confirm that John would fulfill his promise; otherwise he would be expelled from his see. The *dux* Anastasius acted firmly. As soon as he arrived in Jerusalem he cast John into prison, to the joy of the inhabitants of the city, the admirers of the deposed Patriarch Elias. Zacharias, the governor of Palaestina Prima (Festugière 1962b, 79 n. 164), who also happened to come from Caesarea to Jerusalem, secretly entered the jail and advised John to obtain an extension by promising the *dux* to fulfill all his promises in two days' time, provided that he would be released from prison immediately and therefore would not appear to be coming into communion with Severus under compulsion. The *dux* believed him and released him from prison.

The same night the patriarch summoned to Jerusalem the monks from the entire region. The multitude that assembled numbered 10,000 monks along with many inhabitants of Jerusalem. They all gathered in the monastery and church of the protomartyr Stephen outside the city walls, since there was no church in the city large enough to contain the mass of those gathered. This was the Sunday on which Hypatius, the nephew of the emperor, who had recently been released from the captivity of the rebel Vitalian,[28] was supposed to arrive in order to fulfill a vow he had taken during that time. There is no doubt that Zacharias, the governor of Palaestina Prima, came to Jerusalem because of this visit and sought to free John from prison in order not to spoil this important occasion. The *dux* Anastasius also joined the crowd waiting for the distinguished guest in the basilica of St. Stephen, located along the road leading to Jerusalem from the north, the way along which the guest was expected to arrive.

The *dux* expected that John would take advantage of this opportunity to fulfill his promise to accept Severus into communion and ban the canons of the Council of Chalcedon. The event, however, turned into an impressive demonstration in support of Chalcedonian Orthodoxy. John ascended the pulpit (ἄμβων), flanked by Theodosius and Sabas, the leaders of the monks and their heads (οἱ τῶν μοναχῶν κορυφαῖοι καὶ ἡγεμόνες) (*V. Sab.* 56, 151.22), and all those gathered shouted for a long time to the patriarch: "Ban the heretics and confirm the Council!" On the spot the three, unanimously, placed a ban on Nestorius, Eutychius, Severus, Soterichus, and on all those who did not accept the acts of the Council of Chalcedon. Afterwards, when they were about to descend from the platform, Theodosius turned around and called out to the crowd: "If anyone does not accept the four Synods as the four Gospels, he will be placed under the ban."

The *dux* Anastasius did not dare to intervene and, out of fear of the great number of monks, fled to Caesarea. Hypatius, the emperor's nephew, swore to the fathers that he did not share the belief of Severus and that he wanted to enter into communion with them. Afterwards he contributed 100 pounds of gold to the building complex of the church of the Holy Sepulcher: the Anastasis, Golgotha, and the Cross. He gave an additional 100 pounds of gold to the archimandrites Theodosius and Sabas for distribution among the monks of the Holy Land.

---

[28] About Vitalian and his revolt against Anastasius, see the detailed discussion in Charanis 1974. The allusion here is to the disturbances after Vitalian's third attack in 515, when Hypatius was released within the framework of an agreement between Vitalian and the emperor, which led to the lifting of the siege of the capital and to the end of his first revolt. See Charanis 1974, 83–85. About the church of St. Stephen in Jerusalem, see Vincent and Abel 1926, 743 ff.

The mass assembly in the church of St. Stephen took place at the end of 516. In the meantime, the emperor was busy with other matters (516–518): the renewal of the revolt of Vitalian, as a result of the invasion of the Sabirian Huns from the Caucasus, through Armenia, to the border of Cappadocia; and disturbances in Syria between the opponents and supporters of Severus. Because of these concerns, Anastasius, then in the eighty-eighth year of his life, decided to leave the Church of the Holy Land in peace and not to depose John from his see (Festugière 1962b, 81 n. 167; Charanis 1974, 92–94).

It was only after external pressure was relieved that Anastasius returned to his original plan, intending to send a large military force to Jerusalem to send into exile John and the leaders of the monks, Theodosius and Sabas, who had stood with John on the dais. Cyril and Theodore of Petra mention a petition that was sent to Anastasius by Theodosius and Sabas after they had gathered in Jerusalem all the desert monks (ἅπαν τὸ μοναχικὸν τῆς ἐρήμου) (V. Sab. 57, 152–57; Theod. Petr., V. Theod. 60). The petition contained a request not to harm the Church of Jerusalem, the mother of the churches, which received its faith directly from Christ and his Apostles; a complaint regarding the expulsion of Patriarch Elias, priests, and monks; a condemnation of the heresy of Severus and adherence to the four church councils of Nicaea (325), Seleucia (359),[29] Ephesus (431), and Chalcedon (451); and the refusal to come into communion with any of the Aposchists or to accept the head of the Akephaloi, Severus, as a bishop. A copy of this petition was also sent to John II, the new patriarch of Constantinople (after the death of Timothy), who had been consecrated on April 17, 518. This date constitutes a *terminus post quem* for the sending of the petition, while the sequence of Cyril's writings gives the impression that it was sent at a time closer to the assembly in St. Stephen's church.

In his letter of response to the petition of the monks, which according to Theodore of Petra (V. Theod. 60.17 ff) was addressed only to the archimandrite Theodosius, Anastasius accused unnamed priests and monks of having incited the disturbances in Jerusalem under the guise of the defense of the faith. Sabas is not mentioned in this letter, which may be why Cyril does not refer to it.

Theodore of Petra also mentions additional attacks by Anastasius on the Orthodox faith, against which Theodosius took vigorous action (V. Theod. 61.27–70.12) in the sermons he delivered from the pulpit of the Anastasis and in the tours he conducted in the cities of Palestine, together with the other desert fathers, in order to disseminate the Orthodox faith. The emperor was angered by this activity and issued an expulsion order against him, but he died before the order could be executed. Theodore also mentions letters of appreciation sent to Theodosius by Pope Agapetus and by Ephraim, the patriarch of Antioch, for his courageous struggle during the difficult days at the end of Anastasius' reign (ibid. 70.10–12). Theodosius' resoluteness in the struggle for the faith can also be deduced from Cyril's own description of the course of events in St. Stephen's church.

Cyril does not explicitly mention similar activities of Sabas, even though the trip to the exiled patriarch Elias in Aila indicates that Sabas also went forth with his disciples and devotees to support the followers of Chalcedon. The journey to Aila took place close

[29] In general, the supporters of Chalcedon count among the four canonical synods the first Council of Constantinople (381) and not the Synod of Seleucia.

to June 24, 518, together with Stephen, the abbot of the monastery of Euthymius, and Euthylius, the head of the two monasteries of Elias near Jericho (*V. Sab.* 60, 161). This took place during the eightieth year of Sabas' life. Emperor Anastasius died shortly there-after, during Sabas' stay with Elias (July 10, 518). Ten days later Elias died in Sabas' arms, at the age of eighty-eight.

E. The Synod of Jerusalem and the Mission to Caesarea and Scythopolis (Aug. 518)

Anastasius died during the night between July 9 and 10, 518, and was succeeded by Justin, who, in contrast to the religious policy of his predecessor, adopted a clearly pro-Chalcedon policy (Vasiliev 1950, 132–254). He ordered that all church officials who had been exiled should be restored to their places and offices, and in the festive ceremonies held in the capital on July 15 and 16 he declared his loyalty to the Acts of Chalcedon and ordered the restoration of the names of the Chalcedonian patriarchs to the lists in the sacred diptychs from which they had been expunged.

When the letter containing the emperor's orders reached Jerusalem, a tremendous crowd of monks and citizens gathered. The bishops, along with Sabas, assembled for a synod in Jerusalem, and on August 6, in the midst of the general holiday in honor of the new emperor, they read out to the crowd the emperor's orders and the four church councils were recorded in the holy lists. Archbishop John appealed to Sabas, together with the other heads of the desert monasteries, to take the imperial letters to Caesarea and Scythopolis and to record the four church councils in the holy lists there as well (*V. Sab.* 61, 161–63). It is clear, therefore, that this Synod of Jerusalem was not a council of all the bishops of the Holy Land, but rather a home synod attended by the bishops who happened to be in Jerusalem at the time. The bishops of Caesarea and Scythopolis did not attend it.

In Caesarea the visitors were greeted by Bishop John of Choziba (Vailhé 1897–98b, 1903). The warm reception given the delegation in Scythopolis, Cyril's birthplace, is de-scribed in greater detail. Metropolitan Theodosius and the inhabitants of the city went to the church of Thomas the Apostle to receive the visitors, and a festive prayer service was conducted there. The emperor's letter was read in public, and the four church coun-cils were restored to the holy lists. During his visit Sabas resided in the house of the metropolitan and established close ties with many inhabitants of the city, including Cyril's parents.

Cyril does not tell of special events connected with the Christological controversy of the following years, the reigns of Justin I and Justinian. This was a period of grace for the Chalcedonian party, which had been persecuted during the reign of Anastasius. Only close to Sabas' death does he mention an additional event that reflects Sabas' adherence to Chalcedonian Orthodoxy.

F. Religious Debates in the Capital (Summer 531)

In the summer of 531, during the second visit of Sabas to Constantinople (see Chap. 4 below), while visiting Justinian's palace, Sabas did not fear the empress' wrath and re-fused to bless Theodora with a male child because of her Monophysite tendencies (*V. Sab.*

71, 174). In the presence of the emperor Sabas also condemned the heresies of Nestorius and Origen and that of Arius, which was then prevalent in the West (ibid. 72, 176).

At that time a change occurred in Justinian's religious policy (Stein-Palanque 1949, 369–402). Contributing factors to this were both the influence of the Empress Theodora and the spread of a parallel church hierarchy among the Monophysites due to the activity of John of Tella and Jacob bar-'Adai. The persecutions of the Monophysites were stopped, and a policy of reconciliation and dialogue was adopted. The monks from the Diocese of Oriens, who had been exiled, were permitted to return to their places, and eight exiled Severian bishops were invited to the capital by the emperor to participate in a colloquium with the Chalcedonians in order to attain a new formula of union. The bishops came to the capital accompanied by hundreds of monks, and the Monophysite presence there greatly increased (Stein-Palanque 1949, 377–78 and n. 2; Festugière 1962b, 103, n. 233).

The colloquium with the Severians was held only in 532, after Sabas' departure, with the participation of twelve bishops, six from each party, in the presence of a large audience of priests and monks. But already earlier, during Sabas' stay in the capital, the monks who had come with him conducted debates with these Aposchists in the civil basilica in the capital, a famous place of assembly (Janin 1964, 157–60). During the course of the debates it was revealed that among them were supporters of Theodore of Mopsuestia, one of the heads of the Antiochian theology, the teacher of Nestorius and author of one of the "Three Chapters," which were to be condemned by the Council of Constantinople in 553, a few years before the time of Cyril's writing. Leontius of Byzantium, a monk from the New Laura, was prominent in these debates, whereby his Origenist tendencies came to light (see below, Part V, end of Chap. 2A). When their heresy was revealed, Sabas removed them from his entourage and left them in the capital upon his return to Palestine (*V. Sab.* 72, 176; 74, 179).

4

Emissary of the Church of Jerusalem
to the Imperial Court

Sabas went to the capital twice to intercede with the emperor on behalf of the Palestinian Church. On his first journey he dealt with Emperor Anastasius, and on his second, which took place some twenty years later, he faced Justinian. In both instances he was chosen for the mission because of his personal qualifications and close ties with the patriarchs of Jerusalem who trusted him, and not because of any formal office he held in the ecclesiastical hierarchy of Jerusalem. At the same time, it was an indication of the increasing influence of the monastic movement and its leadership in the ecclesiastical establishment of this period. Matters of cardinal economic importance to the Church of Jerusalem were entrusted to him and not to the *oikonomos* (Jones 1964, 902) or to the *apokrisiarios* of the patriarchate.

A. First Journey to Constantinople (Autumn 511–May 512)

Sabas was first sent to the capital in autumn 511 by Patriarch Elias for the urgent purpose of preserving his status as patriarch. In the capital Sabas had three encounters with the emperor in his palace. In the first two meetings Sabas spoke in favor of the patriarch's Orthodoxy, persuading the emperor not to take any punitive measures against him in the wake of the failure of the Synod of Sidon (see above, Chap. 3). Sabas remained in the capital while the other members of the delegation returned to Palestine. The real purpose of his extended stay in the capital was apparently the subject of his third encounter with the emperor, a matter pertaining to the finances of the Palestinian Church. He requested the cancellation of the extra levy (περισσοπρακτία/*superflua discriptio*) imposed on the church of the Anastasis and on other landowners in Jerusalem by the tax contractors (τρακτευταί) and collectors (βίνδικες) of the treasury of Palestine (Festugière 1962b, 72–73 nn. 139–40; Dan 1982, 406–7).

This levy came into being in the following manner: lands that had been deserted by their impoverished owners and lay fallow caused a loss of tax revenue. In order to overcome this loss, the lands were redistributed by the state according to the principle of *adiectio* (ἐπιβολή) among the wealthy landowners, including the Church, in return for which they were required to pay the debts on the lands (*V. Sab.* 54, 145; Stein-Palanque 1949, 209–10; 1959, 28–29; Karayannopulos 1956, 314–15; 1958, 266; Jones 1964, 814–23). The "extra levy" was a debt to be repaid in installments, to which interest was added each year (Stein-Palanque 1949, 194–96). The total amount of the "extra levy" was 100 gold pounds. Patriarch Elias authorized Sabas to intercede with the emperor for the cancellation of this levy, which imposed a heavy burden on the Church of Jerusalem.

In the background were the financial and administrative reforms introduced by Anastasius. Everywhere an exact calculation was made regarding which portion of the taxes would be paid in kind and which portion in gold. Even before his reign a portion of the land tax had to be paid in gold, but this was not done in a systematic manner. Anastasius required that most of the land tax be paid in gold, leaving for the payment in kind only the amount necessary for the maintenance of the army in each province. This was accompanied by an administrative change of great importance, intended to ensure the orderly collection of the land tax. The supervision over the collection of these taxes was entrusted to special officials, *tractatores* and *vindices*. For each province in Oriens one *tractator* was appointed; he was the head of the fiscal administration of the province but was not subordinate to its governor. The *vindices*, who were subordinate to the *tractator*, were appointed for each city and district. These officials supervised the actual collection, which continued to be done by the officials of the provincial governor and by the urban *curiales* (Stein-Palanque 1959, 221; Festugière 1962b, 73 n. 140; Dan 1982, 400–401; Jones 1964, 235–37).

These new arrangements inevitably led to a reexamination of the ownership of land and a redistribution of deserted or fallow land among the large landowners in order to prevent a continual loss of taxes to the treasury. It is not inconceivable that uncultivated areas on the fringes of the desert and within the desert itself, which until now had been considered, for tax purposes, as the areas of the villages on the edge of the desert—such as Machmas, Anathoth, Fara, Lazarion, Beth Abudisson, Metopa, Thekoa, Caparbaricha, Aristoboulias—were now considered as belonging to the Church or to the desert monasteries. Moreover, the villagers themselves encouraged the monks to settle in the desert close to their villages (*V. Sab.* 39, 130).[30] If there is a basis for this proposal, we can gain a better understanding of why Sabas specifically was chosen for this mission, since he was the founder of many of the desert monasteries, several of which had been established by him only a short time before his journey to the emperor, perhaps in the period in which the reapportionment of the fallow land was implemented.

Fourteen years earlier (May 498), Anastasius had cancelled the *chrysargyron* tax, an act that had gained him much popularity.[31] Sabas' appeal to the emperor regarding an exemption from the "extra levy" was therefore made during a period of far-reaching financial reforms. Anastasius initially intended to respond favorably to Sabas' request and had even given an appropriate order to the praetorian prefect (ἔπαρχος τῶν πραιτωρίων) of the East, Zoticus. However, his senior financial advisor at the time was Marinus

---

[30] This suggestion occurred during fruitful discussions with Leah Di Segni, to whom I am indebted.

[31] The translation of this tax is "gold and silver," because it was collected in these coins and not in kind. The tax was instituted by Constantine the Great, and was imposed mainly on city dwellers: craftsmen, merchants, etc. This quinquennial levy was a very heavy burden on these lower and middle classes of urban society. Since the income from it was not great, Anastasius decided to cancel it. The amount that was lost to the treasury was made up by the emperor from the income on crown lands. The cancellation of the tax was received with great joy. A laudatory speech of Procopius of Gaza on the cancellation of the *chrysargyron*, among others, has been preserved. See Stein-Palanque 1949, 204–5; Festugière 1962b, 72 n. 138; Jones 1964, 110; Dan 1982, 406.

the Syrian, the *numerarius scrinii Orientis,* that is, the official in charge of the financial administration of the Diocese of Oriens in the eastern prefecture (Stein 1944, 180; Stein-Palanque 1949, 194–95; Jones 1964, 589). Marinus vigorously opposed Sabas' request and even succeeded, on the spot, in persuading the emperor to withdraw his approval.[32]

This marked the end of Sabas' mission to the capital, which had been extended for more than six months (Autumn 511–May 512). He succeeded in cancelling the emperor's decision to depose Patriarch Elias, but the second purpose of his mission, the cancellation of the "extra levy," was not successful. This levy was partially abolished only by Justin I, Anastasius' successor, after a petition (ἀναφορά) on this matter was sent to him by Sabas and the other desert fathers. It was finally completely cancelled during the reign of Justinian (*V. Sab.* 54, 146–47; Schwartz 1939, 263; Stein-Palanque 1949, 195; Vasiliev 1950, 413).

During his stay in the capital, Sabas renewed ties with the village of his birth. He had the right to distribute as he wished the funds that came to him, and so sent a portion of the 2,000 gold coins[33] that he had received from the emperor in the capital to his village, Moutalaska. The money was for the purpose of establishing a church in honor of Sts. Cosmas and Damian on the site of his parents' house (see above, Part II, Chap. 3B).

After his return to the Holy Land (May 512), he distributed the remainder of the money among his monasteries (*V. Sab.* 55, 147.26–148.5). The manner of its distribution caused resentment among the disciples who accompanied him to the capital, thinking that he demonstrated excessive generosity in this matter, giving money to those who, in their opinion, were not entitled to receive such funds. Although Cyril does not state this explicitly, Festugière (1962b, 74 n. 143) is of the opinion that the monastery of Theodosius as well was included among the recipients. It apparently was Sabas' position as archimandrite of the monks that guided him in the act of distribution. His approach was broader than that of a founder caring only for his own monasteries. It is possible that the underlying intent of this act was to prevent slanderous talk accusing him of deriving benefit only for his monasteries from his ties with the emperor, who had clear Monophysite leanings, and that this in fact was the objection raised by his disciples (cf. Theod. Petr. *V. Theod.* 21, 55).

B. The Second Journey to Constantinople (April–Sept. 531)

1. The Background of the Journey: The Samaritan Revolt[34]

The Samaritan revolt erupted in April or the beginning of May 529 (in the fourth month after the death of Theodosius, Jan. 11, 529; *V. Sab.* 70, 171–72). This was the largest and most serious revolt of the Samaritans against Byzantine rule and the Christian commu-

---

[32] Regarding Marinos the Syrian see *PW* XIV, 1798–1800: "Marinos" (no. 13) (Ensslin); Stein-Palanque 1949, 177–78, 194–96, 204 n. 2; Festugière 1962b, 73–74 n. 141.

[33] In addition to the 1,000 gold coins that he received in his first meeting with the emperor, he received an additional 1,000 coins at the conclusion of his third meeting with him. Theodore of Petra (*V. Theod.* 21, 55; Festugière 1963a, 132) mentions a similar gift by Emperor Anastasius to Theodosius: 30 gold pounds, equivalent to 2,160 gold coins. Theodosius was not included in the delegation sent by Elias from Palestine to the capital.

[34] For the rebellions of the Samaritans see *V. Sab.* 70, 171–73; Montgomery 1907, 98 ff; Stein-Palanque 1949, 287–88; Abel 1952, 355–59; Avi Yonah 1956; Festugière 1962b, 100 n. 22; Winkler 1965; Dan 1982, 282–89; Safrai 1982, 252–64; Rabello 1987, 237–57, 403–22; Di Segni 1988; Dar 1988.

nity. It had been preceded by two rebellions during the reigns of Zeno (484) and Anastasius (498). An additional revolt in the time of Justinian erupted in 555 or 556, and hostile acts also occurred under Justin II, after 572.

The reason for the revolt was the strict religious policy of Justinian, as expressed in the religious legislation of the beginning of his reign (527–528), which prohibited heretics, Jews, and Samaritans from serving in the imperial and municipal administration, and established for them an inferior status in civil law, in disputes with the Orthodox and in matters of inheritance (Linder 1987a, 356–67, 368–69, nos. 56, 58). In another edict (*Cod. Iust.* I.5.17), apparently published in 529,[35] the emperor ordered the destruction of the synagogues of the Samaritans and the abrogation of their right to bequeath or inherit property—clearly an attempt to wipe out this community. An additional reason for the revolt apparently was social-agrarian, which led the Samaritans to attack the estates of the Christians.

Samaritan-Christian relations were also tense in the mixed cities, Neapolis and Caesarea in Palaestina Prima and Scythopolis in Palaestina Secunda. The timing of the revolt was influenced by the first Persian war of Justinian, which was being conducted at the time: in March 529 a joint Persian-Arab force, headed by Al Mundhir, the governor of Hira, penetrated into Syria and almost reached the walls of Antioch.

The revolt erupted in Samaria, spread to Neapolis, and almost reached the borders of Caesarea (Dan 1982, 286). Events of importance also took place in Scythopolis (Di Segni 1988). The rebels caused severe damage to the urban and rural Christian community and to its property, chiefly in the district of Samaria (Dar 1988). Many churches were burned, and entire villages with their farmsteads were destroyed. The dead included Mamonas (or Amonas), the bishop of Neapolis, and some priests. The chief destruction to the Christian community was inflicted in Palaestina Prima, mainly in the area of Neapolis, and to a lesser extent in Palaestina Secunda. This is evident from the report on the damages and the scope of financial aid determined by the emperor to the two provinces, in the ratio of 12:1 (see below).

The revolt was suppressed with bloodshed. According to Procopius, 100,000 Samaritans fell in the revolt; it seems, however, that the number given by Malalas—20,000—is more reliable. Many Samaritans fled to Transjordan, to the Trachon, and even to Persia. The spoils of the Arabs comprised a similar number of young captives, both male and female, who were sold in the markets of Persia and India. The mutual acts of destruction and killing severely damaged the agriculture of the region of Samaria and lowered the incomes of the estate owners from their land, so that they had difficulty in paying taxes as they had previously. The depletion of the Samaritan community therefore caused serious damage to the state income from land taxes.

Arsenius, who had the title of *illustrius* and lived in the capital as a crypto-Samaritan who had converted to Christianity, exerted a great deal of influence upon the emperor

---

[35] The decree itself is undated. It was published between Justinian's rise to power as sole emperor in 527 and November 22, 530, the date of law I.5.20. Cyril (*V. Sab.* 70, 173) maintains that the legislation of Justinian against the Samaritans was the result of their crimes during the revolt and that it was issued due to Sabas' influence, which was brought to bear on the emperor during his stay in the capital. For more about this and about Sabas' visit to Justinian, see below.

and Empress Theodora and came to the aid of his fellow Samaritans (*V. Sab.* 70 and the end of 71, 172–74; Dan 1984, 142–47; Martindale 1980, 152, no. 3). After the Christians of Beth Shean killed his father and his brothers, he succeeded in arousing the anger of the imperial couple against the Christians in all of Palestine, because of the decrease in revenues to the imperial treasury.[36] Many ills (κακὰ πολλά) came upon the Christians as a result of his influence (Procopius, *Anecdota* XXVII, 8–10). It is understandable that in such a situation the Christians were unable to appeal to the emperor with a request for aid and tax concessions for the repair of the damages caused by the Samaritan revolt.

2. Sabas' Journey to Constantinople

In order to counteract the influence of Arsenius in the capital and to obtain the aid of the imperial court to repair the damage caused to the Christian communities, Patriarch Peter and the bishops subordinate to him decided to send Sabas to Constantinople despite his advanced age: Sabas was then in the ninety-second year of his life.[37] Additional monks from among his disciples set out with him, including Jeremias, the deacon of the Laura, and the future head of the laura named after him, and Leontius of Byzantium from the New Laura. The patriarch sent the emperor a letter informing him of the expected arrival of his emissary. Sabas' activities in the capital and the type of aid he requested reflect thorough preparation for the journey and good coordination between him and the patriarch.

3. The First Meeting with the Emperor

Even if Cyril's descriptions are somewhat exaggerated, Sabas apparently was received in a most impressive manner. When the ship in which he sailed approached the waters of the Bosphorus, the emperor sent imperial rowboats to escort it. Similarly, Patriarch Epiphanius (520–535), the *papas* (distinguished priest) Eusebius, and Hypatius, the bishop of Ephesus all went forth from the city to receive him and bring him to the emperor (*V. Sab.* 71, 173–74). Justinian, who regarded him as a holy old man, brought him into the throne room, "behind the curtain," where Sabas delivered to him the petition he had brought. The main purpose of this encounter, however, was to become acquainted with each other. The old man blessed the emperor, and the latter invited him to enter with him the inner rooms of the palace so that he could also bless Empress Theodora and pray that a male child be born to her. Sabas, however, who was aware of her Monophysite tendencies and support of Severus (Stein-Palanque 1949, 376–81; Duchesne 1915), rejected the request.

---

[36] The emperor's anger and the decrees against the Christians were also expressed in the deposition of Bassos, the governor of Palaestina Secunda, in the arrest and execution of the *dux* Theodore because of his failure to repress the rebellion, and in the appointment of Irenaeus as a special emissary and chief commander. See Di Segni 1988, 225.

[37] Cyril states that Sabas set forth on the journey in April of the 8th year of the indiction (Sept. 1, 529–Aug. 31, 530), i.e., in the year after the outbreak of the revolt. This date is accepted by Schwartz (1939, 345), and Di Segni (1988, 225–26 n. 32) also prefers it. Stein (1944), on the other hand, adopts the chronology proposed by Diekamp (1899, 11–15), according to which the journey is to be dated to April 531. In April 530 the revolt had not yet been suppressed, and therefore it was not possible to estimate the full extent of the damage. This and other arguments by Stein seem convincing to me.

Cyril relates that, as a result of his meeting with Sabas and reading the petition delivered to him, the emperor learned of the severe damages suffered by the Christians during the Samaritan revolt and accordingly issued a law prohibiting the Samaritans from assembling, and even cancelled their right to bequeath their property to their relatives or to transfer it to one another as presents. He also ordered that many of them, especially their leaders, be executed. The allusion apparently is to the above-mentioned laws, including *Cod. Iust.* 1.5.17; however, these laws had almost certainly been issued before the revolt, contrary to Cyril's statement, and were among its causes. This is learned from the statements by Procopius of Caesarea (*Anecdota* XI.24–30; XXVII.8–10), according to which the uprising of the Samaritan farmers was a result of the strong feelings of bitterness caused by Justinian's legislation, which limited their rights, especially property rights. At any rate, it is clear that as a result of this meeting with Sabas the emperor adopted a diametrically opposed position toward the Samaritans, and a similar change befell the status of Arsenius, who until then had apparently maintained the way of life of a Christian, although he had never been baptized. Cyril (*V. Sab.* 71, 174.20) relates that the emperor ordered his execution; however, he disappeared for a period of time and then, in order to save himself, went to Sabas, who was still in the capital, and was baptized by him together with all the members of his household.[38] Procopius notes only that he was forbidden to enter the imperial palace, under pressure from Christians who desired to end his influence at the court (*Anecdota* XXVIII.10). Procopius does not mention Sabas' name in this context, but the missing details can be supplied from Cyril.

4. The Second Meeting with the Emperor: the Compensation for Damages Due
   to the Revolt

Sabas received permission to reside in the imperial palace. A few days later, the emperor summoned him to a second meeting in which he offered to Sabas financial aid for his monasteries by providing an allowance for the monks living in them. Sabas wisely rejected this generous proposal, which was not the reason for his mission and which was likely to bring about a decisive change in the structure of the monastic movement and to provide an opening for its consequential enslavement to the emperor. Sabas requested that the funds offered by the emperor be diverted to the repair of the damages caused by the revolt, for the well-being of the residents of Palestine, the Church of the Holy Land, and the See of Jerusalem. He requested for his monks only an improvement of the security conditions in the desert in which they lived. Sabas listed his requests in articles that undoubtedly had been agreed upon between him and the patriarch before the departure of the delegation to the capital.

Sabas had five requests (*V. Sab.* 72, 175):

(1) Granting an exemption from taxes and economic support for the Palestinian Christians who were plundered and had become impoverished during the course of the Samaritan revolt.

(2) Rebuilding all the holy structures (σεβασμίων οἴκων) burned by the Samaritans.

---

[38] Several years later Arsenius went to Alexandria, where he was involved in the disturbances that eventually led to the Council of Gaza (540). He was executed by the governor, and the emperor confiscated his property (Procopius, *Anecdota* 11; Liberatus, *Brev.* 23, 139; Dan 1984, 144–45; Rabello 1987, 268–72).

(3) Establishing a hospital in Jerusalem for the treatment of sick foreigners (ξένοι), apparently pilgrims. This does not refer to the care of the casualties of the revolt and bears no relation to it whatsoever; it deals with the well-being of the Holy City of Jerusalem.

(4) Completing the building and furnishing of the New Church of Mary, which had already been founded by Patriarch Elias (*V. Sab.* 72, 175.13–14). This clause as well obviously bears no direct relation to the revolt. This was a matter within the authority of the patriarch, who requested aid for this from the imperial court.

(5) Construction of a fortress (κάστρον) in the desert, below the monasteries of Sabas (apparently in the area of the Hyrcania valley), as a defense against the invasion of the Saracens. The period was that of the first Persian war, in which the Persians were aided by the Arabs of Hira and other Arab tribes, who had an alliance with them. This situation undermined security conditions in the Judean desert. Some of the Samaritan refugees even reached Persia, where they succeeded in gaining the support of the Persian king and in persuading him to break the peace with the Romans.

Cyril adds that in return for the emperor's granting these requests, Sabas promised him that God would increase his kingdom and add to it all the territory of the western empire. He thereby attributed to Sabas a prophecy regarding the reality of which Cyril was already aware when he wrote his description.

Justinian responded favorably to all the requests (*V. Sab.* 73, 176–78):

(1) He gave Patriarch Peter and the governors (ἄρχοντες) of Palestine royal decrees establishing an exemption from taxes for the ninth and tenth tax years of the indiction (Sept. 1, 530–Aug. 31, 532).[39] The decrees stated that the exemption would be for Palaestina Prima and Palaestina Secunda, in the total amount of 1,300 pounds of gold, and would be divided between the two provinces in proportion to the damage caused to buildings (κτίσματα) in each of them. The allusion was to damage caused to the farm buildings and farms (χωρία) of the Christians that were burned by the Samaritans (*V. Sab.* 70, 172.6; Festugière 1962b, 106 n. 239). The decrees also determined that Antony, the bishop of Ascalon in Palaestina Prima,[40] and Zacharias, the bishop of Pella in Palaestina Secunda, would assess the damages. After their assessment, Palaestina Prima, which included the territory of Samaria, was given an exemption in the amount of 1,200 gold pounds, and the Scythopolis region, in Palaestina Secunda, an exemption in the amount of 100 gold *librae* (ibid. 75, 181). These figures indicate the relative material damage and the scope of the actions of hostility in each of the two provinces.

(2) Regarding Sabas' second request, the bishops appointed to serve as assessors

---

[39] The first year of exemption was therefore the year of the indiction that ended before Sabas' return to the Holy Land (Sept. 531), bringing with him this decision of the emperor. The practice was that the third and last payment for each tax year would be made in the month of May. Schwartz (1939, 345) is of the opinion that it cannot be assumed that the exemption was granted for the tax year that had already ended; however, Stein (1944, 177–78; see also Festugière 1962b, 106 n. 238) cites another example of this procedure, and adds that the retroactive payment of taxes was common even during ordinary times, and it may reasonably be assumed that in the year 530/31 the payment was only partial, due to the revolt which had broken out already in 529.

[40] This Antony was the son of Marcianus and the brother of John, the former patriarch of Jerusalem. The father and his two sons had helped Sabas to establish the monastery of the Cave.

were also given the task of assessing the damage caused to houses of prayer (εὐκτήριοι οἶκοι) which had been burnt, and of deciding upon the compensation to be given for the repairs of each site. It was also determined that these sums would be paid from the public treasury (ἐκ τοῦ δημοσίου λόγου) or by mortgaging the real estate of the Samaritans. The implementation of this section was imposed upon the *comes* Stephen, the proconsul of Palestine. The total sum of the expenses in this clause was not limited, and after the assessment of the damages, the bishops of Palestine received as much gold as was needed for the restoration of the churches (*V. Sab.* ibid.).

(3) The emperor ordered the construction in the heart of Jerusalem of a hundred-bed hospital (νοσοκομεῖον), and provided for the first year of its maintenance a tax-exempt yearly allocation (πρόσοδος) in the amount of 1,850 gold coins (*nomismata*). He also ordered that in the future the hospital would be enlarged to two hundred beds and provided for this purpose a permanent additional tax-exempt allocation in the same amount (on the hospital, see Milik 1960–61, 150–51).

(4) For completing the building of the New (Nea) Church of Mary, on a much larger scale, the emperor sent to Jerusalem an architect named Theodore, and ordered the administrators of the treasury of Palestine (τρακτευταὶ Παλαιστίνης) to provide the gold needed for the construction work. This was a tremendous undertaking.[41] Patriarch Peter supervised the entire project, while the construction itself was supervised, by order of the emperor, by Barachos, the bishop of Bakatha in the district of Philadelphia, who apparently possessed expertise in this work. The construction work lasted for twelve years. The dedication ceremony, which took place on November 20, 543, was also attended by Cyril of Scythopolis, who came especially for this from his city (*V. John Hes.* 20, 216.8–16).

(5) Regarding the establishment of the fortress, a special edict was sent to Summus, the *dux Palaestinae,* whose duties included responsibility for the fortification works in the three provinces of Palestine. The edict ordered him to give Sabas 1,000 gold coins from the treasury of Palestine (ἐκ τῶν Παλαιστίνης δημοσίων) for its construction. He was similarly ordered to station in it a guard of soldiers to be maintained from the public treasury (ἐκ τοῦ δημοσίου λόγου), whose task would be to guard the monasteries of Sabas. Sabas died shortly afterwards. Summus gave the sum to his successor Melitas, who unwisely gave it to Patriarch Peter, who spent it for other needs, and the fortress was never built (*V. Sab.* 83, 187–88).

As was stated above, Sabas rejected the emperor's offer to grant a permanent income to his monks; he did not, however, return to the Holy Land empty-handed. This time too, as on his previous journey, he obtained for his monasteries a grant in gold coins. Cyril does not mention the source of this money. It cannot be ruled out that, despite everything, Sabas received from the emperor himself, in addition to the above-mentioned decrees, which were issued for the well-being of the entire Christian community of Palestine and of the Church of Jerusalem, a contribution for his monasteries, instead of the permanent annual allocation proposed by the emperor (*V. Sab.* 74, 179).[42]

---

[41] Procopius of Caesarea describes at length the construction of the church (*Buildings* V.6). Its ruins were discovered during the archaeological excavations in Jerusalem. See Avigad 1977; 1983, 229–46; Ben-Dov 1985, 233–42; see also Vincent and Abel 1926, 917.

[42] Deslandes 1922 and Meester 1942, 8–9, 102–8 discuss the types of the monasteries according to

Cyril, in a literary vein, emphasizes the piety of Sabas, who stood in the corner reciting psalms while Justinian and the quaestor Tribonian were occupied with the detailed formulation of the decrees. It is clear, however, from Sabas' very mission and the contents of his petition that as a person of action he was acquainted with matters of economics and taxation. He knew how to formulate the request for funds to repair the damage from the revolt and was entrusted by Patriarch Peter to deal with the financial matters of the See of Jerusalem. It is not inconceivable that the selection of the assessing bishops, as well as the supervisor of the construction of the Nea Church, was done in consultation with Sabas, since he and not the emperor might have had personal knowledge of them, being acquainted with their qualifications and reliability. The emperor mentioned them by name in the decrees, and did not leave any choice to the governors of Palestine or of the patriarch. If so, then Sabas' intervention in the formulation of the decrees is much greater than indicated by a cursory reading of Cyril's description.

Despite Sabas' advanced age and the rigors of the journey, he was sent by Peter and the other bishops to publicize the edicts in Caesarea and Scythopolis, the capitals of Palaestina Prima and Secunda, in and near which were the centers of the revolt, where the greatest damage had been wrought. This ensured a reliable assessment of the damages, restoration of the buildings, and punctiliousness in using the funds for the purposes for which they were intended. In this mission, as in the missions to the capital, Sabas was chosen because of his personal qualifications, and not because of any formal office that he held in the church hierarchy.

---

their jurisdictional status. A monastery of an imperial status first occurs in ca. 600, when Maurice bestowed upon the monasteries of Theodore of Sykeon an imperial status. The monastic legislation of Justinian (*Nov.* 5.1, 67.1) gave legal recognition to the ecclesiastical canons 4 and 8 of the Council of Chalcedon, according to which the monks everywhere were put under the authority of the local bishop. Patriarchal status is also mentioned in this legislation, but not an imperial status. Did the emperor intend to give the Sabaite monasteries an imperial status when he offered a permanent annual allocation? Did he intend thereby to extend his direct influence on Palestinian monasticism by interfering in its affairs and dictating the appointment of the next Sabaite abbots? There is no evidence for this.

Part V: Sabas' Successors (532–638)

1

The History of the Great Laura from Sabas' Death to the Muslim Conquest (532–638)

Cyril of Scythopolis is the most important source for the history of the Laura up to 559. The extant sources for the period after this are much sparser.

There was some decline in the status of the Laura after Sabas' death. To a large extent, it was the personality of the head of the Laura that determined its standing. This was the case during Sabas' lifetime, and even more so after his death. At the same time, however, despite the decline, the Laura maintained its senior status among the laurae of Palestine. This status was assured by the heritage of the past, the size of its population, and its financial resources; contributions continued to stream in, even after Sabas' death, out of loyalty to and veneration of his memory. Besides, famous monks such as John the Hesychast continued to live and be active in the Laura. Cyril's writings as well contributed to increase the reputation and ensure the special standing of Sabas' disciples and the Great Laura at the head of the monastic movement in the Holy Land. This situation is reflected in the special role played by the Laura and its monks during the course of the Origenist controversy (see below, Chap. 2A).

Sabas selected Abba Melitas as his successor (*V. Sab.* 76, 182). He led the Laura for five years (Dec. 532–Sept. 537). The decline that occurred in the status of the Laura and its leader in the eyes of the ecclesiastical establishment is reflected in the fact that Patriarch Peter requested and received from him the 1,000 gold coins received from Summus, the *dux Palaestinae,* for the construction of the fortress that was to defend Sabas' monasteries (see above, Part IV, Chap. 4). During Sabas' time the patriarchs had not intervened in the distribution of the funds he had received. As noted earlier, Peter spent this money on other things, and the fortress was never built (ibid. 83, 187–88).

Melitas' successor was Gelasius (Sept. 537–Oct. 546), a veteran monk of the Laura, one of the two Isaurian brothers, architects who came to the Laura in 494 and aided Sabas in constructing the buildings at the core of the Laura and some of the satellite monasteries (his brother Theodulus, who was a priest of the Laura, was already dead). Gelasius displayed a forceful stance against the penetration of the Origenists into the Laura. In 546, when he was of very advanced age, he agreed to the request of the fathers of the Laura and went to the capital to report the actions of the Origenists to the emperor. But due to the wiles of Theodore Ascidas, the leader of the Origenists, in the patriarchate and in the royal palace, he was refused access to the emperor and the patriarch. He died in Asia Minor on his way back to Palestine, in October of that year (ibid. 87, 195; see below, Chap. 2A).

As a result of the dispute between the Origenists and their opponents regarding the appointment of a successor, the Laura remained without a *hegoumenos* for several months. Eventually the Origenists, aided by a contingent of soldiers, succeeded in imposing upon the monks one of their members as the successor. This was George the "Cruel Wolf." This led to the Orthodox monks leaving for other monasteries. John the Hesychast left for the Mount of Olives. George served in this position for only seven months (Feb.–Aug. 547). In the end he was driven out by the Origenists themselves, being charged with revelry and licentiousness (ibid. 88, 195). Upon the counsel of the patriarch, the fathers remaining in the Laura elected Abba Cassianus as abbot.

Cassianus (Sept. 547–July 548), like Cyril, was from Scythopolis. Already during his childhood he had "withdrawn from the world" and had been educated by Sabas. He served as the priest of the Great Laura, and as such he appears among the signatories to the decisions of the Council of Constantinople in 536 (*ACO* III, 36.38, 50.14). Afterwards he was the head of the laura of Souka for eight years. During this period he also founded in Scythopolis the monastery of Zougga. Cassianus was taken from Souka to head the Great Laura. The transfer of a *hegoumenos* from one monastery to another was an exceptional event, indicating the distress encountered by the patriarch and the monks in the election of a suitable candidate acceptable to all to head the Great Laura. Cassianus died after having served in this office for approximately ten months (ibid. 88, 196).

The fathers of the Laura next elected Conon to head it (ibid. 89, 196). He was still the abbot during the time of Cyril's writing. This fact, and not only his excellent actions, undoubtedly influenced Cyril's writings about him. Conon was of Lycian origin (like Gerasimus). From his childhood there he had devoted himself to the monastic life and had excelled in character and piety. He arrived at the Great Laura only after Sabas' death, serving as an example to others in his way of life, simplicity, charming manner, and wisdom. In his time, and under his leadership, the Origenists were defeated, and the community, which had diminished, once again increased (see below, Chap. 2A). Like Sabas, he went on various missions in the service of the patriarchs of Jerusalem. During Peter's time he wrote, at the latter's request, a treatise against the Origenists, and went to the capital on a campaign against them. During Eustochius' time he went on a mission to Ascalon with one of John the Hesychast's disciples, at the beginning of 559 (Garitte 1954, 80).

Abba Conon, *hegoumenos* of Sabas' Laura, is mentioned in one of the anecdotes of John Moschus (*Pratum* 42, 2896). He sent a present to a monk of the laura of Pharan, who was bedridden in the hospital of the patriarch in Jerusalem. This took place during the time of John Moschus' stay in Pharan (568–578). If this is the same Conon who was active in resolving the Origenist controversy, then his term in office as head of the Great Laura lasted more than twenty years.[1] John Moschus began his monastic life in the coenobium of Theodosius in ca. 565 and left Palestine in 604. From ca. 590 until he left he lived, together with Sophronius, in the New Laura (Schönborn 1972; Chadwick 1974;

---

[1] In the list of the Laura's abbots given by Phokylides (1927, 605), the duration of his office is not stated.

Mioni 1974). During the course of this period, they also visited the Great Laura frequently. Besides Abba Conon, he also mentions a few more of its monks: Abba Athanasius (ibid. 3, 2853; 128–29, 2992–93), who had previously stayed in the monastery of Penthucla next to the Jordan and had ties with Abba Athenogenes, the bishop of Petra. He complained to John Moschus about the loss of virtue in those times, as compared with the past (ibid. 130, 2993). Abba Petrus, who was a priest of the Laura (ibid. 11, 2860; 59, 2912); and Abba Stephen "the hairy" (ibid. 53, 2908; 58, 2912). It is possible that Abba Thaleleus of Cilicia, whose career as a monk lasted more than sixty years (ibid. 59, 2912), was also a monk of the Laura. Abba Kallinikos the Great, an anchorite, also lived in it (ibid. 137, 3000).

We do not possess any source later than Cyril's writings that provides detailed information about the history of the Laura. This is the situation until the Persian conquest in 614. In the list of the Laura's abbots there is a gap between the end of Conon's office and the Persian conquest (Phokylides 1927, 605), when it was headed by Nicomedes (see below). Vailhé (1899–1900b, 176) suggested the insertion in this gap of Stephen Trichinas ("the hairy"), mentioned by John Moschus (ibid.). The information about the Laura in the *Vita Theodori Sykeoni* also does not give the name of the Laura's abbot at that time.

Theodore of Sykeon in Galatia (d. 613), who eventually became the bishop of Anastasiopolis in Galatia Prima, had visited Palestine three times. The first time, at the beginning of the second half of the sixth century, he went as a young pilgrim to Jerusalem and the holy places (*V. Theod. Syk.* 24, 24). He made a tour of the desert monasteries and of the anchorites living in the heart of the desert in order to gain close acquaintance with their way of life. He received the monastic habit (σχῆμα) from the abbot of Choziba but did not settle there, returning to his country immediately afterwards (see above, Part III, Chap. 5B). During his third visit, after he had already become bishop (ibid. 62, 55–56), he was seized by a fierce desire to rid himself of the troubles of the office he held and to live in the Holy Land as an anchorite. He settled in the Laura of Sabas (ibid. 63, 56) in the cell of an outstanding monk named Andreas. He would begin the fast preceding Easter starting from Christmas and would pass the entire period in silence, sitting on a small stool. This act aroused the admiration of the fathers of the Laura. He did not remain there long, however, and eventually returned to his bishopric after St. George appeared to him in a dream and ordered him to do so.

Many years before the arrival of Theodore at the Laura of Sabas, one of his three senior disciples, a monk named Evagrius, came to live there (ibid. 47, 44–45).[2] The other two, Arsenius and Andreas, returned to Galatia, after having visited the Holy City as pilgrims, and became hermits. The Great Laura therefore continued to serve in the second half of the sixth century as an ideal, attracting monks from throughout the Christian world who sought the perfect monastic life. The fact that Theodore lived in the cell of another monk suggests certain changes in the norms, as compared to the previous pe-

---

[2] This Evagrius is not mentioned during Theodore's stay in the Laura of Sabas. It is possible that he was no longer alive at the time or that he had gone to another place. It cannot be ruled out, however, that there was an error in the name, and that Andreas is the name of the disciple who remained in the Great Laura. If this is indeed the case, then Theodore lived in the cell of his former disciple when he stayed in the Great Laura.

riod. The abbot at that time apparently was not a personality to be mentioned in a *vita* whose geographical background was so distant from Palestine. The link between the Laura and Galatia Prima is also indicated by the testimony of Antiochus Monachus (see below).

John Climacus (570–649) mentions an elderly Sabaite monk, also named John, who lived in Sinai. Climacus had met him in the early years of his monastic career (late 6th century). Initially he had been a monk in a coenobium in Asia; afterwards he came to the monastery of St. Sabas and then went to the desert of Guda in Sinai, where John Climacus met him (*Scala Paradisi* 85; 89 and in the *prolegomena* to this treatise: PG 88, 608, 720, 721–24; Anastasius Sinaitae, *Narrationes* 6; 32, ed. Nau 1902b, 63–64; 79). It is possible that the reason for this monk's moving to Sinai was that the Judean desert was too crowded, and the monk sought a quieter and more isolated life.

We possess more detailed information about the problems the monks endured during the Persian invasion. The main source on this subject is the letter of Antiochus, a monk of the Laura, who relates the martyrdom of 44 monks of the monastery by the Saracens. The letter (*Ep. ad Eust.*) was sent ca. 620 to Eustathius of Ancyra, the capital of Galatia Prima. Eustathius had been forced to flee from his city with many monks and wander from place to place because of the advance of the Persians in Asia Minor. Under these conditions it was difficult to move around with heavy books, and Eustathius therefore requested in a letter to his friend Antiochus that he send him a small volume of the scriptures to take with him. In his letter Eustathius also refers to rumors that had reached him about a massacre of the monks of Sabas' monastery and asks for more details. Antiochus sent the requested volume (see below) together with a letter relating what had happened in Sabas' monastery during the Persian invasion (see also *Synax. CP.* 689, May 16).

A week before the Persian conquest of Jerusalem (end of May, 614), Arabs came to the Laura and pillaged all the holy vessels of the church. Among the monks there were recluses who had not left the Laura for fifty or sixty years. In the wake of this raid, most of the fathers, including Antiochus (the writer of the letter) and the *hegoumenos* Nicomedes, fled to Arabia, that is, beyond the Jordan. Others (including the monk Strategius/Eustratius; see below) fled to Jerusalem. Those strongest in their faith, however, remained in the Laura. In a second assault the barbarians captured and tortured them in the hope of gaining information about hidden treasures. When they despaired of this, they beat them to death. Forty-four were killed; their memorial day falls on May 16.[3] The monks were therefore not harmed by the Persians themselves but rather by the Arab tribes who arrived with them. We hear similar things about the identity of those raiding the monastery of Choziba, where only one elderly monk was killed, while the remaining monks who were caught were taken captive (*V. Geor.* 31, 129–30). In another place mention is made of the redemption of Christian captives from the Midianites, apparently a term referring to an Arab tribe (Lappa-Zizicas 1970, 276, para. 9).

---

[3] The date appearing in the text in PG 89, 1421–28 is May 15. But in Chap. 4 in *AASS, Maii* III, 613–14, the memorial day is stated in the Greek *menaia* and *synaxaria* as May 16. According to Baronius, the editor, this is indeed the correct date, while May 15 is a copyist's mistake. May 16 is also the memorial day appearing in *Synax. CP.* 689.

The bodies of the forty-four martyrs remained unburied until the return of those who had fled to Arabia. Modestus, the abbot of the monastery of Theodosius, and eventually patriarch of Jerusalem (630–634), also came there from Jerusalem and took part in their burial. After the burial the returnees remained for an additional two months in the Laura. When rumors reached them of further imminent raids, they went to the abandoned monastery of Abba Anastasius ca. 20 *stadia* (ca. 4 km) from Jerusalem (Vailhé 1899–1900a, 515, proposes identifying it with the monastery of Mar Elias), whose monks apparently had fled to Jerusalem. Since it was a coenobium surrounded by a wall, it provided for its inhabitants a greater degree of security than the open Laura. After they had been there a few months, they were encouraged by Modestus, who was in charge of the rehabilitation of the Christian community and its institutions, to return to the Laura. The bravest of the monks, headed by the monk Thomas, returned there immediately, with others joining them later on. Antiochus was among those who returned. The *hegoumenos* Nicomedes aided Modestus in repairing the damage that had been done to the Christians of Palestine. With 1,200 gold coins from John Eleemon he redeemed twenty high-ranking captives, both men and women (Lappa-Zizicas 1970). The monks who remained in the monastery of Anastasius elected as *hegoumenos* over them one Justin, a veteran monk and priest of the Great Laura. Justin enforced the Rule of Sabas in the new coenobium.

The horrors of the slaughter accordingly led to the division of the community. With the support of Modestus, however, the Laura developed once again, and during the time of the writing of Antiochus' letter (620), the situation was again stable. Therefore Antiochus had no difficulty in composing and sending Eustathius the book he had requested. This was the *Pandectes* (= encyclopedia) *scripturae divinitus inspiratae* (PG 89, 1415–1850), comprising *Capitula sive homilias 130,* extracts and summaries of various works.[4] At this time Thomas was already the abbot of the monastery.

The monks of the Laura who found refuge in Jerusalem during the Persian invasion included Strategius/Eustratius, who had written the narrative of the conquest of Jerusalem by the Persians.[5] He was an eyewitness to this event, and would later be among those going into exile in Persia. In chapter 6 of the Greek version (Conybeare 1910, 506 n. 18) and of the Georgian version, which is longer and more detailed than the Arabic ones, a story is related about an anchorite monk named John, who lived with his disciple in a place called Heptastomos (CSCO 203, 11–12). This laura was therefore already deserted by that time, and they were the only ones living in it. He was not harmed at the time of the attacks on the Great Laura, a week before the conquest of Jerusalem, during the second of which the forty-four martyrs were killed. He saw the conquest of Jerusalem

---

[4] This composition inspired the 11th-century author Nicon of the Black Mountain to compose a similar florilegium, comprising 63 chapters, entitled Ἑρμηνεῖαι τῶν Θείων ἐντολῶν τοῦ Κυρίου, or Πανδέκτης, in face of the turmoil caused by the Seljuk-Turkish capture of Antioch and its environs in 1084. Nicon explored the liturgical *typika* of his time, including the Sabaitic one, with which he became acquainted while visiting the monastery. Gerasimus, to whom Nicon addressed his most intimate letters, was a monk at Mar Saba. The Πανδέκτης was translated into Arabic shortly after its composition, by a Sabaite monk, so it seems (Doens 1954; Nasrallah 1969; Taft 1988).

[5] His identity as a Sabaite monk appears in the title of the Arabic manuscripts A and V, in which his name is Eustratius, and in the Georgian version, in which his name is Strategius.

when it happened, from where he was, far from the city, due to his prophetic powers, and he himself was killed at that very moment. His disciple, who succeeded in escaping, returned afterwards and buried him in the tomb of the holy fathers (apparently that of the Great Laura and not that of the laura of Heptastomos).

According to the *Menologium Basilii* (PG 117, 276), Anastasius the Persian[6] became a monk in the Laura of Sabas. However, in the detailed version of his life (ed. *AASS* and Usener; see also Chitty 1966, 160–61), it is stated that he was admitted as a monk to the monastery of Anastasius by the above-mentioned Justin in 620–21, and lived there for seven years. It is possible that the source of the error lies in the ties between the Great Laura and the monastery of Anastasius in its new form, which was settled by refugees from the Laura and which was following the Rule of Sabas.

In the wake of the Persian invasion and the harm that befell the monasteries (the massacre in the Laura was not an isolated incident), many monks fled to the West, founding several Greek-speaking monasteries, including one dedicated to Sabas, in North Africa (which was a Byzantine exarchate). This monastery was established by refugees from the Great Laura. Sabaite refugees later went from Africa to Rome (before 649), where they established a monastery of the same name. This monastery played an important role in the anti-Monothelitic Lateran Council of 649. By the beginning of the ninth century this Greek monastery was the most important monastery of Rome, but gradually it was latinized, a process which reached its completion by the end of the tenth century (Borsari 1951; Ferrari 1957, 281–90; Chadwick 1974, 58; Sansterre 1980, 22–31; 1988).[7]

Eutychius relates that when Heraclius reconquered Palestine from the Persians, he was greeted upon his arrival in Jerusalem, by the residents of the city and by the monks of Al Siq or Siqat, who complained of the conduct of the Jews during the occupation and requested that he punish them for this (*Annals* 241: PG 111, 1089–90; 271: CSCO 471, Scrip. Arab. 44, 128). This term refers to laurae, in this case, so it seems, the Great Laura and the laura of Chariton, the Old Laura.

We possess no information regarding the history of the Laura afterwards and during the Arab conquest. From then on, however, the change of government ushered in a new reality in the life of the Christian community in the Holy Land (Gil 1992, 430–89; Linder 1987b). The history of the Laura during the early Muslim period (638–1099) and the changes that took place in the way of life of the monks during it are a subject deserving thorough research; these matters will not be discussed here (see Phokylides 1927, 253–491; Vailhé 1897, 1899, 1899–1900b; Leclercq 1950). During this era, as security worsened, the Laura shrank toward its center and the number of monks decreased. But despite the deliberate attacks of the Saracens, literary creativity there during this period

---

[6] Anastasius (Magundat in Persian) was the son of one of the magi of King Chosroes II of Persia. During the Persian occupation of territories of the Byzantine Empire he served as a recruit in the army, and was witness to various miracles performed by the Holy Cross which was taken in captivity to the capital, Ctesiphon. When he began to inquire into the matter, he drew nearer to Christianity. Initially he served in Chalcedon and afterwards in Hierapolis, where he retired from the army and "from the world." He came to Jerusalem, converted to Christianity, and received his Christian name, Anastasius. He later came to Caesarea to promote Christianity among the garrison. He was seized by the Persians, exiled to the east, and put to death as a martyr, without denying his faith. His memorial day is Jan. 22. See Flusin 1992.

[7] See also R. Krautheimer et al., *Corpus Basilicarum Christianarum Romae* IV (Rome 1970), 51–71.

reached its peak (Ehrhard 1893; Vailhé 1898a; Blake 1965; Griffith 1986). The most important author who lived and wrote in it was John of Damascus (d. before 753), who wrote in Greek (*BHG* 884–85; Bardenhewer 1932, 51–65; Jugie 1924, 1925; Nasrallah 1950, 137–68; Hoeck 1951; Beck 1959, 476–86; Altaner-Stuiber 1966, 532–56). In addition to his polemical works against the iconoclasts, his ascetical, exegetical, and liturgical treatises, and his hymnography, his chief dogmatic work, *The Fount of Wisdom* (see below), is the first comprehensive exposition of Christian dogma. Another prominent contemporary author was Cosmas Hymnographos, who composed hymns and religious melodies, and eventually became the bishop of Maiumas (ca. 743–760) (*BHG* 394–95; Papadopoulos-Kerameus 1897, 271, 303; Bardenhewer 1932, 173–76). A third prominent, ninth-century *hymnographos* of the Laura was Stephen (not to be confused with Stephen the Thaumaturge); others, less famous, were Sabas the younger, Babylas, Aristoboulos, and Gregory (Vailhé 1898a). To another category of authors belongs Theodore abu-Qurrah (d. 820), most of whose work—about twenty compositions—was written in Arabic and who is considered the first Christian author to write in this language (Graf 1910; 1947, 7–27; Dick 1962–63; Griffith 1979, 1985). Mention should also be made of Leontius of Damascus, the disciple and hagiographer of Stephen the Thaumaturge (the miracle worker) (see below). Along with original literary work, in the Laura there was also extensive manuscript copying and translating from Greek into Arabic and Georgian. Thus, for example, the *Vita Sabae* was translated into Georgian already at the end of the seventh or the beginning of the eighth century (Garitte 1954, 84 n. 1; Linder 1987b, 117–21). On the other hand, Syriac writings of Isaac of Nineveh (7th century) were translated into Greek at the beginning of the ninth century by two monks of Mar Saba named Abraamios and Patrikios (Brock 1984, art. ii, 15).

The monks belonged to three different linguistic groups: Greek, Syriac, and Georgian. Each community had a separate church, and only on Sunday did they all gather for a common rite (Linder 1987b, 121; see also above, Part iii, Chap. 5d).

The most famous of the Laura monks became saints, whose memory was preserved in the liturgical calendar of the Byzantine Church. Some of them died as martyrs at the hands of the Saracens or the Muslim authorities. Their stories provide information about the history of the Laura under the caliphate. In addition to John of Damascus, Cosmas Hymnographos, and Theodore Abu Qurrah, these martyrs and saints included: Michael the Sabaite, a native of Tiberias, who was killed by the Caliph 'Abd al-Malik, between 691 and 705 (*Passio S. Michaelis*, ed. Peeters 1930); John Eremopolites ("the desert-dweller," ed. Halkin 1968), in whose time Nicodemus, who accepted John of Damascus and Cosmas Hymnographos at the Laura, served as abbot; Stephen the Sabaite (Thaumatourgos), who entered the Laura in 734 (*V. Steph. Sab.*); another monk named Stephen, who came to the capital during the reign of Leo III (717–741), after he had been a monk in the monastery of Sabas (*Synax. CP.* 389–90, Jan. 14); and Bacchus, who arrived at the Laura at the end of the eighth century. This monk, whose father had converted to Islam, along with his seven children, rebaptized five of them to Christianity and for this died as a martyr (806) in a place called Fossatum (ibid. 310–12, Dec. 15; *Men. Bas.* 212–13, Dec. 17; *BHG* 209, Dec. 15). The saints of the beginning of the ninth century include Michael the Synkellos (760–846) (*BHG* 1296–97, Jan. 4; *Synax. CP.* 329–32, Dec. 20; *Vita*, ed. Cunningham 1991) and his disciples the brothers Theodore (775–841) and Theophanes

(778–845) (*Synax. CP.* 130, Oct. 11; 349–50, Dec. 27–28; *Men. Bas.* 229, Dec. 28; *V. Theod. Gr.; BHG* 1793), who were sent by the patriarch of Jerusalem Thomas to Constantinople and Rome during the controversy concerning the *filioque* and who later were active in the capital during the iconoclast controversy (see below, Chap. 2c–d). In the course of it the two brothers were condemned, and their sentences, composed in ridiculous iambic verses, were tattooed on their faces, giving rise to their appellation "the tattooed" (γραπτοί) (Vailhé 1901a). Their father Jonas, who was a monk and priest in the Laura, also became a saint (*Synax. CP.* 657, Sept. 21; *Men. Bas.* 67, Sept. 22), as well as Hilarion the Iberian, who lived in the Laura in the middle of the ninth century for seven years (847–854) (*V. Hil. Ib.* 8–10, 246).

In 786 the monastery of Sabas was attacked (Linder 1987b, 113), and in 797 twenty of the Laura's monks, some of whose names are known, were killed by the Saracens. At the request of Basil, the abbot at the time, Stephen Hymnographos, who was an eyewitness, wrote the story of their death (*Pass. XX Mart. Sab.*). The story indicates that at this stage there were still no walls around the core of the Laura. Despite this massacre, many monks continued to live there, among them Michael the Synkellos. If we accept the testimony of the *Commemoratorium* (line 20), there were 150 monks counted there in 808. However, after the death of Harun ar-Rashid in the same year, additional attacks began against the Christian community in Jerusalem and in the desert monasteries. Theophanes cites reports of this in 809 (AM 6301) and in 813 (AM 6305) (*Chron.* 484, 499). In the wake of the second attack, many fled to Cyprus, continuing from there to Constantinople. Among those coming to the capital at this time were Michael the Synkellos and the two brothers Theodore and Theophanes.

The monastery of Sabas continued to be a doctrinal and theological center of great importance during this period as it had been in the past. It was an important iconodule stronghold in both the eighth and ninth centuries (see below, end of Chap. 2d). Parties in the capital looked for its support in other issues as well. Theodore of Stoudios (d. 838: Amann 1946b), the abbot of the most important monastery in Constantinople at that time, in 809 sent a letter to the above-mentioned abbot Basil (letter 221) in which he requested the support of the Sabaite monks in his struggle against the iconoclast patriarch of Constantinople and the "Synod of Adultery," which had sanctioned the second marriage of Constantine VI.

In his monastic reform Theodore of Stoudios adapted, with modifications and adaptations, the Sabaitic liturgical *Typikon*, but as the main advocate of coenobitism, in terms of monastic life and monastic administration, his chief Palestinian source of inspiration was Dorotheus of Gaza, not the Sabaite system (Leroy 1958, 190).

2

Sabas' Followers in Theological Disputes

A. The Origenist Controversy of the Sixth Century

Introduction

Origen (ca. 185–254) was one of the leading church fathers and one of those who provided philosophical foundations for Christianity. He was among the disciples of Clement of Alexandria in the renowned catechetical school there, and from 203 served as a teacher in it. He led an ascetic life and made do with little. He was fluent in the disciplines of Greek wisdom, and was also familiar with the Jewish religious writings. He regarded all these as aids in understanding Christianity properly. His many treatises are concerned with establishing the correct texts of the Septuagint and the Gospels, which are an essential basis for his interpretations of the scriptures, with a defense of Christianity against its opponents, and with the philosophy of the new religion.

From among the three different ways of interpreting the scriptures—literally, ethically, and spiritually—which are equivalents of the body, the soul, and the spirit, Origen regarded the last method, the allegorical, as the main one. His exegesis of the scriptures was written with this approach and frequently examined theological questions. A different, mainly literal approach, characterizes the biblical interpretation of the Antiochene fathers, such as Apollinarius of Laodicea, Diodorus of Tarsus, and Theodore of Mopsuestia. These different approaches were one of the roots of the controversy between the patriarchates of Alexandria and Antioch.

Origen's writings on the philosophy of the Christian religion, especially his book *De principiis* (Περὶ ἀρχῶν), a systematic exposition of Christian doctrine, are the source of the various Origenist controversies connected with his name, which divided Christianity in the following generations. The four books of this treatise have survived only in fragments that were incorporated into the polemics against him (*ODCC* 981–83; *ODB* 1534).

His followers in subsequent generations sought to find in his philosophical teaching support for different theological issues that arose in the wake of the various disputes that divided the Christian Church: the Trinitarian controversy in the fourth century and the Christological controversy in the fifth and sixth centuries. Thus a split in the Orthodox camp between his followers and his opponents came about.

We are not here concerned with the Origenist controversy of the end of the fourth century and the beginning of the fifth, in which a central role was played in Palestine by Epiphanius and Jerome, against John, the bishop of Jerusalem, and Rufinus, and in Egypt by Patriarch Theophilus against the "Tall Brothers" and the disciples of Didymus the Blind and Evagrius Ponticus. This controversy, in which two groups of Latin monks took an active part—one from Bethlehem and the other from the Mount of Olives—did not have a direct bearing upon the later controversy. Our survey, which is devoted to the controversy of the fifth and sixth centuries, will focus mainly on the events in Palestine. A discussion of the theological and philosophical background of the controversy would exceed the scope of this book.

(a) *Information about the Origenists in Palestine in the Fifth Century*

Under pressure from Theophilus, the patriarch of Alexandria (385–412), the Origenist monks of Egypt were expelled. They hoped to find refuge in Palestine, where they had come after being expelled from Nitria (399). In a letter to Theophilus in 400, the bishops of Palestine diplomatically replied to him that it was free of Origenists (Jerome, letter 93). A more aggressive anti-Origenist line was proposed by Dionysius, the bishop of Diospolis (ibid., letter 94). There were Origenists, however, in Palestine as well, in especially great numbers around Caesarea. About the middle of the fifth century, Origenists from that region came to the monastery of Euthymius, who sent them away (*V. Euth.* 26, 39.28). But there is no explicit report that Euthymius took a stand against John, the Origenist bishop of Jerusalem until 416, who most probably came *ex officio* to sanctify and dedicate the church of the Theoctistus monastery in 411, even though this encounter between the two is not mentioned by Cyril, for understandable reasons (ibid. 9, 17).[8]

At about the same time, Antipatrus, the bishop of Bostra (from 455), wrote an important treatise against Origen, which has not survived. During the sixth century, however, it was used by the monks of the Great Laura in their struggle against the Origenists (*V. Sab.* 84, 189). Euthymius maintained contact with Antipatrus, who ordained one of his disciples, Gaianus, as bishop of Medaba (*V. Euth.* 34, 52–53).

(b) *The Controversy of the Sixth Century*

The Origenist controversy burst out again in full force in Palestine only in the sixth century.[9] The freedom of action enjoyed there by the supporters of Origen at the beginning of the century, as compared with Syria, is indicated by the fact that Stephen Bar-Sudaili, a monk from Edessa, found refuge in a monastery close to Jerusalem, after having been forced to flee from his city. This took place between the years 509 and 512 during the time of Patriarch Elias (494–516). Jacob of Sarug wrote him a letter of reproach, and Philoxenus warned two priests from Edessa against his teachings (Duchesne 1925, 158–60; Perrone 1980, 205; Vööbus 1988, 151–60). Stephen Bar-Sudaili was a keen philosopher who presumably spent some time in the Academy of Athens and in Alexandria. He wrote his works, which were known in Palestine, in Syriac.[10] They are also mentioned by John Scholasticus, a leader of the neo-Chalcedonians, and eventually the

[8] My thanks to Leah Di Segni for drawing my attention to this point.

[9] The basic study of this subject is that of Diekamp 1899, which was used by all the other scholars whose works I consulted for the following survey: Duchesne 1925, 156–218; Fritz 1932, 1574–88; Schwartz 1939, 387–408; Stein-Palanque 1949, 392–95, 633–38, 654–69, 683–90; Festugière 1962b, 134–36; Perrone 1980, 203–22.

[10] For the publication of parts of his writings, see M. Frothingham, *Stephan Bar Sudaili the Syrian Mystic and the Book of Hierotheos* (Leiden 1886).

bishop of Scythopolis (538–543), who wrote an anti-Origenist treatise (*scholia*) (Flusin 1983, 25–29), and by George of Scythopolis, who wrote an introduction to the Syriac translation of the writings of Pseudo-Dionysius.

We do not possess any concrete information on whether Bar-Sudaili had any tangible influence upon the activities and beliefs of the Origenist movement that sprang up in the Judean desert. Shortly after he arrived in Jerusalem, however, there are reports for the first time of Nonnus and his group (514). Seemingly this group drew directly from the teachings of Origen, rather than from the teachings of Bar-Sudaili. Two subjects concerned them: the preexistence of the soul prior to the body and the general reformation of the world in the End of Days, when all would be purified through the transmigration of souls and would resemble Christ.

Phase I: From the Beginning of the Origenist Settlement in the New Laura until the
     Death of Sabas (514–532)

The main source for the Origenist controversy in Palestine in the sixth century is the work of Cyril of Scythopolis (Flusin 1983, 76–83). Since this is a hostile source, its testimony should be regarded critically. The New Laura was the bastion of the Origenist monks, and their heresy spread from there, but there was no direct connection between this heresy and the revolts of the monks against Sabas in the preceding years. At the same time, however, we can easily understand that Origenist ideas would be better absorbed by monks who had a broad secular education, and as such tended toward the Origenist teachings of Nonnus in the New Laura. The members of his group were defined by Cyril as οἱ λογιώτεροι, "the more educated" (*V. Cyr.* 14, 230.31; *V. Sab.* 83, 188.18 and note of Festugière 1962b, 118, n. 279). Those rebelling against Sabas were defined by Cyril as οἱ γεννάδες, "the noble" or "distinguished ones" (*V. Sab.* 35, 121.2, 122.21), and they probably received a proper, broad education due to their distinguished lineage.

In 514, when Sabas' disciple Agapetus was elected *hegoumenos* of the New Laura, he discovered in the community four Origenist monks who had been accepted by Paul, his predecessor in the post, which he had held for only six months before fleeing from there to Arabia because of the great burden of his responsibilities in office (*V. Sab.* 36, 124–25). The four were headed by Nonnus, a native of the province of Palestine. The others were Leontius of Byzantium (see below), Domitian, who would eventually become the abbot of the monastery of Martyrius, and Theodore Ascidas. Fearing that their heresy would spread, Agapetus expelled them from the New Laura, with the permission and on the counsel of Patriarch Elias and probably with the blessings of Sabas, his teacher and the archimandrite of the laurites. Those expelled went to the lowlands (πεδίας), the region of Eleutheropolis and Ascalon (which during the time of Epiphanius, at the end of the fourth century, had been specifically an anti-Origenist bastion, and which had now become a Monophysite one, in which the influence of the patriarch of Jerusalem was weak), and continued their proselytizing there. Sometime later, after Patriarch Elias had been deposed (Sept. 1, 516), Nonnus and his fellows came to Jerusalem and requested from the new patriarch, John (516–524), permission to return to the New Laura. The latter summoned Sabas and Agapetus, who emphatically refused. Agapetus went so far as to express his readiness to leave the Laura himself and not to permit the return of the

Origenists. The patriarch accordingly rejected their request, and they returned to the lowlands.

Agapetus administered the New Laura for five years. When he died the monks chose Mamas to head the laura; he secretly accepted Nonnus and his group back into the New Laura (520). They committed themselves to refrain from acting openly in the laura to promote their Origenist ideas. This commitment was maintained as long as Sabas was alive. The Origenist activity at that time was so clandestine that Leontius of Byzantium managed to be included in the entourage of Sabas during his trip to the imperial court in 531. It was only there, incidental to disputes with the Monophysites, that his Origenist philosophy was revealed and he was sent away from Sabas and remained in the capital (*V. Sab.* 74, 179).

Phase II: From the Death of Sabas to the Death of Melitas (Dec. 532–Sept. 537)

After the death of Sabas, Nonnus' group came into the open and began to promote his teachings, not only among the more educated (οἱ λογιώτεροι) in the New Laura but also in the monastery of Martyrius, which was headed at that time by Domitian, one of the members of the group. This also occurred in the laura of Firminus, where Firminus, the founder of the laura, and his successor Sozomen, both disciples of Sabas, had already died. Within a short time the Origenist heresy also penetrated into the Great Laura and the other desert monasteries (*V. Sab.* 83, 187–89). In the Old Laura, Cyriacus resisted Nonnus' attempt to take control of it by the appointment of Peter of Alexandria, one of his group, as the abbot of the monastery. The monks rejected him. A second attempt in which Nonnus sought to appoint another Origenist, Peter the Greek, as abbot of the monastery, also failed. Instead of him the monks elected Cassianus of Scythopolis, from the Great Laura, who served as the abbot of the monastery of Souka from 538 to September 546 (*V. Sab.* 88, 196; Festugière 1963, 48 n. 44).

In the meantime the Origenist lobby had grown in the capital, where it championed the pro-Chalcedonian camp against the Monophysites. Leontius of Byzantium (*V. Cyr.* 14, 232), who had been expelled by Sabas during his trip to Constantinople in 531, was joined by Domitian and Theodore Ascidas, who according to Cyril was the *exarchos* (ἔξαρ-χος) of the monks of the New Laura.[11] With Leontius acting as go-between, the group joined the circle of the priest (πάπας) Eusebius, who enjoyed great influence at the court of Justinian (*V. Sab.* 83, 188–89). In 536 they participated, as the representatives of the monks, in the Constantinopolitan Synod which confirmed the deposition of Patriarch Anthimus. In the wake of their aggressively pro-Chalcedonian stance, the new patriarch, Menas, appointed Domitian as bishop of Ancyra, the capital of Galatia, and Theodore Ascidas as bishop of Caesarea, the capital of Cappadocia (Schwartz 1939, 390–91). As a result of the increase in their power, the Origenist heresy spread throughout all of Palestine.

Phase III: From the Appointment of Cassianus to the Anti-Origenist Decree of Justinian (Sept. 537–Feb. 543)

The Origenist heresy had already penetrated the Great Laura of Sabas during the time

---

[11] For the meaning of this title of Theodore Ascidas, see above, Part IV, n. 10.

of Melitas, Sabas' successor (Dec. 532–Sept. 537). The Origenists were opposed by Gelasius, and immediately upon his appointment as abbot of the Laura, he formed an opposing camp, which included John the Hesychast, Eustathius (a calligrapher of Galatian origin), Stephen of Jerusalem, and Timothy the Gabalenean, who would later go to Scetis in Egypt. They summoned all the monks of the Laura to the church (*V. Sab.* 84, 189–90), where Gelasius ordered read to them the treatise by Antipatrus of Bostra against the teachings of Origen. As a result, an uproar erupted in the church. The leader of the rebels was John of Antioch, deacon and precentor of the Laura, who had been deposed from his position because of his heresy. John had led the group of Origenists in the Laura, which used to meet secretly and enlist additional supporters for their teachings. It also included John the Thunder-Demon, Ptolemaius, and others, and numbered about forty people. As a result of the disorder in the church, the Origenists were expelled from the Laura, and went to the New Laura (Sept. 537), joining Nonnus and Leontius of Byzantium, who had returned there from the capital.

Leontius, who bore a grudge against Sabas for having expelled him from his entourage in 531, attempted to incite the others to go to the Great Laura to destroy it. To this end he gathered into the New Laura Origenists from all parts; however, his attempt to include in this the monks of the monastery of Theodosius, which was headed at the time by Sophronius the Armenian, failed.[12] After mobilizing the people, the Origenists began to collect weapons: plowshares, spades, iron poles, and similar agricultural tools taken from the farmers. Then the rebels headed for the Laura, intending to raze it to the ground. This is the testimony of Cyril, which apparently is exaggerated.

Cyril attributes the failure of the violent campaign to a miracle: despite the early morning hour, darkness fell upon the land, accompanied by thunderstorms—this was probably a cloudy, foggy winter day. The attackers went on their way, and found themselves the following day next to the monastery of Marcianus, close to Bethlehem, quite a distance from the Great Laura, tired and broken. Thus the planned attack failed.

Liberatus (*Brev.* 23, 1046; Duchesne 1925, 170–71; Fritz 1932, 1575) relates that at the beginning of 540, when Pelagius, the *apokrisiarios* (legate) of the pope in Constantinople, passed through Palestine on his way to the Council of Gaza,[13] he received from the monks passages from the writings of Origen which they asked him to denounce in the capital. Pelagius gave them to the emperor, requesting that he thereby attack his rival in the capital, Theodore Ascidas.

Leontius sought other ways to return the expelled Origenists to the Great Laura. He sought the aid of the *papas* Eusebius, the above-mentioned priest of the Great Church of Constantinople, whom he had known from the time he had been in the capital during the colloquia against the Monophysites. On his way back to the capital from the Council

---

[12] At the end of *V. Theod.* by Theodore of Petra, 70.10, there is an addition not included in the original eulogy, which relates that Theodosius was an anti-Origenist. See Festugière 1963, 141 n. 25. This composition, which is mainly a eulogy, was edited before its publication ca. 555.

[13] The Council of Gaza, which was held at the end of 539 or the beginning of 540 (Schwartz 1939, 401 n. 3; Stein 1944, 179; Stein-Palanque 1949, 383 ff; Festugière 1962b, 134–35; Perrone 1980, 206; cf. Diekamp 1899, 42–45), did not deal with the Origenist controversy. Paul, the patriarch of Alexandria, was deposed there, because of his execution of a deacon who opposed him. See Duchesne 1925, 170–96.

of Gaza, Eusebius passed through Jerusalem, and Leontius presented to him the monks expelled from the Great Laura. They complained to him about Gelasius, charging him with splitting the community by expelling them, while he showed kindness to their opponents. According to Cyril, the Origenist controversy, which constituted the background to the expulsion, was not mentioned, and Eusebius was not aware of this; however, it is difficult to believe this. At any rate, Eusebius regarded the act of expulsion as a distortion of justice and as favoritism, and he asked Gelasius to demonstrate the same attitude toward the two camps: either to recall the expelled monks or to expel their rivals as well. He hoped thereby to bring an end to the dispute. As a result of his pressure and after the fathers had conferred, they decided to bring about a certain balance and expel from the Laura a few leaders of the opposing party: Stephen of Jerusalem, Timothy the Gabalenean, and four additional monks who had taken an active part in the gathering in the church that had led to the expulsion of the Origenists.

These expelled monks had no choice but to accept the decree. Since they obtained no relief from the patriarch of Jerusalem, they turned to Antioch, reported to Patriarch Ephraim what had happened, and brought to his attention the treatise by Antipatrus of Bostra. Ephraim convened a council against the Origenists (between 540 and 541) and placed a ban on their opinions (*V. Sab.* 85, 191–92). When the news of this reached Jerusalem, it aroused the ire of Nonnus and his group, and with the help of Leontius of Byzantium, who had once again left the New Laura and returned to Constantinople, and with that of Domitian and Theodore Ascidas, they sought to bring about a break between Jerusalem and Antioch in that Patriarch Peter would expunge the name of Patriarch Ephraim from the holy diptychs. In order to withstand the pressure from the capital, Peter secretly turned to Sophronius the Armenian, the head of the monastery of Theodosius, and to Gelasius, the head of the Great Laura, who, as successors of Theodosius and of Sabas, also were archimandrites of the coenobites and laurites, and forced them to write and send him a pamphlet (*libellus*) against the Origenists (ibid. 191.25–192.2), which would also contain an appeal not to strike Ephraim's name from the holy diptychs, as well as a report on the disorders and irregularities caused by the Origenists. Upon receiving the *libellus* (which was not survived), Peter sent it to the emperor accompanied by a letter in which he described the radical doctrines of the Origenists that were to be denounced. During this period (542 CE), the anti-Origenist struggle was joined by Cyriacus, who returned from his place of seclusion in Sousakim to the Old Laura and lived for five years in the cell of Chariton. John the Hesychast from the Great Laura kept in close contact with him (*V. Cyr.* 11–14, 229–32).

Another anti-Origenist bastion in Palestine was in Beth Shean (Scythopolis): during the years 538–543 the metropolitan John Scholasticus wrote an important anti-Origenist essay, *Scholia in Corpus Areopagiticum* (*CPG* 6852). Cyril of Scythopolis was greatly influenced by the writings of this educated bishop (Flusin 1983, 25–29).

After Justinian received from Peter the *libellus* of the monks and the passages given him by the *apokrisiarios* Pelagius, he published, in January 543, an edict against the teachings of Origen: *Edictum Contra Origenem* (*CPG* 6880; ed. E. Schwartz, *ACO* III, pp. 189–214). Menas, the patriarch of Constantinople, consented to the edict by signing it, together with the other participants in a home synod (σύνοδος ἐνδημοῦσα) convened on the emperor's order, in which a ban was declared on Origen and his heretical doctrine, formulated in ten clauses. The emperor also ordered that the decisions of the synod be sent throughout the empire for the signature of all the other bishops and abbots. Justinian also established that in the future no one would be allowed to be appointed bishop or abbot unless he would first sign the ban against the heretics against Orthodoxy—the leaders of the Monophysites—and against Origen and his heresies. Domitian, now the bishop of Ancyra, and Theodore Ascidas, now the bishop of Caesarea in Cappadocia, were also compelled to sign the edict. But when Domitian learned that there were Origenists who had succeeded in hiding and refraining from signing, he was so grief-stricken that he shaved his beard, cut himself off from the Church, and eventually died in Constantinople of a serious disease. Theodore Ascidas renewed his struggle against the Orthodox, despite his signature, this time from another direction, attempting to denounce the "Three Chapters" (see below).

When the edict against Origen was published in Jerusalem (Feb. 543), it was signed by all the bishops of Palestine (except Alexander, the bishop of Abila) and all the heads of the desert monasteries (*V. Sab.* 86, 192). In protest, the heads of the Origenist movement, monks from the New Laura, withdrew from the Catholic Church,[14] left their Laura, and went to the lowlands (εἰς τὴν πεδιάδα). These were the monks Nonnus, Peter, John (the latter two would eventually become secretaries, *synkelloi*, of the patriarch of Jerusalem), Callistus, Anastasius, and others.

Phase IV: The Strengthening of the Origenists in Jerusalem and in the Desert (543–547)

In the meantime, two of the supporters of the Origenists in Palestine died in the capital: the *papas* Eusebius and Leontius of Byzantium, in addition to Domitian. Theodore Ascidas, however, attained tremendous influence at the imperial palace, being a member of Theodora's entourage. By means of the *apokrisiarioi* of the church of the Holy Sepulcher in the capital, he sent to Peter of Jerusalem a threat that if he did not order the return of the secessionists to the New Laura and appease them, he would take action in the capital to depose him from his post as patriarch. Following his advice, at the same time Nonnus and his group sent a letter to Peter in which they demanded that he publish a declaration cancelling "every ban which was not decreed to the Lord's desire," with the allusion being to the ban against Origen. Initially Peter refused to do so, but since he feared Ascidas' plotting and in an attempt to gain time, he summoned from the coastal lowlands Nonnus and his followers and told them what they wanted to hear, and then they agreed to return to the New Laura (*V. Sab.* 86, 192–93).

When Peter arrived in the capital, with the intent of strengthening his position, bringing with him an additional *libellus* by Gelasius and others in favor of the "Three Chapters," he was compelled by Theodore Ascidas to denounce them and to take as secretaries (*synkelloi*) two Origenists: Peter of Alexandria and John the Round. As *hegou-*

---

[14] These are the words of Cyril. In the region of Eleutheropolis there was an important Monophysite center during and after the Council of Chalcedon; however, the Origenists all supported the Acts of Chalcedon, and in practice were among the leading spokesmen of the neo-Chalcedonian camp in 536. The withdrawal from the Catholic Church of which Cyril speaks is probably to be understood as an attempt to break away from the authority of the patriarch of Jerusalem and not as joining the Monophysites. Cf. also the statement of Cyril in chap. 90, which speaks of the withdrawal of the Origenists from the Catholic Church in the wake of the censure of 553 and the attempts of Patriarch Eustochius to return them to the Church.

menos of the Nea Church, which was dedicated in the same year, he appointed John the Eunuch, the abbot of the monastery of Martyrius.

The degree to which the Origenist teachings had spread among the monks can be learned from the writings of Cyril, who at that time (November 543; see Stein 1944, 172–74) had left his home in Scythopolis on his way to Jerusalem, for the dedication of the Nea Church, and to the desert monasteries. Cyril relates that due to the Origenist plague that had spread among the monks of Jerusalem, his mother ordered him to turn to John the Hesychast, who would serve as his teacher and guide, and prevent him from being carried away by this heresy (*V. Euth.* 49, 71.20–27; *V. John Hes.* 20, 216.11–15).

During that year, despite the anti-Origenist edict of Justinian, under pressure from Theodore Ascidas and his influence in the capital and the imperial court, the Origenists' strength increased in Jerusalem. They now spread their teachings with increased vigor and plotted in various ways against the fathers of the Great Laura. They pursued the monks of the Laura who came to Jerusalem, and caused their removal from the city with deprecatory cries—"Sabaite"—and blows. The Bessoi,[15] who came from the monasteries near the Jordan, came to the aid of the Sabaite monks. Thus street fights broke out in Jerusalem, with the Bessoi, the Sabaites, and the other opponents of the Origenists being repelled and forced to find refuge in the hostelry of the Great Laura. The attackers also fell upon it, smashed its windows with stones, and brutally stoned those dwelling within. In this fighting a Bessic monk named Theodulus especially excelled. He went out by himself, and with blows with a pitchfork succeeded in repelling the attackers, about three hundred in number; in the end, however, he was struck by a rock and died a few days later.

In light of the serious deterioration in the state of affairs, the fathers of the Great Laura implored Gelasius to go himself to the capital and report to the emperor what was happening. Before his departure he assembled the fathers in the church of the Laura and ordered them not to accept supporters of Theodore of Mopsuestia, the author of one of the "Three Chapters." He also expressed his sorrow that, under pressure from Patriarch Peter, he had signed the *libellus* of the monks of the desert in their favor (*V. Sab.* 87, 194.24–25), which the emperor had refused to accept, even imposing a ban on Theodore of Mopsuestia, one of the leading Antiochene teachers.

When Gelasius arrived in the capital, his mission was hampered by Theodore Ascidas, who, relying on Gelasius' signature on the *libellus* against imposing a ban on Theodore of Mopsuestia, took steps so that he would not be received in the palace, by the patriarch, or even in the orphanage where he was supposed to stay while in the capital (Festugière 1962b, 125 n. 292). His mission was therefore futile, and Gelasius encountered closed doors everywhere. Therefore, after a short stay he decided to return to Palestine on foot; on the way, he died in Amorium in Greater Phrygia (Oct. 546).

---

[15] According to Milik (1960–61, end of n. 1), the Bessoi were Iberians (Georgians), while according to Festugière (1962b, 124 n. 291), the Bessoi were descendants of a Thracian tribe who served as a separate unit in the imperial army. Milik's suggestion seems to me more persuasive. In the 5th and 6th centuries there were relatively large numbers of them in Palestine, and they established a monastery in Soubibes near the Jordan (*Pratum* 157, 3025). They constituted an important component in the community of Theodosius' monastery, and one of the four churches of the monastery, in which they prayed in their own tongue, was established for them (Theod. Petr., *V. Theod.* 18, 45). It is related of the three heads of the monastery in Sinai that they knew many languages, including Bessas (Antonini Placentini, *Itinerarium* 37: CCSL 175, 148; 171).

When the news reached the Laura, all the fathers went to the patriarch in Jerusalem, requesting from him a new *hegoumenos*, but on the orders of the *synkelloi* (the Origenist secretaries of the patriarch), they were sent away with blows and insults and were forced to return to the Laura. The Origenists reached the pinnacle of their success, and after many intrigues succeeded in appointing as *hegoumenos* an Origenist named George, whom they brought to the Laura accompanied by a strong military guard (Feb. 547).

In the wake of these events, many of the fathers dispersed to other monasteries. John the Hesychast came forth from his cell of seclusion (τὸ ἐγκλειστήριον) after many years in isolation and went to the Mount of Olives (which ca. 150 years previously had been the Origenist bastion of Rufinus and Melania the Elder). Many left the Laura in his footsteps, scattering throughout the countryside (κατὰ τὰς χώρας). But at the same time a turning point occurred in the fortunes of the Origenists. Cyril mentions that on the same day in which the fathers left the Great Laura, Nonnus, the head of the Origenists, suddenly died (Feb. 547). Following this, a split occurred in this camp, and even in the capital things took a turn for the worse against them (see below).

George served as the head of the Great Laura for only seven months, and was deposed by the Origenists themselves on charges of debauchery and licentiousness (*V. Sab.* 88, 196). Following the counsel of the patriarch, the fathers remaining in the Laura elected as *hegoumenos* Abba Cassianus of Scythopolis, one of Sabas' disciples, who from 538 had served as head of the Old Laura. He also did not live long, and died eight months later (July 29, 548). Abba Conon was elected to succeed him (*V. Sab.* 89, 196).

Phase V: From the Death of Nonnus to the Council of Constantinople
(Feb. 547–March 553)
After the death of Nonnus, a split developed in the Origenist camp between the monks of the laura of Firminus and the monks of the New Laura (*V. Sab.* 89, 197). The former were called by their opponents *protoktistoi* (πρωτόκτιστοι)—believers in the preexistence of the soul—or *tetraditai* (τετραδίται),[16] while the monks of the New Laura were called by their opponents *isochristoi* (ἰσόχριστοι) (equal to Christ), since they believed that at the time of the reformation of the world (ἀποκατάστασις), all people will become equal to Christ (ἴσοι τῷ χριστῷ) and will be redeemed (Festugière 1962b, 127 n. 298; Evagrius Scholasticus, *HE* IV.38), a position denied by the *protoktistoi*.

Theodore Ascidas, formerly a monk of the New Laura, became the patron of the *isochristoi* and appointed many of them as bishops in Palestine. He also appointed Theodore, the head of the New Laura, as the guardian of the cross and metropolitan of Scythopolis. The *protoktistos* camp was headed by Isidore, the head of the laura of Firminus. He formed an alliance with Abba Conon, the head of the Great Laura, against the *isochristoi*, and they went together to Constantinople to act together against Theodore Ascidas (Sept. 552) (Stein 1944, 176–77).[17]

Despite the attacks by Ascidas, this time Abba Conon had the upper hand (*V. Sab.* 90, 198–200). Shortly after their arrival in the capital, Patriarch Peter died in Jerusalem

[16] The source of this name presumably lies in their custom of fasting on Easter, as on Wednesdays. See Festugière 1962b, 127 n. 297.
[17] Chitty 1966, 129 n. 39, erroneously dates the journey to the end of 551, despite his referring to Stein, 1944, who dates this journey to Sept. 552.

(Oct. 552), and the monks of the New Laura crowned as his successor, without authority, Macarius, leading to the outbreak of a riot in Jerusalem. The emperor, who regarded this as a violation of his authority and his position as head of the entire Church, became angry with Ascidas and the *isochristoi,* and ordered that Macarius be deposed (he served a second time, for a period lasting about twenty years, beginning only in 563/4, after he abandoned his Origenist opinions [Evagrius, *HE* iv.39]). Conon and his fellows took advantage of the opportunity, made contact with the emperor (end of 552), and gave him a memorandum listing the main elements of the isochrist heresy (*V. Sab.* 90, 198.14–17). This memorandum (not preserved) was before the participants at the Fifth Ecumenical Council in Constantinople (see below) and guided them in formulating the bans against Origen and his supporters (Evagrius, ibid.). In the meantime Isidore died, but the favor of the emperor toward Conon and the anti-Origenists increased. Under their influence, he appointed as patriarch of Jerusalem Eustochius (Dec. 552–563/4), the *oikonomos* of the Patriarchate of Alexandria, who at the time was in Constantinople.[18] The emperor also ordered the convening in the capital of an ecumenical council to whose participants he sent a letter, *Epistula ad Synodum de Origene* (*CPG* 6886; PG 88.1, 989–93), which includes fifteen chapters of bans against Origen and his disciples, requesting that they confirm them by signature.

Under pressure from the emperor, many of the *isochristoi* were forced to abandon their previous opinions. Especially striking is the case of Theodore, the former head of the New Laura, who in 548 was appointed metropolitan of Scythopolis under pressure from Theodore Ascidas. The change that took place in his views is reflected in the treatise he sent at the end of 552 to Justinian and the archbishops, "Pamphlet of the Errors of Origen" (*Libellus de erroribus Origenis, CPG* 6993; PG 86.1, 232–36), containing twelve chapters (see Perrone 1980, 213–14; Flusin 1983, 20–21). He thereby followed in the path of his predecessor as metropolitan, John Scholasticus. Diekamp (1899) proposed that Theodore took this step in order to ensure his participation in the council that was about to convene in the capital.

Abba Conon sent Eustochius to Jerusalem and requested that upon his arrival he send to Constantinople, as aide, Eulogius, the successor of Sophronius the Armenian (died Mar. 21, 542) as head of the monastery of Theodosius, so that he too would participate in the council about to be convened. Eustochius did so, and also sent with him Cyriacus, from the laura of the "Spring," a Stylite monk named Pancratius, and three bishops who would represent him at the council.

The Fifth Ecumenical Council opened on May 5, 553, after a long delay; its main topic was the issue of the "Three Chapters": the writings of Theodore of Mopsuestia, Theodoret of Cyrrhus, and Ibas of Edessa. About two months previously, in March 553, the bishops who had already arrived in the capital issued, at the request of the emperor, a ban with fifteen canons against Origen and his teachings, *Canones XV (Contra Origenem sive Origenistas)* (ed. J. Straub, *ACO* iv.1, pp. 248–49), within the framework of a special convocation, a home synod (σύνοδος ἐνδημοῦσα). The ecumenical council itself did not,

---

[18] Eustochius fled to Constantinople from Alexandria after having been accused there of embezzlement. See Festugière 1962b, 129 n. 300; Stein-Palanque 1949, 629.

as was stated, deal with the matter of the Origenists, but the participants in the council added their names at the end of canon 11 of the council, which included a long list of heretics, including Arius and Nestorius, upon whom a ban was to be placed.[19] When the decisions of the council reached Palestine, they were ratified in writing and orally by all the bishops except Alexander, the bishop of Abila, who had also refused to sign the previous edict of Justinian against the Origenists in 543. This time Alexander was deposed, and he eventually died in an earthquake in Byzantium.

Phase VI: The Defeat of the Origenists (June 553–Feb. 555)

As a result of the new state of affairs, in which the inhabitants of the New Laura withdrew from the Catholic Church (see n. 14 above), the patriarch unsuccessfully attempted, during the course of eight months, to persuade them to return. Finally, relying on the edicts of the emperor and aided by Anastasius, the *dux Palaestinae*, he expelled them from the New Laura and from the Diocese of Jerusalem (autumn 554), settling in their stead 120 Orthodox monks: 60 from the Great Laura, including John, the former Scholarius, who was appointed head of the community, and 60 from the other monasteries of the desert. These included Cyril of Scythopolis, who was taken from the coenobium of Euthymius on the recommendation of John the Hesychast.

The Origenist controversy in Palestine came to an end with the repopulation of the New Laura. Also in later years, however, during the period of Pope Gregory the Great (590–604), mention is made of the incessant battles between the patriarch of Jerusalem and the Nea monastery, presumably the Nea Laura (Duchesne 1925, 215; for Origenist tendencies in the 6th century in the Gaza area, see Canivet 1965). There is also an echo of the struggle in an anecdote of John Moschus (*Pratum* 177, 3048): a monk who came to the Ennaton (the famous monastery at the ninth mile from Alexandria) seeking to live in the cell of Evagrius Ponticus eventually committed suicide, and John Moschus is not surprised at this, for Origenism leads to a loss of one's way.

(c) *Sabas' Monks in the Origenist Controversy: John the Hesychast and Leontius of Byzantium*

The Origenist struggle in the sixth century erupted beyond the bounds of the New Laura and spread in all directions only after the death of Sabas. Sabas' disciples constituted the front line in the struggle against the Origenists, and the Great Laura was one of the important bastions over which they sought to gain control and almost succeeded. The anti-Origenist treatises written by the desert monks headed by those of the Great Laura, which have not survived, constituted the basis for the two bans against the Origenists. First, the *libellus* of Gelasius and Sophronius the Armenian, written at the request of Peter, the patriarch of Jerusalem, influenced the formulation of Justinian's edict of 543, which contained ten chapters. The letter of the emperor to Menas, which was the basis of this edict, also included citations from Origen's famous treatise Περὶ ἀρχῶν (which is

---

[19] This is the reconstruction of the events proposed by Diekamp 1899, 66–77, and see also Fritz 1932, 1579–88, even though the impression is gained in some of the sources, such as Cyril of Scythopolis (*V. Sab.* 90, 199), Evagrius (*HE* IV.38), and others, that the ban of the Origenists was one of the topics occupying the participants in the council and that it was decided upon there. Indeed, in the protocols of the council there is no evidence of this, and Origen's name is mentioned only at the end of the list of heretics, in the 11th canon of the council.

not extant), which was to be condemned. Apparently these citations were also derived from the memorandum of the Palestinian monks (Fritz 1932, 1578). Second, the *libellus* of Conon influenced the formulation of the fifteen canons of the ban of 553. Flusin (1983, 76–83) proposes the existence of an additional Sabaite composition, which has not survived but is alluded to in Cyril's statements (*V. Sab.* 89, 197.10–13). This was a writ of condemnation (λόγος στηλιτευτικός) against the two Origenist factions which, according to Cyril, was written by a number of people from the Great Laura close to the time of the writing of the *Vita Sabae* (556 CE). In Flusin's opinion (1983, 83), long passages attributed by Cyril to Cyriacus were derived from this composition.

Memoranda regarding the Origenist controversy were sent by the monks to the West as well. All this indicates the scope and depth of the literary-theological creativity of the desert monks, especially those of the Great Laura, the disciples of Sabas. It also indirectly sheds some light on the contents of the library that was at the disposal of the monks in their literary activity (see also above, Part III, Chap. 1E).

John the Hesychast (454–559)
Among the leaders of the anti-Origenist camp, besides the heads of the Great Laura Gelasius and Conon, Cyril mentions the names of Eustathius the Galatian, Stephen of Jerusalem, Timothy the Gabalanean, and John the Hesychast (*V. Sab.* 84, 189). The last was a revered paragon and holy man, the spiritual guide of Cyril, who wrote his biography.

John spent fifty-six of his 105 years in *hesychia* (ἡσυχία) in the Great Laura and was therefore known as "John the Hesychast." *Hesychia* has a double meaning: tranquility and silence. It is like still water, which permits both reflection and looking deeply.[20] It describes a mood of inner tranquility and quietness, which are the consequence of overcoming one's urges. This is an essential requirement for contemplation. The way of life needed to attain this is that of prolonged seclusion in silence in a cell, without leaving it for the church on weekends, as was the custom of regular laura monks. The link with the outside world of the monastery was maintained by means of a disciple or an attendant monk, who would care for the maintenance of the recluse, bring to him the appeals of pilgrims and admirers, and would fulfill various missions for him.[21]

---

[20] Thus in the *Apoph. Pat.*, ed. Nau, *ROC* 13 (1908), 47. See Flusin 1983, 124 p. 43, and above, Part I, n. 40.

[21] The praises of this ascetic method are mentioned by Gregory of Nyssa, Evagrius Ponticus, John Climacus, and others. In Cyril's writings this term and the verb from which it is derived are common mainly in *V. John Hes.* and *V. Euth.*, where it serves to describe the way of life of Euthymius both during the weekdays in his cell and in the desert, during Lent; i.e., *hesychia* does not always mean seclusion for years in a cell. George, the founder of a monastery in Beella near Scythopolis, to whom Cyril sent his composition *V. Sab.*, was also given the title "the Hesychast" by Cyril. See Festugière 1962a; 55 n. 1. Festugière also draws our attention to the fact that Cyril refrained from applying this term to Sabas himself, who was first and foremost a man of action. In the *V. Steph. Sab.*, a *hesychasterion* is a cell of seclusion of an anchorite. In the 14th century there developed on Mount Athos a *hesychia* accompanied by an unceasing repetition of the same prayer in one posture of the body—head bowed, eyes fixed on the heart, and breathing carefully controlled—as a useful means of attaining a vision of the Divine Light. This approach aroused so much opposition that it had to be approved in several church councils that convened in Constantinople. See *ODCC* 644; *ODB* 923–24; and above, Part I, n. 40.

John was born on January 8, 454, in Nicopolis (today Devrighi) in Pontus in the Roman province of Armenia Prima, to a wealthy and noble Christian family whose sons filled important posts in the imperial and urban administration and in the army. In 471, at the age of eighteen, after his parents had died, John began the monastic life in the district in which he had been born. At the beginning of his twenty-eighth year (481), he was ordained as bishop of the city of Colonia, in the same province, but continued the ascetic life of a monk. At the end of nine years in this post, a disagreement broke out between the governor of the province, who was John's brother-in-law, and church officials. John went to Constantinople to deal with church matters, and there, after tending to them, he resolved not to return to his previous post but rather to escape secretly to the Holy Land and live as an anchorite in the desert of the Holy City. After a short stay in Jerusalem he found his way to the Laura of Sabas, guided by a vision.

John arrived at the Great Laura in 491, when he was thirty-eight years old.[22] In 492 he took part with others in building the monastery of Kastellion, and in the second year

[22] There are contradictions in the chronological data adduced by Cyril regarding the first 12 years of John's life in the Laura. In his conclusion (*V. John Hes.* 28, 222), Cyril divides this time into two 6-year periods: a period of service in various offices, and a period of seclusion. A careful examination of the data reveals, however, that this is an artificial division, which does not hold up under examination. The chronology of John's "career" can be reconstructed as follows:

(a) His arrival in the Great Laura: in the first year of Anastasius' reign and the 14th year of the indiction (*V. John Hes.* 5, 204), i.e., between April 11, 491 (the date of Zeno's death) and Aug. 31, 491, the end of the indiction year. Upon his arrival Sabas gave him over to the *oikonomos* of the Laura, and as one of the novices, he would carry water from the stream, cook for the builders, and help them in transporting stones and in the other construction work of the hostelry of the Laura, which was being built at the time.

(b) The first year of his stay in the Laura is to be counted as the first complete indiction year in which he stayed there, i.e., Sept. 1, 491–Aug. 31, 492. In this period he took part in the construction of the monastery of Kastellion (ibid. 6, 205).

(c) In the second year of his stay in the Laura he was elected to serve as the official in charge of the hostelry and the cook of the Laura, a position he held for only one year: Sept. 1, 492–Aug. 31, 493. This was the first year of a new indiction (ibid. 6, 205–6).

(d) For 3 years he lived as a cell dweller: Sept. 1, 493–Aug. 31, 496 (years 2–4 of the indiction) (ibid. 7, 207).

(e) On Sept. 1, 496, he was elected *oikonomos* of the Laura (ibid. 7, 207), a position he filled for three years, i.e., until Aug. 31, 499 (years 5–7 of the indiction). Afterwards, when Sabas failed to ordain him as a priest, he began to live as a recluse.

(f) The first period of seclusion lasted ca. 4 years until the 11th year of the indiction (ibid. 10–11, 209), when in the wake of Sabas' exile to Scythopolis he also went into exile, to Rouba. The date of his retreat to Rouba would therefore be close to Aug. 31, 503. The chronological data given by Cyril regarding the date of the retreat to Rouba indicate that Sabas' attempt to ordain John as a priest was at the beginning of the 8th year of the indiction, and not as Cyril states (ibid. 8, 207) in the 6th year of the indiction. Accordingly, in the preceding paragraph I allocated to John 3 years in the office of *oikonomos* of the Laura, even though Cyril's statements imply that he presumably served in this office only one year.

(g) Six years of seclusion in the desert of Rouba: Sept. 1, 503–Aug. 31, 509 (ibid. 11, 209). He returned to the Laura in the second year of the indiction (Sept. 1, 508–Aug. 31, 509) (ibid. 14, 212).

(h) The second period of seclusion—from the date of the return from Rouba to the time of the conclusion of *V. John Hes.* by Cyril, in the 104th year of John's life (ibid. 28, 222), i.e., between Jan. 8, 557 and Jan. 8, 558, a count of more than 48 years. Cyril, on the other hand, speaks (ibid.) of 47 years of seclusion in a cell. If we subtract from these 48 years the period in which John was forced to go into exile to the Mount of Olives during the Origenist controversy, a period that could have lasted ca. 1 1/2 years, we arrive at the number given by Cyril.

(i) The date of his death: Jan. 8, 559 (Garitte 1954).

of his stay in the Laura he was chosen to serve as administrator of the hostelry and as cook, a position he filled for one year. Afterwards he lived for three years as a cell dweller, and then he was elected steward of the Laura, which he was for three years. This was a period of growth and prosperity for the laura (*V. John Hes.* 7, 207). Sabas, who recognized his good qualities, wanted to ordain him as a priest then, but when John was brought before Patriarch Elias his secret was revealed: since he was not only a priest but even a bishop, he could not be re-ordained as a priest. From then on John was permitted to live in the Laura as a recluse, exempt from coming to the church on weekends and without contact with anyone except his attendant. He lived in this manner for four years.

In the wake of Sabas' exile to Scythopolis during the second rebellion of the monks against him, John also fled from the rebellious community to the desert of Rouba, during his fiftieth year. He secluded himself there in a cave, engaging in extreme asceticism for six years, and ate mainly *melagria* roots and other wild plants. On occasion one of the brothers from the Laura would join him to receive his aid and guidance in this way of life (ibid. 12, 210). After his return to the Laura, in response to Sabas' entreaties, he lived in *hesychia* as a recluse in his cell (ἐν τῷ κελλίῳ καθείρξεως) for some forty-nine years until his death. This long period of isolation was interrupted in February 547 when the Origenists succeeded by a stratagem in having one of their members appointed *hegoumenos* of the Laura (a position from which he was deposed after seven months). John left his cell of seclusion (τὸ ἐγκλειστήριον) and went to the Mount of Olives, with many others leaving the Laura in his footsteps. The duration of this exile is not known; it is clear, however, that when the Orthodox regained control of the Laura, during the office of Conon, John and many others returned.

During the period of his prolonged isolation, John maintained contact with the outside by means of two disciples, Theodore and John, who once went forth on a mission of his to Livias beyond the Jordan (ibid. 18, 215). By means of other emissaries he corresponded with Cyriacus during the Origenist controversy (*V. Cyr.* 11, 229). They also brought him petitions from pilgrims and then took his messages back to them (*V. John Hes.* 23–24, 218–20). He was also visited frequently by Cyril, who heard from him about Sabas and what was happening in the Laura; John urged Cyril to write the *Lives* of Euthymius and Sabas on the basis of the material he had collected (ibid. 20–21, 216–18). Cyril's parents were among his admirers and were accustomed to send him, his disciples, and other monks of the Laura an annual contribution (ibid. 20, 217). Despite Cyril's close relationship with him and his veneration of him, Cyril does not call himself his disciple. This was not his official standing, and furthermore he regarded himself as a disciple of Sabas (Flusin 1983, 29–30).

John was a paragon and source of encouragement and inspiration to other monks who sought his blessing, prayer, and counsel at times of crisis (*V. John Hes.* 22, 218). He was renowned as a holy man who worked miracles, had healing powers (ibid. 21, 218), and was blessed with the gift of prophecy (ibid. 23–24, 218–20). His fame spread. His admirers, who sought his blessing and guidance, included Aitherios, the metropolitan of Ephesus (Festugière 1963a, 25 n. 50), who was acquainted with that chapter of his life when he still was the bishop of Colonia and brought it to the attention of Sabas and the monks of the Laura (ibid. 15, 213). Another admirer was Basilina, a woman of Cappadocian origin and deaconess of the Great Church in Constantinople,[23] who came to him accompanied by one of her young relatives of "the highest" (μειζότερος) rank, who tended toward the heresy of Severus. John succeeded in returning him to the bosom of Orthodoxy (ibid. 23–24, 218–20).

What is the date of John's death? His memorial day is December 7,[24] but this is not the date of his death. The Greek text of his *Vita* published by Schwartz was written between January 8, 557, and January 8, 558 (Flusin 1983, 32), when John was still alive, in the forty-seventh year of his seclusion in a cell after his return from Rouba (ibid. 28, 222). In the Georgian translation of the *Vita*, however, a later addition is preserved, the work of Cyril himself, which is not found in the extant Greek manuscripts, and which indicates that John died on Wednesday, January 8, a date suitable for the year 559 (Garitte 1954). This therefore was his 105th birthday. Like other saints, he could predict the date of his death, a prediction mentioned in Cyril's addition.

John is included in the list of saints of the Church of Jerusalem. He is identified with one of the saints by this name painted in the burial chapel in the monastery of Kastellion (Mader 1937, 44). In the wall inscriptions in the chapel of the dwelling complex attributed to him by local tradition, preserved among the Mar Saba monks (Figs. 36–39), he is mentioned as a saint. The existence in the eighth century of a tradition preserving the site of his cell is evident in the *Vita Stephani Sabaitae* (Garitte 1959, 368).

The struggle against the Origenists was not the only theological struggle in which John took an active part. Cyril (*V. John Hes.* 27, 221) mentions in extremely concise fashion also his struggle against the teachings of Theodore of Mopsuestia—one of the leading Antiochene theologians and commentators—one of the "Three Chapters" denounced by the Council of Constantinople in 553.

Leontius of Byzantium (ca. 485–544)

The primary sources for our knowledge of the positions of the Origenists on various theological questions are the writings of their opponents: Justinian, Theodore of Scythopolis, Cyril of Scythopolis, and others (Flusin 1983, 77). The writings of Nonnus, the leader of the group, have not survived, but one of its outstanding representatives, Leontius of Byzantium, identified with Leontius the Hermit (ἐρημίτης) or the Monk (μοναχός), is the author of several writings against the Nestorians, the Eutychians, the Aphthartodo-

---

[23] The "Great Church" of Constantinople comprised four churches: Hagia Sophia, Hagia Heleni, Hagios Theodore, and the Church of the Virgin, which was built by Empress Verina. These churches shared a common ecclesiastical administration and a common clergy. See Jones 1964, 900–901.

[24] Garitte (1954, 84 n. 1) notes that to most of the Greek manuscripts of *V. John Hes.*, at the end of Cyril's text, a sentence has been added by another hand, which speaks of the death of John on Dec. 7, without mention of the year. Only in the Greek manuscript from Sinai is it stated that the date of death was Jan. 8. Schwartz was of the opinion that the authenticity of the last datum is doubtful. The Georgian translation, however, indicates that this is indeed the date of his death. The Georgian translation apparently was done by a monk of the monastery of Sabas at the end of the 7th century or the beginning of the 8th, when *V. Sab.* as well was translated into this language. The Georgian manuscript cited by Garitte was copied in the 11th century in the monastery of the Cross and is currently preserved in the British Museum.

The date of Dec. 7 as the date of death is also mentioned in the Greek *synaxaria,* along with other dates such as the 3rd, the 8th, or the 9th of December. It apparently springs from the proximity to the date of Sabas' death on Dec. 5 and the desire to establish memorial days close to each other.

cetes (ἀφθαρτοδοκῆται: the followers of Julian of Halicarnassus), and the Severians. Together with Theodore of Rhaithou and Leontius of Jerusalem, Leontius of Byzantium was one of the three most prominent philosophical theologians of the Justinianic period (Grumel 1926; Rees 1940; Richard 1944; Evans 1970). His writings are: *Adversus Nestorianos et Eutychianos* (PG 86, 1268–1316); *Dialogus contra Aphthartodocetas* (ibid. 1316–57); *Deprehensio et triumphus super Nestorianos* (ibid. 1357–96); *Adversus argumenta Severi = Epilysis* (ibid. 1916–45); *Capitula XXX adversus Severum* (ibid. 1901–16; F. Diekamp, *Doctrina patrum de Incarnatione Verbi* [Münster 1907], 155–64). The first three compositions are three books of one treatise, at times listed together under the first title.

Leontius of Byzantium is not to be confused with three other monks and writers of the same name: the Skythian (Gothic) Leontius, whose language was Latin, and who was involved during the years 518–520 in the struggle against the Monophysites in Constantinople and Rome; the Byzantine Scholasticus Leontius, redactor of the composition *De sectis;* and his contemporary, the important theologian Leontius of Jerusalem.[25]

Schwartz (1939, 388 n. 2, and before him W. Rügamer in 1894) rejected the identification of the Origenist Leontius of Byzantium of Cyril of Scythopolis and the hermit author of the above writings, arguing that the latter was not an Origenist. Richard (1947; and see also Evans 1970; Daley 1976), however, showed that the author of the three-book polemic against the Nestorians and the Eutychians was indeed an Origenist and that this treatise was written in 543 or 544 as a (concealed) protest against the anti-Origenist edict of Justinian. Richard also discovered in one of the manuscripts a remark by an early anti-Origenist reader, identifying an anonymous holy man mentioned by Leontius at the beginning of the treatise with Nonnus, the Origenist leader in Palestine (Richard 1944, 34). Leontius died shortly after the completion of this composition.

He was born ca. 485 (Frend 1972, 207) and went into exile from his birthplace (Constantinople) in order to be a monk in Palestine, where he shook off the Antiochene theology of Diodorus of Tarsus and Theodore of Mopsuestia, under whose influence he had been in Constantinople (Richard 1944, 62–63; Rees 1940), and at some point (ca. 520) he joined Nonnus' group.

As mentioned earlier, Cyril relates that Leontius was a member of Sabas' entourage in his second journey to the capital in 531. During debates with the Monophysites and Severians, his Origenist tendency was revealed, and he was sent away by Sabas. Leontius then remained in Constantinople.

Is he to be identified with the Leontius who participated there in the colloquia convened by Justinian between the Chalcedonians and the Severians in the years 532/3 and

[25] The first comprehensive essay seeking to clarify the identity of Leontius of Byzantium was that of F. Loofs, *Leontius von Byzanz und die gleichnamigen Schriftsteller der griechischen Kirche* (Leipzig 1887). Loofs identified all four of the above-mentioned monks bearing this name as one person, a thesis that he defended until his death in 1928, despite its having aroused many objections. The currently accepted opinion is that these are four different persons, although there still is disagreement about several points, e.g., the identity of the Leontius who participated in the colloquia against the Severians in the capital in the year 532/3, and the one who participated in the council of Menas in 536.

For the Scythian monk, see E. Amann, "Scythes (moines)," *DTC* XIV, 1746–53; Duchesne 1925, 59–69. For the Byzantine Scholasticus Leontius, the supposed author, or actually redactor, of *De Sectis*, see M. Richard, "Le traité *'De Sectis'* et Léonce de Byzance," *RHE* 35 (1939), 695–723; S. Rees, "The *'De Sectis,'* Treatise Attributed to Leontius of Byzantium," *JTS* 40 (1939), 346–60. On Leontius of Jerusalem, see below, n. 27.

with the Leontius who appears in the list of Palestinian monks among the participants of the Council of Menas in 536? We shall first examine the reports regarding the colloquia which, according to Zacharias Rhetor (*HE* IX.15, ed. Brooks, 84), continued for more than a year. The minutes have been preserved of only one meeting (Frend 1972, 265) which lasted for three days between six Syrian bishops and five Chalcedonians (one withdrew due to illness) and their supporters, including also a monk named Leontius who was a legate/emissary (*apokrisiarios*) of the fathers of the Holy City (*ACO* IV.2, 170.5).

At the Council of 536 a monk named Leontius was present at all five sessions, and his signature appears also on additional documents connected with this council (see Schwartz 1939, 390–91). Generally he signed as a monk (μοναχός), abbot (ἡγούμενος), and legate (τοποτηρητής; Lampe 1961, 1398) of the entire desert (*ACO* III, pp. 249–50, Λεόντιος 11). Once he signed as *hegoumenos* and monk in the name of his monastery and in the name of all the holy fathers of the desert and the Jordan (ibid. 5.14, no. 117, 50.30). And in one instance, in which there is a lacuna in the Greek text, the Latin translation adds the title *prior* as an equivalent to the Greek *hegoumenos,* and the Greek continuation mentions his authority to speak in the name of all the holy fathers of the desert (ibid. 12 no. 74, 37.1; see also above, Part IV, end of Chap. 2).[26]

Schwartz (ibid.) is of the opinion that each of these instances refers to the Origenist Leontius of Byzantium. This opinion is held also by Evans (1970, 156–59). Chronologically, this is indeed possible, since Leontius of Byzantium stayed in the capital during these years (531–536). Richard (1947, 64–65), however, wonders whether it is reasonable to assume that shortly after his removal from the entourage of Sabas he was appointed representative of the monks of the Holy City to the colloquia in the capital. The Leontius who participated in the Council of Menas was an abbot, while Leontius of Byzantium, so he argues, was not an abbot of a monastery and therefore not the participant in that council (see also the reservations of Duchesne 1925, 167 on this matter), and in his own writings he defines himself as a hermit.

Schwartz proposed that the appointment of Leontius as the legate of the monks of Palestine was given him by the emperor, and not by the monks themselves or the patriarch, and it was the emperor who appointed him as *hegoumenos* of a small monastery near the capital. Countering these conjectures, which cannot be proved, Richard raises an objection, according to which from 532 Justinian and the theologians in his entourage adhered to a moderate neo-Chalcedonian line, while Leontius remained faithful to the old, severe Chalcedonian doctrine; therefore it is strange to assume that the emperor would choose him specifically to represent the interests of the desert monks in these theological debates. Richard prefers to identify the Leontius who was the representative of the Palestinian monks in the capital with Leontius of Jerusalem (1944, 83–88; 1947, 65).[27] This identification is generally agreed upon (*ODB* 1213).

[26] Granič (1929–30, 26) erred in the equation between *prior,* with the meaning of *deuterarios,* and τοποτηρητής. See Du Cange, *Glossarius Latinitatis,* s.v. *prior.*

[27] Leontius of Jerusalem wrote two compositions against the Monophysites and against the Nestorians: *Contra Monophysitas* (PG 86, 1769–1901) and *Contra Nestorianos* (ibid. 1399–1768). As was mentioned, he, together with Theodore of Rhaithou and Leontius of Byzantium, was one of the three most important philosophical theologians of the Justinianic era. His writings were composed during the second quarter of

The Origenists who did participate in the Council of Menas in 536 were Theodore Ascidas, a representative of the New Laura, and Domitian, abbot of the monastery of Martyrius (Schwartz 1939, 391). Afterwards, under the influence of Leontius of Byzantium on the *papas* Eusebius, they were appointed as bishops of Caesarea in Cappadocia and of Ancyra in Galatia, respectively. In the struggle against the Aposchists, the Orthodox Origenists were no less firm than the representatives of the Laura of Sabas at that council.

B. The Monoenergetic and the Monothelitic Controversies

Some thirty-five years after the expulsion of the Origenists from the New Laura, no doubt with the memory of the event still fresh, John Moschus and Sophronius settled there (ca. 590–603). Both lived for a lengthy period in the monastery of Theodosius as well. Their theological stand of staunch Chalcedonism was nourished by the tradition of Sabas and Theodosius. The synodal letter issued by Sophronius upon his elevation to the patriarchate of Jerusalem (634) is a detailed exposition of this stand. This approach is also evident in the *Pratum* as well as in the sermons, poetical and other liturgical compositions of Sophronius (Schönborn 1972, 99–242). In their two joint visits to Egypt (578 and 608), John and Sophronius served as counselors to the Orthodox patriarchs of Alexandria—Eulogius (581–610) and John Eleemon (610–619)—in their struggle against the Monophysites there. In ca. 629 Sophronius went from the monastery of Theodosius to North Africa, where he headed a community of monks, among whom was Maximus, the future theologian and confessor. Sophronius was his teacher in theology and dogma and his spiritual father (Schönborn ibid. 9, 75).

The religious policy of Heraclius, who already in 624 met with the Monophysite leaders, was to attempt a compromise with them in order to achieve a union in the Church of the East in face of the Persian and Arab threats. This policy was aided by Sergius, the patriarch of Constantinople, and Cyrus, the Orthodox patriarch of Alexandria, who suggested in 633 the Monoenergetic formula, which speaks of two natures and a single energy (μία ἐνέργεια) in Christ. Sophronius opposed this formula, traveling to both capitals in order to abolish it. A temporary compromise was achieved with Sergius, but by the end of 638 the *Ekthesis* (Ἔκθεσις) of Sergius and Heraclius was issued, banning the Monoenergetic formula, while setting up instead the Monotheletic formula, which speaks of a single will (ἓν θέλημα) in Christ. The formula was approved at two church councils in the capital (638 and 639). Sophronius died March 11, 639; the formula was not approved by the Monophysites, and the expected union was not achieved. The main opponent of Monotheletism, first put forward by Pope Honorius I (625–638), was Maximus the Confessor. Among the participants of the first Lateran Synod (649), which addressed the Monothelitic heresy, were refugees from the Great Laura, who had settled

---

the 6th century, seemingly between the years 538 and 544, and at any event not later than 548. He may be defined as a neo-Chalcedonian. The topic of the "Three Chapters," which occupied the Chalcedonians beginning in 544, is not reflected in his writings. His description as a Jerusalemite in the title of his compositions indicates that he was born in Jerusalem or spent some time in the city or in one of the desert monasteries close to it; the treatises themselves, however, apparently were written in Constantinople. His secular education in the sciences is evident in his writings; seemingly in his youth he was in contact with the philosophical schools of Alexandria (Richard 1944).

in the monastery of Sabas in Rome. Monotheletism and its adherents were condemned in 680 by the Sixth Ecumenical Council held in Constantinople.[28]

C. The Dispute Regarding the *Filioque*

This dispute, which took place at the beginning of the ninth century, revolved around the addition that the Western Church had introduced into the text of the Creed. According to the original formula, which had been consolidated at the councils of Nicaea (325) and Constantinople (381), the Holy Spirit proceeded from the Father. To this formula was added the word *filioque* ("and from the Son"), implying a double procession of the Holy Spirit from the Father and the Son. Support for this doctrine can be found in the writings of Jerome, Ambrose, and Augustine, and it is also mentioned in the writings of Cyril of Alexandria, while Theodore of Mopsuestia and Theodoret of Cyrrhus explicitly opposed it.

The original formula of the Creed, on the other hand, reflected the Orthodox doctrine according to which the Holy Spirit proceeded from the Father through the Son, and not from the Father and the Son. Paulinus of Aquileia defended the addition of the *filioque* at the Council of Friuli in 796, and from 800 on this version of the creed was accepted throughout the empire of Charlemagne (*ODCC* 423, 512–13).

The introduction of the new formula to Jerusalem in 807 by the Benedictine monks on the Mount of Olives, originating from the Latin West, aroused great tumult and opposition. The struggle was led by a Sabaite monk named John (Vailhé 1901a, 321–25). On Christmas in the year 808 he incited the faithful to drive out the Benedictine monks from the church of the Nativity in Bethlehem. On the following Sunday he once again stirred up a protest against them in the church of the Holy Sepulcher, and compelled them to make a public confession regarding their faith and their version of the Creed.

To support their formula the Benedictines produced proof from the *Regula* of St. Benedict and from the writings of Athanasius and Gregory the Great. This event led to a certain relaxation, but John did not relent. He rejected their arguments and continued to fan the opposition to and hostility against them in Jerusalem and in the monasteries of the desert, thereby causing Patriarch Thomas to send a letter of complaint to Pope Leo III.

In 809 the Benedictine monks turned for aid to the pope, sending him an epistle in which they described the troubles that had befallen them in the previous year due to John the Sabaite, and they requested his aid and guidance: what was the correct version? They also asked him to bring their application to the attention of Charlemagne, adding that they had heard that in the church at his court the *filioque* version of the Creed also prevailed. Two of the Benedictine monks who had accompanied the delegation of Harun ar-Rashid to Charlemagne learned of the addition during their stay at his court and upon their return introduced it to Jerusalem (Dick 1963, 125).

The pope acceded to their request and sent them a detailed document regarding the Creed of the Church of Rome. He sent a copy of this document, which indicates that

---

[28] Beck 1959, 292–94; Schönborn 1972, 9, 75; Frend 1972, 316–53; F. Winkelmann, "Die Quellen zur Forschung des monoenergetisch-monotheletischen Streites," *Klio* 69 (1987), 515–59.

he did adopt the doctrine that the Holy Spirit proceeded from the Father and the Son, to the emperor, along with a letter requesting that he act to ensure their safety.[29]

Charlemagne imposed upon Theodulf, the bishop of Orleans, the task of writing a treatise on the Holy Spirit, and in November of the same year (809), he convened in Aix-la-Chapelle a church council that ratified the double procession of the Holy Spirit from the Father and the Son, the treatise of Theodulf that formulated this doctrine, and the inclusion of the *filioque* in the Creed.

In December 809 the decisions of the council were sent to the pope along with a letter from the emperor. In January 810 Pope Leo III convened a council at St. Peter's in Rome. The decisions of the Council of Aix-la-Chapelle were read to those present, and the doctrine regarding the double procession of the Holy Spirit was ratified, but the pope strongly objected to changing the text of the Creed and of the symbols of Nicaea and Constantinople. This change had not prevailed in Rome until then, and the pope refused to accept the change ratified by the Council of Aix-la-Chapelle. He recommended that the imperial chapel also adopt the formula that prevailed in Rome. In order to emphasize his position, he ordered that the symbols of Nicaea and Constantinople and the original text of the Creed, without the addition, be engraved on two heavy silver tablets which he installed in the tomb of Peter. The churches of France slowly adopted the position of the pope, but later the addition was reintroduced to the prayer text of the Frankish churches, and shortly after the year 1000 it was adopted in Rome as well (*ODCC* 512–13).

After the receipt of the letter of reply from the pope, Patriarch Thomas decided to send a delegation to Rome. The delegation, which included his *synkellos* Michael and his two disciples, the brothers Theodore and Theophanes, as well as a monk named Job, arrived in Constantinople during the reign of Michael Rhangabes (811–813). The results of their mission are not known, but they did not reach Rome, apparently because of the war with the Bulgarians, which threatened security on the roads. In the capital they would later become embroiled in the renewed iconoclast controversy (see below), and they remained there. They would not return to Palestine, which was troubled at the time by recurrent persecutions against the Christian community and the monks. In the capital they appealed to the emperor to act to lessen the yoke of taxes imposed by the Arabs on the Christian community in Palestine (Vailhé, 1901a, 328–32).

The *filioque* controversy between Rome and Byzantium was renewed in 864, during the time of Photius, the patriarch of Constantinople. From that time on the subject became the chief ground of disagreement between the Orthodox Church and the Church of Rome. At the reunion councils of Lyons (1274) and Florence (1439), the acceptance of the doctrine, though not of the addition to the Creed, was imposed on the Greeks as a condition of the short-lived union.[30]

---

[29] These three documents—the letter of the monks to Leo (*Epistola peregrinorum monachorum*), the *Symbola* sent by him to the monks, and his letter to Charlemagne—were published in Le Quien, *Oriens Christianus* III, 347–52. The pope also sent a letter of reply to the patriarch of Jerusalem. This letter and his response to the Benedictine monks have not been preserved, but his position can be inferred from the biography of Michael the Synkellos (Vailhé 1901a).

[30] For the doctrine regarding the double procession of the Holy Spirit and the change introduced in the text of the Creed and the resulting disputes, see at length J. N. D. Kelly, *Early Christian Creeds* (London-

D. The Iconoclast Controversy

The iconoclast (εἰκονοκλάστης, "icon-breaker") controversy that embroiled the Byzantine Empire from the second quarter of the eighth century until the middle of the ninth had two phases. The first phase (726–787) began with the iconoclast edict issued by Emperor Leo III (the Isaurian) (717–741), continued during the time of his son Constantine V (Copronymus) (741–775), and concluded with the Second Council of Nicaea, the Seventh Ecumenical Council (787), which was convened at the initiative of Empress Irene and which cancelled the decisions of the iconoclast council at Hiereia near Chalcedon, which had convened in 754. The second phase (815–843) began with the rise to power of Emperor Leo V (the Armenian) (813–820), continued during the time of Michael II (820–829) and his son Theophilus (829–842), and concluded with the Council of Constantinople in 843. This council, convened at the initiative of Theodora, Theophilus' widow, restored icon veneration.[31]

This struggle concerned mainly the Orthodox Church of the Byzantine Empire, and generated a split between the imperial court and the monks, who were loyal supporters of icon veneration. The struggle had echoes in Palestine as well. In the first phase of the controversy, John of Damascus, the most important theologian of the eighth century, took an active role. During the years 726–729, at the request of Patriarch John V of Jerusalem (706–735 or 745), he wrote three polemical discourses in favor of icon worship (Jugie 1924).[32] In his writings he represented the patriarch of Jerusalem, who at that time also served as acting patriarch of Antioch, for the patriarch had died without leaving a successor. In the year 730/31 a council of the bishops of the East convened in Jerusalem, which imposed a ban on Emperor Leo III. John of Damascus played a prominent role in this council. When the iconoclast council, at which he was condemned, opened in Hiereia (Feb. 10, 754), John was already dead. He had a major role in formulating the Christological significance of the controversy (Noble 1987). His writings provided the iconodules with the theological and doctrinal basis for adhering to their positions, both in the struggle with the iconoclast emperors and in the religious debates with the Muslims and the Jews in areas outside the Byzantine Empire.

His dogmatic work *The Fount of Wisdom* (πηγὴ γνώσεως), the third and main part of which is *De Fide Orthodoxa* (Ἔκδοσις ἀκριβὴς τῆς ὀρθοδόξου πίστεως), an exposition of the Orthodox faith, is a comprehensive and orderly synthesis of Orthodox theology up to

---

New York 1950), 358–67; G. B. Howard, *The Schism between the Oriental and Western Churches, with Special Reference to the Addition of the Filioque to the Creed* (London 1893); P. de Meester, "Études sur la théologie orthodoxe IV," "La *Filioque*," *Revue bénédictine* 24 (1907), 86–103; M. Jugie, "Origine de la controverse sur l'addition du *Filioque* au symbole," *Revue des sciences philosophiques et théologiques* 28 (1939), 369–85; A. Palmieri, *DTC* V (1913), 2309–43; E. Amman, "L'époque carolingienne," in Fliche and Martin 1936–37, 179–84. See also Linder 1987b, 99.

[31] For the iconoclastic controversy in Byzantium see, among others, L. Bréhier, *La querelle des images, VIII–IX siècles* (Paris 1904); E. J. Martin, *A History of the Iconoclastic Controversy* (London 1930); G. Ostrogorsky, *Studien zur Geschichte des byzantinischen Bilderstreites* (Breslau 1929); A. Grabar, *L'iconoclasme byzantin: Dossier archéologique* (Paris 1957); P. Brown, "A Dark-Age Crisis: Aspects of the Iconoclastic Controversy," *EHR* 88 (1973), 1–34.

[32] *De Imaginibus, orationes I–III* = λόγοι ἀπολογητικοὶ πρὸς τοὺς διαβαλλόντας τὰς ἁγίας εἰκόνας, PG 94, 1231–1420. For the critical edition see B. Kotter, *Die Schriften des Johannes Damaskos, III: Contra Imaginum Calumniatores, Orationes Tres* (Berlin-New York 1975).

his time. His sources on the subject of Christology also include the writings of Leontius of Byzantium, the sixth-century Sabaite monk.

Theodore Abu Qurrah made use of John's discourses in favor of icon worship when he wrote, between the years 800 and 812, his treatise in favor of icon veneration (Griffith 1985). This treatise, which had been written when Theodore already served as bishop of Harran, was intended to stop the phenomenon of iconophobia, which had begun to spread in Edessa under the pressure of Muslim and Jewish polemicists. They troubled the Christians, declaring that the veneration of icons was idol worship. The treatise by Theodore, written in Arabic, is not related at all to the iconoclast controversy in the Byzantine Empire. It was written for the needs of the Orthodox Christian community in Edessa and in the other Islamic lands. At the same time, however, the treatise reflects the basic iconodule position of this Sabaite monk, who, from the doctrinal aspect (although not from the chronological one), was one of the prominent and outstanding disciples of John of Damascus. The monastery of Sabas therefore was an iconodule bastion which not only spread its influence throughout the Byzantine Empire, but also strengthened the Christians in Muslim lands in the religious debates in which they were forced to participate.

The Sabaite monks were also active in the second phase of the Byzantine iconoclast controversy. As was stated above (Chap. 1), in 817 Theodore of Stoudios, who headed the iconodule camp in the capital, sent an epistle (no. 16) to the abbot of the monastery of Sabas, in which he requested the support of his monks in his struggle against the iconoclast emperor Leo V. This epistle was also sent to the monastery of Theodosius, and an epistle of similar content (no. 17) was sent to the monasteries of Chariton and Euthymius. The patriarch of Jerusalem, Basil (821–836 or 839), convened a church council there, with the participation of representatives of the patriarchs of Alexandria and Antioch. The council sent Emperor Theophilus an iconodule document. Theophilus, on his part, persecuted in the capital the former Sabaite monks Michael the Synkellos and his disciples Theodore and Theophanes, who took an active part in the struggle on the side of the iconodule camp. Michael was imprisoned; his disciples were sentenced to exile, and the sentence was tattooed on their faces. Theodore died in prison, at age sixty-six, December 27, 841. Michael and Theophanes witnessed the triumph of Orthodoxy in the Council of Constantinople in 843, which restored icon veneration. Theophanes was appointed metropolitan of Nicaea and died in October 845 at the age of sixty-seven. Michael was appointed abbot of the monastery of Chora and *synkellos* of the new patriarch, Methodius. He died January 4, 846, at the age of eighty-six (Vailhé 1901a, 610–42; Cunningham 1991).

Conclusion

The writings of Cyril of Scythopolis are the only available literary sources for Sabas' personality and activities. The purpose of the *Vita Sabae* and Cyril's other writings is, no doubt, to praise Sabas. They should therefore be read with appropriate caution, especially regarding personal issues. At the same time, Cyril's writing is far from the generic laudatory style typical of many hagiographers. His testimony is generally considered to be trustworthy and useful on various subjects if treated with the proper critical approach.

Sabas, a Cappadocian, was acquainted with the monastic tradition of Basil the Great, but he was attracted to a more ascetic life in the spirit of the enthusiastic Anatolian monasticism. He chose to lead this type of life in a place that every monk longed for—the desert of the Holy City. Here Euthymius was his paragon. After living seventeen years in the monastery of Theoctistus, five of them as a cell dweller, Sabas broke all ties with a monastic community and spent five years wandering in the deserts and five more in a cave in the Kidron ravine, where he later established the Great Laura (483).

For forty-nine of his ninety-three years Sabas served as an abbot. His career may be examined under three different but complementary aspects: his activities as a builder and founder of monasteries, as a monastic administrator and legislator, and as a holy man and an ecclesiastical leader. These aspects have been extensively discussed in the three main parts of this study.

Sabas significantly increased the number of monasteries in the interior of the desert. During the century and a half that preceded his enterprise, there were only fourteen monasteries in the Judean desert (six laurae and eight coenobia), only one of which (the coenobium of Theoctistus) was located in the desert plateau; the others were on the fringes of the desert or in the Jordan valley. He and his disciples erected thirteen monasteries (seven laurae and six coenobia), almost all within the desert plateau, not on its outskirts. Other famous monasteries of the past—the monasteries of Euthymius, Theoctistus, and the Old Laura (Souka)—also came under his aegis. As one of the two archimandrites who were nominated by the patriarchs of Jerusalem to control the fervent desert monks, and to integrate them into the ranks of the See of Jerusalem, Sabas' authority and influence spread even beyond his foundations. More than any other of the monastic leaders, he transformed the desert into a city (*V. Sab.* 9, 90.8–10 and 50, 141.9–10). The meaning of this phrase is demonstrated not only by the large number of his monasteries within the desert but also by the appearance, size, and density of the buildings of the Great Laura. Both aspects are illustrated by the new archaeological material.

Sabas was the only one of Euthymius' disciples to establish laurae. He gave a new impetus to laurite monasticism in a period when there was a tendency to transform laurae into coenobia. Such was the case with the laura of Euthymius, which was transformed into a coenobium in 482—a significant event for desert monasticism—and with the laura of Peter the Iberian near Gaza, which became a coenobium after his death in 489. The tendency toward coenobitism was evident in Syria already earlier in the fifth century.

As for the components of a laura, the main contribution of the present study concerns the hermitages. More than sixty dwelling complexes were carefully measured, and some were excavated. A phenomenon previously unknown in Palestinian archaeology was the existence of private chapels or prayer niches in many of the hermitages. The cells generally comprise a single room and a courtyard. In the Great Laura several spacious hermitages were discovered, each consisting of several rooms and a large chapel. Such hermitages, in spite of their size, housed only a single monk or an elderly monk and one or two disciples. These more elaborate complexes are the minority even in the Great Laura. In any case, in light of the archaeological finds of the last twenty-five years in the hermit colonies in Egypt (mainly in Kellia and near Esna), where elaborate and spacious hermitages were excavated, those found in the Great Laura are not unique. Complexes designated for an elderly monk and one or two disciples, or for a small group of two to three monks, are also encountered in these Egyptian sites.

The Sabaite laurae were more organized, orderly institutions than the monastic settlements of Mount Nitria, Kellia, and Scetis in Lower Egypt. In these settlements a monastic tradition took shape, of course, but there were no written regulations. In Palestine, Gerasimus enacted rules for his monks, but only Sabas put his in writing. Life under a rule was a basic principle of Basilian monasticism, which was a coenobitic system. Gerasimus and Sabas applied it to the lauritic style of monasticism. To judge from the extant form of the rules of Gerasimus and Sabas' Rule from Sinai, the regulations were given as short statements. They were not by any means systematic, detailed, or all-embracing legislation. Many unmentioned issues remained to be determined according to ancient tradition or to be interpreted by successive monastic superiors. There was a separate set of rules for the laurites and another for the coenobites. Thus, when political and security conditions changed in Palestine, making impossible the continued existence of lauritic life, and gradually transforming the Great Laura into a coenobium, the coenobitic rules of Sabas were found to be still valid and could be applied.

The coenobia of Sabas, like most of those in the Judean desert, were of moderate size, the majority of them inhabited by a few dozen monks. These communities were of the size recommended by Basil the Great. These were not settlements of hundreds or thousands of monks, like the Pachomian coenobia or the "White Monastery" of Shenoute. Their organizational structure was also quite simple, without the complex hierarchy of the Egyptian or the Syrian coenobia. The way of life combined light work and prayer, in the spirit of the Basilian brotherhood, and was completely different from that prevalent in the centers of work and agricultural production such as the Egyptian monasteries.

The laurae of Sabas and his disciples were on a smaller scale than the monastic settlements of Nitria, Kellia, and Scetis. Monastic life was conducted in accordance with a written rule, and there was no room for the freedom of choice or individuality that was present, for example, in Nitria during the time of Palladius.

The hostels Sabas established in Jericho and Jerusalem served administrative and economic purposes; they were recruitment centers for new monks and branches for exerting Sabaite influence on political and ecclesiastical affairs in Jerusalem. Sabas' greatness, even as a religious leader, was not as a theologian but rather as an administrator. Like Pachomius, he also headed a kind of union or confederation of monasteries, although the structure here was not as hierarchical and well defined as in the Pachomian *Koinonia*. Sabas' Rules—one for the laurae and one for the coenobia—established a uniform way of life in all his monasteries. This preserved the relationship between the monasteries as well as their attachment to him.

For Sabas the first act of foundation was not enough. He continued to care for his monasteries and those of his disciples throughout his life, taking personal measures to ensure their economic subsistence and to embellish their churches.

By examining the modes of administration of the Great Laura and Sabas' other monasteries, it was found that laurae were administered differently from coenobia. A laura was headed by an abbot (ἡγούμενος), assisted by a steward (οἰκονόμος), whose term of service did not last more than three years. This method, in practice in the Great Laura, guaranteed that the steward would not cease from being a cell dweller for more than the determined period. This rotation in office also contributed to building a sense of community, since many monks took a turn in serving in administrative posts.

A coenobium such as the monastery of Theodosius had a different, more hierarchical system of administration. Besides the abbot there was a deputy (δευτεράριος), a distinguished monk who generally succeeded the abbot in office after his death. In case of a coenobium, a lengthy term of service in this position did not mean keeping the coenobite out of his cell. This post came into being toward the end of the fifth century or the beginning of the sixth. In smaller coenobia, such as Choziba, the abbot himself took care of financial and economic matters. He had neither a deputy, nor a steward, but a cellarer to assist him. In the secondary monasteries of Sabas, subjugated to him and to the Great Laura, both coenobia and laurae, there was a dual form of leadership—an administrator (διοικητής) and his deputy.

Pharan was administered at the beginning of the fifth century by a group of monks, "the fathers of Pharan" (*V. Euth.* 8, 16.8), and not by a single abbot. This system of leadership was similar to that existing at about the same period in the anchorite colonies of Lower Egypt. In the sixth century Cyril does not name any abbot of Pharan; neither does the author of the *Vita Charitonis* (a 6th-century monk acquainted with that laura) name any of Chariton's successors. John Moschus, on the other end, does mention the names of some of the laura's fathers.

In his two journeys to Constantinople, Sabas was entrusted with important assignments concerning the well-being of the See of Jerusalem and the welfare of the Christian settlements in Palestine, indicating that he was well-versed in financial matters and taxes. His skills as an able administrator are evident here as well as in his building projects and his monastic regulations.

A detailed analysis of the literary sources, both synchronically and diachronically, has enabled us to define the Sabaite system and to distinguish it from the endeavors of Chariton, Euthymius, and Gerasimus. It is clear that there was both synchronic diversity and chronological development in various realms of monastic life throughout the Byzantine period.

This analysis indicates that the Great Laura was not founded on the model of the laura of Euthymius, that is, the type of Pharan. Rather, Sabas adopted, with modifications, features first introduced by Gerasimus. His innovations do not indicate revolution, but rather a process of evolution.

The comparison between Gerasimus' regulations for the cell dwellers and what we know about the daily life in the Great Laura regarding the diet, garb, and utensils used by monks in their cells indicate that Gerasimus' regulations were stricter than the actual practice in the Great Laura. What for Gerasimus was the norm was a measure of extraordinary asceticism and excellence in Sabas' Laura. This may be explained not by the chronological gap of about one hundred years between Gerasimus' regulations and Cyril's writing, but rather by the fact that the comparison is not between two sets of regulations but between one set of regulations and the lived reality. It is quite possible that the actual way of life of Gerasimus' monks was quite similar to that practiced in the Great Laura. And indeed, according to the *Vita Gerasimi*, his monks had difficulty in supporting the severities that he imposed on them.

The novitiate—a period of probation and preparation in a coenobium prior to being admitted to the laura—was an important institution. In fact, Euthymius required it of both Sabas and Cyriacus, but, unlike Gerasimus and Sabas, he did not establish a special coenobium for this purpose. Gerasimus' laura was erected around his coenobium, where the monks undertook their preparation for lauritic life. But in his system, laurites and coenobites intermingled in the coenobium church during the weekend services. Sabas, on the other hand, kept a complete segregation between the novices and the cell dwellers. The construction of the Small Coenobium at some distance from the laura prevented any association between the two groups. Thus instruction in accord with Sabas' regulations was guaranteed from the very beginning. This preparatory course, which lasted ten years or more, also guaranteed that only experienced, educated, and mature monks (at least thirty years old), entered the Laura. These were monks who had proven themselves in their way of life and who had undergone profound and vast theological instruction. There is no wonder, therefore, that the Great Laura and the other Sabaite institutions became important intellectual centers of theological and literary activity.

Priests and deacons were important components of Euthymius' first disciples, and he himself was from a young age a member of the church establishment. Sabas' recoiling from ordination to the priesthood, which he initially prevented (in the years 483–490) for both himself and his monks, indicates that from the very beginning his Laura was established in a different manner from that of Euthymius.

At Pharan and in the laura of Euthymius, the Eucharist was celebrated only on Sunday. Gerasimus adopted the Egyptian monastic practice of celebrating the Eucharist both on Saturday and Sunday. Sabas also introduced this practice into his monasteries, from at least 490, after being ordained to the priesthood and changing his negative opinion on ordination for monks. But unlike Gerasimus, Sabas instructed that an all-night vigil (ἀγρυπνία) in the church for the entire community should be held between Saturday and Sunday. This was an important liturgical innovation of Sabas, and became one of the most recognizable features of the Sabaitic-Palestinian liturgical *Typika* in future generations.

Another liturgical innovation introduced by Sabas was the date of Lent. Whereas Euthymius had gone off to the desert on January 14, Sabas, delayed the date of his departure to the desert by a week, following St. Antony's memorial day on January 17 and that of St. Euthymius' on January 20 (*V. Sab.* 22, 106). This alteration, which shortened the stay in the desert by a week, arose from Sabas' desire to celebrate together, within the Laura, these two important monastic feasts. Another, no less significant, innovation of Sabas was five days of fasting per week instead of the six prescribed by Euthymius. This change resulted from the frequency with which the Eucharist was celebrated.

We do not hear of Sabas delivering to his monks exegetical lectures on the scriptures, as Pachomius did to his. But although he was not a distinguished theologian, he became, due to his experience and ascetic way of life, an authoritative guide, as did other monastic founders. His authority was not only a result of his written rule but also of his personality and his veneration as a holy man. He was a superior, a guide, and a shepherd (*V. Sab.* 16, 100.6). This was not the case with his successors. After Sabas' death, not the abbots but other distinguished monks, such as John the Hesychast or Cyriacus of Souka, were the spiritual fathers and attracted pilgrims and admirers.

Sabas was worshiped as a holy man and a miracle worker during his lifetime and after his death. His admirers included both lay people and ecclesiastical officials, ordinary people and nobles, from Palestine and from other provinces, including Constantinople. All made donations to his instititions as tokens of gratitude for his consultation and healing and as a means of venerating his memory. He also received generous donations from the emperors Anastasius and Justinian in his two visits to the capital. During these visits he established lasting relations with the Orthodox party there. This ceaseless stream of donations was the factor that ensured the existence of the Sabaite institutions during his lifetime and after his death.

The physical layout of Sabas' monasteries and the increase in the number of his monks, his enterprise as founder and settler of the desert, his function as archimandrite, the administration assigned to each monastery and the way of life dictated by his Rule, the missions he undertook for the welfare of the Palestinian Church—all contributed to the flourishing of the monastic movement in his lifetime and increased its influence on the See of Jerusalem, with the Great Laura in a position of leadership. The system that he established remained viable for the generations to come, guaranteeing the continued existence of the Great Laura and its continuous activity under the Muslim regime.

Despite various influences, both local and from abroad, a unique pattern developed in the Sabaite monasteries, different from that in the earlier laurae of Pharan type or the urban monasteries. This pattern, which was dictated by the regulations and the physical and organizational infrastructure delineated by Sabas, provided the Sabaite monks with a high degree of self-consciousness and a deep theological foundation. This was a lively monastic society with religious fervor, which flourished physically and ideologically during Sabas' lifetime and after.

The Sabaite monks played a prominent role in the various theological controversies in which they were involved. They composed doctrinal treatises that supplied the required theological articulation for the triumph of Orthodoxy in Sabas' time and in later generations. This awareness of theological issues and involvement in the definition of Orthodoxy are characteristic features of the Sabaite monks and of the Great Laura, not only of a few prominent individuals. Sabaite monks were active in Byzantium and Rome in promoting and defending Orthodoxy.

In later years the Sabaite monks also considered it their sacred duty to supply translations of church books to increasing numbers of Arabic-speaking Christians, as well as to the Orthodox Christians in Georgia. Such was the nature of the literary activity in the scriptorium of Mar Saba and of the affiliated monasteries in Sabas' time and later, when the Great Laura actually served as the intellectual center of the See of Jerusalem.

The later contribution of the Sabaite-Palestinian monastic rite to the development of the Byzantine liturgy should be mentioned as well. As the prayer book of an ancient Greek and Orthodox center of the Holy Land, the Sabaitic liturgical *Typikon* had a special appeal to reformers of the Byzantine monastic liturgy in later generations. The early Sabaitic *Typikon*, which was redacted by Sophronius after the devastation of Christian institutions by the Persians in 614, and later by John of Damascus, was adopted by Theodore of Stoudios, supplanting the former akoimetic rite that prevailed at that monastery earlier. After being modified by absorbing some cathedral Constantinopolitan elements, the Stoudite *Typikon* of the ninth and tenth centuries was adopted by Athanasius the Athonite. It was later supplanted by the neo-Sabaitic synthesis formulated in Palestine during the eleventh and twelfth centuries, after the disturbances caused to monastic life there by Arab incursions and the deliberate devastation caused by al-Hakim in 1009. This neo-Sabaitic *Typikon*, in which a prominent place is still given to the *agrypnia*, was known in the monasteries of Constantinople already in the twelfth century and was adopted on Mount Athos in the fifteenth century. From Athos it spread throughout the Orthodox world under the influence of Athonite hesychasm. The Athonite redaction of the neo-Sabaitic *Typikon* became the definitive liturgical synthesis of the Byzantine and Russian rite (Arranz 1976, 1982; Egender 1975; Taft 1988).

Sabas' veneration among the Serbians is best revealed by the example of Sava of Serbia (1175–1235), the founder and organizer of the autocephalous Serbian Church. Born as prince Rastko, the youngest son of the grand župan Stefan Nemanja, the founder of the Serbian state, he fled at a young age to Mount Athos, where he became a monk and took the name of the great Palestinian monk he admired. Sava founded the Serbian monastery of Hilandar on the holy mountain and visited Jerusalem twice (1230, 1234). On his first visit he restored to the Sabaite monks the church of St. George at Acre, which had served for generations as a hostel for pilgrims and was confiscated by the Latins during previous crusades. Sava bought the church from the Latins and returned it to its original proprietors, adding a substantial amount of gold. While later visiting the monastery of Mar Saba, he was given, as a measure of honor and gratitude, a staff believed to have been used by St. Sabas and two precious icons of the Virgin. One of them, known as "the Holy Virgin of the Three Hands," he later placed in his monastery of Hilandar (Matejić 1976; Velimirovich 1989). Serbian monks also played an important role in the later history of Mar Saba (Vailhé 1899–1900b).

Bibliographical Abbreviations

I. Periodicals, Dictionaries, Series, and Primary Sources

AASS *Acta Sanctorum.*

AB *Analecta Bollandiana.*

ACO *Acta Conciliorum Oecumenicorum*, 4 vols. in 13, ed. E. Schwartz, Strassburg-Berlin-Leipzig 1914–40; vol. 14, ed. J. Straub, Bonn 1970.

Acta Anast. Pers. *Acta sancti Anastasii Persae*, ed H. Usener. Bonn 1894. See also Flusin 1992, vol. 1.

ADAJ *Annual of the Department of Antiquities of Jordan.*

AIBL *Académie des Inscriptions et Belles-Lettres, Comptes rendus.*

AJA *American Journal of Archaeology.*

An. St. *Anatolian Studies.*

Ant. mon., *Ep. ad Eust.*

Antiochus monachus, *Epistola ad Eustathium*, PG 89, 1421–28 (*AASS*, Maii III, 613–14).

Apoph. Pat. (alphabet. coll.)

Apophthegmata Patrum, PG 65, 71–440 (Codex regius 2466 = MS Paris gr. 1599), supplemented by J. C. Guy, *Recherches sur la tradition grecque des Apophthegmata Patrum*, 2nd ed., Subsidia Hagiographica 36, Brussels 1984. Fr. trans. J. C. Guy, *Les Apophthègmes des Pères du Désert*, Begrolles 1966; Eng. trans. Benedicta Ward, *The Sayings of the Desert Fathers*, CS 59, London 1975.

Apoph. Pat. (anon. coll.)

Apophthegmata Patrum, ed. F. Nau, "Histoire des solitaires égyptiens" (Gr. text and Fr. trans.), *ROC* 12 (1907), 43–47, 171–89, 393–413 = *Ap.* 1–37, 38–62, 63–132; 13 (1908), 47–66, 266–97 = *Ap.* 133–74, 175–215; 14 (1909), 357–79 = *Ap.* 216–97; 17 (1912), 204–11, 294–301 = *Ap.* 298–334, 335–58; 18 (1913), 137–46 = *Ap.* 359–400; 10 (1905), 387–417, to be inserted after *Ap.* 132 (MS Coislin. 126). Fr. trans. J. C. Guy, *Les Apophthègmes des Pères du Désert*, Begrolles 1966. Eng. trans. Benedicta Ward, *The Wisdom of the Desert Fathers*, CS 59, London 1975.

Apoph. Pat. (systematic coll.)

Apophthegmata Patrum; systematic collection, a Latin version by Pelagius and John, PL 73, 851–1052. J. C. Guy, *Les Apophtègmes des Pères: collection systématique*. Chapitres I–XI. SC 387, Paris 1993. Fr. trans. J. Dion and G. Dury, *Les Sentences des Pères du Désert*, Solesmes 1966; also L. Régnault, *Les Sentences des Pères du Désert: nouveau recueil*, Solesmes 1970.

Ariel *A Review of Arts and Letters in Israel.*

Armenian Jerusalemite Lectionary

see Renoux 1961–62.

BA *Biblical Archaeologist.*

BAR *Biblical Archaeology Review.*

Barsanuph et Jean de Gaza

        Correspondance; Recueil complet traduit du grec par Lucien Régnault et Philippe Lemaire ou du Géorgien par Bernard Outtier. Solesmes 1972.

Basil, *Ascetica*   Basilius Magnus, *Ascetica*, PG 31, 619–92; 869–88.

Basil, *Ep.*   Basilius Magnus, *Epistulae*, ed. and Fr. trans. Y. Courtonne, *Saint Basile, Lettres,* I (Epp. 1–100), Paris 1957; ed. and Eng. trans. R. Deferrari, *Saint Basil: The Letters,* 4 vols., LCL, London-Cambridge, Massachusetts, 1926–36, repr. 1950; PG 32, 220–1112.

Basil, *Moralia*   Basilius Magnus, *Moralia.* PG 31, 691–869.

Basil, *Reg. brev.*   Basilius Magnus, *Regulae brevius tractatae.* PG 31, 1080–1305.

Basil, *Reg. fus.*   Basilius Magnus, *Regulae fusius tractatae,* PG 31, 889–1052. Eng. trans. Monica Wagner, *Saint Basil: Ascetical Works,* New York 1950, 223–337.

Basil, *Small Ascetikon*

        Basilius Magnus, *Ascetikon,* Latin trans. by Rufinus, PL 103, 487–554.

BASOR   *Bulletin of the American Schools of Oriental Research.*

Bessarione   *Publicazione periodica di studi orientali.*

BHG   *Bibliotheca Hagiographica Graeca.*

BIFAO   *Bulletin de l'Institut Français d'Archéologie Orientale.*

BO, ed. Assemani, J. S.

        Bibliotheca Orientalis, 4 vols., 1719–28. Rome.

BSAC   *Bulletin de la société d'archéologie copte.*

BSEG   *Bulletin de la Société d'Egyptologie, Genève.*

BTS   *Bible et Terre Sainte.*

BZ   *Byzantinische Zeitschrift.*

CCM   *Cahiers de civilisation médiévale.*

CCSL   Corpus Christianorum, Series Latina.

CH   *Church History.*

CMH   *Cambridge Medieval History.*

Cod. Iust.   *Codex Iustinianus,* ed. P. Krüger, Berlin 1877; 10th ed. 1929 (*Corpus Iuris Civilis* II).

Comm. Cas. Dei   *Commemoratorium de Casis Dei vel Monasteriis,* ed. T. Tobler and A. Molinier, *Itinera Hierosolymitana* I, 299–305. Eng. trans. C. M. Watson, *PEFQSt* 45 (1913), 23–33.

Con.   John Cassian, *Conlationes XXIV,* ed. E. Pichery, vols. I–III, SC 42, 54, 64, Paris 1955, 1958, 1959; ed. M. Petschenig, CSEL 13, Vienna 1886. Eng. trans. E. C. S. Gibson, *A Selected Library of Nicene and Post-Nicene Fathers,* 2nd Series, vol. XI, New York 1894; repr. Grand Rapids 1973.

CPG   *Clavis Patrum Graecorum.*

CS   Cistercian Studies.

CSCO   Corpus Scriptorum Christianorum Orientalium.

CSEL   Corpus Scriptorum Ecclesiasticorum Latinorum.

Cyril of Scythopolis

        Opera, ed. Schwartz 1939. Fr. trans. Festugière 1962a, b, 1963a; Ital. trans. Baldelli and Mortari 1990; Eng. trans. R. M. Price, Kalamazoo 1991.

DACL   *Dictionnaire d'archéologie chrétienne et de liturgie.*

DCB   *Dictionary of Christian Biography,* ed. W. Smith and H. Wace, 1877–87.

DDC   *Dictionnaire de droit canonique.*

De Sync.	*De Syncletica in Deserto Iordanis*, ed. B. Flusin and J. Paramelle, *AB* 100 (1982), 305–17.
DHGE	*Dictionnaire d'histoire et de géographie ecclésiastique.*
DOP	*Dumbarton Oaks Papers.*
Dorotheus of Gaza	
	Dorothée de Gaza, *Oeuvres spirituelles;* introduction, texte grec, traduction et notes par Dom L. Régnault et Dom J. de Préville, SC 92, Paris 1963. Eng. trans. of *Discourses and Sayings*, Erica P. Wheeler, CS 33, Kalamazoo, Michigan 1977.
DS	*Dictionnaire de spiritualité.*
DTC	*Dictionnaire de théologie catholique.*

EAEHL	*Encyclopedia of Archaeological Excavations in the Holy Land.*
Eastern Saints	John of Ephesus, *Lives of the Eastern Saints*, ed. and trans. E. W. Brooks, PO 17–19. Paris 1923–26.
EHR	*English Historical Review.*
EI	*Eretz-Israel:* archaeological, historical and geographical studies.
Enc. Catt.	*Enciclopedia Cattolica.*
ENDF	*Échos de Nôtre Dame de France de Jérusalem.*
EO	*Échos d'Orient.*
Epiphanius, *Panarion*	
	Epiphanius Constantinensis episcopus, *Panarion seu adversus LXXX haereses*, ed. K. Holl, 1–33: GCS 25, 151–464; 34–64: GCS 31; 65–73: GCS 37. Leipzig 1915–31.
ESI	*Excavations and Surveys in Israel.*
Eutychius, *Annali*	
	M. Breydy, ed. and trans., *Das Annalenwerk des Eutychios von Alexandrien*, CSCO 471–72, Scrip. Arab. 44–45, Louvain 1985; PG 111, 907–1156.
Evagrius Ponticus, *Practica*	
	Capita practica ad Anatolium, PG 40, 1219–51. Eng. trans. J. Eudes, CS 4, Kalamazoo, Michigan 1964.
Evagrius Scholasticus, *HE*	
	Historia ecclesiastica, ed. J. Bidez and L. Parmentier, London 1898; repr. Amsterdam 1964.
Expug. Hier. (Arab.)	
	G. Garitte, ed., *Expugnationis Hierosolymae A.D. 614, Recensiones Arabicae* A, B, CSCO 340–41, Scrip. Arab. 26–27, Louvain 1973; C, V, CSCO 347–48, Scrip. Arab. 28–29, Louvain 1974.
Expug. Hier. (Georg.)	
	G. Garitte, ed., *La Prise de Jérusalem par les Perses en 614*, CSCO 202–3, Scrip. Iber. 11–12, Louvain 1960. Eng. trans. F. C. Conybeare, "Antiochus Strategos' Account of the Sack of Jerusalem in AD 614," *EHR* 25 (1910), 505–17.

GCS	Die griechischen christlichen Schriftsteller.
Georgian Jerusalemite Lectionary:	
	see Tarchnischvili 1960.
Georgian Palestinian Lectionary:	
	see Garitte 1958.

HL	*Historia Lausiaca:* see Palladius, *HL.*

HM	*Historia Monachorum in Aegypto*, ed. and Fr. trans. A. J. Festugière, Subsidia Hagiographica 53, Brussels 1971. Eng. trans. N. Russell, *The Lives of the Desert Fathers*, CS 34, London-Oxford 1980.
HM (Rufinus)	*Historia Monachorum*, PL 21, 387–461; ed. Eva Schulz-Flügel, Berlin-New York 1990.
HPh	*Historia Philotheos:* see Theodoret, *HPh.*
IEJ	*Israel Exploration Journal.*
ILN	*Illustrated London News.*
Inst.	John Cassian, *De institutis coenobiorum*, ed. J. C. Guy, SC 109, Paris 1965; ed. M. Petschenig, CSEL 17, 3–231, Vienna 1888.
Itin. Eger.	*Itinerarium Egeriae. Égérie, Journal de voyage*, ed. P. Maraval, SC 296, Paris 1982; *Itinerarium Egeriae*, ed. E. Franceschin and R. Weber, CSCL 175, 35–90, Turnhout 1965.
JAOS	*Journal of the American Oriental Society.*
JEA	*Journal of Egyptian Archaeology.*
JEH	*Journal of Ecclesiastical History.*
Jerome, *Ep.*	Hieronymus, *Epistulae*, ed. J. Labourt, *Saint Jérôme, Lettres*, Paris 1949–55.
John of Ephesus, *HE*	
	Historia ecclesiastica pars tertia, ed. and trans. E. W. Brooks, CSCO, Scrip. Syr. III.3, Paris-Louvain 1935–36. Eng. trans. R. Payne Smith, *The Third Part of the Ecclesiastical History of John Bishop of Ephesus*, Oxford 1860.
John Malalas, *Chron.*	
	Johannes Malalas, *Chronographia*, ed. L. Dindorf, Bonn 1831.
John Malalas, *Frag.*	
	Johannes Malalas, *Fragmentum*, ed. C. de Boor, *Excerpta historica iussu imperatoris Constantini Porphyrogeneti confecta. Excerpta de insidiis*, Berlin 1905 (= T. Mommsen, *Hermes* 6 [1872]).
Joshua Stylites	*Chronicle*, ed. and trans. W. Wright, Cambridge 1882.
JPOS	*Journal of the Palestine Oriental Society.*
JRS	*Journal of Roman Studies.*
JSAI	*Jerusalem Studies in Arabic and Islam.*
JTS	*Journal of Theological Studies.*
Koinonia	I–III: see Veilleux 1980–82.
LA	*Liber Annuus Studii Biblici Franciscani.*
LCI	*Lexikon der christlichen Ikonographie*, ed. E. Kirschenbaum and W. Braunfels, 8 vols., Rome-Freiburg-Basel-Vienna 1968–76.
LCL	Loeb Classical Library.
Le Muséon	*Revue d'études orientales*, Louvain.
Levant	*Journal of the British School of Archaeology in Jerusalem.*
Liberatus (archdeacon of Carthage), *Brev.*	
	Breviarium causae Nestorianorum et Eutychianorum, ed. E. Schwartz, *ACO* 2.V, pp. 98–141; also PL 68, 969–1050.
Men. Bas.	*Menologium Basilii*, PG 117, 19–614.

Miracula	Antonius Chozibitae, *Miracula beatae virginis Mariae in Choziba, AB* 7 (1888), 360–70.
MUSJ	*Mélanges de l'Université Saint Joseph, Beyrouth.*
Nili, *Narr.*	Nili Monachi eremitae, *Narrationes,* PG 79, 589–693.
Nov.	Imp. Iustinianus, *Novellae,* ed. R. Scholl and W. Kroll, Berlin 1898; 4th ed. 1912 (*Corpus Iuris Civilis* III).
Nov. (ed. Lingenthal)	
	Imp. Iustinianus, *Novellae,* ed. C. E. Zachariae von Lingenthal, Teubner, Leipzig 1881–84.
OC	*Oriens Christianus.*
OCA	*Orientalia Christiana Analecta.*
OCP	*Orientalia Christiana Periodica.*
ODB	*Oxford Dictionary of Byzantium,* ed. A. Kazhdan et al., New York-Oxford 1991.
ODCC	*Oxford Dictionary of the Christian Church,* 2nd ed., Oxford.
Or. Syr.	*L'Orient Syrien.*
Palladius, *HL*	*Historia Lausiaca,* ed. C. Butler, Cambridge Texts and Studies VI.1 and 2, Cambridge 1898–1904. Eng. trans. W. K. Lowther Clarke, *Translations of Christian Literature,* ser. I, Greek Texts, London, S.P.C.K. 1918; R. T. Meyer, *Ancient Christian Writers* 34, Washington 1965.
Palladius, *HL* (Syriac)	
	R. Draguet, *L'Histoire Lausiaque,* CSCO 389–90, Scrip. Syr. 169–70; CSCO 398–99, Scrip. Syr. 173–74.
Pass. Mich. Sab.	P. Peeters, "La passion de S. Michel le Sabaite,"*AB* 48 (1930), 66–77.
Pass. XX Mart. Sab.	
	Stephanus Sabaitae, *Passio XX Martyrum Sabaitarum, AASS* 20 Mart., III Mart., Paris 1865, 165–78; R. P. Blake, "Deux lacunes comblées dans la 'Passio XX monachorum Sabaitarum'," *AB* 68 (1950), 27–43.
Paul El., *V. Theog.*	
	Paulus Elusinus, *Vita sancti Theogenii,* ed. J. van den Gheyn, *AB* 10 (1891), 78–118.
PEFQSt	*Palestine Exploration Fund, Quarterly Statement.*
PEQ	*Palestine Exploration Quarterly.*
PG	Patrologiae Cursus Completus, Series Graeca, ed. J. P. Migne.
PL	Patrologiae Cursus Completus, Series Latina, ed. J. P. Migne.
Plerophoria	John Rufus, *Plérophories. Témoinages et révélations contre le Concile de Chalcédoine; version syriaque et traduction française,* ed. and trans. F. Nau. PO 8.1 (1912), 11–183.
PO	Patrologia Orientalis, ed. R. Grafin and F. Nau.
POC	*Proche-Orient Chrétien.*
Pratum	Iohannes Moschus, *Pratum Spirituale,* PG 87.3, 2847–3116. Fr. trans. M. J. Rouet de Journel SC 12, Paris 1946.
Pratum (add. Mioni)	
	E. Mioni, *Pratum Spirituale,* OCP 17 (1951), 83–94 (MS Marcian. Cl. 11, 21).
Pratum (add. Nau)	
	F. Nau and L. Clugnet, eds., "Vie et récits d'anachorètes (IVe–VIIe siècles)," *ROC* 7 (1902), 604–17; 8 (1903), 91–100; 10 (1905), 39–56 (MS Paris. gr. 1596).

Pratum (add. Nissen)
> Th. Nissen, "Unbekannte Erzählung aus dem *Pratum Spirituale*," *BZ* 38 (1938), 354–76 (MS Berlin. gr. 221).

Procopius of Caesarea
> *Wars, Buildings and Anecdota*, ed. and trans. H. B. Dewing, LCL, 7 vols., London 1914–40.

PW
> *Paulys Real-Encyclopädie der classischen Altertumswissenschaft*, neue Bearbeitung von G. Wissowa.

QDAP *Quarterly of the Department of Antiquities of Palestine.*

Qedem Monographs of the Institute of Archaeology of the Hebrew University of Jerusalem.

RAC *Reallexikon für Antike und Christentum.*

RAM *Revue d'ascétique et de mystique.*

RB *Revue biblique.*

REA *Revue des études arméniennes.*

REB *Revue des études byzantines.*

REG *Revue des études grecques.*

RHE *Revue d'histoire ecclésiastique.*

RHR *Revue de l'histoire des religions.*

ROC *Revue de l'Orient chrétien.*

RQ *Römische Quartalschrift für die christliche Altertumskunde und für Kirchengeschichte.*

RQH *Revue des questions historiques.*

Rufinus, *HE* Rufinus Aquileiensis, *Historia ecclesiastica,* GCS 9.ii, 957–1040; PL 21, 465–540.

Sabas, *Typikon of Sinai*
> E. Kurtz, ed., *BZ* 3 (1894), 167–70.

SC Sources chrétiennes.

Scala Paradisi Joannes Climacus, *Scala Paradisi,* PG 88, 631–1164. Eng. trans. L. Moore and M. Heppell, New York 1959; C. Luibheid and N. Russell, New York 1982.

Socrates, *HE* Socrates Scholasticus, *Historia ecclesiastica,* PG 67, 29–842. Eng. trans. *Nicene and Post Nicene Fathers,* II.

Sozomen, *HE* *Historia ecclesiastica,* ed. J. Bidez and G. C. Hausen, GCS 50, Berlin 1960. Fr. trans. of books I–II: A.-J. Festugière, SC 306, Paris 1983; Eng. trans. *Nicene and Post Nicene Fathers,* II.

SP *Studia Patristica.*

SR Science et religion.

St. Mon. *Studia Monastica.*

Synax. CP. *Synaxarium ecclesiae Constantinopolitanae, Propylaeum ad AASS Novembris,* ed. H. Delehaye. Brussels 1902.

Theod., *De Situ* Theodosius, *De Situ Terrae Sanctae,* ed. P. Geyer, CCSL 175. Turnhout 1965.

Theodoret, *HE* Theodoretus episcopus Cyrrhensis, *Historia ecclesiastica,* ed. L. Parmentier, GCS 19. Leipzig 1911.

Theodoret, *HPh* *Théodoret de Cyr, Histoire des moines de Syrie,* ed. P. Canivet and A. L. Leroy-Molinghen, 2 vols., SC 234, 257, Paris, 1977–79. Eng. trans. R. M. Price, CS 88, Kalamazoo, Michigan 1985.

Theod. Petr., *V. Theod.*

> Theodorus Petraeus, *Vita sancti Theodosii*, ed. H. Usener, Leipzig 1890. Fr. trans. Festugière 1963a, 81–160.

Theod. Stud., *Ep. 221*

> Theodorus Studita, *Ep. 221*, ed. R. Devreesse, "Une lettre de S. Théodore Studite relative au synode moéchien (AD 809)." *AB* 68 (1950), 44–57.

Theoph., *Chron.*   *Theophanis Chronographia* (AD 284–813), ed. C. de Boor, Leipzig 1883. Eng. trans. of AM 6095–6305 (AD 602–813), H. Turtledove, *The Chronicle of Theophanes,* Philadelphia 1982.

TS   *La Terra Santa.*

TU   Text und Untersuchungen zur Geschichte der altchristlichen Literatur.

V. Ab.   Cyrillus Scythopolitanus, *Vita Sancti Abraamii,* ed. E. Schwartz, Leipzig 1939, 243–49; P. Peeters, "Historia S. Abramii ex apographo arabico,"*AB* 24 (1905), 349–56. Fr. trans. Festugière 1963a, 69–79.

V. Alex.   *Vie d'Alexandre l'Acémète,* ed. E. de Stoop. PO VI.5 (1911), 658–701.

V. Char.   *Vita Charitonis,* ed. G. Garitte, "La vie prémétaphrastique de S. Chariton."*Bulletin de l'Institut Historique Belge de Rome* 21 (1940), 16–42.

V. Cyr.   Cyrillus Scythopolitanus, *Vita Sancti Cyriaci,* ed. E. Schwartz, Leipzig 1939, 222–34. Fr. tr. Festugière 1963a, 35–51. For the Georgian version see Garitte 1962.

V. Dan. Styl.   *Vita Sancti Danielis Stylitae,* ed. P. Peeters, *AB* 32 (1913), 121–214. Ed. and Eng. trans. E. Dawes and N. H. Baynes 1948.

V. Euth.   Cyrillus Scythopolitanus, *Vita Sancti Euthymii,* ed. E. Schwartz, Leipzig 1939, 3–84. Fr. trans. Festugière 1962a.

V. Geor.   Antonius Chozibitae, *Vita Sancti Georgii Chozibitae. AB* 7 (1888), 95–144, 336–59; 8 (1889), 209.

V. Ger.   *Vita Sancti Gerasimi anonyma,* ed. C. M. Koikylides, 1–11. Jerusalem 1902.

V. Hil.   Hieronimus, *Vita Hilarionis,* ed. J. P. Migne. PL 23, 29–54.

V. Hil. Ib.   "Saint Hilarion d'Ibérie," ed. P. Peeters. *AB* 32 (1913), 243–69.

V. Hypatii   Callinicus, *Vita Hypatii,* ed. G. J. M. Bartelink, SC 177. Paris 1971.

V. John Eremopolites

> *Saint Jean l'Erémopolite,* ed. F. Halkin. *AB* 86 (1968), 13–20.

V. John Hes.   Cyrillus Scythopolitanus, *Vita Sancti Ioanni Hesychastesis,* ed. E. Schwartz, Leipzig 1939, 201–21. Fr. trans. Festugière 1963a, 9–33.

V. Mel. Jun.   *Vita Melaniae Junioris,* ed. D. Gorce, SC 90, Paris 1962. Eng. trans. Elizabeth A. Clark, *The Life of Melania the Younger,* New York 1984.

V. Mich. Sync.:   see Cunningham 1991.

V. Pach.   A. Veilleux, *Pachomian Koinonia I: The Life of Saint Pachomius.* Kalamazoo, Michigan 1980.

V. Petr. Ib.   John Rufus (Beit Rufina), *Vita Petri Iberi,* ed. R. Raabe (Syriac text and German trans.). Leipzig 1895.

V. Porph.   Marcus Diaconus, *Vita Porphyrii,* ed. H. Gregoire and M. A. Kugener (Gr. text and Fr. trans.). Paris 1930.

V. Sab.   Cyrillus Scythopolitanus, *Vita Sancti Sabae,* ed. E. Schwartz, Leipzig 1939, 85–200. Fr. trans. Festugière 1962b.

V. Steph. Sab.   Leontius Damascenus, *Vita Stephani Sabaitae, AASS,* Julii III, 531–613 (ed. 1723); 505–84 (ed. 1867); G. Garitte, "Le début de la Vie de S. Étienne le Sabaite retrouvé en arabe au Sinai," *AB* 77 (1959), 332–69. Ital. trans. C. Carta, *Leonzio di*

Damasco, Vita di. S. Stefano Sabaita (725–794), Jerusalem 1983; Georgian recension: see Garitte 1954a.

V. Steph. Sab. (Arab.)

Leonzio di Damasco, Vita di Stefano Sabaita; testo arabo edito e tradotto da Bartolomeo Pirone. Cairo-Jerusalem 1991.

V. Sym. Sali   Leontius Neapolitanus, *Vita Symeoni Sali Confessoris*. PG 93, 1669–1748.

V. Theod.   Cyrillus Scythopolitanus, *Vita sancti Theodosii*, ed. E. Schwartz, Leipzig 1939, 235–40. Fr. trans. Festugière 1963a, 53–61.

V. Theod. Gr.   Symeon Logotheta Metaphrastes, *Menologium seu Vitae Sanctorum*, 26 December: Theodorus Graptus. PG 116, 653–84.

V. Theod. Syk.   A. J. Festugière, ed., *Vie de Théodore de Sykéon*, Subsidia Hagiographica 48, Brussels 1970. Eng. trans. E. Dawes and N. Baynes 1948.

V. Theog.   Cyrillus Scythopolitanus, *Vita Sancti Theognii*, ed. E. Schwartz, Leipzig 1939, 241–43. Fr. trans. Festugière 1963a, 62–68.

V. Tych.   *Vita Tychonis*, ed. H. Usener, *Sonderbare Heilige I, Der Heilige Tychon*, 111–49. Leipzig 1907.

V. Xen.   *Vita Sancti Xenophontis et Sociorum* (MS Florentinis), ed. A. Galante. *AB* 22 (1903), 383–94.

V. Xen. (Metaph.)   *Vita Sancti Xenophontis* (*apud* Symeon Logotheta dictus Metaphrastes). PG 114, 1013–44.

VC   *Vigiliae Christianae*.

Zacharias Rhetor, *HE*

Historia ecclesiastica, ed. and trans. E. W. Brooks, CSCO, Scrip. Syr. III.5 and 6, Paris-Louvain, 1919–24. Eng. trans. F. J. Hamilton and E. W. Brooks, London 1899.

ZDPV   *Zeitschrift des Deutschen Palästina-Vereins*.

ZKG   *Zeitschrift für Kirchengeschichte*.

II. Secondary Works

Abel, F. M.
     1952   *Histoire de la Palestine* II. Paris.

Adam, A.
     1952   "Grundbegriffe des Mönchtums in sprachlicher Sicht." *ZKG* 65, 209–39.

Adnes, P.
     1969   "Hésychasme." *DS* VII, 381–99.

Altaner, B., and Stuiber, A.
     1966   *Patrologie*, 7th ed. Freiburg-Basel-Vienna.

Amadouni, G.
     1985   "Le rôle historique des hiéromoines arméniens." *OCA* 153, 279–306 (= *Il monachesimo orientale, Atti del Convegno di Studi Orientali*. Rome.

Amand, D.
     1949   *L'ascèse monastique de Saint Basile: Essai historique*. Maredsous.

Amand de Mendieta, E.
     1955   Le Mont-Athos. Paris.
     1957   "Le système cénobitique basilien comparé au système cénobitique pachômien." *RHR* 152, 31–80.

Amann, E.
1946a   "Théodore de Scythopolis." *DTC* XV.1, 286–87.
1946b   "Théodore le studite." *DTC* XV.1, 287–98.
Andreu, G., Castel, G., and Coquin, R.-G.
1980   "Sixième campagne de fouilles aux Kellia (1979–80): Rapport préliminaire." *BIFAO* 80, 347–68.
Andreu, G., and Coquin, R.-G.
1981   "Septième campagne de fouilles aux Kellia (avril 1981). Rapport préliminaire." *BIFAO* 81, 159–88.
Anon.
1974   "Communion, frequency of." *ODCC*, 322.
Arranz, M.
1976   "Les grands étapes de la liturgie byzantine: Palestine-Byzance-Russie." In *Liturgie de l'église particulière, liturgie de l'église universelle*, Bibliotheca Ephemerides Liturgicae, Subsidia, 43–72. Rome.
1980   "N. D. Uspensky: The Office of the All-Night Vigil in the Greek Church and in the Russian Church." *St. Vladimir's Theological Quarterly* 24, 83–113, 169–95.
1982   "L'office divin, II: En Orient." *DS* 11, 707–20.
Ashbrook Harvey, S.
1990   *Asceticism and Society in Crisis: John of Ephesus and the "Lives of the Saints."* Berkeley.
Avigad, N.
1977   "A Building Inscription of the Emperor Justinian and the Nea in Jerusalem." *IEJ* 27, 145–51.
1983   *Discovering Jerusalem*. Nashville, Tennessee.
Avi-Yonah, M.
1956   "The Samaritan Revolt against the Byzantine Empire." *EI* 4, 127–32 (Hebrew with English summary on p. IX).
1966   *The Holy Land: From the Persian to the Arab Conquest*. Grand Rapids, Michigan.
Bagatti, P. B.
1938   "Il monastero del Nebo e gli antichi monasteri della Palestina." In *Atti del 4° Congresso internazionale di archeologia cristiana*. Vatican City, II, 89–110.
1954a   "Antiche iconi palestinesi." *TS* 30, 107–11.
1954b   "Hircania—Castellion." *TS* 30, 311–15.
1961   "Tre grandi capi di monaci palestinesi nei sec. V–VI." *TS* 37, 4–7.
1962   *L'archeologia cristiana in Palestina*. Florence.
1968   "Un'inedita chiesa al Qasr el-'Abd presso Tequa—probabile monastero di Romano." *LA* 18, 288–300.
1971a   *The Church from the Gentiles in Palestine*. Jerusalem.
1971b   *The Church from the Circumcision*. Jerusalem.
1971c   "La Laura di Suka sul Wadi Kareitun." *TS* 47, 336–45.
Baldelli, R., and Mortari, L., trans.
1990   *Cirillo di Scitopoli: Storie monastiche del Deserto di Gerusalemme*. Abbazia di Praglia.
Baldi, D.
1952–53   "I santuari mariani di Terra Santa." *LA* 3, 219–69.
Baramki, D. C., and Stephan, St. H.
1935   "A Nestorian Hermitage between Jericho and the Jordan." *QDAP* 4, 81–86, pls. LII–LIV.

Baras, Z., et al., eds
    1982   *Eretz Israel from the Destruction of the Second Temple to the Muslim Conquest, I: Political,
                Social and Cultural History.* Jerusalem (Hebrew).
Bardenhewer, O.
    1914–32   *Geschichte der altkirchlichen Literatur.* Freiburg im Breisgau; repr. Darmstadt 1962.
Bardy, G.
    1937   "Basile (règle de Saint)." *DDC* II, 218–24.
Barison, P.
    1938   "Ricerche sui monasteri dell'Egitto bizantino e arabo secondo i documenti dei pa-
                piri greci." *Aegyptus* 18, 29–148.
Barrois, A.
    1930   "Une chapelle funéraire au couvent de Saint Euthyme." *RB* 39, 272–75.
Baumstark, A.
    1920   "Wandmalereien und Tafelbilder im Kloster Mâr Sâbâ." *OC* n.s. 9, 123–29.
Baynes, N. H.
    1947   "The *Pratum Spirituale.*" *OCP* 13, 404–14. Repr. in his *Byzantine Studies and Other
                Essays,* 261–70, London 1955.
Beck, H. G.
    1959   *Kirche und theologische Literatur im byzantinischen Reich.* Munich.
Beck, E.
    1956   "Zur Terminologie des ältesten syrischen Mönchtums." In *Antonius Magnus,* Studia
                Anselmiana 38, 261–62. Rome.
    1958   "Ascétisme et monachisme chez S. Ephrem." *Or. Syr.* 3, 253–98.
    1960   "Ephrem." *DS* IV, 788–800.
Bell, D. N., trans.
    1983   *Besa, The Life of Shenoute,* CS 73. Kalamazoo, Michigan.
Bell, H. I.
    1917   *Greek Papyri in the British Museum* V. London.
Ben-Dov, M.
    1985   *In the Shadow of the Temple: The Discovery of Ancient Jerusalem.* Tel Aviv.
Besse, J. M.
    1900   *Les moines d'Orient antérieure au concile de Chalcédoine.* Paris.
Binns, J. E.
    1989   *Cyril of Scythopolis and the Monasteries of the Palestinian Desert.* Ph.D. diss. London.
                Unpublished.
Blake, I.
    1969   "El Kuseir: A Hermitage in the Wilderness of Judaea." *PEQ* 101, 58–93.
Blake, R. P.
    1950   "Deux lacunes comblées dans la 'Passio XX monachorum Sabaitarum'." *AB* 68,
                27–43.
    1965   "La littérature grecque en Palestine au VIII siècle." *Le Muséon* 78, 367–80.
Blau, J.
    1962   "Über einige christlich-arabische Manuskripte aus dem 9. und 10. Jahrhundert."
                Le Muséon 75, 101–8.
Borsari, S.
    1951   "Le migrazioni dall'Oriente in Italia nel VII secolo." *Parola del passato* 17, 133–38.
Bottini, G. C., Di Segni, L., and Alliata, E., eds.
    1990   *Christian Archaeology in the Holy Land. New Discoveries: Archaeological Essays in Honour
                of Virgilio C. Corbo* OFM. Jerusalem.

Bousset, W.
1923a   "Das Mönchtum in der sketischen Wüste." *ZKG* 42, 1–41.
1923b   *Apophthegmata: Studien zur Geschichte des ältesten Mönchtums.* Tübingen.
Brehier, L.
1937   "La politique religieuse de Justinien." In Fliche and Martin 1937, 437–82.
Brock, S.
1973   "Early Syrian Asceticism." *Numen* 20, 1–19. Repr. Brock 1984, art. I.
1984   *Syriac Perspectives on Late Antiquity.* London.
Brooks, E. W.
1893   "The Emperor Zeno and the Isaurians." *EHR* 8, 209–38.
Brown, P.
1971   "The Rise and the Function of the Holy Man in Late Antiquity." *JRS* 61, 80–101.
             Repr. in his *Society and the Holy in Late Antiquity*, 103–52. Berkeley-Los Angeles 1982.
1982   "Town, Village and Holy Man: The Case of Syria." In his *Society and the Holy in Late
             Antiquity*, 153–65. London-Berkeley-Los Angeles.
1987   "The Saint as Exemplar in Late Antiquity." In J. S. Hawley, ed., *Saints and Virtues*,
             3–14. Berkeley-Los Angeles-London.
Brunot, A.
1975   "Les laures du désert de Juda." *BTS* 169, 7–16.
Bundy, D.
1991   "Jacob of Nisibis as a Model for the Episcopacy." *Le Muséon* 104, 235–49.
Butler, E. C.
1898–1904   *The Lausiac History of Palladius*, 2 vols., Texts and Studies VI.1 and 2. Cambridge;
             repr. Hildesheim 1967.
1911   "Monasticism." In H. M. Gwatkin and J. P. Whitney, eds., *Cambridge Medieval His-
             tory* I, 521–42. Cambridge.
Cabrol, F.
1915   "Monasticism." *Encyclopaedia of Religion and Ethics*, 781–97. Edinburgh.
Cachelli, I.
1951   "Laura." *Enc. Catt.* VII, 958–60. Rome.
Cameron, Averil
1978   "The Theotokos in Sixth-Century Constantinople." *JTS*, n.s. 29, 79–108. Repr. in
             Cameron 1981, art. XVI.
1981   *Continuity and Change in Sixth-Century Byzantium.* London.
Canivet, P.
1965   "Dorothée de Gaza, est-il disciple d'Évagre?". *REG* 78, 336–46.
1969   "Catégories sociales et titulature laïque et ecclésiastique dans l'*Histoire Philothée* de
             Théodoret de Cyr." *Byzantion* 39, 209–50.
1975   "Contributions archéologiques à l'*Histoire des moines de Syrie*." *SP* 13 (= *TU* 116),
             444–60.
1977   *Le monachisme syrien selon Théodoret de Cyr.* Paris.
Canivet, P., and Leroy-Molinghen, A. L.
1977   See Theodoret, *HPh*, vol. I.
1979   See Theodoret, *HPh*, vol. II.
Castel, G.
1979   "Étude d'une momie copte." *Hommage à la mémoire de Serge Sauneron* II, 121–43 and
             pls. Cairo.
Cauwenbergh, P. van
1914   *Étude sur les moines d'Égypte.* Paris-Louvain.

Cavallera, F.
1922   *Saint Jérôme: Sa vie et son oeuvre* I–II. Louvain-Paris.
Chadwick, H.
1974   "John Moschus and His Friend Sophronius the Sophist." *JTS*, n.s. 25, 41–74.
Chadwick, O.
1968   *John Cassian*, 2nd ed. Cambridge.
Charanis, P.
1971   "The Monk as an Element of Byzantine Society." *DOP* 25, 61–84.
1974   *Church and State in the Later Roman Empire: The Religious Policy of Anastasius the First (491–518)*, 2nd ed. Thessalonike.
Chitty, D. J.
1928a   "Two Monasteries in the Wilderness of Judea." *PEFQSt* 60 134–52.
1928b   "The Church of St. Euthymius at Khan el-Ahmar, near Jerusalem." *PEFQSt* 60, 175–78.
1929   "The Wilderness of Jerusalem." *The Christian East* 10.2, 4–80.
1930   "Excavations at the Monastery of St. Euthymius, 1929." *PEFQSt* 62, 43–47; 150–53.
1932   "The Monastery of St. Euthymius." *PEFQSt* 64, 188–203.
1952   "Jerusalem after Chalcedon, AD 451–518." *The Christian East* II, n.s. 1, 22–32.
1966   *The Desert a City*. Oxford.
1971   "Abba Isaiah." *JTS* 22, 47–72.
Clarke, W. K. L.
1913   *St. Basil the Great: A Study in Monasticism*. Cambridge.
1925   *The Ascetic Works of Saint Basil*. London.
Cohen, R.
1977   "Monasteries." *EAEHL* III, 876–85. Jerusalem.
Compagnoni, P.
1978   *Il Deserto di Giuda*. Jerusalem.
Conder, C. R., and Kitchener, R. E.
1883   *The Survey of Western Palestine, III: Judaea*. London.
Conybeare, F. C.
1910   "Antiochus Strategios' Account of the Sack of Jerusalem in AD 614." *EHR* 25, 502–17.
Coquin, R.-G.
1982   "Huitième campagne de fouilles aux Kellia (avril 1982). Rapport préliminaire." *BIFAO* 82, 363–77.
Corbo, V.
1951   "Il Romitorio dell'Egumeno Gabriele." *TS* 26, 202–7.
1955   *Gli scavi di Kh. Siyar el Ghanam e i monasteri dei dintorni*. Jerusalem.
1958a   "L'ambiente materiale della vita dei monaci di Palestina nel periodo bizantino." In *Il monachesimo orientale* (= *OCA* 153), 235–57. Rome.
1958b   "Finalmente identificata—La Laura Eptastomos?". *TS* 34, 85–88.
1958c   "Il cenobio di Zannos ed il piccolo cenobio della Grande Laura ritrovati nel Wadi el-Nar." *TS* 34, 107–10.
1958d   "Come abbiamo ritrovata la Laura di Geremia." *TS* 34, 169–72.
1960   "Ritrovati gli edifici della Laura di Firmino." *TS* 36, 137–41.
1962   "La Nuova Laura identificata con Kh. Tina." *TS* 38, 109–13.
1989   *Herodion I: Gli edifici della reggia-fortezza*. Jerusalem.
Couret, A.
1869   *La Palestine sous les empereurs grecs*. Grenoble.

Couret, M.
1897   "La prise de Jérusalem par les Perses en 614." *ROC* 2, 125–64.
Cox, P.
1983   *Biography in Late Antiquity: The Quest for the Holy Man*. Berkeley.
Cunningham, M. B., ed. and trans.
1991   *The Life of Michael the Synkellos*. Belfast.
Dagron, G.
1970   "Les moines et la ville: Le monachisme à Constantinople jusqu'au Concile de Chalcédoine (451)." *Travaux et mémoires* 4, 229–76.
Dahari, U.
1982   "The Sinai Monasticism in the Byzantine Period in the Light of Archaeological Excavations." In U. Lachish and Z. Meshel, eds., *South Sinai Research 1967–1982*, 36–47. Tel Aviv (Hebrew).
Daley, B.
1976   "The Origenism of Leontius of Byzantium." *JTS*, n.s. 27, 333–69.
Dalman, G.
1904   "Der Pass von Michmas." *ZDPV* 27, 161–73.
1905   "Das Wadi es-Swenit." *ZDPV* 28, 161–75.
Dan, Y.
1982   "Eretz Israel in the Fifth and Sixth Centuries." In Baras et al. 1982, 265–99; and "The Byzantine Administration," ibid., 387–419 (Hebrew).
1984   *The City in Eretz Israel during the Late Roman & Byzantine Periods*. Jerusalem (Hebrew).
Dar, Sh.
1988   "Archaeological Evidence for the Samaritan Revolts in the Byzantine Period." In Jacoby and Tsafrir 1988, 228–37 (Hebrew).
Daumas, F.
1967   "Les travaux de l'Institut Français d'Archéologie Orientale pendant l'année 1966–67." *AIBL*, 438–52.
1968   "Fouilles et travaux de l'Institut Français d'Archéologie Orientale durant l'année 1967–68." *AIBL*, 395–408.
1969   "Rapport sur l'activité de l'Institut Français d'Archéologie Orientale du Caire au cours des années 1968–1969." *AIBL*, 496–507.
Daumas, F., and Guillaumont, A.
1969   *Kellia I—Kom 219. Fouilles exécutées en 1964 et 1965, fascicule I: Texte; fascicule II: Planches*, Fouilles de l'Institut Français d'Archéologie Orientale du Caire 28. Cairo.
Dawes, E., and Baynes, N. H.
1948   *Three Byzantine Saints*. Oxford.
Dekkers, E.
1957   "Les anciens moines cultivaient-ils la liturgie?". *La Maison-Dieu* 51, 31–54.
Delau, V.
1899–1900 "Monastères palestiniens du cinquième siècle." *Bulletin de littérature Ecclésiastique* 1, 233–40, 269–81.
Delehaye, H.
1948   "Byzantine Monasticism." In *Byzantium*, 136–65 ed. H. N. Baynes and H. Moss. Oxford.
Dembinska, M.
1985   "Diet: A Comparison of Food Consumption between some Eastern and Western Monasteries in the 4th–12th Centuries." *Byzantion* 55, 431–62.

Deslandes, S.
1922   "Une question de droit canonique: De quelle autorité relèvent les monastères ori-
            entaux?". *EO* 21, 308–22.
Devos, P.
1980   "Cyrille de Scythopolis: Influences littéraires: Vêtement de l'évêque de Jérusalem."
            AB 98, 29–32.
1983   "Une nouvelle Égérie." *AB* 101, 43–70.
Dick, I.
1961   "La passion arabe de S. Antoine Ruwah, néo-martyr de Damas (†25 déc. 799)." *Le
            Muséon* 74, 109–33.
1962–63   "Théodore Abuqurra, évêque melkite de Harran—la personne et son milieu."
            POC 12, 209–23, 319–32; 13, 114–29.
Diekamp, F.
1899   *Die origenistischen Streitigkeiten im sechsten Jahrhundert.* Münster in Westfalen.
Di Segni, L.
1988   "Scythopolis in the Samaritan Revolt of 529 CE." In Jacoby and Tsafrir 1988.
1990a   *Cercare Dio nel deserto: Vita di Caritone.* Comunità di Bose.
1990b   "The Life of Chariton." In V. L. Wimbush, ed., *Ascetic Behavior in Greco-Roman An-
            tiquity: A Sourcebook*, 393–421. Minneapolis.
1991   *Nel deserto accanto ai Fratelli. Vite di Gerasimo e di Giorgio di Choziba.* Comunità di Bose.
Di Segni, L., and Hirschfeld, Y.
1986   "Four Greek Inscriptions from Hammat Gader from the Reign of Anastasius." *IEJ*
            36, 251–68, pls. 33–35.
1987   "Four Greek Inscriptions from the Monastery at Khirbet Ed-Deir in the Judean
            Desert." *OCP* 53, 365–86.
Dmitrievskij, A. A.
1890   "Die Klosterregeln des hl. Sabbas" (russisch). *Trudy der Kiewschen Geistlichen Akade-
            mie*, 170–92.
1895   *Opisanie liturgičeskich rukopisej* I. Kiev.
1917   Vol. III. Petrograd.
Dölger, F.
1940   "E. Schwartz, *Kyrillos von Skythopolis.*" *BZ* 40, 474–84.
1953   *Der griechische Barlaam-Roman, ein Werk des H. Johannes von Damaskos.* Ettal.
Doens, I.
1954   "Nicon de la Montaigne Noire." *Byzantion* 24, 131–40.
Draguet, R.
1944–45   "Le chapitre de *HL* sur les Tabennésiotes, dérive-t-il d'une source copte?". *Le Mu-
            séon* 57 (1944), 53–145; 58 (1945), 15–95.
1946   "L'*Histoire Lausiaque*, une oeuvre écrit dans l'esprit d'Évagre." *RHE*, 321–64.
1948   "Réminiscences de Pallade chez Cyrille de Scythopolis." *RAM* 98–100, 213–18.
1949   *Les Pères du Désert.* Paris.
Dublanchy, E.
1911   "Communion fréquente." *DTC* III.1, 515–22.
Du Cange, C.
1688   *Glossarium ad scriptores Mediae et Infimae Graecitatis*, Leiden; repr. Paris-Leipzig 1905.
1883–87   *Glossarium Mediae et Infimae Latinitatis*; repr. 1954.
Duchesne, L.
1909   *Early History of the Christian Church* III, Eng. trans. C. Jenkins. London.
1915   "Les protégés de Théodora." *Mélange d'archéologie et d'histoire de l'École Française de*

Rome 35, 57–59. Rome.
1925   *L'Église au VIe siècle*, Paris.

Dühr, J.
1953   "Communion fréquente." *DS* II.1, 1234–50.

Dumont, P.
1955   "Vie cénobitique ou vie hésychaste dans quelques 'typica' byzantines." In *L'église et les églises* II, 3–13. Chevetogne.

Egender, N.
1975   "Introduction: Formation de l'office." In *La prière des heures: Hôrologion, La prière des églises de rite byzantin* I, 25–49. Chevetogne.

Ehrhard, A.
1893   "Das griechische Kloster Mar-Saba in Palestina." *RQ* 7, 32–79.

Evans, D. B.
1970   *Leontius of Byzantium: An Origenist Christology,* Dumbarton Oaks Studies 13. Washington.

Evelyn-White, H. G.
1932–33   *The Monasteries of the Wadi'n Natrûn: Part II, The History of the Monasteries of Nitria and Scetis.* New York, 1932; *Part III, The Architecture and Archaeology.* New York 1933.

Farmer, W. R.
1957   "Soundings at Khirbet Wadi ez-Zaraniq." *BASOR* 147, 34–36.

Federlin, L.
1902–7   "Recherches sur les laures et monastères de la Plaine du Jordain et du Désert de Jerusalem." *La Terre Sainte.* Paris. 19 (1902), 129–32, 152–56, 166–68, 181–84; 20 (1903), 117–20, 132–34, 148–50, 168–71, 180–82, 196–99, 215–18, 232–34, 263–66, 278–79, 299–301, 309–11, 328–31, 342–46, 360–62, 372–75; 21 (1904), 7–10; 24 (1907), 177–85.
1909   "Mémoire sur les Paremboles." In R. Génier, *Vie de S. Euthyme le Grand,* 104–11. Paris.

Ferrari, G.
1957   *Early Roman Monasteries: Notes for the History of the Monasteries and Convents at Rome from the Vth through the Xth Century,* Studi di antichità cristiana 23. Vatican City.

Festugière, A.-J.
1959   *Antioche païenne et chrétienne.* Paris.
1962a   *Les moines d'Orient, III/1: Les moines de Palestine* (Cyrille de Scythopolis: Vie de Saint Euthyme). Paris.
1962b   *Les moines d'Orient, III/2: Les moines de Palestine* (Cyrille de Scythopolis: Vie de Saint Sabas). Paris.
1963a   *Les moines d'Orient, III/3: Les moines de Palestine* (Cyrille de Scythopolis: Vie des Saints Jean l'Hésychaste, Kyriakos, Théodose, Théognios, Abraamios; Théodore de Petra: Vie de Saint Théodose). Paris.
1963b   "La Vie de Sabas et les tours de Syrie-Palestine." *RB* 70 (1963), 80–92.

Finkelstein, I.
1985   "Byzantine Monastic Remains in the Southern Sinai." *DOP* 39, 39–75.

Fitzgerald, S. M.
1939   *A Sixth Century Monastery at Beth-Shan.* Philadelphia.

Fliche, A., and Martin, V., eds.
1936–37   *Histoire générale de l'Église depuis les origines jusqu'à nos jours, III: De la paix constantinienne à la mort de Théodose,* by J.-R. Palanque, G. Bardy, and P. de Labriolle. Paris

1936. Vol. IV: *De la mort de Théodose à l'avènement de Grégoire le Grand*, by P. de Labriolle, G. Bardy, L. Bréhier, and G. de Plinval. Paris 1937.

Flusin, B.
1983   *Miracle et histoire dans l'oeuvre de Cyrille de Scythopolis*, Études augustiniennes. Paris.
1992   *Saint Anastase le Perse et l'histoire de la Palestine au début du VIIe siècle*. Paris.

Frances, D. J.
1963   "Mar Saba." *TS* 43, 80–85.

Frazee, C. A.
1981   "St. Theodore of Stoudios and Ninth Century Monasticism in Constantinople." *St. Mon.* 23, 27–58.
1982   "Late Roman and Byzantine Legislation on the Monastic Life from the Fourth to the Eighth Centuries." *CH* 51, 263–79.

Frend, W. H.
1972   *The Rise of the Monophysite Movement*. Cambridge.

Fritz, G.
1932   "Origenism." *DTC* XI.2, 1565–88.

Furrer, K.
1880   "Nachtrag zu Baurath Schicks 'Die alten Lauren und Klöster in der Wüste Judä'." *ZDPV* 3, 234–36.

Galatariotou, C.
1987   "Byzantine Ktetorika Typika: A Comparative Study." *REB* 45, 77–138.

Garitte, G.
1941   "La Vie prémétaphrastique de S. Chariton." *Bulletin de l'Institut Historique Belge de Rome* 21, 1–42.
1954   "La mort de S. Jean l'Hésychaste d'après un texte géorgien inédit," *AB* 72, 75–84.
1954a   "Un extrait géorgien de la Vie d'Etienne le Sabaite." *Le Muséon* 67, 83–90.
1957   "Réminiscences de la Vie d'Antoine dans Cyrille de Scythopolis." In *Silloge bizantina in onore di Silvio Giuseppe Mercati*, 117–22. Rome.
1958   *Le Calendrier Palestino-Géorgien du sinaiticus 34 (xe siècle)*. Brussels.
1959   "Le début de la Vie de S. Étienne le Sabaïte retrouvé en arabe au Sinai." *AB* 77, 332–69.
1962   "La version géorgienne de la Vie de S. Cyriaque par Cyrille de Scythopolis." *Le Muséon* 75, 399–440.
1971   "La Vie géorgienne de Saint Cyriaque et son modèle arabe." *Bedi-Kartlisa* 28, 92–105.

Genier, Fr. H.
1909   *Vie de St. Euthyme le Grand, AD 377–473*. Paris.

Giet, S.
1941   *Les idées et l'action sociales de S. Basile*. Paris.

Gil, M.
1992   *A History of Palestine 634–1099*. Cambridge.

Goldfus, H.
1990   "Khallet ed-Danabiyeh: A Desert Monastery." In Bottini et al. 1990, 227–44.

Gordini, G. D.
1961   "Il monachesimo romano in Palestina nel IV secolo." In *Saint Martin et son temps*, Studia Anselmiana 46. Rome.

Gough, M.
1964–65 "The Monastery of Eski Gümüz." *An. St.* 14 (1964), 147–64; 15 (1965), 157–64.
1985   *Alahan: An Early Christian Monastery in Southern Turkey*. Toronto.

Gouillard, J.
    1946   "Théodore le sabaïte." *DTC* XV.1, 284–86.
    1969   "Un 'quartier' d'émigrés palestiniens à Constantinople au IXᵉ siècle?". *Revue des Études sud-est européennes* 7, 73–76.

Graf, G.
    1910   "Die arabischen Schriften des Theodors Abû Qurra Bischofs von Harran (ca. 740–820)." *Forschungen zur christlichen Literatur- und Dogmengeschichte* 10, 1–20.
    1913   *Des Theodor Abû Kurra Traktat über den Schöpfer und die wahre Religion*, Beiträge zur Geschichte der philosophie des Mittelalters, Texte und Untersuchungen 14.1, ed. C. Bäumker. Münster.
    1944   *Geschichte der christlichen arabischen Literatur, I. Band: Die Übersetzungen*, Vatican City.
    1947   *II. Band: Die Schriftsteller bis zur Mitte des 15. Jahrhunderts.* Vatican City.

Granič, B.
    1929–30 "Die Rechtsstellung und Organisation der griechischen Klöster nach dem justinianischen Recht." *BZ* 29, 6–34.

Gray, P. T. R.
    1979   *The Defense of Chalcedon in the East.* Leiden.

Grégoire, A.
    1904   "La Vie anonyme de S. Gérasime." *BZ* 13, 113–35.

Gribomont, J.
    1953   *Histoire du texte des Ascétiques de S. Basile*, Bibliothèque du Muséon 32. Louvain.
    1957   "Le monachisme au IVe siècle en Asie Mineure; de Gangres au Messalianisme." *SP* 2 (= *TU* 64), 400–416. Berlin.
    1959   "Eustathe le philosophe et les voyages du jeune Basile de Césarée." *RHE* 54, 115–24.
    1961   "Eustathe de Sébaste." *DS* IV.2, 1708–12.
    1965   "Le monachisme au sein de l'Église en Syrie et en Cappadoce." *St. Mon.* 7, 7–24.
    1980   "Saint Basile et le monachisme enthousiaste." *Irénikon* 53, 123–44.

Griffith, S. H.
    1979   "Some Unpublished Arabic Sayings Attributed to Theodore abû Qurrah." *Le Muséon* 92, 29–35.
    1985   "Theodore Abu Qurrah's Arabic Tract on the Christian Practice of Venerating Images." *JAOS* 105, 53–73.
    1986   "Greek into Arabic: Life and Letters in the Monasteries of Palestine in the Ninth Century: The Example of the *Summa Theologiae Arabica*." *Byzantion* 56, 117–38.
    1988   "The Monks of Palestine and the Growth of Christian Literature in Arabic." *The Muslim World* 78, 1–28.
    1989   "Antony David of Baghdad, Scribe and Monk of Mar Saba: Arabic in the Monasteries of Palestine." *CH* 58, 7–19.
    1989–90 "Images of Ephraem: The Syrian Holy Man and His Church." *Traditio* 45, 7–33.
    1991   "Singles in God's Service: Thoughts on the Ihîdāyê from the Works of Aphrahat and Ephraem the Syrian." *The Harp* 4, 145–59.
    1992   *Theodore Abu Qurrah—The Intellectual Profile of an Arab Christian Writer of the First Abbasid Century.* Tel Aviv University, the Dr. Irene Halmos Chair of Arabic Literature.

Grohmann, A.
    1963   *Arabic Papyri from Hirbet el Mird.* Louvain.

Grossmann, P.
    1979   "The Basilica of St. Pachomius." *BA* 42, 232–36.

Grumel, V.
   1926   "Léonce de Byzance." *DTC* IX.1, 400–426.
   1937   "Acémètes." *DS* I, 169–75.
Guérin, V.
   1869   *Description géographique, historique et archéologique de la Palestine, III: Judée*. Paris.
Guillaumont, A.
   1962   *Les "Kephalaia Gnostica" d'Évagre le Pontique et l'histoire de l'Origénisme chez les Grecs et chez les Syriens*, Patristica Sorbonensia 5, 124–70. Paris.
   1965   "Premières fouilles au site des Kellia (Basse-Égypte)." *AIBL*, 218–25.
   1977   "Histoire des moines aux Kellia." *Orientalia Lovaniensia Periodica* 8, 187–203. Repr. in his *Aux origines du monachisme chrétien*, 151–67. Abbaye de Bellefontaine 1979.
Guy, J. C.
   1961   *Jean Cassien: Vie et doctrine spirituelle*. Paris.
   1964   "Le centre monastique de Scété dans la littérature du Ve siècle." *OCP* 30, 129–47.
Halkin, F.
   1930   "L'*Histoire Lausiaque* et les *Vies* grecques de S. Pachome." *AB* 48, 257–301.
   1968   "Saint Jean l'Érémopolite." *AB* 86, 13–20.
   1973   *Saints moines d'Orient*. London.
Halloun, M., and Rubin, R.
   1981   "Palestinian-Syriac Inscription from 'En Suweinit." *LA* 31, 291–98.
Hanslik, R.
   1972   *Klosterregeln im Mönchtum des Östens und Westens von Pachomius zu Benedikt von Nursia*. Vienna.
Hausherr, I.
   1936   "Barsanuphe." *DS* I, 1255–62. Paris.
   1956a   "L'hésychasme, étude de spiritualité." *OCP* 22, 5–40, 241–85.
   1956b   "Comment priaient les Pères?". *RAM* 32, 33–58, 284–79.
Hefele, C. J., and Leclercq, H.
   1907   *Histoire des Conciles*, I–III. Paris.
Hendriks, O.
   1960   "La vie quotidienne du moine syrien." *Or. Syr.* 5, 293–330, 401–31.
Hermann, T.
   1926   "Zur chronologie des Kyril von Skythopolis." *ZKG*, 318–39.
Heussi, K.
   1936   *Der Ursprung des Mönchtums*. Tübingen.
Hintlian, K.
   1976   *History of the Armenians in the Holy Land*. Jerusalem.
Hirschfeld, Y.
   1985   *Archaeological Survey of Israel: Map of Herodium (108/2) 17–11*. Jerusalem.
   1987   *The Judean Desert Monasteries in the Byzantine Period: Their Development and Internal Organization in the Light of Archaeological Research*. Ph.D. diss. Jerusalem.
   1989   "La vie quotidienne dans les monastères"; "Les Laures du désert judéen"; "Les monastères cénobitiques." *Le Monde de la Bible* 68, 10–32.
   1990   "List of the Byzantine Monasteries in the Judean Desert." In Bottini et al. 1990, 1–90.
   1992   *The Judean Desert Monasteries in the Byzantine Period* (with a detailed bibliography of the author's previous publications on this topic). New Haven-London.

Hirschfeld, Y., and Birger, R.
   1986   "Chronique archéologique: Khirbet ed-Deir (désert de Juda)—1981–1984." *RB* 93, 276–84.

Hirschfeld, Y., and Schmutz, T.
   1987   "Zur historisch-geographischen Entwicklung der mönchischen Bewegung in der Wüste Judäa." *Antike Welt* 18, 38–48.

Hoeck, J. M.
   1951   "Stand und Aufgaben der Damaskenos-Forschung." *OCP* 17, 5–13.

Holum, K. G.
   1982   *Theodosian Empresses: Women and Imperial Dominion in Late Antiquity.* Berkeley.

Honigmann, E.
   1956   "Juvenal of Jerusalem." *DOP* 5, 211–76.

Humbertclaude, P.
   1932   *La doctrine ascétique de saint Basile de Césarée*, Études de théologie historique. Paris.

Hunt, E. D.
   1973   "Palladius of Helenopolis: A Party and Its Supporters in the Church of the Late Fourth Century." *JTS*, n.s. 24, 456–80.
   1982   *Holy Land Pilgrimages in the Later Roman Empire, A.D. 312–460.* Oxford.

Hussey, J. M.
   1939   "Byzantine Monasticism." *History*, n.s. 24, 56–62.
   1967   "Byzantine Monasticism." *CMH, IV: The Byzantine Empire*, pt. 2, 161–84. Cambridge.

Husson, G.
   1979   "L'habitat monastique en Égypte à la lumière des papyrus grecs, des textes chrétiens et de l'archéologie." In *Hommage à la mémoire de Serge Souneron* II, 191–207. Cairo.

Jacoby, D., and Tsafrir, Y., eds.
   1988   *Jews, Samaritans and Christians in Byzantine Palestine.* Jerusalem (Hebrew).

Janin, R.
   1929   "Michel le Syncelle." *DTC* X.2, 1710–11.
   1930   "Arménie." *DHGE* IV, 291–304.
   1949   "Cappadoce." *DHGE* XI, 907–9.
   1953   "2. Césarée." *DHGE* XII, 199–202.
   1956   "2. Colonia." *DHGE* XIII, 326.
   1964   *Constantinople Byzantine*, 2nd ed. Paris.
   1969   *Les églises et les monastères de la ville de Constantinople, Géographie ecclésiastique de l'empire byzantin 3*, 2nd ed. Paris.
   1975   *Les églises et les monastères des grands centres byzantins, Géographie ecclésiastique de l'empire byzantin 2*. Paris.

Jargy, S.
   1952   "Les origines du monachisme en Syrie et en Mésopotamie." *POC* 2, 110–24.
   1954   "Les premiers instituts monastiques et les principaux représentants du monachisme syrien au IV siècle." *POC* 4, 106–17.

Jerphanion, G. de
   1925   *Une nouvelle province de l'art byzantine: Les églises rupestres de Cappadoce.* Paris.
   1931   "La chronologie des peintures de Cappadoce." *EO* 30, 5–27.

Jones, A. H. M.
   1964   *The Later Roman Empire: 284–602.* Norman, Oklahoma.
   1971   *The Cities of the Eastern Roman Provinces*, 2nd ed. Oxford.

Jugie, M.
   1924   "La Vie de Saint Jean Damascène." *EO* 23, 137–61.
   1925   "Jean Damascène." *DTC* VIII, 693–708.
Julien, M.
   1901   "À la recherche de la grotte de l'Abbé Jean." *ENDF* 8, 205–18.
Karayannopulos, J.
   1956   "Die kollektive Steuerverantwortung in der frühbyzantinischen Zeit." *Vierteljahr-schrift für Sozial- und Wirtschaftgeschichte* 43, 289–322.
   1958   *Das Finanzwesen des frühbyzantinischen Staates.* Munich.
Kasser, R.
   1967   *Kellia 1965: Topographie générale, mensurations et fouilles aux Qouçoûr Isâ et aux Qouçoûr el-Abîd; Mensurations aux Qouçour el-Izeila*, Recherches Suisses d'archéologie copte 1. Geneva.
   1972   *Kellia: Topographie*, Recherches Suisses d'archéologie copte 2. Geneva.
   1980   "Aux origines du monachisme copte: Fouilles de l'Université de Genève aux Kellia (Basse-Égypte)." *BSEG* 3, 33–38.
   1982   *Survey archéologique des Kellia (Basse-Égypte): Rapport de la campagne 1981*, EK 8184: Projet International de Sauvetage Scientifique des Kellia. Fascicule I: Texte; fascicule II: Planches. Louvain.
   1984   *Le site monastique des Kellia (Basse-Égypte).* Louvain.
Kasteren, V. P. van
   1890   "Aus der Umgegend von Jerusalem." *ZDPV* 13, 76–118.
Kazhdan, A.
   1990   "Kosmas of Jerusalem: 2. Can We Speak of His Political Views?". *Le Muséon* 103, 329–46.
Kazhdan, A. and Gero, S.
   1989   "Kosmas of Jerusalem: A More Critical Approach to His Biography." *BZ* 82, 122–32.
Kelly, J. N. D.
   1975   *Jerome: His Life, Writings and Controversies.* London.
   1977   *Early Christian Doctrines*, 5th ed. London.
Keyes, C. F.
   1982   "Charisma: From Social Life to Sacred Biography." In M. A. Williams, ed., *Charisma and Sacred Biography*, 1–22. Chico, California.
Khitrovo, B. de
   1889   *Itinéraires russes en Orient.* Geneva.
King, G.
   1982   "Preliminary Report on a Survey of Byzantine and Islamic Sites in Jordan 1980." *ADAJ* 26, 85–95.
Kirchemeyer, J.
   1962   "Le moine Marcien (de Bethléem)." *TU* 80, 341–59.
Kirsten, E.
   1954   "Cappadocia." *RAC* II, 861–91.
Kister, M. J.
   1981–82   "On a Fragment of a Private Letter of the First Century A.H." *JSAI* 3, 237–40.
   1982   "On an Early Fragment of the Quran." In *Studies in Judaica, Karaitica and Islamica presented to L. Nemoy*, 163–66. Ramat-Gan.
Knowles, D.
   1969   *Christian Monasticism.* London.

Koch, H.

1933   *Quellen zur Geschichte der Askese und der Mönchtums in der alten Kirche.* Tübingen.

Koikylides, C. M.

1901a   Τὰ κατὰ τὴν Λαύραν καὶ τὸν χειμάρρον τοῦ Χουζιβᾶ. Jerusalem.

1901b   Ἡ κατὰ τὴν ἔρημων τῆς ἁγίας τοῦ θεοῦ ἡμῶν πόλεως λαύρα Θεοδοσίου τοῦ Κοινοβιαρ-
           χοῦ. Jerusalem.

1902   Αἱ παρὰ τὸν Ἰορδάνην λαύραι Καλαμωνὸς καὶ ἁγίου Γερασίμου καὶ οἱ βίοι τοῦ ἁγίου
           Γερασίμου καὶ Κυριακοῦ τοῦ ἀναχωρητοῦ. Jerusalem.

Krumbacher, K., Ehrhard, A., and Gelzer, H.

1897   *Geschichte der byzantinischen Literatur,* 2nd ed. Munich; repr. 1958.

Kühnel, G.

1984   "Wiederentdeckte monastische Malereien der Kreuzfahrerzeit in der Judäischen
           Wüste." *RQ* 79, 163–88.

Kurtz, E.

1894   "A. Dmitrievskij, 'Die klosterregeln des hl. Sabbas'." *BZ* 3, 167–70.

Labriolle, P. de, et al.

1937   *Histoire générale de l'Église depuis les origines jusqu'à nos jours* (ed. Fliche and Martin),
           IV: De la mort de Théodose à l'avènement de Grégoire le Grand. Paris.

Lackner, W.

1982   "Zwei Membra Disiecta aus dem *Pratum Spirituale* des Joannes Moschos." *AB* 100,
           341–50.

Ladeuze, P.

1898   *Étude sur le cénobitisme Pakhômien pendant le IVe siècle et la première moitié du Ve.*
           Louvain.

Lafontaine, G.

1973   "Deux vies grecques abrégées de S. Sabas." *Le Muséon* 86, 305–39.

Lampe, G. W. H.

1961   *A Patristic Greek Lexicon.* Oxford.

Lappa-Zizicas, E.

1970   "Une épitome de la Vie de S. Jean l'Aumônier, par Jean et Sophronios." *AB* 88,
           265–76.

Lassus, J.

1947   "La vie monastique et la culte des ascètes." In *Sanctuaires chrétiens de Syrie*, 264–88.
           Paris.

Lease, G.

1980   "The Fourth Season of the Nag Hammadi Excavation." *Göttinger Miszellen* 41,
           75–85.

Leclercq, H.

1924   "Archimandrite." *DACL* I.2, 2739–50.

1925   "Cénobitisme." *DACL* II.2, 3047–3248.

1929   "Laures palestiniennes." *DACL* VIII.2, 1961–88.

1934   "Monachisme." *DACL* XI.2, 1774–1947.

1944   "Reclus." *DACL* XIV.2, 2149–59.

1950   "Sabas." *DACL* XV.1, 189–211.

1953   "Vigiles." *DACL* XV.2, 3108–12.

Leipoldt, J.

1903   *Schenute von Atripe und die Entstehung des national-ägyptischen Christentums,* TU 25.1.
           Leipzig.

Lemerle, P.
 1979   *The Agrarian History of Byzantium.* Galway.
Leroy, J.
 1954   "La vie quotidienne du moine studite." *Irénikon* 27, 21–50.
 1958   "La réforme studite." *OCP* 153, 181–214.
Lialine, C.
 1960a   "Monachisme oriental et monachisme occidental." *Irénikon* 22, 435–59.
 1960b   "Érémitisme." *DS* IV.1, 936–53.
Liddell, H. G., and Scott, R.
 1982   *A Greek-English Lexicon.* Oxford.
Liguori, A. M.
 1936   "Le laure di Palestina: Pagine sparse di cenobitismo orientale." *TS* 16, 3–76.
Linder, A.
 1987a   *The Jews in Roman Imperial Legislation.* Detroit.
 1987b   "The Christian Communities in Jerusalem." In J. Prawer, ed., *The History of Jerusa-
              lem: The Early Islamic Period (638–1099).* Jerusalem (Hebrew).
Lombardi, P. G.
 1958–59   "Alcune questioni di topografia." *LA* 9, 272–82.
Longo, A.
 1965–66   "Il testo integrale della *Narrazione* degli abati Giovanni et Sofronio, attraverso le
              Hermêneiai di Nicone." *Rivista di studi bizantini e neoellenici* 12–13, 223–67.
Macdonald, B.
 1980   "The Hermitage of John the Abbot at Hammam 'Aqra, Southern Jordan." *LA* 30,
              351–64, pls. 59–70.
MacKean, W. H.
 1920   *Christian Monasticism in Egypt to the Close of the Fourth Century.* London.
Mader, A. E.
 1928   "Sechsunddreißig Heiligengemälde in einer Gräberhöhle von Hirbet el-Merd in
              der Wüste Judä." *Das Heilige Land* 72, 33–52, pl. I.
 1929   "Conical Sundials and Ikon Inscription from the Kastellion Monastery on Khirbet
              el-Merd in the Wilderness of Juda." *JPOS* 9, 122–35.
 1937   "Ein Bilderzyklus in der Gräberhöhle der St. Euthymios-Laura auf Mardes (Chir-
              bet el-Mard) in der Wüste Judä." *OC* 34, 27–58, 192–212.
Magen, Y., and Talgam, R.
 1990   "The Monastery of Martyrius at Ma'ale Adumim (Khirbet el-Murassas) and Its
              Mosaics." In Bottini et al. 1990, 91–152.
Mango, C.
 1980   *Byzantium: The Empire of New Rome.* London.
 1991   "Greek Culture in Palestine after the Arab Conquest." In G. Cavallo, G. de Gre-
              gorio, and M. Maniaci, eds., *Scritture, libri e testi nelle aree provinciali di Bisanzio*, Atti
              del Seminario di Erice, 18–25 settembre 1988, 149–60, Centro Italiano di Studi
              sull'Alto Medioevo. Spoleto.
Marcoff, M., and Chitty, D. J.
 1929   "Notes on Monastic Research in the Judaean Wilderness 1928–1929." *PEFQSt* 61,
              167–78, pls. I–IV.
Marin, E.
 1903   "Acémètes." *DTC* I, 304–8.
Marti, K.
 1880   "Mittheilungen von Baurath C. Schick über die alten Lauren und Klöster in der

Wüste Judä." *ZDPV* 3, 1–43.

Martin, M.
  1966a   "Laures et ermitages du désert d'Égypte." *MUSJ* 42, 183–98.
  1966b   "Les ermitages d'Abû Daraǧ." *BSAC* 18, 139–45.
  1971   *La Laure de Dêr al Dik à Antinoë*. Cairo.

Martindale, J. R.
  1980   *The Prosopography of the Later Roman Empire* II. Cambridge.

Matejić, M.
  1976   *Biography of Saint Sava (of Serbia)*. Columbus, Ohio.

Mateos, J.
  1961   "La vigile cathédrale chez Égérie." *OCP* 27, 281–312.
  1963   "L'office monastique à la fin du IVe siècle: Antioche, Palestine, Cappadoce." *OC* 47, 53–88.
  1967   "The Origins of the Divine Office." *Worship* 41, 477–85.
  1971   *La célébration de la parole dans la liturgie byzantine*, OCA 191. Rome.

Mayerson, P.
  1975   "Observations on the 'Nilus' *Narrationes*: Evidence for an Unknown Christian Sect?". *Journal of the American Research Center in Egypt* 12, 51–74.
  1976   "An Inscription in the Monastery of St. Catherine and the Martyr Tradition of Sinai." *DOP* 30, 375–79.
  1988   "Justinian's Novel 103 and the Reorganization of Palestine." *BASOR* 269, 65–71.
  1993   "The Meaning and Etymology of the Word μαν(ν)ούθιον," in M. Heltzer et al., eds., *Studies in the Archaeology and History of Ancient Israel in Honour of Moshe Dothan*, 195–98. Haifa.

Meester, P. de
  1937   *Règlement des Bienheureux et Saints Pères Sabas le Grand et Théodose le Cénobiarque pour la vie des moines cénobites et kelliotes*. Lille.
  1940   "Les typiques de fondation (Τυπικὰ κτητορικά)." *Atti del V Congresso Internazionale di Studi Bizantini (Roma 20–26 settembre 1936) (= Studi bizantini e neoellenici* 6), 489–508. Rome.
  1942   *De monachico statu iuxta disciplinam byzantinam*, Statuta selectis fontibus et commentariis instructa. Vatican City.

Meimaris, I.
  1978   "The Hermitage of St. John the Chozebite, Deir Wady el-Qilt." *LA* 28, 171–92.
  1986   *Sacred Names, Saints, Martyrs and Church Officials in the Greek Inscriptions and Papyri Pertaining to the Christian Church of Palestine*. Athens.
  1989   *The Monastery of Saint Euthymios the Great at Khan el-Ahmar in the Wilderness of Judaea: Rescue Excavations and Basic Protection Measures 1976–1979*. Athens.

Meinardus, O.
  1965–66 "Notes on the Laurae and Monasteries of the Wilderness of Judaea" II. *LA* 16, 328–56.
  1966b   "Anachorètes modernes en Palestine." *RB* 73, 119–27.
  1966c   "Wall-Paintings in the Monastic Churches of Judaea." *OC* 50, 46–55.
  1968–69 "Historical Notes on the Laura of Mar Saba." *Eastern Churches Review* 2, 392–401.
  1970   "A Study of the Relics of Saints of the Greek Orthodox Church." *OC* 54, 130–278.

Menabde, L.
  1968   *Centers of Ancient Georgian Culture* (Eng. trans. D. Skvirski). Tbilisi.
  1980   *Seats of Ancient Georgian Literature* II. Tbilisi (Georgian).

Mensbrugghe, A. van der
  1957   "Prayer-time in Egyptian Monasticism (320–450)." *SP* 2 (= *TU* 64), 435–54.
Meshel, Z.
  1973   "The Landscape Units of the Judean Desert." *Teva Vaaretz* 15, 116–19 (Hebrew).
Milik, J. T.
  1953   "Une inscription et une lettre en araméen christo-palestinien." *RB* 60, 526–39.
  1960   "Notes d'épigraphie et de topographie palestiniennes." *RB* 67, 354–67, 550–91.
  1960–61   "La topographie de Jérusalem vers la fin de l'époque byzantine." *MUSJ* 37, 127–89.
  1961   "The Monastery of Kastellion." *Biblica* 48, 21–27.
Mioni, E.
  1951   "Il *Pratum Spirituale* di Giovanni Mosco." *OCP* 17, 61–94.
  1974   "Jean Moschus." *DS* VIII, 632–40.
Monneret de Villard, U.
  1925–26   *Les couvents près de Sohâg (Deyr el-Abiad, et Deyr el-Ahmar)*. Milan.
  1927   *Description général du Monastère de St. Siméon à Aswan*. Milan.
Montgomery, J. A.
  1907   *The Samaritans*. Philadelphia.
Morison, E. F.
  1912   *St. Basil and His Rule: A Study in Early Monasticism*. Oxford.
Murphy, F. X.
  1945   *Rufinus of Aquileia (345–411): His Life and Works*, Catholic University of America, Studies in Mediaeval History, n.s. 6. Washington.
Murphy, M. G.
  1930   *Saint Basil and Monasticism*. Washington.
Muyser, J.
  1937   "Le samedi et le dimanche dans l'Église et la littérature copte." In T. Mina, *Le Martyre d'Apa Epima*, 89–111. Cairo.
Nasrallah, P. J.
  1950   *Saint Jean de Damas: Son époque, sa vie, son oeuvre*. Harissa.
  1969   "Un auteur antiochien du XIe siècle: Nicon de la Montagne Noire (vers 1025–début du XIIe s.)." *POC* 19, 150–61.
Nau, F.
  1902a   "Note sur la date de la mort de Saint Jean Climaque." *BZ* 9, 35–37.
  1902b   "Le texte grec du récit du moine Anastase sur les saints Pères du Sinaï." *OC* 2, 58–89.
  1907   "Histoire des solitaires égyptiens." *ROC* 12, 43–69, 171–89, 393–413.
Nautine, P.
  1963   "Épiphane (saint) de Salamine." *DHGE* XV, 617–31.
Nesbitt, J. W.
  1969   "A Geographical and Chronological Guide to Greek Saint Lives." *OCP* 35, 443–89.
Nir, D.
  1965   "Geomorphological Map of the Judean Desert, 1:100,000." *Scripta Hierosolymitana* 15, 5–29.
Noble, T. F. X.
  1987   "John Damascene and the History of the Iconoclastic Controversy." In *Culture and Society in the Middle Ages: Studies in Honor of R. E. Sullivan*, 95–116. Kalamazoo, Michigan.

Noret, J.
1968 "Ménologes, Synaxaires, Ménées: Essai de clarification d'une terminologie." *AB* 86, 21–24.

Olphe-Galliard, J.
1953 "Cénobitisme." *DS* II.1, 405–10.

Oppenheim, P.
1931 *Das Mönchskleid im christlichen Altertum.* Freiburg im Breisgau.

Orestano, R.
1956 "Beni dei monaci e monasteri nella legislazione Giustinianea." In *Studi in onore di Pietro De Francisci* III, 563–93. Milan.

Ovadiah, A., and de Silva, C. G.
1981 "Supplement to the Corpus of Byzantine Churches in the Holy Land." *Levant* 13, 220–61.

Palanque, J. R., Bardy, G., and de Labriolle, P.
1936 *Histoire général de l'Église depuis les origines jusqu'à nos jours* (eds. Fliche and Martin), III: *De la paix constantinienne à la mort de Théodose.* Paris.

Palmer, A.
1990 *Monks and Masons on the Tigris Frontier.* Cambridge.

Palmer, E. H.
1881 *The Survey of Western Palestine: Arabic and English Name Lists.* London.

Papadopoulos-Kerameus, A.
1897 Ἀνάλεκτα Ἱεροσολυμιτικῆς Σταχυολογίας IV; repr. Brussels 1963.

Pargoire, J.
1899 "Les débuts du monachisme à Constantinople." *RQH* 21, 67–143.
1907 "Acémètes." *DACL* I.1, 307–21; "Archimandrite." DACL I.2, 2739–50.

Patlagean, E.
1977 *Pauvreté économique et pauvreté sociale à Byzance 4ᵉ–7ᵉ siècles.* Paris.

Patrich, J.
1983 "The Survey of Mar Saba Map." *ESI* 2, 65–66.
1984–89 "Caves Survey in the Judean Desert." *ESI* 3 (1984), 61–62; 6 (1988), 66–70; 7 (1989), 62–64.
1985 "Deir Mukelik: Greek Inscriptions." *ESI* 4, 21.
1986 "The Caves Encampment of Simon Son of Gioras in the Ravine Called 'Pheretae'". *Ninth World Congress of Jewish Studies* B.1, 21–26. Jerusalem (Hebrew).
1987 "The Last Hermit: Elia, the Monk from Ain Fara." *Teva Vaaretz* 29.7, 32–33 (Hebrew).
1988 "Hermitages of the Great Laura of St. Sabas." In Jacoby and Tsafrir 1988, 131–66 (Hebrew).
1988a "Caves Survey in the Judean Desert." *ESI* 6, 66–70.
1989 *The Monastic Institutions of Saint Sabas: An Archaeological-Historical Research,* Ph.D. diss. Jerusalem (Hebrew).
1989a "Hideouts in the Judean Wilderness." *BAR* 15.5, 32–42.
1989b "Chronique archéologique: Réfuges juifs dans les gorges du Wadi Mukhmas." *RB* 96, 235–39, pl. xv.
1989c "Caves Survey in the Judean Desert." *ESI* 7, 62–64.
1989d "The Aqueducts of Hyrcania." In D. Amit, Y. Hirschfeld, and J. Patrich, eds., *The Aqueducts of Ancient Palestine,* 243–60. Jerusalem (Hebrew).
1990a "The Cells (*ta kellia*) of Choziba, Wadi el-Qilt." In Bottini et al. 1990, 205–26.

1990b   "The Sabaite Laura of Jeremias in the Judean Desert." *LA* 40, 295–311, pls.
             XXXVII–XL.

1991   "The Sabaite Monastery of the Cave (Spelaion) in the Judean Desert." *LA* 41,
             429–48.

1993a   "Hyrcania." In E. Stern, ed., *The New Encyclopedia of Archaeological Excavations in the
             Holy Land.* Vol. 2, 639–41.

1993b   "Chapels and Hermitages of St. Sabas' Monastery." In Y. Tsafrir, ed. *Ancient
             Churches Revealed,* 233–43. Jerusalem.

1994   *Archaeological Survey of Israel: Map of Mar Saba (18-12).* Jerusalem.

Patrich, J., Arubas, B., and Agur, B.
1993   "Monastic Cells in the Desert of Gerasimus near the Jordan." In F. Manns and E.
             Alliata, eds., *Early Christianity in Context. Monuments and Documents,* 277–96. Jeru-
             salem.

Patrich, J., and Di Segni, L.
1987   "New Greek Inscriptions from Theoctistus Monastery in the Judean Desert." *EI*
             19 (Avi Yonah Volume), 272–81 (Hebrew with Eng. summary on p. 81*).

Patrich, J., and Rubin, R.
1984   "Les grottes de el-'Aleiliyat et la Laure de Saint Firmin." *RB* 91, 379–87.

Pattenden, P.
1975   "The Text of the *Pratum Spirituale.*" *JTS,* n.s. 26, 38–74.

Payne, R. M.
1981   *Christian Worship in Jerusalem in the Fourth and Fifth Centuries: The Development of the
             Lectionary, Calendar and Liturgy.* University Microfilms. Ann Arbor, Michigan.

Peeters, P.
1905   "Historia S. Abramii ex apographo arabico." *AB* 24, 349–56.

1911   "S. Romain le néo-martyr († 1er mai 780), d'après un document géorgien." *AB*
             30, 393–427.

1913   "S. Hilarion d'Ibérie." *AB* 32, 236–69.

1930   "La Passion de S. Michel le Sabaïte." *AB* 48, 65–98.

1931   "La première traduction latine de 'Barlaam et Joasaph', et son original grec." *AB*
             49, 276–312.

1936   "Une vie copte de S. Jean de Lycopolis." *AB* 54, 376–81.

1955   "Saint Théoctiste moine Sabaïte et martyr (†797)." *AB* 73, 373–74.

Peña, I., Castellana, P., and Fernandez, R.
1980   *Les reclus syriens.* Jerusalem.

1983   *Les cénobites syriens.* Jerusalem.

Peradze, G.
1937a   *An Account of Georgian Monks and Monasteries in Palestine as Revealed in the Writings of
             Non-Georgian Pilgrims.* Hertford.

1937b   "An Account of the Monks and Monasteries in Palestine." *Georgia: A Journal of Geor-
             gian and Caucasian Studies* 4–5, 181–246.

Perrone, L.
1980   *La Chiesa di Palestina e le controversie christologiche.* Brescia.

1988   "'Eis ton tes hesychias limena': Le lettere a Giovanni di Beersheva nella corrispon-
             denza di Barsanufio e Giovanni di Gaza." *Mémorial Dom Jean Gribomont,* 463–86.
             Rome.

1990   "Il deserto e l'orizzonte della Città: Le storie monastiche di Cirillo di Scitopoli." In
             Cirillo di Scitopoli, Storie monastiche del deserto di Gerusalemme, trans. R. Baldelli e L.
             Mortari, Scritti monastici 15, 11–90. Abbazia di Praglia.

Perrot, C.
1963   "Un fragment christo-palestinien découvert à Khirbet Mird (Actes des Apôtres X, 28–29, 32–41)." *RB* 70, 506–55.
Petit, L.
1925   "Jean Climaque." *DTC* VIII, 690–93.
Petrides, S.
1900–1   "Le monastère des Spoudaei à Jérusalem et les Spoudaei de Constantinople." *EO* 4, 225–31.
1910   "Spoudaei et Philopones." *EO* 7, 341–48.
Phokylides, J.
1927   Ἡ ἱερὰ Λαύρα Σαβᾶ τοῦ ἡγιασμένου. Alexandria.
Piccirillo, M.
1988   "The Mosaics at Umm er-Rasas in Jordan." *BA* 51, 208–13.
Pierri, P. G.
1947   "Nel Deserto di Giuda." *TS* 22, 12–15.
Pringle, D.
1981   "Some Approaches to the Study of Crusader Masonry Marks in Palestine." *Levant* 13, 173–99.
Quasten, J.
1963   *Patrology* III. Westminster, Maryland.
Quibell, J. R.
1912   *The Monastery of Apa Jeremias.* Cairo.
Rabello, A. M.
1987   *Giustiniano, Ebrei e Samaritani* I. Milan.
1988   Vol. II. Milan.
Ramsay, M.
1890   *The Historical Geography of Asia Minor.* London.
Rauschen, G., and Altaner, B.
1931   *Patrologie: Die schriften der Kirchenväter und ihr Lehrgehalt,* 10th–11th ed. Freiburg im Breisgau.
Raz, E.
1979   "The Geography and Geology (of the Judean Desert)." In S. Ben Yosef, ed., *Israel Guide: The Judean Desert and the Jordan Valley.* Jerusalem (Hebrew).
Rees, S.
1940   "The Life and Personality of Leontius of Byzantium." *JTS* 41, 263–80.
Régnault, L.
1981   "Les Apophthègmes des Pères en Palestine aux Ve–VIe siècles." *Irénikon* 54, 320–30.
Renoux, A.
1961–62   "Un manuscrit du Lectionnaire arménien de Jérusalem (Cod. Jerus. arm. 121)." *Le Muséon* 74, 361–85; 75, 385–98.
Řezáč, G.
1958   "Le diverse forme di unione fra i monasteri orientali." *OCA* 153, 99–135.
Rhetore, J.
1897   "La prise de Jérusalem par les Perses." *RB* 6, 458–63.
Richard, M.
1944   "Léonce de Jérusalem et Léonce de Byzance." *Mélanges de science religieuse* 1, 35–88.
1947   "Léonce de Byzance, était-il origéniste?". *REB* 5, 31–66.

Riess, V.
1892   "Das Euthymiuskloster, die Peterskirche der Eudokia und die Laura Heptastomos in der Wüste Judä." *ZDPV* 15, 212–33.

Rochcau, V.
1978   "Saint Siméon Salos, ermite palestinien et prototype des 'Fous-pour-le-Christ'." *POC* 28, 209–19.

Rodinson, M.
1961   "De l'archéologie à la sociologie historique: Notes méthodologiques sur le dernier ouvrage de G. Tchalenko." *Syria* 38, 170–200.

Rodley, L.
1986   *Cave Monasteries of Byzantine Cappadocia.* Cambridge.

Rot, I.
1969   "The Geology of the Northern Judean Desert." *Teva Vaaretz* 11, 11–114 (Hebrew).

Rousseau, P.
1974   "The Formation of Early Ascetic Communities: Some Further Reflections." *JTS* 25, 113–17.
1985   *Pachomius: The Making of a Community in Fourth-Century Egypt.* Berkeley-Los Angeles-London.

Rubin, R.
1982   "The Laura Monasteries in the Judean Desert in the Byzantine Period." *Cathedra* 23, 25–64 (Hebrew).

Ruppert, F.
1971   *Das pachomianische Mönchtum und die Anfänge klösterliche Gehorsams.* Münster-schwarzbach.

Rusch, W. G.
1977   *The Later Latin Fathers.* London.

Sabrames, D.
1962   *Zur Soziologie des byzantinischen Mönchtums.* Leiden-Cologne.

Safrai, Z.
1982   "The Samaritans." In Baras et al. 1982, 252–64.

Salem, G.
1966–67 "The Monastery of St. Sabas, and the Return of the Relics." *Eastern Churches Review* 1, 41–46.

Sansterre, J. M.
1980   *Les moines grecs et orientaux à Rome aux époques byzantine et carolingienne (milieu du VIᵉ s.–fin du IXᵉ s.).* Brussels 1980.
1988   "Le monachisme byzantin à Rome." *Settimane di Studio del Centro Italiano di Studi sull'Alto Medioevo* 34, 391–407. Spoleto.

Sauneron, S.
1967   "Fouilles d'Esna (Haute-Égypte): Monastères et ermitages." *AIBL*, 411–18.
1969   "Les 9ème et 10ème campagnes archéologiques à Esna: Les ermitages du désert." *BIFAO* 67, 103–12.

Sauneron, S., and Jacquet, J.
1972   *Les ermitages chrétiens du Désert d'Esna, I: Archéologie et inscriptions; II: Descriptions et plans; III: Céramique et objets; IV: Essai d'histoire.* Paris.

Schick, R.
1987   *The Fate of the Christians in Palestine during the Byzantine-Umayyad Transition, A.D. 660–750.* Ph.D. diss. Chicago 1987.

Schiwietz, S.

1913   *Das morgenländische Mönchtum II: Das Mönchtum auf Sinai und in Palästina im vierten Jahrhundert*. Mainz.

1938   *Das morgenländische Mönchtum III*. Mainz.

Schneemelcher, N.

1962   "Epiphanius von Salamis." *RAC* 5, 909–27. Stuttgart.

Schneider, A. M.

1931   "Das Kloster von Koziba." *RQ* 39, 297–332.

1938   "Das Kalamon Kloster in der Jerichoebene." *OC* 13–14, 39–43.

Schönborn, C. von

1972   *Sophrone de Jérusalem: Vie monastique et confession dogmatique*. Paris.

Schwartz, E.

1939   *Kyrillos von Skythopolis*. Leipzig.

1940   "Zur Kirchenpolitik Justinians." *Sitzungsberichte der bayerischen Akademie der Wissenschaften zu München, Philosophisch-historische Abteilung* 2, 32–81.

Sellers, R. V.

1953   *The Council of Chalcedon: A Historical and Doctrinal Survey*. London.

Smith, W., and Wace, H., eds.

1877–87   *Dictionary of Christian Biography*, 4 vols. Boston.

Stein, E.

1944   "Cyrille de Scythopolis: À propos de la nouvelle édition de ses oeuvres." *AB* 52, 169–86.

Stein, E., and Palanque, J. R.

1949   *Histoire du Bas-Empire* II. Paris.

1959   *Histoire du Bas-Empire* I, 2nd ed. Paris.

Stone, M. E.

1984   "An Armenian Pilgrim to the Holy Land in the Early Byzantine Era." *REA* n.s. 18, 173–78.

1986   "Holy Land Pilgrimage of Armenians before the Arab Conquest." *RB* 93, 93–110.

Strobel, A.

1967   "Die Charitonhöhle in der Wüste Judä." *ZDPV* 83, 46–63.

Stroumsa, G. G.

1983   "Gnostics and Manichaeans in Byzantine Palestine." *SP* 18, 273–78.

Tachiaos, A. E.

1966   "Le monachisme serbe de saint Sava et la tradition hésychaste Athonite." *Hilandarski zbornik* 1, 83–89.

Taft, R. F.

1978   *The Great Entrance, OCA* 200. Rome.

1982   "Praise in the Desert." *Worship* 56, 513–36.

1984   *Beyond East and West: Problems of Liturgical Understanding*. Washington.

1986   *The Liturgy of the Hours in the East and West*. Collegeville, Minnesota.

1988   "Mount Athos: A Late Chapter in the History of the Byzantine Rite." *DOP* 42, 179–94.

Talbot, A.-M.

1987   "An Introduction to Byzantine Monasticism." *Illinois Classical Studies* 12, 229–41.

Tarchnischvili, M.

1955   *Geschichte der kirchlichen georgischen Literatur*. Rome.

1960   *Le grand lectionnaire de l'église de Jérusalem (V–VIII siècles)*, CSCO 188–89, Scrip. Iber. 9–10; CSCO 204–5, Scrip. Iber. 13–14. Louvain.

Tchalenko, G.
1950   "La Syrie du Nord: Étude économique." *Actes du VIe Congrès International des Études Byzantines*, II, 389–97. Paris.
1953–58   *Villages antiques de la Syrie du nord*, 3 vols. Paris.
Testore, C.
1950   "Communione eucaristica." *Enc. Catt.* IV, 135. Rome.
Thierry, N.
1978   "L'archéologie cappadocienne en 1978." *CCM* 22, 3–22.
Thomsen, P.
1940   "Kyrillos von Skythopolis." *Orientalistische Literaturzeitung* 43, 457–63.
Tobler, T.
1853–54   *Topographie von Jerusalem*, I–II. Berlin.
Toumanoff, C.
1966   "Armenia and Georgia." *CMH* IV.1, ed. J. M. Hussey, 593–637. Cambridge.
Tsafrir, Y.
1971   "Monasticism at Mt. Sinai." *Ariel* 28, 65–78.
1975   *Zion: The South-Western Hill of Jerusalem and Its Place in the Urban Development of the City in the Byzantine Period*. Ph.D. diss. Jerusalem (Hebrew).
1984   *Eretz Israel from the Destruction of the Second Temple to the Muslim Conquest, II: Archaeology and Art*. Jerusalem (Hebrew).
Tzaferis, V.
1991   "Early Monks and Monasteries in the Holy Land." Δελτίον τῆς Χριστιανικῆς Ἀρχαιολογικῆς Ἑταιρείας, Περίοδος Δ΄, Τόμος ΙΕ 1989–90. Athens.
Vacandard, E.
1910   "Carême." *DTC* II, 1724–50.
Vailhé, S.
1897   "La Laure de Saint Sabas." *ENDF* 5, 112–23, 135–44.
1897–99   "Les premiers monastères de la Palestine." *Bessarione* 3 (1897), 39–58, 209–25, 334–56; 4 (1898–99), 193–210.
1897–98a   "Saint Théognius, Évêque de Béthélie." *EO* 1, 380–82.
1897–98b   "Les saints Kozibites." *EO* 1, 228–33.
1897–98c   "La Laure de Souka ou la Vieille Laure." *Bessarione* 3, 50–58.
1897–98d   "La Laure et le couvent de Saint Euthyme." *Bessarione* 3, 210–25.
1898a   "Les écrivains de Mar Saba." *EO* II, 1–11, 33–47.
1898b   "Le monastère de S. Théoctiste." *ROC* 3, 58–76.
1898c   "Les Laures de St. Gérasime et de Calamoun." *EO* 2, 106–19.
1898–99   "La Nouvelle Laure." *Bessarione* 4, 198–209.
1899   "Le monastère de Saint Saba." *EO* 2, 332–41.
1899–   "Répertoire alphabétique des monastères de Palestine." *ROC* 4 (1899), 512–42; 5
  1900a   (1900), 19–48, 272–92.
1899–   "Le monastère de Saint Saba." *EO* 3, 18–28, 168–77.
  1900b
1900–1   "Saint Dorothée et saint Zosime." *EO* 4, 359–63.
1901a   "Saint Michel le Syncelle et les deux frères Grapti, Saint Théodore et Saint Théophane." *ROC* 4, 313–32, 610–42.
1901b   "La prise de Jérusalem par les Perses en 614." *ROC* 4, 643–49.
1901–2   "Jean Mosch." *EO* 5, 107–16.
1902–3   "Sophrone le Sophiste et Sophrone le Patriarche." *ROC* 7, 360–85; 8, 32–69, 356–87.

| 1903 | "Jean le Khozibite et Jean de Césarée." *EO* 6, 107–13. |

1903   "Jean le Khozibite et Jean de Césarée." *EO* 6, 107–13.
1904   "Souka ou la Vieille Laure." *ROC* 9, 333–58.
1905   "Saint Abraham de Cratia." *EO* 8, 290–94.
1906   "Date de la mort de S. Jean Damascène." *EO* 9, 28–30.
1910   "Formation du Patriarchat de Jérusalem." *EO* 13, 325–36.
1910a   "Cyrille de Scythopolis." *DTC* II, 2581–82.
1911   "Les Philopones d'Oxyrhynque au 4ᵉ siècle." *EO* 14, 277–78.
1912   "Acémètes." *DHGE* I, 272–82.

Vailhé, S., and Petrides, S.
1904   "Saint Jean le Paléolaurite, précédé d'une notice sur la vieille laura." *ROC* 9, 333–58, 491–511.

Van den Gheyn, J.
1891   "Saint Théognius, évêque de Bétélie en Palestine." *RQH* 50, 559–74.

Van Elderen, B.
1979   "The Nag Hammadi Excavation." *BA* 42, 225–31.

Van Roey, A.
1975   "Remarques sur le moine Marcien." *TU* 115, 160–77.

Vasiliev, A. A.
1942–43   "The Life of St. Theodore of Edessa." *Byzantion* 16, 165–225.
1950   *Justin the First*, Cambridge, Massachusetts.

Veilleux, A.
1968   *La liturgie dans le cénobitisme pachômien au IVème siècle*, Studia Anselmiana 57. Rome.
1980–82   *Pachomian Koinonia I–III*, CS 45–47. Kalamazoo, Michigan.

Velimirovich, N.
1989   *The Life of St. Sava (of Serbia)*. Crestwood, New York.

Venables, E.
1877   "Basil of Caesarea." *DCB* I (repr. 1967), 282–97.

Vincent, H., and Abel, F. M.
1914–26   *Jérusalem Nouvelle*. Paris.

Vircillo-Franklin, C., et al., trans.
1982   *Early Monastic Rules: The Rules of the Fathers and the Regula Orientalis*. Collegeville, Minnesota.

Vogüé, A. de
1980   Foreword to *Pachomian Koinonia* I (Veilleux 1980).

Vööbus, A.
1951   "The Origins of Monachism in Mesopotamia." *CH* 20, 27–37.
1958a   *History of Asceticism in the Syrian Orient* I, CSCO 184 (14). Louvain.
1958b   "Die Rolle der Regeln im syrischen Mönchtum des Altertums." *OCP* 24, 385–92.
1959   "Sur le développement de la phase cénobitique et la réaction dans l'ancien monachisme syriaque." *Recherches de science religieuse* 46, 401 ff.
1960a   *History of Asceticism in the Syrian Orient* II, CSCO 196 (17). Louvain.
1960b   *Syriac and Arabic Documents Regarding Legislation Relative to Syrian Monasticism*. Stockholm.
1961   "The Institution of the *benai qeiāmā* and *benat qeiāmā* in the Ancient Syrian Church." *CH* 30, 19–27.
1970a   *Syrische Kanonessammlungen: Ein Beitrag zur Quellenkunde*, CSCO 307, 317, Subsidia 35, 38. Louvain.
1970b   "Syrische Verordnungen für die Novizen und ihre handschriftliche Überlieferung." *OC* 54, 106–12.

1982   *The Canons Ascribed to Maruta of Maipherqat and Related Sources*, CSCO 439–40, Scrip. Syr. 191–92. Louvain.

1988   *History of Asceticism in the Syrian Orient* III, CSCO 500 (81). Louvain.

Walters, C. C.
1974   *Monastic Archaeology in Egypt.* Warminster.

Warren, H. B. de
1937   "Le travail manuel chez les moines à travers les âges." *Vie spirituelle* 52, 80–123.

Weigand, E.
1914   "Das Theodosioskloster." *BZ* 23, 167–216.

Wilkinson, J.
1977   *Jerusalem Pilgrims before the Crusades.* Surrey.

Winkler, S.
1965   "Die Samariter in den Jahren 529/30." *Klio* 43–45, 435–57.

Winlock, H. E., and Crum, W. E.
1926   *The Monastery of Epiphanius at Thebes*, Part I. New York.

Wright, G. R. H.
1961   "The Archaeological Remains of el-Mird in the Wilderness of Judaea." *Biblica* 42, 1–21.

Indices

Index of Monasteries

Index of Persons

Index of Places and Peoples

General Index

Errata

Page	For	Read
304, line 40	Eutychius	Eutyches
305, line 22	Eutychius	Eutyches
307, line 29	Eutychius	Eutyches
396, line 42	Eutychius, patriarch of Jerusalem	Eutyches